Survey Research in the United States

Survey Research in the United States

Roots and Emergence 1890–1960

Jean M. Converse

UNIVERSITY OF CALIFORNIA PRESS

Berkeley • Los Angeles • London

Chapters two and seven are adapted and extended from material published previously as "Attitude Measurement in Psychology and Sociology: The Early Years," chapter one in Charles F. Turner and Elizabeth Martin, eds., *Surveying Subjective Phenomena*, vol. 2 (New York: Russell Sage Foundation/Basic Books, 1984), and "Strong Arguments and Weak Evidence: The Open/Closed Questioning Controversy of the 1940s," *Public Opinion Quarterly*, no. 48 (1984), pp. 267–282.

University of California Press
Berkeley and Los Angeles, California

University of California Press, Ltd.
London, England

Library of Congress Cataloging-in-Publication Data

Converse, Jean M., 1927–
    Survey research in the United States.

    Includes index.
    1. Sampling (Social sciences)—History.   2. Social surveys—United States—
History.   I. Title.
HA31.2.C66   1986   300'.723   85–24500
ISBN 0–520–05399–0

Printed in the United States of America
1   2   3   4   5   6   7   8   9

To Once and Future:
Marian and Edward, Peter and Tim

Contents

Acknowledgments

The collective generosity of many people made this study possible. I am especially indebted to the individuals whom I interviewed for their considered reflections on survey research and social science and for their many helpful suggestions. I am also grateful to many others who answered queries and suggested ideas, informants, and source materials. The list of these gracious individuals is long:

Rebecca Adams, Tony Asmann, Gladys Baker, Allen H. Barton, Richard H. Baxter, Wolfgang Beck, Joe Belden, Tracy R. Berckmans, Yvonne Blotner, Norman Bradburn, Jerome S. Bruner, Martin Bulmer, Don and Ellen Cahalan, Angus Campbell, Charles F. Cannell, David Caplovitz, Mary Elizabeth Carroll, Dorwin P. Cartwright, Richard Centers, Donna Charron, John A. Clausen, John Colombotos, Leonard S. Cottrell, Jr., Leo Crespi, Helen Crossley, James A. Davis, W. Phillips Davison, Thelma A. Dreis, Otis Dudley Duncan, David Easton, Jack Elinson, Raymond Fink, Marjorie Fiske, Lloyd A. Free, George H. Gallup, Charles Y. Glock, Martin Gold, Edith Gomberg, Roe Goodman, Morris H. Hansen, John S. Harding, Albert H. Hastorf, Philip M. Hauser, Ernest R. Hilgard, Esther and Joseph Hochstim, Helen and Herbert H. Hyman, Richard Jensen, William G. Jones, Mara Julius, George Katona, Daniel Katz, Elihu Katz, Patricia L. Kendall, Leslie Kish, Evelyn Kitagawa, Andie L. Knutson, Sheldon J. Korchin, Edward O. Laumann, Jane and Rensis Likert, Elizabeth Martin, Marlene Mayo, Robert McCargar, Sandy McKay, Robert K. Merton, Warren E. Miller, Michael Minor, Louis Moss, Hans Mueller, Judith P. Murphy, D. Morgan Neu, Ann Pasanella, Herbert Passin, James H. Ricks, David Riesman, Theresa F. Rogers, Burns Roper, Sydney Roslow, Peter H. Rossi, Naomi Rothwell, Merrill Shanks, Clara Shapiro, Paul B. Sheatsley, Phyllis Sheridan, David L. Sills, Eleanor Singer, M. Brewster Smith, Mary Spaeth, Garth Taylor, Charles F. Turner, Ralph W. Tyler, H. Ashley Weeks, Robert P. Weeks, Robin M. Williams, Jr., Ann Schuetz Zanes, and Pearl Zinner.

A number of individuals made useful critical comments on various parts of the manuscript: Allen H. Barton, Martin Bulmer, Don Cahalan, Charles F. Cannell, Dorwin P. Cartwright, Otis Dudley Duncan, Jack Elinson, Charles Y. Glock, Patricia L. Kendall, Francis Keppel, Leslie Kish, William Kruskal, Louis Moss, Stanley Presser, Howard Schuman, Paul B. Sheatsley, Tom W. Smith, Charles F. Turner, and Stephen B. Withey. Comments by the anonymous reviewers of the National Science Foundation and the University of California Press were also very helpful. One's counselors are rarely of unanimous mind, but I profited greatly from the quality and the diversity of their criticisms. These readers are, of course, innocent of those errors of judgment, interpretation, or omission that remain in the manuscript.

To the keepers of records and archives who made their treasure easily accessible, I feel very indebted. My special thanks go to Adye Bel Evans, librarian of the Institute for Social Research, University of Michigan, who was ever-patient and resourceful in tracking down elusive materials. F. Thomas Juster, Director of the Institute for Social Research, authorized my use of archival materials. Through Norman Bradburn and Robert T. Michael, successive directors of the National Opinion Research Center, and Patrick Bova, librarian extraordinary, I was given gracious access to NORC archives and documents. By permission of the Harvard University Archives and Ann Stouffer Bisconti, I consulted Samuel Stouffer's professional papers at the Nathan Pusey Library, Harvard University. Patricia L. Kendall authorized my use of Paul F. Lazarsfeld's interviews in the Oral History Collection, Butler Library, Columbia University, and the Oral History Research Office granted me permission to use the George Gallup interview in the same collection. Allen H. Barton and Phyllis Sheridan pointed me to a special collection of materials from the Bureau of Applied Social Research at Columbia. Marion E. Jemmott, Secretary of Columbia University, authorized my use of the University Archives, and Sarah Vos of that office was especially helpful in my search for materials. The American Association for Public Opinion Research granted me permission to use interviews with George Gallup, Elmo Roper, and Archibald Crossley. The Bentley Historical Library of the University of Michigan made available the professional papers of Rensis Likert. The Department of Special Collections of the Joseph Regenstein Library, University of Chicago, granted me permission to use the collected papers of Louis Wirth and Ernest W. Burgess.

I would also like to thank the knowledgeable and helpful archivists in three collections: Michael T. Ryan and Daniel Meyer of the Department of Special Collections, Joseph Regenstein Library, University of Chicago; Mary Jo Pugh and Nancy Bartlett, Bentley Historical Library, University of Michigan; and specialists at the National Archives in Washington, D.C., and the Washington National Records Center in Suitland, Maryland: Richard Crawford, Mike Miller, Donald Mosholder, Edward J. Reese, Gibson B. Smith, and Helen Ulibarri.

This project was supported by fellowships of the Earhart Foundation of Ann Arbor, Michigan, and research grants of the National Science Foundation (SES 78–11490 and SES 80–28385). I am grateful to Antony L. Sullivan, Director of the Earhart Foundation, and Ronald Overmann, Assistant Program Director of the History and Philosophy of Science Program, National Science Foundation, for their support, encouragement, and good counsel. Stanley Holwitz, Assistant Director of the University of California Press, Los Angeles, and Shirley Warren, Principal Editor, brought their special competence, patience, and good cheer to this endeavor.

Finally, I owe special thanks to Michigan friends and colleagues: to Howard Schuman, for his facilitation of this project and his suggestions at many points over the long course and expansive growth of this manuscript; to Philip E. Converse, A. F. K. Organski, and Stanley Presser for their special encouragement; to Patricia Preston, Michael Bourgon, and James Caffrey for their patient and efficient labors in permission and verification.

J. M. C.

August 1986

Abbreviations

Note: In a few cases where confusion may occur, the name of an individual associated with the organization is included.

AAA	Agricultural Adjustment Administration
AAAA	American Association of Advertising Agencies
AAAS	American Association for the Advancement of Science
AAPOR	American Association for Public Opinion Research
AIPO	American Institute of Public Opinion (Gallup)
AJS	*American Journal of Sociology*
APA	American Psychological Association
APSR	*American Political Science Review*
ASA	American Sociological Association
ASR	*American Sociological Review*
BAE	Bureau of Agricultural Economics, USDA
Bureau	Bureau of Applied Social Research, Columbia University (Lazarsfeld)
COGSIS	Committee on Government Statistics and Information Services
DPS	Division of Program Surveys, BAE, USDA (Likert)
FERA	Federal Emergency Relief Administration
GSS	General Social Survey, NORC
HICOG	High Commissioner for Germany
ICD	Information Control Division
IESS	*International Encyclopedia of the Social Sciences*
IJOAR	*International Journal of Opinion and Attitude Research*
IRSS	Institute for Research in Social Science, University of North Carolina (Odum)
ISR	Institute for Social Research, University of Michigan

ISRR	Institute of Social and Religious Research (Rockefeller)
JAP	*Journal of Applied Psychology*
JASA	*Journal of the American Statistical Association*
JASP	*Journal of Abnormal and Social Psychology*
JSP	*Journal of Social Psychology*
MMB	Modern Military Branch, National Archives
MRLF	*Monthly Report on the Labor Force* (later Current Population Survey)
NA	National Archives and Records Service
NAS	National Academy of Sciences
NES	National Election Study, Center for Political Studies, ISR
NIH	National Institutes of Health
NIMH	National Institute of Mental Health
NORC	National Opinion Research Center, University of Denver and later University of Chicago
NRC	National Research Council
NSF	National Science Foundation
OFF	Office of Facts and Figures
OMGUS	Office of Military Government, United States
ONR	Office of Naval Research
OPA	Office of Price Administration
OPOR	Office of Public Opinion Research (Cantril)
ORC	Opinion Research Center (affiliate of NORC)
ORR	Office of Radio Research (Lazarsfeld)
OSRD	Office of Scientific Research and Development
OWI	Office of War Information
OWI Surveys Division	Successor to Polls Division (Wilson)
Polls Division	Division of Extensive Surveys, OFF/OWI, renamed OWI Surveys Division in 1943 (Wilson)
POQ	*Public Opinion Quarterly*
PSU	Primary sampling unit
Research Branch	Research Branch, Morale Division, US Army (Stouffer)
RG	Record Group, National Archives
SCAP	Supreme Command Allied Powers, Japan
SES	Socioeconomic status
SHAEF	Supreme Headquarters Allied Expeditionary Force

SRC	Survey Research Center, University of Michigan; University of California, Berkeley
SSRC	Social Science Research Council
Surveys Division	Division of Extensive Surveys, OFF/OWI (Likert)
USDA	United States Department of Agriculture
USIA	United States Information Agency
USSBS	United States Strategic Bombing Survey
WNRC	Washington National Records Center, Suitland, Maryland
WPA	Works Progress Administration (1935), Work Projects Administration (1939)
WPB	War Production Board

Introduction

Themes and Perspectives

This book is about the historical development of "survey research"—an instrument that serves as something of a social telescope in the social sciences. In the pages that follow, social scientists consider other metaphors for this new instrument: should it be called a social microscope, perhaps, or a spectroscope, or a "demoscope" or social barometer for recording the ups and downs of political and social tensions all over the globe? The image of the "far-seeing" telescope is more apt than the others, for one uses the survey telescope to scan some rim of the social world, without any real hope of resolving great detail, looking instead for large shapes of social geography, movements of populations, flows of information, opinion, and feeling.

The survey has ancient ancestors. As a straight population count to raise taxes or muster soldiers, the survey can be traced back at least 2,000 years and probably much further. The more complex survey of our own time has been forged in the twentieth century as an instrument of special power for viewing mass populations in industrialized societies, especially in their character as social facts, political publics, and economic markets. It is an instrument serving some purposes of three basic constituencies: elites, social scientists, and the mass public.

Elites are intensely interested in the survey's yield of information for prediction, planning, profit, and control; for mustering mass support for political programs; and for mobilizing resources to contend against other elites.[1] Social scientists use the sample survey for gathering descriptive data, for making inferences to populations, for building blocks of social theory, and for advancing their own disciplinary and intellectual career interests. Finally, the mass public consumes survey data as something of a mirror of its own time, of its national political opinions, beliefs, and experiences.

1

Polls and surveys took root in Western societies that were becoming economically industrialized and urbanized, increasingly literate, and politically democratic—for good reason. Industrial society offered the technology and transportation that made a mass constituency accessible to interview in the first place. (Polls and surveys continue to spread to nonindustrialized countries, but they are not a home-grown product there, where physical and cultural conditions offer much resistance and expense.) The literacy distributed by mass public education and the mass media has made a national public intellectually accessible as sources and as consumers of poll/survey data. Most important, a democratic governmental structure has made it politically strategic for powerful groups to gather, assess, represent (or misrepresent), try to influence, and invoke mass opinion.

There is much to support Beniger's contention that survey research developed as business and government became technically able to communicate to mass audiences and then grew interested in "receiving feedback from this same audience, in order better to control its behavior." As he writes, survey research arose

> [not] from a need to speak one's mind . . . but rather from the need to find out what is on people's minds—whether they intend to speak them or not. Attitudinal research arises not out of any need of the holders of attitudes, that is to say, but rather from the needs of an audience interested in the potential exploitation of those attitudes.[2]

The needs referred to are those of business and government. That survey research did not well up from The People seems pretty certain. Yet it is also the case that polls and surveys have been a natural for democratic political systems, consonant with and reflective of official democratic structures and values. American elites cannot simply and safely pursue their own ends by force or intimidation, without paying some heed to "the holders of attitudes" in their mass constituencies. Whether such elites are seen as the vanguard of democratic reform and liberation or as the oligarchic rear guard of manipulation or repression depends on one's ideological tastes, utopian hopes, and judgment of the constraints of social reality. In any case, surveys are not useful to established elites alone, as public opposition to the Vietnam war demonstrated, to cite one case. It seems likely indeed that polls and surveys have become as acceptable, ubiquitous, and significant as they have in American life because they can serve some purposes of all of the major constituencies—established elites of business and government, aspiring political elites, scientific experts, and large parts of the mass public. On to more specific assumptions.

The history of survey research, like that of the sciences in general and of the arts as well, can be seen from one of two perspectives: internalist and externalist. Now that survey research has achieved a niche in university culture, survey researchers tend to view their own activity from an internalist perspective—that is, as theory and data-driven work carried out by scientists themselves—rather than from an externalist approach, which treats science as still another form of human culture that is most explicable in terms of its economic, political, and social contexts.[3]

Survey researchers know well enough that they are affected by their external environment. Like all sophisticated social scientists, they try to see the openings and dead ends of the funding environment, but they generally perceive these factors as the surround of their work rather than as the core of their scientific enterprise. They see their work as originating and cumulating in the unique intellectual values of the logic of ideas, the marshaling of data, the canons of evidence—the internal structure of science.

While survey research has taken on something of the character of a quasi-discipline rather than a full-fledged scientific discipline—an argument I shall make in the course of this book—its life history provides an example of the internalizing course of scientific disciplines conceptualized by Kuhn. In that analysis, the content of a science in its early years is close to commonsense concepts and needs of external, practical life. As the science matures, its content is increasingly shaped by the communication of scientists themselves, who become organized into a social system of their own, insulating each other from the language, problems, and—if they can manage it—the pressures of other realms. In Kuhn's view, the internalist perspective is eminently successful not because it actually does fully explain scientific development but because scientists become insulated in their own disciplinary cultures and thus usually *think* that it does.[4] (When Daniel S. Greenberg put together his study *The Politics of Pure Science*, for example, some of the objects of his research were appalled: How in the world could there be a politics of science?[5]) In this book I have tried to blend something of both the internalist and externalist perspectives. My account starts in the wider world of affairs and gradually focuses on the smaller world of science. In one sense, it becomes progressively narrowed and increasingly internal in the course of three sections in the book.

Organization of This Book

In part one (1890–1940), I have traced the origins of polls
and surveys to three "ancestors," two of which were engaged in the practical concerns of business and politics and one in university science. Toward the end of these years, with the crisis of the Great Depression, vast
new surveys of national scope were mounted by federal agencies to assess national problems. The power of the new public opinion polls, by
Gallup and the others, was not lost on certain actors in the federal
administration nor on certain academic social scientists interested in attitude measurement. Survey researchers generally assume an internalist
interpretation of these beginnings, seeing their ancestors in science as
having been more weighty than those in either politics or business. I see
the genealogy as the other way around.

Relegating these fields to the role of ancestor requires a brief apology,
for their importance in their own right is thereby diminished. In the account of social surveys, for instance, I consider certain phases of their
evolution up through the New Deal, but I do not follow the full story of
social fact-gathering on up through 1960. With the exception of some
developments of special relevance to survey research, such as probability
sampling, I quite neglect the history of the U.S. Census as a subject in itself. Likewise, with commercial research. I have selected material about
market research and opinion polls to show their commanding influence as forerunner, indirect facilitator, and sometime (uneasy) ally of survey research. Their wider political and cultural importance is thereby
slighted, and their history truncated. The appearance of scientific ancestors is even briefer. The specific focus on attitude measurement is restricted largely to the 1920s and 1930s, although that field has of course
thrived and burgeoned ever since. The history of inferential statistics is
left largely unexplored, except—again—for those innovations bearing
on probability sampling.

To excuse such shabby treatment of ancestors, I offer only my sense
that fair treatment would open the horizon to a whole new cast of characters and events, perhaps requiring some three or four other books. To
justify the concentration on such a small part of the forest, I offer only
the conviction that survey research has become an intellectually powerful and influential part of the scientific terrain. I will proceed to a preview of parts two and three without such extended caveats.

In part two, which spans the years from 1935 to 1945, we see the process by which the example of the polls and the funds of the federal gov-

ernment facilitated the development of survey research. A protosurvey style of research came to the national scene on the arm of a government growing massively in power and responsibility, mandated first by the Great Depression and then by World War II. In the war years, especially, the expanding agencies of Washington were charged with gathering subjective data—opinions and morale factors that were deemed of consequence to the war effort. A shared community of interest between federal administrators and social scientists lasted for the duration. At the end of the war, congressmen suspicious of the Roosevelt administration and wary of outsiders' information about their own constituencies broke it up, cutting opinion research out of the federal budget.

The wartime experience served to enlarge the potential pool of academic talent for survey research. When most of the Washington social scientists went back home to their universities, some took with them a new professional interest in surveys as well as new technical expertise in putting such surveys together. As we shall see, they later came to share with scientists in general a new system of extracting financial support from the federal government.

Part three (1940–1960) was the period of establishment of survey research in the university. Social scientists interested in survey methods came to academic life (or came back to it) with experience in applied empirical research before and during World War II. As a group, most of the survey researchers were bent on trying to shed these externalist beginnings in order to join the community of scholars and chart an internalist future. Yet they felt the strain between the two cultures, needing the money of applied business and government while desiring the prestige and freedom of basic science.

Their organizations were a poor fit for academic life. Their "number crunching" violated the sensibilities of humanists and of theoretically inclined social scientists, and it threatened the security of the individual scholar. Their organizational division of labor evoked—and still does evoke—the noisy image of knowledge "factories." (While a physical telescope is understood to require capital investment and a complex division of labor, the same cannot be said for social telescopes.) The researchers required more money than universities or foundations were able or willing to find, and their reliance on clients outside the academy raised issues of business and government control of new knowledge itself and threatened the tranquillity of the life of the mind. While the researchers often felt on the financial edge, beleaguered, and vulnerable, to some of their colleagues they appeared imperial, aggressive, and too rich by half.

Their organizations were not perceived as resources for the university
as a whole, on the order of museums, libraries, or (later) computer installations, but were felt by many as threats to the established university
order.

The struggle of these researchers to establish a place in the university
(and the university's struggle with them) is intertwined with two other
stories: the researchers' efforts to consolidate some professional nucleus
of their own, and their efforts to gain acceptance and influence in the
established disciplines of social science. These subjects will take us, finally, to an evaluation of the contributions of the new survey organizations and an assessment of the particular powers and limits of survey research itself.

On Sources, Designs, and Second Thoughts

To construct this history, I have used archival documents,
published and unpublished materials, and interviews—not structured
survey interviews permitting quantifiable data, but informal ones without such a yield. I should have used both. Some more pieces of comparable quantifiable data would have enhanced this study, just as the definition of a sample and population would have. The unstructured
interviews nevertheless have offered rich detail, interpretation, and useful links to documentary evidence. After the more extensive interviews
have been fully edited and authorized, I hope to deposit transcripts of
them in the archive being created by the University of Chicago and the
American Association for Public Opinion Research. They are accounts
provided by scientists of fine mind and superb training who are deeply
interested in their work, alive enough to good professional gossip and
intrigue, rich in their appreciation of others' research, and sometimes
quite modest about their own. As Harry Levin recently observed, "There
is an inevitable compulsion to make a lifetime of research appear orderly, as though one interest led naturally to another"[6]—and that tendency may be even stronger in individuals' accounts of their research organizations. But most of my informants tried to resist the compulsion,
too, as they gave some room to accident, error, incongruity, and comedy
as well as to the sobersided pursuit of orderly plans. Most would surely
be delighted by a foreign scholar's recent struggle to express his appreciation for empirical research: "Why, I have learned that it is the very
basement of social science!"

The quality of my own interviewing was inevitably variable. I interviewed some people too early, before I had read certain key writings or before I had defined certain parts of the study well enough to hone my questions down to the most cogent ones. In some cases, nevertheless, I managed to bring the right questions to the right person, and in all cases I learned a great deal about survey research from my informants, all of whom were gracious and helpful. I have listed them in the Acknowledgments.

One of my major objectives in personal interviewing was to try to scale the walls of the research organization I knew best, the Survey Research Center/Institute for Social Research at the University of Michigan, where I have been affiliated for the last ten years in various modest research and writing roles. I was intent on trying to absorb some of the local culture of the other founding survey organizations, notably the Bureau of Applied Social Research and the National Opinion Research Center. Whether I learned enough to escape the local culture and attain a more general perspective on the field is an evaluation that I myself cannot make.

Part One

The Ancestors: 1890–1940

1

The Reformist Ancestor of Policy: The Social Survey

> The study of history allows one to make a conscious choice of ancestors.
>
> *Marvin S. Becker*

The English Social Survey

The Choice of Ancestors

Any man who wrote seventeen books in as many years in his spare time surely deserves to be a founding father of something. At the turn of the century, the indefatigable Charles Booth (1840–1916) produced a landmark study of social conditions, *Life and Labour of the People in London* (1889–1903),[1] the first English "social survey" of huge proportions. The intellectual lineage of American survey research has sometimes been taken back to Booth, but in these short accounts the line of descent is not very clear.[2] How was the line transmitted to these American survey researchers, who began to function in the 1930s and used the name in the 1940s? Is the link to Booth through surveys a loose linguistic one, available because so many connotations have been given the multipurpose word *surveys* over its long life? Or is there a more substantial line of intellectual influence and succession?

Indeed, there is, first, a linguistic connection. The naming of social surveys as such was made in direct analogy to the surveying of land, and they were qualified as social to indicate that these were surveys of people rather than agricultural or geological surveys and also to distinguish broad-based data collection about human beings from the "bare enumeration" of official census collection.[3] And, as we shall see, the linguistic connection is still a live one.[4]

The second reason that Booth is an ancestor of choice is that of drama and clarity. There he is at the turn of the century, astride a monument, a huge survey of the largest city in the world, which he conducted with the help of a small staff (which included Beatrice Potter Webb) but in enormous part by himself. At the time, Booth was engaged in the owning and managing of a thriving international steamship company that sometimes took him abroad, and so much of his survey work had to be conducted at night and on weekends. He spent his own money on the project—33,000 English pounds. He took to the political lecture circuit on behalf of old-age pensions because of his empirical findings. At the same time he lived a family and personal life, with a wife and children, friends, political and business colleagues at hand, correspondence with those afar.[5] He wrote on and on for publication—not only the seventeen volumes mentioned but other books as well. Booth was a man "obsessed," as Abrams has put it, gathering "an avalanche of facts."[6] Booth thus has a certain mythic proportion that is pleasing in venerable forebears.

In his lifetime, this made for renown and influence. The Booth survey, along with other late Victorian work, was an example of thoroughness and scientific authority to American activists who wanted to establish objective "scientific facts" to help power social change. An American social survey movement of widespread, fervent fact-gathering about social problems was conducted at the state and local level by laymen and professionals, but it showed some influence from Booth. In the 1930s, under the impetus of the Great Depression and the New Deal, surveys of national scope were undertaken by social scientists in government, not without some of the same hope and fervor of effecting social change through applied science that characterized surveys in the Victorian and Progressive eras. The national work added important technical capacities to the survey.

Booth's ancestry thus has some reality for survey research, but it should nevertheless be viewed in the context of two qualifications. First, for the scientific roots of survey research—even in its specifically factual inquiry—Booth's social survey is not the only ancestor of choice. The census survey of population and official government statistics is another. Tracing that lineage would take us back at least to the first national census surveys of population (in the United States, 1790, and in England, 1801) and back to predecessors in the 1600s in work on epidemics, vital records, life tables for insurance companies, and other quantitative studies done in England and Europe. We shall not proceed either that far back or that wide, and we shall largely neglect the history and development of the United States Bureau of the Census, except where it impinges on the history of probability sampling.[7]

Second, we should note that Booth did not *invent* surveys of social conditions. The poor had been a worry as well as a fascination in England for centuries, and counting them was of importance in assessing the problem and in assigning responsibilities. In 1601 the Elizabethan Poor Law established the principle of workhouses and charged parishes with the responsibility for raising taxes for poor relief. There was some empirical research into the incidence of poverty and other social conditions from the seventeenth to the nineteenth century,[8] but the industrialization and urbanization of the nineteenth century—the new visibility of poverty in congested cities and the menace of epidemics—spurred fact-gathering and reform efforts in both England and the United States. A systematic effort to ground the argument in descriptive statistics was made in both countries midcentury as the new statistical societies of the 1840s undertook sanitary surveys of health and housing conditions by house-to-house canvass.[9] In the United States, surveys of social conditions were conducted by letter and questionnaire to businesses and by house-to-house canvass carried out by police, settlement-house workers, insurance agents, students, agricultural agents, and religious workers. But none of these had the scope of Booth's project at the turn of the century.[10]

The Booth Enterprise

THE SOCIAL CONTEXT

The English social survey and its American counterpart were the "factualizing" branch of a broad social movement that spanned the Atlantic roughly from the 1880s to World War I. In late Victorian England, a congeries of wealthy philanthropists, charity workers, Marxists, single-taxers, trade unionists, Fabian socialists, liberals, workers of the new settlement houses, physicians and health workers, evangelists of the new Salvation Army all reflected their various concerns about the plight of the poor and fear of their revolutionary threat. Solutions were cast in fervent programs for Christian evangelism and in fervent debate about the rival prescriptions of capitalism and socialism.

Booth undertook his inquiry in this context, with policy and influence in mind, intent on being "scientific"—that is, unbiased and objective—and graphic in his presentation. Along with a businessman's deep respect for numbers, Booth also had a novelist's eye for individual character and detail, and he animated his quantitative treatment with sprightly street scenes and memorable characters, which made his work accessible to a large audience. "Mr. Booth's inquiry," as it came to be called, was well

known long before the complete edition of 1902–03, for he had presented preliminary findings to the Royal Statistical Society in two papers
(1887–1889). When he published the first volume in 1889, it sold out
quickly and was widely reviewed in a "chorus of praise," with only some
negative criticism. Booth was soon elected president of the Royal Statistical Society (1892–1894) and later served on royal commissions investigating social conditions. The universities of Cambridge, Oxford, and
Liverpool all conferred honorary degrees on him, and the government
made him a Privy Councillor.[11]

It has long been thought that Booth was directly inspired to his inquiry by a skeptical reaction to the claims of the Social Democratic Federation, a Marxist group, that one Londoner in four was living in misery.
But if this was not the specific stimulus, the issue of who and how many
the poor were was given new salience in the 1880s, and Booth responded
to this.[12] Within the first two years of his work, he concluded that one
Londoner in three was living in poverty. The London poor were not a
ragtag group of beggars and drunkards who refused to work but instead
comprised well over a million people—a whopping 30.7 percent of the
population—in the richest city in the world. These people were living
below a "Line of Poverty" that Booth quantified as a "regular though
bare" income of eighteen to twenty-one shillings a week for a "moderate"
family. Those he defined as the poor struggled to obtain the necessities
of life; the very poor, who had even less income and less certainty, lived
in a state of "chronic want" or outright "distress."[13] They were poor less
because of drink and depravity, indulgence and improvidence—popular
hypotheses that the problem was one of individual morality rather than
of social or economic conditions—and more because they lacked enough
work or because they were overwhelmed with sickness, debt, injury, or
too many mouths to feed. The efforts of private charities and public authorities to help the poor get back on their feet were largely unavailing,
Booth concluded. As to the churches, their ministry was largely irrelevant to both the material needs and spiritual condition of the poor.[14]

THE BOOTH METHOD: AN EFFORT AT ENUMERATION

Any appraisal of Booth's survey of London inevitably pays tribute to the
sheer size of his inquiry—"monumental" is the relentless adjective—but
his significance for survey research stems more from two of the four volumes of the poverty series than from the seventeen-volume work as a
whole, which encompasses studies of industries and religious influences.

For the seven volumes dealing with religion, Booth found no means of classifying and quantifying the voluminous detail he obtained from interviewing almost 1,800 informants and from the questionnaires of hundreds of other church workers.[15] The volumes abound in colorful vignettes and observations that have their own fascination, but they do not have the definition and classification of the poverty work. For his five volumes on industry, Booth lacked data on individual income, and he was not able to link the aggregate data on the wage structures of industry with the data on household income of his poverty series. As the Simeys have put it, the poverty and industry series were "allowed to run in different directions, the first toward a deeper understanding of the nature of poverty as a social phenomenon, the second nowhere in particular."[16]

It is important to note that Booth's work did not incorporate the new correlation analysis of Karl Pearson and G. Udny Yule, innovations of 1895–99, nor did his data collection incorporate systematic sampling, which Arthur L. Bowley applied to the social survey in 1912–13.[17] By Booth's invention of a *poverty line* and his conversion of it into a poverty map of London, color-coded for eight economic levels, he nevertheless captured in summary form enormous amounts of information. The poverty work alone is indeed deservedly called monumental.

For this work, Booth and his assistants used a variety of methods, consulting existing statistics, conducting interviews with informants, and making countless observations of real conditions. Booth himself became a "participant observer" when he rented a room in the houses of relatively poor Londoners. The most important procedure was what Beatrice Webb called "the method of wholesale interviewing,"[18] in which Booth and his assistants spent enormous numbers of hours in essence interviewing the interviewers, the so-called school board visitors.

The visitors were attendance officers who had visited families personally, many over long periods of time, asking questions and making observations. Booth used the visitors in effect as a field staff. He had not set them to their initial task, so he could not standardize their observations, and he remained dissatisfied that he lacked a fully objective indicator of poverty and had to rely instead on the visitors' opinions. But he had confidence that their opinions were not biased, coming as they did from visitors of every kind of experience and persuasion, and he made persistent efforts to check their impressions against other findings. Collectively, they had great physical coverage as well, encompassing 80 percent of London.[19]

For some 3,400 streets in the East End of London, Booth condensed

the visitors' information into notebooks of standardized format that captured the particulars for each house: the residents' occupations, the
number of occupants per room, the number of children, and the class
category (i.e., income and general situation). Booth defined, classified,
and tabulated the information by individual household. When he expanded his inquiry to London as a whole, he deemed the family-by-fam-
ily inquiry too lavish in time and made notebook entries of a more summary fashion, as shown in the following example:

> Colour for map: purple [meaning a mixture of classes]
> Houses: number scheduled 109; unscheduled 0
> Character: two to eight rooms, let in tenements
> Number of children aged three to thirteen: 231
> Description of street: Struggling poor, mostly casual. Few in regular work.
>   Porters in meat market, slaughtermen, brick. lab. car men, etc.[20]

Booth's concern was with enumerating these social conditions as thoroughly as he could and then replicating the data informally from whatever other sources he could find. Analytically, his method was limited to
simple hypotheses about the extent of poverty and its purported causes
presented in percentage tables, but the quantitative study, with new data
of such great scope, was dramatic and authoritative.

The Rowntree Variations: An Effort at Representative Case Study

When B. Seebohm Rowntree (1871–1954) was inspired directly by
Booth's work to replicate the findings on poverty in 1899, he saw two
choices. One was to conduct an "extensive" study from diverse records
(census, health, charity records, etc.) and to try to assess from them the
incidence of poverty for the whole of the United Kingdom. It would be
better, he decided, to undertake an "intensive" study of a provincial
town, and he chose his native city of York in the judgment that this
"might be taken as fairly representative of the conditions existing in
many, if not most, of our provincial towns."[21] Canvassing the working-
class districts of York was a very substantial labor, but it was feasible. Like
Booth, Rowntree aspired to mass enumeration and internal replication
through the use of multiple methods. He published *Poverty: A Study of
Town Life* in 1901.[22]

   Acknowledging Booth's example and advice, Rowntree divided the
population into income classes, establishing a poverty line, color-coding
the streets for their class levels, drawing a "drink map" that identified all

public houses in the city. Like Booth, Rowntree availed himself of many kinds of information, digging out existing statistics as well as creating new data. For example, he weighed and measured schoolchildren of the working classes; he made new counts of churchgoers all over York on two Sundays; and he also made counts of men, women, and children entering a certain pub every hour from dawn until late at night. He counted privies and middens, measured rooms and yards, evaluated light and air. Somewhat to his surprise, Rowntree found that the incidence of poverty in York was virtually the same as the percentage that Booth had found in London—28 percent in York were "ill-housed, ill-clothed, and under-fed."[23] Rowntree's procedures were close enough to Booth's to convince him that the two estimates were very comparable, but his deviations from Booth's practice made for a leaner treatment of the subject—a single volume, and more incisive.

Rowntree operationalized the poverty line more precisely as the level of income insufficient to buy the necessary food, shelter, and supplies to maintain physical efficiency. Calling especially on bulletins published by the U.S. Department of Agriculture (USDA), Rowntree defined a standard of nutrition that would enable an individual to do moderate physical labor, constructed a model weekly diet that would provide that kind of energy, and then assessed the costs of buying the requisite food (mostly starch). It was an austere regime: it included no fresh meat, as this was much too expensive, and it was thereby more Spartan than the diet provided in local workhouses for able-bodied paupers.[24]

In estimating the necessary "household sundries," including clothes, Rowntree undertook an important second departure from Booth's procedures because he used respondents' own judgments. In this one instance, Rowntree provided the following paraphrase of the question he asked:

What in your opinion is the very lowest sum upon which a man can keep himself in clothing for a year? The clothing should be adequate to keep the man in health, and should not be so shabby as to injure his chances of obtaining respectable employment. Apart from these two conditions, the clothing [is] to be the most economical obtainable.[25]

Rowntree and his helpers obtained information from "a large number of working people," many of whom "knew what poverty meant, and had learnt by hard experience what could be 'done without,' and how to obtain most cheaply that which was absolutely necessary." Rowntree trusted

the validity of their consumer judgments about prices, shopping, durability, and value, but apparently he did not trust the self-report of income, using more regularly his knowledge of averages for a given industry or factory or else employers' figures.[26]

The Changing Word and a Definition

These two studies of poverty at the turn of the century quickly became
well known, classics in their own time, and in England they came to be
called social surveys—at least by the publishers, if not by the authors.[27] If
Rowntree used the term, it was surely only in passing. Booth himself
used the word *survey* essentially to mean *an overview*, which was a standard meaning of the word in English and American dictionaries of the
time.

The verb *sur-vey'* (as well as the noun *sur'-vey*) was derived from Latin
and from the Old French *survoir*, and by the 1600s the word was already
rich with meanings. It meant *seeing over*, in the sense of a broad view or
scan (as in "to stand on a hill and survey the surrounding country," as
Webster put it in his 1838 edition for Americans). It also carried another
(faintly contradictory) extension of the word *oversee*, with the meaning of
examining in detail, scrutinizing close up, inspecting (as well as supervising). There was another connotation, that of counting or measuring, establishing value or extent. A survey of agriculture counted acreage,
crops, orchards, livestock, farm buildings, and fences. One might make
a survey of a ship's stores or munitions; of roads or bridges; or of land,
seacoasts, and harbors, to measure the surface of the earth.[28]

In Booth's time, the survey did not specify or imply specific modes or
instruments of data gathering, such as interviews or questionnaires. Indeed, as we have seen, the early social surveys used a mélange of techniques—the more the better—to gather data: questionnaire, interview,
letter, direct observation, participant observation, systematic counts of
observed behaviors, physical examination and measurement of houses
and human beings; family budgets of income and expenditure; and aggregate data on population, migration, births and deaths, health and disease, wages, and prices.

The word *survey* was nevertheless an apt one for both Booth's and
Rowntree's work, because their activity reflected three meanings that
had become conventional. First, their work had scope and mass in an
overview, or comprehensive vision, of the whole. Second, it involved the

detailed examination of particulars—the profusion of cases and the individual observations or answers. And finally, the overview was composed from the details by counting, or measuring. To put it still another way, the two conducted surveys because they collected brief case histories in great abundance, and by classifying and counting them they converted the detail into quantitative summaries that provided the comprehensive view. A survey therefore counted cases—*many* cases, enough to provide a view of the whole. This, then, is the Booth tradition of surveys.

The survey tradition is also sometimes traced to the work of Frédéric Le Play (1806–82), the French mining engineer who conducted studies in family budgets, systematic observation, and personal interviewing almost a half-century before Booth and Rowntree did their work.[29] The Le Play family monograph stands as a better example of the case study, however, designed to be "representative" of a whole class of families in a given region or nation. The approach of Le Play and his followers was "intensive," as they obtained copious detail about a family's income and expenditures (as well as their health, religion and conventions, family history, etc.) by living with the family for days or weeks and filling out an exhaustive schedule of observations and questions. Le Play aspired to grand design in studying and understanding all of society through the income and outgo of the individual family economy, in a scheme classifying types of societies and types of workers. His six-volume work *Les Ouvriers Européens*, first published in 1855, inspires the adjective *monumental*, just as Booth's does, not only because of the number of volumes but also, perhaps, because Le Play planned 300 family monographs. He may have actually conducted that many himself, although he published only 36 in the first edition of *Les Ouvriers* and 57 in the second.[30]

In later European practice, the instrument of the household budget itself usually featured a continuous record kept over a period of time. In the United States, the income-outgo record was more often recalled and reported to a survey interviewer. The family budget method—not the Le Play monographs, but the income/expenditure record—was used widely in the United States from 1869 on and had a strong impact on government statistics, especially in the construction of cost-of-living indices.[31] Here we shall consider the family budget not as a method entirely distinct from a survey but as one of the instruments by which survey data have been gathered.

The word *survey* is sometimes used so vaguely and broadly as to cover almost the whole empirical waterfront of social science, and it is confus-

ing to stretch the definition that far. Surveys can be distinguished fairly
clearly by where they are collected and how they are organized. First,
surveys are conducted with a strong sense of place; they are taken *out
there*, in the field, among real-world events and people. This feature
serves to distinguish surveys from laboratory experiments, which bring
situations and people in to an artificial environment that permits controlled conditions, and from clinical interviews, which are usually conducted in the professional's setting, not the client's.

Second, surveys are now distinguishable from the whole general class
of statistical data because they are permanently organized and analyzed
by the individual record. The individual in question is most often an individual human being, but it need not be, either in principle or in practice. It can be an *individual something else*—a school board, a highway accident, a community, a two-person friendship, a family, a corporation, or
(most often) a household—and still be a piece of survey data, if the data
are collected for each unit and the integrity of the individual record is
maintained.

At the risk of belaboring the obvious, it may help to offer an imaginary example: "The average milk consumption of residents of the Denver metropolitan area is 0.83 glasses per day." Is this an estimate based
on survey data? There is no way of telling, as the answer depends on the
unit of analysis. If milk sale figures were obtained from dairies or industry associations, duly totaled, and then divided by the number of Denver
residents, the results are aggregate, not survey, data. If, however, reports
of milk drinking were obtained from an enumeration or a sample of
Denver residents and a mean was calculated from the total consumption
reported, we would indeed consider the results to be survey data.

Grouped and individual data offer very different advantages.
Grouped data are generally much cheaper to collect, for in principle it
would not be impossible to determine the rate of "0.83 glasses per day"
through a telephone call or two to a dairy association. But these data
would soon be exhausted. Individual data, however, would be much
richer to analyze. As expensive as it would be to find the required Denver residents to ask them about their milk drinking, one would surely
stay out in the field long enough to ask them about many other things as
well, which would provide the stuff of additional variables and analysis.

Nowadays, to the general public and to some scholars it is probably
the interview that is a chief defining characteristic of surveys. But the
more basic property is the organization of data by individual record. In-

dividual data can be gathered in the familiar forms of the (structured) interview, the written questionnaire, or other written forms distributed in person or by mail, in which respondents are asked questions. Individual data can also be gathered by an investigator making systematic observations or taking measurements, without necessarily asking questions of persons at all, or by combinations of these forms. By this definition, the survey is a very general term that includes census enumerations and opinion polling and does not necessarily involve sampling. Historically, a *sample* survey is a relatively new variant.

To summarize the general definition and the early technical practice, we can say that at the turn of the century the survey already had the following features:

Fieldwork: The survey was conducted in the natural world of events, objects, and people rather than exclusively in the artificial or "arranged" world of the laboratory or clinic or in the statistical world of existing records.

Scope: The survey undertook comprehensive coverage of some domain, providing an overview of the whole.

Detail: The survey's overview was based on the examination of detailed cases.

Quantification: At least some of the detail was summarized by quantifying some of the case material.

Individual unit of analysis: Data were collected, organized, and analyzed by individual records.

These five characteristics link the social surveys of Booth and Rowntree at the turn of the century to the American survey research that took shape thirty to forty years later. But the English social surveys were actually less defined and more catholic in their tastes, using not only field data but statistical records as well, not just individual records but also aggregate data—they used, in fact, everything the surveyors could think of to achieve that "overview." Some of the early American versions of the English social survey did the same thing. In one important American translation the survey was nothing less than a whole social movement dedicated to putting science ("the facts") in the service of social reform. The survey as a specific technical instrument evolved in the United

States in a second stage, as the social survey movement itself evolved politically and intellectually.

The American Social Survey

The Social Survey as a Community Reform Movement

The social survey in the style of Booth generated publicity and imitation
in American reform circles of philanthropy, settlement-house work, and
Progressive politics. Just as in England, there was mounting concern in
the United States about the effects of industrialism and urbanization.
This concern was heightened by the great immigrations from abroad
and by the streams of migrants to the city from the American farm. Misery of new visibility in the crowding of city slums and in the harsh conditions of factories evoked the beginning of both the Social Gospel of
Protestantism and the political movement of the Progressives. There was
agitation for ameliorative legislation and regulation, the ferment of
"muckraking" journalism, and a continued outpouring of articles and
books, such as Campbell's *Prisoners of Poverty*, Riis's *How the Other Half
Lives* and *Children of the Poor*, and Hunter's *Poverty*.[32] Booth's study of the
London poor spoke to an aroused audience of activists in the United
States. Soon after the publication of the first volumes of his poverty series, the work was reviewed enthusiastically in such American magazines
as *Nation, Outlook*, and *Century Magazine* and in such scholarly journals as
the *Annals of the American Academy of Political and Social Science* and the *Political Science Quarterly*.[33] Certain reformers and social scientists set out to
apply Booth's methods to document the facts of American poverty.

The *Hull House Maps and Papers of 1895* was an early such effort.
Working cooperatively with a federal investigation of slums in large cities, Hull House workers went door-to-door in a small section of Chicago,
constructing from their data maps of nationality and wages and a series
of articles. They took pride in their kinship with Booth's study:

> The great interest and significance attached to Mr. Charles Booth's maps
> of London have served as warm encouragement; and although the eyes of the
> world do not centre upon this third of a square mile in the heart of Chicago
> as upon East London when looking for the very essence of misery, and al-
> though the ground examined here is very circumscribed compared with the
> vast area covered by Mr. Booth's incomparable studies, the two works have
> much in common.[34]

In the next year, 1896, the sociologist W. E. B. DuBois undertook, almost single-handedly, a study of the Philadelphia Negro, in a prodigious labor that was even closer to Booth's survey. DuBois acknowledged the influence of both Booth and Hull House. Like Booth, DuBois immersed himself in the life of the city, living in the black section, attending meetings and churches, conducting systematic observations, counting, tabulating, and integrating new data with historical records, vital statistics, and census data. He also obtained field data from a house-to-house canvass of a central district in the city that historically had been the center of the Negro population. Using six different kinds of schedules—for family, individual, home, street, institution, and house servants—DuBois ordered data into many tables and also into many effective colored maps, in the Booth manner. The canvass put DuBois in contact with nearly 10,000 residents of the central ward, about a quarter of the city's black population.[35]

The examples of Booth and Rowntree were of importance to American activists, who made of the American survey a more sprawling affair of community participation than their predecessors had done in England.[36] The survey movement in the United States became a vehicle for bringing reformers, scientists, and citizens together to take stock of their communities' living and working conditions (as in Booth's *Life and Labour*) and for designing programs for improvement. "Surveys" were undertaken to study both a community as a whole and a wide range of conditions and institutions, such as schools, nutrition, sanitation, housing, recreation, wages, unemployment, registrations of births and deaths, crime, vice, and so on. The studies were carried out by civic volunteer groups, church organizations, local and state government agencies, social scientists and their students.[37]

The social survey as a community reform movement began to flourish with the Pittsburgh Survey, of which Paul Kellogg, a journalist and social worker, was director. The Pittsburgh Survey proceeded from a journalistic venture of the new magazine *Charities and The Commons*, which had come into existence through a merger in 1905 of the *Charities* magazine of the New York Charity Organization and *The Commons*, a publication of the Chicago settlement-house movement. Now representing a more national scope, the new magazine sought a way of getting more national publicity and coverage, and in 1906 it published a piece on slum conditions in Washington. The article inspired some Pittsburgh citizens to request a similar feature on their city.[38] Thanks to various funds, especially those from the newly founded Russell Sage Foundation, the Pittsburgh

Survey was launched in 1907. This was not a house-to-house canvass or
questionnaire study of city residents. Rather, it was an effort to provide
an inventory and an overview of the state of the city, for which the investigators were omnivorous in their methods of data collection. Within a
few years, the survey published six volumes on investigations into the
steel industry, housing, family life, typhoid, child-helping institutions,
and other major social studies.[39]

THE SPREAD OF THE MOVEMENT AND COMMUNITY PARTICIPATION

The survey experience was important enough to the people who directed it in Pittsburgh that they changed the name of the magazine with
which they had been affiliated: in April 1909, *Charities and The Commons*
was rechristened *The Survey*.[40] *Charities* harked back, the survey directors
felt, to a tarnished image of a "Lady Bountiful" dispensing baskets of
alms to the "deserving" poor and dispensing adages of moral reform to
the "undeserving" who were given to drink, vice, and extravagance.

In 1912, Kellogg wrote with satisfaction that the survey movement
was burgeoning beyond the capacity of existing organizations and
professionals to deal with it. After Pittsburgh, there had been an important survey in Buffalo of the Polish section, paid for by the city itself; a
quick overview of the state of Kentucky; a series of community surveys in
Rhode Island and New Jersey; and a set of specialized surveys in Syracuse. Churches, especially the central board at the Presbyterian Church,
were conducting surveys of church and material resources in several
states, and sociologists were surveying the rural community.[41]

Also in 1912, the Russell Sage Foundation set up the Department of
Surveys and Exhibits to help in organizing and publicizing the surveys
and in eliciting community participation. The Pittsburgh Survey had
capped its efforts with an exhibition in the Carnegie Institute in the winter of 1908, featuring wall maps, enlarged photographs, housing plans,
and other pictorial displays. Combined with information from other cities, the Pittsburgh exhibits were taken on tour to several cities. The efforts to make the Springfield Survey of 1914 an educational experience
for the community were still more massive. More than 900 local volunteers helped to mount the exhibit, which was held in the armory for ten
days. The exhibit was prefaced by promotional activity of all sorts—a
"survey question box" in the state *Register*, essay contests, leaflets carried
by children, free transportation to the show. Some 15,000 people attended.[42]

Sociologist Carl C. Taylor wrote approvingly in 1919 that "the ultimate form" of the survey exhibit would undoubtedly include the *pageant*. With such a highly dramatic piece of technology, he wrote,

> the community surveyed and the social workers and citizens of the community will for the first time see a . . . community in miniature . . . pass before their eyes . . . the actual interwoven, living tensions, forces and factors of their common life even more distinctly than the expert investigators saw it at the beginning of their investigation. When this stage is reached, as it surely will be, scientific knowledge and social consciousness will have become mutual cause and effect.[43]

Changing the community's consciousness was indeed the ultimate aim. The social workers and other social scientists who became committed to the survey approach believed that participation of the community was essential. By participating in gathering, publicizing, and dramatizing the facts, citizens were to become sensitized to the problems of their community and aroused to undertake a program for their solution.

THE COUNTRY LIFE MOVEMENT

The survey movement for improving towns and cities had a counterpart in the Country Life Movement. Reformers in the Progressive era were concerned with stemming the tide of migration to the cities, not only because it threatened more waves of urban crowding, poverty, and squalor but also because it endangered "the rural way of life." They worried that urban migration was sweeping from the American farm the more ambitious, the more intelligent, and the young. The Progressive reformers had various prescriptions for revitalizing country life: making farming practice more efficient through machine cultivation and cooperative marketing practices; reducing the drudgery and isolation of farm life by providing rural electrification, running water, roads, and mail delivery; making the rural school and church new centers of social organization and culture; and trying to combine farming with village life to make a new form, "rurban" life.[44]

The Progressives valued nature, the land, and the yeomanry as sources of social stability, family life, and strong individual character. The reformers were largely urban themselves, and they were sometimes mocked in political cartoons as trying to milk cows in their Prince Albert coats and top hats. But the leadership had come from farm backgrounds and had strong personal attachment to maintaining and improving the rural life they remembered, valued, and, to a certain extent, sentimentalized.[45] The Country Life Movement was not entirely without rural representation, however, especially through the state agricultural experiment stations and extension work and probably to a modest extent through some rural churches. In an effort not only to improve agricultural yields but also to sustain the rural community and improve farm life, scientists in the experiment stations and agricultural colleges gathered voluminous quantities of survey data in the 1910s and 1920s.

The Country Life Movement started around the turn of the century, but it received a special impetus in 1907 (the same year that the Pittsburgh Survey started its work), when President Theodore Roosevelt began to organize the Country Life Commission. This commission was chaired by Liberty Hyde Bailey, then dean of the New York State College of Agriculture at Cornell University (1903–1914). For more than a decade, Bailey had been practicing and preaching the need to broaden the state agricultural experiments beyond work with plants and animals (for greater yields, control of pests, soil enrichment, etc.) to include surveys in agricultural conditions and practice. As he wrote in 1908, there was need of a "thorough-going study of the exact agricultural status of every state," including the study not only of crops, soil conditions, drainage, waterpower, and livestock but also of the educational and social conditions of rural life. Bailey had conducted attitude surveys to gather information about the farm situation.[46]

Bailey and his colleagues on the commission wanted to do a "detailed survey," but there was neither time nor money.[47] Instead, they held hearings and meetings in thirty different places and sent out a "circular" to some 550,000 rural residents. They received well over 100,000 replies and many additional letters, which they had encouraged. Their questionnaire may well have been the first quality-of-life study done with individual subjective indicators—or at least the first such study of this magnitude—and it tried to track satisfaction with twelve realms of farm life with these questions:

> I. Are the farm homes in your neighborhood as good as they should be under existing conditions?
> II. Are the schools in your neighborhood training boys and girls satisfactorily for life on the farm?
> III. Do the farmers in your neighborhood get the returns they reasonably should from the sale of their products?
> IV. Do the farmers in your neighborhood receive from the railroads, highroads, trolley lines, etc., the services they reasonably should have?

V. Do the farmers in your neighborhood receive from the United States postal service, rural telephones, etc., the service they reasonably should expect?

VI. Are the farmers and their wives in your neighborhood satisfactorily organized to promote their mutual buying and selling interest?

VII. Are the renters of farms in your neighborhood making a satisfactory living?

VIII. Is the supply of farm labor in your neighborhood satisfactory?

IX. Are the conditions surrounding hired labor on the farms in your neighborhood satisfactory to the hired man?

X. Have the farmers in your neighborhood satisfactory facilities for doing their business in banking, credit, insurance, etc?

XI. Are the sanitary conditions of farms in your neighborhood satisfactory?

XII. Do the farmers and their wives and families in your neighborhood get together for mutual improvement, entertainment, and social intercourse as much as they should?

And a final question:

What, in your judgment, is the most important single thing to be done for the general betterment of country life?[48]

In 1908, many farm families expressed dissatisfaction with the economic arrangements of farming and with the rural schools provided for their children. Women, especially, also scored the social isolation and the lack of modern sanitation and labor-saving conveniences, such as running water. Although the commission did learn this much from its questionnaires, which were tabulated by the Census Bureau, it was prevented from learning much more—as well as from doing anything. Congress swiftly put it out of business by failing to appropriate even the $25,000 that President Roosevelt had requested to enable the commission to finish its data collection and prepare a more thorough report. The Secretary of Agriculture, James ("Tama Jim") Wilson, had taken particular umbrage at the commission's inquiry because it had bypassed the department and was interpreted as a political threat. Wilson feared that it aimed to replace him in the next Republican administration (that of President Taft), which was just taking office when the commission made its preliminary report in 1909. He demanded that the questionnaires be filed with the Department of Agriculture, and some were duly delivered. Later, during Woodrow Wilson's presidency, another Secretary of Agriculture had the questionnaires burned as useless.[49]

The Country Life Commission of 1908–09 was thwarted, but Congress and the Department of Agriculture echoed some of its recommendations in improvements for rural life and in greater appropriations to the states for experiment stations and extension activities.[50] At least as early as 1915, the department undertook its own quality-of-life studies, especially of farm women.[51] In 1919, a new section for research into rural life was created in the department under the direction of Charles J. Galpin, a leading rural sociologist who advocated "rurbanism." (This research section was named the Division of Farm Population and Rural Life, and social surveyor/sociologist Carl C. Taylor was a longtime director.)[52] In 1924, the Purnell Act gave federal support to expanding experiment-station research into sociological surveys and attitude studies.[53]

The surveys of farming were broadly of three types. In one, data on acreage, crops, yields, and so on were gathered by mail from large sets of voluntary crop reporters.[54] In another, the "surveys of farm management," agricultural agents went to farms to gather data from farmers' records or recollections.[55] A third kind of survey dealt with farm living, including not only housing, sanitation, and health but also activities, time budgets, preferences, attitudes, and opinions. For example, how much time did the women spend carrying water and tending kerosene lamps? How many miles did farm men walk behind crude farm implements? How many farm families had radios, books, and magazines, and how much time did they spend in such leisure activities? What did farm youth do for recreation? Did farm families go to church? What kind of social life did they have?[56]

All these subjects were of interest to Congress, which put a good deal of legislation into the service of sustaining American families on the farm. They were of interest to manufacturers of farm machinery and labor-saving conveniences, as well as to advertisers and publishers looking to the rural market.[57] They were also of interest to religious leaders who looked to the rural church as a source of community organization, and to social scientists, especially rural sociologists and agriculturalists, who conducted much of this research. An American Country Life Association, formed just after the First World War, in 1919, attracted rural sociologists and ministers especially and published its annual proceedings as well as a monthly magazine, *Rural America*, for decades. In 1936, a new journal called *Rural Sociology* provided a new vehicle of communication and publication for rural specialists. Some of its contributors had by this time taken their professional and human concern for rural life—now devastated by the Great Depression—into survey work for the New Deal, which we shall turn to shortly. But first we shall consider briefly one more dramatic development of the survey movement.

The most extravagant ambitions to emerge from the survey movement were those advanced by the Interchurch World Movement. This was a large coalition of 140 different boards, representing about thirty-five Protestant denominations. Formed in the United States after World War I, with the financial blessings of John D. Rockefeller, Jr., the coalition had as its purpose no less than a survey of the world—it aimed to "undertake a scientific survey of the world's needs from the standpoint of the responsibility of evangelical Christianity" and then to develop a program to meet those needs. Surveying the world was not going to be cheap. A World Survey Conference in 1920 projected a tentative budget for the whole movement, to be provided by the participating denominations for five years' work, of over $1.3 billion.[58]

Within the first year the grandiose plans were under way. In each state of the union, a full-time paid executive was functioning to select and train personnel who would conduct a survey in every county of that state. While some experienced surveyors joined in the task, roughly three-quarters of the state supervisors were clergymen who at one time or another had been rural ministers. They were conversant with the rural church environment, surely, but were not experienced in surveying that milieu. The county supervisors were generally younger ministers, schoolteachers, professors, or graduate students who took the survey work for academic credit in sociology courses. In 1920–21, a survey was in progress in more than 2,400 of the nation's 3,000 counties.[59]

The project was an enormous effort to apply *sociological* concepts to the study of community and church, an extension of the survey's focus on the community to a national and international scale. The fact that the surveyor was to define the community as a trade center rather than as an administrative unit complicated the data-gathering task, because census data and other statistics were not available for a community defined in this way. Much information had to be dug up anew. The surveyor of a given community was equipped with a questionnaire prepared by a conference of thirty experts. While most of the questions seem not to have survived, we do know a few of the questions along with the general scope of their content. Surveyors were to gather data on the following subjects: the major industries and agricultural activities of the community; the condition of the roads; the facts of taxation; school administration, financing, and attendance; the presence and conditions of other institutions, such as hospitals, asylums, and homes for the aged; and the community's material resources, social organization, leadership, and participation, as well as those of the churches. There was also a section on the "social mind" of the community. Certain questions from that section, such as "Do all the people of the community mingle together freely without class distinction?" and "Is the moral tone of this community improving?" were dropped from a later effort to salvage some of the Interchurch work because it was thought that these focused too much on "opinion" and "too little on fact."[60] The surveyors' task was indeed imposing.

According to the sociologist Edmund De S. Brunner, who worked on the project, Interchurch workers surrendered to the seductive argument (which will sound very familiar to contemporary survey researchers) "As long as we are getting so much information, we might just as well get this too," and they produced a huge survey schedule numbering more than 500 questions.[61] But length was not the only issue; standardization was another, probably the much more formidable, one. Gathering information of this scope would have taxed the statistical resources of any community and the ferreting ability of even the best-trained surveyors. As it was, the task was beyond the capability of many of the survey teams, and a good half of the data collected proved to be almost useless, insufficiently standardized or coherent with other data to warrant even initial tabulation, much less further study. The administrative problems of data collection were massive, but the movement as a whole came to a virtual collapse from the force of political controversy, denominational splits, and financial overextension. Finally, in 1924, the directors filed for voluntary dissolution of the association, a denouement that the *Literary Digest* captioned "Cooperation's Greatest Failure."[62]

In 1921, a committee had been formed to salvage what it could of the Interchurch surveys. The committee soon became the Institute of Social and Religious Research (ISRR) and was funded by John D. Rockefeller until 1934, when it went out of existence. ISRR published some of the Interchurch data: a monograph on each of three counties, and a larger volume, *The Town and Country Church in the United States* (1923), which used data surviving from 5,500 churches in 1,979 counties. Regrettably enough, however, the vast schedules that proved so ponderous to administer were deemed too lengthy to publish.[63]

During its fourteen years, ISRR sponsored about 75 research projects, from which some 100 publications were developed. While church studies still bulked large, a sizable minority of the publications dealt with other topics, such as rural sociology, race relations, and education. ISRR supported some landmark projects, notably the Lynds' *Middletown*, the Hartshorne-May Character Education studies, and the Race Relations Survey on the West Coast.[64] Professional social scientists dominated the research of this new organization, whereas ministers had provided most of the Interchurch personnel, and it thus marks a transition between the reformist social survey and social scientists' social research. Robert E. Park, in fact, who was director of the so-called Race Relations Survey, broke with ISRR when his dispassionate approach proved unacceptable to the reform goals of the sponsors.[65] In several publications, ISRR presented methods of the reformist social survey, and in other work it reflected new currents in sociology and psychology that showed a sensitivity and awareness of scientific measurement.[66]

The Protean Survey "Method"

In 1957, many years after the social survey movement had waned, Brunner noted that rural sociologists' first research studies "used the survey method in its simplest form":

> They went to the field, asked questions and tabulated answers. The universe was usually a single community, all households were enumerated, and the product was statistically oriented and descriptive.[67]

This kind of survey does not seem to have been that general. Brunner's own surveys included examples in which households were not enumerated and data about the community were gathered principally from expert informants. Many of his contemporaries took it for granted that what they were doing was "the survey method," but they were doing different things.

First, the term *survey method* was used to refer rather grandly to the surveyors' use of *"the" scientific method* as they gathered "the facts." The context here was that of science as a form of knowledge, constructed of hard, objective measurements rather than of slippery opinions, private emotions or intuitions, or exaggerated political hopes. As Shelby Harrison later put it, surveys were to provide the "correcting power of facts, which must be gathered as carefully and faithfully as the truth-loving scientists in any field gathers them."[68]

A second, quite different application of survey methods was that of *community organizing*. In Kellogg's summary of what was signal and distinct about the Pittsburgh Survey, he listed six "methods," the first and last of which dealt with the division of labor between imported expert and native community participation. Professional investigators were brought in first to cooperate with local leaders and then, at the last, the professionals turned over the reins to local people to carry the work into the future, especially in institutional and legislative change.[69]

To other surveyors, survey methods meant a third aspect, namely the *topic or subject matter* along the lines of which the factual inquiries were to be conducted. M. C. Elmer developed his University of Chicago dissertation on social surveys into a handbook, *Technique of Social Surveys*, published in 1917. It set forth the committees that should be formed after preliminary investigations, the additional lines of inquiry, and ways of encouraging local volunteer participation. The great bulk of the book presented the topics of information that comprehensive surveys should pursue to provide a social diagnosis.[70]

The methods that social surveys had on hand for the task of making the empirical translation—methods in the fourth sense, that of *instruments of data collection* or *procedures of data analysis*—were actually quite modest as we see the matter now. Analyzing or interpreting data was rather a vague proposition at the time. Elmer had counseled his readers in *Technique of Social Surveys* to delve into two great stocks of information: the official statistics of the Census, health records, prison rolls, school records, and reports of state boards and commissions (the list of possibilities soon grew large); and the unofficial data gathered from organizational records and reports, interviews with officials, and relevant laws at every level.[71] How to select and organize this information, however, was not a rich subject of explication (although Elmer was himself an experienced surveyor). With some exceptions, the procedures were apparently seen as those of intelligent common sense, not warranting much detailed explanation.

By 1929, George A. Lundberg, not a surveyor but a sociologist very interested in quantitative methods, contended that there was no such thing as a "survey method":

> Since the form of inquiry known as the social survey is nothing but a more or less closely coordinated series of investigations or researches into related problems, all methods and principles of observing and recording data . . . may properly be applied to the survey.[72]

While it is surely fair to say, with Lundberg, that the social survey was not in itself a method of measurement or analysis—it was a patchwork of different kinds of data, collected by different means and processed in different ways—it is nevertheless true that the social surveyors did use certain instruments of choice (especially, the schedule and the scorecard) for the creation of new data in the field and worked to improve their design.

INSTRUMENTS OF DATA COLLECTION

The basic instrument for creating new data was the *schedule* (or *card* or *blank*). This listed topics of information, rather than fully worded questions, which were often designed to be answered with a check mark or a number:

Was the house of stone ____ brick ____
wood ____ shack ____?
Number of rooms? ____ windows ____ occupants ____
lights ____ privies ____ toilets ____
connections to sewers ____
Number of outbuildings ____
Number of stock animals ____[73]

And the physical facilities were appraised in considerably more detail.

Some surveyors aspired to an inventory of cultural life as well, as excerpts of this home card show:

6. Number Papers: Daily ____ Local ____ Others ____
Number Magazines ____
Number Books in Library ____
7. Musical Instruments: Piano ____ Organ ____
Phonograph ____ Others ____
8. Games: Card Games ____ Caroms ____ Checkers ____
Dominos ____ Number Toys ____
9. Athletic Equipment: Swing ____ Punching Bag ____
Football ____ Baseball ____ Tennis ____ Other ____
14. Number Chickens ____ Horses ____ Cows ____ Autos ____
15. Pets (number): Cats ____ Dogs ____ Rabbits ____
Others ____
(To be filled by visitor) House ____ Yard ____
Interior ____[74]

The primary function of the schedule was to systematize the survey-or's own observations and, whenever possible, to render them quantita-tive, free of that "personal equation" that surveyors were at pains to avoid. F. Stuart Chapin, a statistically sophisticated and influential soci-ologist of the time, was one who saw in the schedule an analogy to the telescope and the spectroscope for increasing both the range and the de-tail of social observation.[75] Some of this detail will strike contemporary readers as sheer fussiness, as in this checklist for clothing:

    spotted ____ dusty ____ torn ____ worn ____
    patched ____ mussed ____ wrinkled ____

But the social surveyors were nothing if not earnest about trying to es-tablish the facts. And Chapin's point was that qualitative generalities and judgments could be specified with a "tolerable degree of objectivity."[76]

The *schedule* in the hands of the social surveyors was an instrument for making observations *or* for conducting interviews with respondents, or a mixture of both. It was an all-purpose term that we have inherited and modified as *interview schedule*. Surveyors also made use of interviews in two other ways: (1) informant-interviews, by which facts were ob-tained about conditions in a community, business, agency, or church, and (2) case-history interviews, which were gathered and then counted and compared along some dimensions, thus providing a "casemounting" that represented a merger of the case study and statistical methods.[77]

Scorecards were another effort to quantify with indices that would per-mit standardization and comparison. John R. Commons (on the staff of the Pittsburgh Survey and later a distinguished political economist) de-vised a Dwelling House Score Card, published in 1908, which featured a maximum of 100 possible points by the weighting of points added and subtracted for desirable and undesirable features. This method of quan-tifying qualitative observations, now so familiar in rating athletic and ar-tistic competitions, was one that Commons borrowed from ratings used for stock animals, and it was apparently new to social science.[78] At least, in 1920 Chapin treated this and the C. A. Perry scorecard "Measure of the Manner of Living" (published in 1913) as innovations in measure-ment. (Chapin's own socioeconomic status scale derived from the same tradition of interviewer observations.)[79] Scorecards came into use for rat-ing sanitary conditions, neighborhoods, health conditions, schools, play-ground and recreational facilities, prison conditions, and many other topics, including church facilities and functioning.[80]

THE ISSUE OF SAMPLING

Bowley's application of sampling theory to the survey does not seem to have had much impact on actual practice in the United States until the 1930s.[81] Chapin's 1920 text made use of Bowley's 1910 text on statistics and his 1915 social survey, and it presented in brief form a treatment of sampling error and some brief rules for stratified and random sampling. But even his conceptualization of sampling as a method of field investigation intermediate between the casework technique appropriate to the individual and the complete enumeration suitable for study of the entire community left the vague inference that enumeration was still the more perfect form.[82]

Certain American surveyors were sensitive to the problem of generalizing or estimating from their data collection. In the Pittsburgh Survey, for example, Byington collected family budget data with an awareness of the problem of bias—underrepresenting families who did not have the skill or intelligence to keep their own household accounts—and provided assistance to those who could not carry out the task. Other surveyors sought "typical" conditions in a "typical" city, as in the case of Springfield. The "partial canvass" was a still more common form of purposive sampling, a house-to-house canvass of a portion of the city selected to be "representative" of *something*.[83] Kellogg and other major writers on "survey methods," such as Aronovici, Elmer, and Fry, recommended this as a practical measure for cities with slender budgets for their surveys *and* as a political strategy for remaining credible and persuasive by sampling "good and bad conditions alike, the well-to-do, the middling-to-do, and the poor."[84] Activists in the Country Life Movement felt some of the same tension. They wanted the grave problems of farm life to be understood and acted upon politically, but they also wanted to dramatize the good things of farm life and attract people back to the family farm.[85] Real advances in the application of sampling to the survey were not made in the early local reform movements. Statisticians, as well as sociologists and psychologists who were statistically trained, made applications later, especially in surveys conducted by the federal government.

THE DECLINE OF THE LOCAL MOVEMENT

Social surveys were conducted in profusion before the Great Depression. The Russell Sage bibliography of surveys is often cited to make that point, for the authors located no fewer than 2,775 different studies that had been published by January 1, 1928 (most of those collected were published between 1907 and 1928). More than 150 general or community social surveys were located, mostly in the United States, with a few as far afield as Peking, Constantinople, and Prague. The great majority of the citations were "specialized" surveys on topics ranging from alms, blindness, and charities to vice, wages, and zoning, with surveys of schools the most numerous topic of all.[86] Many of these surveys were carried out without the éclat, evangelism, or community participation of the Pittsburgh or Springfield variety, being factual investigations conducted by individual or small groups of economists, sociologists, social workers, or other professionals working in state or local government agencies or in colleges. These surveys provided not only facts for liberal reform politics but also basic statistical information for state and local units of government.

The Russell Sage bibliography definition of a *survey* was the broad one of the era that swept in virtually all kinds of empirical investigations. As an estimate of survey research in the narrower sense of individual data gathered in the field, this bibliography is surely an underestimate, for it gives only very partial coverage to the vast number of such surveys conducted by members of the state agricultural experiment stations and agricultural colleges noted in Bercaw's bibliography. Nor does it overlap entirely with items of the comparable period listed in Faith Williams's annotated bibliography *Studies of Family Living in the United States* (1935), which is dominated by surveys.[87] As a fact-gathering operation, the social survey indeed spread all over the land.

As a movement in applied science, the social survey presents some failures and some successes. The Interchurch Survey clearly came to grief, for example, but it took another, more modest form in its successor organization, ISRR, which sponsored some durable social research. The Country Life Movement failed to prevail against the forces of an industrializing, mechanized agriculture that ultimately overwhelmed the family farm and relentlessly reduced the farm population—in fact, certain wings of that movement actually contributed to the process. However, it created data that aided in the political process of upgrading rural life, especially in the provision of rural health facilities, the consolidation of rural schools, the building of roads, and the extension of mail service. It also provided a vehicle of professional organization for rural sociologists, some of whom continued in the broader national studies of rural life during the depression.[88]

The fervor of the Progressive movement was interrupted by the First

World War. By the end of the 1920s the local movement was swamped by the Great Depression, which diminished the supply of funds from the local community as well as support from national organizations and foundations. In 1929, the Russell Sage Foundation provided advisory help in forty to fifty cities in the United States; in the next two years, the number fell to below thirty.[89] The American farm sector was devastated by the Great Depression because it had not fully recovered from the depression of 1920–22, which hit when foreign agriculture had recovered from the war and became competitive once again. Funds available to the experiment stations shrank, just as all other funds did.[90]

The Great Depression demonstrated dramatically that the enormous magnitude of certain social problems—most notably, unemployment, migration for jobs, and the need for relief—dwarfed the resources of a single community. As Steiner observed,

> The futility of perfecting local administrative machinery when our whole economic structure seemed to be breaking down has stood out as an inescapable fact which saps the enthusiasm of local leaders. Communities alone seem powerless to stem the tide of approaching economic disaster.[91]

During the first two years of the depression, local communities were expected to undertake the burden of providing emergency unemployment relief, a task that proved to be far beyond their capacity. As state and federal resources were mobilized, especially the Federal Emergency Relief Administration (FERA), local practice was governed by federal policy.

The interpretation of some activists was that the social survey declined because the seductive wiles of the "sociological charmer" had lured social surveyors from their rightful path of social diagnosis into social research for science's sake.[92] The decline of the movement was probably affected much more by national political and economic factors. But, indeed, prominent academic sociologists such as Park and Burgess had withdrawn from the evangelism of the survey movement.[93] Chicago sociologists still conducted so-called surveys, but these were now studies in human ecology. Students were sent into the "city as a laboratory" to study hoboes, ghetto dwellers, and rooming-house residents as well as the distribution of gangs, vice areas, and suicides. The intention was not activist, and a basic handbook for conducting social research in the University of Chicago style tried to dissociate these "sociological" surveys from the social survey.[94] This was indeed part of an effort by sociologists to carve out a disciplinary area of scientific inquiry which was distinct from the immediate reform purposes of social workers.[95]

The social survey slowed as a local movement, but it had generated great quantities of social data. While the surveys were fragmented in small, local studies and were utterly unequal to the tasks of national inquiry, estimates, or planning, they were of use in the local, state, and regional domains as basic descriptive statistics that had not been gathered before. Social scientists continued to participate in a successor to the social survey movement when they were employed in the burgeoning New Deal agencies as economists, sociologists, demographers, and statisticians. Their highly applied research projects were concerned with the same fact-finding for social diagnosis, now in a wider canvass and with greater urgency. Some of the utopian hopes for applied social science of the Progressive era were echoed in the New Deal, as fact-finding for policy decisions flourished with national initiatives and federal funds disbursed to state projects. Writing in the 1960s, Loomis and Loomis recalled the fervor of researchers who were especially concerned with the desperate plight of the farmers:

> Present-day uses of studies continue their day-to-day usefulness to government, but nothing in today's governmental scene equals in urgency the record set in the depression years of the 1930s for utilization of social science. . . . Perhaps only the urgency of the civil-rights movement now matches what many rural sociologists saw then as their mission.[96]

The American Sample Survey

Surveys in the Federal Government

The Hoover administration (1929–1933) determined that there was a need to gather information about the economic and social conditions of the whole nation.[97] In 1929 the president called upon a group of social scientists to consider national social trends in the United States. Under the chairmanship of the economist Wesley C. Mitchell and the staff direction of the sociologists Ogburn and Odum, the group put together a two-volume report. Contributors included some of those active in the social survey movement, such as Fry, Kolb, Woofter, Steiner, and Odum. By the time the committee had published *Recent Social Trends* in 1933, the Hoover administration had been turned out of office. The successor Roosevelt administration undertook in that very year a larger and more coherent program in fact-gathering about the state of the nation, which was now mired in economic depression.[98]

Social research projects mushroomed under Roosevelt's New Deal, especially in research conducted under the auspices of the Federal Emergency Relief Agency of 1933–35, and such projects continued under the successor agency, the Works Progress Administration (WPA) (1935–43). Approximately 2,000 of the more than 5,000 research projects sponsored by FERA/WPA bore on social topics. The "survey" was still a number of things—almost anything empirical. It referred to research in general (investigation, study, and research were synonyms) as well as to a specific mode of data collection (for which census, canvass, and questionnaire-study were synonyms). It referred to data aggregated in existing records and to individual data gathered in the field. It denoted the preliminary overview of the physical and social environment of the community and, in the same study, the specific information about individual schoolchildren that was recorded on individual cards.[99]

A more technical definition, however, was implicit in survey work undertaken in the Division of Social Research of the WPA by statistically trained sociologists such as Dwight Sanderson, Paul H. Landis, T. J. Woofter, Thomas C. McCormick, Carle C. Zimmerman, and others, many of whom had been practicing the survey of individual record in agricultural experiment stations. Their work during the New Deal showed three technical features: (1) a sensitivity to the measurement process; (2) an effort for national coverage and estimates by "representative" sampling; and (3) the beginning of the extension of the social survey to the study of attitudes.

The Individual Record and New Attention to Measurement

Although there were variants on the practice, the survey of the mid-1930s in this branch of the federal government meant field data based on the individual record. The Division of Social Research conducted at least sixteen large regional or quasi-national surveys between 1933 and 1938 on rural relief problems, especially. All involved some collection of individual field data. In the published monographs, there was almost always scrupulous care taken in a "methodological note" that reported how the study was done, how the sampling was conducted, what questions were asked, and, in a few cases, how the interviewers were instructed—although there was little description of the field staff itself, and little focus on question wording per se.[100]

The material that field-workers were after was considered straightforward, matter-of-fact, obtainable by topics listed on the schedule in abbreviated form. It was apparently not a worry that such no-nonsense items as years of education, kind of occupation, or number of farm acres under cultivation might vary with nuances in wording, and in fact there was not always a clear distinction between a fully worded question addressed to a respondent and a topic directed to the interviewer. The following questions, for example, were duly reported in a monograph from the division:

> 1. Why did you leave the community where you last maintained a settled, self-supporting residence?
> 2. Why did you select one particular place, to the exclusion of other places, as your destination?

which surely sound (for all the rather elevated language) as though they were addressed directly to the respondent. On the schedule itself, however, which the authors reproduced, the topics were actually directed to the interviewer:

> Q6. Last place in which the family lived a settled, self-supporting life; that is, the place at which family group mobility began. _____
> Q7. Reasons for leaving. State fully all the circumstances that caused the family to leave the town entered in Question 6.

> Q8. Destination at time of leaving place entered in Question 6.
> a. State ____ City or County ____
> b. Reasons for selection of this place _____[101]

It is not finally clear from this study just how the questions were actually asked.

This kind of interview schedule should not be seen as sloppy questionnaire construction. It represented, rather, a different notion of what an interview was to be. The conception of a survey question as a fully standardized stimulus was not a feature of the social survey, even in its application during the New Deal, for reasons of principle and practice. The practical fact was that the interviewers in these New Deal projects were often professional social scientists who trusted themselves to make judgments (but would not trust such discretion to interviewers of lesser education). Certain schedules were indeed worded to be read by the interviewer exactly as written, but in general the principle of standardized wording came more from psychologists, who brought to their interest in attitude study the canons of the experimental tradition. Social scientists generally thought of attitudes and opinions as more fragile and vulnerable to the way in which the question was asked. Matters of fact were thought to be more hardy, more resistant to forms and wording fashions of asking questions. Well into the 1970s, in fact, the wording of questions dealing with demographic or "background" variables probably remained less specified than wording for questions of attitude, requiring (or allowing) the interviewer to exercise more judgment and initiate more probing.[102]

Toward Probability Sampling

SOME OF THE INTELLECTUAL GROUND: KIAER, BOWLEY, NEYMAN, FISHER

With the application of probability theory to survey work, the *sample* survey gradually came into the parlance and practice of American social scientists, starting in the late 1930s. It came into American use from two sources: surveys of population and experiments in agriculture. Probability theory had been available since the eighteenth century, but extensive applications of practical sampling problems in social and economic surveys did not engage statisticians until the late nineteenth century. In the very years during which Booth was laboring to enumerate London's poor, the director of Norwegian statistics, Anders N. Kiaer (1838–1919), was arguing for the use of sampling in official government statistics, a development described in some detail by Seng and also by Kruskal and Mosteller, and on which I rely heavily here.[103]

Kiaer is credited with earning respectability for the practice of sampling among world statisticians. In a series of presentations and debates at the turn of the century, he brought to the forum of the International Statistical Institute (ISI)—many of whose members were responsible for national censuses—a description of his "representative method," which he was using in Norway in conjunction with census data. The debate that he inspired turned on sampling itself: whether this kind of "partial investigation" had merit compared to the full census enumeration, on the one hand, or to the "ideal" or "typical" case studies of few or even single cases, on the other.[104]

In the first days of this debate with statisticians, Kiaer by no means prevailed. Opponents warned that this was a "dangerous" doctrine and argued that a sample could never replace full coverage. Kiaer agreed that a partial investigation of this sort could not supplement census information unless it was "representative," by which he meant, as Seng put it,

> a partial inquiry in which observation was made on a large number of units distributed throughout a country or territory so that their totality would form a miniature of the whole country or territory.[105]

Representativeness was deemed more important than sample size, although Kiaer was also at pains to collect substantial numbers of interviews at each level and to stratify roughly by urbanicity and by economic categories. In his main investigation of 1894, 20,000 town dwellers and 60,000 rural residents were interviewed and another 40,000 interviews were conducted in a special investigation of working-class members.[106]

Trying to get results that would resemble those of the census in geographic scatter, urbanicity, major industry, and income levels, Kiaer used systematic selection from lists or directed interviewers to make judgmental selections of households which would show a range of values in addition to the "average" ones. When the resulting sample statistics on age, sex, occupation, and so on compared reasonably well with the census figures, Kiaer had practical evidence that his procedure worked. When he found his results discrepant, he added or subtracted sample data to beef up deficient categories or to trim them down to the desired proportions.[107] His procedure was closer to what was later called "purposive selection" in order to distinguish this method from the "random selection" methods of probability design, but in Kiaer's day the distinction had not yet been clearly made. Proceeding by "validation," Kiaer of course had no means of estimating sampling error.

The contribution of Arthur L. Bowley (1869–1957) was to undergird the design for surveys he conducted with some probability theory. A statistician-economist at the London School of Economics, Bowley had been stimulated by discussions of the "representative method" at the ISI meetings. In a 1906 address to the British Association for the Advancement of Science, he argued that sampling precision could and should be assessed with reference to Edgeworth's central-limit theorem, which stated that mean values taken successively from a large distribution of values showing almost any shape (whether normal or not) would themselves be distributed normally. Thus, the error within which a sample value estimated a population value could be assessed by the standard deviation of that sampling distribution if all elements in the population had an equal chance of selection. Bowley made a bolder case for sampling than Kiaer had, arguing that samples could substitute entirely for censuses.[108]

When a group of citizens in the town of Reading approached Bowley for advice on how best to investigate working-class living conditions, he recommended the "application of the pure method of sampling" as an economy of time and money. Bowley was moved by the same social concern that Booth and Rowntree had felt, and he set out to measure the incidence of families living below the poverty line in the tradition of their work, making certain refinements. From the investigations conducted in four towns in 1912–13, published as *Livelihood and Poverty*, Bowley and Burnett-Hurst concluded that the most pervasive cause of poverty was not unemployment or irregularity of work but desperately low wages (drink and "depravity" were not even contenders in this analysis).[109]

In deliberations of the ISI in 1925, Bowley was associated with the view that "representative" sampling could be conducted by either random selection methods or purposive ones. Bowley's views have been interpreted somewhat variously—George Snedecor, in 1939, found that Bowley had neither recommended nor used the method of purposive sampling, and he interpreted Bowley's explication of it as reducing it in practice to stratified random sampling. Bowley, for his part, felt that he had not given equal support to both methods but had instead damned purposive sampling "with very faint praise."[110] A subcommittee of which Bowley's report was a part, commend a resolution, adopted by ISI, which set forth both methods as legitimate.[111]

Neyman resolved the ambiguity. The work of Jerzy Neyman (1894–1981), a Polish statistician who later came to the United States, is considered fundamental to modern probability sampling. In a 1934 paper, "On the Two Different Aspects of the Representative Method: the Method of Stratified Sampling and the Method of Purposive Selection," Neyman distinguished clearly between random and purposive selection, and he made the case that purposive selection should be redesigned as stratified random sampling to yield unbiased results. The paper is widely regarded as a veritable fountain of new statistical ideas: confidence intervals, optimal allocation of the sample to various strata, cluster sampling, basic notions of multistage probability samples.[112] While the paper addressed an audience of technical sophistication, an example Neyman used both in it and in 1937 lectures at the Department of Agriculture Graduate School—which helped to circulate his ideas among government statisticians—provides a vivid instance of the perils of purposive selection.[113]

This was the story of Gini and Galvani, two Italian statisticians who, faced in the late 1920s with the need to dispose of the census of 1921 in order to make room for the new batch, decided to make do with a sample of the old data which would serve as a miniature. They chose 29 "representative" districts (out of 214) that on a dozen variables resembled the averages displayed by the census. When they later worked with these sample data, however, as Neyman put it, "all statistics other than the average values of the controls showed a violent contrast between the sample and the whole population."[114] Gini and Galvani despaired of drawing a sample that reproduced the population in all its characteristics. Neyman agreed that their mission was hopeless but pointed out that they should have despaired of purposive selection, not random methods. Through the force of Neyman's demonstration, according to Kruskal and Mosteller, "purposive sampling lost its appeal"—at least in these realms of statistical expertise. Probability sampling was translated into effective national designs in the U.S. government in the late 1930s and early 1940s. As we shall see, purposive sampling of the "quota control" variety continued to thrive in commercial research well into the 1940s and 1950s.[115]

R. A. Fisher (1890–1962), geneticist, biologist, mathematician, and statistician, was another giant in the succession of Galton, Karl Pearson, Egon Pearson, Edgeworth, Yule, and others of this brilliant era in English statistical invention.[116] By 1915, Fisher had already published the sampling distribution of the correlation coefficient and had made other statistical discoveries, and Karl Pearson offered him a position at University College. Pearson and Fisher were to become locked in a lifelong feud—Fisher was already aggrieved in those early years because he felt that Pearson had simply taken over his solution to the correlation coefficient without consulting him—and Fisher took a job at the Rothamsted agricultural experiment station instead. Here, from 1919 to 1933, his career flourished, especially in work in genetics (making links between Darwin's evolution and Mendel's genetics) and in the design of experiments, including his invention of the analysis of variance.[117]

Fisher's great contribution to probability sampling was made in this period, when he introduced into experimental design the principle of randomization. As Chang has noted, Fisher's work in agricultural experiments in the 1920s and Neyman's argument in the 1930s against purposive selection were part of the same battle for randomization in experiments and surveys.[118] Major principles of the rational design of experiments had already been known and used before Fisher's innovation—replication, factorial design, and blocking (which is analogous to "stratification" in sampling).

Randomization was new. Fisher introduced it after he had developed the analysis of variance, a technique that was a major breakthrough in assessing the impact of agricultural experiments. Prior to Fisher, the effects of agricultural experiments, or "treatments," had been imprecise: there were only a few replications of a given treatment, they were conducted on a compact set of plots that would provide the same soil conditions, and error in the mean for the treatment was estimated from the deviations from the mean shown by yields of the individual plots. The analysis of variance technique made it possible to pool the estimates of error of different treatments and to partition the components into the systematic variation "between" treatments and the random variation "within." Randomization of the assignment of plots to experimental treatments was essential to insure that they were all subjected, with equal probability, to all other sources of variation which were extraneous to the treatment and which would also be operating in the experiment.[119]

The experimental principles of randomization, stratification, and subsampling in complex designs (to save travel costs, for example, over great agricultural holdings, as in clustering) all had applicability to sample surveys where replication was not generally possible. Fisher himself did not publish on these applications, but he nevertheless had great influence on their development and diffusion through his personal contact and consultation with workers in the field. Clapham, Yates, Cochran, and others influenced by Fisher pursued the applications to survey sampling. In the United States, Fisher's influence was felt especially at the Statistical Laboratory at Iowa State University, Ames.[120]

SAMPLING EXPERIMENT AND PRACTICE
FOR THE FEDERAL GOVERNMENT

The Statistical Laboratory was founded in 1924, as Henry A. Wallace (later Secretary of Agriculture), Snedecor, and Charles Sarle were instrumental in getting it established with state funds. In the 1930s, the Department of Agriculture called upon the laboratory to conduct special research into agricultural yields and sampling. Agricultural statistics were collected at the time through mail questionnaires to farmers and through some experiments and estimates using various kinds of physical samples. Crop yields, for example, were estimated for market forecasts by crews that proceeded by automobile along a highway, with a meter recording the frontage of crops. At a predetermined interval, the crew stopped, and a sampler took a certain number of steps into the field to avoid border effects, placed a frame down on the ground, and collected the grain that fell within the frame. Area sampling of human populations assumed that people could be sampled in something of the same fashion by associating each person with a unique space or area.

In 1936, the Bureau of Agricultural Economics (BAE) sponsored a conference on sampling at the Statistical Laboratory and mapped out an ambitious program of research into agricultural sampling. The first experiment in area sampling of farm households was undertaken in the winter of 1938–39, with interviews conducted at 800 Iowa farms by students under the direction of Raymond J. Jessen. The data obtained were farm statistics—crop production, livestock, farm receipts, expenditures, land values, and so on—and certain estimates proved to be more accurate than those obtained by traditional methods, vindicating the experimental work. The Statistical Laboratory under Snedecor, with Jessen, Arnold King, William G. Cochran, and others, played an important role in sampling theory and experiment.[121]

In Washington, meanwhile, the other center of sampling activity, area sampling was already under way, although it apparently had not yet been given that label. When federal workers were trying to assess the effects of the depression and design programs to ameliorate them, the census of 1930 had been of little help. Those data did not address the urgent new problems at hand and were limited by tradition, time, and money to factual questioning; furthermore, the census was out of date.

The federal workers had two other basic choices: they could sample the populations defined by existing records (e.g., the population of people shown by record to have applied for or received relief), or they could locate people by sampling from maps or areas. The samplers did both, as the needed information dictated, and there were nettles in each direction. Available records did not necessarily provide the information desired, or the ways in which they were organized were later found to confound sampling procedures. For its part, area sampling posed the especially formidable problem of a field staff that was to be distributed and supervised across the nation, and the FERA/WPA surveys showed this constraint vividly. In the monographs, maps identified states in which investigators were either unable to gain the cooperation of local officials or else lacked the time and money to assemble and train staff. In their early studies, the investigators sometimes sampled first and then tried to decide what population it was that they must be investigating.[122]

Duncan and Shelton, in *Revolution in United States Government Statistics 1926–1976* (1978), distinguish four stages of sampling in these years, with complete enumeration at one end and full probability sampling at the other. In between were "intuitive" sampling (stage two), conducted without any apparent knowledge of laws of probability, and "structured" practice (stage three), which showed cautions against obvious biases and some knowledge of probability theory. The sampling procedures of the reformist social survey had clearly been "intuitive," while the surveys of the 1930s by the federal government were essentially "structured" in their compromise mix of probability and purposive elements, a distinction that was not yet entirely clear even to government professionals in the 1930s.[123]

Statistically sophisticated social scientists were brought to the task of constructing national samples in good part through a committee organized by Stuart A. Rice. At the invitation of Frances Perkins, Franklin D. Roosevelt's Secretary of Labor, and other cabinet members, the Committee on Government Statistics and Information Services (COGSIS) was put together by Rice, then president of the American Statistical Association, and by the Social Science Research Council (SSRC).[124] Unemployment clearly was a massive social problem, but exactly how many people were out of work was difficult to measure: estimates varied wildly, from 3 million to 15 million.[125] Unemployment had been assessed in three different wordings in census collections since 1890, none of them satisfactory, and in 1920 the question had been abandoned. It would in time become abundantly clear that assessing unemployment or the state of "looking for work" was not only a problem in sampling or an exclusively factual problem but that there was also a strong subjective or attitudinal component in the measure.[126]

Samuel Stouffer served on COGSIS in 1934–36 and brought to it stimulation in statistics and sampling from his recent period of study in England. In a project to remedy his deficiency in statistics—he had been an undergraduate English major and sometime editor of his father's newspaper in Iowa—Stouffer had spent several months in England in 1931–32 on an SSRC fellowship, where he had personal contact with statistical giants of the time, Karl and Egon Pearson, Fisher, and Bowley.[127] Stouffer had already been influenced by ideas of correlation and regression. A generation of sociologists, such as William F. Ogburn, Howard Odum, Frank A. Ross, Chapin, Woofter, and Rice (most of whom had been trained at Columbia, when Franklin H. Giddings was chairman of the Department of Sociology there) had all been applying such statistical concepts to aggregate data, and Stouffer had worked directly with Ogburn at the University of Chicago in the late 1920s.[128]

At COGSIS, Frederick Stephan, Calvin L. Dedrick, and Stouffer experimented with probability sampling on unemployment. They were in search of the most feasible way to conduct a national survey, and among other things they tested three different sampling units (household, building, and block) against schedules of a complete census.[129] This testing, done in 1933–34 and called the Trial Census of Unemployment, demonstrated the practical feasibility (and efficiency) of probability sampling by individual household before Neyman's theoretical work was known in the United States.[130] Stouffer soon learned of the Neyman article, however, for he referred to it in a 1935 piece of his own, in a context showing that the issue of purposive selection had not been instantly laid to rest:

> there is not agreement . . . on the wisdom of selecting the constituents of the sample in each sub-group by deliberate consideration of the merits of each case instead of by chance. Good arguments can be presented for and against the procedure. . . . Such unsettled problems are among the most interesting and important in all social research. The latest and perhaps the most searching contribution to the subject of representative sampling is a mathematical paper by Neyman.[131]

SOCIAL SURVEYS AND SAMPLE SURVEYS

Stouffer's 1935 article, "Statistical Induction in Rural Social Research," itself provides something of a watershed between the old social survey and the emerging sample survey. His discussion of sampling and inference was organized here around an examination of Brunner and Kolb's 1933 book *Rural Social Trends*, the second in a series studying 130 villages which was designed as a purposive sample of American communities, an ambitious project sponsored by the Institute of Social and Religious Research.[132]

Brunner and Kolb designed their study by asking individuals and organizations in thirty-three states to submit the names of incorporated villages that they considered "representative of the agricultural areas of their states." A village had to be nominated by at least two sources before it was included in the sample.[133]

Stouffer was respectful of their practical problems but critical of their loose judgmental approach to sampling. His own interest in *attitude* surveys was also visible in his questions:

Did villagers feel in 1930 that their communities were more and more becoming stagnant waters . . . or were the villagers feeling new satisfactions in village life, new enthusiasms for the roles?[134]

In *Rural Social Trends*, Brunner and Kolb did not treat questions about morale in American villages, except indirectly. In fact, they did not construct their study on the individual record at all, much less on the attitudes of individuals. This was indeed the surviving social survey of the community of the 1910s and 1920s, now being projected on a national canvas—not the large-scale sample survey of the individual record that was taking shape in the 1930s.

The surveys constructed in the early New Deal years of "structured" rather than full probability samples were not generally called "sample" surveys. Not at first. Rather, they simply incorporated various efforts at probability sampling along with field data and individual records, and more technically ambitious sampling became implicit in the definition of the survey. The National Health Survey of 1935–36, the New York City Youth Survey, the set of youth surveys undertaken by the Office of Education in 1935, and various surveys of the WPA, especially those concerned with unemployment—these were all sample surveys, although they were labeled simply as surveys. There were other sample surveys that received neither term, such as the Study of Consumer Purchases.[135] The Enumerative Check Census of 1937 was another variant. A 2 percent sample of postal routes was drawn first, and questionnaires were then distributed to a "census" of all households on the route to "check" figures against a national voluntary report of unemployment. The 1939 Sample Survey of Unemployment had the new name, as well as a still closer approximation to area probability sampling. By the late 1930s, a *survey* was very likely to be a sample survey.

Toward Attitude Surveying

THE INTEREST IN SUBJECTIVE MEASURES

Social surveyors intent upon getting "the facts" had sometimes felt the force of attitudes, especially in the rural context.[136] Some of the broad-scale national and regional surveys undertaken during the 1930s included some attitude questions (e.g., in studies of youth and their job plans and of migrants and their reasons for moving), but no major surveys of truly national scope were conducted of American attitudes in this period.[137]

Researchers in government, industry, and social science felt the lack of subjective measures, and they made inferences from elite or indirect measures of subjective states of the nation. For example, the work commissioned by President Hoover, *Recent Social Trends*, included a content analysis by sociologist Hornell Hart which showed sweeping change among Americans over the course of the twentieth century in attitudes toward religion, science, sexuality, divorce, and so on. But who had been changing—large groups in the national population, or an elite that wrote the books, magazine articles, and newspaper editorials that Hart used? There was, of course, no telling.[138]

An influential industrial group tried to generalize to the nation from a different elite: newspaper editors. In 1934–35, the National Industrial Conference Board circulated long questionnaires on political attitudes to newspaper editors, asking them to answer the questions as they thought their communities would.[139] Social scientists, too, wanted subjective data on a national scale. When Stouffer and Lazarsfeld worked together in 1936 on a study of the American family during the depression, they had only aggregate data of various kinds (such as divorce rates, relief payments, and migration rates), and they felt keenly the lack of subjective self-report from families themselves. They looked forward to public release of some data gathered by the Gallup Poll.[140]

THE DIVISION OF RURAL ATTITUDES AND OPINIONS

In 1935–36 a small interviewing outfit was established in the Department of Agriculture to try to tap farmers' attitudes. This project was the brainchild of Assistant Secretary M. L. Wilson, who shared with Secretary Henry A. Wallace (and other New Dealers) an ardent advocacy of democratic political philosophy, a commitment to national planning, and strong hopes for applied science to effect social change.[141] Wilson was especially concerned about farmers' attitudes because the complicated new farm programs of the New Deal required widespread understanding and cooperation from the farmers themselves. One basic program for which Wilson had labored since about 1930 was acreage control ("domestic allotments" or "agricultural adjustment"), which meant restriction of the harvest to a size for which an effective demand was estimated. The model was industry's control of supply in response to demand, and farmers were paid subsidies to cut back on certain crops. This was a vast undertaking, involving the department in contractual relations with some six and a half million farmers. On practical as well as philosophical

grounds, Wilson wanted the department to keep in touch with this constituency.[142]

Wilson felt that the intangible barriers to social change bred of attitudes and customs were even more complex and intractable than the
tangled and complex economic problems facing the farm sector. It was
this analysis that drew him to new currents in social psychology and anthropology, as well as to the opinion polls—ideas that he tried through a
series of projects to bring into the department.[143] One of these projects
was the interviewing outfit, which Wilson began to organize in the spring
of 1935.

Wilson saw the interviewing work as a leading edge of social science,
for which he had bright but patient hopes. As he wrote to interviewers in
1936 and 1937,

> I think that we in Washington are always apt to shoot entirely too high and to
> assume that the mass of farmers are thinking about the same as we are think-
> ing.[144]

> I feel that the work which you [interviewers] are doing is very much like fight-
> ing Indians on a frontier far in advance of human understanding and social
> science, and that before we can make as great progress as we hope for in ad-
> justing the conditions of man to the age of science we shall have to do more
> about the processes which produce the opinions and attitudes on the part of
> individuals.[145]

The field operation was actually tiny. By 1937 or 1938, there were
only a half dozen interviewers. Most were specialists in agriculture. Jay
Whitson, for example, had been a farm reporter; Gladys Baker had just
finished her Ph.D. at the University of Chicago on the history of the
county agent; Shep Wolman was a graduate of social work.[146] They went
out in their cars, crisscrossing their regions—one person in the corn-
and-hog counties of the Midwest, another in the cotton areas of the
South, and so on—striking up conversations with farmers in as natural a
fashion as they could. They were advised to pick farms through some
sort of system—for example, every tenth—but they were "scouts," not
samplers, and their interviews were also informal. They carried no
schedules, although they usually had topics they were expected to get to
if they could do so in a natural way. When the conversation came to an
end, the interviewer drove on down the road and wrote up narrative reports of what he or she had learned. Carl C. Taylor suggested that the interviewers' reports be analyzed by types of attitude and background fac-

tors, and such tabulations were made.[147] The most important reporting, however, was done in person. Every few months, the field-workers were called to Washington for a week or more of "seminars" with top officials in the department.[148]

While the great focus of the work seems to have been on farm problems and remedies, the fact that farmers were also *voters* was not lost on the department. When Wilson joined one of the interviewers in the field in 1936, he noted this tally from their visit to twenty-three farms:

48 Roosevelt votes
 6 Landon
 3 Undecided[149]

He later noted that "most of both the women and the men that we saw in our interviews knew why they were for Roosevelt."[150] In at least a few other instances, there is evidence that interviewers were picking up voting information, perhaps in incidental ways. Republican congressmen would surely not have taken the news calmly, for there was also suspicion on Capitol Hill that the department might try to mobilize farmers as voting troops for Roosevelt's third term or for a Wallace candidacy.[151] This may account for the fact that the narrative reports have not been found in the National Archives in those files in which they would most logically have been preserved, and which include copious references to the dispatch and receipt of these reports. They may have been deemed too "sensitive" to keep.

Even before the Gallup Poll was syndicated, Gallup's work was of interest to administrators in the Department of Agriculture. Gallup was from Iowa, like Secretary Wallace himself as well as certain other department administrators, and his work was especially salient to the department and to its own project in opinion research. As administrator Howard Tolley later put it,

> The public opinion poll was a development in the social sciences as important to us in Agriculture as if a chemist had found a new compound like DDT. If it worked for Gallup, why would it not work for us? We wanted a try at it.[152]

Note that Tolley, himself an economist, did not distinguish opinion polls *from* social science, as many other academic social scientists later would. In 1938, Wilson asked Gallup to give one of a series of lectures on democracy that he had organized in the Graduate School of USDA. (The lecture program included Ruth Benedict, Thurman Arnold, Charles A. Beard, James K. Pollock, T. V. Smith, and others.)[153]

Academic studies in attitude measurement and commercial work in opinion polling were *both* of great interest to agricultural administrators like Wilson and Tolley, who were trying to incorporate an understanding of the subjective realm into their programs for farm life. They did not make the separation that academics later did. Contemporary survey researchers have come to feel greater kinship to their "internalist" ancestry in academic attitude measurement than to their "externalist" roots in commercial research, but both are of importance, and we shall consider their development in chapters two and three.

2

The More Elegant Ancestor of Science: Attitude Measurement in Psychology and Sociology

> If we want to know how people feel: what they experience and what they remember, what their emotions and motives are like, and the reason for acting as they do—why not ask them?
>
> *Gordon W. Allport*

> If, say the behaviorists, you wish to know what a person is doing, by all means refrain from asking *him*. His answer is sure to be wrong, not merely because he does not know what he is doing but precisely because he is answering a question and he will make the reply in terms of you and not in terms of the objective thing he is doing.
>
> *E. C. Lindeman*

The Approach to Attitudes in Psychology and Sociology

The Concept of Attitude

The study of attitudes and their measurement began to flourish in academic social psychology in the early 1920s, before the advent of the new opinion polls in 1935, and such study became a key piece of the mosaic that would later become survey research. Attitude measurement had nothing like the prestige of experimental psychology. The experimentalists, in fact, thought that things had gone rather too far even by the mid-1920s, when they took a stand at their annual meeting in 1926:

> Resolved, that this meeting deplores the increasing practice of collecting administrative or supposedly scientific data by way of questionnaires; and that the meeting deplores especially the practice under which graduate students undertake research by sending questionnaires to professional psychologists.

The psychologist reporting on these meetings even suggested that the maturity of a science might be measured inversely by the number of questionnaires it sponsored.[1]

Studies of attitude (and other uses of the questionnaire) went on, to be sure. Survey researchers from psychology would later identify with the disciplinary tradition of attitude measurement, confident that they were not studying mere opinion, even when it was sometimes difficult for outsiders to tell the difference or when some researchers themselves used the terms *opinion* and *attitude* interchangeably. Ultimately, survey research would be omnivorous, taking everything it could get of an individual record—attitudes, opinions, facts, information, behaviors, beliefs, experiences, personality measures, and even physiological measures—but attitudes were an early focus of survey research.

W. I. Thomas is credited with introducing the concept of attitude into social psychology in 1918–20, in his work (with Florian Znaniecki) *The Polish Peasant in Europe and America*.[2] Thomas's definition was a loose one, referring to a state of consciousness, a potential activity toward or away from some object of value. It was vague on a number of points, and other definitions subsequently abounded. Gordon Allport, for example, collected sixteen definitions in 1935. Classification of types of attitudes was also a busy enterprise.[3] In a sense, the concept of attitude became a hopeless catchall, but it simultaneously stimulated much empirical work. Much of the utility of attitudes probably proceeded from what they were *not*.

First, attitudes were not *instincts or traits* of personality.[4] Attitudes were bred of continuous experience in the social world rather than laid down by biological structure. As Rice pointed out, "Since human experience is infinitely varied, attitudes are regarded as variables, and hence theoretically subject to measurement."[5] They could be measured over space, over time, within individuals, across groups, and, as Thomas and Znaniecki conceptualized, they could be used to analyze the interaction and integration between groups and individuals and between culture and personality.

Second, attitudes were not just *ideas, beliefs, or ideologies*—not just an intellectual matter. The light cast by Freud, Jung, and Adler on the purportedly rational made such constructs seem simplistic in their neglect of feelings and unconscious motivations. In Gordon Allport's discussion, it was the influence of Freud especially that resurrected attitudes, and "endowed them with vitality . . . longing, hatred and love, with passion and prejudice . . . with the onrushing stream of unconscious life."[6]

Attitudes were close to the nerve and the bone, and everyone could have them. Yet, third, they were not just *feelings*—they had some cognitive structure, and yet they had energy, or "color." They were a mix of the affective and cognitive, and as cognitions they could be reflected upon, as well as reported to or observed by inquiring social scientists.

Nor, fourth, were they merely *opinions*. Attitudes had something of "deep structure." They were somehow underlying. While they were not so deep, usually, as the Unconscious, which might animate rationalization, illusion, and neurotic adjustments and not permit fair reporting at all, they were not so superficial as opinions, which might be too specific, transient, or intellectualized, without any particularly integrative role in personality or behavior. For many researchers, however, opinions would serve as a verbal indicator of underlying attitudes. Finally, attitudes were not simply *behavior*, although they had something important to do with it and especially with purposive human action. Some social scientists argued, in fact, that behavior should be considered as the only meaningful indicator of underlying attitudes.

In 1930, the sociologist Read Bain pointed to a veritable grab bag of terms that were often used loosely, vaguely, or interchangeably: *attitude, opinion, trait, wish, interest, disposition, desire, bias, preference, prejudice, will, sentiment, motive, objective, goal, idea, ideal, emotion, instinct*. Bain did not even mention some other candidates, such as *habit, belief, feeling, judgment, value, ideology*, or *stereotype*.[7] The confusion was not surprising. Political scientists gathering in 1925 could only agree, after protracted debate, that opinions were not necessarily rational processes or conscious choices but should be sufficiently clear to "create a disposition to act" if circumstances were favorable.[8] And attitudes were a richer, more mysterious matter than that!

Still, from a contemporary vantage point, it does not seem quite so chaotic now as Bain contended. At least there was one emergent order, as psychologists and sociologists pursued the study of attitudes in their different fashions. This was not a perfect split—there was variability within each group[9]—but psychologists started out on their study of attitudes with disciplinary traditions in laboratory experimentation or mental testing, while sociologists brought to their inquiry a tradition in fieldwork or statistical analysis of aggregate data. Representatives of the two groups took different paths to four aspects of the study of attitudes: *techniques* of measurement, the *subjects* used, the *settings* in which the studies were conducted, and preferred *indicators* of attitude.

Psychologists used questionnaire data that permitted quantification, most often obtained from students; their classroom setting had some properties of the laboratory; and they inquired into verbal measures, especially opinions, as attitudinal indicators. Sociologists who were interested in attitudes tended to place more reliance on personal interviews and case-history methods; they sought out subcultures in the adult population; their setting of choice was the community rather than the classroom; and they sought behavioral indicators (at least as supplements to opinions) that could be observed directly or that had been recorded publicly or even recounted personally.

Attitudes in the Psychologists' Domain

QUESTIONNAIRES

The psychologists' enthusiasm and skill for the study of attitudes came naturally. For some, it provided a way to apply rigorous quantification to *subjective* meaning and mental life, which had been excluded from the stimulus-response experimental work of behaviorism.[10] For others, it may have provided an extension of the tradition of mental measurement, which had burgeoned in psychology after the development of Binet's intelligence tests in 1905, for the testing of school children, vocational testing, and employee performance, as well as in the IQ testing of army recruits in World War I.[11] In 1935, Gordon Allport, noting a new enthusiasm for attitude measurement, wrote that he had the impression that "militant testing, having won victories on one field of battle, has sought a new world to conquer."[12] In any case, psychologists working with attitude measures published a great volume of studies in the 1920s and 1930s in such journals as the *Journal of Abnormal Psychology*, the *Journal of Social Psychology*, the *Psychological Bulletin*, and the *Psychological Review*, as well as in journals of personnel and industrial psychology.

STUDENT SUBJECTS

"That attitude studies have so frequently been limited to students is a misfortune that we shall have many occasions to lament," wrote Murphy, Murphy, and Newcomb in their 1937 revision of a 1931 review of the attitude literature.[13] That being said, they did not, in fact, lament much. The 1931 review had described fifty-five studies of attitude in some detail. Only five dealt with respondents who were all members of the adult population outside the college community; forty-five dealt exclusively with students. In his important 1935 review, Gordon Allport summarized various studies without even indicating that they were based exclusively on college students or on school children. It is important to note that the subject matter of the great bulk of psychological attitude research in this era was not the college experience itself, for which students would have of course been essential. Daniel Katz's study, *Student Attitudes*, for example, was unusual in that regard.[14] Students were being used most often as surrogates for people-in-general. Rather than being a source of widespread visible regret, this was assumed to be a fact of research life.[15]

In his 1932 presidential address to the American Psychological Association, Walter R. Miles considered the problem. He said that while the use of student subjects was limited, there were also problems with adult groups, because researchers could rarely do test-retest reliability or even make the instruments long enough for correlations by halves or by odd-even tests of reliability: "Doubtless this is in fact the chief reason why we regard adequate selection of adult subjects as treacherous." Miles was hopeful that representative groups could be built up from clubs, lodges, and social groups of one sort and another who would be willing to serve the purposes of science if group goals were rewarded by the scientists.[16]

Some psychologists got beyond the classroom in person or by mail,[17] but more stayed put, where they worked with a set of complex questionnaires and attitude scales that virtually required this kind of hothouse environment. There were three critical requirements for the use of these instruments, which students in the classroom provided. First, one needed people with some *talent* for attitudes—literate, comprehending, articulate, and self-conscious to some extent about their intellectual, political, and moral positions; people, in sum, who were trained in having attitudes. Students were being stimulated by the very intellectual content of their college experience to consider issues of war, peace, the church, prohibition, business and labor, and the like. Students also did not pose problems of academic translation—that is, they did not require the simplified wordings, less abstract ideas, and concerns and situations that were closer to common experiences among the broad public.

Second, one needed people with the *time and tolerance*, and students could be—gently—imposed upon.[18] Authority relations of the classroom could help insure that most students would cooperate in the request for data, and as a rule the form was the one entirely familiar to students, the paper-and-pencil test.

Third, and of commanding importance, compared to the cost of finding other people, using students was indeed *inexpensive*. That these subjects in the college classroom helped provide for low-cost research almost goes without saying. The newly established great foundations began to fund research projects in social science in the 1910s and 1920s, but this was still an era in which social scientists were likely to embark on research projects with very small grants or even at their own expense.[19]

LABORATORY SETTINGS

With these resources, psychologists conducted relatively *pure* tests of attitudes where such attitudes would be found in abundance—it was not unlike conducting epidemiological studies in hospitals—and where conditions were similar to those of a laboratory with regard to the degree of control. A single investigator could manage the test, specifying the time, place, duration, number of people, and the invariant wording of questions, without risk that the respondents or interviewers would change things once they were out of reach of the investigator. Psychologists wrote up their results in good experimental fashion, explaining the conditions under which the test was given, along with tests of reliability and such indications of validity as they could muster. Often, they reproduced at least a portion of the test questions, if not the entire instrument.

OPINIONS

The use of verbal indicators by psychologists meant in theory that underlying attitudes were to be inferred from the opinion indicators gathered by questionnaire. In practice, the opinions themselves were often of commanding interest, and many investigators used the two terms synonymously. Asking opinions directly represented an implicit confidence that respondents were capable of giving reasonably faithful accounts of their own opinions under the admittedly contrived conditions of a written questionnaire. Psychologists paid tribute, indirectly, to the essential validity of the subjective realm and to the value of their own instruments for studying this realm. Sociologists were more inclined to doubt both assumptions.

Attitudes in the Sociologists' Domain

INTERVIEWS AND CASE HISTORIES

The quantitative side of academic sociology in the 1920s was being tended for the most part by demographers or other statistically trained professionals, who worked with census data or election statistics, or by ecologists, who studied physical-cultural distributions. Most sociologists becoming interested in attitudes were not yet as well trained in quantitative techniques. They tended to work intuitively with interviews of an unstructured sort, without standardized questionnaires or standardized interview schedules, using life histories (written or recounted), letters, diaries, and other personal documents on the qualitative side of life.

Various sociologists urged the integration of the statistical and case-history approaches to data so that insight could be stimulated by the qualitative material and hypotheses could be verified by statistical analysis of *other* data.[20] In truth, a more adequate integration of the two methods would have involved gathering case studies in profusion, organized along standardized dimensions so that the *same* collection of data could have been classified, quantified, and then analyzed statistically. But who had the resources to gather data of this sort? The enduring debate in sociology about case history versus statistics (qualitative versus quantitative) reflected very directly the kinds of data resources that were available at the time: the small numbers of case histories that could be gathered by social scientists themselves, and the large numbers of official government statistics that were available at the library. The fit between the two, however, was terrible, certainly for scientists interested in attitudes, because there were no "statistics" in subjective measurement.

SUBCULTURES

Sociologists and their wing of social psychology also used students in the classroom for the study of attitudes, but more often than psychologists they sought out other groups as well. The disciplinary concerns of sociologists with groups, communities, social structure, status, culture, and personality directed them to try to learn the attitudes of various groups such as immigrants, Orientals on the West Coast, hoboes, lumberjacks, ministers, delinquents, and farmers, finding in the study of attitudes the link between the individual and the culture.[21]

REAL-WORLD SETTINGS

Social scientists interested in these communities and groups naturally had to go out into their worlds to find them. For a study of farmers' attitudes in 1925, Zimmerman selected 45 Minnesota farmers from each of nine towns by setting out north, south, east, and west from the center of town and taking every farmer on each road until he located a quarter of the number needed. He collected all kinds of data about farm conditions in the area as well as about the individual farmer's experiences, verbal attitudes, the farmer's own explanation of his views, and other people's insights into that farmer's situation. Zimmerman appears to have worked with informal interviewing that was structured enough to permit tabulations of all 345 farmers on certain issues and to analyze attitudes that had been bred of experience as opposed to those of traditional ideology.[22]

LaPiere explored French and English racial attitudes by roaming widely in both countries, going up and down the social ladder in first-, second-, and third-class railroad cars and restaurants and striking up conversations where he could, doing so with over 700 people altogether. Where it seemed natural to insert it into the conversation, he asked a question about reaction to Negroes. In France he asked about welcoming a Negro into one's home; only the upper-class French showed much prejudice. In England he asked a different question, about allowing white and black children to play together. He apparently did so because he found racial antipathy so much more widespread and intense in England that the question he had used in France would have produced no variation; it would have yielded an invariable no.[23] The studies by Zimmerman and LaPiere were imaginative explorations, but they were not the stuff of laboratory conditions, nor were they scrupulous accounts of the procedures used, experimental norms important to psychologists. They nevertheless had an advantage of breadth because they *were* conducted outside the laboratory-classroom.

BEHAVIORS

A later LaPiere study conducted in the early 1930s has become a classic study in discrepancy between behaviors and opinions (or, at least, between behaviors and self-perceptions). In a mail questionnaire, LaPiere asked a set of innkeepers whether they served Chinese guests, and almost all who answered said no. In fact, however, they already *had*, for LaPiere and a Chinese couple had been duly served in almost all of the places to which he later sent the questionnaire.[24] There were few such experiments in behavior/opinion by either sociologists or psychologists at the time.[25] In general, sociologists were less inclined to trust opinions, and they tended to use behavioral indicators of four basic kinds: (1) personal *observation* of individuals or groups, in the "participant observation" mode conceptualized by Lindeman and practiced in the Chicago field studies;[26] (2) statistical analysis of *recorded* behaviors such as votes cast, taxes paid, magazine articles published, and churches joined;[27] (3) *personal histories* of behavior and experience, as recalled and obtained by personal interview and life-history documents;[28] and (4) attitude scaling of *hypothetical or anticipated* behavior, which was a special concern of Emory S. Bogardus. Attitude scaling took quite different forms in sociology and psychology.

Attitude Scaling

A SCALE FROM EACH SIDE OF THE AISLE:
BOGARDUS AND ALLPORT

In 1924, when the psychologist Floyd H. Allport made his clarion call to sociologists to repudiate "group mind" theories and instead to explain group phenomena through a social psychology of the individual, the sociologist Bogardus made something of a rejoinder in the *American Journal of Sociology*. If there was a "group" fallacy, there was also an "individual" one, Bogardus cautioned, and Allport risked it if he was bent on measuring individuals apart from their group relationships. Social psychology could not be based exclusively on the social behavior of individuals, Bogardus argued; it must study the "intersocial stimulation" that occurs between members of a group, and gives an individual attitudes, a sense of values, personality itself. In that exchange, the two scholars did appear to be rather talking past each other; at least, it was not at all clear from Bogardus's brief discussion how he might differ from Allport in actual research conduct.[29]

In the following year, it became clear. In 1925, each scholar published an attitude scale, and there was indeed a difference between the scales. The contrast is of special interest to the history of survey research, because the two approaches to the measurement of attitude captured one facet of a doctrinal dispute between psychologists and sociologists about a proper survey research. The dispute, which may even persist to this day, certainly animated a debate about the theory and practice of survey research during its formative years.

Bogardus, a University of Chicago Ph.D., went on to the University of Southern California and remained there throughout a long and productive career as journal editor, activist, scholar, text writer, and teacher. His degree had been in psychology, with a dissertation on industrial accidents and fatigue. He was, however, strongly influenced by the Chicago sociologists, especially W. I. Thomas, and throughout his career Bogardus identified himself as a sociologist.[30] Allport had taken his degree at Harvard, with a strong background in experimental psychology. He later took a position at Syracuse University, where, under his aegis, social psychology and attitude study flourished. Allport would be credited with putting social psychology on a new footing of scientific rigor. When the *Public Opinion Quarterly*—which would become the single most important vehicle for publication in survey research—was founded in 1937, Allport wrote the lead piece for the first issue.[31]

Bogardus was an early representative of the sociologists who tried to use individual units of analysis in social psychology, and later in survey research, to study "contextual effects" of community settings and group memberships. He devised his Scale of Social Distance after a suggestion by Robert E. Park, in the interest of understanding both structural relations and status and cultural accommodations and conflicts—mainline sociological concerns at the University of Chicago.[32] The scale was a measure of attitude toward groups, but it was *behavioral by self-report*, for respondents were to explain what they thought they themselves would do rather than what they believed or advocated as policy. The Allport scale focused on the measurement of attitudes through *opinions*, especially political ones, which he related to measures of personality.

The Bogardus scale was simple in language and conception. People were to decide, on the basis of their "first feeling reaction," how they would respond to various groups along a seven-point scale of nearness/distance (to what level of association would they admit Armenians, Chinese, French, Koreans, Negroes, Russians, Turks, and other groups):

1. to close kinship by marriage
2. to my club as personal chums
3. to my street as neighbors
4. to employment in my occupation
5. to citizenship in my country
6. as visitors only to my country
7. would exclude from my country[33]

Bogardus set the categories in a logical order that he assumed was cumulative: in steps one through five, at least, an individual espousing the first, most intimate level would be expected to admit groups to the other four, less intimate ones.[34]

The task of recording social distance was doubtless more difficult than

Bogardus imagined, requiring imaginative projection of one's own behavior to a long list of groups (in one discussion of the method, he offered thirty-nine, many of which were surely unknown personally to the respondent).[35] Hartley's later work would in fact demonstrate that a few students would register their attitude to wholly imaginary groups inserted into the list.[36] But Bogardus's scale itself was straightforward and clear, certainly as compared to some of the complex opinion statements that would clutter questionnaires. Also, the variable had analytic meaning, showing variability by age, sex, occupational group, and the like. Through much personal interviewing, Bogardus satisfied himself that the written "recording," or scale, method reflected attitudes expressed in much fuller form in person. In his study *Immigration and Race Attitudes*, he administered the social distance scale to 1,725 respondents from various parts of the country; 700 of these respondents were also interviewed.[37]

The Allport scale (which he developed with D. A. Hartman) assumed much knowledge of political issues. It asked college students to react to propositions on seven topics, which included the League of Nations, the Ku Klux Klan, and prohibition. The scale was constructed from personal opinions written by sixty students, which were then sifted, selected, and arranged independently by six judges (college teachers) in logical order from one extreme position to the other. The average rank assigned by the judges was the final rank order accorded to each statement. The scale was not designed to be cumulative; students were asked to select the *one* statement on each issue that best represented their own opinions.

The scales varied in their length and complexity. Attitudes toward President Coolidge, for example, were arrayed on a ten-point scale that ranged from "Coolidge is perfectly fitted for the office of President of the United States" to "A man such as Coolidge is bound to bring with him a corrupt government." On other scales, the steps were veritable portmanteaus of propositions, as shown in clusters from the five-step scale on attitudes toward the distribution of wealth. At one end of this scale were these propositions:

> The wealth of this country is at present distributed fairly and wisely. Wage earners get a perfectly fair deal. The poor are necessarily poor because of low mentality, and lack of ambition and thrift. . . .

And so on, through three other provisos. At the other end of the scale was this set:

Concentrated wealth gives great power which should belong to the government alone. The amassing of fortunes beyond a certain limit should be *prohibited by law*, and the money returned to the people. There should be very heavy income and inheritance taxes, rapidly approaching 100 per cent for the greater fortunes.[38]

And so on, again, through three more clauses for this scale step.

When the scales were administered, students were also asked to indicate on a five-point scale the degree of *certainty* and the level of *intensity* with which they held these opinions (the two proved to be virtually the same), in what appears the first use of intensity measures in data analysis.[39] Allport and Hartman graphed the distributions of both the opinions and the intensity measures, and they concluded that the "atypical" groups on the ends of the opinion distributions held their views more strongly than those in the middle, and that on other personality measures the groups on the ends tended to resemble each other more than either resembled the middle ranks. This presaged the study of authoritarianism of the Left, as well as of the Right, as Daniel Katz has noted.[40] Both the Bogardus social distance scales and the Allport-Hartman opinion scales occasioned much interest in certain sociological and psychological circles and were cited regularly in attitude studies and in reviews of the attitude literature.[41]

In the journal that Bogardus himself edited, *Sociology and Social Research* (originally the *Journal of Applied Sociology*), social distance studies flourished, not surprisingly. Numerous articles by Bogardus and others used the social distance measures of racial groups, religions, occupations, communities, parents and children.[42] There also appeared the beginnings of further analytic development in the "sociometric" potentialities of the scale and in the concept of the "social distance margin" for expressing how discrepant two groups' attitudes were toward each other.[43] But in Bogardus's journal there were just the beginnings of data analysis. A good deal of the social distance work published here was data-free, impressionistic, or conceptual—Bogardus himself was given to writing essays on social distance—and the inquiry remained something of a regional specialty for sociologists. While the *American Journal of Sociology* reviewed Bogardus's books with regularity, "social distance" was not a topic by which articles were cataloged in either the first *AJS* index (through 1935) or the second (through 1947). When eight articles from the early period under discussion here (through 1935–36) were reclassified under "social distance" in a 1965 index, only one dealt with a Bogardus-type scale.

This article, by Stuart C. Dodd, was on social distance measures taken in the Near East. Curiously, Dodd acknowledged a debt to Thurstone methods of scale constructions (which we shall consider presently) but did not mention Bogardus, from whom the measure's substance and form were obviously derived. If modern readers can recover from the startlement of proceeding in five scale steps (designed to be *equidistant*) from the intimacy of marriage partner to the sudden ferocity of wishing an entire group killed off, they will find the article quite contemporary in certain respects. Dodd's scale read as follows:

> If I wanted to marry, I would marry one of them.
> I would be willing to have [one] as a guest for a meal.
> I prefer to have [one] merely as an acquaintance to whom one talks on meeting in the street.
> I do not enjoy the companionship of these people.
> I wish someone would kill all these individuals.[44]

Dodd offered some interesting observations and hypotheses about social distance measures. For example, he found that religious groupings generated greater social distance than nationalities or economic classes, and he administered measures on all three types of groups to student subjects who themselves represented major categories within each. He suggested that cross-cultural indices of mobility could be derived from social distance measures, and he offered some general predictions about how these measures would behave in highly stratified as well as in more open societies.

Dodd did fail to herald the future in one critical respect. Lavish in his algebraic notation, he did not present one jot of data in support of the notions he presented. The article is nevertheless conceptually interesting, and it suggests some implications for data analysis of the Bogardus-type measures of attitude which few other sociologists were making at the time.

If Bogardus saw such implications, he may not have been entirely sympathetic to them. The scale was his most original contribution, but he saw it as a preliminary or superficial "recording," especially suitable for group administration and requiring the additional richness of the case-history methods of sociology, notably interviewing.[45] For one thing, he did not place full reliance on respondents' self-knowledge—or not enough, at any rate—so direct measurement was not completely attractive to him. He doubted that the great mass of people understood their own experience well enough to provide primary data. Without naming the authors, Bogardus commented that the Merriam/Gosnell study *Non-Voting* (1924) was probably bootless because nonvoters were being asked to explain why they did not get to the polls, and chances were slim that they really knew. He relied instead on the unstructured interview, cast in a clinical mode, stressing rapport and "mental release," and on the written life history to yield insight to the investigator. As to large-scale analysis, Bogardus went to the trouble of incorporating mass data into his race and immigration study. The Race Relations Survey in which he participated had been an ambitious effort to reach many people. But large numbers were not essential, he felt. By the "method of personal experience," he thought, one case could be "proportionately as vital as a million" if it brought something new to the researcher's mind that illuminated new understanding of the whole.[46]

When he joined colleagues in a 1931 festschrift to W. I. Thomas, Bogardus's contribution, "Attitudes and the Mexican Immigrant," did not make use of the scale of social distance nor of any systematic quantitative material. It was an essay of generalizations about how Mexicans adapted to American culture. In its nonquantitative emphasis, it was typical of most of the other contributions to the book by former students and collaborators of Thomas, such as Park, Faris, Young, Burgess, Thrasher, Znaniecki, and Steiner. The editor, Kimball Young, explained that while the authors did not discount the statistical method, most had found that the material in their analysis of social progress and social structure did not, so far, really lend itself to statistical treatment and was indeed qualitative.[47]

The polar choice for sociologists was still case histories versus statistics. Young pointed to other work in progress that was promising in its effort to "devise methods of treating certain aspects of social attitudes by statistical techniques,"[48] and he referred to the psychologists Floyd Allport, May, and Thurstone and the sociologist Rice, but not to Bogardus. His social distance actually had the potentiality of extending Chicago-style sociology into a more quantitative social psychology, but he appears not to have had the aspiration himself. The social distance measures persisted, however, and very probably influenced a good deal of question-writing in survey research on hypothetical behavior, especially in race relations.[49] But neither the self-reported behavioral properties nor the cumulative properties of his rather homely, merely logical scale were topics of wide interest or appreciation on the part of leading sociologists in this early period.[50] The quantification of attitude study flourished with questionnaires and scales of opinion indicators in the hands of psychologists.

Floyd Allport's study of attitudes flourished more vigorously than did Bogardus's brand in two ways. First, Allport's students, such as Katz and Schanck, used opinion indicators to explore attitudes toward institutions,[51] the contrast between "public" and "private" attitudes[52] (from which Allport developed the concept of "pluralistic ignorance"), and the application of stereotype to race prejudice.[53] These were genuine contributions to data analysis. Second, and more important for our purposes here, Allport's attitude scales flourished in their transformation by L. L. Thurstone, a psychologist at the University of Chicago. Thurstone became aware of both the Bogardus and Allport endeavors, but when Allport wrote to him seeking counsel on psychological measurement, Thurstone's interest was captured. He credited Allport with pioneering studies that directly inspired his own work in scaling.[54]

Thurstone Scales

Thurstone had been involved in psychophysical measurement—that is, the discrimination of "just noticeable differences" in weights, shades of gray, changes in handwriting—and he had come to think of it as quite a trivial enterprise. After all the hairsplitting, as he later wrote, he had never yet seen a psychologist who really cared a rap about any particular person's *limen* (threshold of discrimination). At any rate, it is clear that he himself no longer cared. However, stimulated by Allport's work, Thurstone thought that the "new psychophysical toys" might be put to another interesting use, after all.[55]

The crux of his efforts was the search for a true metric, an attitude scale with units of equal value all along a favorable-to-unfavorable continuum. The most elegant application from his psychophysical repertoire would have been the method of *paired comparisons*, in which judges compared every opinion statement with every other one and the measure of dispersion in the judgments was used to allocate statements to scale positions.[56] But this was a tedious business. In the scale that Thurstone and Chave devised for attitudes toward the church, they asked judges to assign a value to 130 statements. Had they used the method of paired comparisons, this would have required 8,385 separate judgments for one judge—$(n \times [n-1])/2$—and they used 300 judges! Not only were the judgments an enormous chore but in addition the various calculations to assign statements to scale positions after the judges had done their work represented a vast enterprise. Instead, for the church scale, Thurstone and Chave used a simpler method for judging, and even at that the construction of the scale took the better part of a year, as Thurstone told Gordon Allport.[57]

The method they used was that of "equal-appearing intervals." Judges were asked to sort opinion statements into eleven piles that seemed to them to represent equal distances of favorability. The statements were propositions of the following sort:

> I believe church membership is almost essential to living life at its best.
> I believe in what the church teaches but with mental reservations.
> I think the church is a parasite on society.[58]

In this particular scale, they were 130 strong. The scale value of each item was the mean value assigned by the 300 judges, modified by statistical criteria for detecting items that were ambiguous (high dispersion around the median) or irrelevant (judged not to measure the same dimension), which were dropped. The original list of statements was winnowed down to a final list of 45 statements about the church. These statements constituted a "more or less uniformly graduated series of scale values," although various Thurstone-type scales were shorter, with statements numbering in the twenties.[59]

Although the scale was obviously not a full interval scale and had other problems as well, which Thurstone recognized,[60] it was not merely a conventional rank order. Within limits, items could be added or subtracted without changing the values of other items in the scale; in a conventional rank order, such changes risked changing the values of many other items.

The Thurstone invention, quite awesome even now for its ingenuity, had an enormous influence. In the late 1920s and early 1930s, there was a flurry of scale-building in the Thurstone style (especially the equal-appearing interval scale) on such subjects as war, race, law, God, the professional training of social workers, prohibition, Germans, the U.S. Constitution, capital punishment, patriotism, censorship, communism, birth control, Sunday observance, and many others.[61] Bogardus revised his own scale in response to the Thurstone technique by enlisting judges to assess an enlarged set of statements.[62]

The issue of whether attitudes *should* be studied through opinion indicators was not of great moment to Thurstone. He saw his scales as a verbal index of attitude, limited as any index was, and as no more a representation of a full and complex attitude than a measure of a man's height was a rendering of the "whole" man. Opinions were surely no certain clue to conduct, Thurstone noted, but if people should intentionally distort their attitudes, one would at least be measuring the attitude they were trying to make people *believe* they had.[63] He also pointed to the fact that people could disguise their real attitudes by dissembling behavior, just as they could disguise their real attitudes by faking opinions. (The earnest quest by others in later years for validating opinions through measures of behavior certainly did not take Thurstone's stance of detachment about such matters.) In any case, Thurstone avowed, opinions/attitudes were of great interest in themselves, a proposition with which many academic psychologists obviously agreed.

Critique and Application

RICE AND STOUFFER

The sociologists Rice and Stouffer had catholic tastes in research that drew them to consider psychologists' quantitative measures. Rice used subjective opinion questionnaires in classroom studies, on the one hand, and objective behavioral methods of recorded votes, on the other. Stouffer tested the equivalence of the psychologist's classroom questionnaire and attitude scale with the sociologist's case history.

Although Rice's research interests were in politics, such that he is now sometimes taken for a political scientist, he did indeed take his degree in sociology, at Columbia under Giddings. In the first few years of his career, Rice might have been taken for a psychologist as well, for he wrote a questionnaire for the psychologist Henry T. Moore and inquired into students' expectations about marriage and children.[64] While most of his research bore on political topics, it had a strong methodological interest. He did a retrospective study of attitude change from students who had heard William Jennings Bryan's lecture against evolution. He conducted an actual "panel" measurement of change in students' attitudes in the course of the 1924 election. In a nonverbal measure, he studied students' visual stereotyping of people appearing in newspaper photographs. He isolated interviewer bias operating in attitudes toward prohibition when respondents' recorded views closely mirrored the interviewers'. He compared legislators' attitudes obtained by questionnaire with those of their constituents as indicated by votes. (All of the studies just mentioned were collected in a book published in 1928.)[65]

Had he pursued these research interests, Rice might well have exerted more influence on the measurement of attitudes. As it was, he grew wary of subjective data obtained by direct measurement and turned his attention back to electoral statistics, on which he had done his dissertation. He advocated the study of behavioral patterns to infer attitudes through the following sources: voting records and other behaviors, such as patterns of attendance at movies, lectures, and sermons; participation in organizations; gate receipts for sports events; radio programming; and a host of other such cultural indicators of "public attention."[66]

Rice's critique of Thurstone scaling was a trenchant one, not only for the judging process but also for the typical practice of measuring attitudes through opinions. Constructing scales and measuring attitudes with them were increasingly difficult, Rice wrote,

> once we leave the classroom, the discussion club and the other small, comparatively infrequent and highly selected groups that enjoy having experiments tried upon them. Such groups already have developed ways of making their attitudes articulate. It is the more numerous work-a-day groupings of society, which are inaccessible to his controlled measurements, about whose attitudes the social scientist is in the most need of information. Students may be required, good natured academicians may be cajoled, and sundry needy persons may be paid to sort cards containing propositions into eleven piles. But it is difficult to imagine securing comparable judgments, or satisfactory measurements in the final application, from bricklayers, business men, Italian-Americans, nuns, stevedores, or seamstresses.[67]

The validity of a scale was open to question, Rice added, unless a random sample of the group to be measured served as the judges constructing the scale.[68] He also voiced this skeptical view:

> Perhaps the attitude scale, like other scales employed in science, is valid only within the middle ranges of its phenomena—in other words, among persons whose intellectuality and knowledge are neither too great nor too small.[69]

Most fundamentally, he felt that continued devotion to Thurstone scaling risked a spurious accuracy, a more refined statistical treatment than the basic data really warranted when its validity and representativeness were still in question.

Stouffer found the Thurstone scales attractive enough to test their equivalence to the qualitative case histories that were more congenial to the Chicago sociologists. Linking of the two methods was the subject of Stouffer's 1930 dissertation at Chicago. Students were asked to write an essay on their personal experiences and their attitudes toward prohibition law and personal drinking, which a small set of academic judges then rated on a five-point scale of favorability toward prohibition. The judges agreed closely with one another as well as with a pair of judges who were active in pro- and antiprohibition politics, respectively, and the rating scores of the essays correlated highly with students' scores on a Thurstone-type scale on prohibition. So it all worked well.

The results favored the use of the scale over case histories, as Stouffer pointed out, for it could be administered in perhaps fifteen minutes. In the time it would take to analyze a handful of case histories, one could gather up several hundred indices of attitude. Stouffer also recommended the use of questionnaires over case histories in another study, for the same reason. He nevertheless thought life histories were indispensable for two purposes: the initial formulation of direct questions, and the interpretations of the meanings of relationships after their magnitudes had been determined statistically.[70] Stouffer's test of a Thurstone scale was a limited one, dealing with a narrow topic, and the subjects were the obliging student population. The results nevertheless commended the more quantifiable procedure on practical grounds.

By the early 1930s, as a line formed at his door asking for still more scales on still more attitudes, Thurstone himself had begun to grow weary of the whole enterprise. Few petitioners showed any interest in the basic theory of attitude measurement. He later recalled that he had picked up a dozen or more attitude scales that were in preparation and thrown them in the wastebasket, and that thereafter he had discouraged any further work on the matter in his laboratory.[71] Thurstone then moved on to factor analysis. His achievement in scaling commanded influence and prestige long after he himself had had enough, however, and it remains a classic in attitude measurement.[72]

THE LIKERT REVISION

Rensis Likert's dissertation in 1932 was an alternative to Thurstone scaling, designed to make judges unnecessary. The method, called "summated rating," used scaled items such as these:

An American committing a crime in Shanghai should be tried by a Chinese judge.

Strongly Approve	Approve	Undecided	Disapprove	Strongly Disapprove
(5)	(4)	(3)	(2)	(1)

Negro homes should be segregated from those of white people.

Strongly Approve	Approve	Undecided	Disapprove	Strongly Disapprove
(1)	(2)	(3)	(4)	(5)

Should there be a national referendum on every war?

Yes	?	No
(4)	(3)	(2)

How much military training should we have?

(a) We need universal compulsory military training.

(b) We need Citizens' Military Training Camps and Reserve Officers' Training Corps, but not universal military training.

(c) We need some facilities for training reserve officers but not as much as at present.

(d) We need only such military training as is required to maintain our regular army.

(e) All military training should be abolished.[73]

About 200 items on various topics were mingled in the questionnaire (and no numbers were attached to the choices), and they were later grouped according to the subject matter of the various scales. What has come to be called the Likert-type item (the Strongly Approve/Strongly Disapprove form) was not the only form of question that he used, as the examples indicate.

The Likert method bypassed judges by administering a battery of items to subjects and afterward analyzing their suitability for the scale by the criterion of internal consistency, familiar in psychometrics, which had not apparently been applied to attitude measurement before.[74] Likert obtained high correlations between his scales and the Thurstone scales, and he also obtained generally higher reliabilities with fewer items.[75] There were various efforts in this period to simplify the Thurstone judging process and to mass-produce scales by finding all-purpose items.[76] Likert's alternative was a serviceable one, although it lacked the theoretical coherence and elegance of a Thurstone scale. In constructing his scale, Likert initially made the items comparable for scoring by transforming the percentages obtained for each alternative into a "sigma" value of a normal distribution. He repaired to the simpler, arbitrary scoring (one through five) when he found that it yielded nearly identical results.

The Likert revision implicitly raised an important question about the conduct of large-scale empirical research. Did one stay with measures of theoretical elegance and clarity if they were more costly and yet no more illuminating in practice of quantitative data than simpler tools were? The Likert scale argued no, and the method came into widespread use despite some later debate about its comparability to Thurstone[77]—Hall, for example, used it in morale measures of unemployed men, and Rundquist and Sletto adapted it to a study of personality[78]—and it also became a classic in attitude measurement. Virtually any review of attitude literature after 1932 would include a reference to Likert's work as well as to Thurstone's.

Likert's scale was one of the instruments used in a broader project of Gardner Murphy's which addressed the "perennial altercation between quantitative and qualitative sociologists":

> The issue is to be settled, we believe, not by debate, but by much sober presentation of qualitative and quantitative data in conjunction, in the modest hope that in time ways of combining the two sorts of information will become clearer in studies like the present.[79]

The effort of Murphy and Likert to convert "subtle and fleeting subjective factors" into objective measures was at once more ambitious and less successful than Stouffer's study of attitudes toward prohibition.

From students' written histories of their lives and the development of their social and political beliefs, Murphy and Likert tried to code *three* different attitudes bearing on political radicalism, and they had only a tiny pool of reasonably complete autobiographies (an *n* of 9) which was the study's low point (the high point of the quantitative analysis using the Likert attitude scales and personal background data was 377). Other ambitious efforts to integrate qualitative materials and quantitative ratings had practical difficulties, too, for they were limited to that small set of students who volunteered for the ten hours of writing and paper-and-pencil tests *and* who stayed the course: twenty-five at Columbia University and sixty at the University of Michigan. The investigators felt that they had failed to exploit fully the autobiographical materials and had also failed to quantify variables of the "rather intangible and personal sort," especially the personalities of parents and the students' reading habits, the two factors that students themselves reported as being most influential.[80] The authors' candid analysis of their problems is in fact one of the special virtues of this book, providing an illuminating record of problems in design and measurement. One other feature of their methods illustrates how difficult it was to take complex attitude measurement out of the college classroom.

Attitude Surveys Outside the Classroom: On the Utility of Interviewers

Attitude Change after College

After about five years, in late 1934, Murphy and Likert conducted a "retest" of their student subjects (who were, of course, now out of college) and incorporated their findings into *Public Opinion and the Individual* (1938). This seems to have been the first panel measurement of attitude change taken over such a long period.[81]

The mail-questionnaire results showed some evidence of change. Certain relationships that had been of some importance during the respondents' college years had flattened out (for example, the positive relationship between grade point average and radicalism). "Life has attenuated the forces which seem to be of major importance at the college level,"[82] the authors noted, but they had few means of exploring why this was so. Was it the depression in general, they wondered? Personal hardship? Five years of growth? Other factors? Other interactions? There was suggestive evidence that the depression, as a general social and political force rather than as a specific personal hardship, was a determining factor, but the researchers lacked data to explore the matter further. The response rate was high after a lapse of five years—49 percent of 262 students returned the mail questionnaire—but the form itself was an important obstacle to analysis.

For example, in answer to the question "Please indicate the chief things which have changed your views," students who had grown more conservative gave explanations of this variety:

Growing older.
The lack of "intellectual honesty" of all Communists causes my lack of tolerance towards them.
Education. Experiences in life. Trial and error experiences.
A month of traveling third class in Russia.[83]

The answers were often elliptical, incomplete, and scattered on various dimensions. The authors concluded that the questionnaire at a distance was a weak instrument for gathering such open-ended materials, and they looked forward to the next steps in attitude research, such as better methods of the diary and the interview and "means of formulating more penetrating and revealing questions."[84] Other researchers working with subjective measurement of the adult population were in search of the

same thing. Some who could afford it were finding that personal interviewing had advantages.

Industrial Psychology

Attitude scales generated interest in applied psychology as well as in academic social psychology, but industrial psychologists were also looking
for simpler, more all-purpose instruments. J. David Houser's studies of
employer and employee attitudes used unstructured interviews on the
one hand and a "question blank" method on the other.[85] In the latter,
the interviewer asked standardized questions and then coded the answer
on the spot into categories memorized in advance by the interviewer. The
categories were those that Houser deemed to be at equal intervals of
feeling from hostility to enthusiasm. In response to a question about
opportunities to learn on the job, for example, the interviewer was to
listen attentively to the employee's response and then to convert it men-
tally into one of these "type" responses, which had a numerical value.
For example, this was a low-ranked item:

> 1. Don't think I'm getting along at all! I'm in a fierce rut! No chance to
> learn! There's no encouragement at all to try to learn or go ahead.

And this was a high-ranked item:

> 5. The company certainly does encourage me and offers me every oppor-
> tunity to develop and make progress. I'm sure I am being given every chance
> I could be.[86]

One could well wonder why these fully detailed categories were not
simply given directly to the respondents, who could then decide for
themselves where their attitude best fit. Houser, however, was concerned
about the lack of communication between employees and employers, especially the latter's insensitivity to employees' attitudes and morale. The
interviewing situation was to provide communication—written questionnaires would not have been as appropriate—as well as a mechanism by
which to summarize attitudes in quantitative fashion.

In the case of the Hawthorne experiments of 1927–32, interviewing
came to take on an unexpected therapeutic purpose, as it seemed to
provide insight to the respondents themselves as well as to investigators.
After industrial output increased steadily under experimental conditions
at Western Electric's Hawthorne Works in Chicago, *no matter what*—for

example, even when the liberalized rest breaks and lunch hours were withdrawn—there were clues that styles of supervision might be an important factor. Participants in the experimental room expressed great pleasure at being out from under the pressures of harsh bosses of the regular plant. A program of interviewing was instituted to look into workers' attitudes about working conditions and supervision in particular, and in the period from 1930–32, half of the plant personnel were interviewed (more than 21,000 people). The masses of data gathered were rather perplexing to analyze, but it was clear that the very free-flowing, nondirective interviewing yielded much information about the workers' attitudes toward the company and about their personal lives off the job, which workers were pleased to discuss.[87]

While the Hawthorne studies made the most massive use of unstructured interviewing, other studies of attitude commended the use of interviewing over the exclusive use of written questionnaires or elaborate scaled measurements—when there was enough money. First, there was the matter of *reward*. As the Hawthorne experiments demonstrated, if there was no danger of being identified or punished for unpopular opinions, it was clearly more satisfying to tell one's opinions to a sympathetic listener than to a piece of paper.[88]

Second, there was the matter of *information about the situation*. Interviewers could answer questions, determine whether questions were understood, note problems, smooth over difficulties posed by an ungainly question, and report on the respondent's understanding and on the adequacy of the questions. Bingham and Moore recommended that interviewing be used to supplement mass questionnaires when it was too expensive to use interviewers exclusively.[89]

Third, there were *opportunity costs* to consider. To measure an attitude toward a company in all its Thurstone precision might well take up much of the available time and yield information on only one attitude. Kornhauser and Sharp reported being asked repeatedly why they had not used Thurstone-type attitude scales in their studies at the Kimberly Clark Corporation. They explained that they had used the informal but "guided" interview based on a set of topics as well as questionnaires of the "cruder, shot-gun" approach because, while they learned things with less precision, they learned more things.[90] As a fourth consideration, when research was conducted out of the bounds of the classroom or the industrial plant, interviewers were valuable for the plain purpose of *finding people*.

The Chicago Surveys

Some of the young political scientists in Charles E. Merriam's department at the University of Chicago used interviewers for these purposes
when they could, in both their studies exploring psychological attitudes
and cognitions and those exploring sociological and political variables in
complex research designs. Leonard D. White and Harold F. Gosnell, in
particular, did pioneering survey work in the 1920s at Chicago.

In *The Prestige Value of Public Employment in Chicago* (1929), White investigated the perceived status of jobs in government versus private industry, along with other measures and ratings of the respective efficiency,
honesty, and courtesy of workers in the public and the private sectors.
The study was a mixture of the fieldwork and the classroom traditions,
for written questionnaires were administered to small groups as well as
to individuals under the supervision of an interviewer. White's procedures were not unlike those used by Bogardus in the same years. In at
least some situations, the interviewer delivered questions orally. White
tried to put together a "representative" mix of occupational groups—
housewives, clerks, businessmen, professionals, and skilled and unskilled
workers—and ranges of age, education, and nativity. Students were a
substantial group, but the largest single group was composed of people
in business jobs. (In analysis, White did some weighting of demographic
groups by their known proportion of the Chicago population.)[91]

The decision to rely more on written materials than on personal interviewing was based on a field staff that was limited to virtually a one-
man operation: over the course of nine months one research assistant
collected about 3,800 schedules—over 80 percent of the data—while
White and four graduate students collected about another 900. Understandably, White abandoned the idea of personal interviewing "for fear
the interviewer would soon build up a pattern into which, perhaps un-
consciously, would be fitted the responses made to him"; and it is also
small wonder that administering the questionnaire to groups in addition
to individuals became a procedure of choice.[92]

The respondents gave city hall and public employment very poor report. On twenty occupations, only two of the city hall occupations showed
higher prestige than their counterparts in private business. Political authorities were castigated for graft and corruption. City administration
fared better—the health department and civil service did well, in fact—
but government workers generally got pretty disastrous marks on honesty, courtesy, and efficiency. In a separate content analysis of almost

1,000 press clippings of the same period, White and his students found in six Chicago newspapers a mild tendency toward negative coverage of city services; the health department got the most positive treatment.

Two other findings remain of special interest. First, the perception of government status was inversely related, on the whole, to the status of the groups: the less well educated, those with lower income, and the foreign born were more approving of the city sector than were groups of higher socioeconomic status. (White also speculated that public service was given a more positive evaluation in Europe.) Second, the attitudes could not be related to personal experience with the city government. When respondents were asked, "Have your own dealings with public employees and officials been satisfactory?" only a minority (24%) expressed clear dissatisfaction.[93] White's research design clearly allowed for analysis beyond simple comparisons by occupational group.

This patchwork design—a motley of groups, many assembled "on loan" from their workplaces; data obtained mostly from brief paper-and-pencil work contained on a single Hollerith card; a tiny staff of graduate students—poses a sharp contrast to the sheer elegance and scope of the national probability sample design and extended field staff that began to emerge in the 1930s. But within the practical constraints that White and his students faced, one must admire the ingenuity and sophistication of their survey—enriched by a prestige index of private and public occupations, fifteen different measures of their perceived functioning, and nine-point scales, as well as a content analysis of press coverage.

Gosnell's work in this period is even more impressive. Gosnell conducted two notable surveys in the 1920s: *Non-Voting: Causes and Methods of Control* (1924), and *Getting Out the Vote: An Experiment in Stimulation of Voting* (1927).[94] Both used complex research designs and a mixture of mass personal interviewing and written questionnaires. *Non-Voting*, a study of the Chicago mayoral elections in 1923, was a form of mass/elite design: informants who were very involved in politics (prominent political figures, precinct committeemen) were questioned about the phenomenon of nonvoting, and large groups of nonvoters were themselves questioned.

The efforts to obtain elite data by questionnaire suffered difficulties, however. Gosnell wrote to political experts asking them to indicate on a checklist the most common reasons that people did not vote, but many of the precinct committeemen marked nearly *all* of the reasons on the list, and only a few tried to give them any rank order. (Gosnell realized too late that he should have asked respondents for a rank ordering.)

Only one noble soul among the 3,800 committeemen who had been sent the questionnaire responded with an elaborate analysis of what he knew about nonvoting. Gosnell found that personal interviewing was much more fruitful with the political expert group, even though it did not lend itself to statistical analysis.[95] Altogether, Gosnell obtained opinions from 300 expert informants.

From 6,000 nonvoters selected by quota sampling to be "representative" of census categories, Gosnell obtained data by personal interview. He also compared the characteristics of the nonvoters with those of 5,000 voters. Graduate students carried out the personal interviewing with a schedule that involved much field coding—that is, interviewers were equipped with a list of possible reasons for not voting, which they checked off whenever the respondent volunteered any of them. The interviewer was instructed to let the respondent do as much of the talking as possible, to summarize their comments by the use of the checklist when it provided a good fit, and to note any additional reasons or detailed explanations when the checklist options did not suffice. By far the single most frequent reason volunteered by the respondents was general indifference to the election or to politics overall (33%); 11 percent expressed disapproval that women, newly enfranchised, *should* vote; and about the same percentage were diffident or ignorant about the procedures of registering and voting. A recheck on reasons for nonvoting was included in a follow-up study, and it showed much the same patterns.[96]

The follow-up, *Getting Out the Vote*, was a combination survey and experiment—perhaps the first field experiment in the social sciences outside of psychology[97]—which tested the differential effect on voting of mailed reminders to register and vote. Chicago data were gathered for the presidential election of 1924 and for a city election of 1925. First, graduate student interviewers made a complete canvass of residents in twelve areas in Chicago (most of them precincts) which had been selected for the range of their demographic characteristics. The households of those areas were then separated geographically into experimental and control groups, and the experimental groups were sent nonpartisan postcards with exhortations and information about registration and voting. Residents who had not registered by a certain date were sent another, more graphic reminder, in the form of a cartoon. Finally, the effect of the experimental treatment was assessed by consulting official precinct lists to determine who had registered and voted.

The overall impact of the experiment was to increase registration of former nonvoters by 10 percent. The experiment was less successful where strong party organization was already active in promoting registration. It was also less successful among more educated voters, who were already more informed, interested, and likely to vote. The measured level of political information was in fact directly related to voting itself and inversely related to the effectiveness of the experiment.[98] Based on both studies, Gosnell's strong recommendation was to urge that registration procedures be simplified and routinely publicized to all residents.

Gosnell's measures of information in this study are of special interest. First, interviewers were equipped with the general schedule on the following page,[99] which in its use of topics rather than exact question wording resembles some of the schedules we saw in chapter one.

Then, respondents' knowledge of government (line 23) was obtained by another questionnaire. Respondents who could read it were sometimes asked to fill it out themselves, but usually this took so long "that the interviewer was compelled to resort to the method of direct oral questioning."[100] Gosnell considered the first ten questions to be very simple ones:

1. Who was the father of our country?
2. Who is the president of the U.S.?
3. Where does he live?
4. Who was president before him?
5. If the president dies in office, who takes his place?
6. What does Congress do?
7. How many states are there in the U.S.?
8. What is the name of our state?
9. Who is the chief executive of this state?
10. Where does he live?

He considered the next ten to be rather more technical but nevertheless of the sort that naturalization examiners asked:

11. Was the Constitution adopted by a vote of the people?
12. Does Congress make all the laws in this country?
13. Who is your congressman?
14. Who are the senators from Illinois?
15. How are the judges of the Supreme Court of the U.S. chosen?
16. Can a person who commits a crime be arrested in a state other than that in which the crime was committed?
17. Can the Constitution be changed?
18. Who is the chief executive of this city?
19. Who is your alderman?
20. What is the only crime the Constitution defines?

A STUDY OF CITIZENSHIP
Schedule for Interviewing Adult Persons*

1.	Date	Filled by
2.	Dist. No.	Name
3.	Sex	
4.	Color	Date of naturalization
5.	Cit. status	
6.	Yrs. a citizen, if naturalized, yrs. in U.S., if alien, and yrs. in Chicago, if native born	
7.	Occupation Employer Bus. Ad.	
8.	Country of birth	
9.	Country of birth of father of mother	
10.	Place (1. Urban) of birth (2. Rural)	
11.	Age in yrs.—Date of birth	
12.	Age on arrival in U.S.	Date of arrival
13.	Yrs. elapsing between arrival and declar.	Date of declaration
14.	Time elapsing between 21 yrs. (or later arrival) and petit.	Date of petit.
15.	Marital condition	
16.	Children	Name of school
17.	Sp. [Language spoken]	
18.	Yrs. in U.S.	Witness
19.	Yrs. in Ill.	Address
20.	Yrs. in dist.	Witness
21.	Pol. contacts	Address
22.	Reads and writes Eng.	(1. Y.) Paper read (2. N.)
23.	Knowl. of govt. (1. Insuf.), (2. p.), (3. f.), (4. g.), (5. e.).	
24.	Years in school in U.S. abroad	
25.	Voting record in Regis. N.-V. last seven elections Not regis. file no.	
26.	Economic status	
27.	Reasons for coming to Chicago	
28.	Explanation of citizenship status	

*[Codes for marital status, nationality, language spoken, etc. were included on the schedule.]

Gosnell's measure of political knowledge now seems remarkably ambitious, longer and with a greater range of difficulty than anything survey researchers would be likely to ask in the 1980s—out of reluctance, perhaps, to devote that much time in the interview to such a measure but also out of concern not to appear patronizing to the best informed or challenging to the least informed. We learn from Gosnell's summary data that approximately 5 percent of the respondents failed to answer any of the questions, 35 percent answered half or fewer of the items correctly, and the remaining 60 percent answered more than half correctly.[101] Could these results be replicated in our own era?

Of equal interest to the history of survey research is the question of whether the studies themselves, in their magnitude, would be conducted now with only the resources that White and Gosnell had on hand in the 1920s. To imagine that task is to appreciate the accomplishment. These projects were huge. The interviews and questionnaires were brief, but in all three studies the n was on the order of 5,000 to 6,000. The administrative and technical arrangements would have been formidable enough for a permanent professional staff; for a floating graduate student group, with only some professional support, they now seem quite daunting. Anyone who has directed survey fieldwork with either professionals or students knows what a large order this all was, especially the Gosnell studies, which involved more complexity, elaborate coordination, and close timing. These ambitious studies by White and Gosnell were made possible by the resources of the Local Community Research Committee (launched by funding of the Laura Spelman Rockefeller Memorial), but it should be remembered that these were projects, not continuing research organizations, and much of the organization thus had to be one-time and improvisational. It is in this context that one should read the following excerpt from Gosnell's introduction to *Getting Out the Vote*:

> The tremendous amount of work involved in making the observations set forth below will have been justified if some small advance has been made in the application of more exact methods to the study of electoral problems.[102]

Bulmer has recently written that these Chicago surveys have been neglected in historical accounts of survey research:

> Chicago sociology was more quantitative than it is usually presented as being, but by and large survey research was unusual. But when one turns to political science, the department headed by Charles E. Merriam poses a real challenge.

Why has it been overlooked? Merriam was a leading proponent of the science
of politics; Chicago became its center. Indeed, in the history of the scientific
social survey in America . . . [monographs by White and Gosnell] in the 1920s
prefigure many later developments, yet they do not figure prominently in
histories of survey research.[103]

Political scientists have credited the pioneering character of the early
Chicago work, but they have ordinarily done so in the context of the
"behavioral revolution" in the discipline, of which survey research was
one part.[104] Somit and Tanenhaus, for example, in their history of political science (which Bulmer cites) credit Merriam with having inspired
new attention to methodology and quantitative work in the discipline
(less by his own research example than by exhortation, encouragement,
and efforts at interdisciplinary organization), and they note the innovative empirical work of Gosnell, White, Harold Lasswell, Herbert Simon,
Quincy Wright, V. O. Key, Jr., Gabriel Almond, David Truman, and of
other political scientists associated with Merriam at Chicago. Others,
such as Almond, Eulau, and Campbell, Converse, Miller, and Stokes,
acknowledge Gosnell's contribution to survey research more specifically.[105] The lacunae that Bulmer detects seem to represent an inatten-
tion by latter-day *sociologists* to Gosnell's early work.

Gosnell nevertheless was not a continuing influence in the shaping of
survey research. He was a productive scholar, but he did not focus on
the survey instrument. His fascinating book *Machine Politics: Chicago
Model* (1937), for example, is based on his own rich culture and personal
participation in politics, personal interviews with political figures, and
content analysis of the press, census data, and election statistics.[106] Gosnell did not create a "school" or a research organization, which would
have resonated his influence. It is probably significant that he left Chicago, just as Lasswell did, and Almond attributes both departures to the
same reason:

> Under the presidency of Robert Maynard Hutchins, the hospitality of the
> University to the empirical social sciences had notably cooled. Merriam's de-
> partment came under criticism on grounds of "number crunching" and "psy-
> chologizing," as well as internal recruitment. . . . While Lasswell had tenure,
> as did Gosnell, both men left the inhospitable University—Lasswell in 1938
> [and Gosnell, in the 1940s, for government service]. Merriam himself was
> approaching retirement and was unable to defend his younger men.[107]

Gosnell was enthusiastic about the new public opinion polls of 1935
as well as a discerning critic of their technical problems, and he sensed

their importance for American political institutions. In countries dedicated to democratic theory, he wrote, polls would take a place alongside familiar devices such as the initiative, referendum, recall, legislative hearing, and the commission of inquiry as another instrument for ascertaining the will of the people.[108] To take just a single, very concrete example, the use of polling criteria in 1980 to decide which candidates could participate in the nationally televised presidential debates makes Gosnell's view seem prophetic indeed.[109]

In a political science text in the late 1940s, Gosnell and Merriam's discussion of the polls noted that social scientists were slow to recognize the practical applications of (quota) sampling methods for the study of public opinion and slow to find ways of financing the applications.[110] This is rare tribute in this period to the fact that the conduct of large-scale survey research was not only a complex intellectual task but that it also took some money-raising genius. Gosnell's own labors with large surveys in Chicago may well have given him a special appreciation for the entrepreneurial achievements of Gallup, Roper, and Crossley.

In the 1920s and early 1930s, the collective intellectual achievements of social scientists interested in attitude measurement were imaginative and substantial. In the classroom, they designed instruments of considerable elegance. They tried to simplify them for use with groups in the broader population, tinkering with written questionnaires and interviewing in various combinations. They classified attitudes and constructed attitudinal indices and tried to link these to the study of personalities and cultures. They explored prejudice, attitude change over time, "public and private" attitudes, and opinion and behavioral indicators. They looked for links between individual or qualitative insight and quantitative evidence. Their work proliferated quantification of the subjective realm of human experience and expanded the ranks of social psychologists who wanted to explore it.

Their work was nevertheless limited by its sampling. Even the range of variation in attitude available to study was circumscribed by the use of student groups, and when researchers broke out of academic environments, they put together groups from the adult population in the patchworks we have observed. That limitation was linked to another: that of organization. The social psychologists proliferated "small" science, projects directed by one or two individuals, assisted at best by a few graduate students. The work necessarily lacked scope and continuity because academic researchers simply did not have the necessary money and institutional capacity.

The federal government began to develop large-scale research in the mid-1930s, as we have seen, and the opinion pollsters did so in another way in the same period. By the time the new national polls came on the scene in 1935, academic social psychologists who had been working with attitudes and opinions tended to feel that they knew a good deal more about the matter than the pollsters did, and some came to take special umbrage at the high speed and superficial approach of the pollsters. The academic specialists doubtless did know more about the complexities of attitude measurement, but the pollsters had two interrelated resources that the social scientists did not: they offered *national* data on opinion, which until their advent had essentially been unavailable, and they found *funding* for work of this expensive scope. With these resources the polls quickly became of interest to some government officials. Social scientists were later recruited into governmental attitude/opinion work because national opinion polling (more than attitude measurement) was seen to have obvious political and administrative utility. Like it or not, the academic survey researchers owed a good deal to the pollsters. It is to their development that we will turn in chapter three.

3

The Most Direct Line, Business: Market Research and Opinion Polling

Applied psychologists in particular are . . . likely to resent the dating of everything in public opinion polling from the 1935 reports of Roper and Gallup.

Donald G. Paterson

The Two Routes to Public Opinion Research

The most immediate ancestors of survey research were the election pollsters of 1936, George Gallup, Elmo Roper, and Archibald Crossley, who correctly forecast the Roosevelt reelection and stayed in the business. All three were market researchers who became straw-vote journalists. Because they all wore two hats, two somewhat different accounts of public opinion polling exist. One account stresses journalism. In this chronicle, the polls of the mid-1930s proceeded directly from a century of various American straw votes, of which the *Literary Digest* poll was the most famous and long-lived but was finally seen as ill-starred when it trumpeted a Landon victory for 1936.[1] In that year, the polls of a new genre conducted by the trio soared into public prominence with forecasts of Roosevelt's reelection and eclipsed the *Digest*, which soon thereafter sank into bankruptcy and oblivion—"hooted out of the business," as one historian recently put it, with only partial accuracy.[2]

Another branch of the family traces opinion polls to market research, which extended research on consumers' preferences for commercial *products* to their preferences on public *issues*. As a prominent market researcher, Frank R. Coutant, put the matter in the 1940s, "We [in the market research field] have not borrowed methods from polling, as some people think. They have borrowed from us."[3] The applied psychologist Henry C. Link was another important spokesman for this view of the ancestry. He claimed priority for the field in general:

The fact that much of this early [market] research was devoted to the study of people's opinions about magazines, about food products, about soaps and many other things of everyday life should not obscure its great importance to the field of public opinion research. After all, opinions are opinions. It may be that opinions on political and social issues are more important than opinions about automobiles, cigarettes, coffees . . . [but] the techniques of obtaining opinions reliably were furthered by the comparatively non-partisan nature of the commercial field.[4]

Link also claimed priority for his own public opinion poll, which had been established in 1932, three years before the polls of Gallup and Roper.

There is truth to both of these accounts, but Coutant was correct: market researchers knew much more about research methods than journalists did. The technical methods of the new polls of 1935 had indeed been developed in market research, a field in which well-trained and sophisticated businessmen, psychologists, economists, and statisticians all played an important part.[5] The journalists certainly knew how to raise *money* for the work, as they harnessed the engine of political campaigns— the interest, excitement, controversy—in the service of boosting media circulation with preelection straws. Election forecasts later provided the horse-race excitement (with presidential popularity questions designed to generate some of that excitement between elections).[6]

Election forecasts also offered the advantage—and risk—of validating methods generally. If the new pollsters could call the winner, this should inspire public confidence in their work as a whole. The pollsters were much more heavily engaged in market research than in this new opinion polling experiment. *New York Times* finance writers reported in 1936 that the business community had been following the new polls with great interest, mindful of the implications for business forecasts in the accuracy of the political forecasts.[7] The famous trio of Gallup, Roper, and Crossley constructed the new opinion polls in a merger of the two fields, using methods of market research and financing them with the money and publicity of election straw-vote journalism.

Market Research and the Methods

The Early Organizations

Market research into consumer preferences goes back to at least the 1890s—the psychologist Harlow Gale at the University of Minnesota used questionnaires to study reactions to advertising in 1895[8]—and there were very probably earlier efforts because advertising agencies emerged as independent organizations in the United States by the mid-nineteenth century. Substantial beginnings of consumer research departments in industry or independent organizations are dated to the decade 1910–1920.[9] In 1911, Charles Coolidge Parlin was made director of a research department in the Curtis Publishing Company, which published the *Saturday Evening Post*, the *Ladies' Home Journal*, and *Gentleman Farmer*. He remained head of the Division of Commercial Research there for some thirty years and was influential in inspiring similar departments in major industrial firms such as Swift and Company and U.S. Rubber.[10]

Parlin's advice to carmakers in 1915 expressed very succinctly the rationale for market research. He pointed out that the game of selling cars had to change. Production had soared in the past years from an annual crop of 20,000 cars to some 400,000, an increase of over 2,000 percent. People who already had the money and desire to buy the cars produced had largely done so. Now the manufacturer had to find a new group of consumers and heed what they wanted in cars. In order to rationalize mass-production industries—that is, to organize investment and sales—it was now necessary to anticipate and help create consumer preferences and to feed them back into the design and manufacturing process. The market henceforth, Parlin explained, would be strongly influenced by national business conditions, national advertising of brand names, and a national network of distributors and salesmen.[11]

While the total dollar expenditures in market research were very small in the decade from 1910–20 (*Printers' Ink*, the advertising trade magazine, estimated that no more than $50,000 was actually spent on market research in 1910),[12] some organizations in academic-commercial collaboration were beginning. In 1911, the Harvard Graduate School of Business established the Bureau of Business Research, which became receptive to the psychological aspects of market research. Paul T. Cherington, later Roper's senior partner in the *Fortune* quarterly survey, taught at the Harvard School of Business from 1908 to 1919; he taught one of the earliest courses in marketing, and in 1911 he began work on the consumer research field.[13] Harvard became an influential force for intellectual organization of the field in sampling and analysis.[14]

A nucleus of professional organization was formed. In 1915, the psychologist Walter Dill Scott became the first president of a new association of practicing advertising professionals and teachers of marketing, and Paul Cherington became the second. It was this group that ultimately became the American Marketing Association, which published the *Journal of Marketing*.[15] The *Journal of Applied Psychology*, founded in 1917, covered a number of applied interests—industrial psychology, counseling, mental testing, vocational guidance—and became a vehicle for both survey and experimental data bearing on consumer research problems.

The earliest consumer research focused on consumers' reactions to products and to advertising, especially advertising in magazines, newspapers, billboards, and direct mail. Leading publishing houses undertook research to demonstrate to their potential advertisers who and where their readership was and what products these readers would be likely to buy. Not only Curtis but also others such as Crowell (*Better Homes and Gardens, Successful Farming*), McFadden (*True Story* and many others), Meredith (*Liberty Magazine*), and Funk and Wagnalls (*Literary Digest*) conducted market research.[16]

Newspapers did early work into distribution and consumption patterns in their areas. As early as 1913, the *Chicago Tribune* sent out mail questionnaires on the subject of why certain foods were purchased.[17] Starting in 1922, the *Milwaukee Journal* for many years conducted an annual study of consumer purchases, selecting every third household in a canvass of the Milwaukee area.[18] When radio networks began to spread in the 1920s, research into radio listening followed quickly. The study of radio's advertising impact and audience listening preferences became research specialties of Daniel Starch (a Harvard psychologist and commercial researcher who became research director for the American Association of Advertising Agencies [AAAA] in 1924)[19] and of Archibald Crossley (who in 1930 inaugurated the Cooperative Analysis of Broadcasting, which conducted telephone interviews for a large group of advertisers).[20]

Growth of the field proceeded in the 1930s, in some part from the spur of the Great Depression on business to make advertising and sales methods more cost effective.[21] The federal government, especially the Department of Commerce, began providing important new sources of data, such as the first Census of Distribution in 1929 and the Census of Business in 1935, for assessing competition and potential customers.[22] *Business Week* estimated the commercial research business at an annual $4 million enterprise in the fall of 1936.[23] By the mid-1930s, leading firms included Crossley, Inc.; Cherington, Roper, and Wood; Market Research Corporation of America; Ross-Federal Service; Houser Associates; A. C. Nielsen; and Clark-Hooper, among others.[24] While market research of the 1930s was not based exclusively on survey data, it relied on them substantially.[25] With survey methods, market researchers in the 1930s made an easy and logical extension to the measurement of public opinion on economic, political, and social issues.

State of the Art, 1920s–1930s: Issues in Data Collection

SAMPLING

Elmo Roper claimed for "advertising men" a pioneering role in sampling in the 1920s,[26] and there is *a* truth to his claim. Market research sampling was informal, rule-of-thumb, and fraught with judgment throughout and was thus a measurable distance from true probability sampling. But in the 1920s, market researchers were trying to draw samples after their fashion more regularly than their counterparts in the social survey movement or in academic attitude measurement were in theirs.

There is a bit of evidence that market researchers were actually less troubled by problems in their sampling procedures than they were by quandaries of question writing.[27] In many circumstances, market researchers were satisfied that they could get good information—often as good, and sometimes better, and certainly at cheaper cost—from special groups of people than from actual samples. Relying on methods that had no standing in sampling theory, they trusted their own practical experience before more formal sampling theory got some currency in the 1930s.[28]

Panels and juries. Elite groups provided special information when large-scale research was deemed too costly or when their expertise was of special value. General Motors, for example, used a panel of "motor enthusiasts" to project future trends. GM also gathered the "deliberative" reactions of a sample that had been given special information about the pros and cons of an issue and then compared them with the "spontaneous" reactions of a regular sample that had been given no such information.[29] GM used various special groups to assess the "ultimate trend of public thinking" that the company felt would emerge when the general public had become more familiar with the issue.[30]

"Panels" in market research were akin to consumer "juries"—a constituted group of people who were willing to taste things or cook them, try products, listen to radio programs, or answer questions, sometimes by being brought into a studio or a firm, sometimes by reacting individually in their own homes, and often by answering by mail. The word *panel* had evolved in courts of law. Before there were "panels of jurymen," a panel was a small piece of anything, a strip of parchment, and finally a slip or roll of parchment "on which the sheriff entered the names of jurors and which he affixed to the writ."[31] The legal panel came to mean the jury itself. Consumer juries sometimes made judgments on behalf of other people, for instance, on which advertisements would be most effective or which products most salable. Panels more often spoke for themselves. But consumer panels, like jurymen, usually served for a time.

One major purpose of panels was economy: finding a group of people who would be willing to carry out their tasks over a period of time was cost effective. In certain studies, this time period was designed as a means of measuring change. For example, in a CBS pantry check of products, an interviewer visited the homes of housewives in the panel over a period of weeks to observe which brand names had appeared and disappeared and then queried respondents for details about these consumer decisions.[32] Certain radio-listening panels were required to listen over a period of time to cover the installments of the program. Gathering up a panel in these instances saved the trouble and expense of finding new people all the time—locating, recruiting, explaining, and following up.[33] Paul Lazarsfeld later transported the term *panel analysis* from market research into survey research, changing its meaning in the process to the study of change through the repeated measurement of the same individuals.[34]

Experience with larger publics: quota samples. When market researchers reached out beyond juries and panels, it was not always crucial to get cross sections of the national population. Often they wanted "cross sections of the prosperous," in any case; the truly poor population (which also involved most of the black population) was effectively ignored.[35] Likewise, geographic coverage of the nation was not always necessary if goods were of such a character as to appeal to certain regions more than to others or to urban more than to rural areas. The larger market organizations had a "nationwide" capacity, meaning that they had interviewers on call in various key cities throughout the country and could construct regional and economic quotas from cities and regions to "represent" the nation in an informal sense.[36] But much early consumer research was local.

The practice of market sampling of this period was described very

generally in 1924 by Cherington, then head of research for the J. Walter
Thompson advertising agency.[37] For house-to-house inquiries, there was
need of some system of selection which would also serve to provide comparability in analysis. Cherington described as practicable the procedure
of one firm (probably his own). This so-called ABCD system described
quotas for income. Interviewers were instructed to select respondents in
certain percentages from the following groups:

> Class A. Homes of substantial wealth above the average in culture that have
> at least one servant. The essential point, however, in this class is that the
> persons interviewed shall be people of intelligence and discrimination.
> Class B. Comfortable middle-class homes, personally directed by intelligent
> women.
> Class C. Industrial homes of skilled mechanics, mill operators, or petty trades
> people (no servants).
> Class D. Homes of unskilled laborers or in foreign districts where it is difficult
> for American ways to penetrate.[38]

Cherington had a similar classification for selecting retail stores.

Even this weak reed introduced some system in the field procedure
which was an improvement over "man-on-the-street" interviews or talks
with customers in any retail store and which could provide some record
of where interviewers had been. Such quotas were often combined with
others for region, city size, sex, and age groups, with proportions of each
ascertained from census data.[39] The same kinds of quotas were the basis
of the pollsters' samples in the mid-1930s.

Market researchers were trying to make commonsense applications of
sampling theory. As Crossley pointed out later, "Mostly, we do not even
have lists to work with. If we are covering a small town, the same effect
is achieved by going up and down every street and taking every fourth
house, for example." This procedure accomplished only part of the job,
because callbacks were not routine.

> But when you have three million square miles of the United States to cover,
> the problem is not so simple. Not being able to achieve randomization easily
> in our everyday work, we try to manufacture it by examining its component
> parts to see what they are and how they are put together. This brings us to
> what we call selective sampling. We select so many in each part of the country,
> so many in each population group, etc. Selective sampling in some form has
> brought us a long way. It is almost universally used in marketing research
> today.[40]

Gallup, especially, later became associated with the term *micro-America*,[41] but market researchers before him were making simpler applications of the same idea that Kiaer had argued for at the turn of the century (chapter one).

Market researchers determined sample size by a process they called "stabilizing" or "cutoff" sampling, which deemed that there were enough cases when successive estimates of a mean or a proportion began to "settle down," no longer changing "very much" from additional batches of interviews. Early in the interviewing season, a new batch of questionnaires might make the overall estimate bounce from ten to, say, twenty-five or thirty. Later, however, if overall estimates were relatively impervious to new increments, showing modest wobbles of this kind—

| 20.1 | 19.7 | 20.8 | 22.9 | 19.9 |

—sampling would probably be suspended. How much the variability had to be minimized was, of course, a matter of how much a client was willing to pay.[42] Theodore H. Brown of the Harvard Business School pointed out in 1935 that samples were often carried out to a huge size and tiny variability that were unnecessary.[43]

Market researchers who were dissatisfied with the cumbersomeness of the stabilizing procedures were receptive to the efforts of the Harvard Business School to circulate sampling theory and practice in the business research community.[44] Brown's tables of sample size and the standard error for simple random sampling were much cited in market circles of the 1930s and in opinion research circles in the 1940s.[45]

Researchers merged old practice and "new" theory by using sampling theory to determine sample size and to assign confidence limits, while continuing to use quota methods to gather their data.[46] But even statisticians, who had brought more sophistication to sampling than had many market researchers, did not find the practice an outrage. In 1935, it was seen as an accommodation to a set of formidable practical problems.[47] Even five years later, the Princeton statistician S. S. Wilks discussed the combination of probability and quota methods at some length in an article for *Public Opinion Quarterly*, and he did indeed set confidence limits on estimates produced from quota data. Wilks did not see probability sampling as a practical option for the national opinion polls.[48] Market researchers and pollsters were entirely unprepared to shift their practice to probability sampling when certain government and academic social scientists took up that banner later, in the 1940s.

STANDARDIZING THE MEASUREMENT PROCESS?

Interviewing. What was the proper scope, responsibility, and competence of the market interviewer? In principle, there were two poles. At one, an expert interviewer, knowledgeable about the field in question, obtained information through "conversationalizing" a set of topics, generally without using a questionnaire and also without taking notes on the interview until after leaving the scene. Respondents were likely to be manufacturers and business executives, sometimes distributors and dealers, and, less often, consumers. As we have seen, it was this kind of interviewing that the "scouts" in the USDA practiced.

At the other pole, a "questionnaire" interviewer asked a small set of written questions and noted answers on a questionnaire blank. These interviews, usually very brief—just a few questions or a very few minutes—were conducted in homes, stores, and even on street corners. Questionnaire interviewers were not expected to know much about the subject at hand, and the use of the brief questionnaire was thought to require rather minimal training or instructions.[49]

In practice, a good deal of the market literature of the 1920s and 1930s placed the interviewer in some sort of middle ground of freedom and responsibility, with questions less standardized and the scope of the job rather more variable than we assume today. There was concern that trying to standardize the interview more fully might interfere with the communication process. Would respondents talk freely if interviewers went around carrying questionnaires and taking notes on the spot? Or was it necessary to muffle the mechanics of data collection, requiring interviewers to ask questions from memory in a natural-seeming way and take notes after the interview, in private? Should interviewers stick to the exact wording of a questionnaire, or should the resourceful interviewer use written questions more as a guide than as a harness, with freedom to devise new questions or elaborate on old ones as insightful understanding of the situation might suggest? By the mid-1930s, such issues in the standardization of measurement in the field were lively.

Those who favored showing the questionnaire and taking notes on the spot were represented by the prominent researcher R. O. Eastman, with this perspective:

> We want to dignify the study from the beginning and get a serious, interested attention. When the impression is made on persons giving information that these facts are wanted for a very serious purpose, the answers we get are dependable.[50]

In Eastman's view, the conversational approach was *too* conversational. At the other extreme, the informality of the interview was stressed as a great advantage in putting the respondent at ease and eliciting maximum information, which displaying the questionnaire or taking notes would inhibit.[51]

Some authorities agreed on a kind of compromise procedure in which an interviewer was to commit to memory *all* of a short questionnaire as well as the opening questions of a long one, so that the mechanics could be subdued if necessary. Percival White suggested the techniques of writing topics on an "old envelope," which could be taken casually from a pocket, or of the "magazine method" of writing the questions in brief on a magazine cover, placing a copy of the complete questionnaire within the pages. If the respondent seemed to be tolerant of the mechanics, the interviewer could pull out the full form of the questionnaire and take notes as well.[52]

Quality control. White's 1931 book *Marketing Research Technique* leaves us the most complete account of market interview training and supervision in this period. His Market Research Corporation of America was a leading organization, and it probably represented some of the best technical practices of the early 1930s. White's interviewing staff incorporated both *resident* interviewers, who worked in their own communities across the country, usually on a part-time basis, and *traveling* interviewers. The latter were attached to headquarters and worked on studies in the vicinity, but they also moved across the country on assignments that required tight coordination or offered special problems. The more demanding the interviewing assignment, White felt, the greater need there was to dispatch a small group of this interviewing elite or perhaps even a single interviewer. The traveling interviewers also acted on occasion as supervisors. Resident interviewers generally involved less overhead for the firm—they did not have travel and living expenses of the road; they could gather data more quickly; and they were usually willing to work part-time. The traveling staff, however, brought the advantages of mobility, information from headquarters, and special experience. It was not unusual in other firms, too, for even one or two interviewers to do hundreds of interviews.[53]

Market researchers wanted for their interviewing staff the same magic combination that survey researchers have wanted ever since: people bright with ability and energy who are willing to work for rather drab wages. White's list of qualities desirable in an interviewer is little more than a litany of virtues that would serve nicely for almost any work in the world: intelligence, perseverance, judgment, honesty, personableness, courteousness, physical stamina, and so on.[54] Specific hiring practices tell us something more about market research field staffs. White reports that some firms found college students, especially those taking classes in marketing or psychology, to be effective interviewers; other firms avoided students as risks in confidentiality, judgment, and supervision. Especially for full-time work and for interviewing of business executives and dealers, men were more common as interviewers than they have become in survey research. Women were commonly hired for part-time work interviewing consumers.[55]

Training of interviewers under the best of conditions meant personal instruction at firm headquarters, practice interviews, and supervised interviewing in the beginning, but this kind of program must have been a rarity. In White's firm it was available only to interviewers hired in the immediate vicinity of headquarters; for the rest of the staff, far-flung across the country, training was conducted by mail, and supervision for the most part was too.[56]

Interviewer cheating was a concern.[57] When Coutant and Doubman reported in 1935 that fake questionnaires were well under control ("A man who is not strictly honest in attending to his duties or in recording his results cannot hope to escape detection, for check backs and comparisons with other investigators' work is part of the routine"), they must have been bluffing. These authors approved of telling interviewers as little as possible about a study so that they would be "in no position to fake acceptably," even if they should be "so misguided as to try."[58] Other writers were more candid. Link noted rather gracefully that paying field interviewers by the piece was likely to "affect the accuracy of the information obtained," and the pressure of meeting a daily minimum quota of interviews would do likewise.[59] Others stressed the value of conducting routine checks. Some consumer questionnaires obtained respondents' names, addresses, and, often, telephone numbers as well, abandoning the value of anonymity in order to permit verification.[60] White admitted that these various remedies had no prospect of entirely stamping out the problem, writing that

> faking by an interviewer is hard to prevent if he really desires to deceive. . . .
> An investigator with two hundred consumer interviews to report can make
> fifty calls and spread the results of these over the one hundred and fifty faked
> reports of calls which were not made.[61]

White placed some faith in questionnaire design itself. If comments were reported and if some open questions asked the respondents' personal experiences with products, the range and variety of real experience would soon exceed the creative imagination of the interviewer: it would be easier to *make* interviews than to *fake* them (a view that still has some currency in contemporary survey research).[62] White meant business. In some interviewer instructions of his firm, preserved in the American Marketing Society/Association text, there is this pointed warning: "If your questionnaires do not give full comments, we cannot pay you for the work."[63] In 1938, Roper indicted "careless fieldwork" as one of the three major weaknesses of market research.[64] The solitary work of interviewers, their minimal training, the skeletal supervisory staffs, the supervision by mail, the short factual questionnaire—most of these factors were likely to increase the chances of error and of possible deception.[65] The best market researchers continued to worry about this problem and to take steps to try to control it—and opinion researchers would too.

Interviewer effects. With interviewers often charged with much responsibility and discretion, it is not surprising that there was little systematic work or study of interviewer effects or bias in early market research. Market researchers were aware, nevertheless, of possible social desirability effects—they were called matters of "pride," "vanity," and the like—and they also cautioned interviewers against suggesting answers, products, or brand names.[66] There appears to have been fair confidence that simple (usually, written) injunctions would serve to sensitize interviewers and to deter them from bad practices. Firms matched interviewers and respondents by age group and sex, on occasion, on the theory that this would facilitate communication and diminish bias.[67] Others thought that keeping interviewers relatively uninformed about study purposes and sponsors would help control bias. Coutant and Doubman reported that it was general practice to give questionnaire interviewers

> a minimum of information as to why the study is being made. . . . When investigators know too much about the study, they may unconsciously guide the answers and counteract the value of the material obtained.[68]

This viewpoint is still common in contemporary survey research.

Mail questionnaires. Experienced market researchers of this period had few illusions about mail questionnaires. They expected returns of 10 to 20 percent at best, and Starch even estimated the range at from 1 to 10 percent. They also knew that people who returned the questionnaires were likely to be different from those who did not—"more intelligent or more aggressive or more obliging or better to do," in Starch's view.[69] Others stressed differential return by interest in the product or topic and the higher mail responses by *users*.[70]

General Motors' consumer research, under Henry B. Weaver's direction, experimented with mail questionnaires and made concerted efforts to boost return rates with questionnaires that were attractive, graphic, and striking. The questionnaires themselves were not necessarily short—they were sometimes substantial booklets containing up to 100 items—but the questions were vivid and were simple to answer. Respondents were to check their choice of three or four drawings—automobile hoods, fenders, and interior styling, for instance—and they sometimes had a chance, in the category of "other," to draw in their own suggestion. GM's pictorial questions got wide attention in the field.[71] Link considered GM's market research department to be probably the best in the country.[72]

QUESTIONNAIRE DESIGN AND WORDING:
NORMS OF PRACTICE[73]

Open and closed questions. Closed questions carried the largest load of information by questionnaire interviewers and mail questionnaires, such as yes/no, multiple choice, and checklists. What the utility of open questions was generally and how many there should be to leaven the closed questionnaire were matters of interest and comment in the field. Starch advocated including a few open questions so that those interviewed would be "free to give an unimpaired response in their own language." These questions could also serve as a "check" against the same questions asked in closed form, as in this example:

A. What do you think is most important in putting money into any investment? (Put down exactly what the person says.)
B. Which of the following points do you consider most important? Number these in the order of importance 1, 2, 3, 4:
Rate of interest
Safety
Makes me save
Can turn into cash at any time

Starch thought to use the two forms of the same question more as a guide to interpretation than as any more systematic test of consistency.[74] Jenkins's intent for the open question was much the same: to use such answers, along with the unsolicited comments, as a way of getting the respondents' own ideas in a form relatively free from the researcher's own preconceptions or predetermination of the answer, and also as a means of pretesting questions.[75]

The greatest use of open questions was to probe the reasons why consumers liked or bought certain products. These were considered valuable questions in part because they could furnish ideas for advertising copy—"reason why" copy was a standard ingredient of advertising material—as well as more general information on product design.[76] Some "why" questions were difficult, such as those asking the respondent to reconstruct his or her own purchasing history and motivation, as in "Why have you never used . . . ?" "How did you happen to start buying . . . ?" when the consumer might not have the faintest idea of what inspired a certain purchase, especially if it was a habit of long standing.[77] But other "why" questions involved a more straightforward reporting of tastes and preferences, likes and dislikes—at least, *ostensibly* more straightforward. Contemporary survey researchers will doubtless see in such questions a vaguely defined frame of reference, which would practically insure a clutter of miscellaneous answers that would be difficult to classify. A coding sheet preserved by White provides an unwitting example of just this problem. Among a list of eighteen reasons for cigarette preferences were these categories: mild, no aftereffects, price, smooth, uniformity, premiums, aroma, habit, and blend.[78] The miscellany does not impose even preliminary boundaries between, say, economic matters (price, premium) and sensory experience (aroma, mild, etc.). The answers to these questions may have provided some words for "reason why" copy, but they provided many vague, useless answers, too.[79]

Archibald Crossley took pride in an open/closed combination that he developed to rank-order magazine preferences in market research for the *Literary Digest*.[80] The simple graphic device shown in figure 1 was "reinvented" on at least two later occasions as a measure of intensity—in the 1940s, apparently in connection with Gallup data, and, more recently, in the 1960s and 1970s, when the National Election Study used a thermometer to measure respondents' feelings toward political and social groups.[81]

Simplified versions of scales and rank-orders that had been developed in attitude measurement in the classroom and laboratory were exported to the consumer field on a limited basis. Likert-type items are cited by White in what was probably a study conducted by Lazarsfeld.[82] Rank-ordering of items was a practice that underwent some change in this period, as we shall see shortly.

On question taboo. Researchers' concern with the personal interaction

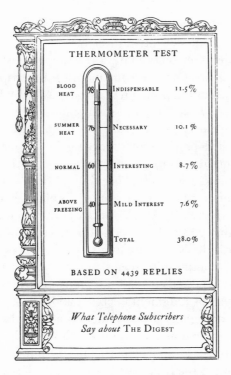

THERMOMETER TEST

BLOOD HEAT	98	INDISPENSABLE	11.5%
SUMMER HEAT	70	NECESSARY	10.1%
NORMAL	60	INTERESTING	8.7%
ABOVE FREEZING	40	MILD INTEREST	7.6%
		TOTAL	38.0%

BASED ON 4439 REPLIES

What Telephone Subscribers Say about THE DIGEST

Fig. 1. The *Literary Digest* Thermometer, 1925

of the interview made them very chary of asking anything that seemed too "personal." In the 1920s and 1930s, basic demographic questions were often considered intrusive. Questions not only of age (deemed especially sensitive for women) and income (thought to be touchy for both sexes) but also even of occupation and home owning were often thought to be tactless. When interviewers were to get such information, they were often instructed to be as deft and subtle about it as they could be.

In an example from White, the interviewer was given a short checklist of seven occupational groups and told to use it cautiously:

> It would not be tactful to ask the lady outright what her husband does, but you might ask her to indicate to what general class her husband belongs; and then read to her the list of occupations, checking the one she designates.

As to home owning, the last item on the questionnaire, the interviewer was charged with framing the question "diplomatically" or with finding a way to get it "imbedded in conversation."[83] Matters of income and education were thought to be best left to the interviewer's considered guess.

On rare occasions, the interviewer was to estimate intelligence or cultural level. But inquiring into education directly was apparently just as taboo as asking respondents' income: in most cases, it was just not done.[84] Interestingly enough, we find the contemporary prescription for asking the so-called ticklish question in a text as early as 1919: put it last.[85]

Experiments in wording. The stress on standardized delivery of the question—reading the question exactly as it was written—was exerted especially by applied psychologists working in the market field, who brought with them the canons of laboratory experiment and experience in intelligence testing, where it had been found that "a small variation in wording made it impossible to compare results obtained on the same test by different interviewers."[86] This norm from the laboratory ran somewhat counter to that governing interviewer behavior in the field, where adjustment to individuals and situations was seen as necessary and desirable. A kind of compromise seems to have been common in which interviewers were expected to read questions as written and yet to innovate around them as judgment decreed, adding, skipping, rearranging, interpreting, and generally carrying out a good deal of hand fashioning. The standardization of questions itself was rather imperfect, but there was interest in testing by experiment just how much specific differences in wording actually changed answers.[87]

Some ingenious experiments in question wording were conducted during this period. In the early 1920s, Poffenberger experimented with the language and comprehensibility of questions in laboratory experiments with students and also with adult consumers. Housewives proved able to consider soberly both the epicure's way of baking ham and the Igorots'—the latter being a group of tribes in the Philippines which included headhunters—and Poffenberger demonstrated in other wondrously foolish examples that if advertisers' woefully unintelligible copy were incorporated into consumer survey questions, respondents would dutifully answer them.[88]

Open/closed experiments were published by the J. Walter Thompson agency in its house organ in 1926. In a study of magazine readership, only 19 percent of the respondents named exactly the same magazines in an open question that they had chosen on a checklist three weeks earlier. Differences by occupational group were not significant, but the mere fact that data on this issue were presented indicated a sophisticated curiosity about whether changes in question form could affect the association among variables as well as differences in marginals.[89]

Jenkins's commercial and experimental work satisfied him that one solution to the problem lay in providing a *complete* checklist of all items most frequently volunteered in open-ended questions. (Jenkins used college student subjects and their opinions on fraternity life.) When he presented the full list of fifteen reasons obtained from pretests, there was little difference in the rank-order of the answers that resulted in both closed and open forms. When he proved a "mutilated" list, however, from which he had cut off the five front-running items, there were sharp differences, even though respondents were especially requested to give "other" reasons if they wished.

This striking experiment, published in 1925, appears to have been the earliest one of its kind. Jenkins used these data to counsel researchers to build "complete" checklists from pretests or to run parallel forms of the questions in the same questionnaire in the kind of check that Starch had advocated.[90]

Toward simplifying questions. There is evidence of effort over the course of the 1920s and 1930s to make questions easier for respondents to answer. Starch's 1923 text was an early and influential one, but his questions were difficult. First, he asked respondents to make *very fine discriminations*, as in this question:

> What do you consider most important in buying boys' and children's clothing? (Rank in the order of importance)
>
> | | |
> |---|---|
> | Material | Comfort |
> | Durability | "Wear like Iron" |
> | Union Made | Price |
> | Style | Reputation of the firm |
> | Tailoring | Fit |
> | "Satisfaction or Money Back" | Maker's guarantee |
> | guarantee | Merchant's guarantee |

as well as other long rank-orders. By the 1930s, such laundry lists were in disfavor, with lists of a maximum of three to five items recommended. Rating scales of complexity also came under criticism.[91]

Second, Starch asked respondents for *introspective accounts* of influences and motivation, which inspired stringent criticism in the 1930s. In a laboratory procedure that became quite well known, Starch asked a set of students to assess reasons for their own behavior in general by assigning a score from zero to ten to a towering list of forty-four "motives." (Hunger got the top score, with instinct for "teasing" the lowest.)[92] While he did not apparently put consumers to such an arduous task, Starch nevertheless expected them to introspect into influences on their purchases. Link, among others, found such introspective questioning and lists of instincts entirely useless. He urged market researchers to abandon inquiry into "*what [people] think they think*," and ask them, instead, what they *did*, what they bought, where and when.[93]

Third, Starch asked people to recall *large stores of detailed information*: for example, how much it cost to "completely clothe a boy for one year," which involved summarizing purchases and costs for eighteen kinds of articles over that year. Or, he asked how many pounds of raisins a consumer had bought this year and how this compared with purchases of a year or two earlier. Starch himself simplified some of his procedures over these years.[94] Poffenberger, in contrast, was critical of questions that inevitably committed respondents to a "large element of guessing"; Reilly cautioned against asking respondents to make estimates over a long period or to make complex calculations; and Brown specifically warned against asking for expenditures over a long period of time—and the examples in the texts of these writers bore out these precepts.[95]

White, editorializing in 1936 in *Market Research*, the magazine he edited in the 1930s, wrote with exasperation of the federal Study of Consumer Purchases because it was so long, tedious, detailed, and "blunderingly prepared"—it was, he charged, the work of the "inexperienced."

> The respondent is supposed to know the number of quarts of oil which he has bought during the year and have an account of the money he has spent for bridge and ferry tolls.

Anyone who actually kept such minutely detailed records, in White's view, would be "so abnormal that their reports might not be representative of the public in general."[96] And market researchers had been learning from experience to scale down the difficulty of survey questions.[97]

Issues in Data Analysis

The analytic raking, sifting, storing, and recombining of variables was relatively brief and simple in market research of this era. It was not yet very rich in methods for constructing and elaborating variables or for tracing their impact on each other. Tabulation itself was something of moment. Keypunch machines and counter sorters were available to the larger firms of this period, but it was not until the late 1930s that verifying machines were in any considerable use, so errors were difficult to detect.[98] Hand tabulation was more practical in many situations, especially when there were few cross-tabulations.

That data analysis was not yet a richly elaborated set of procedures was apparent in the attention urged upon the incidental comments made by respondents on a questionnaire or in an interview. Interviewers were counseled to cherish and heed these "asides" for insight. Such counsel was surely sensible, but it was also revealing of how little developed the classification and analysis process was. One example of the new idea provided by an incidental comment was, in fact, to look at the data by age![99] With a few exceptions, the classifications that survive in the textbook literature are miscellaneous descriptive categories without analytic interest, by no means the stuff of new variables that could be put into service for further analysis.

Gallup's early readership research showed some analytic interest. He classified the content of a large set of magazine advertisements into nine different thematic "appeals," and he then asked consumers which of the advertisments they recalled seeing. Advertisers had used appeals to economy in the largest number of advertisements and appeals to sex and vanity in the smallest number. In the attention consumers remembered giving to the ads, that rank-order was almost turned on its head.[100]

J. David Houser's consumer research also got beyond simple description in analytic comparisons of attitude and behavior. In a 1935 "state-of-the-art" piece for the *American Marketing Journal*, Wheeler applauded Houser's approach to data along the "second dimension," by which he meant attitudinal measures controlled on behavior indicators.[101] Lazarsfeld's work in market research inspired even more enthusiasm among his contemporaries. Wheeler found in Lazarsfeld's approach to subjective data "the most promising development in the interpretive phase of marketing research."[102] By 1935, Lazarsfeld was a prominent participant in the market research community and was already making a visible mark on its practice, a development that will concern us in more detail in chapter four.

Statistical treatment of data was covered very briefly by leading texts. For example, they discussed various measures of central tendency (means, median, mode) in fair detail and measures of dispersion somewhat less. The treatment of correlation or, very rarely, regression was likely to be very brief indeed, and readers were referred to statistical texts by Yule, Chaddock, Mills, Sechrist, Ezekiel, and others.[103]

In the early 1930s, Brown reported on the use in *non*survey marketing research of a profusion of indexes and on the growing use of multiple

correlation to assess business activity and potential markets.[104] Whether
there was as much statistical sophistication in the survey sector is not clear
from the evidence I have consulted. There are clues, though, that the
summarization of data was in practice very simple. Coutant and Doubman, in fact, recommended that researchers confine their presentation
to averages and percentages.[105] The fact that White strongly recommended using not only marginals but cross-tabulation as well is instructive:

> Simple tabulation often fails to bring out essential facts. For example, 3,000
> replies from users might indicate that economy, convenient size, and attractive
> container were of equal importance as reasons for purchasing a certain prod-
> uct. If respondents were arranged according to income groups, the results
> might be quite different, the low-income group showing preference because
> of economy and convenient size, and the high-income group because of the
> attractive container.[106]

It was also recommended that market researchers use cross-tabulations
with other variables such as region, business size, individual nationality,
social position, and age.[107]

The reigning advice was to trust large obvious differences. Weaver,
whose prestige in the field was considerable, disparaged results of "hairsplitting fineness" which were "accurate down to the last decimal place";
he sought strong, obvious differences that held up across time, as sound
guides to policy and practice. One should not worry about whether the
consumer vote came in at 75 percent or 95 percent, he wrote; action
based on such numbers would doubtless be the same in either case.[108]

ACADEMIC-BUSINESS TENSION

The counsel of simplicity was designed to reconcile some of the tension
between academic and business needs and culture, which one would expect on a theoretical level[109] and which surfaced occasionally in the market literature. Businessmen's need for quick, practical counsel made
them impatient with what they saw as an academic penchant for complexity and unintelligibility, as in this reaction:

> The standard of research reports in academic circles is, in many instances,
> not applicable to practical business use. I do not mean to question academic
> standards or the comprehensive form in which findings are published. With-
> out a doubt, a more comprehensive statistical and detailed analysis is neces-

sary; but from the standpoint of business it is imperative to present the findings in a form which can be used to reach the busy business executives. . . . The power of simple expression seems to be a lost art with many expert research men.[110]

The same impatience with academic style was apparent in Coutant's wry solace to business colleagues in the American Marketing Society that they should not be discouraged if they did not have Ph.D.s in psychology: "Many of the psychologists haven't even a B.A. in advertising economics."[111]

Academics who were not involved in commercial research were suspicious of business money and control, wary that scientific norms of disinterested inquiry might be compromised by business needs for competitive advantage and secret work. Academics who combined teaching with applied work experienced tension within the university community on this score.[112] Hollingworth, of Columbia, a prominent figure in the development of the psychology of advertising, reflected some years later on the disdain that some of his colleagues had expressed for business financing of research. One colleague had whispered to another at a professional meeting, "Did you know that Hollingworth received funds for his caffeine experiments?" Not without irony, Hollingworth noted that he, "Judas," had "never been able to secure research subsidies from any sources except the hard-headed businessman."[113]

For social scientists interested in research, contract work for business (rather than business subsidy) was a likely source of funds. Outside of direct university support, there were only three major possibilities: government contracts or employment; private-foundation grants, which were available to social science but only in small amounts, rather thinly sprinkled; and business. The first public opinion research was an extension of market research conducted for business by psychologists, an effort that grew out of a project of academic psychologists to turn profits from applied research into the conduct of basic research.

Public Opinion Research in the Psychological Corporation

Surveys begun in 1932 within a consortium of psychologists were "nationwide" polls of public opinion that were organized before Gallup and Roper published theirs. These surveys have a valid claim to being the "oldest existing poll of public opinion and buying habits."[114] The psychologists were a part of the Psychological Corporation, which had been

put together by James McKeen Cattell, the first psychologist to be named
to the National Academy of Sciences.[115] As his colleague R. S. Woodworth later described the origins,

> It irked Cattell that the support of scientific research should be dependent on
> the favor of administrators and politicians. Time and again he urged that it
> would be much more logical if a fraction of the economic gain from research
> should be turned back as a matter of right to the scientific fraternity for the
> support of further research. In founding the Psychological Corporation . . .
> his hope was—and it is being realized—that applied psychology might pay its
> own way and earn at least a part of the funds needed for its advancement.[116]

Members of the Psychological Corporation were to charge a proper
fee for applied services (such as standardized psychological tests, vocational guidance materials, and industrial counseling) for which the corporation would act as a clearing house, and they were to split the profits
with the corporation, which could then sponsor psychological research.
By 1923, 170 psychologists—nearly half the members of the American
Psychological Association—were stockholders.[117]

That true profits did finally materialize (in the late 1930s, after some
struggle) was credited to Link, among others. Link was a Ph.D. in psychology from Yale, who joined the corporation in 1930 and added an
enterprise that had not been part of the original design, the Market Surveys Division.[118] Surveys were conducted by graduate students and undergraduates under the supervision of psychology professors in various
schools across the country. This network was limited to urban areas but
served as an approximation of a national field staff.

Link's division became known especially for its Psychological Sales Barometers, which gathered continuing (quarterly) information on the
changes in consumers' purchases of brand-name products, and for its
Triple Associates Test of consumers' knowledge of advertising slogans.
The latter was an extension of the paired association tests between brand
names and commodities that had been conducted by psychologists as
early as 1917, usually with students.[119] Link added the advertising slogan
and the task of matching it, as in "What brand of coffee advertises 'Look
for the date on the can?'" to the product (here, coffee) and to the firm
(say, Chase and Sanborn). It was a modest but useful addition: if consumers were responding to advertising slogans but mixing up brand
names, a manufacturer might be spending a part of his advertising budget in support of his competitors. And in any case, it was a test of the
diffusion of the slogans themselves.

In the two devices (the barometers and the associates test), Link argued, was an appropriate use of behavioral psychology. The theory of instincts and methods of introspection had already fallen into the rearguard of psychological thought, but Link criticized their vestigial or implicit influence in market research questions that asked respondents themselves to explain their own motivations. But their preferences were another matter. By learning how consumers themselves reacted to products and advertising, Link hoped to illuminate relationships between opinions and behavior. In no time at all, he was asking not only for opinions about products but also for opinions about public issues and business corporations, which were of interest to his clients.[120]

The "nationwide poll of urban public opinion and buying habits," the Psychological Brand Barometer—the "brand" was later dropped from the title in the 1940s—was established before the 1935 pollsters' work, and Link later stressed both the kinship with Gallup and Roper and his priority before them. He took pride in working entirely by personal interview when Gallup was still experimenting with the combination of mail and personal interviews, as well as in developing two other features of the barometer: first, the assigning of interviewers to designated areas rather than allowing them complete freedom to find their own quotas, in contrast to Gallup's field practice; and second, the use of a large set of interviewers, each one of whom would conduct twenty-five or fewer interviews. Making smaller field assignments per interviewer was a contrast to that part of market research that still used two or three interviewers, each conducting hundreds of interviews.[121] It may have involved making something of a virtue of necessity, for a limited number of interviews was probably all that one could ask of students (who were not being paid at all for their work, until 1934, and then only very modestly). But Link saw that the distribution of interviewing had the probable advantage of reducing interviewer bias.[122]

Link's public opinion work had two purposes, one of which was *polling* of a limited sort—limited, that is, to questions of particular interest to his corporate clients, such as consumers' views of the New Deal (unemployment relief, farm allotments, the National Recovery Act) and to questions bearing on corporate "image" and public relations. Link was in fact taxed by the psychologist Leonard W. Doob with being pro–big business in his interpretations, which he probably was.[123]

Link wanted his polling data to go beyond mere description to substantive research in psychology. This aspiration was unrealized, although Link did conduct some research into survey methods and also encouraged pretesting of questionnaires, standardization of measurements, and diffusion of sampling ideas. Like all market researchers of the era, he used quota sampling, but his division helped to circulate some sampling theory in market circles and stressed that the cumbersome "stabilizing" procedures were unnecessary. Under the direction of psychologists Irving Lorge and Philip Corby, the division conducted a demonstration in 1934 showing that the successive "stabilizing" estimates from many subsamples conformed to the theoretical binomial distribution.[124]

Link and his colleagues were convinced that personal interviewing had to be tightened up and questions read exactly as written. Their backgrounds in educational measurement and industrial testing made them sensitive to the problems of wording changes which were likely to occur when interviewers *thought* that they were reciting questions from memory.[125]

In the methodological research during the 1930s, Link was struck by "how much the form of the question has to do with the answers obtained and how precarious is this matter of measuring public opinion."[126] The division conducted and published split-ballot experiments in wording and question order which may have been the first such experiments on a large scale. While neither Link nor the pollsters succeeded in going much beyond ad hoc explanations for wording effects, this is not very surprising: theory for wording effects has proved difficult to construct in the almost fifty years since the early experiments of the corporation.

In the 1940s, Link's own interest in methodological experiment seems to have waned. He concluded that most wording effects were rather minor and that the basic problem in question design was that of framing, through the trial and error of pretesting, a question that was "worded simply enough that it could be understood" and that dealt with "a problem on which people were well informed"[127]—a commonsense approach that would hardly spur much further investment in methodological research. Link also sided with pollsters in the view that single questions could measure public opinion as reliably and validly as the multiple questions and attitude scales being advocated by academics.[128]

His hope of fusing the business and the science of market research appears to have dimmed some with time—probably as his disappointment grew that neither opinion polling nor market surveys commanded the respect of the scientific community which he felt they both deserved. On the occasion of the Barometer's fifteenth anniversary in 1947, he expressed great regret that surveys like the Barometer, the Gallup, Crossley, Roper and other polls are not more widely recognized as the peculiar instruments of psychological research.[129]

Recognition had languished, he felt, because the superficial distinction between basic and applied research was playing the profession false, obscuring to many psychologists the research potential of surveys in attitude and behavior.

Link was surely right. Market research remained low caste in the profession (and probably lower than other applied psychologies) in the period of concern to us here. Link was not well placed to bridge the commercial and academic worlds. The network of Psychological Corporation psychologists served to get the fieldwork done, but it did not stamp market research with the theoretical generality or the professional prestige of basic science, although it did provide individual psychologists with new or additional experience in survey work.

Link considered "consumer surveys and their off-shoot, polls of public opinion" as "one of the most important developments in the field of scientific psychology,"[130] but he valued the consumer surveys more highly. He saw in them greater technical virtuosity and theoretical promise for dealing with attitude/behavior problems in many different ways and not just at election time, when the opinion polls undertook their only test of validity. He regretted the greater appeal that public opinion work seemed to have for psychologists.[131] While members of his division made the extension from opinions about products to opinions about issues, they did not succeed in making their work into vehicles for ambitious projects in research, and they did not have the institutional capacity for (or perhaps the interest in) full-scale national polling. Public opinion polling appeared to the public to emerge from the straw vote and election forecasts of commercial journalism.

Straw Votes and the Money

The Pollsters of 1936

ARCHIBALD CROSSLEY (1896–1985)

The three men who became famous pollsters after the election of 1936 were established market researchers. Archibald Crossley was an acknowledged leader; George Gallup had become well known in the field; and Elmo Roper, newest to the national scene, was in partnership with Cherington, who was eminent in academic and business circles for his work in advertising and market research.[132]

Crossley went into the market field in 1918. Fresh from his Princeton graduation, he landed a perplexing assignment to set up a research department. In not knowing what such a department did, Crossley was not much more ignorant than his employer, who had learned only that some of his competitors were offering clients a new service, "research." Crossley did succeed in setting up such a department, and later, from 1922 to 1926, he applied his new experience in the research department of the *Literary Digest* (without responsibilities for the *Digest Poll*). Quite apart from its poll, the *Literary Digest* was a leading advertiser and conducted a good deal of market research, especially into the market provided by telephone subscribers.[133]

In 1926, Crossley founded his own market research firm, Crossley, Inc., in Princeton, New Jersey, and New York City, and in 1930 he developed the Cooperative Analysis of Broadcasting (CAB) for the Association of National Advertisers.[134] The Crossley Radio Survey, or Crossley Report, published monthly reports based on telephone interviews conducted in 50 broadcasting cities, detailing the size of the radio audience by hours and by days of the week, the composition of the listening audience by age, sex, and buying power, and the popularity of stations and programs. The 1930 study won the Harvard award for the year's most outstanding example of commercial research. In 1931, the reports broadened coverage to include another 100 towns. In addition, Crossley had published a book in 1930 on market research, *Watch Your Selling Dollar!*[135]

By the time he was asked to conduct an election poll in 1936 for the Hearst newspapers, Crossley was a leader in the market field, with much experience in radio, readership, and other market research. While he used telephone interviewing for radio-listening studies, Crossley, along with Roper, relied exclusively on personal interviewing for election forecast work. Crossley built up a set of interviewer quotas for a national sample and a system of reporting based on approximately 30,000 interviews every two weeks.[136] He did not think the market would bear a third poll of public opinion outside of the presidential campaign season, so he stayed with market research exclusively. In recent years, Crossley has been revered and honored as something of a "grand old man" of opinion and election polling: linked as one of the famous trio, he has been invited to comment on developments in the field in *Public Opinion Quarterly* and in the councils of the American Association for Public Opinion Research (AAPOR). He has been more widely recognized by professionals for his pioneering work in market research, for which he also has been specifically honored.[137]

ELMO ROPER (1900–1971)

Elmo Roper proceeded into market research after his jewelry business failed in the 1920s, before the crash of 1929. When he shifted to selling stock to other jewelers, he became skeptical of their certitude about the jewelry market. Roper carried out an informal kind of market research that took him across the country to talk to dealers and customers, and he brought back information that moved a Detroit jewelry manufacturer to restyle his line. When Roper recounted his travels to Richardson Wood, then with the J. Walter Thompson advertising agency in New York, Wood was enthusiastic. He was eager to have Roper meet Cherington, who taught marketing at Harvard Business School and who had until recently been the research director at J. Walter Thompson. From these contacts developed, in 1934, the marketing consulting firm of Cherington, Roper, and Wood, Inc.[138]

It was Wood who had the idea of making a survey for *Fortune* magazine to inform the business community on consumer buying intentions, preferences, and attitudes on certain issues. Henry Luce, the publisher, was interested. Roper's old contacts in the jewelry business were helpful as he traveled about the country recruiting a national field staff. The first quarterly survey was published in the spring of 1935. Its content reflected the initial market interest a good deal more than did Gallup's poll, which in the beginning concentrated exclusively on political and social issues. The *Fortune* survey continued to publish a few questions on major purchase intentions and brand-name preferences. Like Crossley, Roper acknowledged the direct lineage to market research, commenting in later years that "published public opinion research came out of marketing research—absolutely directly."[139]

Wood, more interested in writing than in market research, left the partnership in 1936, later becoming an editor of *Fortune*. Within a couple of years, Cherington and Roper parted company. It was an "unnatural partnership," Roper later observed, in part because of the age difference between the two men of almost twenty-five years and in part, too, because of their different perspectives on the financing of the firm. It was probably also a source of friction that Roper became more fascinated with the details of the survey than Cherington did. When the partnership was dissolved, Roper apparently succeeded in keeping most of the old clients. The firm became Elmo Roper, Inc., and continued its work in market research as well as in public opinion polling and presidential forecasts. In 1938, the quarterly survey became monthly.[140]

Roper's articles on the survey appealed to a more sophisticated and educated audience than Gallup's did. The articles were longer, analytically more interesting, with more cross-tabulations and interpretation. Roper apparently brought some of the analytical instincts of the academically trained social scientist to his column, but he did not bring the credentials of advanced degrees, and he was not without some defensiveness on this matter. In later years, Roper would enjoy mocking academic pretensions and woolly-mindedness. While none of the pollsters was pleased with receiving academic criticisms of their work, Roper in particular bristled at negative comments beamed from the ivory tower.[141]

The publication of the Gallup Poll came a few months after the first *Fortune* survey, but Roper and his associates knew that Gallup was not simply "copying" their work. The start-up time for such a venture was considerably longer than that would allow, Roper knew, and Gallup had in fact been doing direct experimental work on election forecasts since 1933–34 and other relevant survey work for still longer.[142]

GEORGE GALLUP (1901–1984)

Gallup traced his own first contact with opinion work to a summer job he had taken while in college, probably during the summer of 1922, conducting house-to-house interviews on people's reactions to the *St. Louis Globe-Democrat*. Gallup thought the questions were too general and did not seem to capture much more than the "proper" preferences for editorials and national and international news. He recalls this experience as having been a basic spur to his Ph.D. dissertation in applied psychology at the State University of Iowa in 1928: "An Objective Method for Determining Reader Interest in the Content of a Newspaper," which came to be called the "Gallup Method." In this simple procedure, one presented a respondent with yesterday's newspaper and went through it column by column to learn which articles the respondent reported having read and how much of each article. Gallup had tested the method for both reliability and validity in a series of small experiments, and he proceeded to draw a quota sample of 1,000 in the Des Moines circulation area of the *Des Moines Tribune and Register*.[143]

In later years Gallup reflected that three factors had provided the "spontaneous combustion" that flared into a poll: first, he had an interest in journalism and public opinion, in which he had taught a course at the State University of Iowa; second was the method of study he had developed for his dissertation; and third was the political activity of his wife's family. By a strange fluke and a Roosevelt landslide that swept Iowa Democrats into major state office for the first time since the Civil War, Gallup's mother-in-law was elected secretary of state in Iowa in 1932. She had been put on the ballot as an honor to her husband, who had run for governor on the Democratic ticket in 1926 but had died at the end of the campaign. Ola Babcock Miller did no campaigning—the race was deemed hopeless for a Democrat—but to the family's consternation and amazement, she won the election and in fact went on to reelection, with increasing majorities. Gallup dated his own interest in applying his readership survey methods to political polling from the time of this brush with electoral politics.[144]

The arrangements by which Gallup wrote his dissertation in 1928 suggest that he should have listed still a fourth factor that helped to ignite the "spontaneous combustion," that of his business acumen and entrepreneurial skill. Gallup, whose talent for business had been apparent even during his childhood and youth, had his dissertation financed by Gardner Cowles, Jr., the Des Moines newspaper publisher who would later start *Look* magazine. He later combined this talent with academic credentials and responsibilities when he finished his Ph.D. and went to Drake University (in Des Moines) as head of their department of journalism, a job that also gave him access to the newspaper world.

Gallup continued readership studies of metropolitan newspapers and national magazines, which pointed to the large reading audience for comic strips, photographs, and obituaries and the small following for editorials and international news. By 1931 he had attracted enough attention in the advertising world that Lever Brothers signed him on as a consultant. By 1932, after a year as a professor of journalism at Northwestern University, he accepted a job as director of research for the advertising agency of Young and Rubicam. During evenings, weekends, and lunch hours, Gallup began work on the operation that would become the Gallup Poll. The first syndicated column, "America Speaks," appeared in October 1935.[145]

In the course of his career, Gallup built up various market research activities and firms, but he kept these separate from the public opinion polling with which he would become identified worldwide—in some languages, a "Gallup" came to mean a public opinion poll.[146] In the United States, reports of the poll appeared two and three times a week in such major metropolitan dailies as the *Washington Post*, the *New York Times*, the *Los Angeles Times*, the *Cincinnati Enquirer*, and the *Detroit News*.[147] Gallup himself also published in the popular press, in advertising trade magazines, and, soon after the election of 1936, in the scholarly press of social science. He also wrote several books.[148] Gallup become the foremost spokesman for "The New Science of Public Opinion Measurement," as he entitled a pamphlet first released in 1938. He also promptly began working to develop international affiliates, a network that ultimately numbered more than twenty-five polling organizations.[149]

Gallup thus had membership in both the academic and business worlds. He named his poll the American Institute of Public Opinion (AIPO) and based it in Princeton, New Jersey, across the street from the main campus entrance of Princeton University—not without awareness that a Princeton address might help to encourage the return of mail questionnaires, which were a heavy component of his earliest polling.[150] Although the institute was never a nonprofit organization, its name always had that ring, and in certain ways it actually came to perform some public service functions, as we shall see. It was also Gallup, in particular, who emphasized the polls of 1936 as a new chapter in straw-vote journalism rather than as a new chapter in market research.

The Straw-Vote Tradition

GALLUP'S CHRONICLE

Gallup became an informal historian and popular interpreter of the polls, more than either of his peers did, and he emphasized the background history of straw votes. In part, this was simply a matter of personal past, for Gallup had a professional identity in both journalism and market research. It was also a matter of presentation. Gallup's capsule history of polling shows the new polls of 1935–36 bringing *science* to the straw vote: the "Straw Vote Era," as he later wrote of it, stretched back as early as 1824; the "Modern Polling Era" started in 1933, when Gallup began experimenting with polls on issues and candidates; and the real "turning point" was 1936, when the three new polls, using the "same scientific approach," forecast a Roosevelt victory.[151]

Straw-vote journalism had been as much a venture in advertising and publicity for the parent newspaper or magazine as a venture in serious election forecasting. Its methods were simple. Pollsters often carried straw ballot boxes into crowded places—theaters, train stations, stores, busy street corners—and gathered as many ballots as quickly and conveniently as they could. (The *Farm Journal* conducted a door-to-door canvass, but it worked only in rural areas.) Other straws used return coupons published in newspapers, a direct borrowing from advertising, or mail ballots sent out to names available from published lists, especially telephone directories.[152] Journalists using straw-vote methods had not picked up the culture of their neighbors in market research, certainly not in sampling, and they lacked sophistication about problems in mail questionnaires, personal interviewing, field organization and supervision, question design, and data analysis.

The methods that Gallup and the others brought to polling were indeed those they had been using in their market research, although their new sampling labors seem to have been considerably more ambitious. In the congressional elections of 1934, Gallup experimented with various correlates of voting behavior to construct a national quota sample—in fact, he reported making fifty-four nationwide polls in that quest.[153] All three pollsters used slightly different but fairly complex quota formulas, involving up to six variables, to design their national samples.[154] In later years, the adjective *scientific* was sometimes put in quotation marks by others to mock the pollsters' claim—a practice that the pollsters naturally came to resent a good deal—but in 1936 the word *scientific* was applied to polls as a serious label to distinguish the careful construction of their quota samples from the fashion of gathering straw votes wherever these might be found.[155]

THE CHALLENGE TO THE *LITERARY DIGEST*

In a July 1936 column, Gallup threw down the gauntlet to the *Digest*, predicting that it would come to grief in November with a forecast of Landon by 56 percent. In a letter to the *New York Times*, the editor of the *Digest* spluttered at Gallup's cheek: never before had anyone had the effrontery to tell the *Digest* what their poll was going to show before it had even started polling.[156] The editor did not really address Gallup's brief; he simply invoked the *Digest*'s record. Gallup had explained that he could predict the *Digest* results because AIPO collected *part* of its data from the same sources the *Digest* used—lists of telephone subscribers, automobile owners, and registered voters. These were lists in which the upper economic levels were much better represented than the lower levels, particularly in the rate of return, for, as Gallup explained, "People at the upper level are more inclined to answer [mail] ballots than people at the lower end of the economic scale." Lower-income groups, the ones that the *Digest* was missing, were heavily for Roosevelt; to reach them, Gallup pointed out, it was necessary to go beyond the *Digest*'s lists and beyond their mailings, to personal interviewing.[157]

Gallup had daring. He sold his column with a money-back guarantee that his would be a better forecast than the *Digest*'s, and he urged subscribing newspapers to run the two polls side by side.[158] The *Digest* poll had become something of an institution in American politics and journalism. There were many polls in the United States—Claude Robinson located eighty-five different polling operations for his 1932 dissertation—and the great majority of them were local or regional. Of the very few with pretensions to national coverage, the *Digest* was the largest and most famous for several reasons. The magazine had grown impressively since its founding in 1890, reaching a circulation in the 1920s of nearly 2 million—the highest circulation yet for a newsmagazine. This was in part a result of the poll itself, which had served its advertising purposes admirably, with the straw-vote return ballot accompanied by a subscription-order return.[159] The mailing list to which the *Digest* sent ballots and publicity had grown to over 20 million by 1930, and at its zenith of effectiveness about 5 million ballots were returned. In its biggest years, the poll had a special staff of 400 clerks just to tabulate the millions of incoming ballots. The *Digest* was also well known for its several polls on single issues, particularly for its ballots in 1922, 1930, and 1932 on that very lively law, Prohibition.[160]

The *Digest* laid claim to "uncanny accuracy" in its election polls, and congratulated itself regularly on its amazing record. The *Digest* even came to misremember its record somewhat and took credit for predicting Wilson in 1916, citing its poll of labor leaders, which favored Wilson, when its largest poll that year had shown Hughes the winner.[161] Its tabulation of the ballots did reflect the wins of the Republicans Coolidge (1924) and Hoover (1928), and of the Democrat Roosevelt (1932). Politicians came to watch the *Digest* count uneasily. They were fearful of bandwagon effects and were quick to charge error or even chicanery in the *Digest* procedures when their party was behind.[162] Likewise, prohibitionists became increasingly critical and distrustful of the polls, which recorded a rising sentiment for repeal.[163]

Sophisticated, disinterested observers knew that the *Digest* results were less impressive than the magazine claimed. In 1924, for example, the *Digest* Poll had shown LaFollette coming in second, when in fact he proved a very slow third runner. It had long been apparent that the Republicans were overrepresented in the poll. Because the *Digest* data showed a cross-tabulation between current vote intention and past presidential vote—these two questions plus state residence were the total sum of information gathered by the poll—this overrepresentation was easy to see. The *Digest* was cautioned repeatedly by sophisticated poll watchers. But the editors shrugged off technical criticism as easily as they did the politically motivated attack, and they made no changes to reduce or adjust their biases.[164]

Gallup's own forecast showed Roosevelt taking 54 percent of the major party vote and 477 electoral votes. Both were underestimates, for Roosevelt got 61 percent and 523 electoral votes, so Gallup's forecast was not splendid. It was in fact considerably less accurate than he had hoped when he set out to name the winner and to "predict figures accurate within three points for all doubtful states and for all other states that have sizable populations."[165] His error ranged as high as 28 percent for Arizona and 24 percent for Minnesota, with a median error of 12 percentage points overall. Gallup's error on this first try was in fact the largest it would ever be.[166] But his try was more ambitious than *Fortune*'s, which was not considered a major poll at the time because it made only a national prediction, and it was closer to the mark on electoral votes than Crossley's forecast was. It was also bolder than the efforts of either *Fortune* or Crossley.

The Crossley forecast was muted, probably by Hearst policy. It, too, gave Roosevelt 54–55 percent of the popular vote, but the last two pre-election reports were clouded with imprecision: 159 electoral votes were placed in the Roosevelt column but "might shift." Headlines kept alive the hopes of Landon supporters in ways totally unwarranted by the data, as in this cheerful headline: "Roosevelt in lead but Crossley Poll finds Landon victory quite possible." Hearst was fiercely anti-Roosevelt and apparently very fearful of a bandwagon effect.[167]

The *Fortune* quarterly survey did not actually publish a straight-out forecast. Rather, it presented in October the results of a four-point attitude scale that ordered sentiment about a Roosevelt reelection from a high approval of "essential for the good of the country" to a low of "about the worst thing that could happen to this country."[168] With a small percentage of "Undecideds" excluded, these results showed pro-Roosevelt

sentiment at 61.7 percent. This amounted to a forecast and was captioned as showing Roosevelt "the favorite," but it was nevertheless somewhat tempered by qualifying prose. The *Fortune* pollsters had actually
asked a more direct forecast question in October, and the results, with
the "Don't Know" and "Not Ascertained" responses excluded, were much
the same. But because a huge 28 percent of the sample had refused to
commit themselves in that survey, the editors did not publish these results until after the election.[169] Later, in a 1940 *New Yorker* profile of Gallup, it was written that the editors of *Fortune* had not really believed their
results in 1936. *Fortune* hotly denied this, demanding an apology from
the *New Yorker*, and it pointed to its attitude scale results as proof.[170] *Fortune* had actually claimed these results as an official forecast immediately
after the 1936 election, in *Printers' Ink*. Without naming names, *Fortune*
compared its 1 percent error with the 7 percent of both Gallup and
Crossley and with the 19 percent of the *Digest*.[171] *Fortune* quickly took on
the mantle of the most accurate poll of all, but it had not quite made the
dare that Gallup had *before* the election.

The *Digest* forecast, wildly off, showed a tally for Landon that was
quite as Gallup had said it would be. Gallup missed it by only 1 percent.
Back in July, Gallup had also diagnosed three reasons for the forthcoming *Digest* failure: sampling frame bias that favored middle- and upper-
income groups; response bias, inevitable in mail questionnaires, that favored the same groups; and a new class-political party alignment that
made the force of these long-standing biases quite fatal.[172] Though the
political realignment theory has been refined and enriched by recent
historical scholarship, Gallup's theory of the *Digest's* failure has not been
improved upon in any major way.[173]

SAMPLE SIZE AND THE DUAL OBJECTIVE

The size of the *Digest* samples has come to seem almost preposterous in
our own time, as we have become accustomed to estimating national populations within a small sampling error with multistage samples of 1,500–
2,000. The *Literary Digest* misforecast has sometimes been analyzed as
having provided in 1936 a sudden new learning experience for research
in sample size. While the highly publicized event doubtless contributed
to *popular* understanding of the principle of sampling and awareness that
huge size would not correct for sample bias, it was not news to the research community. Market researchers had come to know full well that
huge mail samples were unnecessarily big and almost inevitably biased

in composition. Gallup wrote in early fall 1936 that in most fields of commercial research, a national sample of 3,000–4,000 was found to be entirely adequate. Roper's national sample was only 4,500 cases.[174]

The size of the *Digest* samples always represented advertising objectives. If the *Digest* poll editors knew anything much about sampling, as market researchers did—and nothing in the published poll betrays any such knowledge—they did not apply it. The *Digest* stayed in the rear guard methodologically, using much the same methods it had started with in 1916, learning almost nothing from market research. When it cut the poll's mailing list sample in half, from 20 million to 10 million (in 1934–35), sample design was not apparently at issue. The purpose was to save money, for the magazine was in severe financial trouble.

The *Digest* was not "hooted out of the business" simply because its 1936 forecast failed; it had been struggling a good three years to find a way to *stay in* the business. The size of the magazine was shrinking, and its circulation had fallen to half of its high-water mark of the 1920s. *Time* magazine, in particular, which had entered the field in 1923, had cut into the *Digest*'s circulation and its advertising revenues.[175] The great embarrassment of the misforecast obviously provided another weight on an already sinking magazine. The *Digest* was sold to new publishers in June of 1937; early in the following year, a new version of the magazine went into bankruptcy.[176]

Polling as Democracy and as Science

THE OPTIMISTIC CONCEPTION

In the new public opinion research that succeeded the *Literary Digest*, there was not only the appeal of scientific work but also the attraction of purposeful, public-spirited work in a context of political optimism and democratic idealism. While the depression of the early 1930s had made for enormous suffering, the effects of which were by no means spent when the polls of 1935 appeared, the politics to deal with it was bred of a belief that national problems would prove soluble. Faith in the benign effects of the truth of science and the virtue of democracy was expressed in more confident and more clarion tones than it has tended to be in the 1970s and 1980s. This belief was an animating spirit in the reform politics of the New Deal, as we have seen, and it was a strong current in the commercial, governmental, and academic work in public opinion.

Pollsters saw themselves as innovators who would defend a democratic faith with new methods of conveying the popular will. They saw their role as providing a continuous measurement of public opinion which would supplement and strengthen the normal operations of representative government and protect it from the domination of lobbyists and special interests. Writing in 1937, Crossley sounded the democratic thesis of polling:

> In the next four years, the country will be faced with many important issues. . . . Will [Congress] be swayed by pressure groups with false presentations of public opinion? Or will it seek by scientific sampling to give American voters the opportunity to express themselves on their views and needs of the day? . . .

> Scientific polling makes it possible within two or three days at moderate expense for the entire nation to work hand in hand with its legislative representatives, on laws which affect our daily lives. Here is the long-sought key to "Government *by* the people."[177]

Gallup was the most prominent and tireless spokesman for this conception of polling. The views he published in the late 1930s would remain remarkably unchanged throughout his career. Polling was democracy in action, he wrote, reflecting the theory that the people had political sovereignty and the collective intelligence by which to find solutions to their common problems. While given individuals might be ignorant or confused about political issues, Gallup noted, he nevertheless shared Theodore Roosevelt's faith that, in the aggregate, the "plain people of the United States" would make less of a mess of governing themselves than a small elite would in doing the job *for* them. Gallup saw in polling the spirit of Jeffersonian democracy and the process of New England town meetings. Polling would *not*, he argued, make representative democracy all too direct or turn elected representatives into mere puppets, because people realized that they did not have "the time or the inclination or the competence" to concern themselves with all the problems that confront political leaders.[178]

As it grew more exact, the "new science" was to provide the instruments by which the collective horse sense of Americans could be relayed to the leaders of government. Gallup was fond of citing and quoting the political theorist James Bryce, who was indeed a fine background figure for the new polls:

> A fourth stage [in the evolution of public opinion] would be reached, if the will of the majority were to become ascertainable at all times, and without the

need of its passing through a body of representatives, possibly even without the need of voting machinery at all . . . the [completely efficient] machinery for weighing or measuring the popular will from week to week or month to month has not been, *and is not likely to be, invented.*[179]

The pollsters were here to say that it *had* been invented and that it could serve the public good.

Gallup began his experiments in polling in 1933–34, in the very season when Adolf Hitler was conducting some of *his* experiments in public opinion, with the great use of radio propaganda to manipulate public opinion and the use of mass plebiscites to legitimize the seizure of power. Gallup did not make the connection; he saw in Hitler only a foe of democracy bent upon destroying the popular will. Gallup cited Walter Lippmann's 1922 *Public Opinion*, but he rather ignored the "dark" view of democracy that Lippmann brought from his experiences in advisory councils of the peace conference after World War I and the American rejection of the League of Nations: the doubt that the common man brought the requisite understanding and information to the tasks of democratic political participation.[180]

Gallup's view of democracy did not anticipate that corrupt leaders or aggressive pressure groups might effect their will by manipulating public opinion or capitalizing on public confusion or ignorance. The very conception of public opinion he popularized did not address either conceptually or politically the structure and differentials of power; it dealt with simpler notions of a kind of classical democracy of one person/one vote—and one opinion.

In these matters of confidence, Gallup was hardly alone. The full implication of Hitler was surely not apparent to most Americans until the experience of World War II, and possibly even beyond. (That American political power in high places might be seriously abused was probably not entertained widely among American intellectuals until the McCarthy era of the early 1950s.) Nor was there good reason to see in Gallup's optimistic, democratic theory of polling mere rationalization for personal advantage.

Gallup was a brilliant publicist, and he has been rewarded in the marketplace for his abilities. His articulation of polling as applied democracy and applied science was surely a fusion of the public interest as he saw it and private gain as he planned it. There is no compelling reason to think, however, that this motivation was any more opportunistic than that affecting social scientists who became interested in the field by reason of intellectual interests, political idealism, or their own good sense that these instruments could be used in the advancement of the public good as well as in a personal career. The democratic conception was shared by businessmen and professors; the scientific aspirations, however, would later divide many of them.

THE CLAIM TO SCIENCE

Just recently, in 1979, Gallup and Roper were admitted to one of the halls of fame of social science by being included in the new biographical volume (no. 18) of the *International Encyclopedia of the Social Sciences*, edited by David L. Sills.[181] When the first seventeen volumes were published in 1968, Gallup and Roper did not qualify for biographical inclusion because they were still alive, but their work was given a brief treatment, a paragraph dealing with their 1936 victory over the *Literary Digest*.[182] Had a biographical volume been published in these early years, would they have been admitted to the company? It seems unlikely. It would take some years—some crises, some rancorous debates, and some changes in methods as well—before social scientists would grant a secure place to the pollsters as pioneers in public opinion research.

Before 1936, academically trained social scientists had not been much interested in the straw polls. There was Robinson's dissertation in 1932 and articles by Crum of Harvard and Willcox of Cornell, but most of the interest had been journalistic and political.[183] After 1936, more interest was sparked in both academic life and in government, especially in the polls' continuous measurement of opinion on public issues. It is impossible to know what a scientific consensus was at the time. Instead, we have evidence that the polls commanded interest and enthusiasm in some quarters but uneasiness and skepticism in others, especially about the pollsters' claims that their polls represented a "new science." Certain academic social scientists had already established a stake of their own in attitude measurement, which was a good ten years old, and compared to the methods of that field—item reliability, batteries of questions on one issue, indices, and scales—the measurement of public opinion in these new polls was superficial indeed, however much it improved upon the antediluvian methods of the old straw polls. The psychologist Leonard W. Doob, for one, dismissed the whole lot—the polls of the Psychological Corporation, Gallup, and *Fortune* and the market surveys of private industry—as a technique that had "grown popular in a democracy which is curious concerning its future and alert to capitalize [on] trends for commercial purposes," but which as a "measuring gadget at the moment is almost worthless as a contribution to a systematic science, no matter how useful it happens to be for practical living."[184]

The polls were practical and interesting, but could they be defended as the stuff of science? Scientific theory was not really at issue here—the pollsters were not making that claim—but scientific measurement was. Poll procedures in data collection as well as in data analysis would give some social scientists pause. Were single closed questions on complex issues the stuff of scientific measurement? Note, for instance, these questions of Roper's:

> Has your cost of living in the past year gone up, down, or stayed the same?
> Do you feel more secure or less secure than you did a year ago?
> Do you believe that in general labor is fairly or unfairly treated in this country today?
> What foreign country do you feel most friendly toward (a checklist of nine)?[185]

Or take these questions of Gallup's, asked in 1935–37 and representing a wide range of issues but a narrow format of yes/no, favor/oppose, or three alternatives:

> Do you favor or oppose the Agricultural Adjustment Act? (p. 9, Favor 41%)
> Do you favor an amendment to the Constitution to regulate minimum wages? (p. 28, Yes 72%, New York State only)
> Should the distribution of information on birth control be made legal? (p. 4, Yes 70%)
> What do you think is the ideal family size? (p. 43. Largest percentages were 32% for 2 children, 32% for 3).
> Do you believe in the death penalty for murder? (p. 45, Yes 61%)
> Do you think there will be another world war? (p. 65, Yes 73%)
> In strict confidence and at no expense to you, would you like to be given, by your own physician, a blood test for syphilis? (p. 66, Yes 87%)
> In your opinion is the cost of living higher, lower, or about the same compared to a year ago? (p. 73, Higher 86%)
> Do you expect general business conditions to be better or worse in the next six months? (p. 75, Better 64%)
> Do you think Henry Wallace has done a good job as Secretary of Agriculture? (p. 79, Yes 69%, Farmers only)[186]

A spirited argument on survey questions that developed in the 1940s will concern us in some detail in chapter seven. Here, suffice it to say that questions very much on the order of these early poll offerings are still visible in academic as well as commercial opinion research.[187]

What of sampling? Social scientists were not, on the whole, very critical of the quota sample itself until the mid- and late 1940s. Those who were involved in survey work themselves accepted the practicality of the quota sample, as we have seen. And pollsters have been credited at the time, and since, with stimulating more public understanding of the principle of sampling.[188]

Field procedures were undeniably rough-hewn. Paul Sheatsley, whose later career at the National Opinion Research Center (NORC) was prefigured by the rather chance event, happened to get a job as a Gallup interviewer in 1937. His instructions were brief and entirely conveyed by mail, and he recalls that aside from them he was very much on his own:

> The interview was very simple. Just the front and back of a single page, and it took about ten or fifteen minutes. I remember in those days the way I would fill my relief quotas was to walk around town until I saw a WPA construction gang and I would get them on their lunch hour, three or four men sitting around eating their sandwiches and drinking their beer. I'd pull out my questionnaire and say, "Do you approve or disapprove of a treaty with Germany?" or whatever it was, and then I'd say, "How about you, and you, and you?" I got four interviews very quickly that way. I would go to parks, good places to find people, mothers with their children, old men sitting around in the sunshine. I would go to train terminals and bus stations. You couldn't find many A-level people this way, so you'd have to screw up your courage and go through a fancy part of town and try to figure out which house looked the most approachable. This is the way the sampling and the interviewing went.[189]

The simple nature of the results was another matter on which some scientists were loath to confer the imprimatur of science. The new polls were shaped in some good part by the structure of their financing and constrained by the journalistic needs to be interesting, intelligible, and simple enough to appeal to readers in the mass—and to appeal promptly while the campaign was in progress or the issue was at least still somewhat warm. Poll analysis, if it could be called that, was simple indeed: marginal results and a few cross-tabulations. Breakdowns by region and political party were about the sum of Gallup's analysis in the first year. Journalism, surely—but science?

From another, more practical standpoint, there were two interrelated questions. Were poll data "scientific" enough to be useful to social scientists who wanted mass subjective measures in the pursuit of social action or social theory? And could social scientists make polling data better? Some social scientists saw the promise and opportunity in the polls. Stouffer, Lazarsfeld, Hadley Cantril, M. L. Wilson and Howard Tolley, Bingham and Moore, Merriam and Gosnell, V. O. Key, Jr., and many others all saw immediate interest and long-term potential in the polls.

Some of their ilk felt that their own interest and experience in empirical research gave them some special purchase to improve on the collection and analysis of poll/survey data. The particular efforts, before the war, of Lazarsfeld, Cantril, and Likert to do just that will concern us in chapter four.

Part Two

The Prewar and Wartime Generation: 1935–1945

4

The Prewar Years: Academic Entrepreneurs and Survey/Poll Data

Scientists have become fund raisers, recruiters, coordinators, negotiators, and trouble shooters. . . . However marginal many of these roles and institutions may seem to the closed social system of science, as traditionally defined, they are now integral parts of research. Yet these are roles for which the professional norms of science give little guidance and to which recruits into science are rarely introduced during graduate education.

Saad Z. Nagi and Ronald G. Corwin

The Early Bridging

The applied science of market and opinion research added new prospects to the professional lives of Paul Lazarsfeld, Hadley Cantril, and Rensis Likert, stimulating new interests, aspirations, jobs, and plans. These three men differed substantially as individuals, as we shall see, but they were linked by certain threads. They knew each other, worked on some of the same projects, and affected each other in various ways. All three, by their own lights, saw opportunity and high purpose in market survey and opinion poll data; in their different ways, they created and directed new organizations that collected and analyzed survey data. All three saw a mission for social science and had some genius for raising money. They inspired confidence, activated other people's imaginations about the potential of research, and undertook bold, ambitious projects.

Other social scientists in academic life—Merton, Floyd and Gordon Allport, Stouffer, Newcomb, Katz, and others—also made distinguished intellectual contributions to survey measurement, and many other talented people with academic training were pursuing careers in govern-

131

ment or business surveys. The trio of focus here is of special interest because they were the first survey research "entrepreneurs" who made important links between academic culture and the applied research of business and government.

If they had come to professional maturity during the 1960s, when research funding prospects were more munificent, they might well have stayed in academic work entirely. In the 1930s and early 1940s, before social science had much funding and under the pressure of the depression, the rise of fascism, and a world war, all three looked outside as well as inside the academy for their professional opportunities. They all found value, affinity, or opportunity in market research or polls and surveys—before many other academics did. At the time of the new polls, in 1936, Lazarsfeld was thirty-five, Likert was thirty-three, and Cantril was thirty. All three were already experienced social scientists, intent upon careers in research *and* already fascinated by problems and potentialities of subjective meaning and experience.

Cantril had the least varied research experience, but he was probably the best situated at the moment. An assistant professor at Teacher's College, Columbia, he was in the mainstream of academic life. He had just published (with Gordon W. Allport, his major professor at Dartmouth and Harvard) a major study of radio, *The Psychology of Radio*, based on experimental data and some poll data.[1]

Both Likert and Lazarsfeld were directing research projects. Likert was working in industrial psychology, directing research into morale factors for an institute of life insurance companies which was based in Hartford, Connecticut. Lazarsfeld, who had come to the United States from Vienna in 1933 on a Rockefeller fellowship, was directing a government-funded research project at the University of Newark which provided jobs to unemployed youth. He had already done contract research in Vienna for several years in an organization he had created and directed in connection with the University of Vienna department of psychology.

Lazarsfeld, Likert, and Cantril were all interested in improving upon market research and the polls, convinced that they and their colleagues could bring to attitude/opinion research more depth, breadth, validity, and technical power and that they could integrate it into social research of broader compass. They took different stances toward the polls, as they saw differing opportunities and problems in the polls' capacity for large-scale data collection. In one of his organizational roles, Lazarsfeld became a *client* of the American pollsters, using their existing data for secondary analysis and employing their field staffs for the collection of new data. Cantril entered into collaboration with Gallup as a virtual *partner*, using AIPO data in the conduct of policy and methodological research. Likert, in time, when he directed a unit in government with a national capacity of its own, became something of a *competitor* of the polls. We shall consider the careers of each in turn.

Paul F. Lazarsfeld (1901–1976)

The Background of the Vienna Experience

Lazarsfeld received his Ph.D. in applied mathematics from the University of Vienna in 1925, and for a time he combined teaching at a *gymnasium* with research assistance in the university's department of psychology (or "psychological institute," as it was called in European convention). At the latter, he worked for the psychologist Professor Charlotte Bühler, who was conducting research into life histories and life phases. From this project Lazarsfeld wrote a monograph on youth employment, which has apparently not been translated into English.[2] He later recalled that around 1927—dates vary slightly—he got the idea of establishing a center for applied research: the application of psychology to social and economic problems was the literal translation.[3] Applied market research was an American import to Vienna which Lazarsfeld had learned of from one of his students (unnamed) who was doing some interviews for an American market researcher.[4]

Lazarsfeld's research organization, the Wirtschaftspsychologische Forschungsstelle, was an adjunct organization, without official standing in the university, but it had the moral support of Professor Karl Bühler, a well-known psychologist who served as president of the board, and of other people well placed in government, business, or academic life who served as board members. It also provided research jobs and experience for students. Marie Jahoda and Hans Zeisel were among those working with Lazarsfeld. Zeisel has recalled the experience as an intellectually exciting one that posed some challenges in landing research contracts in the first place—about as easy as selling the idea of a bicycle to someone who had never heard tell of such a machine—and in trying to stay solvent. (Years later, Zeisel asked an associate what her most vivid recollection of the enterprise was: "I remember coming to find you one time to tell you that I had not received any salary for four weeks. You said, 'Well, four weeks isn't very long.'"[5])

Most of the work of the Vienna center appears to have been contract work for business firms, but the most ambitious project from the Vienna period was a community study that had been commissioned by a labor union in 1931, when great waves of depression unemployment had washed across Europe. The small mill town of Marienthal, not far from Vienna, began to suffer heavy unemployment in the late 1920s. By 1930, the plant had been demolished, and the community, as the researchers discovered, took on the atmosphere of a ghost town, with residents deprived by poverty and dispirited by idleness.

Marienthal (1933), by Jahoda, Lazarsfeld, and Zeisel,[6] was not a survey. It was participant-observation research in the community that teems with data of different kinds and sizes: government statistics, newly created data from personal interviewing, family files (for 478 families), family diaries, life histories (of 62 individuals), time budgets (for 80 persons), meal records (kept by 40 families for one week), records of observations and of "overheards" in public bars, and so on.[7]

Community studies in the Marienthal mold did not become a major research theme in Lazarsfeld's work. Nor did his involvement in socialist politics—or in any politics, really—transplant with him when he came to the United States in 1933 and then, as Austrian fascism deepened, stayed permanently.[8] He did bring with him a fascination with data analysis and a view that market research could enrich basic scientific inquiry. While on his Rockefeller fellowship, he tried to find out everything he could about what was going on in both market research and academic social science. At Columbia, he went to see Robert S. Lynd, whose community study *Middletown* had been published in 1929. He traveled to see other people who had been doing empirical work, such as Luther Fry at Rochester, William McDougall at North Carolina, and John Jenkins at Cornell. He volunteered at the Psychological Corporation in New York, where Link was directing the Psychological Brand Barometer.[9] He spent two months at the University of Pittsburgh's Retail Research Institute doing market research studies. He became well known in commercial research circles in New York through contact with George Gallup, Percival White, and many others. The American Marketing Society commissioned him to write four chapters of their book *The Technique of Marketing Research*.[10] In fact, most of what we know about the market research work of the Vienna research center comes from reflections on it that Lazarsfeld published in the United States during the period from

1934 to 1937. The examples, insights, and analytic strategies, which draw heavily on the Vienna days, provide some enduring themes of Lazarsfeld's work.[11]

Writings on Market Research: Small Samples and Psychological Insights

In these early articles, Lazarsfeld applied to consumers' decisions such psychological theories as Freudian repression, Adlerian feelings of inferiority, and introversion/extroversion. A study of milk drinking, for example, suggested the applicability of repression:

> Milk is closely connected with early childhood experiences, which are most apt to be repressed because all the desires operative at this phase are still "unsocialized." Many people, therefore, might keep away from any change of their milk-drinking habits in order not to come too near those repressed realms of their past experience.

Lazarsfeld also found great utility for market research in a "psychological attitude" that seized upon "significant" detail:

> The way a man enters a room, the speed or hesitation with which he makes a remark, the books he looks at first when he approaches a shelf—all of these, to the psychologist, offer indices of a man's aims, problems and habits.[12]

The early market research articles were dotted with one concrete detail or vignette after another, some of which recurred in other articles and turned up again much later, in a retrospective by Hans Zeisel entitled "The Vienna School of Motivational Research" (1968), as hallmarks of that research style.[13]

As Zeisel summarized the Viennese school's rule for psychologically correct questioning, he called up an example that Lazarsfeld was fond of, the study of flower buying. The rule Zeisel explained was that of stressing the concrete, *specific* purchase, not merely the commodity in general. He noted that when respondents were asked why they bought flowers in general, they stressed such matters as beauty and fragrance; when asked about the specific flower or plant they bought, however, they described their choice from another point of view, namely, how little care was required. Lazarsfeld noted that he and his associates counseled their client to advertise a certain flower as "the *grateful* flower that would flourish with a minimum of care and cultivation." In 1934, however, Lazarsfeld had identified the *place* of questioning as the key variable: people spoke about the care of flowers when they were interviewed in their own gardens.[14]

The woman buying shoes was another evocative vignette. An interviewer reported how uncomfortable an informant in the shoe store seemed, sitting there in her stocking feet, probably thinking about runs in her stockings or how ugly her feet looked, and yet unable to leave because the salesperson had taken command of her shoes. After the interviewer's report, the researchers went back to other interviews and found "distinct traces of this inferiority complex" that was especially likely to flare up when people were buying shoes.[15] Zeisel used the vignette to stress the role of unconscious motivation, the limits of the subjective account by the degree of self-awareness, and thus the need for what came to be called "motivation research"—that is, underlying motives, observation of involuntary actions, and free association of ideas and concepts.[16]

Lazarsfeld made psychologically vivid and intriguing interpretations that were not tightly tied to a single idea and could indeed be pulled from one case and made to serve as a vivid example of another. The fact that interpretations were used rather freely in both Lazarsfeld's early articles and in Zeisel's much later reprise of their work is, in one sense, simply an indication of how rich in implications the details of human behavior can be when imaginatively reconstructed and arranged by gifted social scientists (or by artists of any kind). There is little evidence of tempering these insights or interpretations in the fires of replication, but this was a beginning—a period of discovery for Lazarsfeld himself— of the possibilities of psychological theory in interpretations of market research. And Lazarsfeld never lost his respect or fascination for the power of the "qualitative" hunch or flash of insight to start the process of analysis.[17]

The Analytic Mode

Lazarsfeld's particular genius was in the fusing of the intuitive and the analytic. It has been appreciated by sociologists as a resolution of the qualitative and the quantitative, the integration of the case history and the statistical approach.[18] From the standpoint of Lazarsfeld's own biography, this fusion seems to represent a union of clinical ideas of psychology and quantitative ideas of applied mathematics. Lazarsfeld's quantitative work is commonly referred to as *methods*, in implied contrast to *theory* (the dichotomy that has so concerned sociologists). It is probably more accurate to consider Lazarsfeld's great gifts as an analyst of data rather than as a methodologist, but he himself accepted the latter designation. His interest in methods involved him in research design—the designs of questions, index construction, and panel analysis.

QUESTIONNAIRE OR INTERVIEW DESIGN

Lazarsfeld wanted to undergird consumer research with more intellectual elegance, which would give it more scientific power. He saw consumer purchase as a special case of human decision, behavior, or "action," a complex activity that had structure, parts, dimensions, correlates, determinants, and so on and that was entirely worthy of analysis. Subjective measurement of consumers' reasons was under suspicion in market research at the time as part of the broad reaction of behavioral psychology against introspection. As we have seen in chapter three, the introspective analysis of "motives," such as those used by Starch in his early work, came under criticism (e.g., Link's objection to asking people "what they think they think"). The proliferation of motives in the Starch mode did not interest Lazarsfeld, but he argued for the validity of subjective measurement; people *could* explain the reasons for their own behavior and preferences, he contended, if the dimension was clearly identified.[19] Using a three-part system—an Object, a Self, and Others—to account for the purchase, Lazarsfeld outlined questioning to illuminate the *attributes* of the articles, the *impulses* or tendencies operating on behavior from within the individual, and the *influences* brought to bear on the purchase from outside the individual.

The ideas were presented most fully in his 1935 article "The Art of Asking Why in Marketing Research," which got attention at the time and has since become a classic.[20] In this article, Lazarsfeld explained that finding out "why" was often hampered by the use of a standardized questionnaire, which he opposed at the time:

> Traditional opinion is that a question should be so worded as always to insure the same reaction on the part of all those interviewed. We advocate a rather loose and liberal handling of a questionnaire by an interviewer. It seems to us much more important that the question be fixed in its *meaning* than in the *wording*. This new emphasis places the responsibility on the interviewer for knowing exactly what he is trying to discover and permits him to vary the wording in accordance with the experience of the respondent.[21]

Lazarsfeld's confidence in the trade-off—that one could be sure of fixing the meaning if one allowed the wording to be flexible—was shared in the 1930s and 1940s by other social scientists who did interviewing themselves or who entrusted it to elite interviewers in small-scale studies. It was not shared by pollsters doing large-scale studies conducted by large, nonprofessional interviewing staffs, nor later by social scientists who undertook research of this scope.

The use of detailed questions. Lazarsfeld's basic purpose for classifying reasons into the dimensions of *why* was to be exhaustive about all possible determinants of action, and these could be pursued with a series of "detailed" or interlocking questions that were used, almost detective-style, to track down reasons for some behavior or opinion. This was the beginning of a long battery of questions of varying formats designed to detect evidence of the influence of advertising on the purchase of face powder:

> How long have you been using that particular brand?
> How long did you know about it before you started using it?
> What specific things did you know about it before you started to use it?
> (IF SPECIFIC ANSWER IS OBTAINED) . . . How did you happen to be familiar with the name?[22]

Lazarsfeld did not say how respondents reacted to this kind of questioning. Certainly, they had to be taking their purchase of face powder with considerable seriousness to answer such a long battery of questions. It seems unlikely to have been a fruitful line of inquiry for more casual shoppers. In any case, this use of detailed questions seems to reflect the possibilities of small-scale informal work more than it does the constraints of mass surveys.

Classification. Lazarsfeld urged market researchers to use questions of various formats to elicit "psychological raw material, contributed by all of the respondents" and to use classification schemes that would lead to "true conclusions." One of his chapters, included in the 1937 book *The Technique of Marketing Research*, "Psychological Technique of Classification," is the clear precursor of an article that he and Allen H. Barton wrote in 1951.[23] Two of the four rules of classification were virtually the same in 1937 and 1951:

> A. General categories of coding should be divided into specific categories. (This was called "articulation.")
> B. Code categories should be mutually exclusive and exhaustive. ("Logical correctness.")

The other two rules were also quite equivalent in the two versions, but in 1951 they changed in the examples offered, the scope and richness of the rules, and the sharpening and clarity of meaning:

C. Coding should provide some organic structure. It should capture the logic of the situation or the process being studied.
D. Coding should reflect the respondent's own frame of reference or definition of the situation.

The examples in the two versions addressed different audiences. The 1937 version addressed the market community with a stockpile of examples from consumer research (e.g., beer, radios, magazines, commercial laundry, advertising, motor oil, fruit juice, dress shops, pullover sweaters). In 1951 only one vivid consumer remained: the woman choosing cosmetics survived in very much the same language. The analytic thrust had become more elaborate in 1951, as five different "structural schemes" were presented by which to classify materials when true theoretical models were not available, but the basic ideas of 1937 remained. Anyone who works with designing survey questionnaires will find both articles worthwhile. In 1937, the first article was without rival.

Analysis using the classification. The best exposition of Lazarsfeld's analysis by "typological reduction" from this period appears in the 1937 monograph written with Stouffer, in an appendix entitled "Notes on the Logic of Generalization in Family Case Studies."[24] This was a procedure by which to reduce the plethora of detail of case histories and to create new variables. Their example reduced detailed answers on a number of questions to two variables, the *exercise* of authority in the family and the *acceptance* of authority, and it then combined them to form the following nine logical types:

	Acceptance of Authority		
	(High) Complete	(Medium) Normal	(Low) Reluctant
Exercise of Authority:			
Strong	1	2	3
Normal	4	5	6
Weak	7	8	9

These were further reduced to four types of authority, in these combinations:

Complete Authority:	1 and 2
Simple Authority:	4 and 5
Lack of Authority:	8
Rebellion:	3 and 6

There were no instances of 7 and 9—complete or reluctant acceptance of authority that was weakly exercised—but logically there might have been, and this logical device would have suggested them.

The fourfold table. In the same appendix, Stouffer and Lazarsfeld presented fourfold tables illustrating the construction of variables from case histories which were then tested for statistical relationships. Lazarsfeld later credited Stouffer with stimulating this mode of analysis:

> We were sitting there [at a restaurant, talking with another person about a study]. Sam got impatient. He didn't know quite what it was. So he took a napkin, on the tablecloth, like that . . . [and] drew a fourfold table (on the tablecloth). Sam has neither before or later on ever written or talked about it. I was absolutely fascinated by this device. I'd never heard about it before. Immediately I began to think what the implications of such could be, and my first papers which had to do with fourfold tables are a complete outgrowth of that. Sam used it, but didn't pay any attention.[25]

Lazarsfeld's basic scheme for causal analysis, which he explained in more detail in later work, was set forth in this monograph with Stouffer. He was to make much use of this kind of analysis in his voting studies, and we shall return to it in chapter nine, when we will consider more broadly the work of the Bureau of Applied Social Research.

INDEX CONSTRUCTION AND SUBJECTIVE MEASUREMENT

Lazarsfeld's work in radio research in the United States in the 1930s shows his penchant for index construction. In the two issues of the *Journal of Applied Psychology* which he edited in 1939 and 1940, as well as in his book *Radio and the Printed Page* (1940), various indices were under discussion by Lazarsfeld and his coworkers:

> an index of "radio-mindedness" (Ollry and Smith/Lazarsfeld)
> an index of "standard of reading" (Lazarsfeld)
> three indices of attitude toward radio (Sayre)
> index construction from case studies (Lazarsfeld and Robinson)
> rating scales on popular songs (Weibe)
> the "interchangeability" of indices (Lazarsfeld)[26]

The "standard of reading" was an index that Lazarsfeld constructed as a substitute for reading ability (which he could not measure) from four variables: education, economic status, amount of reading, and level of reading. He dichotomized all four and summed the plus signs for a scale ranging from zero to four:

Formal education	+ Completed high school or went to college
	− Did not complete high school
Economic status [rated by interviewer in the familiar market classes]	+ "A" and "B" homes
	− "C" and "D" homes
Amount of reading	+ Three or more magazines read fairly regularly
	− Two or less magazines read fairly regularly
Level of reading	+ Read a book during the last month
	− Did not read a book during the last month

These were rough-and-ready procedures, to be sure, with nothing to commend their combination except common sense—that is, there was no indication of the relationships among these variables. Lazarsfeld's operations on these field data were simply an effort to increase the quantitative yield of questions.[27]

His 1939 article "The Interchangeability of Indices in the Measurement of Economic Influences" is of special interest here. Lazarsfeld's thesis was that economic status could be measured in a number of ways—owning a car or a home, having a phone, type of occupation, economic level, and others—and still show much the same relationship to a psychological variable, such as voting. He found from some poll data, for example, that while the proportion of respondents in a given economic level varied from some forty to sixty percent depending on the indicator, the percentage of the Republican vote did not vary greatly. Lazarsfeld sounded a note of caution about the generality or importance of these findings when he said, "Many tests must be made to find out when the interchangeability of indices is possible and when not."[28] Yet in 1940 he also gave the findings the status of a "rule of the interchangeability of indices."[29] The fact of the immediate matter was sturdily practical: the data did not offer the measure of reading which Lazarsfeld really needed, so he improvised a rough substitute from the sphere of radio,

on which much more research had been done. But this was also a root
of his "latent structure analysis," which he considered for many years, in
which all manifest indicators were seen to have probabilistic relationships
to underlying dimensions. (See also chapter seven.)

Some of the articles Lazarsfeld selected for inclusion in the *Journal of
Applied Psychology* were very rough-cut diamonds indeed, simply because
he and his coworkers fell heir to collections of data which lacked the
variables they needed to fine-cut and sharpen.[30] Lazarsfeld got data
where he could—from the *Woman's Home Companion* panel of reader-
editors, from the Book-of-the-Month Club, from Roper, from Gallup,
from Market Analysts Inc., who interviewed 765 visitors to a state fair,
from magazine circulation figures and radio listening-time estimates,
and from high school students willing to serve as a panel of radio listeners. One can visualize Lazarsfeld and his troupe as a bunch of indus-
trious scavengers, finding data in all sizes and shapes, carrying them back
to their offices in boxes, crates, baskets, and quart jars, and then setting
upon their analysis.

It was a practical quest but also a matter of fascination and conviction,
for, as Lazarsfeld explained, he wanted to show how much value remained in data of all sorts—public opinion polls, accident figures, business statistics, or whatever—and also how well simple statistical procedures could illuminate the psychological implications of these mass
surveys. Lazarsfeld's ingenious scavenging and substituting expressed a
variant of E. Y. Harburg's marvelously wry love song: when Lazarsfeld
was not near the data he loved, he loved the data he was near.

Lazarsfeld brought from this period an enduring confidence in the
usefulness of subjective measurement. He thought it was always likely to
be of value and certainly better than no data at all. As he and Stouffer
put it pointedly in 1937,

The writers believe that a careful collection of opinions is far superior to
pseudo-scholarly tabulations of the type of statistics which have only a remote
relationship to the special problem under investigation.[31]

In the 1930s, Lazarsfeld especially regretted the lack of subjective and
retrospective measures of the influence of radio:

It would have been very easy, even in a mass survey, to ask those people who
reported a change in opinion and also reported listening to the speech, the
following question: "Do you think that the speech has had anything to do with
your change in opinion?" We are quite positive that this special group of lis-

teners and shifters for which the question was appropriate, would have been able to give an intelligent answer, but somehow such questions still conflict with the convictions of many students in social research.[32]

By "students of social research," Lazarsfeld clearly meant the behaviorists in psychology and sociology.

While he became a sociologist in the 1940s, by his faith in the subjective realm of respondents' own self-report and the investigator's "depth" interpretation Lazarsfeld showed a continued affinity with some psychologists—not with the experimentalists, but with the clinicians (or novelists), because of their ability to fathom or fashion the "deep structure" of human experience from the everyday details of human biography. Lazarsfeld's involvement in Charlotte Bühler's project in autobiographies and life phases seems to have been a far more enduring heritage from Vienna than his socialist politics were.

PANEL ANALYSIS

Lazarsfeld's interest in panel analysis apparently dated from his early years in the United States. As we have seen, the major purpose of panels in market research was usually not to measure change over time but instead to save money in the present.[33] Lazarsfeld transported the term from market research into the study of opinion and gave it new connotations as a measure of change. In a 1938 article, "The 'Panel' as a New Tool for Measuring Opinion," Lazarsfeld and Fiske still reflected more of the dominant market research concern with saving time and money than they did a concern with measuring change.[34]

In the *Journal of Applied Psychology* series, three articles used data collected from the same panel of 500 high school students who had served as a pool of respondents for various research projects, but only one study showed concern with change measures.[35] Lazarsfeld's own article on change in this set involved retrospective measurement. It was a series of questions in a single Gallup Poll of October 1937, asking respondents how they had felt about an issue in August. Lazarsfeld later cited this article twice in a rather confusing context, suggesting that it was a panel. In this period, he seems to have used the term *panel* to mean both retrospective measurement and repeated measurements taken over time in the same individuals.[36]

By 1940, the measurement of change had become for Lazarsfeld the chief attraction of the panel design. He now had some experience with panel reinterviewing—a disappointing 54 percent reinterview of a Gallup sample, but a fine 88 percent reinterview of a sample of A. B. Blankenship's—and he was aware of such problems as common mortality rates of about one-third, losses that tended to be disproportionately from respondents of a lower cultural level or with lesser interest.[37] He had been planning to do a large-scale panel that would illuminate attitude change over time in a way that the one-shot polls could not. In 1940 he embarked on the first major survey panel study, for which Elmo Roper's firm did the fieldwork, the election study in Sandusky (Erie County), Ohio.

In these few years in the United States, Lazarsfeld had not fully fashioned a transition from the small empirical works of market research to mass survey data, but he had accomplished a great deal in his intention to sweep up neglected empirical data and enrich the power of market research and polling. By this time, Hadley Cantril had taken another approach to the improvement of polling, having fashioned a collaboration with Gallup that gave him direct access to AIPO data both for the analysis and the design of questions. In 1940, Cantril brought together a group of colleagues and students in a small organization at Princeton, the Office of Public Opinion Research (OPOR), to analyze poll data and conduct methodological experiments. Lazarsfeld and Cantril had themselves been collaborators in radio research for a brief period, but by 1940 they had gone their separate ways of trying to weave into poll/survey data some structure and texture from social science.

Hadley Cantril (1906–1969)

Of social scientists with a professional interest in the psychology of attitude, Cantril was one of the most enthusiastic about the polls' present activity and future promise. He sensed their importance, and he encouraged cooperative research ventures between pollsters and social scientists and undertook some himself. For an academic, Cantril was unusually skilled and successful in maneuvering in the circles of wealth and power. Tall, good-looking, charming, a commanding presence, he had an unfailing ability to "be important," as some of his colleagues later reflected, and a striking ability to find funds.[38] He put these resources to work in finding ways to work with poll data. Perhaps more than any other social scientist before (and during) the war, he bridged the gap between commercial polling and social science.

In principle, such a promoter might well have been a political scientist rather than a psychologist, for public opinion had long been of concern to political theorists.[39] It would have been unsurprising to find political scientists burrowing into the mounds of data (national and, soon, international data) which the pollsters were collecting. Indeed, certain political scientists were interested—Harold Gosnell, Harold Lasswell, Harwood Childs, and Peter Odegard, for example—but they were not typical of the discipline. Cantril wrote later that in the fifteen years during which he archived poll data at Princeton University, when dozens of scholars had had tabulations run for their own analyses, it was psychologists, sociologists, and some economists who came. "Oddly enough, not a single political scientist (except one graduate student) ever darkened the door of the Office of Public Opinion Research between 1940 and 1955."[40]

Poll data, even if largely political rather than psychological, could provide national scope to the study of opinions and attitudes, and Cantril saw the possibilities before many of his colleagues did. In his intellectual memoir, *The Human Dimension* (1967), he recalled the beginning of his interest:

> When I read in 1935 about the surveys being launched and reported in the newspapers by George Gallup, and saw the *Fortune* surveys begun by Elmo Roper and his associates and by Archibald Crossley, I felt that here was a new instrument the social scientist, particularly the social psychologist, had better look into. The survey technique seemed to hold potentialities for the study of genuine problems, for learning how people look at things, and for understanding better than we did why people of various backgrounds, interests, loyalties, and information levels hold the opinions they do.[41]

Certain early interests of Cantril's academic career now make his gravitation to polling seem a natural.

Cantril's Early Interests

"EVERYDAY LIFE"

Cantril's 1932 doctoral dissertation, "General and Specific Attitudes," addressed a psychological controversy of the time which turned on disentangling "attitudes" from "traits"—for example, the degree to which specific preferences, such as whether one would rather meet a pope or a president, were correlated with general attitudes about the religious realm or the political. It built on the work of Gordon Allport and P. E.

Vernon, *A Study of Values* (1931).[42] That Cantril would have a special taste for poll data is suggested even more by his lengthy 1934 article "The Social Psychology of Everyday Life."[43] Here, he urged psychologists to start with a human problem and devise appropriate methods to explore it rather than cutting it to the size and shape of the laboratory methods they had on hand.

By "everyday life," Cantril meant fads and fashion, gossip and rumor, friendship and conflicts, suggesting a welter of questions. For instance, how did the standards of "good taste" vary in different groups? Was it true, as Kant observed, that married people grew to look alike? Did unemployed people tend to think environment more important than heredity? To what extent did a woman take an interest in clothes because of competition with other women? Why were people interested in scientific discoveries that were entirely incomprehensible to them? Did the radio have any influence in modifying language? How did industrial psychologists in the United States and the Soviet Union differ in their assumptions? And so on. Cantril listed a potpourri of research projects— about 185, in fact, which differed greatly in their scope and specificity— and grouped them into almost forty different substantive topics, many of which he found had been largely neglected.

While this collection included political topics, it was clearly much broader, and this may have influenced Gallup's occasional choice of topics. In the Gallup Poll, over the years there has been a sprinkling of poll questions bearing on culture and personality, more than in Roper's poll or, later, in that of Louis Harris. Some of these questions were clearly designed for a client's immediate practical interests (such as travel preferences and plans) rather than for any long-term interest of Gallup's or Cantril's in social history, but they serve the latter purpose quite admirably. Whether they reflect Cantril's interest or influence is not clear, but they were surely similar to the interests Cantril expressed in the 1934 article. For example:

What do you think is the greatest invention that has ever been made? (1947) (Highest mention, electric light and electrical appliances.)

Generally speaking, whose life is more difficult—a man's or a woman's? (1946) (30 percent of men and 18 percent of women answered a *man's* life; 47 percent of men and 61 percent of women answered a *woman's* life.)

(Asked of married women) What is the chief fault of your husband? (1946) (Highest mention, thoughtlessness.)

(Asked of married men) What is the chief fault of your wife? (1946) (Highest mention, nagging.)

(Asked of parents) Do you approve or disapprove of spanking children? (1947) (Parents who were not spanked as children approved by 38 percent; parents who were spanked as children approved by 81 percent.)

If you could have been present and seen any one event in the whole history of the United States—which event would you like to have seen? (1947) (Highest mention, signing of Declaration of Independence.)

Are you going to make any New Year resolutions? (1947) (Of those planning) What will they be? (Highest mention, Improve own disposition, be more understanding, control temper.)

What do you argue about most with your husband (wife)? (1948) (Highest mention, money.)

Can you locate the following ten states on this outline map of the United States—California, Texas, Pennsylvania, New York, Illinois, Ohio, Michigan, New Jersey, Massachusetts, and Missouri? (1948) (Correct answers by education: grade school 4 percent, high school 6 percent, college 8 percent.)

What is your favorite first name for a boy? For a girl? (1948) (Highest mentions: John, William . . .) (Mary, Elizabeth.)[44]

Cantril's broad sense of the "psychology of everyday life" puts in relief the narrow political focus of most early poll questions.[45] In Cantril's own case, he did not actually undertake research into most of these cultural questions. During the Second World War, his own survey work bore largely on politics. However, his later work (in the 1950s and beyond) did show the broader interest in human experience, as he undertook studies of human aspirations and the quality of life in a number of different countries, using a "self-anchoring scale" by which to make cross-cultural comparisons.[46] Cantril's early study of radio listening with Allport, published in 1935, showed some of this interest in "everyday life."

In the radio study, the bulk of the empirical work was based on laboratory experiments, most of them conducted in the Harvard Psychological Laboratory, with a few done in a Boston radio station. The laboratory work was supplemented with a questionnaire collected from a quota sample of 1,075 people from several communities.[47] The purpose of the questionnaire was to find out what kinds of programs people preferred: sports, recipes, church music, dance music, political speeches, and so on, through a checklist of forty-two items, the frequencies of which were ordered by age and sex. Respondents were also asked for other, more detailed preferences (voices, jokes, music, speeches) as well as the effect of radio listening on other leisure-time activities. There was no integration of the two kinds of data, but the mere use of them was unusual at the time, and Cantril used the two again when he supplemented detailed interview findings with poll results, especially Gallup data, in his widely read book *The Invasion from Mars* (1940).[48] By this time, Cantril had become professionally involved with both Gallup and Lazarsfeld, associations that would prove to be of consequence for survey research.

THE GALLUP CONNECTION

In 1936, before the November election, Cantril had been dispatched by the *New York Times* to interview Gallup about the new polls. Cantril was impressed. The article that came from it reflected several themes that Gallup would repeatedly stress: the intellectual heritage of James Bryce; the "scientific" polls that sampled a cross section of the population versus "practical" polls that depended on vast coverage (e.g., the *Literary Digest*); the readjustments required because of incomplete returns; the function of polling for two-way democratic communication, especially to correct for the influence of pressure groups; and the guarantees of the pollsters' integrity. Cantril's account was indeed sympathetic:

> The polls now best known to the public are unquestionably honest, yet their sponsors are constantly accused of some partisan or social bias, or some selfish and hidden motive. . . . Most critics fail to realize . . . that the very life of public polls depend[s] in the last analysis on their proved reliability.[49]

Cantril did not subscribe to all of Gallup's views, however. Unlike Gallup, he credited the existence of a bandwagon, for example ("By creating the illusion of universality it helps the wavering citizen to jump on the bandwagon"). Cantril also wrote that while issues were inevitably oversimplified in democratic politics, polls cut away still more of the subtlety and complexity. He pointed to other difficulties as well as to other advantages. Cantril later recalled the meeting itself as cordial and fruitful; Gallup, he said, was "delighted to have a social scientist take his work seriously and offered his facilities at cost for any research I might want to do."[50] The offer was appealing. And Cantril remembered the chance to dig into the Gallup data as one of the chief attractions of joining the faculty at Princeton University, where he accepted an offer in 1936.

At Princeton, Harwood L. Childs, a professor of political science, was trying to set up an academic institute for research into public opinion. Cantril joined with him in 1937 as one of four founding editors to establish the journal *Public Opinion Quarterly*. Cantril also began to make considerable use of Gallup data. His association with Gallup remained cordial and fruitful, unlike his collaboration with Lazarsfeld.

The Radio Project with Lazarsfeld

THE ORIGINS

It is not without irony that Lazarsfeld and his students came to consider 1937 as the founding date of the Bureau of Applied Social Research, the organization at Columbia University which Lazarsfeld officially directed for more than a decade and which he always inspired intellectually, whatever his title. Official publications of the Bureau do likewise. The founding project was really a project initiated by Cantril and Frank B. Stanton, research director (and later president) of CBS. Within two years, by the fall of 1939, it had indeed become Lazarsfeld's. In the way in which a forceful personality is often described as "filling a room," Lazarsfeld "filled" the Cantril-Stanton project.

Cantril and Stanton had obtained a two-year Rockefeller Foundation grant for $67,000 to study the psychological and cultural impact of radio. They offered Lazarsfeld the job of directing the research while they took roles as associate directors, and the Princeton Radio Research Project was launched in the fall of 1937, with the three principals in three places in close proximity. The grant was administered through Princeton University, where Cantril was, and where Lazarsfeld was given a formal research appointment. The project was directed at the University of Newark, where Lazarsfeld was, making the radio project part of the ongoing work of his research center. Much of the actual work was done in New York City, where Stanton was. When University of Newark officials asked Lazarsfeld to vacate his headquarters because they needed the space for other uses, he took the project to New York, to a building on Union Square. By the spring of 1939, he had obtained a Rockefeller renewal, and the radio project officially became an organization, the Office of Radio Research (ORR) (later renamed the Bureau of Applied Social Research).[51] Lazarsfeld continued to collaborate with Stanton, but he and Cantril had a falling-out.

Cantril promptly obtained another Rockefeller grant to establish the

Princeton Office of Public Opinion Research (OPOR) in 1940—it seems unlikely that the parallelism of the two names was coincidental—and did no more research into radio. It would have been at least as plausible for Cantril to have dated his organization, OPOR, from 1937, rather than from 1940, as he did. If OPOR had flourished as the Bureau did, expanding in the ranks of loyalty, élan, and a sense of its own history, perhaps Cantril *would* have.

THE CONTENTION

Cantril left no public account of the rift with Lazarsfeld. In his memoir, *The Human Dimension*, he leaped over the Lazarsfeld-radio experience without a word, proceeding nonstop in two sentences from his 1936 meeting with Gallup and his move to the Princeton faculty to his 1940 application for funds to set up OPOR. It was well known to his contemporaries that Cantril considered Lazarsfeld his arch rival and that he made invidious distinctions between OPOR and Lazarsfeld's shop.[52] Lazarsfeld, for his part, did leave an account in his memoir. There were struggles over money and program, he recalled:

> Cantril was correctly strict about budgetary arrangements, since the university held him accountable. I did not make life easy for him, because I often exceeded the Princeton budget, sure that I would cover the deficit with additional income from some other source. By and large, this worked out all right.[53]

Not from Cantril's perspective. The two scholars had grand battles over money, according to Marjorie Fiske, who was working with them; Lazarsfeld keenly resented Cantril's overseeing role, and Cantril felt very disturbed by the financial chaos.[54] The research program also became an issue because Lazarsfeld veered away from the experimental work that Cantril had expected to do toward secondary analysis of poll data, without shaping a new plan for research. The Rockefeller Foundation people asked Lloyd A. Free to join the staff of the Office of Radio Research as an editor to move the project along, and Free worked for some months to bring *Radio and the Printed Page* to publication.[55] Financially and intellectually, Lazarsfeld's directorship was clearly not a tidy affair. By his own description, it was a "policy of research improvisation guided by available material and personal interests and contacts."[56] It was not

everyone's cup of tea, and it was certainly not Cantril's. In future research endeavors, these two strong personalities kept their distance.

From the period of their radio work together, Lazarsfeld produced the
work already noted. Cantril, for his part, produced some articles and,
with Hazel Gaudet and Herta Herzog, the book *The Invasion from Mars*
(1940).[57] This was an analysis of panic experienced by radio listeners who
thought that Orson Welles's adaptation of H. G. Wells's *The War of the
Worlds* was the real thing, that the Martians really had arrived. The "invasion" event of mass panic itself was interesting to social scientists, and
the book was dramatic and appealing. It was reviewed favorably and was
later excerpted in the Newcomb and Hartley volume *Readings in Social
Psychology* (1947).[58] Setting forth, first, the script of the Welles radio
drama, it proceeded to an analysis based on detailed interviews with 135
persons, most of whom were selected because they were known to be
upset by the program and because they could be reached easily. Four
interviewers conducted intensive case histories of the respondents' reactions, using a schedule of questions which they were free to use as a
guide. The estimate that something on the order of 1 million people
were frightened by the broadcast was made from Gallup data.[59]

The very urgency and transiency of the event pressed the researchers
hard, and their book combined journalism with psychological concepts
rather than with anything more rigorous. Cantril and his collaborators
were well aware of the problem, disclaiming any pretense to sampling in
method or to generality in conclusions, but they did try to link their
findings at certain points to a broader context. They made comparisons
with a CBS survey. They also used Gallup data to assess the size of the
listening audience, and they reported the results of a Gallup question
bearing on job security in support of the interpretation that "unsettled
conditions" contributed to vulnerability to suggestion and thus to panic.[60]

Cantril proceeded immediately in the text to the observation that two
Gallup questions asked in the same ballot showed a discrepancy between
respondents' identifications of their social class and their economic class.
(Cantril was contributing questions to Gallup during the 1940s, so this
may have been one of his own.) Cantril later pursued this observation in
an article, "Identification with Social and Economic Class,"[61] showing that
people were more likely to see themselves as "lower class" in economic

terms than in social terms. This concern with measures of social class appears to be the beginning of the idea developed by Cantril's student Richard Centers, in a study of subjective and objective indicators of social class which has become a classic, *The Psychology of Social Classes: A Study of Class Consciousness*.[62] This is a good example of meaning yielded by treating indices not as "interchangeable" but as discrepant in analytically interesting ways.

Cantril was influenced by Lazarsfeld's analytic style during this period, specifically concerning the technique of index construction which coded open-ended answers for their apparent presence or absence of certain characteristics (insecurity, lack of self-confidence, religiosity, etc.), and he credited Lazarsfeld heavily in the introduction to *The Invasion from Mars*:

> The author's greatest indebtedness is to Dr. Paul Lazarsfeld [for] innumerable suggestions for analysis and interpretation . . . an invaluable intellectual experience. Because of his insistence, the study has been revised many times, each revision bringing out new information hidden in the statistics and the case studies.[63]

It seems likely that Cantril turned from radio research to a concentration on public opinion research in some part because of his dispute with Lazarsfeld. In any case, *The Invasion from Mars* was Cantril's second, and last, substantial involvement in radio research. It was indicative of his interest in suggestibility and mass movements, a subject he pursued in his 1941 book *The Psychology of Social Movements*, in which he called upon considerable poll data.[64] Before the war, Cantril became engaged in attitude/opinion research to improve the technical methods of polling and to use its content for government policy.

Policy Research for the Government

Cantril became involved in government intelligence work with his colleague Lloyd A. Free, who, as noted earlier, had edited the Lazarsfeld book on radio. Free, a Stanford-trained lawyer, had become attracted to public interest broadcasting, State Department work, and opinion polling, and he became a lifetime collaborator of Cantril's. Before and during the war, research projects involved them both in some clandestine surveys abroad for the U.S. government and some discreet relays of poll opinion at home to President Roosevelt's staff.

In 1940, Free conducted the first public opinion survey in Brazil, an intelligence operation disguised as market research, which tried to determine how to reach Brazilians by short wave when the country's leadership was siding with the Axis powers. He and a crew of twenty interviewers made their way up the Brazilian coast by commercial boat—when they could get reservations (they sometimes had to wait on shore for as long as a month). Over the years of collaboration with Cantril, Free was to direct many such international undertakings in survey research in Nigeria, Panama, Italy, Yugoslavia, Cuba, and other countries. (His monograph on Cuba in 1959 showed widespread support there for Castro—good reason, indeed, *not* to mount a Bay of Pigs invasion.) Free estimates that ultimately he and Cantril sampled one-third of the world's population.[65]

In domestic policy work before the war, Cantril designed poll questions of special interest to President Roosevelt. Cantril had no field staff himself in these early years, but the AIPO facilities were available and Cantril dispatched national poll results to the White House staff. This quiet work for the White House is more explicable if one remembers, as Karl and Katz point out, that until 1939 the president had no discretionary funds at all with which he could commission the gathering of information without the approval of Congress.[66] The information for Roosevelt (during the war and probably before) was financed by Listerine heir Gerard B. Lambert.[67]

Cantril (or Gallup) asked a variety of interventionist/isolationist questions of the following sort:

> Which of these two things do you think is more important for the U.S. to try to do: to keep out of war ourselves or to help Britain, even at the risk of getting into war? (May 29, 1941: 58 percent, Help Britain)
>
> Should the United States go into the war now and send an army to Europe? (Sept. 17, 1941: 8 percent, Yes)[68]

In a "tree diagram" that became well known, Cantril showed that questions on U.S. involvement in the war varied enormously according to the contingencies expressed in a given question. That tiny 8 percent, for instance, who wanted to send an army over in the fall of 1941 swelled to 76 percent when it was a matter of sending aid to Britain even if this ran the risk of U.S. involvement. The Cantril/Gallup trend data during 1939–41 showed a rising ride of willingness to *risk* war in order to help Britain and a rising belief that the United States would indeed get into it.[69]

In his analysis, Cantril tried to make a very close correspondence between specific events of the war and opinion change, which is unconvincing, but the rapid upward movement of various interventionist indicators is unmistakable. He also showed some interesting properties of prewar opinion, such as the greater intensity associated with interventionist than with noninterventionist sentiment; the evidence of cognitive structure and consistency in multiple measures of opinion; and a number of interesting generalizations about national morale (e.g., that high morale was more closely associated with an expectation of victory than with a sense of righteousness of cause). These Cantril-Gallup data from the prewar period were continued during the war and remain a fascinating historical document.

The trend data were published in *Public Opinion Quarterly*. By 1940–41, Cantril and Free together had made an impact on the journal, for Free had become editor of *POQ* for a year at Cantril's urging and had tried to expand the subscription lists beyond the academic community, particularly by giving coverage to polling, public relations, and advertising. Free instituted the section entitled "The Polls," which has remained a continuing feature of the journal ever since.[70] The Cantril-Free influence on the journal was decisive in making it especially responsive to poll/survey data and in extending its scope beyond academic realms. Both Free and Cantril operated comfortably in elite levels of business and government, in close touch with Gallup, Lambert, Rockefeller, and others. These contacts were valuable for the funding of Cantril's various research activities during the war.

Rensis Likert (1903–1981)

We have already had occasion (in chapter two) to consider Likert's early work in attitude scaling and in a panel study. Subsequent phases of his career, to which we turn now, involved him more directly in polls and surveys. After completing his doctorate, Likert took a teaching position at New York University, where he also participated in the Psychological Corporation, acting as its New York representative and secretary of the board of directors and working with the network that conducted surveys with student interviewers. Likert recalled an instance in which some graduate students at NYU who were deeply involved in one of the Psychological Corporation surveys (a study of attitudes toward the Veterans' Bonus Bill) recruited a large group of undergraduates to help with interviewing. At this, the word went out from the department chairman to all members of the department that no one was to employ students in outside projects without the chairman's express permission.[71] Likert refused to comply, and he left NYU. He did some market research in an advertising firm and some teaching at Sarah Lawrence College before accepting a job directing research for a life insurance institute in Hartford, Connecticut (the Life Insurance Sales Research Bureau) in December 1935.[72]

Research in Industry

The psychologist Leonard W. Ferguson later evaluated the major publication resulting from Likert's research at the life insurance institute, *Morale and Agency Management* (1940), by Likert and Willits, as one of the pioneer works of research in organizational motivation and morale. Ferguson considered it "the backbone of much individual company effort to motivate and enhance the morale of their sales organizations."[73] Although these morale studies apparently had wide circulation within the insurance industry, they were not published in professional journals or by commercial publishers. The morale work is of interest to us here for two reasons: it shows Likert's early interest in organizational theory, and it also shows his continued concern with measurement.

In the morale reports, organizational ideas were conveyed through examples from history and literature. The leadership styles of Napoleon and Robert E. Lee were contrasted: Napoleon was seen as a quintessential "boss" whose troops hated him and cheered only upon command, and Lee was seen as a leader who inspired loyalty and sacrifice because his soldiers felt his concern for them.[74] Such images were congruent with counsel elsewhere in the reports for managers to be concerned about their subordinates as individuals, to be generous in giving public recognition to them, and to resist the temptation to act like a "big shot."[75] This was indeed the "human relations" school of organization rather than the bureaucratic or physical efficiency model of rationalized tasks. It was more suffused with psychological values, the importance of interpersonal contact, moral concern with individuals, and a rather simple model of encouragement and praise. These basic ideas were at the root of Likert's organizational theory, which he later developed into a sophisticated model of communication, group structure, styles of supervision, and the process of conflict resolution.[76]

The methodological work he conducted in the insurance field reflected the use of both interviewing and questionnaires in industrial psychology in the work of Houser and others (chapter two). Likert used the two in an experiment that was another variant on the qualitative/quantitative comparisons that he and Murphy had worked on for *Public Opinion and the Individual* (see chapter two). The life insurance experiment was a more limited and successful one, not unlike the Stouffer dissertation of 1930, except that this venture used personal interviews rather than written materials.

Life insurance agents' attitudes were sought qualitatively in personal interviews developed conversationally around a set of topics. Some dozen topics were covered in interviews with 292 agents, scored independently by research staff members on a morale rating from one to five, and then averaged by agency. A second set of morale measures was obtained by a mail-back questionnaire that each agent was asked to fill out anonymously. (The return rate was two-thirds.) These morale scores were also averaged by agency, which was almost always known from the postmark. Agency scores on the two measures were quite comparable (with a rank-order correlation of .85).[77]

Certain features of the mail-back questionnaire are of interest. First, it was called "the ballot" in an obvious reference to voting and very probably to Gallup polling as well, for Gallup was cited appreciatively in the reports in support of the fact that the researchers had sampled rather than enumerated agencies in the association:

> During the 1936 presidential election campaign an intelligent young research man named Gallup directed the interviewing of only a few hundred thousand voters about their choice of candidates. He had carefully selected these voters to give him a true cross section of all the people. From his results he predicted the outcome of the election with astounding accuracy. Today his name is a household word, and his public-opinion polls are in every man's conversation.[78]

Indeed, in this period Likert shared in the quota sampling of market research, praised Gallup's work, and addressed an audience in the Department of Agriculture which found sampling itself to be an implausible notion.[79]

Second, this questionnaire was considerably more like public opinion polling than the Murphy/Likert attitude study of the classroom: it was short (19 rather than 200+ questions), the language was colloquial, and the results of the experiment commended the "quantitative" or closed measure for ease and efficiency, just as Stouffer's work had.

Why, then, in a very few years, did Likert advocate the more qualitative approach of interviewing with open-ended questioning when he directed a public opinion unit in the federal government? The job that Likert took in 1939 with the Department of Agriculture was important. Over the span of about five years, Likert worked in three quite different realms, each grittier than the last: classroom, insurance agency, and the world of the working farmer. The farther Likert got from the classroom, the more he and his associates had to *learn* about what was going on in the particular subculture, and the less constraint there was on the respondents to *tell* them—in writing. Likert himself later wrote that the general public could not be pressed into the service of attitude measurement the way students were and asked to adapt their own thinking to the dimensions set forth by the experimenter.[80] It is also the case that when Likert arrived at Agriculture, research with farmers was being conducted in the very informal "cracker-barrel" tradition.

Government: The Division of Program Surveys

On September 1, 1939, Likert became director of the small interviewing unit that M. L. Wilson had organized in USDA in 1935–36 (see chapter one). The "scouting" operation had given enough satisfaction to the department that it was upgraded and placed in a larger unit that was charged with planning and research, the Bureau of Agricultural Economics (BAE). There had been growing interest in making the interviewing yield more information. However fascinating the scouting reports were, it was difficult to generalize from them, and in any case they were not always in agreement. Wilson and others in Agriculture consulted with various social scientists about how to proceed in program and personnel: Floyd Allport, Leonard S. Cottrell, Jr., Jerome Bruner, Cantril, and others were consulted.[81] Robert S. Lynd was also a special source of advice. His book *Knowledge for What?*, a fervent advocacy for interdisciplinary social science in the service of social problem-solving, was highly regarded in USDA. When Lynd was consulted about the new division, he recommended Likert for the director's job; he also told Likert about the job opening, and Likert applied.[82] (Lynd was in fact almost as facilitative for Likert in 1939 as he was for Lazarsfeld.) The organization was renamed the Division of Program Surveys because its mission was to conduct surveys into farmers' experiences and opinions about the programs of USDA, such as domestic allotments, soil conservation, farmer resettlement, tenant purchase, and the like.

ADAPTING TO NEW MEASUREMENT PROBLEMS

Early in his job at Program Surveys, Likert expressed some interest in trying to make use of scale measurement of various sorts, such as the Sewell and Chapin scales of socioeconomic status, but there is no sign that he expected to bring his own attitude scales to the farm. For the mission of Program Surveys, attitude measurement in the college classroom tradition would surely have been a folly. Furthermore, personal interviewing was the reigning tradition when Likert arrived. The "scouts" were ardent advocates not only of personal interviewing but also of a very intuitive and nonstandardized form of it. As Likert wrote, "Considerable effort has gone into trying to learn what these people really feel by avoiding artificially focused alternatives as the basis for noting their responses."[83] Likert's role in the beginning was to work within the tradition of informal methods and to try to "reform" them with some system and structure. In his efforts to create some standardization, we can see some of the same problems that Lazarsfeld faced in moving from small-scale to large-scale measurement and analysis.

Likert contrasted his views about question wording with those of Gallup:

> It is not necessary, as is sometimes thought, for every interviewer to use precisely the same words in asking a given set of questions. The words may vary so long as the question in each case represents exactly the same idea.[84]

This was a view that Lazarsfeld had advocated in his "Why?" piece of 1935. The freedom that Likert espoused was actually a new stage of constraint for the interviewers, who had not been using written questions at all. He hoped to achieve a balance between standardization and flexibility by providing written questions that allowed for variation in their wording under certain circumstances. Interviewers, to be sure, were cautioned against rephrasing questions in ways that would generate bias. The following, for instance, was not the thing to say:

> Mr. Jones, I noticed the new terraces in that field of yours over there. Am I right in believing that you like them very much, not only because they keep your soil from washing but also because the water they hold back will increase your crop yield?[85]

Interviewers were also cautioned to avoid biasing chitchat or "emotionally charged words."

These instructions, however, were fair proof of the responsibility that the interviewers had at this time. Avoiding emotionally charged words, for example, would later be seen as the responsibility of the researchers or study directors who wrote the interview schedule. Indeed, pollsters already saw it as their responsibility.

The new regime of greater standardization at Program Surveys was not without conflict. A good deal transpired between the interviewers and Likert's second-in-command, Bela Gold (who had worked with Lynd on the second *Middletown* study). Two or three of the scouts transferred out of Program Surveys, in fact, feeling that the new emphasis on standardization and quantification was uncongenial, sometimes more distorting than translating of the spirit of their reports.[86]

The interviewers felt that they were being "layered" as well. Intervening between them and the top officials of USDA was a new set of supervisors and interpreters—Likert and Gold—and a new process that depersonalized their contribution. Some of the old-style interviewers stayed on, but they were not entirely reconciled to the ways of the new regime. Their situation was being affected by changes at the very top, in any case. Secretary Wallace's direct interest and contact with BAE waned as he became involved in the campaign of 1940 for the vice presidency. M. L. Wilson did not replace him as secretary, becoming instead the head of the Extension Service of Agriculture. The top administrators who had taken a direct interest in the personal reports of the scouts now had other aspirations and responsibilities.

SURVIVING AND EXPANDING

The first year of Program Surveys had begun rather inauspiciously, for within a month of the new administration Likert announced that the division was broke, its modest appropriation of $30,000 having been virtually exhausted before his arrival. Additional funds were garnered from BAE, however, and the work went forward. During that first year, Program Surveys conducted studies for various agencies and programs within the department—the AAA, the Farm Credit Administration, the Forest Service, Extension, the Food Stamp Plan, the new homestead communities, a study of forest fires being deliberately set in a backwoods farm community, and others. (For the most part, a single interviewer seems to have been responsible for a given study.)[87] The work was going well enough that Secretary Wallace coauthored an article for the spring 1940 *Public Opinion Quarterly* which publicized the new division.[88]

After that first year, expansion was Likert's motif. As the first annual report argued, there was need of more interviewing; coverage was wanting in the Appalachian states, the Eastern corn belt, and other areas; samples needed to be larger, so that analytic breakdowns could provide statistically reliable results; and more agencies within Agriculture needed the services of Program Surveys. The very conception of farm problems was too narrow, in fact. Likert argued that farm problems and reactions needed to be seen in the larger context of national and international problems that affected agriculture and had meaning in their own right, such as national morale.[89] Indeed, the day that Likert had taken the Program Surveys job was the day that Hitler invaded Poland and the Allies declared war. While the mission for Program Surveys was born of peacetime problems in Agriculture, it soon came to reflect concern with American defense and, later, involvement in the war.[90]

In its second year, Program Surveys did indeed expand to an appropriation from BAE of just under $100,000. BAE's contribution to the budget never exceeded that amount by much during the lifetime of the division.[91] It was through "entrepreneurial" work that Likert sought with other federal agencies outside of Agriculture that Program Surveys expanded its function, funds, and reputation. The first of these was the Office of Facts and Figures (OFF), headed by the poet and Librarian of Congress Archibald MacLeish.

The Bureau of Intelligence within OFF was charged with learning the state of American opinion on many matters of national morale and defense. Program Surveys' association with it began shortly after OFF was established in October 1941. It was the entry of the United States into the war after the Japanese attack on Pearl Harbor that made the association an important one. Waldemar Nielsen, the field director of Program Surveys, explained the process a year later for new interviewers coming into Program Surveys:

On the night of December 7 a hasty conference was held in the Washington office. Program Surveys interviewers scattered at such points as Reidsville, North Carolina; Okmulgee, Oklahoma; and Norfolk, Virginia, were summoned to a meeting at Memphis, some of them driving all night to get there. They flew to the West Coast in time to experience Los Angeles' first full-fledged blackout, and began interviewing. Most of them had had little urban interviewing experience, and they were obliged to proceed with extreme caution because of the intense emotional state among a people just roused to war.

The resulting report on "Immediate Developments after Pearl Harbor," rushed into the hands of administrators on December 14, gave evidence that here was an organization which could carry on a new type of social research with remarkable speed and versatility. Moreover, it was able and eager to undertake problems of a national scope, providing information about public reactions which no other federal agency was prepared to secure.[92]

Program Surveys was by no means set up to dispatch interviewers routinely with this speed and urgency, but it was indeed alone in the government opinion research field.[93] Wartime would spawn a number of government projects in public opinion work, but Program Surveys was already in existence at the outbreak of the war, and at that time it had a unique capability for national government work. During the war years, it would expand its mission well beyond the Department of Agriculture.

5

The Wartime Experience in Policy Research

Certainly, the social sciences will never have the opportunity to delude themselves that the support coming from the federal treasury is for the pursuit of truth unrelated to social utility.

Don E. Kash

The Influx to Washington

In World War II, government officials needed information about the "home front" just as surely as they needed information about the military conduct of the war. Wartime involved massive mobilizations of people and resources, new programs and regulation, and a new need for civilian understanding, cooperation, and support. With polls and surveys, administrators were able to monitor wartime rationing, the sales of war bonds, cooperation with price controls, absenteeism in war plants, the currents of national hope and worry, the morale of soldiers—and they learned something of enemy morale, too, for that matter.

Opinion polls were not the only source of information: there was traditional cloak-and-dagger spying, radio monitoring, content analysis of the press, interviews with the well-placed, unobtrusive "overheards" of the "man in the street," and letters from special panels who reported on their own areas. All of these methods were implemented at one time or another within various divisions of the Office of War Information (OWI).[1] But *surveys* were used by the federal government during the war on a new scale. The new or newly expanded agencies were engaged not only in opinion/attitude research (they gathered facts and inquired into behaviors) but they also placed an emphasis on the subjective measures, and we will often refer here to opinion/attitude research. *Survey research*, a broader term for this work which also includes factual, behavioral measures, seems to have come into first use late in the war years.[2]

The social scientists who became involved in opinion/attitude research in World War II were a part of a vast wartime migration into governmental work. The federal civil service itself ballooned in the early years of the war, growing at a rate of 97,000 employees per month in 1941–42, and it included substantial numbers of social scientists.[3] The survey enterprise was small by contemporary standards. Several hundred researchers, at most, were at work in a handful of agencies. The following three agencies produced the bulk of the work: the *Research Branch* of the Division of Morale, U.S. Army (1941–45), directed by Samuel Stouffer; the *Surveys Division of OWI* (1942–44), directed by Elmo C. Wilson; and *Program Surveys* of USDA (1939–46), directed by Rensis Likert.[4] They produced something over 1,000 specific reports of surveys prepared under crash-program deadlines and in great haste.[5] These organizations were small ones, deep in labyrinths of their federal organizations. Early in the war, Program Surveys swelled briefly to a staff of around 180–200, but this was an all-time maximum, and the number was cut back to less than half that before the end of 1942. At its peak, the total professional and clerical staff of the Research Branch in Washington numbered just less than a hundred.[6]

The new researchers were in another sense a very small world, especially in the beginning. The few knowledgeable people with experience in commercial, academic, or governmental survey work were in great demand (to help each other, especially), and were linked in webs of frequent contact. Lazarsfeld, for example, who had worked on a project with Stouffer during the depression (see chapter one), served as a consultant to Stouffer's Research Branch, as did Likert, Cantril, Merton, Mosteller, Guttman, and Stanton. Lazarsfeld, Cantril, and Stanton also served as consultants to the Bureau of Intelligence in OWI, along with Gallup, Roper, Franzen, and others. The position of top command in the Bureau of Intelligence was held first by Gardner Cowles, the Iowa publisher (later of *Look* magazine) who had supported Gallup's dissertation in 1928. The ubiquitous Cantril served throughout the war on the board of trustees of the newly established National Opinion Research Center (NORC) along with Gordon Allport, Stouffer, and others. Harry Field had worked with the Gallup organization for several years before branching out on his own in 1939 and then founding NORC in a university setting in 1941. Wilson, who had worked with the Roper organization before the war, directed polling in the Bureau of Intelligence and arranged with Field to have NORC's New York branch do the fieldwork. And so on. Most of those who had major responsibilities for wartime opinion research were, at some time or other, working for or advising one another in this small world.[7]

The Interdisciplinary Process

Among social scientists, the wartime research might well have been the special preserve of political scientists. They too made their way into wartime Washington, but reportedly they found governmental research jobs rather hard to come by. For one thing, training in statistical skills was not yet widespread in political science. Sociology and psychology both offered larger stocks of professionals with some training in handling quantitative data (sociologists, in the analysis of aggregate statistics and psychologists, in the analysis of experiments or of attitude measurement). They also offered disciplinary content of special interest to government in wartime: matters of "depth" such as motivation, "morale," propaganda, and the influence of attitudes on behavior.[8]

This wartime enterprise was a new interdisciplinary endeavor. In the 1920s, Charles A. Merriam had sought to interest political scientists in the measurement and analytic tools of psychology and statistics. But these behavioral/attitudinal studies were largely limited to local studies: there were no funds for inquiries of a massive national scope. Harold Lasswell's work in the 1920s and 1930s was another effort at interdisciplinary fusion, as he applied clinical ideas to politics.[9] These earlier, self-conscious efforts of disciplinary cooperation tried to graft a set of ideas and techniques from one disciplinary field onto the research problems of another. In wartime Washington, some degree of fusion was accomplished by *migration*, as social psychologists moved into the realm of politics and plied the trade of attitude measurement for the first time on a mass scale. The wartime work in the service of government had the effect of providing a new group of social scientists with on-the-job training in survey research at government expense. After the war, they helped to make it a new field of research with academic, scientific credentials.

Divisions of the Realm

Congress commissioned no surveys during the war, but it appropriated funds to programs of the administration and the armed forces that dealt with morale in three realms:

military morale	(Research Branch, 1941–1945)
civilian morale	(various agencies, with some overlapping responsibilities, 1941–46)
foreign morale	(U.S. Strategic Bombing Survey, 1945)

Before any of these projects were established, the president and his staff quietly arranged for access to polling information on civilian attitudes.

The Presidential Sector

Cantril was already acting as something of a free agent before the war in providing public opinion data to President Roosevelt and in working on other secret government projects. During the war years, Cantril directed a succession of research organizations—partly real, partly paper—that permitted both public and secret opinion research.[10] The Office of Public Opinion Research (OPOR) was the completely public and visible one, and it persisted from 1940 to 1955, providing during its early years an administrative home for the analysis of poll data. As we have noted, in 1941 and 1942 these data were provided by Gallup, who made duplicate punch cards available to Cantril at cost and also put into the field questions designed by Cantril. A small group of graduate students, new Ph.D.'s, and faculty members worked as part-time associates at OPOR. Daniel Katz was there briefly in the early 1940s (as the most senior scholar), and others, such as John Harding, Mosteller, Harold Rugg (who went on into an organization in the Gallup empire), and Frederick Williams (who went on to military work in opinion research).

OPOR itself never had a field staff, but this was something of a technicality, for the Research Council, Inc., a nonprofit organization incorporated by Cantril in 1942, the headquarters of which were the same as those of OPOR, did have a field staff and analysis program in 1943–1945.[11] It was paid for out of the private pocket of Gerard B. Lambert (see chapter four). Through this organization, an increasing number of surveys were conducted and put into the pipeline to the White House during the war. Under the auspices of OPOR, Cantril and Gallup continued to collaborate publicly in various kinds of experiments.

Military Morale: The Research Branch

THE ORIGINS

In the winter and spring of 1941, the idea of opinion/attitude work in the army was in the wind, having originated in at least three places. In April 1941, Roper wrote to General George C. Marshall, the Army Chief of Staff, offering to help:

It is our thought that the selective sampling method can well be employed in the present Army for the purpose of providing you, and the Army generally, with a good deal of information as to the likes and dislikes, preferences and pet peeves of the men as regards the food they eat, the clothing they wear, the quarters they occupy, and the routine they are called upon to undergo.[12]

Roper was also hopeful of providing a "running thermometer reading" of morale in the military.

Some plans were already in motion within the military to do something similar. A new Morale Division was established in March 1941, reviving one that had been set up just before the armistice of World War I and discontinued shortly thereafter. And in February 1941, another organization, the Special Studies Group in Army Intelligence, G-2, was making plans for morale studies. In late summer the G-2 group and some of the people who would soon take major roles in the Morale Division's Research Branch (Stouffer, among others) cooperated in presenting a planning survey at Camp Lee, Virginia. The Research Branch was established officially on October 28, 1941, within the Morale Division, and it conducted its first survey the day after Pearl Harbor. (The Morale Division was later renamed the Information and Education Division.)[13]

All these plans were ruled out in principle when Roper's plan was rejected by the army. In a memorandum drafted for General Marshall's signature, the *civilian* nature of the operation was deemed a threat to army discipline and leadership. Secretary of War Stimson issued an order in May 1941 to all theaters and all commands expressly prohibiting polls. Yet through some legerdemain, a few months later the Research Branch was indeed conducting polls or surveys.[14]

"The full story of how the War Department changed from a position of flat opposition to such research [to considerable and public use] should some day make instructive reading," Stouffer wrote a few years later, not without suggestions of intrigue.[15] While archival records may well not disclose the "full story," they do reveal some adroit maneuvering. The social scientists who had been planning research into army morale were well aware that polling of soldiers had been declared out of bounds; they continued, nevertheless, defining their work as *not polling* because they would avoid direct questionnaires and proceed instead by the usual form of an investigation.[16] By the time the first planning survey was conducted (December 8–10, 1941), however, those "indirect" questions had yielded to another sort, such as these:

Do you feel proud of your company?
___ Yes, very proud.
___ Yes, rather proud.

___ I have no particular feeling about it.

___ No, not proud.

___ No, I'm ashamed of it. (Q42)

Is there any help you would like to get from officers that you don't get now?

___ Yes.

___ ?

___ No.

What kind of help, if any, would you like? (Q54A and B)

When you came into the Army, how did you feel about the war?

___ That the U.S. should help defeat Germany, even if it meant war.

___ That the U.S. should help defeat Germany, but stay out of the war.

___ That the U.S. should stay out of the war, even if Germany won in Europe.

___ Had no opinion. (Q77A)

If you have any remarks to add to this survey, please write them here as fully as you like. (Q118)[17]

By the time of this survey, Research Branch staff had decided to use a written questionnaire instead of personal interviewing, except with those soldiers whose literacy was too low. Their written questions were clearly of the sort found in the standard polling repertoire: simple Yes/ No, or degrees of Yes/No, small scales, checklists, and occasional short answer. There would be differences in the measurement and analysis purposes to which these closed questions would be put—scaling, in particular, was not characteristic of polls—but from the questionnaire itself Secretary of War Stimson might have been hard pressed to imagine why this enterprise was legitimate, given his ban. When a second "planning survey" came into his hands, in summer or fall of 1942, he did indeed conclude that it was *not* legitimate.

General Osborn went into operation, and showed to Stimson some of the Research Branch's work. One report particularly interested the secretary. It showed beer drinkers in the army as a little better adjusted than non–beer drinkers. Stimson had been doing battle with some congressmen who wanted to ban the sale of beer at army posts, and he requested copies. Up to this point the work of the branch had languished because of delays and shortages of funds and personnel. Osborn's astute crisis management did not by itself change the fortunes of the Research Branch, but it helped a good deal. Stimson did not insist that his ban against polls be enforced, and logjams began to break up in the United States. By the fall of 1942, General Eisenhower had authorized work in Europe, thanks in some part to Roper, who had aroused his interest. Other theaters followed in 1943 and 1944.[18]

SPECIAL CONDITIONS OF THE MILITARY ENVIRONMENT

Research in the army always proceeded against the obstacles of bureaucratic authority and tradition. But in a few respects, it offered some advantages over the civilian agencies. For one thing, making contact with respondents was relatively simple. Ordinarily, one officer and one enlisted man were sent to a camp, where the officer dealt with administrative arrangements and the enlisted man trained a small temporary staff from among local enlisted men to administer the questionnaire. Then the enlisted men selected for the sample were simply ordered to report to a central place, such as a mess hall, where in groups of twenty-five to fifty they filled out a questionnaire. While the compulsory nature of participation might have been a problem, branch staff were satisfied that their respondents showed high levels of cooperation, interest, and candor. Williams recalls that in combat areas, "many of the usual research problems of acceptance and rapport melted away":

> One's sheer presence under such conditions was itself sufficient to bring acceptance. Soldiers were more than willing to talk to a concerned and interested interviewer—or to fill out questionnaires if enemy fire did not require immediate attention.[19]

There was a second advantage in the clarity of command. General Osborn, a direct commission from civilian life, was a polished, aristocratic, millionaire businessman, a personal friend of the president, and he had had the support of General Marshall from the beginning—all of which made for considerable political effectiveness. He also knew research. He had published in demography and had served on various scientific counsels (SSRC and others). In the judgment of Harold F. Gosnell, who studied the wartime agencies, Osborn took the time and care to choose staff members who got along well together.[20] In the comparable civilian agency, the OWI Domestic Branch, as we shall see, there was more divided authority, more confusion and competition.

There was a third, closely related, advantage in being insulated from competition with the commercial polls. Many more Research Branch staff came from university than from business experience, but the realms were not in any case institutionally pitted against each other—as they were, in effect, for a short time in the civilian agencies. Stouffer himself duly credited the pollsters for innovation in the field of opinion/attitude research, and he later played a diplomatic role between pollsters and social scientists.

Attitude research in the army required the exercise of tact, maneuver, and pressure. Regular army officers were often skeptical, convinced that they knew the attitudes of the men in their command better than any poll or survey would. Units could *request* research on local problems; if they were *asked* to cooperate in cross-section surveys, they had the right to refuse. Though the cooperation was sometimes grudging and narrowly construed—General MacArthur, for instance, was one who gave very limited cooperation—no unit did flatly refuse, and this was credited to support from on high, especially from generals Marshall and Eisenhower, and to the talent and perseverance of Osborn and Stouffer.[21]

Stouffer's behavior convinced members of his staff that he was a good match for the army, for all its rules and rigidities. He remained a civilian in fact and in spirit. He was enormously enthusiastic, with a walk that was almost a run, a capacity to stay up most of the night feeding punch cards into the counter sorter, and a passion for social science data.[22] As M. Brewster Smith recalls Stouffer in this wartime period,

> I think he internalized an image of himself from his newspaper editing days in Iowa as *The Front Page*. The ruffled clothes, the ashes, the eternal cigarette. . . . Sam traded beautifully on a studied innocence of military protocol. He was a good fit for the director of the Research Branch . . . lots of chutzpah, enormous energy, indefatigable, lots of imagination, always trying to promote his officers meteorically for the good of the work.[23]

Stouffer wrote after the war that the branch's work was not conducted to further social science:

> The Research Branch was set up to do a fast, practical job; it was an engineering operation; if some of its work has value for the future of social science, this is a happy result quite incidental to the mission of the Branch in wartime.[24]

The mission of ascertaining the state of "morale" meant in fact a grand miscellany of practical matters. What about food, clothes, leave policy, promotion? Who was getting VD? Malaria? What kinds of books should be stocked in the post library? Could psychological crack-up in combat be predicted? Were most men doing jobs in the army which they had been trained for? Did being taught to "hate" the enemy help in combat? Did contact between whites and blacks increase or decrease racial tension? And so on. Within a few years after the war, key staff members and consultants of the Research Branch would publish the four-volume *Studies in Social Psychology in World War II*, two volumes of which, entitled *The American Soldier*, were based on the survey work. That any work as coherent as *The American Soldier* could ultimately be assembled from the miscellany was a triumph.

Members of the Research Branch took some real pride in carrying out the specific tasks, and they felt that their findings were heeded in many instances. For example, to address the low morale of combat infantrymen, the army created a special combat badge and gave the job special publicity. The branch helped in the development of a psychoneurotic inventory that was used in U.S. induction centers. And the branch's estimates of how many soldiers would go to college after the war under a G.I. Bill were used in projecting the costs of such a veterans' benefit.[25]

Stouffer also concluded that work of the branch had influenced army policy at a deeper level in at least two instances. One of these involved the point system for army discharge, a remarkably democratic departure from traditional top-down decisions of the military. The Research Branch had recommended that men be discharged after war individually, on the basis of credit earned for time in the army overseas, the soldier's age, and number of children. Most important, the soldiers themselves were to assign the priorities through opinion surveys. Although the army did not incorporate the Research Branch plan in every detail, it did so in large part. While the rate at which men were discharged after the war aroused discontent, the point system itself, as a principle of equity, was generally given good marks. President Roosevelt backed it publicly as a democratic solution. Stouffer was convinced that there might well have been an "*explosive*" morale situation "if men whose sacrifice was small had been released by the millions, ahead of men whose sacrifice had been greatest."[26]

Rank and its privileges was another issue on which Stouffer felt that the branch had affected policy, at least in some part. The branch had abundant evidence that enlisted men deeply resented the social caste system in ways that probably lowered morale. After the war, veterans' complaints about officers who were incompetent, corrupt, or self-centered were given enough publicity in the press that special hearings were held by a board headed by General Doolittle. Branch data were made available, and Stouffer felt that these had some influence on the recommendations that enlisted men be treated in ways reflecting "advanced concepts in social thinking" and "recognition of the dignities of man." He knew that similar recommendations had been made after the First World War, so he was not naive about the impact that the Research Branch had made. But he was satisfied on this issue and on a broader plane that the branch had helped in showing government that social science indeed had something practical and useful to offer.[27]

Civilian Agencies: Polls and Surveys

THE ORIGINS

In the civilian agencies concerned with government information, organizations with overlapping responsibilities vied for leadership. A special competition developed between two small organizations deep within one of these major wartime agencies. A Polls (or Polling) Division, reflecting considerable commercial influence, and a Surveys Division, reflecting more academic influence, were both placed in the same major agency. In principle, they were to complement each other; in fact, they became competitors for a brief but significant time because of confusion at higher levels.

Just before and during the war, there were many cooks trying to serve up official government information. In addition to the departments of State, War, and Navy, five other multiagency organizations had diffuse responsibilities and ambitions to dispense information, monitor propaganda, maintain secrecy, coordinate the media, and promote national morale. One of the organizations in the foreign information field was headed by Col. William J. Donovan's group, which was responsible for much of the globe. On the domestic front, there were three major agencies that had some major responsibility, and Archibald MacLeish headed one of these. In one part of the bureaucratic forest, Col. Donovan had expected to provide the president with national *polls* in the course of his global information-gathering duties, and he began to make arrangements with Gallup and Roper. In another, MacLeish thought he had responsibility for a "home intelligence" service provided by government *surveys*. In the confusion, government got both.[28]

The president decided on MacLeish's plan and appointed him as head of the new office to coordinate government information, the Office of Facts and Figures (OFF), in October 1941. But by this time, Donovan had already made plans and promises that MacLeish found difficult to undo: consultations with the commercial pollsters; an understanding with Elmo Wilson (lately of Roper's firm) that he would head up a governmental polling organization; another with Harry Field's new National Opinion Research Center (NORC), which was just setting up shop, to do the fieldwork; and still another, that Roper would provide Field with the temporary loan of some interviewers. MacLeish let these arrangements stand as the Polls Division in OFF's Bureau of Intelligence. He also proceeded to contract with the Division of Program Surveys in Agriculture for it to wear another hat as a Surveys Division in OFF. He put both Polls and Surveys (along with other divisions) in the Bureau of Intelligence, under R. Keith Kane, a lawyer from the Department of Justice.[29] This was the structure of authority:

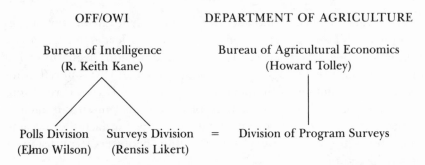

OFF/OWI   DEPARTMENT OF AGRICULTURE

Bureau of Intelligence   Bureau of Agricultural Economics
(R. Keith Kane)   (Howard Tolley)

Polls Division   Surveys Division   =   Division of Program Surveys
(Elmo Wilson)   (Rensis Likert)

Kane, who was not experienced in survey work, had the advice of a group of consultants which included Roper, Gallup, Stanton, and Franzen from the commercial world, and Paul Lazarsfeld, Cantril, and Cottrell from university experience.[30] As bureaucratic changes continued at the top, MacLeish's OFF was absorbed and replaced in June 1942 by the new Office of War Information (OWI), headed by the well-known journalist Elmer Davis. But for a brief time, Polls and Surveys stayed in place—and competitive.[31]

THE PERILOUS CIVILIAN ENVIRONMENT: RESEARCH ORGANIZATION

The two opinion research groups in the Bureau of Intelligence had their differences in research methods, organization, and costs. It complicated Kane's life that Program Surveys had a *double* life: as the Surveys Division, it was subordinate to Kane's overall direction; as Program Surveys of the Department of Agriculture, it was out of Kane's jurisdiction entirely. When Likert's group started doing some exciting new work for the Department of the Treasury on people's wartime financial situations—Treasury was concerned about boom times and the need to hold inflation in check—Kane felt that Likert's entrepreneurial forays amounted to insubordination. For his part, Likert felt that Kane's organizational structure was blocking the communication between researchers and their clients which was vital to the conduct of research. The other division, Polls, did not pose these problems, and it turned out survey data for less cost.[32]

Elmo Wilson, in the view of his supporters, ran a shop that was more orderly, efficient, and reliable in meeting deadlines and budgets than Surveys. Wilson was admired for his administrative ability. He was not considered a sophisticated research methodologist—his university training had been in history, journalism, and political science, and his research experience had been in market research—but he was seen as bringing an intelligent and practical approach to the time-pressured tasks at hand, as well as much personal charm and a sensitive regard for the welfare of his staff.[33] Likert was considered by his supporters to be sophisticated in research, imaginative, buoyant and bold about its future, and a developer of talent. Deemphasizing status and organizational hierarchy, he operated with much informal consensual decision making and decentralization. He encouraged Leslie Kish, for example, to become the division's first sampler, even though Kish had not yet taken a course. "You'll learn," Likert said, and Kish did. But he also allowed two field supervisors to come into Washington and direct a study themselves—and they did not learn, or at least not enough.[34] Whether Likert's division was the scene of organizational innovation or confusion was, in some measure, a matter of taste. Robert MacLeod referred humorously to the contending groups as the Neat-Reliables and the Sloppy-Valids and stood comfortably with the Sloppy-Valids.[35] And there was great élan in Likert's group because they felt that they were pioneering in new applications of social science.

The competition turned centrally on comparative costs. The greater costs of the Surveys Division was an important matter, for Kane's Bureau of Intelligence was vulnerable to congressmen carrying a very sharp budgetary ax. Under the force of internal disputes and external pressures, as of November 1942 the contract with Program Surveys was canceled. The Polls Division stayed on as the only OWI opinion research group, and its name was changed—confusingly—to the OWI Surveys Division.[36]

PRACTICAL AND POLICY CONTRIBUTIONS

Wilson's OWI Surveys Division continued for another year and a half (1942–44), contracting some of its fieldwork to OPOR, more to NORC. NORC continued work for governmental agencies during the war after

OWI Surveys was cut, producing the data for some 160 reports on war-time issues—gasoline rationing, victory gardens, tin salvage, perceptions of government information programs, attitudes toward our allies and our enemies, information and purchase of war bonds, absenteeism in war plants, and so on. Some of these reports were published after the war.[37] Through its work with various agencies, NORC did not specialize in any given program, but it took a role in studying and improving survey methods (see chapter ten). Program Surveys, for its part, tried to replace the OWI work it lost in contracts with other agencies such as the Office of Price Administration (OPA) and the War Production Board (WPB). Its most significant work turned out to be for Treasury and the Federal Reserve Board, starting with the war-bond surveys.

During the war, social scientists were involved in evaluating two basic approaches to selling war bonds. One was the mass advertising, mass media approach, for which the War Advertising Council provided much nearly free campaign material in the form of posters, print, and radio. The OWI Surveys Division assessed the effect of this information campaign. The most dramatic effort was the series of radio marathons by the popular singer Kate Smith, who made a number of very successful all-day, all-night appeals in song and talk, urging the public to help "Bring the Boys Home" by buying war bonds. The book *Mass Persuasion* (1946), by Merton, Fiske, and Curtis, analyzed a radio marathon of 1943, a project suggested by Lazarsfeld. (See also chapter nine.)

The other approach applied social psychology of interpersonal influence. A Program Surveys project under the direction of Dorwin Cartwright provided strong, sturdily replicated evidence to Treasury that bond sales increased with personal solicitation in the workplace and the neighborhood. This research validated the effectiveness of a vast network of state and local organizations of volunteers and a system of war-bond sales quotas. Both OWI Surveys Division/NORC and Program Surveys produced a substantial volume of surveys that were used by wartime administrators.[38] But Congress, as we shall see, was not enthusiastic about governmental polls.

Enemy Morale: The Strategic Bombing Survey

APPLIED RESEARCH OF A NEW COMPLEXITY: ORIGINS

By 1944, Congress had made its hostility to survey work unmistakably clear. In November of that year, the administration and the military showed their confidence. Plans were made for survey researchers to move quickly into occupied Germany (and later Japan) in the wake of victory to assess what effect saturation bombing had had on enemy morale. Among other methods, they would interview civilians. It was an exciting assignment, of great ambition and significance.

The United States Strategic Bombing Survey (USSBS) was a "survey" in both the old and the new styles: data of many kinds were assembled to provide detailed information in profusion as well as a massive overview of the field—in this case, the bombed landscapes of Germany and Japan. Its purpose was to assess the role of air power in future military strategy and defense spending. The USSBS was a large organization, created at the formal initiative of the president, and it ultimately produced more than 300 reports dealing largely with the physical, industrial, and economic effects of bombing. The Morale Division, a small part of the project, produced three reports on the effects of bombing on civilian morale. Some of the questions it addressed were of great strategic and public interest—for example, did bombing help shorten the war? The morale of Britishers, after all, was said to have increased under German bombing. Could our bombing also have had the wrong effect of *stiffening* Axis morale, especially by arousing rage at the Allies, even delaying unconditional surrender?[39]

THE FOREIGN ENVIRONMENT AND TECHNICAL PROBLEMS

After each surrender, the Morale Division went into the field, first in Europe (May–July 1945) and then in Japan (November–December), with a national cross-section sample stratified by city size and bomb tonnage dropped. Over several weeks, 3,000–4,000 individuals were brought to a regional headquarters and personally interviewed in their native language on their recall of experiences and attitudes during the war.[40]

The morale survey appears to have had the same kind of political support from on high that the Research Branch did, and its support was perhaps even more effective. In the judgment of the executive officer of the Morale Division, the presidential auspices helped the morale project "to enter the military scene on a relatively high level of prestige," and the social scientists in this venture adapted to military coordination better than some others had.[41] But practical and technical problems abounded in this formidable task, especially in the less familiar environment, Japan. Respondents were sampled from official lists (police, rationing), but Japanese streets were not named, and the houses were not numbered. Special cadres of Japanese-Americans were brought from the United States for the interviewing; questionnaires were retranslated back into English for coding in the United States. Special efforts were made in question-naire design to try to encourage candor. There were all kinds of new problems, but the Morale Division brought together much talent, with new experience in adapting to the requirements of mass research ap-propriate techniques in scaling, open-ended questioning, probability sampling, and sophistication in research design.[42]

THE CONFUSING IMPLICATIONS

If bombing the British raised their morale—and that notion has come under much suspicion—the bombing of the Germans and the Japanese did *not* raise theirs.[43] The reports of the USSBS and even the Morale Division reports in particular are still cited now and then to argue that bombing of those magnitudes did not really "work" as a practical matter: it is argued that either it had little or no effect on morale, or it had the wrong effects by inspiring resistance, or it had unnecessarily strong ef-fects because it was used in prodigal amounts that were far beyond any reasonable definition of military usefulness. Certain morale researchers themselves have come to feel that their findings and counsels of mod-eration have been neglected, because bombing in the Korean and Viet-nam wars was used in far greater amounts than it had been in World War II.[44] It seems likely that these varying interpretations of the morale surveys reflect the very complexity of the findings, such that most gen-eralizations would invite cavil and perhaps some moral uneasiness about this particular applied research. To consider these problems we shall review briefly the reports themselves.

RESULTS AND METHODS

The situations in Germany and Japan were vastly different, and the re-spective studies were different too. There were general similarities, in that both studies defined levels of bombing in two ways: first, as an ob-jective estimate of gross bomb tonnage, or damage to the *city* in the sam-ple, and second, as a subjective report by the respondent of the *personal* experience of having been in a bombing raid (Japan) or of having suf-fered personal loss from bombing, such as property loss, injury, or death of family members (Germany).[45] As dependent measures of morale, both studies used *attitude* questions (which concerned willingness to surrender, loss of confidence in leaders, certainty that the Allies would win, weariness with the war, increased fear and anxiety, etc.) and self-reported *behavior* questions (such as absence from work, neglect of fire-fighting duties, and "black listening" to Allied radio). Both studies analyzed such questions individually and used some of them in a morale index.

The two reports concurred in the most basic conclusion that strategic bombing contributed substantially to the disruption, deprivation, and dispiriting of civilian life, increasing weariness with the war, despair of victory, and willingness to surrender. Both reported, as well, that enemy civilians tended to blame their own governments more than they did the Allies for the severity of their suffering under bombing. Otherwise, however, it is difficult to generalize from the two studies, in part because the two measures of bombing behaved somewhat differently in the two countries.

Germany and diminishing returns. In Germany, the bombing had been massive, and it was close to ten times the ration that was dropped on Japan—1.4 million tons, as compared to 160,000. German morale continued to suffer from the onslaught, but at diminishing rates. There was an "onset effect" as bombing started, but with repeated attacks on the same community, morale effects leveled off. At the heaviest levels of bombing, there was even a suggestion of morale upturn on several indicators. As the morale report concluded, "Continuous heavy bombing of the same communities did not produce decreases in morale *proportional* to the amount of bombing."[46]

Bombing severity as a *personal* measure of loss, however, did *not* show diminishing returns:

> When personal involvement, in terms of casualties in the immediate family or property loss, is taken as a measure of the severity of raids, there is a marked decline in morale as the degree of involvement increases. There is little evidence of diminishing returns and no tendency for morale to improve at the levels of greatest personal involvement. Personal involvement is clearly the most sensitive measure of the severity of raids for the individual, and is more closely related to changes in morale than the other measures reported.[47]

Why did the vast increases in *city* tonnage show only modest declines in morale? Two major reasons emerge from the reports. First, there were diminishing rates of personal damage from increased tonnage, for which there was a physical basis. The maximum destruction to cities was caused by incendiary bombs, but after a time, much of what *could* burn already had. Then explosive bombs were used heavily, but some of them inevitably landed in rubble, so "losses per ton of bombs decreased materially as time went on."[48] Second, there was probably a composition effect. In the samples of heavily bombed cities, evacuees were usually missing—people who were likely to have had much personal loss and low morale—and their absence probably helped to "improve" morale measures in their cities.[49]

The emphasis of the report was on the diminishing returns of city tonnage, not on the personal variable, and this was probably so for several reasons. It was presumably the more unexpected finding, which called for explanation. Analysts were probably also concerned about unnecessary losses of American life and resources in wasteful bombing. Further, they apparently became convinced that bombing could be conducted in a more restrained, somewhat more humanitarian way and still achieve the military objective of depressing civilian morale. But the policy recommendation of the report itself was not particularly humanitarian, for it explicitly recommended not less bombing but more widely scattered attacks:

> These observations on the diminishing returns from heavy bombing point to the practical conclusion that the maximum *morale* effects of dropping a given tonnage of bombs on Germany would have been attained by lighter raids as widely distributed as possible, rather than by concentrated heavy bombing in limited areas.[50]

A policy of dispersing more widely the same amount of city tonnage would by all odds have *increased* the personal losses, as more bombs would have fallen on fresh targets rather than on evacuated rubble. Was this the intended spirit of the report? The later judgment of social psychologist Herbert Hyman, who served in the Morale Division, suggests not. Hyman felt that air strategists should have learned from the report of diminishing returns in Germany that "the *prolongation and expansion* of bombing did not serve the Allies' goals," and he felt that this counsel of moderation had been put straight to the government, in "remarkably candid reports by a government agency of a government excess."[51] The recommendation for the lighter but wider scatter of bombs remains somewhat ambiguous, nevertheless. A direct criticism of bombing policy was made much more clearly in the Japanese report. The findings from Japan were rather different too, however, and they limit the generalizations that can be supported by both studies.

Japan and uniform effects. Patterns of diminishing returns on morale damage are faint, at best, in the Japanese data. The city tonnage/damage measure of bombing did not show the "onset effect" that the German data had shown: the results were mixed, with the lightly bombed communities showing now higher, now lower levels of morale than the unbombed. Nor did morale effects regularly level off at the highest levels of bombing. In general, city bombing was a steadier predictor of morale effects in Japan than it had been in Germany.[52]

The Japanese data also offered another surprising fact: those who had the personal experience of being in an air raid showed lower morale than the unbombed, but on the whole the differences across a dozen morale measures were not large. The smallest difference showed in this comparison: 80 percent of the personally bombed reported a lowered work capacity, but 76 percent of the unbombed did too.[53] Analysts were impressed that bombing apparently had a more general than differential effect on morale.

Could this relatively flat effect have meant that the bombing in Japan had little effect on morale? No. Such a conclusion about a level of bombing which had killed close to 1 million people—by the survey's estimate, 900,000 were killed in Japan, and 305,000 were killed in Germany—defied common sense, and it also flew in the face of plentiful evidence from interviews that bombing had been a terror, a continuing worry, and an exacerbation of miseries coming from other quarters. The report concluded that for a variety of reasons—Japan was so small, the attacks were so concentrated, the bombers so continually in view crisscrossing the sky at will, and air-raid protection virtually abandoned by the government— bombing affected almost everyone, whether they had been personally bombed or not. Bombing failed to show specific, differential effects because it showed such massive, uniform ones.[54]

Military defeats, population bombing, and great privations in the economy had all been effective enough, in fact, that the atomic bombing of Hiroshima and Nagasaki was deemed unnecessary. The Japanese report by the Morale Division was straightforwardly critical on the point. Japanese morale had been plummeting so disastrously that in May 1945 the governmental "politics of surrender" were already in motion. The report judged that the atomic raids hastened those politics but not by much: without atomic bombing Japan would almost certainly have surrendered within ten to fifteen weeks of the time that it did.[55] A major USSBS report from the office of the chairman on the effects of the atomic bombing, however, gave a rather different emphasis: "The atomic bombings considerably speeded up these political maneuverings [for peace] with the [Japanese] government" by providing an opportunity to break the political deadlock within the government, and they could be seen as having saved Japan from further useless slaughter and destruction.[56]

The lesson of the morale studies themselves—even without such other USSBS studies with implications for morale—is not as clear as some may have hoped at the time or concluded since. Morale damage to Germany, after all, did not stop; it proceeded at diminishing rates. It would have been greater if personal losses had been greater, and those losses presumably would have been greater in turn if bombing had been scattered more widely—as the Japanese bombing was, in effect, by virtue of a number of political and geographic factors in addition to the bombing itself: Japan received a veritable rain of bombs on a small area. This type of bombing produced modest differential effects because it affected almost everyone, whether they had been personally bombed or not, in a way that less massive bombing probably would not have. In any case, if military strategists who greatly escalated the tonnage of strategic bombing in later years were relying upon the morale studies of World War II for counsel, they must have learned their "lessons" from judicious selection within these reports, not to mention the many other reports of USSBS.[57]

Policy Research and the Exodus to University Science

Dismantling Governmental Opinion Research

During and immediately after the war, Congress gradually cut the wartime survey organizations out of the federal budget. The domestic branch of OWI lacked the support from the top (notably from the president) that army morale research received from important generals. Davis, head of OWI, was not himself a great enthusiast of opinion research generally, but he supported it and tried unsuccessfully to protect it from the depredations of budget cutters. Opinion research was a very small part of a large agency, however, with manifold and confusing responsibilities, which came under very enthusiastic congressional attack. Davis had his hands full.[58]

Congressmen, especially Republicans, were wary of the administration's use of wartime information and intelligence, suspicious of social control and policy changes, and suspicious that it all had as much to do with helping Roosevelt to win a fourth term as with helping the Allies win the war. They took special umbrage, for example, at an OWI publication entitled *Victory*, which in their view lauded the commander in chief and the New Deal much more than was seemly. Some Southern congressmen were outraged by the OWI pamphlet *Negroes and the War*, which praised the contributions of the black soldier.[59] OWI's information/propaganda work came in for much more attack than its information/research did, but Congress was no champion of the polls in any case. Such information as we have about congressmen's attitudes in general in this period suggest that they felt they knew their constituencies better than any survey could discover and that they wished to protect their own expertise from such rival incursions[60] (rather like certain regular army officers, in fact!). The specific efforts of certain congressmen to cut away opinion research became very visible.

After a sizable political storm in 1943, OWI's Bureau of Intelligence was abolished by Congress, the whole domestic branch of OWI itself having narrowly escaped with its life—its budget in tatters, a third of its former size.[61] Wilson's OWI Surveys Division within the bureau had been preserved by having been carried off to another part of OWI. But in May 1944 this fragment too was cut away from the OWI budget for 1945—it was desirable but not necessary, Congress concluded.[62] Had Wilson been on the scene, he could conceivably have rounded up some support to save the operation, at least temporarily. But in spring 1944, he was in Europe organizing within the Supreme Headquarters Allied Expeditionary Force (SHAEF) a "combat survey" team that landed on the beaches of Normandy some three weeks behind the invasion troops to survey a sample of the French population.[63] When OWI tried to get its Surveys Division restored a year later, Congress was unmoved:

> A year ago the committee determined, after searching inquiry, that such surveys did not serve a purpose worth the amount expended and this year has reviewed the matter but does not believe substantial disadvantage has resulted from the lack of such surveys during 1945 and therefore has again not provided for the Division.[64]

The amount was a trifle: $128,530, three-tenths of 1 percent of the OWI budget of $35 million, the vast part of which was for OWI overseas. The trifle was cut to zero. On August 31, 1945, as the war had ended on both fronts, OWI itself was disbanded.

Program Surveys was the last to go, abolished August 1, 1946. Congress had been on the point of prohibiting *all* surveys, but the Department of Agriculture managed to preserve a remnant organization that was restricted to the quieter knitting of market and agricultural studies. Congress had been especially exercised about a "cultural survey" in Mississippi critical of race relations matters, conducted not by Program Surveys but by another division in Agriculture. This survey was a descendant of the old social survey movement in its political activism, its focus on the community, its anthropological rather than polling techniques, and in its director, Carl C. Taylor, a sociologist who had done his dissertation on the social survey movement in 1919 (see chapter one). In this case, the diffuse meanings of the word *survey* had political consequences. All surveys with obvious political potential were scrapped.[65]

Congress looked with more favor on survey research in foreign countries. In Germany, after the war, an opinion survey section was established in the Office of Military Government, United States (OMGUS) under the direction first of Frederick W. Williams and then of Leo P. Crespi. At the end of the occupation, this survey unit became the Reactions Analysis Staff, Office of Public Affairs, High Commissioner of Germany (HICOG) (1949–55). In Japan, the anthropologists Herbert Passin and John W. Bennett had major responsibility in what became the Public Opinion and Sociological Research Division of the Civil Information and Education Section of the Supreme Command, Allied Powers, Japan (SCAP) (1946–51). These activities were absorbed by surveys conducted worldwide by the United States Information Agency (USIA) in the early 1950s.[66]

This successive dismantling of domestic survey agencies represented the cumulating judgment of Congress that the administration either did not need or could not be trusted to conduct research into opinions/attitudes of the American public. Government continued to need survey data, and it got them by contract and through some small projects surviving in government. But the *official* institution of governmental opinion research was an experiment that was largely over by the time the war was. In 1945 Julian Woodward thought the setback was temporary:

> Sooner or later the government itself will have to go into the polling field and provide both its administrators and its legislators with adequate and sound information on what the public thinks. Eventually this sort of information will become as necessary as census data and will be provided by an agency with a reputation for unbiased research equal to that now enjoyed by the present Census Bureau.[67]

But his judgment was not prophetic. Instead, subjective measures in survey research flourished not in government but in academic and commercial enterprises.

The Naive Model

The implicit model of applied research in wartime opinion work was a fairly simple one. It was not unlike Gallup's "civic" model: a government that wanted to know the will of the people as a guide to intelligent policy; a citizenry of great common sense that had important things to say; strong links of democracy uniting them in much community of interest— *if* research kept the information flowing through the system. The wartime researchers did not use that rhetorical language, but the assumptions were very similar. Researchers could provide to governmental administrators information they needed from the public about their preferences, attitudes, and behavior in order to carry out the consensual goal of winning the war.[68] Some of the research conducted during the war was really quite like this, as certain administrators welcomed and used the findings of research.[69] Although wartime research was hardly without frustrations in bureaucratic complexity, overall the wartime researchers were proud of trying to put attitude/opinion/morale research in the service of government, and there was dedication and excitement about the importance of this work for victory and democracy and for social science.[70]

The model nevertheless was very oversimplified: blandly democratic, rather blind to power, confident that government and citizens shared a vast community of interest. In the course of their wartime work, survey researchers, who surely knew intellectually that the model was too simple, got some personal experience in that fact. As we have seen, congressional suspicions and battles whittled away their budgets and acted, in effect, to drive the new researchers out of Washington and back into business or the university. The civic model now looks particularly weak in the case of the bombing surveys.[71]

Richard Jensen has argued that the political battles that coursed around wartime opinion research were instrumental in taking "the politics" out of an emerging survey research:

What was lost in the synthesis, at least from the 1940s to the late 1960s, was a sense of politics itself, and the value of social science in policy formation. The polls thus came full circle, from avid search for new techniques that would *enhance the democratic prospect*, however defined or distorted, to an avid search for techniques that would analyze homo politicus with the political part dropped.[72] [Italics added]

It is worth asking whether the survey researchers, at least during World War II, were ever quite "in" politics in the sense that Jensen seems to have in mind. V. O. Key, Jr.'s observation seems cogent here: that the emerging survey research yielded little insight into the workings of government or politics during its first couple of decades because it was so largely the work of social psychologists and sociologists.[73]

In any case, an expectation that scientific opinion research could *simply* "enhance the democratic prospect" seems so profoundly apolitical that it was bound to fail. Gallup continued to enunciate the civic model and to practice a version of it, but it has required him to ignore the vast political uses of polls and surveys by elites. It stands in some contrast to the elite or power model as set forth in Harold D. Lasswell's book *Politics: Who Gets What, When, How* which was published in 1936, the same year in which Gallup "won" his first major election.[74] Gallup's assumptions, more than Lasswell's, underlay the applied opinion research of wartime.

It also appears that when Congress wanted the survey researchers out, they were largely ready to go. They went rather gladly, it seems, their patriotic service completed, ready to resume their former careers and willing to abandon political wars for which as scientists or businessmen they were untrained and which they were not very motivated to fight under peacetime conditions. Not unlike other art forms requiring sustained concentration, research of the kind that social scientists wanted to do—as thorough, as complex, as coherent, as continuing—was not very feasible in the heat of the political kitchen. Social scientists going back to their universities hoped to get on with scientific advance.

Stouffer probably spoke for many of his colleagues in wartime governmental research when he reflected that their wartime work had been a long-term investment for science: if scientists did not come out into the world of practical affairs now and then to show what they could "do," they could not expect the public to support their basic research. He said this when the day-to-day chores of the Research Branch were over and he himself was back in university work, but he was surely right.[75] Federal funding of social science in universities was a direct outgrowth of the war, as we shall see.

Certain survey researchers who went back to university teaching and research felt that they had learned something new under the sun, by extending the reach of attitude studies to national scope, and they thought that there should be a place for this work in the university. Many of their colleagues saw it as rather indistinguishable from the work of the pollsters, but the new researchers saw it as far richer in substance and in scientific potential. In their view, survey research could not only cope with practical problems but could also help to lay the foundation for new generality in science. Some hoped to lay claim to a distinctive *inter*discipline in survey research. This aspiration involved two questions: How much scientific innovation had they really accomplished during the war years, and how clearly could their work really be distinguished from that of commercial polls? The wartime researchers had been working on both those questions during the war itself.

6

The Wartime Experience
in Science (I)

> Although it may still be fashionable in some academic
> circles to speak condescendingly of "mere gadgeteers," it
> has become increasingly clear to me that research in social
> science, lacking these gadgets, would be no less sterile
> than research in medicine lacking microscopes and clinical
> thermometers.
>
> *Samuel A. Stouffer*

Contributions in the Context of Polling

The School of Practical Experience

"During the recent war, social scientists had an unprecedented opportunity to contribute their skills and knowledge," Lazarsfeld and his colleagues noted later, and they surely spoke for many who had taken pride
in the wartime work of their discipline.[1] Social scientists also *learned* a
great deal from breaking out of academic life. As Robert Ford recently
said about life in the Research Branch:

> Sam would give you a problem of concern to someone somewhere in the War
> Department, and you would pursue it all the way from the first perplexity to
> the final report. How could you conceptualize the problem? How could you
> approach the measurement? You learned how to interview. Then you learned
> how to draft a questionnaire, to pretest it, to get it into production, to draw a
> sample, to lay out the fieldwork, to get it into machine summary, to ask for
> intelligent tabulation (not to run everything against everything else). Then
> the hard work started. What do you make of what you have? All your aca-
> demic training was now on the line, I felt that nowhere else in America could
> I have been part of such an important group in the light of my academic
> background.[2]

The wartime survey researchers did the course. They were passionate
pretesters of questions; they interviewed, coded, ran the machines, constructed the tables, wrote the reports. Among them they interviewed

soldiers and civilians all over the world—as noted in chapter five, they moved into France just three weeks behind the D-Day invasion forces to interview civilians; they flew into Germany and Japan right after the armistices; and throughout the war they surveyed American troops in Iceland, Panama, Italy, the Philippines, the major theaters of the Pacific—all over, including bases in the United States. Interviewing troops in combat was not common, but Robin M. Williams, Jr., recalls that one rifle company filled out questionnaires "during sporadic shelling by German 88s."[3] The researchers also conducted many thousands of interviews with the American civilian population in all parts of the United States. For some of the more sheltered academics, this domestic field experience was probably no less exotic, as they tried to learn how to convert or extend their methods into ways that would work with mass publics. The social scientists for the first time faced the pollsters' world— that is, simple questions in plain language, short interviews, far-flung field staffs, large-scale group research, competitive costs, and reports written for laymen, as well as the great advantage of funds that permitted large staffs and surveys of national scope.

During wartime survey research in civilian work, there was more direct contact between academic social scientists and commercial researchers than there had been before. The academics in wartime survey research had a special historical debt to polling, like it or not, but they also wanted to demonstrate to the world of affairs that they could add to the practical utility of opinion polling as well as to demonstrate to their scientific peers that they could add to its scientific worth. They were indeed intent on improving on polling.

While the pollsters and social scientists often had much in common, there was strain in the coalition when pollsters needed the prestige of science for protection and the scientists wanted it for distinction. In the first instance, when pollsters came under political attack for their election forecasts, they needed science as a shield to blunt the charges of malicious bias or incompetent error. Social scientists tended to distrust election forecasting as a rather trivial as well as dangerous enterprise, and they genuinely believed that the polls needed major scientific overhauls. On occasion, they withheld the shield of science and proffered instead their own verbal sword of scientific criticism, putting more distance between themselves and the pollsters.

Even those social scientists who had good working and personal relationship with the pollsters sometimes distinguished their work carefully as being superior to opinion polling, albeit mildly and tactfully.

Stouffer, for example, who was very supportive, credited the pollsters' and market researchers' contribution and urged social scientists not to exaggerate their own. Even so, he saw the Research Branch work as representing a significant scientific advance over polling and some of its "glaring" defects.[4] Lazarsfeld, too, who had much cordial contact in the business world generally, introduced his panel study as "further progress" upon opinion polling, and later (in 1948) he explained that this work should not be confused with polling because it was part of a "new discipline" that was broader and more basic.[5]

Had social scientists in wartime research, especially those working on problems in morale, put together a new domain of inquiry, with distinctive theory, methods, examples, and disciplinary continuity? Not really, and the practitioners did not really lay claim to being a full-fledged discipline in the social sciences. Rather, they saw their work as a new field for quantitative research—a complex kind of group research that could offer new capacity to existing disciplines and interdisciplinary work; empirical data closer to "real life" than laboratory experiments or aggregate statistics; the potential for generalizing results to large populations; and a rich source of new data with which to test and construct social theory.

The Claim to Innovation: Criteria

In what ways could the survey work be said to constitute a new field? Four criteria of innovation are especially relevant to the emergence of a scientific discipline or *interdiscipline*:

1. Theory
2. Research methods, instruments, design
3. Good examples, as in achieved texts demonstrating the use of research methods in developing concepts
4. Social organization for communication and continuity

The first item on the list has usually concerned social scientists the most. In the sense of "grand theory," we can dismiss it almost out of hand. During the war there were no bold theoretical developments—no wholly new conceptions of social structure, individual psychology, or economic or political functioning to please the theorists of those fields, and no domain or theoretical core that would stake out a new intellectual preserve *distinct* from those traditional disciplines. There was more evidence of change in the other three areas, which we shall consider in more detail.

Instruments and Methods

Question Design and Interviewing

Two kinds of survey questioning were developed in the wartime survey work: Guttman scaling and open questioning. Both had been initiated before the war, but in the practical situation they were given new form and broader application.[6] Both were in part efforts to convert or extend methods of small-scale research into instruments practical for mass publics. Louis Guttman had hoped initially to construct a factor analysis for qualitative data, but he proceeded to work on single-factor, unidimensional *scaling* for such data.[7] In this work he addressed both the field of attitude measurement and the practical problems of polling. Open questioning also tried to bridge social science and polling, by trying to apply concepts and techniques borrowed from *clinical psychology* to get beneath the superficiality of the single poll question and enrich survey information. The researchers working on the two techniques both avowed their intention of improving upon pollsters' methods.

The two "schools" of questioning tackled exactly the same problem: the meaning of questions to respondents. Suchman's explanation of the purpose of Guttman scaling was in fact precisely the purpose of open questioning:

Did different people interpret the question differently?
Was it double-barreled?
Was the subject matter too complex or technical to be understood?
Did the question contain some unforeseen implication?
Was the question wording simple enough to be understood?
Did the interviewer change the original meaning of the question?
Did the context in which the question was asked affect its meaning?[8]

Neither technique by itself came close to answering that long list of questions. Each showed certain strengths and limitations, some of which were associated with the respective modes of administration, with written questionnaires being used for Guttman scaling and personal interviews being used for open questioning.

GUTTMAN SCALING

The construction of a Guttman scale was not an easy procedure, but it was more feasible for mass administration than Thurstone scaling, which might require some twenty or thirty questions on a single topic. A Guttman scale, after due pretesting of a number of items, could be winnowed down to six or seven items, or even to three or four, offering the obvious advantage of leaving more time in a given questionnaire or interview for other topics. A perfect Guttman scale ordered individuals on ranks on a single dimension, or at least a closer approximation to a single dimension, than other scales had.[9] A Guttman scale was a rank-order, *cumulative* scale similar in certain respects to the Bogardus social-distance scales first developed in the 1920s (see chapter two). Bogardus had established his scale points *a priori*; Guttman established his scale points in part by judgment of the scale's manifest content and in part empirically, by observing which questions actually formed a scale.

The classical expositions of Guttman scaling illustrate the cumulative property with reference to physical measurement in this way:

1. Are you over six feet tall?   Yes ___ No ___
2. Are you over five feet six inches tall?   Yes ___ No ___
3. Are you over five feet tall?   Yes ___ No ___

A person answering the first question Yes would also answer the other two questions Yes. From the rank-order of such a scale, one would know exactly how a person responded to each of the items. The pattern of those responses on a "scalogram" would show as a parallelogram:

Rank order of respondents	Score	Says Yes to item			Says No to item		
		1	2	3	1	2	3
1	3	x	x	x			
2	2		x	x	x		
3	1			x	x	x	
4	0				x	x	x

In a perfect Guttman scale, the order of the items was established by the order of their popularity.[10]

The physical example was clear but oversimple, because attitudes of course rarely presented themselves in these convenient hard shapes and regular sizes. In practice, Guttman scales were often constructed of items that showed much less difference in manifest content—close to "synonymous" items, on occasion. Those presented as illustrations by the Research Branch were of this sort, for example, the items used to measure attitudes toward officers:

How much did you personally like your officers?
1. Very much
2. Pretty much
3. Not so much
4. Not at all

In general, how good would you say your officers were?
1. Very good
2. Fairly good
3. About average
4. Pretty poor
5. Very poor

When you did a particularly good job, did you usually get recognition or praise for it from your officers?
1. Always
2. Usually
3. Rarely
4. Never

Items of this sort usually did not form a scale if all the answer categories were maintained as discrete units or were collapsed into favorable and unfavorable dichotomies on some uniform basis (for example, Always and Usually vs. Rarely and Never). But these questions, along with several other similar items, were found to scale (within acceptable limits) with various favorable/unfavorable cutting points of the following type:

Favorable	Unfavorable
Personally like:	
1. Very much	2. Pretty much
	3. Not so much
	4. Not at all
How good:	
1. Very good	4. Pretty poor
2. Fairly good	5. Very poor
3. About average	
Good job:	
1. Always	3. Rarely
2. Usually	4. Never[11]

Such cutting points (most often, dichotomies) could be located by manipulating the "scalogram," a physical board designed by Guttman for use in the Research Branch. A visual aid, the scalogram offered an alternative to the prodigious labor of computing correlations of every item with every other item in a large set, for it enabled one to see in a shorter time how each item related to others and to the whole. The board provided holes in 100 rows for persons and 100 columns for answer categories, and each respondent's answers were recorded by distributing metal shot in holes in the board. Because slats in the board could be shifted to change the position of rows and columns, thus changing the position of respondents and the cutting points (combining answer categories), the board could be manipulated to reveal a scale pattern if one existed. (There were other criteria for scalability, such as answers showing a range of marginals and a random scatter of error.)[12] The scalogram technique was seen as a great time saver—after training, a clerk could be expected to test scalability for a set of ten to twelve items answered by 100 respondents in about eight hours[13]—but the overall investment was a large one.

Intensity measures and a zero point. In a special use of Guttman scaling, the Research Branch addressed the nettlesome problem of question wording in work directed especially to pollsters, with their penchant for the single question. As Edward Suchman later explained,

> Public opinion analysts and other workers in the field of attitude measurement have long been aware of the problem of question "bias." There are numerous cases on record in which differently worded questions dealing with the same issue have produced different percentages of the population apparently "opposed to" or "in favor of" the issue being studied. Slight changes in the question wording, in the order of presentation of the answer categories, in the position of the question in the questionnaire, and many other factors known to all pollsters may affect the findings of one's poll.

Thus, Suchman continued, searching for an ideal "unbiased" question was a bootless quest; what was needed was "some *objective* method of dividing the respondents into the *same* proportions pro and con *regardless of question wording.*"[14]

This procedure involved first devising a set of items that scaled and then attaching to each a question measuring intensity. For example, in the questions concerning attitudes toward officers, each question was followed by an intensity question such as this one:

> How strongly do you feel about this?
> 1. Not strongly at all
> 2. Not so strongly
> 3. Fairly strongly
> 4. Very strongly
> 0. No answer[15]

The joint distribution of content and intensity scores was then plotted. The technique was inspired directly by a 1944 article by Daniel Katz (who had been a student of Floyd Allport's), and it showed some lineage to the Allport/Hartman scales of 1925.[16] These had shown that extremes of political opinion on a left/right continuum were associated with greater intensity than were opinions in the middle (see chapter two). Guttman and Suchman's joint distribution of content by intensity answers showed the same U-shaped or J-shaped curve of rising intensity at the extremes of favorable/unfavorable reactions to content. The lowest point of the curve established the so-called zero point, or region of indifference. Different sets of questions (worded differently and dichotomized differently) showed essentially the same curve. Thus, those to one side of the region of indifference could be reported as Favorable and those on the other, Unfavorable.[17]

The polls seem to have largely ignored what Suchman and Guttman offered as a "solution" to question "bias." Not surprisingly. What would it have meant, precisely, to report that Americans were *X* percent for and *Y* percent against "intervention" or "conscription" or the like, as a generalized attitude, without reference to the specific and contingent content of what *kind* of "intervention"—where, how much, at what cost, and to whose lives and fortunes?

The repeated intensity measure after each question of substance would have been a disadvantage as well. The Research Branch staffers actually expected the pollsters to use Guttman scaling for *selecting* poll items for two or three or even single poll questions on a given topic. (Unlike many other social scientists, Stouffer did not read the single question entirely out of court, noting that it was sometimes useful.)[18] Other social scientists in the mid- and late 1940s (such as Cantril) were urging pollsters to specify the contingencies of their questions, and pollsters were somewhat more responsive over the years to that counsel. Gallup, for one, remained convinced that scaling in general did not thrive much outside the college classroom.[19]

Applications and Criticisms. While Guttman scaling did not affect polling practice much, it was nevertheless a substantial and exciting new development for social scientists. In the decade after the war, there were many reports of use, adaptation, and experiment with Guttman scaling in leading social science journals (*American Journal of Sociology, American Sociological Review, Sociometry, Psychological Review, Psychological Bulletin, Journal of Social Issues*, and, especially, the two attitude/opinion journals *Public Opinion Quarterly* and *International Journal of Opinion and Attitude Research*). And Guttman scaling swiftly took a place in the classic literature on scaling. Much of the postwar work was based on students and other small groups, but use was made of it in survey research, too, in various articles and in two important books: Campbell, Gurin, and Miller's *The Voter Decides* (1954) and Stouffer's *Communism, Conformity, and Civil Liberties* (1955).[20]

There was also trenchant criticism and some spirited debate about Guttman scaling in the postwar decade which raised important questions about its applicability to mass survey measurement. For example, Festinger judged that the monotony of several very similar questions argued against their use in the personal-interview setting. Steiner provided evidence that four or five items selected for practical reasons from a longer Guttman scale might not show the same rank-order when they stood alone. Peak's 1953 article summarized a number of reservations and criticisms.[21]

Certain limitations to use were well recognized in the 1940s by Guttman himself: the fact of the "relativity" of scales, meaning that items scaling in one group or at one time might well not scale at another, and—a crucial fact—that most areas of interest to survey researchers did not scale at all in the Guttman mode. For a researcher to learn that a given attitude content conforms to a Guttman scale has come to serve even more as a discovery about that domain than as a handy methodological tool. Some of the hopes and claims for Guttman scaling have come to look too sanguine—survey researchers continue to worry about question wording and to consider realms that do not scale in the Guttman mode—and its use seems to have diminished in recent years. But it nevertheless stands as an innovation of importance for adapting scale measurement to the requirements of survey research.[22]

Lazarsfeld's scaling model. Late in the war, Lazarsfeld developed latent structure analysis, another scaling model, in the course of his consulting work with the Research Branch, but it was not put into the practical use in those early years that Guttman scaling was. (The first publication of Lazarsfeld's model was in the fourth volume of *The American Soldier* series, *Measurement and Prediction*, 1950.) The basic idea was similar to, and a generalization of, the basic idea of factor analysis (i.e., that a "latent variable," or underlying trait, could be inferred back from the response patterns to a set of questionnaire items), except that the observed variables of latent structure analysis were qualitative rather than quantitative. Guttman scales chose cutting points to minimize scalogram errors, as we have noted; Lazarsfeld chose particular item responses *a priori* on the basis of their manifest content and then worked out the theoretical probabilities for each pattern of response expected from the model (for instance, the probabilities for four dichotomous items of the response patterns of Yes/Yes/Yes/Yes, Yes/Yes/Yes/No, Yes/Yes/No/Yes, etc.). Through a complex series of "accounting equations"—as many equations as there were different response patterns—Lazarsfeld determined latent parameters, and he used them to work out the frequencies of the response patterns that would be expected if the model fit perfectly. Comparing these with the observed frequencies provided him with an evaluation of the model for the latent variable (not an actual statistical test, which he did not have). If the two were close, fine; if not, the analyst could either look around for another model or, if the original model still seemed theoretically compelling, check closely for errors in either the theory itself or in the indices chosen for the original empirical work.

This was a milestone in scaling theory, but latent structure analysis did not have much impact on actual practice in survey research until the present era of mathematical models and complex computer programs. (In recent years Lazarsfeld's latent structure analysis has been applied and extended by Leo Goodman and Clifford Clogg.)[23] In the war years of concern to us here, Guttman scaling and open questioning had wider application and influence.

THE OPEN-CLOSED DEBATE

The origins. The debate about questioning and interviewing was a vigorous one during the war years, although it is not very visible in published literature. In his 1946 review, McNemar wrote that the lines of debate had become clouded with "emotional cultism," but he named no names. Lazarsfeld deemed the controversy important and fierce enough to warrant a truce. His 1944 article "The Controversy over Detailed Interviews: An Offer for Negotiation," has become a classic in the sparse literature on question design, but it named just enough names to be confusing.[24] In the context of chapter five, it will be no surprise to learn that the contenders were Wilson's Division of Polls and Likert's Division of Program Surveys (both located in the Bureau of Intelligence, administered by R. Keith Kane). In the spring of 1942, Kane had asked Lazarsfeld, who was then his consultant, to study the situation and bring back a recommendation. The 1944 article, which appeared in *Public Opinion Quarterly* (*POQ*), was a revision of that 1942 report.

The practice of open interviewing. Open interviewing as practiced by Program Surveys was in part an effort to endow the old "scouting" interview with more structure and standardization. Likert tried to replace the word *open* with the term *fixed question/free answer* in order to stress that the questions were written with the alternatives unspecified, but this label was not taken up much by others.

The technique involved five features. The interview was to be as close as possible to a natural conversation with, first, much *verbatim transcription*, even of those answers that might have been coded on the spot. For example, the following kind of question became a staple item in the repertoire of Program Surveys:

> Would you say you are better off or worse off financially now than you were before the war?

Answers could have been recorded by putting a check mark next to one of these answers:

___ Better
___ Worse
___ In between; some ways better; some ways worse
___ Don't know

Interviewers in the Polls Division would have done this. The Surveys interviewers instead took down the exact words of the respondent, or as close to it as they could manage.[25] The dual purpose of preserving the actual words was to learn whether the questions had been understood by the respondent and to determine precisely the meaning of the respondent's answer.

The *probing* for detail and clarification constituted a second important feature of the style, serving both purposes of understanding and meaning. This was the most artful feature of the technique, requiring the most educated judgment and the avoidance of biasing questions, which in turn made *interviewer training* a third and especially important part. The interviewer training was adapted directly from Rogerian clinical psychology. In 1942, Likert arranged with Carl Rogers, who was then at Ohio State and was well known for nondirective techniques of psychotherapy, to assist in training interviewers. Staff members Charles F. Cannell and Victor C. Raimy worked with the interviewers and focused especially on the use of neutral, nondirective probes, such as "How do you mean?" and "Can you tell me more about that?"—even expectant pauses and silences. The theory was duly therapeutic in origin: interviewers were to help respondents overcome diffidence and blocks to communication:

they were to accept and understand respondents' feelings and ideas without suggesting or biasing.[26] The application to the survey situation was novel in that it assumed that a more complex psychology was operating in the interview setting and also in that it institutionalized more training to handle the interviewing than market researchers or pollsters had.[27]

A fourth feature of the open style was that interviewers were generally *well educated*, with college or professional degrees.[28] Not until 1943 did Program Surveys start using part-time interviewers whose education was generally less. This was, of course, an economy move. Surveys did not deal easily with the budgetary implications of open interviewing until after the contention with Polls had run its course.

All this abundant narrative material required, finally, *coding* of a more elaborate kind than that required for closed questions. Most codes used by Program Surveys were what they called *listing* codes, aimed at inductively isolating major categories and subcategories.[29] These generally had more logical structure than most commercial coding did, but they still had less than what Lazarsfeld had explicated as desirable in principle in his articles of the late 1930s (see chapters three and four). Program Survey staffers were restless about not fully exploiting their open materials in richly analytic codes, and they hoped to release personnel from day-to-day pressures to work on the problem, a hope that proved to be largely forlorn.[30]

Open-ended materials were also used to supplement statistical summaries with the local color of respondents. On occasion, three or four interviews would be excerpted and forwarded to a client agency as one of several reports on the topic, and reportedly agencies often took as much satisfaction from these as from statistical summaries. Program Surveys and the Research Branch in the army both frequently used quotations from respondents to illustrate types of answers or persons. Program Surveys staff were familiar with Guttman scaling but appear to have made modest, if any, use of it.[31]

The sum of these five interlocking features of questionnaire-interviewing design took more time and money than parallel methods of the Polls Division did. Program Surveys, which was developing its own probability sampling, was later able to argue that the cost of its more expensive interviews was offset by its smaller national sample (around 2,000). But in 1942, Surveys was not yet conducting probability samples on a national basis. The Polls Division was using larger national samples of 5,000 and more, with an interview of roughly half the length of the Surveys interview.[32]

What people argued about was whether the more expensive model of Program Surveys was worth the extra cost. The debate apparently never focused on coding and its reliability. Program Surveys studied their own coding and kept records that showed a good deal of variability in measures of reliability of open coding, but the criticism of Survey's work seems to have been more budgetary than methodological. More surprisingly, Program Surveys staffers did not publish on coding principles and practice until well into the 1950s,[33] and coding does not seem to have been treated, ever, as a fully professional (or analytic) task, in this or in any other survey organization.

The course of the conflict. By June 1942, the Program Surveys group had developed a vigorous ideology about the strengths of their interviewing methods and the weaknesses of the "restricted-response interview characteristic of the Gallup Polls." The most doctrinaire versions provided an encomium of praise for the open question and a catalog of criticism for the closed (polling) type. Open-ended questions were seen as natural, full, free, conducive to rapport, enhancing of respondent participation, and revealing of meaning, context, centrality of opinion. Polling interviews were seen as straitjackets—rigid, artificial, incomplete. It was granted that time and expense were greater for the open style, but no other difficulties of that style were set forth.[34]

In short order, the two divisions were showing some different results. In the same season, for example, both studied attitudes toward the Japanese, a subject that bore on the impending plan to relocate West Coast Japanese in internment camps.[35] In February 1942, NORC conducted the fieldwork for the Polls Division, interviewing nearly 800 citizens on the West Coast with closed questions. One question asked, "Taking all the Japanese aliens around here as a whole, which of these statements comes closest to the way you feel we ought to treat them?" Of four alternatives on a card, the first was, "Put them all together in camps someplace where they can be closely watched."[36] The report concluded that West Coast residents took a serious view of the threat from the Japanese, and many (some three-fourths of the Southern Californians in the sample) favored relocation camps.

Surveys conducted a small "exploratory" study in February 1942, based on about 100 interviews and using open questions of this sort:

What do *you* think should be done with the Japanese people here?
Do you mean Japanese aliens or American-born, or both?
Should we tighten up or ease up in our treatment of the Japanese (aliens, citizens)?

Their West Coast residents were certainly less concerned about Japanese *citizens* than about Japanese *aliens*, and many knew little or nothing about the issue, in any case. Only 19 percent suggested that Japanese (aliens and citizens) be put in internment camps.[37]

By the following month, there had been contention enough that Lazarsfeld was reviewing questionnaires from the two divisions for Kane. There is evidence that Lazarsfeld was very critical of the intensive interview work but that he also hoped to save it.[38] At the very time that he was preparing his report in June 1942, Surveys went on the offensive to demonstrate the merit of its methods with another "aliens study," on Germans and Italians. This time Surveys asked exactly the same questions that Polls had and followed them with open-ended probes. The Polls report, entitled "The Problem of Enemy Aliens along the East Coast," had concluded that German aliens "were regarded as a real menace" by a considerable number of people. Surveys, in a very small replication in one city, concluded that respondents felt "little sense of danger or threat from German or Italian aliens," and that most of what concern had been expressed flowed from general intolerance rather than from fears for national security. Lest anyone miss the point, the Surveys Division affixed a provocative pair of quotation marks to its report title, "The 'Problem' of Enemy Aliens on the East Coast."[39]

The Lazarsfeld report. In two reports of June–July 1942, Lazarsfeld warned that the current ways of the two divisions were wasteful:

> People are asked whether they are for or against price fixing. Likert gets 84 percent and Wilson gets 89 percent. They are asked whether they approve the government's conduct of the war. Likert gets 74 percent approval, and a Gallup Survey which I used for comparison gets 74 percent. . . . I do not hesitate to state [that there] is not one table in any of the general studies reported by the Survey[s] Division which could not be paralleled by a table gained from the Polling Division. In the great majority of cases the results will be essentially identical.[40]

In his judgment, the Likert group was by no means gathering up the riches they should from their open materials, because, in fact, they had really been making "polls instead of 'Likert studies'"—unkindest cut, no doubt, for this group intent upon distinguishing their methods from those of the polls.

Lazarsfeld set forth a program for cooperation between the two divisions. On an eight-week timetable, Surveys was to gather two sets of open-ended interviews of about 300 cases each, in the beginnning as pretests to help in the construction of the main questionnaire and at the end to help in the exploration of analytic problems. In the middle, Polls was to conduct a "regular poll" with about 3,500 respondents, using mostly closed questions. The two divisions could alternate in writing the reports.

Likert and his close associates thought that Lazarsfeld's plan would "layer" them as a junior outfit, consigning them to pretest and pilot studies while Wilson's Polls Division would be entrusted with the "real" studies.[41] Likert's group resisted the plan—and lost. With fifteen days' formal notice, their contract with OWI was officially terminated as of November 15, 1942. This meant that their existence as the "Surveys Division" was dissolved, although they of course continued their existence as Program Surveys in the Department of Agriculture. At the time, their resistance to Lazarfeld's compromise plan was seen as stubborn by some and understandable by others,[42] but it may have actually prolonged by a few years their survival as an organization in the federal government. Likert's Program Surveys endured with a smaller budget but in the greater shelter of the Department of Agriculture until 1946. Wilson's Polls Division was subject to the greater political buffeting suffered by OWI, and by 1944 his division had fallen entirely to the congressional budgetary ax. If Likert's organization had won the competition of 1942 and remained under contract to OWI, it might well have been dismantled in 1944, too.

After Program Surveys had been cut from the OWI budget, the surviving Polls Division (confusingly renamed the *OWI* Surveys Division) used a certain combination of open and closed questions that reflected the spirit of Lazarsfeld's suggestions more closely than either of the two competing divisions had shown in 1942,[43] though it did not incorporate Lazarsfeld's hopes for intensive use of open-ended reinterviewing at the analysis stage. (*Mass Persuasion* [1946], by Merton, Fiske, and Curtis, did, in the so-called "focused interview," which was used on a smaller number of the total interviewed with a poll questionnaire.[44] See chapter nine.)

A slight retrenchment. Even by 1944, less than two years after Program Surveys had been fired by the Bureau of Intelligence of OWI, there was interest among the staff in modifying the practice of open interviewing. Staff members had learned that questions could be *too* open and undefined, and because the contest with Polls had subsided, they were no longer under quite the same pressure to defend a doctrinaire position.[45] Program Surveys had also been feeling the pinch of costs, which had been a central part of the argument from the beginning. In a cost-saving move, part-time interviewers with less education and experience were added to the field staff in the latter part of 1943. These staff members found it difficult to handle the fully open interview.[46]

In the new situation, Lazarsfeld's recommendations became more attractive. Both Cartwright and Campbell, in fact, commended to the whole Program Surveys staff the 1944 Lazarsfeld article that had been developed from the 1942 report. In that article, Lazarsfeld argued that of six different uses for the open-ended question, four could be handled very well by various kinds of closed questions (scales, typologies, checklists, projective tests), with open questions being indispensable only for discerning influences and clarifying relationships.[47] Campbell's 1945 memo was a strong invitation to abandon the hard ideological line and use open questioning selectively, where it had special value.[48]

Program Surveys did use some closed questioning, but it also continued to use and refine open questioning, and it stayed publicly identified with that hallmark. Likert, especially, continued to champion it.[49] In a 1946 paper, Campbell granted that the "many successful applications of polling methods" were convincing evidence that open interviewing was not essential for all kinds of surveys, but he nevertheless saw it as the wave of the future. And his discussion of it here echoed the old rivalry, as he referred to the "aliens study" controversy without specifically identifying the "sides" and as he offered suggestions for ways in which the pollsters could improve their craft: undertaking intelligent pretesting; using multiple questions; examining one or two issues with some thoroughness instead of a "quick scratching of six or eight"; devising questions on the basis of a study design rather than "concocting isolated questions for their headline value"; and adapting Guttman scaling and intensity measurements.[50]

Many years later, Campbell and Cartwright both reflected that Program Surveys probably stiffened in its advocacy of the open question *because* it got caught up in competition with the Polls Division and with the polls generally. Program Surveys had been evolving in the direction of greater standardization in 1940 and 1941, and the competition probably slowed that process.[51] It seems likely that Program Surveys continued to rely very heavily on open questioning in many situations where enough had already been learned to warrant the use of more interlocking closed questions—not all, but some—and this might in turn have permitted more cumulative work, more ambitious research design, and more data analysis. There was not really time during the war for sustained analysis, but there might have been after the war, if the data themselves had been more cumulative: designed to serve more interesting purposes and reduced for more manageability. The work of Stouffer's Research Branch would have profited from *more* use of open, intensive interviewing to explore servicemen's own perceptions and reasons, and the staff had indeed hoped to do more such work.[52] Program Surveys might well have benefited from *less*.

Area Sampling

DEVELOPMENTS DURING THE WAR

The debate on survey questions and interviewing had little guidance in theory. However clear the polling problem was—superficiality, oversimplification—there were no generally applicable, broad-gauge solutions. The efforts were *always* intimately involved with the costs of large-scale fieldwork: the level of talent available for modest wages, the procedures of training and supervision which could be communicated at a distance, and the ranges of desirable or enforceable standardization. The theoretical fuzziness of the problem of survey questions lent itself then to individual strong opinions and organizational ideologies, and it may still.

In sampling there were also strong opinions and organizational ideologies, with costs of overweening importance, especially to those not in government work. Here, however, there was guidance of theory. During the 1930s, as we have seen, statisticians working in the Department of Agriculture and in the Bureau of the Census, especially, made applications of probability theory to the design of national samples of the American population (see chapter one). The national quota samples of the pollsters had been built pragmatically, without foundation in theory and without means of assessing the accuracy with which the samples estimated population parameters.

Area sampling, the alternative, was the first substantial American contribution to sampling, the theoretical foundations of which had been European (see chapter one), and it became something of an American specialty.[53] It was a complex form of probability sampling which proceeded in multistage fashion. First, a list or sampling frame was constructed, not of individuals but of all component areas in a geographic space. The areas were stratified, most often by size, and the largest cities were made strata of their own, so that all were included in the sample. After the area units were selected at any stage, the units of the next stage were identified, listed, and then selected. At the last stage of selection, the area in question was small, and only at this point were all the dwelling units listed in selected segments (perhaps a part of a city block or a very small rural area). From these small segments a small cluster of dwelling units was sampled.[54]

During the war years, Morris H. Hansen and William N. Hurwitz in particular (both of the Bureau of the Census) made innovations and refinements that are widely regarded as having completed the fundamental building blocks of modern area probability sampling. Some of their key work developed from the stimulation of working on the *Monthly Report on the Labor Force* (*MRLF*). This survey, which had been initially designed by Frankel and Stock in the WPA Division of Research, used stratification and what would soon be called *clustering* of households selected from county primary sampling units. This was close to a strict probability sample, though there were some compromises. (Households, for instance, had a different probability of selection in densely populated areas than in sparsely populated ones.) The sample was serviceable, nevertheless, and was probably the best design in the federal government at the time. In the first years of the sample's use (starting in 1940), its estimates were often considered better than the Census enumeration, which underestimated unemployment.[55] When WPA was discontinued in 1942, Census took over the sample, broadening its scope from unemployment to work-force estimates for wartime and postwar planning and changing its name to the *MRLF*. (In 1947, it was renamed again the Current Population Survey.)[56]

Hansen and Hurwitz extended the theory of *clustering*, showing that the increases in sampling variance which resulted from increasing the size of clusters (reducing their number) were related to the intraclass correlation coefficient. This provided a means of calculating losses in efficiency from using clusters (highly desirable to reduce interviewers' travel costs), losses that were shown to be different for various characteristics and different cluster sizes. Hansen and Hurwitz also developed theory for selecting primary sampling units (PSUs) with *probability proportionate to measures of size*, instead of with equal probability for selection for PSUs. This permitted the selection of clusters at the final stage of selection which were approximately equal in size—a distinct advantage in planning costs and field assignments—while an equal probability of selection was maintained, overall, for all dwelling units in the population.[57] By 1946, Hansen and Hurwitz had also devised a method for getting unbiased estimates from mail surveys (by selecting a subsample of nonresponders to interview), and they and W. Edwards Deming had begun to deal with nonsampling errors.[58]

THE EMERGING CRITIQUE OF QUOTA SAMPLING

As these new strides in probability sampling were made, pollsters began to come under criticism for their quota methods. The criticism was quite new. Both Gallup and Roper had published articles on their quota sampling in the *Journal of the American Statistical Association* before the war,[59] and various well-placed, even distinguished, social scientists had expressed supportive interest in their work. In 1938, Stuart A. Rice, for example, then chairman of the federal government's Central Statistical Board, noted Gallup's "representative sample census" as a hopeful development:

> To the extent that [Gallup] is able to master the problems of sampling which he encounters, his statistical findings may summarize American attitudes and opinions more accurately than do elections or any other method yet devised.[60]

Others shared that cautious optimism. Gosnell concluded his 1937 review of election forecasts on this upbeat note: "Gallup was just beginning to discover how to weight his samples more properly. Undoubtedly he can do a better job next time."[61] The statistician Frederick F. Stephan in 1939 viewed quota sampling as a practical accommodation to certain problems, as did others.[62]

The Katz election reviews provide a useful benchmark for the emergent criticism. In the first review of the 1936 election, Katz and Cantril noted that Gallup and Crossley forecasts had actually been rather wide of the mark, and they explored ten possible sources of error, two of which bore on sampling. But they criticized only the practical problems of constructing a miniature population, not the very principle of judgmental selection. They considered both random and quota sampling as "sound" ways of "using a sample procedure to produce a miniature group representative of the larger group from which it comes." They saw quota control as subject to the advantages and disadvantages that shortcuts were heir to but not as a method flawed at its very core.[63] Katz's review of 1940 did not tax quota sampling, but in his 1944 election article he criticized the pollsters for not having kept up with important new developments in sampling. By the mid-1940's, samplers had broken new ground in theory and application, and knowledgeable social scientists such as Katz had gained experience in probability designs.

SOME LEADING APPROXIMATIONS

The Research Branch. By Stouffer's own postwar evaluations (1950), the Research Branch was not on the cutting edge of sampling during the war. Early in their research experience, in fact, Stouffer and his colleagues had concluded that question wording was probably a more worrisome source of bias and error than were either sampling or mode of administration (written questionnaire)—an order of priority which many market researchers and pollsters had observed in the 1920s and 1930s and which the Guttman/Suchman work addressed.[64]

The Research Branch practiced a mix of purposive and quasi-random methods that it found serviceable enough. The initial selection of army units was done on a purposive basis (in Stouffer's view, the greatest threat to the generality of their findings was posed at this stage), and within units soldiers were selected by systematic methods and ordered to appear to fill out the questionnaire.

It was a "sampler's dream," in the ideal case, as Stouffer pointed out, but practicalities regularly intruded to threaten the vision. In principle, army units could have been selected randomly within the strata set up by branch and type of unit, but in fact there were not enough field staff to allow the kind of geographic scatter that would have predictably resulted. Costs were an issue, just as in civilian and commercial realms, and for most cross-section surveys taken in the United States, Research Branch personnel visited no more than some twelve to twenty installations.[65]

Moreover, field commanders understandably tried to cooperate with the researchers in ways that did not disrupt their own responsibilities. Field commands often wanted to make the selection of respondents themselves, which Branch personnel were at pains to prevent: local commanders might select every *n*th man who was *not* off on training maneuvers, or away at rest camp, or the like. The composition of the duty roster from which selections were made was usually at issue, in any case, for units varied widely in their practice. Sometimes, of course, these design defects were not apparent until after the data had been collected, and on occasion the data had to be discarded and a whole survey of another unit organized from scratch. Stouffer noted that in the course of the war, as experience grew, there was increasing confidence in the feasibility of "cutting corners" in sampling with no serious loss to the ultimate reliability of the findings.[66] Certainly, the debate about area versus quota sampling did not reverberate in the military as it did in civilian realms.

Program Surveys. Program Surveys played a much more visible role in the application of area sampling. After the division "went national," at the time of Pearl Harbor, it set out early in 1942 to construct samples along probability lines. Likert had come to the division in 1939 with the culture of market research's quota sampling, but there was great interest in area sampling in the Bureau of Agricultural Economics (BAE), and Likert came to share it. He delegated Leslie Kish and J. Stevens Stock to design the first probability sample for Program Surveys.

From the first, the division took the selection of the household out of the hands of the interviewers in direct application of probability methods. Sampling instructions were quite complex, however, and they left listing and systematic selection to the interviewers. During the years from 1942 to 1945, the prelisting of city blocks and segments was gradually extended to all urban dwellings. At the last, within the household, the final selection of the individual was made by a *quota* procedure. Interviewers were to keep a cumulative tally that showed the number enumerated and the number interviewed in six categories (males and females in three age-groups), and over the course of the interviewing days they were to maintain the same ratio of interviewed to enumerated in all six classes. If any of these ratios fell out of line with the others, the interviewer was instructed to choose respondents by category to bring the ratios back into balance. Callbacks were a mix of probability and practicality, for as a rule the interviewer made a total of two calls before going on to the next dwelling unit and trying there twice.[67] In 1946, Kish designed a selection table that completely eliminated these vestiges of interview selection by quotas within the household.[68]

Early in the war, *grid* sampling was used in the rural areas. Interviewers were usually equipped with a county map on which two sets of intersecting parallel lines had been drawn to form a grid, or else they were given instructions on how to draw the grid themselves. Sampling points were established by the intersection points of the lines. A certain number of farm households that were located closest to the sampling points were selected for the sample, and within these, respondents were chosen by the same age-sex quotas. It became apparent that the grid sampling biased selection in favor of the larger farms, which were more likely to be touched by grid intersections. This form of sampling was replaced by the more rigorous Master Sample of Agriculture, which was developed in 1943–44 at Likert's initial suggestion.[69]

The Master Sample of Agriculture. The Master Sample was a joint venture of BAE of Agriculture, the Statistical Laboratory at Ames, Iowa, and (in time) the Bureau of the Census. It was designed to permit sampling of both agricultural products and farm population.[70] Through the use of county maps, aerial photographs, and the highly detailed Sanborn maps (that showed farm buildings), built-up urban areas were excluded, and rural county areas were segmented into "count units."[71] Some 3,070 maps were prepared, one for each county, designating sample areas that yielded a sample of about 300,000 farms, about one-eighteenth of the total in the country.

While its initial costs were high, the Master Sample was expected to be economical in the long run because the plan was for various federal agencies to use it. In the eyes of later critics, it was a costly experimental design that did not really pay off, for it never received the anticipated heavy use by federal agencies. In its elaborate mapping and detail, it took so much time and money in preparation that many parts were already out of date by the time it was completed.[72] In the context of 1945, however, for Program Surveys it provided a much better rural sample than the grid sampling of 1942, and it took the division further along the road to probability sampling, which Likert, especially, had enthusiastically endorsed.[73]

THE DEBATE: CONGRESSIONAL HEARINGS

The political contention. "The area samplers initiated the present controversy," Norman C. Meier pointed out later, citing immediately the congressional hearings of 1944 on the Gallup Poll. Meier, then at the State University of Iowa and a close associate of Gallup's, implied that the "controversy" was premature, launched before the empirical facts were in.[74] Gallup thought so, too.

Gallup was called on the congressional mat to explain why he had again underestimated the Democratic vote in 1944, as in 1940: in some two-thirds of the forty-eight states, the polling forecast was less than the actual election tally of Democratic votes. The estimates for New York State were of special concern. Gallup's adjustments (a complicated set of weights that tried to take into account turnout, trends, different sources of data, varying degrees of competence among local field staff, etc.) were jiggered this way and that in the months before the election. For New York, the final forecast read 49.5 percent, when the final real vote gave Roosevelt 51.8 percent. Congressmen and consultants both criticized Gallup's failure to point out publicly that there had *been* any adjustments, and they resisted his defense that journalistic requirements did not permit such technical detail. They felt that he could have said *something* quite simple in the reports and could have made the full technical details available on request.

A similar issue about technical information became a lively one in Program Surveys in 1946. Certain members of the staff, particularly Kish and Campbell, wanted to publish information about response rates routinely in their reports to the government, to pioneer in scientific disclosure. Others argued that response rates were not well understood by laymen and would be misinterpreted, especially because no one else (in governmental work or outside) was publishing these rates.[75] Program Surveys published response rates in 1946, but the concerns of those who resisted were not wholly unlike those that Gallup had expressed in 1944.

Gallup explained his procedures in written and personal testimony, made copious records available to the committee, and defended the great practical values of polls and their scientific foundation. Election forecasts were of no particular importance, he stressed, but they provided an "excellent testing ground for new methods and techniques in the field of public opinion measurement." Sampling was of the essence, he explained: business and industry were spending hundreds of millions of dollars to sample public opinion in order to avoid still more costly mistakes; in fact, government, he was sure, had fallen behind.[76]

The hearings were not without some displays of suspicion and of defensiveness on the part of congressmen about their own expertise. Congressman Clarence J. Brown was particularly active, and he wanted Gallup to know that he himself knew a thing or two about politics in Ohio![77] Overall, the hearings left Gallup's nonpartisan integrity intact. However, the thrust of a technical report, submitted by sampling experts, was that in matters of science and especially in sampling it was Gallup who had fallen behind.

Scientific scrutiny. The technical committee serving the congressional committee was composed of Morris Hansen and Philip M. Hauser of Census, Louis Bean of the Bureau of the Budget, and Likert of Program Surveys. Their report duly praised Gallup in a general way: for pioneering in sampling and polling, for inspiring public interest in poll results, for experimenting in methods, and for having "made relatively effective use of scientific survey technique . . . in contrast to earlier polling attempts such as the *Literary Digest* poll."[78]

While it now sounds as though they were damning Gallup with faint praise, this was probably not their intent at the time. The report nevertheless focused on defects—in sampling method, sample size, interviewer training and field supervision, and the use of personal judgments in adjustments to the raw data. The criticism was not harsh or intemperate, but it was unqualified, confident, and—surely—missionary in its intent. Only pollsters were likely to object, especially because little praise was given to their new sampling experiments.

Gallup expected some credit for adapting the experimental "*area* or pinpoint sampling" from a Census model as an experimental supplement to his regular quota controls. In forty areas, interviewers had been directed by rule to every *n*th household rather than allowed to pick individuals by quota type wherever they found them. This was not *area sampling* as the technical consultants were using the term, however, for the choice of Gallup's areas had been made by the old purposive selection models that Neyman's work had begun to put to rest. Gallup had selected five states as "barometers" to try to forecast the election because over many elections these states had voted for the winner. He also had studied eight areas within each state that had also been regularly on the winning side, and he called these the "pinpoints."[79]

The committee pointed out the weaknesses of the quota sampling, which had carried the major burden of forecast, and criticized "pinpoint" sampling for various defects, especially its purposive selection.[80] The report implied, in conclusion, that these defects in Gallup's procedure were really quite unnecessary, for "Methods superior both to the quota method of sampling and the pin-point method of sampling, as used, were available and could have been utilized."[81]

Why Gallup failed to use these methods when they were so accessible as well as so superior was not broached in the report, which was in fact quite mute on the issue of the costs of converting to probability sampling: the expenses for travel, new detailed maps, retraining of interviewers accustomed to quota sampling, recruitment of new interviewers better able to carry out these new procedures, supervision, the new training documents, and the many other changes involved in reweaving a complex web of new organizational practice. The inference was that Gallup should dally no longer with imperfect quota sampling or minor experimental departures from it but should proceed with dispatch to the new, superior methods.[82] In his direct testimony, Gallup suggested, not without wryness, that this might not be quite so easy.[83]

There were, indeed, still some problems confronting governmental samplers, and they might have been mentioned if common cause with Gallup had been their major intent. The Research Branch, for example, also drew its units purposively. Program Surveys was still practicing within-household selection by age-sex quotas. The Census Bureau, for its part, had only recently dismantled some quota structure that had been built into the design of the Sample Survey of Unemployment/*MRLF*. The focus of the technical report was on principles rather than practicalities, however, and on the differences between Gallup and governmental practices rather than on similarities. In fact, in federal sampling practice, there was work that was still under construction and places where the paint was still quite fresh.

Protecting the infant discipline. At the last, the technical consultants moved to protect public opinion research in general from the criticisms they had been levying at Gallup's electoral work. Forecasting elections, especially close ones, they pointed out, was an "unnecessarily severe test of the accuracy of public-opinions polls on other issues" and should not detract from the value of "public-opinion surveys on general social, political, and economic matters."[84]

There is reason to think that Gallup and his staff felt that the technical consultants had thrown them to the wolves. This is conjecture, without documentation of Gallup's personal reactions at the time. Under the intense political criticisms of 1944, it seems reasonable to think that Gallup would have welcomed some scientific support. Cantril, in fact, provided some.

At the very height of public criticism, in November 1944, Cantril conducted a poll on public opinion polls which appeared in *Public Opinion Quarterly*. A majority of the 56 percent of the OPOR sample who said that they had heard of public opinion polls (Gallup was the best known by overwhelming proportions) gave them pretty good marks—for accuracy in forecasts, honest reporting, providing useful information to legislators, and other virtues.[85] By all odds, Gallup was probably somewhat inured to political criticism, which had become a campaign ritual, but public criticism from professionals was newer. The ranks of qualified professionals had been broadening during the wartime governmental research, and they were trying to shape polling methods in new, more sophisticated ways. Since the last election, more social scientists had come on the scene who had interesting things to say on these matters, and there was also more to be said.

While Gallup did not apparently react publicly to the criticism of 1944, his close associate, Edward Benson, did. In the winter 1944–45 issue of *POQ*, acrimony flared up in an exchange between Benson and Daniel Katz bearing on Katz's third analysis of the polls' quadrennial forecasts, published in the same issue.[86] The *POQ* editor noted that basic questions about polls' honesty and political value had never before been raised "so widely, so persistently, and with so much rancor as in the months surrounding the bitter election of 1944."[87] Benson was probably tired of it.

Katz's 1944 article was actually more laudatory than the Technical Committee's report had been in that he praised AIPO for experimenting in "pinpoint" sampling. However, he criticized the basic premise of the barometer principle. Benson defended it, saying that "the selection of areas on the basis of past political record is the soundest procedure for sampling in an election."[88] While there were other intellectual disagreements, Benson's bitterness was visible over the academic-commercial divide, as he charged Professor Katz (irrelevantly) with ignorance of practical affairs. Katz still withheld the laurels of science, insisting again that despite some experiments the polls had relied largely on old quota sampling and the usual interviewing methods.[89]

A year later, Benson and two coauthors had their own last word, in their *POQ* article "Polling Lessons from the 1944 Election," reiterating their claims to innovation. They conceded the desirability of adapting area sampling to private polling, *if* methods could be found which did not unduly increase costs over the quota methods then in use.[90]

This continued to be the main theme of pollsters for the next several years: area sampling was a good thing, in principle, if costs could be brought down. The area samplers, such as Hansen and Hauser, argued that raw costs or number of interviews per dollar was poor bookkeeping; rather, the efficiency of sample designs should be assessed in terms of "reliability of results obtained per dollar." Quota methods, they explained, were acceptable under certain circumstances—if rough estimates were useful, if "important decisions" did not hang on the results, if "the price to be paid for using a sample whose accuracy can be measured may not be justified."[91] Quota samplers continued to argue that the price rarely was.

Research Design

After the war, especially, some governmental researchers pointed to their wartime record in research design, which had permitted tests of hypotheses, and noted it as a major improvement over polling.[92] The way in which poll results were typically reported conveyed *implicit* hypotheses that standard demographic variables such as age, sex, region, socioeconomic status (SES), and group membership should predict opinions of many kinds. This convention of polling was probably an inheritance of quota sampling, as market researchers and pollsters used for their reporting of results the categories they had used for their samples. Otherwise, the polls made no real pretense to research design. Survey researchers in governmental work tried to cast their practical problems into these scientific shapes when they saw the chance—which occasionally appeared in both military and civilian opinion work. During the wartime period, the two most interesting research designs were incorporated in the government's bombing surveys of 1945 and in the panel analysis of *The People's Choice* (1944).

The morale survey of USSBS was the last important project in governmental survey research during the war. From the standpoint of design, it was also the most ambitious. A talented group of social scientists was mustered for the task, under the direction of Likert, who took leave from Program Surveys to direct the Morale Division. They used techniques that had been refined in the course of wartime work—recent advances in probability sampling, open questions that had been made more precise, trained interviewers, pretesting to test the candor of enemy respondents, content analysis of captured mail to conduct other tests of validity.[93]

It was not possible to construct a truly experimental design, because bombing itself had obviously not been conducted on a random basis; it had been targeted on industrial areas and population centers, and there were too few cities of any size that had *not* been bombed to permit experimental comparisons. In several respects the research design was nevertheless complex, and some of its features, such as objective and subjective measures of the bombing experience, have already been referred to in chapter five. Other features of the design tried to anticipate problems of recall and candor and to test validity. While retrospective measurement was a largely irremediable disadvantage—respondents were asked not only how they felt and acted during the war but also when their feelings and actions had changed, and this put great burdens on memory—efforts were nevertheless made to test validity of the subjective data by making comparisons with documents, with captured German mail, and with interviews of foreign laborers forced to work in Germany during the war. To encourage candor, the special precaution was taken in Germany of using two questionnaires, one of which did not make direct references to bombing until very late in the interview.[94]

The morale researchers tried to design their instruments and procedures to test a variety of hypotheses concerning the effect of bombing on morale. They used a number of intervening variables, such as air-raid protection, social solidarity, Nazi party membership, class position, and others. They also left good documentation of their questionnaires and sampling procedures. The morale researchers were better equipped to assess the morale effects of bombing as a psychological, attitudinal variable than as a set of behaviors, a focus that has reportedly made the

morale reports less interesting to military officials.[95] While the researchers did ask about *self-reported behaviors*, such as absenteeism from work,
reduced capacity to work, and "black listening" to Allied radio, they
could not learn much from these retrospective measures about how the
bombing changed the ongoing daily economic, personal, and family lives
of the victims or about the degree to which bombing disrupted the labor
force.

The morale data were, of course, analyzed with the cross-tabulations
of the counter sorter that was the workhorse of this era. It seems that
they have never been reanalyzed with the powerful computer routines
that have become available in the 1970s and 1980s. However, given the
difficulties of the data collection and classification of the materials in the
first place, reanalysis might not be very illuminating. The morale studies
nevertheless stand as a remarkable achievement for the time. The bombing surveys were the first major instance of the incorporation of survey
research (including large-scale subjective measurement) into an inquiry
by national commission, which would in later years become common in
governmental studies of crime, race, education, and other broad social
problems.

The panel study of the 1940 election by Lazarsfeld, Berelson, and
Gaudet, *The People's Choice* (1944) was the other major example of complex research design in this period, and it was an enormously influential
book. Its appearance during the war was happenstance, however, rather
than an event reflecting wartime collaborations or policy, and we shall
consider it in detail in chapter nine.

7

The Wartime Experience in Science (II)

Good Examples of the Practice

Gauging Public Opinion
A Research Canon and Collaboration

From the wartime work in survey research, two major books and a number of articles were produced. In 1944, Cantril and his associates at OPOR published a volume of experiments on survey methods. Although their enterprise was not funded directly by the government but rather by a Rockefeller Foundation grant and other entirely private monies, these funds represented a government interest in their polling work in the context of urgency about American defense and wartime activities. Cantril was interested in both the policy and scientific aspects of polling.

The set of articles stitched together as *Gauging Public Opinion* (1944) was an admitted miscellany, but Cantril expressed high hopes that it would "advance the science of polling" by its effort to "bring together for the first time in one volume some idea of the serious problems encountered in every phase of the polling operation." He hoped to discourage vague and unsupported criticism while encouraging "more solid criticism by those who sympathize with the basic problems at hand."[1]

In his academic role, Cantril tried to make a bridge *between* commercial pollsters and academic social scientists, but he was probably in greater sympathy with the pollsters than with many of his academic colleagues.[2] He saw OPOR as a research and polling organization, peculiarly well placed to conduct research that would in the long run improve polling, and he collaborated with Gallup to that end. That the collaboration across the two cultures was successful on the whole must be credited to Cantril's contact and friendship with the pollsters, especially Gallup, and to his own sympathy as an "insider." Cantril's OPOR might have become a leading model for opinion research—with pollsters doing most of the actual opinion studies and academics consulting on research into the practice—but it was short-lived as a full-fledged research organization. It endured after 1945 for ten more years, but only in a skeletal form. Its most substantial accomplishment was *Gauging Public Opinion*.

THE RANGE OF THE CONTENT

If one wished to read the volume as evidence of the frailties of polling—and, as we shall see, the "outsider" psychometrician McNemar wished to—*Gauging Public Opinion* offered abundant material. The lead chapter, "The Meaning of Questions," by Cantril and Fried, used actual examples from polls to point up "almost a dozen pitfalls that must be avoided if the results obtained in surveys of public opinion are to be reliably interpreted."[3] Rugg's chapter showed that poll samples overrepresented upper occupational groups. Stock's chapter on sampling pointed to some outrageous interviewer error.[4] The book was not by any means an attack on polling. Cantril and Rugg's illustrations of poor question wording came not only from Gallup's AIPO, Roper's *Fortune*, and NORC but also from their own organization, OPOR. This tactful inclusion, in particular, combined with the spirit of the whole book, showed that this was indeed the counsel of sympathetic researchers who were in it with the others. The point was not to indict polling but instead to learn from experiment some principles that would improve the field as a whole.[5]

The book had some manifest weaknesses—for instance, the lack of Ns in tables, the ad hoc explanations, the failure to set forth the scope of the experiments—but it covered a more ambitious research agenda than the scatter of articles of the past had. It treated question wording, interviewer training, mode of administration, measures of intensity, refusals, and a number of other subjects. It made some recommendations (more open questions, batteries, contingencies, personal training of interviewers) which were useful for their being supported, at least in part, by research findings. And the collaboration itself was noteworthy.

THE UNUSUAL COLLABORATION

There would soon be other edited volumes bringing together articles by governmental, academic, and commercial survey researchers.[6] But Cantril presided over an academic-commercial collaboration that gathered data across organizations that were in at least a partly competitive relationship with one another. The chapter by Rugg comparing interviewer performance in AIPO ("untrained") and NORC ("trained") provides a special illustration of the collaboration. The experiment and the findings were not very striking: NORC interviewers were seen to show one set of virtues and AIPO interviewers another, and such differences as Rugg found were ascribed to the greater interviewing competence of women versus men rather than to NORC's training versus AIPO's lack of it.

While there was much critical comment on polling practices offered in *Gauging Public Opinion*, it was temperate and evenhanded. When an organization was associated with error, the focus was on the problem of the field rather than on a given practitioner's folly. If the comparisons of the NORC and AIPO interviewers had revealed anything really outrageous about either organization, it seems likely that the study would not have been published, but such speculation is not at all meant to disparage Cantril's genuine interest and accomplishment in organizing research across poll organizations. The fact that the experiment was carried out at all was noteworthy.

This kind of research does not seem to have been undertaken again in this period.[7] The very university organizations that might plausibly have taken leadership in continuing such work did not—at least, not work of the sort that gave control of data and interpretation to third parties. Presumably, they did not do so because they did not have sufficient security to risk invidious comparison and criticism. Cantril and the polls did indeed suffer some scorn at the time for their efforts; the enterprise may have been riskier than they had anticipated.

THE MCNEMAR REVIEW

In 1946, Quinn McNemar, a psychometrician of considerable reputation and a self-styled "outsider," published a hypercritical review, "Opinion-Attitude Methodology," a study that had been funded by the Social Science Research Council (SSRC). He had "reluctantly agreed" to do the study "at the request of a number of social scientists who believed that a critique of the opinion-attitude methodologies should be made, preferably by someone without prior or vested interests."[8] That astringent tone pervaded the monograph. A major section of it treated the attitude/opinion field as consisting of two wings: scale measurement of attitudes by psychologists and sociologists on the one hand and "opinion gauging" by journalists on the other.

While the review was an ambitious and valuable summary of a large number of studies, its acerbic tone was unfortunate. Also, it understandably aroused resentment because in it McNemar seized upon weaknesses that other authors had *avowed* in a scientific spirit (such as low correlations, poor question wordings, perplexing results) as though these were his own indicting discoveries. This was his approach to the Cantril volume and to the polls generally (as well as to attitude measurement, as we shall see), for McNemar used the OPOR research findings to construct a catalog of errors and shortcomings. He cited the "tree," for example, in which Cantril had argued for surrounding questions "with varying contingencies just as it usually is in everyday life"[9] in a criticism that now seems captious and even naive:

> Cantril shows that "interventionist sentiment" between May and September 1941 showed an apparent variation from 78% down to 8% mainly as a function of the questions asked. Which is the correct percentage? No one knows.[10]

Katz's 1946 article, "The Interpretation of Survey Findings," was also very critical of polling practice, but it offered a more judicious and useful approach to the problems of analyzing opinion data.[11]

McNemar's role notwithstanding, Cantril spanned the opinion/attitude divide in the mid-1940s. Had these academic-commercial collaborations endured as viable organizations, supported by large-scale foundation or government grants, Cantril would probably be seen today as a principal founder of polling/survey research. As it is, he was surely an important figure in its beginning years.

The American Soldier

THE WARTIME SYNTHESIS

The single most important product of wartime survey work was *Studies in Social Psychology in World War II*, published in four volumes in 1949–50. This work was the fruit of sustained reanalysis and writing after the war. With funding from SSRC, Stouffer, Carl I. Hovland, Guttman, Lazarsfeld, and small groups of their wartime colleagues took time out to review and reanalyze their work in the Research Branch.[12] The two volumes of greatest interest to us here, volumes 1 and 2, together entitled *The American Soldier*, were a special demonstration of how findings of "basic" scientific interest could be wrested from applied survey work.

Work of the Research Branch was not published along the way. There was not the time, tranquillity, or intellectual coherence under the gun of deadlines for practical decisions. Lazarsfeld's argument that "trivial" practical problems could be just as stimulating of science as "dignified" inquiry into mainline matters was supported by the army research experience—*if* one acknowledged that mining the scientific gold required another expedition *afterward*, under less pressured conditions, at substantial additional cost. Lazarsfeld's own review of *The American Soldier* acknowledged in a footnote that "the service nature of the whole enterprise was not hospitable to more abstract considerations,"[13] one of Lazarsfeld's rare references to applied research as a constraint. Stouffer himself did not *recommend* the applied setting:

> The very fact that *The American Soldier* has received a certain amount of acclaim may mislead not only students but also their elders, who may be in important positions in universities or foundations, into thinking that the kind of atmosphere in which our work was done is exceptionally favorable for social science.

> Most of our time was wasted, irretrievably wasted, in so far as any contribution to social science was concerned. Sometimes a study like whether men preferred Coca-Cola to Pepsi-Cola or whether they preferred nuts in their candy bars may have had a neat technical twist, but ordinarily it did not, or if it had we just did not have time to investigate. As director of the professional staff, I was always facing a dilemma. In order to help the Army, or to help "sell" research to the Army, I had to be concerned first and foremost with what was immediately wanted or purchasable. When I supported longer range studies, I ran the risk of being suspect of trying to exploit our situation for social science and on several occasions was severely censured by superiors. When we coopted our best analysts to direct quick studies which practically and politically seemed of much tactical importance, I faced justifiable resentment from these analysts when they found the studies frustrating. Sometimes nerves were taut on both sides.[14]

THE ROLE OF THE APPLIED

Stouffer's endorsement of applied work was less thoroughgoing than Lazarsfeld's, but he had healthy respect for it and credited the work of the pollsters more admiringly than some of his academic colleagues did:

> Public opinion research owes more to the practitioners who were out to make money than it owes to the academicians. The problems the practitioners encountered in questionnaire design, in sampling, and in interviewing have stimulated much of the methodological interest in improvement of the techniques.[15]

The urgency of practical problems, Stouffer continued, which was often death to reflection and formulation of a scientific proposition, nevertheless often brought life to science itself. In any case, it was essential in order to elicit public support.

Stouffer was further convinced, along with Lazarsfeld, that practical emergencies could spur the discovery of generalities and principles of scientific import, citing the work of the pseudonymous "Student" (W. S. Gossett) for the Guinness brewery and R. A. Fisher's practical problems in agricultural experiments. (Stouffer recalled Fisher's having said that the genesis of a very general theorem was "The rabbits came in and ate up two degrees of freedom, and I had to do something about it.")[16] The main goal, a conviction that Stouffer also shared with Lazarsfeld, was to keep the scientist shuttling back and forth between theory and data, in touch with ideas yet mastering research techniques by which to explore them.[17]

CONTRIBUTIONS TO THEORY?

The army's overriding need was for fast, practical research results. Of the hundreds of topics that the Research Branch investigated, only a fraction were selected for detailed analysis after the war. Of "theory on the grand style," Stouffer warned, *The American Soldier* had nothing to offer, and he anticipated that sociologists intent upon grand theory would probably not even define "the sometimes fumbling efforts which many of us made" for organizing and conceptualizing data as real theory at all, unaccustomed as they were to the exploring and testing of theory through data analysis.[18] He also tried to meet the coming criticism of humanists:

> One book by Ernie Pyle . . . or Bill Mauldin, one drama like *A Bell for Adano* or *Command Decision*, it will be said, gives one more of a sensitive feeling for the "realities" of World War II than any collection of statistics. . . . No one can doubt that the "feel" of a hurricane is better communicated through the pages of Joseph Conrad than through the Weather Bureau's statistical records of the barometric pressure and wind velocity. But it is no reflection on the artistry of Conrad to point out that society also finds uses for a science of meteorology.[19]

Stouffer was right on both counts: the historian Arthur M. Schlesinger, Jr., said just that about Mauldin's famous book of drawings of soldiers in the war, and certain sociologists lamented that *The American Sol-*

dier was too "psychological" and atheoretical.[20] Stouffer argued that there was nevertheless a mine of data, "perhaps unparalleled in magnitude in the history of any single research enterprise in social psychology or sociology," and some of the veins had high-yielding ore for social science.[21]

With data gathered from individuals largely by written questionnaires, Stouffer and his colleagues tried to capture some of the dynamic influence of group membership and context on individual perceptions, attitudes, opinions, morale, adjustment, and behaviors. Though they had few means of measuring group process directly, through tireless replication and imaginative analysis, they were able to cast some light on the interplay between individual and group characteristics.

For example, they found that the primary group enforced certain standards of behavior (flag-waving patriotism, for instance, was taboo) and provided emotional support for enduring the stress of combat.[22] They found that officers were quite dissatisfied with their own chances for promotion but thought (mistakenly) that enlisted men were quite satisfied with theirs.[23] They could account for differences between combat veterans, replacements in veteran units, and entirely "green" units in terms of the psychological climate of the group.[24] They found that psychological distance between officers and enlisted men narrowed and feelings of solidarity increased when units were in the front lines—but only up to a point. Men did not become more favorable to their officers with longer combat experience; they may have become slightly less favorable, in fact, as enlisted men who survived combat and stayed on were likely to be more battle seasoned than some of their officers were.[25] They found that favorable attitudes toward racially desegregated units in the army rose with experience with desegregation.[26]

One of the most striking findings of the study concerned differential satisfaction with chances for promotion. Soldiers of low education and lower expectations thought the prospects for promotion were quite good, while the better educated were the most critical. This was one of the early demonstrations of the power of the concept of expectations. Particularly surprising was the finding that emerged in a comparison of the military police and the air corps. Across levels of rank and education, the MPs thought the promotion chances a good deal better than their counterparts in the air corps did, although in fact the "chances of promotion in the military police were about the worst in any branch of the Army" and those in the air corps were high.[27] Typically, the authors of this chapter (Suchman, Stouffer, and DeVinney) subjected the pattern to replication in other branches, with other data. Across a broader set of comparisons, the pattern was less striking but nevertheless apparent:

> For a given rank, longevity, and educational level, the less the promotion opportunity afforded by a branch or combination of branches, the more favorable the opinion tends to be toward promotion opportunity.[28]

The interpretation involved *expectations* and *relative deprivation*, both of which illuminated many findings in the study. The air corps was a branch of high prestige with a lively rate of promotion, and its members came to have a high level of expectation for promotion. Because the majority succeeded, a man who failed to make the grade was likely to feel the disappointment more keenly. In contrast, a man in the military police who did not earn a promotion had more company for his misery—two-thirds of his fellows were in the same boat. Men evaluated their own success relative to the *rate* of promotion in their own unit.

Stouffer took some pride in the new concept, *relative deprivation*, which made intelligible a number of puzzling results. One anomalous finding, for example, had driven some of the Research Branch staff almost to distraction: Northern blacks stationed in the South had reason to be discontent; generally, they wanted to be in the North and they resented the discrimination in the South. Nevertheless, they showed a level of personal adjustment to the army that was equal to or better than that shown by blacks stationed in northern camps. Research Branch analysts delayed their report for over a month as they searched for errors in the data that might explain this paradox.[29] They came to trust the explanation of relative deprivation or relative status, with its inference that black soldiers in the South were comparing their lot to black civilians there and felt better off. Black soldiers in the North, meanwhile, were apparently comparing themselves to civilians there. Northern black civilians were generally making more money than they ever had in their lives, and so the soldiers did not feel better off and, in fact, sometimes felt worse off.[30]

Relative deprivation was a conceptual discovery introduced *after* the research had been conducted to help explain discrepancies and puzzles, and it was not measured directly. There was little direct evidence of who it was that army personnel had in mind in their social comparisons or of why they felt certain resentments or reactions. For light on these matters, researchers had to rely on closed questions and scales and open-ended comments that were volunteered by only a minority of soldiers. Had the

concept been anticipated, more relevant questioning on social comparisons and psychological identifications could have been incorporated into
the design. That the authors of *The American Soldier* distilled as much
intellectual coherence as they did from the mass administration of short,
written questionnaires that were dedicated primarily to practical matters
was the remarkable fact. Merton and Kitt pointed out in a review-analysis
that relative deprivation could be seen and extended in the more general
terms of reference-group theory, and they noted other findings in *The
American Soldier* that could be reconceptualized as reference-group concepts.[31]

THE IMPACT

It is difficult for the most enthusiastic supporter of quantitative methods in
the social studies to overvalue the contributions of these four volumes to social
science in general and to social psychology in particular. The contributions
are both profound and numerous.[32]

Many reviewers shared Katz's enthusiastic judgment, but *The American
Soldier* was also disappointing and disturbing to critics such as Alfred
McClung Lee, Nathan Glazer, Arthur M. Schlesinger, Jr., and others.
Daniel Lerner, who collected and analyzed the reviews, noted that many
of the hostile reviewers in particular actually said very little about the
book itself, being moved instead to reflections on "modern" social science. The book was greeted, and deservedly so, as an exemplar of the
"new social science," the "modern method"—not only by the publicists
for Princeton University Press, but also by social scientists, humanists,
members of the military, and journalists.[33] Volume 3 dealt with experiments in the effect of army training films and other instructional materials, and volume 4 dealt with scaling theory (Guttman's scale analysis
and Lazarsfeld's latent structure analysis) as well as with Star's psychoneurotic inventory and Clausen's prediction studies of soldiers' postwar
plans. Volumes 1 and 2 were the most ambitious demonstration to date
of survey research.

Lazarsfeld and Merton gave particular support to *The American Soldier*—Lazarsfeld to its data analysis, and Merton to its theoretical potential. Lazarsfeld wrote an "expository review" of the two volumes as the
lead article for the fall 1949 *POQ*. In it, he summarized the major findings chapter by chapter and elucidated the major concepts. He also dealt
with the "obviousness" of the findings by contrasting them with the pre-

dictable propositions of cliché and convention.[34] Lazarsfeld's enthusiasm for the book could hardly have been clearer:

> As he approaches the last pages of these two volumes, the reader develops a feeling of frustration. Here was gripping and seemingly inexhaustible reading material which suddenly comes to an end, like a novel of which only the first chapters are available. Why was a war necessary to give us the first systematic analysis of life as it really is experienced by a large sector of the population? As Stouffer is about to turn out the lights he remarks, "What happened afterwards is a story which must be told someday from data other than that assembled by the Research Branch."
>
> Where, O Lord, will they be coming from?[35]

The following year, Merton and Lazarsfeld edited a book of further reflections, *Continuities in Social Research: Studies in the Scope and Method of "The American Soldier"*. The book included the Merton-Kitt chapter on reference group theory and a chapter by Kendall and Lazarsfeld, "Problems of Survey Analysis," which used instances and illustrations from *The American Soldier* to elucidate a logic of analyzing attribute data. The Kendall-Lazarsfeld article was the single most important codification of survey data analysis of this period.[36]

In Stouffer's own contribution to the volume, "Some Afterthoughts of a Contributor," he expressed some prides and some regrets about *The American Soldier*, offering this final judgment about survey work in general:

> Finally, I think that *The American Soldier* will have a dangerous influence on future research if the survey methods on which it relies for so much of the data are regarded as the ideal. . . . I would trade a half dozen Army-wide surveys on attitudes toward officers for one good controlled experiment.[37]

The fact that Stouffer held the controlled experiment in such high regard made him skeptical of survey results, vigilant to find approximations to experiments in the natural setting, and insistent on replications. As John W. Riley, Jr., noted in his review, where else but in *The American Soldier* could one find a single chart that summarized the comparisons of 8,554 pairs of percentages?[38] M. Brewster Smith has suggested that Stouffer may have been somewhat overimpressed by experiments, as he minimized the limitations peculiar to experimental design in his attention to those posed by survey design. The survey work, which he himself did so well, did not impress him as much as did the experimental work, for which he apparently did not have the same talent.[39]

The small Laboratory of Social Relations that Stouffer founded and directed at Harvard (1946–1960) was the site of his work in small-group experiments and scaling, not a survey organization. After the war, he undertook no more research administration on the grand wartime scale. For the single major piece of survey work he published after the war, *Communism, Conformity, and Civil Liberties* (1955), Stouffer used NORC and Gallup for data collection.[40] His greatest contribution to survey research remained his work during wartime, when the army had embarked on the most ambitious program ever in applied social science, with its review and synthesis sponsored by SSRC–Carnegie. Stouffer's example has not been heeded much in one respect, that of the patient replication, perhaps in part because, as Lazarsfeld asked, where would social scientists ever find such data riches again?

THE WORK OF THE CIVILIAN AGENCIES

From the wartime civilian agencies, there was no comparable product— in effect, no *"American Civilian"* that synthesized survey methods and findings of consequence about the American public in wartime. The task would probably have been an even more formidable one than that shouldered by the army researchers. Despite the very miscellaneous character of the work conducted by the Research Branch, it nevertheless had the advantage of some administrative coherence under Stouffer, who had overall responsibility for the professional staff. It also offered a semblance of a "closed" universe that permitted some actual experimental work and some survey work of quasi-experimental design in comparisons across kinds of units, degrees of combat experience, length of service, hierarchy of ranks, and the like.

The civilian work, in contrast, was administratively dispersed among different agencies of the government, some of which were in contention, as we have seen. They used various methods and different samples, and there was diversity enough there, even without considering the work of the commercial polls and Cantril's OPOR. (The best records of wartime public opinion are provided by Cantril's trend articles and by the published compilation of Gallup polls.)

The sheer scatter of the organizations and their data were an obstacle to trying to round up the money and the people for a project in reanalysis after the war. Furthermore, those groups most likely to have undertaken such a project had other needs at the time: both NORC and Program Surveys were trying to survive a conversion to peacetime work and keep their organizations going. NORC had the added strain of Harry Field's death in 1946 and the need to find a new director. It is surely significant that one of the wartime research organizations for the government synthesized *The American Soldier* and that two other groups sustained postwar organizations—and that none of the three did both. The closest anyone got to accomplishing both was Lazarsfeld as an individual, since he contributed to the Stouffer project in postwar synthesis while keeping his own organization going at Columbia.

There were some "good examples" of analysis from the civilian data gathered for the government, but these tended to be shorter articles in professional journals. They lacked the analytic scope of *The American Soldier*, and they did not circulate as broadly in the greater intellectual community. In 1949, Cartwright judged that, for social psychology, at any rate,

> the general conclusion is inescapable that the great bulk of the practical research conducted during the war has not and will not contribute directly to the extension of any empirically testable conceptual scheme.[41]

He found noteworthy accomplishments, however, in the invention and refinement of research instruments and in the application of existing concepts. His own article, "Some Principles of Mass Persuasion: Selected Findings of Research on the Sale of United States War Bonds," was actually a good example of application and stands as the single most substantial analysis of data from the war-bond studies, Program Surveys' most ambitious wartime contract.

The striking finding from the war-bond studies was a very durable one. It held up "in every [publicity] drive, in every income bracket, in every occupational group, [and] in every section of the country," as shown in table 1,[42] excerpted from table 3 in Cartwright's article.

With personal solicitation generally showing yields of triple or better, the findings were decisive, handsomely supporting the personal solicitation drives that were mounted in both World Wars I and II on intuitive or commonsense grounds.[43]

Given the great attention to mass-media publicity in World War II, however, it cannot have been entirely obvious in advance that personal solicitation would prove so powerful. Advertising, both print and radio, was lavished on the war-bond drives of World War II. An estimated $12

TABLE 1

SOME RELATIONS BETWEEN PERSONAL SOLICITATION
AND BUYING OF WAR BONDS

	Percent of persons who bought extra bonds			
	2d Loan Apr. 1943	3d Loan Sept. 1943	4th Loan Jan. 1944	5th Loan June 1944
Not personally solicited	12	18	25	22
Personally solicited	47	59	63	66
N	1358	1583	1441	1925

million worth of advertising was devoted to the second drive, and almost four times that, some $42 million worth, on the seventh drive. The massive publicity campaign spread the word about the campaign itself: in 1941, 97 percent of the adult population reported to the Gallup Poll that they had heard of "defense bonds and stamps."[44]

Mass Persuasion: The Social Psychology of a War Bond Drive, by Robert K. Merton, Marjorie Fiske, and Alberta Curtis (1946), was a study by the Bureau of Applied Social Research of one aspect of that publicity campaign, the eighteen-hour radio marathon conducted by the popular singer Kate Smith. This was Smith's third all-day drive, and it was credited with selling some $39 million worth of war bonds. (See chapter nine.) So the two approaches worked together, Cartwright noted: an effective publicity campaign first, followed by the personal solicitation that greatly increased the number of buyers over that inspired by publicity alone.

Publicity campaigns in themselves were rarely very effective, Cartwright observed, and he theorized that their results were lackluster because information led to certain behavior only if three major conditions were realized: first, that a particular cognitive structure was created; second, that a particular motivational structure was created; and third, that the first two structures together took control of a particular behavioral structure. These broad principles were linked with a number of subpropositions—for example, that persons interpreted new information in ways to ward off changes in their cognitive structure or that the essential feature of the solicitation was in requiring potential buyers of war bonds to come to a decision.

Cartwright concluded that most campaigns of mass persuasion were likely to fail because few could harness the requisite mechanisms, especially the monopolizing of the channels of communication or the orchestrating of the total set of influences in the same direction. (This interpretation was not unlike the "limited effects" model of media influence developed at the Bureau and in studies by NORC; see chapters nine and ten.)

The very stability of attitudes toward war bonds themselves was a case in point. The large part of the American public (two-thirds) remained steadfast in their belief that the purpose of war bonds was to finance the war by buying supplies for the fighting troops, despite much government publicity that inflation control was a major goal. The bond studies provided good warrant for concluding that from barrages of government publicity, people selected or distorted messages to conform to their existing cognitive structure.[45]

Other wartime research showed new power and problems in survey techniques. For example, a Katz-Hyman article on absenteeism and morale in war plants, conducted through the OWI Surveys Division and NORC, identified the actual incidence and the determinants of absenteeism. The mass media and poll questions had made the problem seem enormous and the cause a lack of patriotism, or worse. The study found that levels of absenteeism were lower than reported and had rather complex causes, especially in-plant conditions inducing poor morale and some problems in community facilities. There was little evidence of blunted patriotism or disillusion with the war effort. The research design was noteworthy: a special sample of war plants in various industries was constructed to permit some experimental comparison, and there was an integrated use of various kinds of information and instruments—structured interview schedules, informal interviews, and official records.[46]

Hyman's 1944 article "Do They Tell the Truth?" was an important study of validity, which was also based on OWI Surveys Division work. It dealt with validation in the absenteeism study and with two other actions, redemption of war bonds and display of government posters, which also had prestige value. Discrepancies of self-report from actual records were shown to vary by income group and subject matter. People of higher income, for instance, were more likely to deny that they had redeemed their war bonds, and differential distortion of the absenteeism record was associated with different plant locations.[47]

The Hilgard-Payne article "Those Not at Home: Riddle for Pollsters," based on data from the Office of Civilian Requirements, showed how results could vary by the number of callbacks and how much distortion might arise from relying entirely on the most accessible people. (For instance, 22 percent of respondents reached on the first call were employed outside the home, compared to 54 percent on the third and later calls.)[48]

Other research reports were published from the wartime data, but overall the civilian work generated an interesting scatter rather than the consolidated work produced by the researchers in the army.[49] In the efforts for new social organization during and immediately after the war, researchers in the civilian and commercial agencies were the more active.

Social Organization

Public Opinion Quarterly

In the years from 1944 to 1946, there were major efforts to bring the commercial and academic wings of opinion research together in cooperative work, in three important areas: publication, technical methods, and professional association. In 1944, the first was accomplished by expanding the board of editors of *Public Opinion Quarterly* to involve the most prominent commercial and academic (or governmental) figures in opinion research. Whose idea this was is not clear, and the archives of *POQ* were not carefully preserved along the way.[50] It seems likely that Cantril and Bruner—who was managing editor of *POQ* for the year 1943–44—were instrumental.[51]

Starting in 1944 and continuing in the following year, the board was expanded to about thirty members, who included major figures in commercial as well as academic worlds concerned with public opinion: Walter Wanger of film; Frank Stanton of CBS; Eugene Meyer of the *Washington Post* (and Gallup's first subscriber); the trio of famous pollsters, Gallup, Roper, and Crossley; and some of their colleagues, such as Richardson Wood, Claude Robinson, and Henry Durant. The academic wing was represented by such continuing members as Cantril, Katz, Lasswell, and Odegard and such new members as Lazarsfeld, Likert, Bruner, Harry Field, and Gordon Allport. Stouffer was a conspicuous omission from the notables of the wartime period, and because he would have been such a natural choice one suspects that this was his own decision. (He had a major role in other efforts in this period to engage both commercial and academic researchers in common cause.) It was during the first years of this "fusion" board of *POQ* that the disputatious exchange between Benson and Katz was published. While the tone was by no means a common one in that journal—sharp rejoinders have been more common in such mainline disciplinary publications as *APSR* or *ASR*—it suggested that there might well be some rocky places in the road to collaboration between commercial and academic opinion research.

The Joint Committee on Technical Problems

The second major cooperative venture was launched jointly in 1945 by the National Research Council of the federal government and the Social Science Research Council (SSRC), then under the chairmanship of Donald Young. This was the Committee on the Measurement of Opinion, Attitudes, and Consumer Wants, chaired by Stouffer. S. S. Wilks served as vice chair, and many familiar names served on the committee, among them Cantril, Lazarsfeld, Likert, Crossley, Roper, and Stanton. The committee's name clearly identified three branches of research: the pollsters interested in opinion, the academics interested in attitudes, and the market researchers interested in consumer wants.[52] Stouffer was a logical choice to chair the committee, since he was a talented, respected, effective, and hardworking social scientist with rich experience in the Research Branch which bore very directly on these technical matters. He also had maintained cordial relationships with both academic and commercial researchers.[53]

The committee met for the first time in September 1945, and there was no dearth of interesting problems to consider: interview effect, validity, the scaling of intensity of opinion, product testing through consumer research, advertising research. Sampling was the the most urgent. Many organizations were using sampling methods, the committee observed, and controversy was abroad between the proponents of one method and another—meaning, of course, between quota and area sampling. The executive committee (Stouffer, Wilks, Stanton, and Likert) was charged with formulating a plan to study the sampling reliability of the various methods, at once.[54]

Within a few months, a project had been organized, money had been obtained from the Rockefeller Foundation ($43,800), Frederick F. Stephan had gone to work as staff director on June 1, 1946, and the committee's first project was under way, with promises from various survey organizations to provide data that would permit comparison of various sampling methods. There were other plans in the works: preparation of a "primer" of survey methods for the special use of market researchers; a study of the efficiency of panels, a study of interviewing, and a program of fellowships through which university teachers could intern with survey organizations. These projects all awaited funds.[55] The prime concern was sampling, but by the following year three projects had crystallized as the major concerns of the committee: sampling, interviewing, and the panel. What happened to these plans will take us into the postwar years of later chapters.

A Professional Association in Prospect

The third enterprise in common cause was the 1946 conference at Central City, Colorado, organized by Field, Don Cahalan, and others at NORC. From this conference grew, the following year, the American Association for Public Opinion Research (AAPOR), a professional association that was to merge commercial and academic opinion research (and the academic kindred, governmental researchers). When NORC sent out a conference call in 1946, there was enough interest that almost seventy-five participants came, some fifty from outside Denver (which was an out-of-the-way station in those days, when air travel was not yet common and the train from New York took about three days).

The keynote discussion at Central City by Gallup, Stuart Dodd, and others was on public opinion and international affairs, reflecting the conviction and hope of Field (and many others) that public opinion study could contribute to world peace. Dodd discussed his hopes for a worldwide agency that could use surveys as a "demoscope" to study people all over the globe in their subjective and objective aspects (opinions, habits, migrations, etc.). Other panels set forth topics that would enjoy long runs on the agenda of the survey research field as a whole: ethical and technical standards, and problems in sampling, interviewing, question wording, and validity. The commercial wing provided the largest share of panelists (twenty-two commercial, twelve academics, five governmental, one not ascertained). But there was a goodly mixture among participants, and the committees that were organized at the meetings for future planning and action were carefully constituted to reflect the three realms.

The panel on sampling, not surprisingly, provided the liveliest encounter. Morris Hansen used the forum to try to clarify some confusions about area sampling as well as the loose terminology that had prevailed in the congressional hearings of 1944. There were two kinds of area sampling, he explained: quota area sampling, which involved purposive selection, and random area sampling, which did not. While quota methods could be serviceable enough in certain circumstances, only random selection provided the requisite theory for measuring the precision of estimates and the yield of information per dollar spent.

The other three panelists nevertheless held the line for quota sampling, arguing for more time, more research, and more cost accounting. Norman C. Meier, in a spirited defense of quota sampling, doubted that area sampling had any claim to inherent superiority in general or any "peculiar magic" for opinion work, however satisfactory it might be in Census Bureau projects or crop estimates. The proof, he said, had to be in the pudding of experimental tests, and a recent one in Iowa City had commended the quota procedure. (Hansen cautioned that one successful quota sample was never a guarantee that the next one would also be successful.) Lucien Warner of Time-Life, Inc., reported that their purposive selection samples were performing well. Elmo Wilson, formerly of OWI Polls and now the director of research for CBS, reported that in recent experiments their quota samples had done better on opinion/ attitude items than on factual ones. (Hansen said that there was no reason to expect such differences.) Wilson felt that opinion polls still had reason to hold to quota methods, given the problem of costs, the need for speed, and the lower level of accuracy they required, as a rule, because they were exploring differences among groups rather than making population estimates.

The session was not conclusive, for indeed there were sensible concerns supporting each side.[56] Hansen's own role was that of an explainer, not a debater. The process by which the Bureau of the Census itself was gradually converted to probability sampling has been credited in good part to Hansen's temperate, peacemaking style and administrative effectiveness.[57]

The panels on standards featured a fair consensus on several matters: that high standards should be set; that polling organizations needed to regulate their industry; that the public had to be educated to recognize and demand good polling practice; and, finally, that there be an association of polling organizations, such as that being planned by the trio of pollsters, with an auditing committee. This set of goals was incorporated into the resolutions passed at the close of the conference, and a standards committee was set up to help Crossley, Roper, and Gallup in establishing the new association of polling agencies.[58]

The standards committee was a proper triumvirate of interests—Wilson from commercial, Hansen from governmental, and Henry David from academic life. Julian Woodward, formerly of OWI Polls and now with the Roper Organization, Inc., stressed that a standards committee should have real power and responsibility and that violators should be expelled from the association. By *standards*, Woodward meant adequate sampling methods, competent interviewing staff, well-designed questionnaires, and high ethical standards—a program of great ambitiousness and one for which, with the exception of sampling, almost no objective criteria existed.[59] Forty years later, what constitutes a well-designed questionnaire, for instance, arguably remains as much a matter of intuition, specific experience, and sophisticated folklore as theory supported by empirical evidence. As we shall see, the issue of standards would prove an explosive one in the following year, threatening to destroy AAPOR before it had even come into official existence.

Central City was full of excitement, promise, and interesting shoptalk. Jack Elinson was asked to tell the group about Guttman scales; Valerie Tamulonis reported on her experiments in question wording using NORC and AIPO data; Theodore Lentz discussed the "acquiescent" who agreed with contradictory propositions, and the need to explore how changes in question wording affected relationships, not just marginals.[60] Not everyone of note was there. Stouffer was not there (although Elinson represented the Research Branch and its successor, the Troop Attitude Research Branch), nor were any of his colleagues who would coauthor *The American Soldier*. Neither was Lazarsfeld. Nor anyone from Program Surveys, such as Likert, Campbell, or others, for that summer and fall they were regrouping at the University of Michigan. But something important was happening. All these people made it to the conference the following year.

By the time of the Central City meeting, World War II had been over for nearly a year, but the purpose of the conference was to consolidate the experience in polls and surveys that had burgeoned during the war and to create a full-fledged merger in a professional association. The major accomplishment of Central City was the fact of the meeting and the decision to get on with it and meet again.

The Exodus to the University: II

The Imperfect Union

The Central City conference was called in the belief that academic and commercial researchers labored in neighboring plots of the same vineyard. There were influential social scientists as well as pollsters who shared that belief. Gordon Allport, for example, in 1945 saw polling as "probably the greatest advance made by social science during the present century."[61] In the same year, Pendleton Herring anticipated progress in public opinion research during the next decade with leadership "in the capable hands of Hadley Cantril, Elmo Roper, George Gallup, Samuel Stouffer, Rensis Likert and their numerous fellow workers."[62] (Herring, a political scientist, was at Harvard at the time, but he joined the Carnegie Corporation the following year, and in 1948 he became president of SSRC.)

In 1946, cooperation between the two groups had advantages for both *if* it succeeded in enhancing the scientific prestige of the field. Both groups had something to gain, but the risks were unequal. Social scientists' less public errors held no particular threat to pollsters, but as the congressional hearings of 1944 had made clear, if the pollsters—who led a more dangerous life with their electoral forecasts—"lost" an election, academics in opinion research could share in the defeat.

Certain social scientists kept some distance from the polls, wishing to appeal to their academic reference group. After the war, and even during it, those who wanted to continue doing empirical research in a university setting wanted to show that their work was a considerable advance over straight polling. There were some risks in making these claims to distinction, risks made vivid in McNemar's treatment of attitude research in wartime work. In certain sections of the McNemar report, it was the academics' ox that was gored. In an extended rejoinder to McNemar's punishing treatment of his work, psychologist Herbert S. Conrad finally complained, "Has not social science enough to contend with from biased critics outside its ranks, without supplying 'free ammunition'?"[63] (Gallup must have asked himself the same question about the technical report in the 1944 hearings.)

McNemar was at particular pains to show that nothing about the wartime work augured well for the future of attitude research. Even in sampling, he argued, there had been only modest gains, for the important developments had been made before, not during, the war (a conclusion he left as self-evident). He saw some hope in Guttman scaling and open questioning, advocating in fact greater use of the latter,[64] but he wanted it known that the work of the government agencies constituted, at best, "minor advances." He left no doubt about whom he meant: he named the organizations of Program Surveys, OWI Surveys, NORC, and the Research Branch and the individuals Likert, Kane, Woodward, Wilson, Katz, Stouffer, Cottrell, and Hovland. He also raised this question:

> Certain individuals in these agencies have given such loud acclaim to their interest in and work on methodological problems that some social scientists

have been quite optimistic about the contributions to techniques which might emerge from this extensive work. Can it be said that these agencies have developed and perfected techniques which will aid in the solution of problems in the attitude-opinion field?[65]

The answer was, of course, No. McNemar hoped he was wrong, but he saw no reason for optimism about "war-born advances in the attitude-opinion field of research."[66]

The wartime researchers themselves were not, apparently, dismayed. Cartwright recalls the reaction among Program Surveys people as somewhat dismissive: "If one were as perfectionist as McNemar, who would ever get the work out?"[67] McNemar was probably not a "representative" critic, but he represented the most resistant of academic peers and a risk for survey researchers. If they laid claim to innovation over and above the methods of polling, they would be challenged by academic colleagues, who scrutinized such claims with great seriousness. Such critics were likely to bring little experience in the problems of applied research to temper their sense of what *could* be accomplished under high pressure and rush deadlines and what might constitute, thus, an innovation of consequence. Nor were they likely to appreciate how these applied experiences could enrich the scientific academic perspective with "outside world" realities.

It was this appreciation that many social scientists took back to their university careers after the war, and it changed some of their professional directions and research interests. From that sharing of the wartime experience also came an informal network of friendships and associations, which gave life and meaning to the formal organizations we have considered here. The weavings of informal association were probably the most important form of "social organization" which survey research developed from the war.

The Informal Network: The Enlargement of the Small World

The "sociometry" of the wartime associations was richest within the research organizations themselves. John A. Clausen has expressed the feeling in the Research Branch:

> Ours was a dense network. We worked incredibly long hours, side by side in less than ideal working conditions, and when we celebrated, we celebrated together with an intensity that still produces a warm glow in the recollection of forty years past.[68]

The same sense of kinship, fond association, and high purpose pervades the recollection of participants in the OWI-NORC and Program Surveys as well—feelings bred especially of the urgency and commitment of the wartime mission, the youthful energy and zeal of many of the participants, and the intellectual excitement of the immersion in new, hands-on research experience in an atmosphere of group effort and informal give-and take.

The alumni of the Research Branch did not stay together as a group after the war, but as they dispersed they carried with them a professional experience of great value and an enduring social network.[69] In Clausen's recent survey of Research Branch participants (twenty-four of the twenty-seven persons he reached returned questionnaires, and a number wrote letters as well), many reported their wartime experience as formative for their postwar careers, and very few indeed found the experience negative. People reported having developed new technical skills, new interdisciplinary stimulation, and new research interests, such as race and military sociology. And Clausen feels that there was more:

> [There was] the sense of doing something significant, something that would have pay-off value. Such research need not be applied, but for many of us the wartime experience may have fostered a somewhat different orientation to research, a greater concern with human welfare.[70]

The largest single group from the Research Branch took major roles in health and mental health research projects after the war, notably, Suchman, Shirley Star, Elinson, Ira Cisin, Nathan Maccoby, Dean Manheimer, Irving L. Janis, Felix Moore, and Clausen himself. A nucleus that worked in the Veterans' Administration for a short time after the war (Moore, Clausen, Robert N. Ford, and W. Parker Mauldin) also added recruits to the health research field. The use of survey research was a natural for work in epidemiology and in health attitudes and services, and a number of Research Branch alumni became survey specialists.[71]

Clausen notes one other career direction taken by some Research Branch alumni and consultants, that of foundation executive. Clausen feels that the contacts and recruiting of General Frederick Osborn opened up to people in the Research Branch new contacts and opportunities. Charles Dollard, Young, Cottrell, Leland DeVinney, William McPeak, and Mauldin all took major executive roles after the war in such foundations as Carnegie, Russell Sage, the Ford Foundation, and the

Population Council, and Clausen had major responsibilities at the National Institute of Mental Health (NIMH).[72] Tracing the detailed "sociometry" of these informal associations after the war is beyond our scope here, but it seems certain that the "small world" that had experience and sympathy for survey research before the war was expanded greatly by the wartime experience. The enlarged culture of talent and interest in surveys did not make it *easy* to consolidate and develop survey research in the university during and after the war, but without these resources it would probably have been well-nigh impossible.

Part Three

Migrations to the Universities: 1940–1960

8

General Perspectives and Anticipations

> The mechanism of technological transfer is one of agents,
> not agencies; of the movement of people among
> establishments, rather than the routing of information
> through communication systems.
>
> *William H. Gruber and Donald G. Marquis*

The Primary Organizations

Three research organizations developed survey research as an instrument and organization of university science: the Bureau of Applied Social Research at Columbia University (often called "The Bureau"), the National Opinion Research Center (NORC), originally at Denver and later at Chicago, and the Survey Research Center (SRC) at the University of Michigan. The Bureau was not designed specifically as a "survey" organization (as the other two were), but Lazarsfeld and others there concentrated on survey work and gave the instrument new power. All three organizations originated in some part outside the university and then moved onto the edges of an academic community, setting up a small colony of empirical researchers.

As we shall see in the chapters to come, each of these organizations has some claim to innovation and contribution in survey research.[1] Lazarsfeld and the Bureau are widely credited with having spearheaded a new era of quantification in the discipline of sociology—a role that was related to and yet is separable from Lazarsfeld's innovative role in survey research. In the latter, more interdisciplinary, venture, he was also a formative influence. But in the chapters that follow, the three early research organizations are seen to have originated with some degree of independence in three applied realms.

Thus, we see that in 1939–40, Lazarsfeld brought his foundation grants and *market research* contracts onto the borders of Columbia University sociology. In 1941, Field took his own years of experience in *commercial polling* and a try at nonprofit polling onto the University of Denver campus as an independent nonprofit corporation. In 1946, Likert and his group took the nucleus of their prewar and wartime organization in the federal *government* onto the margins of social science at the University of Michigan. Furthermore, it would seem that while the leadership of these individuals was essential, it would have been largely unavailing without a new pool of talent and new sources of governmental support, which dated, essentially, from World War II. It is difficult to imagine, in fact, that any of these organizations would have survived for very long without new people and new money.

In considering the genesis, problems, and persistence of these organizations, we shall be guided by four questions. First, what were the resources that the new arrivals brought to the universities? Second, why were their universities relatively resistant to providing any substantial support? Third, why did these particular organizations, and not others, succeed by continuing into the postwar period (1946–1960)? And, finally, what did each contribute to survey research as an academic specialization and instrument of social science?

Some New Resources: The Heritage of the War

The Expansion of the Pool of Talent

Problems in applied work have stimulated scientific work that probably would not have emerged from the social roles or the intellectual culture of the university-based disciplines themselves.[2] Survey research offers a case in point. The New Deal attracted social scientists to government projects in applied science, some of which used and developed large-scale surveys (see chapter one). With the advent of World War II, as we have seen in chapters five through seven, the government's research needs and its manpower policy brought social scientists out of the academy again in new numbers to work on various social research projects. In what was partly a direct response to the new opinion polls of 1936, a number of government units worked on polls and surveys, especially to study wartime morale. At the end of the war, the government let these social scientists go as Congress cut away their agencies and their jobs. Most of the academic migrants probably had intended to stay only for the duration and willingly migrated *back* to their academic careers. But they went back with new resources: they had received on-the-job training in practical survey problems, work that was not generally available (or desirable) in the disciplinary channels of the university social sciences.

During the war they had been part of a network of academic, governmental, and commercial researchers, sometimes working in the same agency. The broad network crossed disciplinary lines—sociology, experimental psychology, social psychology, rural sociology, statistics, economics, anthropology, agricultural sciences, political science, journalism. It crisscrossed such realms of business and industry as opinion polling, market research, advertising, and the media as well as such permanent government agencies as the Bureau of the Census, the Federal Reserve Board, the armed forces, and the Treasury.

After the war, some of the social scientists with this applied and interdisciplinary experience wanted to continue this kind of work in the university setting, so there was a new pool of potential practitioners. Still others became new sympathizers or users and clients after the war. In only one case did a small group of scientists—Likert and several of his colleagues—actually move together from Washington to create a new university organization. Lazarsfeld's and Field's organizations had both been founded before the war. Stouffer's government organization did not survive after it. Smaller governmental survey units also closed down, and their participants dispersed. Cantril's university organization at Princeton survived only in reduced form. But the wartime experience generated and distributed new scientific experience and culture in survey work.

The practice of survey research took on some new luster during the war from three sources. First, it changed technically as social scientists searched for new precision and lent new technical complexity, as we have seen in chapters six and seven. Second, it clearly proved its usefulness during patriotic wartime service. After the war, when Stouffer, Likert, and others spoke of the great uses of survey research, they had real instances to offer. The "point system," the bond surveys, and other projects were fair proof not only that polls and surveys *could* be useful to a democratic government, as the commercial pollsters had forcefully argued, but also that they *had* been. Third, the fact that the wartime research had been conducted *by scientists* in new large numbers gave greater credence to Gallup's claim that there was indeed a "new science of public opinion measurement"—under construction, anyway. After the war, there were various signs of increased professional interest in and respect for opinion/attitude/survey research.

New Funds and a New System of Funding

THE NEW MONEY

After the war, the social sciences gradually obtained access to federal support. The money was a direct inheritance from wartime operations. Before the war, federal funds for research had been allocated principally to the government's own agencies. After the war, the government began to allocate vast new funds to research in industries and universities. Federal officials had become convinced that basic research was very likely to have practical payoffs in the long run. It was the wartime experience of contracting with physical scientists for weapons development—rockets, the proximity fuse, radar, and, especially, the atomic bomb—that had converted the bureaucrats to faith in basic science. The ways of federal funding that had been devised during the war were adapted for postwar service.

The model was the wartime research network, the Office of Scientific Research and Development (OSRD), established in 1941, coordinated by Vannevar Bush and James B. Conant. Through this organization, the federal government contracted for R&D projects with scientists who remained in laboratories under industrial or university control, or some semblance of it. (The Los Alamos project on the atomic bomb, for example, was officially under the direction of the University of California, although it was shrouded in military secrecy and was under military administration.) At the end of the war, Bush proposed a new form of the OSRD system to encourage peacetime basic research, which took shape as the National Science Foundation (NSF). Bush was not the first advocate—Senator Harley Kilgore of West Virginia had pushed a different concept of an NSF since early in the war, one that encouraged more applied research—and in part because of these rival proposals, the creation of NSF languished until 1950. Social science was not included for several years. Certain congressmen were hostile to the inclusion, and one wing of physical scientists was also opposed.[3]

Before NSF was established, however, the military agencies began to fund basic social research. The navy led in the support of the social sciences, establishing in 1946 the Office of Naval Research (ONR), which funded both physical and social science research upon the advice of special review panels of scientists.[4] The army, air force, and Department of Defense followed the navy's example within a few years. The nurture of basic science was a small part of the "mission-oriented" research in military and other governmental agencies, but it was a welcome part, and all three of the new survey organizations made use of basic grants or applied contracts with these agencies. SRC launched a program in human relations in industry (later, organizational behavior) with grants from ONR. NORC's program of research into community disasters was begun with money from the army's Chemical Center. The Bureau undertook a study of major cities of the world, funded by the air force.[5]

The National Institutes of Health (NIH) were greatly expanded after the war, and they made funds available for new buildings as well as for research grants. NORC was able to get NIH funds to help with a new building in the late 1950s. By the mid-1950s, social scientists had established a small hold on one of the foothills of NSF, as some modest and gingerly grants were awarded to the most "physical" of the social sciences—physical anthropology, for example. By 1958, social science was considered legitimate enough that an Office of Social Science was incorporated into the NSF structure.[6] While the great bulk of all these federal monies went to R&D in the physical sciences as well as to some in the life sciences, the small share accorded to the social sciences was something of munificence in that rather threadbare world.[7]

THE NEW SYSTEM

The new funds were channeled to scientists by a new system of peer review. Federal officials who were not scientists needed advice in selecting research grants on their scientific merits, and they duly created "review panels," or advisory commissions, of qualified scientists. In this arrangement, grants and contract money were allocated to scientists *outside* the government by their colleagues on the *inside*—not really inside government employment but rather inside the network of advisers recruited by the bureaucrats. This was a remarkable new system that contributed substantially to the growth of social science research.[8] Henry Riecken, an influential social scientist who participated in the new system in NSF and SSRC positions, likened the new role of the advisory scientists to that of industrialists serving on commissions regulating their own industry.[9] Government R&D funds to colleges and universities increased tenfold in the years from 1945 to 1959, to an annual $1 billion.[10]

The share to social sciences developed only gradually, so while this money did not help the research organizations to enter the university environment immediately after the war, it later helped them to hang on and to grow. The new organizations were *permitted* on—or more properly, near—the college campus, but they were not seen as particularly wise intellectual or financial investments. They inspired enthusiastic support among some academics, but among certain administrators they seem to have been viewed with caution. Among some faculty, they were viewed with positive alarm.

The Resistance of Universities

The Cautions of the Administrations

The new organizations were *outsiders*, in effect *foreign bodies* trying to graft themselves onto the university organism, as Rossi has pointed out, and they were not entirely easy to absorb.[11] It is a limit of the present inquiry that it provides only occasional glimpses of the "foreign body" problem as seen by central university administrators and department heads. In part, this is because relevant documents are more difficult to obtain. (University and departmental decisions affecting personnel, for example, are not generally very accessible.) Interviewing of administrators has been less feasible, as well, in part because many of the relevant figures have died. In great part, the angle of vision here is that of the researchers who were trying to colonize on university territory. Where I have found specific evidence or strong inference of administrators' perspectives, I have included them.

Why the resistance? First, for social science, the survey organizations were *big*. Before World War II, most faculty research in the social sciences used data available in libraries or data gathered from small projects conducted in the classroom or the local community. Such data could be handled by a professor with the aid of an assistant or two or of a classroom of students. True, there had been exceptions. In business schools in the 1910s and 1920s, there had been research organizations that were funded essentially by industrial contracts, and they were probably somewhat larger. In the 1920s the Laura Spelman Rockefeller Memorial, under Beardsley Ruml's direction, made substantial grants to the interdisciplinary Local Community Research Committee at the University of Chicago under the aegis of Park, Burgess, Merriam, Gosnell, Thurstone, and others. The memorial also made grants establishing the Institute for Research in Social Science at the University of North Carolina, founded by Howard W. Odum.[12] Nevertheless, academic research organizations overall remained small, of a scale that did not disturb the traditional structure of the university (i.e., the hierarchy of deans and departmental chairmen and, within each department, a ranking of professors, associates, and assistants, but finally a *collegial* relationship, making for much autonomy among individual scholars).

These new organizations in the 1940s involved at least a small entourage of student-employees and at most a veritable "army" of interviewers dispersed across the nation. This was the first instance of "big science" for sociology and social psychology in the university setting, and it did not fit into the traditional structure. What was to be the relationship of such an organization to the disciplinary departments? An equal entity? A subordinate? Should the center be represented in the division of the social sciences? What of the professional staff directing the research? Were they to be members of a department? And if so, did the department or the research center do the hiring and firing? What of tenure? These and other questions were hardly insoluble problems, but the answers did not follow straightforwardly and logically from traditional academic organization. They required negotiation, the creation of new administrative structures, new rules and understandings, and individuals able to put it all together.

Ben-David has pointed to the "virtually unlimited possibilities for the establishment of new fields" in the academic setting and the usefulness of the academic department in the encouragement of that diversity:

> New specialties could easily be accommodated and nurtured within existing departments—which always had a considerable degree of heterogeneity—until they were strong enough to operate independently.[13]

He cites here the case of statistics, which developed in a number of different departments for some two or three decades before a department of statistics eventually took shape in the United States after the war (at the University of North Carolina, in 1946–47).[14]

These new research organizations were a different proposition, however. While small-scale "surveys" using questionnaires or interviews had been conducted in various departments, such as those of psychology, sociology, social work, and education, they were modest ventures, without much technical pretension or scope, and they did not require permanent social organization. Large-scale surveys were conducted outside the university. To conduct them within the university required personnel and funds that no single department could muster (without some special endowment) or else required strong interdisciplinary cooperation to finance, create, and share in a common facility, and such cooperation was not forthcoming. Survey research was, in effect, too big to grow up in the interstices of the disciplines. It could be capitalized and sustained only with the funds available to foundations, business and industry, or government—funds from outside the university.

Second, the problem of *money* was a complex one. The amounts were trifling in comparison to the sums being laid out for investment in the physical sciences, but they were, nevertheless, substantial sums for social science and so were a source of possible conflict within a university community. For example, in its first year at the University of Michigan, the Survey Research Center (SRC) operated on a budget of funds from outside the university of somewhat over $230,000—small by latter-day standards, to be sure, but at the time this was more than four times the university's allocation to the department of sociology for salaries and operating expenses for the same year.[15] The sum was thus large enough to raise new questions of equity and power.

There were more immediate money problems involving overhead, or indirect costs—the costs of general administration, accounting, legal services, libraries, buildings, maintenance, and so on. Early federal support of university research paid only the direct costs of salaries, supplies, and equipment. Beginning in 1947, the military agencies developed a formula for paying certain indirect costs at certain rates; when NIH and NSF began to pay as well, their rates were much lower. In 1956–57, for example, Columbia University reasoned that it lost well over $200,000 through the reimbursements from NIH; Harvard saw its losses as close to half a million dollars. The problem was somewhat alleviated in 1958–60, as NSF raised its rates to 20 percent and began experimenting with institutional grants, but it was by no means solved.[16] The survey organizations' view of the problem was that they had *their own* costs of central administration, accounting, maintenance, and so forth, and they (not the central administration of the university) should receive the government reimbursements for indirect costs as a matter of financial need and moral right.

The new organizations confronted university administrations with still another sort of financial worry. The universities could not endow these organizations, but what was the moral and legal obligation of the university if the research center did not meet its contract deadlines or did not collect from its clients? Would researchers lobby for loans or grants from the university? Would they seek the financial security and acceptance of teaching and tenure? These issues became lively in all three university settings (Columbia, Chicago, and Michigan). That the universities themselves could ultimately enjoy some gain in money and reputation from these facilities that attracted distinguished social scientists was not at all clear in the beginning.

Third, there were *political* risks involved in having clients from outside the university. A university, as the seat of learning and culture for the whole society, could not afford to be seen as the hired hand of profit-making institutions or as the special pleader of certain political or intellectual interests. The university could be tarred with the brush of bad publicity, charges of partisanship in politics, or hucksterism in business, and it risked being caught in the cross fire of others' deadly quarrels. What justification was there for trafficking in these realms of money and power? Actually, the big universities were becoming far more deeply involved in these realms through research in the physical sciences, the prodigious capitalization and costs of which were borne by the federal government, sometimes in concert with industry. But the social sciences were viewed with more caution and apprehension as making universities more vulnerable to political attack, and the survey organizations posed special threats to academic detachment in their obvious similarity to polling. The survey researchers actually hewed to a careful political neutrality, avoiding election forecasts, avoiding political clients, seeking funds for their election studies from disinterested foundations. Signs of university uneasiness appeared in all three settings, even so.

Finally, the issue of *administrative control* was a complex one that intertwined the other three factors. Universities have always been cordial to gifts from wealthy donors and their institutional offspring, tax-exempt foundations, to fund new buildings, laboratories, endowed chairs, and scholarships. But universities have labored to keep control over these funds. The historian Veysey reminds us that the university has had variable success in getting that money without strings: early in the twentieth century, especially, certain powerful donors kept their hands firmly attached to their money, personally supervising the university project and even interrogating aspiring professors on their intellectual, moral, or religious fitness to receive endowed funds.[17] Outside sponsors might well have absolutely no designs on a university, but outside funding of research nevertheless raised the issue. After the war, federal agencies' support of university research in vast new amounts raised the specter of governmental domination of university policy.

What happened in fact was that central *university* control did indeed diminish, but not in the fashion feared—not because federal agencies actually threatened academic freedom by dictating the direction of research, but because university scientists and the federal agencies dealt directly with each other, bypassing university administrators. Federal funds to the universities in this period came to represent a substantial subsidy to higher education—an estimated one-fifth of university funds were being provided by the federal government—but university administrators had less control over its allocation than they wished.[18] By the mid-1950s, they sought more control over federal largesse, pressing for "block" or institutional grants from the government, which they themselves could allocate to various sectors of the university community, not just to research.[19] Federal grants to social science research finally made these organizations far more attractive to university administrations than they would have been otherwise, but the groups did not have that kind of money when they came.

Conflicts Between Business and Academic Culture

Applied money for social research in the university setting raised tensions and antipathies. An applied *contract* posed the issue of proprietary research, the results of which could not be published in journals (or contribute to science) because the data were owned by the clients that had paid for them. Even when applied research was not so hedged about, it differed in other ways from traditional academic research in that it was to be delivered on a targeted deadline and constructed to be immediately useful to the client. An academic research *grant*, however, did not have to be relevant to immediate decision making, and its deadlines could be more elastic. It was designed by the researcher to explore questions deemed to be of consequence to scientific theory and truth in the long run.[20]

The survey researchers sought grants above all. When they made do with contracts, they hoped to combine the best of both worlds, trying to satisfy their clients' short-term applied goals while also capturing something of value to basic social science. The hope was that there was a business use lying at the surface of the project and a scientific revelation lying at the depths. (Such a combination would also reconcile the conflict between the teacher's responsibility to help students learn and the researcher's need to have students work.) There was, nevertheless, an underlying tension that was not entirely resolved, and it was quickened when the contract involved market research for Madison Avenue, the liquor industry, the automobile industry, and other exemplars of the high-consumption money culture.[21]

The academic culture of science (and scholarship) has long had *a vein of asceticism*. It has been organized around the exchange of recognition and honors among scientific peers (what Storer has called "competent response") more than around the exchanges of money or power.[22] This is an idealization, to be sure, and some (perhaps many) academic scientists in this period chafed at their low salaries as compared to those of other groups.[23] Nevertheless, scientists and scholars generally have been expected to be dedicated to long hours and diligent work without high pay. Academic life has stood in some *opposition* to cultures of money and power, as an alternative to reigning values of material success.

In nineteenth-century America, as Charles E. Rosenberg has traced the process, science represented a kind of renunciation of material values, a chance to devote oneself to the collective and continuous creation of the "cathedral" of knowledge, which offered something of the life of the spirit:

> Science, like religion, offered an ideal of selflessness, of truth, of the possibility of spiritual dedication—emotions which in their elevating purity could inspire and motivate, could legitimate the needs of particular individuals to achieve and control—but in a context seemingly far-removed from the sordid compromise implied by most other careers.

Adding to the fund of human knowledge was seen as "selfless, indeed spiritual . . . transcending mere personal ambition."[24] Rosenberg quotes a man who identified with scientists for their high calling, unlike the "base votaries of Mammon."[25]

That particular language is now antique, but William F. Ogburn's sense of mission, expressed in 1929, was not unlike it in spirit:

> The happy ending for a scientific sociology will be its achievement. It will be necessary to crush out emotion and to discipline the mind so strongly that the fanciful pleasures of intellectuality will have to be eschewed in the verification process. . . . It is not necessary for a scientist to be a scientist all of the time. He can temporarily shut the door to his laboratory and open for a while his door to the beauty of the stars, to the romance of life, to the service of his fellow men, to the leadership of the cause, to the applause of his audience, or to the adventure in the great out-of-doors. But when he returns to his laboratory he will leave these behind; although there is a beauty, a romance, a service, a leadership, and an adventure of a kind to be found sometimes in the laboratory.[26]

Science still represents something of an alternative to material success. The difference is more muted now and less distinct, very probably in good part *because* of the financial presence of business and government in the "big science" of the university. Indeed, Storer sees the asceticism of science being diluted in our own time, with scientists increasingly likely to be attracted by political influence in Washington, the affluence of travel, the status of large research grants, and higher salaries, too. In the 1960s, Storer predicted that the culture and practice of "pure" science would be increasingly displaced by that of applied work.[27] The resistance to business culture by academics was visible in 1945–60 (as it is now, still), when the survey organizations were relying in some part on funds from business and industry. In 1950, for example, the managing executive of the Carnegie Corporation of New York, Charles Dollard, a social scientist himself, reminded sociologists of their pure motives in 1950 when he spoke at their national meetings:

> Scholars and teachers have chosen of their own free will to compete for rewards less tangible and more abiding than money. They cannot have their cake and eat it too.[28]

But the new research organizations did require money in new, large amounts—not "profits," properly speaking, but something very like it: a surplus above subsistence to sustain administrative expenses and a complex division of labor, to allow for capital growth, and to provide for long-term security for key personnel and for the organization per se. This took flows of money that were new to social-science circuits—not to distribute greater personal wealth in the ordinary sense, but money, nevertheless, which had effects on the distribution of status as well.[29] The need for money of new magnitudes thinned the insulation of the scientist from "the temptations of the marketplace."[30] Certainly, it did so in the eyes of wary academic colleagues.

Alfred McClung Lee, for example, worried in 1947 that new commercial opportunities were opening up for sociologists both in industrial jobs and in commercial sponsorship of academic work. He was fearful that a "privately subsidized research system" could become imbedded in departments of sociology, replacing the teaching and academic research objectives with "commercial incentives."[31] Jessie Bernard expressed concern for the more subtle influences of business culture in a letter to Stouffer after the 1950 meetings of the Eastern Sociological Society:

> I do not wish to seem to attribute "guilt by association" to anyone, but it does seem worth mentioning that the kind of research technicians Lazarsfeld proposes to turn out will associate with businessmen (their best customers), they

will be consulted by businessmen, they will be inestimably useful to business-men. They will, inevitably, view their profession in terms of its relation to businessmen. They will command the best salaries, they will have status and prestige, they will in large measure influence the course which research will take. . . . It seems dangerous to me to allow research customers to have too much to say about research trends. Baconian scientists have been promising administrators just this kind of service for a century; but now I for one begin to have misgivings.[32]

Lazarsfeld, who was particularly dependent on business contracts in the early years of the Bureau, chafed at the antibusiness orientation of students.[33] In later years he continued to chide his colleagues for failing to realize the intellectual potential of conducting research for and about business.[34] Lazarsfeld sought (and preached) the scientific value of com-mercial work for the testing of instruments, the training of students, and the pursuit of theory. The Survey Research Center (SRC) did some work for clients in business and industry, especially the car companies, but it was more dependent on government contracts in its earliest years and emphasized the value of its work for government.

Management was another difference. The research groups' need for a bureaucratic division of labor and for management of it also went against the grain of academic culture. Business and industry acknowledge man-agerial talent as a valuable and scarce commodity, and they accord it the highest ranges of pay and power in an organization. Scientists as a group do not. Nor do they consider the innovation and direction of organiza-tions as being as truly creative as businessmen do.[35] While in universities the top administrators are usually paid the highest salaries, the premium paid to them is not large, and scientific disciplines rarely confer upon its administrators the most valuable coin of its culture—prestige, honors, and prizes, the most valuable of which provide an enduring place in the history of science. Yet administration is obviously crucial in research or-ganizations. The enclave for scientific work must be protected from in-cursions; it must be tended, in day-to-day matters of routine; staff must be recruited and developed; the organization's future must be consid-ered and insured through vision and prudence. And, of course, it must be founded in the first place in the exercise of some daring, risk taking, zeal of mission, and arts of persuasion and communication which create followers, friends, and allies—and it must be kept alive with the lifeblood of money and of recognition or prestige.[36]

The new survey organizations absolutely required some central direc-tion and management, but none of them quite operationalized a new role that endowed these numerous responsibilities and functions with prestige and honor. The directors were torn between their duties as businessmen to raise money for their research center and their duties as academic scientists to help build the "cathedral."

The need for *communication with laymen* was another conflict between the cultures of applied and basic science. "Pure" scientists have not needed a mass audience—that is, they have needed "critical" successes rather than "good box office." And in fact they have had something to lose from being popular: their peers might see them as abandoning the hard, high road on the frontiers of knowledge for the low road of a vulgar fame conferred by the undiscerning, or as "selling out" for money.[37] But organizations trying to appeal to clients in the practical world had to understand their needs and requirements; they had to offer a useful product; and they had to be intelligible to laymen. In effect, they had to advertise—but subtly, in the service of science, lest they lose their academic legitimacy and the esteem of colleagues.

The *quantitative work* of the survey researchers was perhaps the worst sticking point for some of their university colleagues. It aroused the intellectual distrust of many, including scholars who were hostile to or untrained in numbers, a group that included social scientists as well as humanistic scholars. Quantitative work already had a firm place in psychology and economics, but the "soft" data of subjective measures in social psychology were not trusted in either discipline. In sociology, theorists had the place of honor, and quantitative work was often distrusted as mindless, without foundation in theory or much promise of making the connection. (Rural sociology had an empirical tradition, but as a largely applied science serving clients of low cultural prestige, it commanded a low position on the academic totem pole of the "cow colleges.") In political science there was still little quantitative work, as political theory and the study of political institutions were mainline enterprises.

Quantitative work was criticized for many sins—for being antitheoretical and barren of intellect ("dustbowl empiricism"); for triviality ("If you can count it, it isn't worth counting"); for illiteracy, deliberate obscurantism, and mumbo jumbo; for a malicious or mindless "scientism"; for mechanical reductionism; for displacement of the individual scholar; for pretentious explication of the obvious; for prodigal waste of money.[38] Quantitative social science was not easy to "do" or to appreciate for those who had spent a professional lifetime in the arts and humanities, with no interest in statistics or data analysis, or for social scientists whose training was in theory and in the broad culture of the social sciences.

Those who had taken the time to become skilled in quantitative work often did not bring comparable shares of humanistic learning and culture or a broad knowledge of the history or theory of even their own disciplines. The sociologist Pitirim Sorokin thought the new emphasis on quantitative work was obsessive, and he called the new practitioners "quantophrenics"—with special reference to Stouffer and Lazarsfeld. C. P. Snow's analysis in his book *The Two Cultures* was not wholly inappropriate for the American university after World War II. In protesting quantification, academics were engaged most vigorously in a form of what has been called "boundary work."[39] There is no doubt that quantification posed a kind of democratic threat to those members of the academic elite who had spent a lifetime of patient and brilliant individual scholarship. Peterson has reflected on the excitement that students began to feel about empirical work in a later phase of the "behavioral revolution" in political science:

As graduate students, you began to feel that maybe you could make a contribution *too*. You didn't have to sit in your study chair reading the great books and waiting prayerfully—maybe for a lifetime—for some Great Thought to strike like a thunderbolt. You could put together some smaller ideas, gather data, and try to test them. You could start to labor in the vineyard, humbly, with the hope that it might help![40]

The disciplines were divided internally by the new waves of quantification of subjective measurement which were hitting sociology and social psychology and which would soon hit political science. It is impossible to know now exactly how the fields as a whole were divided, but forceful spokesmen in various fields pointed to the vulgarisms and oversimplifications of applied work, particularly market research and polling.

Objections from the Disciplines

The criticism from psychologist Quinn McNemar is one we have already seen (chapter seven). It may well still stand as the most-cited psychological critique of the emergent survey research, a highly respected monograph despite its arrogant tone and sometimes captious criticism. In a paper delivered at the 1947 sociology meetings, University of Chicago sociologist Herbert Blumer levied a criticism that would be an enduring one in his discipline: public opinion researchers treated society as if it were "a mere aggregation of disparate individuals" instead of an organic whole of interacting, interrelated parts.[41]

This atomism was appropriate in certain situations, Blumer argued, as when individuals in the mass were "casting ballots, purchasing toothpaste, going to motion picture shows, and reading newspapers," and it accounted for the successful use of sampling in consumer research. But in Blumer's view these matters did not bear on public opinion, the organic structure of which defied sampling. Blumer named no individuals or organizations in his paper, but members of both Likert's and Lazarsfeld's group thought that they were being singled out for attack.[42] Stouffer, as Blumer's former colleague at Chicago, was probably also his quarry.[43]

C. Wright Mills's criticism from a sociological perspective was even more thoroughgoing. He addressed in particular the work of the Bureau (with which Mills had been associated in the mid-1940s), not for quantitative data per se, for he also used them to support his analysis in *White Collar* and *The Power Elite*, but for a series of deficiencies bred of intellectual, conceptual impoverishment. *Abstracted empiricism*, as he termed it, was divorced from substantive concerns with society, from historical and comparative perspectives. In its focus on single community samples, it constricted research to an artificially narrow range of variation, and in its concentration on individual respondents, it obscured social structure and highlighted "psychologism." The preoccupations of the abstracted empiricists took on an empty formalism:

> Those in the grip of the methodological inhibition often refuse to say anything about modern society unless it has been through the fine little mill of The Statistical Ritual. It is usual to say that what they produce is true even if unimportant. I do not agree with this . . . I wonder how much exactitude, or even pseudo-precision, is here confused with "truth"; and how much abstracted empiricism is taken as the only "empirical" manner of work . . . surely it is important when some of the most energetic minds among us use themselves up in the study of details because The Method to which they are dogmatically committed does not allow them to study anything else. Much of such work, I am now convinced, has become the mere following of a ritual—which happens to have gained commercial and foundation value—rather than, in the words of its spokesmen, a "commitment to the hard demands of science."[44]

From political science came a book by Lindsay Rogers, *The Pollsters*, written before the 1948 election and published in 1949. The title evoked Frederic Wakeman's attack on modern advertising published in 1946, *The Hucksters*. (The term *pollsters* has since shed much of this early pejorative connotation, in its widespread use as a neutral term.) Rogers's treatment was a more popular, more caustic, and technically less sophisticated one than the others just cited. He reflected on themes of special interest to political scientists: the theory of representative government versus direct democracy, the organization and impact of pressure groups, the nature of publics and public opinion, and the problem of measurement. All of these, in Rogers's view, made polling a pretentious, arrogant, and finally quite hollow enterprise. In this case, there was no mistaking the target: the "tycoons and their academic acolytes" who made up a "large and important American industry." Also, Rogers cited in largely negative fashion the work of Gallup, Roper, Cantril, Cottrell and Eberhart, Katz, Likert, NORC, and, for good measure, all 200 people attending the Second International Conference on Public Opinion Research at Williamstown in 1947. Stouffer's Research Branch commanded some praise in a footnote for having collected "much useful information during the war," thereby escaping the general opprobrium.[45]

From some colleagues in the humanities came criticisms of deep concern about social science generally and new quantitative research in particular. The historian Arthur M. Schlesinger, Jr., inveighed against the new research projects and organizations in a 1949 review of *The American Soldier*:

> The champions of "social science" today. . . . Bursting onto university campuses after the war, overflowing with portentous if vague hints of mighty wartime achievements (not, alas, to be disclosed because of security), fanatical in their zeal and shameless in their claims, they persuaded or panicked many university administrations into giving their studies top priorities. Needless to say, they scored an even more brilliant success with the foundations. Certain foundation directors even decided that virtually all their funds for research in the social sciences should be expended on projects of the "social science" variety; the individual scholar, so far as they were concerned, was through.[46]

Schlesinger thundered at the "social relations hucksters" and their "remorseless jargon," "research by committee," "the fetish of 'interdisciplinary' projects," and the proliferation of "gadgets," all subsidized by foundations "carrying to triumphant completion their ancient hope of achieving the bureaucratization of American intellectual life." Schlesinger made vivid indeed the individual scholar's sense of siege and frustration as quantitative research in the social sciences got attention and funds.[47]

Other humanists such as Joseph Wood Krutch worried with somewhat less stridency that those "obsessively concerned with statistical studies of the human condition" were leading us all to "assume that whatever is measurable must be significant and that whatever cannot be measured may as well be disregarded."[48] The first Kinsey Report, *Sexual Behavior in the Human Male* (1948), was on Krutch's mind.[49] Lionel Trilling shared the same concern in his review of the Kinsey book, noting that the "sexuality that is measured is taken to be the definition of sexuality itself."[50] (The Trilling review still makes splendid reading, especially for its critique of the report's naive bias in favor of "the natural.") Certain humanists felt under intellectual siege by what they perceived to be an aggressive and intrusive social science, bent on arrogating for its domain the most ineffable and deeply felt human emotions and experiences. At least some things shall elude scientific capture, Krutch noted, when he answered his own rhetorical question, What *cannot* be made the subject of scientific experiment?

> "Happiness" is something which falls almost completely outside the purview of science. Its various degrees cannot be measured. The conditions which produce it cannot be controlled. We cannot demonstrate that an individual man either is or is not happy. In fact, his emotional state cannot even be safely inferred.[51]

Perhaps not, but social scientists would soon be intent on trying to do so. Lazarsfeld, in fact, had already put that subject, the measurement of personal happiness, on the research agenda.[52]

The new survey organizations were obviously not without allies and supporters in their universities and disciplines, or they would still be *outside* now. There was a source of support in the current of optimism about the social sciences generally and about the role they could play in solving some of the human problems, perhaps especially some problems (such as weapons and war) that were aggravated by the physical sciences. Conant's presidential address to the American Association for the Advancement of Science in 1947 noted that immediate assistance could be expected from social psychologists, sociologists, and anthropologists, especially in areas involving human tensions and in the humanizing of industry.[53] The "human tensions" project of UNESCO reflected the same hope that opinion/attitude research could make a contribution to world peace.[54]

Within the particular universities, there were several friends and allies. For example, Lynd's help was critical to Lazarsfeld's joining Columbia in 1940.[55] Lazarsfeld could hardly have had a more valuable colleague, friend, and ally in sociology than Merton, who took an official role in the Bureau in 1943. The founding of NORC had the sympathetic support of board members Cantril, Stouffer, Gordon Allport, and certain administrators at the University of Denver. At Michigan, psychologist Donald Marquis was an extremely valuable ally. As chairman of the local department, he was bent upon upgrading and expanding, and as president of the American Psychological Association he was a disciplinary "influential" who believed that large-scale group research was essential to the growth of the social sciences.[56] These and other academics were indispensable to the rooting of these new organizations on at least the margins of university terrain.

Innovation and the Research Entrepreneurs

Intellectual Migration from the Margins

"Marginality" as a source of innovation has been a very general hypothesis for some time. The "marginal man" was a cultural hybrid with experiences in two worlds, which he tried to straddle, feeling identities and affinities with each and caught by pressures and conflicts between them. The image bore especially on the experience of the immigrant, with a negative emphasis on the strains of adjustment to contradiction and cultural conflict.[57]

Recent use of the concept in the history and sociology of science has been more specified and more upbeat, stressing the innovation through intellectual-occupational migration. Ben-David and Collins, for example, have accounted for the appearance of experimental psychology as a "role hybrid" of philosophy and physiology in Germany. Wundt, in particular, who had waited seventeen years for recognition and advancement in the field of physiology, moved into philosophy, where the status was lower but the opportunities were more abundant. There, to maintain his scientific standing, he practiced the experimental methods of physiology.[58] Both interpretations of marginality have some applicability to Lazarsfeld's career.

Lazarsfeld thought of himself at Columbia as a "marginal man" straddling two cultures—he was an immigrant Jew in an American WASP university as well as a scientist bent on trying to wrest social theory from contracts for commercial business[59]—but his location in Vienna had been marginal in a certain sense, too, as it straddled academic life and research for business. The European university system was one of scarcity, providing professorial chairs in short supply, and motion up a career ladder was made possible largely by death of the superior. In Vienna, Lazarsfeld had not been well placed and had no research opportunities of his own, being still in his twenties, so he created a research organization on the edges of the university.[60]

His disciplinary move suggests the Ben-David/Collins thesis more particularly. In joining the Columbia department, Lazarsfeld became a sociologist. He did so, he later wrote, because he found more kindred spirits there, more appreciation for his experiences in market research. Psychologists were less interested, he felt, because applied psychology had low status in the discipline.[61] (It seems unlikely that his contacts were representative of the respective disciplines as a whole, for market research and applied work in general have probably had, if anything, even *lower* status in sociology.) It seems likely that Lazarsfeld shifted to sociology in some recognition, whether conscious or not, that his quantitative skills and orientation would have greater scope there, where they were rarer, than they would in psychology, where students were already being trained in quantitative work and statistical analysis. Lazarsfeld may well have sensed that he could make a greater contribution and gain greater recognition in the field of sociology. If so, he was probably correct.

Lazarsfeld's move into sociology was an instance of migration between disciplines, but his straddling of the realms of *business* and *academic life*, first in Vienna and then in the United States, was of greater significance for survey research. Survey research did not grow up in the interstices of academic disciplines but developed in cross-fertilization of research conducted in the realms of business, government, and the academy. Intellectual migration across the margins of these cultures describes not only the travels of Lazarsfeld but also those of Field and Likert.

Field entered academic life directly from business experience with the Gallup enterprises. He looked to an academic setting to provide freedom from the pressures of the marketplace so that technical methods could be improved and public confidence in polls enhanced. In the brief time he directed NORC, Field felt the pressures of "marginality" himself, as he tried to upgrade public opinion research in a university setting. (See chapter ten.)

Likert was also on the edges of academic life. Had his academic career thrived at New York University, he very probably would not have had experience in market, industrial, and then government research. Had he remained within the academy throughout the depression, it seems very unlikely that he would have had the same impetus to create a new research organization on university ground—and certainly not to export it from the federal government.

Still, the concept of marginality has its limits for explaining the origin and growth of these organizations, for they almost *had* to be built at the margins. There was almost nothing in the university environment that would have encouraged "spontaneous generation." The organizations were too big, too expensive, too applied, too interdisciplinary or too intercultural in spirit to have grown up from within. Academics whose careers had been spent exclusively in a university department would not have had the relevant experience. Their administrative experience (if any) would have been as departmental chairmen or deans, and their research experience (if any) would have been in the traditional mold of small, low-cost operations favoring the use of student subjects and graduate-student assistants.

These organizations were carried into the academy, but why did these organizations (and not others) succeed in grafting themselves onto the university organism? And how did they succeed in *growing*? Of course, not everyone was interested in even trying. Stouffer, apparently, was not. His research administration during the war was an enormous success, he was very well connected to likely sources of funds (such as the Carnegie Corporation), and there is every reason to think that some of his wartime associates would have been glad to have joined him in a postwar survey organization in an academic environment. Instead, Stouffer turned to small-scale research in his Laboratory of Social Relations at Harvard. (Why he did not want to continue is beyond our purview; possibly, he had had enough research administration headaches to last a lifetime.) But some people *did* want to direct social research organizations, and to consider their differential success we can repair to two other concepts that are of some—though by no means definitive—help, both bearing on personal gifts and ideas of the new research entrepreneurs.

Institution Building

THE ZEAL OF INDIVIDUALS

Another theory of innovation stresses the role of the individual zealot: young, intense, highly committed, with the faith and energy critical in overcoming the resistance of the conservative, old, and entrenched.[62] This is not a perfect fit. When they undertook their university organizations, these men were not all young. Lazarsfeld was when he started his research center in Vienna at around age twenty-six. In 1939–40, when he moved his radio project onto Columbia's campus, he was thirty-nine; in the same year, Field was forty-three and Cantril was thirty-four; and in 1946, Likert was forty-three. They were all zealots, however, and that is surely the more critical component: high physical energy, a missionary spirit about their views of science, and a resilience in the face of obstacles or disappointment.

Their actual views differed. Likert brought a certitude and a sense of mission that applied (and basic) science would "help to answer the crucial human problems of the modern world." He wrote repeatedly about the sample survey interview as "one of the fundamental research tools of all the social sciences."[63] Cannell has recalled Likert's fervor: "He had no doubts, no sense of ambiguity; he knew that the people in that room or the next client he talked to *absolutely needed* social science to help solve their problems."[64]

Field's sense of mission, which was that public opinion research could serve both democracy and world peace, seems quite similar to Likert's. Field believed that worldwide public opinion research could be used to detect and then to harmonize tensions on the world scene, and he tried to get UNESCO to incorporate into its charter a commitment to this kind of research.[65] He had left the commercial business of polling, apparently at a considerable loss in pay, precisely to try to develop such potentialities for polling. The record is thinner on Field, simply because his life was so much shorter and his role as founder-director at NORC was quite brief. We therefore have less to go on in interpreting his "institution building."

Lazarsfeld's case is very clear. His prodigal energies and interests were bent on building social science, not so much to have science serve the practical world as to have problems of the practical world serve the long-run goals of science: testing new methods, building theory, training scientists. Lazarsfeld was a missionary campaigner for support from business, foundations, government, the university—anyplace—with a considerable genius in finding it.

Cantril's vision for social science seems to have reflected hopes for both basic and applied developments. He was very interested in improving the survey instrument—and scornful, finally, of the small scope and unreality of the psychological research of the laboratory—but he was perhaps more interested in the applications of survey work. Sharing

Field's interest in measuring world tensions, for example, Cantril directed UNESCO's exploratory project in 1948 on that topic. He also made major career investments in policy research using surveys.[66]

All of these people, in their various ways, were convinced that social science research was a human imperative, deserving of unstinting support from all quarters of the society. Those who succeeded seem to have incorporated a second, related idea.

THE LEADERSHIP FUNCTION

Over the course of his career, Lazarsfeld tried to conceptualize the research director's role. His formulation of the "managerial scholar" conveyed the notion that a research administrator had to continue to be a researcher, that is, a "working" executive but one who also did the "worrying."[67] Glock (of the Bureau), Campbell (of SRC), and Clyde Hart (of NORC) all wrote from personal experience about research administration and the functions necessary to sustain their organizations.[68] It may well be that those organizations that thrived did so because of the still more intangible "leadership" function (the subject of theory by Barnard, Selznick, and others): making of the organizational purpose itself an incentive for participation and activity.[69]

Lazarsfeld, Likert, and Field did indeed have a specific "institutional" mission that they felt and conveyed to the members of their organizations. This was not only a vision of science but was also a very particular sense of why the organization was essential to the scientific mission. It is clear that the students who thrived at the Bureau felt that they were not simply being trained for their professional careers but that they were also part of a movement, a mission to build social science. The professionals in Likert's group had something of the same feeling—they were not simply making a living or developing their own careers but were also bringing their adventures on the high seas of wartime interdisciplinary research to the landlocked departments and to students who needed to learn empirical research.

It may be that Cantril's organization did not thrive after the war because he himself did not have that particular idea, that institutional mission. He was an imaginative, talented scientist, a good writer, and a good speaker who was committed and excited about social science and who conveyed that sense. He also established an academic organization in survey research. But he may well not have seen the one as a vehicle of the other nor felt an institutional mission himself. If he *had* had an institutional mission, the developing of talent and loyalty for the organization might have come more naturally.

While this is speculation, Cantril's record of troubled collaborations provides some tentative support for it. Cantril's closet collaborator and lifetime friend, Lloyd Free, who recalls his relationship with Cantril as almost perfectly harmonious, has been puzzled by the problems that were often occasioned by Cantril's other collaborations and suspects that Cantril aroused envy.[70] This is not to say that the other director-founders were without their battles. Likert jousted with the pollsters, and Lazarsfeld had his difficulties with Theodor Adorno and C. Wright Mills. But Cantril seems to have had more such skirmishes.

The lack of a specifically institutional mission may account for the fact that while Cantril's career as a policy researcher continued to rise, his organization did not. After the war, OPOR itself continued as a very small operation, largely devoted to the archive of polling data which Mildred Strunk compiled under Cantril's direction. In 1955, Cantril and Free were each awarded a lifetime research grant of $1 million from Rockefeller to conduct policy research—a spectacular achievement in research financing, and one which may still be unmatched by any other researchers.[71]

This view of the leadership function suggests a commonality across the very different executive styles and beliefs about organizations which Likert and Lazarsfeld, in particular, displayed. (Again, too little is known about Field to be sure, although there are suggestions that he was closer in spirit to Likert's style than to Lazarsfeld's.) Lazarsfeld was a director in something of the European mold—"Herr Director," Cantril said—but Lazarsfeld had more humor, charm, and personal magnetism than Cantril's term usually conveys, more characteristics of the Viennese stereotype than of the German.

Even so, there was some truth to Cantril's characterization. Lazarsfeld apparently *expected* to direct a laboratory in the German tradition of university science, where students were to work and study as apprentices carrying out the research agenda of the master scientist and funds were provided by a combination of university, state, and federal subsidies. Lazarsfeld admired Charlotte Bühler's strong direction of her laboratory, conducted under clear hierarchical authority (rather than with the collegial individualism of university scholars). Lazarsfeld's own style at the Bureau was of the intellectual dominance of apprentice-students. Many students bloomed under this kind of direction, but some felt the need to escape it. As we shall see, the Bureau's influence spread in part as its alumni were *dispersed*. Conversely, the influence of Likert's Michigan organization was enhanced as it grew, *absorbing* new staff.[72]

From early in his career, Likert espoused democratic organization and consensual leadership. His ideas on the subject went back to the 1930s when, in his morale research for the insurance industry, he became convinced that decentralized authority was important to enhance individuals' initiative, satisfaction, and identification with the work and the organization. We have seen evidence of these beliefs in his wartime organization (chapter seven). A democratic theory of organization and productivity, which stressed communication up and down a organizational pyramid rather than direction from the top down, became a lifetime research interest for Likert.[73] The two organizations were thus very different in structure, but both were obviously effective *as organizations*. Each director clearly believed that his organization had a unique collective mission that could not be achieved by individual scholars alone.

The Research Entrepreneur

THE RIGHT WORD?

The term *research entrepreneur* has come into some currency for the combination scientist-businessman who is professionally trained to do scientific research but who must raise the money to finance it. The term does not quite convey the full responsibility and scope that Lazarsfeld tried to suggest with his term *managerial scholar*, but no single term has seemed entirely apt. Some of the likely words have come from business— and for academics the connotations have not been quite right.

Research management has been a possibility, for instance. But in their own eyes, scientists have sought not to be managed but facilitated. They have wanted other people to take care of the distracting matters of research organization so that they could get on with their work. Neither that term nor the term *administration* has connoted any competence in scientific research itself, which has been a crucial component of the leadership role. Other aspects of the function have been still more difficult to label. *Salesmanship*, for instance, has clearly been involved in the obtaining of research money, but for academics the word has had a negative connotation of manipulation or exaggeration. The term *political skills* has also had this connotation.

Whatever this process is called—this art of persuasion, evangelism, the reading of the funding market, the lining up of support—it has obviously been essential to the garnering of money and acceptance for the foreign bodies in the university's midst. But labeling it has been difficult. *Promoters, operators,* and certainly *hustlers* have all been used ironically among academics to lend a certain tarnish to these political skills of fundraising and organizing.[74]

THE DUAL REQUIREMENTS

There was some tension between the two roles that these entrepreneurial directors carried out as internal institution builders and external ambassadors in search of funds. As Shepard has expressed the conflicting claims on the directors,

> The present-day scientist who would be both "pure" and "applied" can be likened to an actor who plays to two audiences simultaneously, each with a different taste in shows.[75]

And the directors reflected the tension. Lazarsfeld felt it when he made speeches to businessmen to promote the uses of social research. As he reflected in later years,

> Of course you have to have a large number of examples from studies, and you have to be a little bit irresponsible, in the sense that it has to sound amusing. I always put it—I knew it at that time—that I would be horrified if any of my colleagues at Columbia would have heard me talk in those meetings. . . . You didn't even need to repeat yourself too often, because there is a mountain of studies—honest results, but it paid at the dinners or a lunch speech.[76]

Lazarsfeld was surely using the word *irresponsible* puckishly to refer to the liberties of oversimplification which one can and probably must take in informal speeches where there is a need to be entertaining and dramatic. Yet he was reflecting seriously on the tension between the requirements of the business clients and those of his university colleagues.[77]

Whether Likert also experienced that tension is not clear, but some of his *colleagues* felt it when they listened to him address an audience of clients. Two of his close associates compared notes many years later:

> I have so many times sat and listened and said to myself, "If he were giving me that pitch, I would get up and leave." But you know, those people would just sit there with their mouths open, lapping it up and thinking, "Oh, this man is just marvelous!" Did you ever have that experience?

Oh, yes, people would come up to me afterwards and say, "Isn't Dr. Likert a fine man! Isn't he a wonderful person!" He had something to sell, and he was for new ideas when they were valid in some sense. The optimism was essential, I think.[78]

THE AGILITY AND IMPROVISATION

The founding entrepreneurs had to juggle the demands of their clients for *useful* work and those of their colleagues and students for scientifically *interesting* work, and university administrators demanded the while that the organization be *solvent*. The last was probably the most difficult, as in any fledgling business. The university research business was new for the social sciences, and what the optimal financial structure was for surviving and flourishing was an unknown. Where the clients were to come from was not very clear, either. All three of the founders had experience that was relevant but could not have been sufficient. The new organizations developed through some trial and error as the "entrepreneurs" did their best to get as much grant support as they could—they were all in search of substantial endowment, but never got it—and sought contract money for the rest.

In the struggle for solvency, the directors labored to put the best possible face on their outstanding debts and to instill hope for the prosperity and achievements still to come. A hopeful tone colors reports written to authorities (boards or university superiors) and actually makes it rather difficult to establish the true chronicle of what happened when. A given project, for instance, is sometimes announced as ready for publication, in fact already sent to the printer, and then later it is announced all over again as ready for publication; works in hand are sometimes grouped with works in mind, quite as though there were no essential difference between them; financial projections are ever sanguine. In these optimistic reports there was probably some strategic *method* for keeping other officials confident that the organizations were going to thrive. There was also conviction. If these men had not had an expansive faith in their organizations, all three could doubtless have made a substantial living in far more comfortable ways.

Very recently, another successful research entrepreneur reflected on how applied research centers should enter a university: "To be effective in the long run," the research group should come into the university only under clearly understood conditions of "mutual respect and reciprocity"—especially, academic rank for the center's director and key staff and for the several departments, research training, and dissertation data.[79] Perhaps in our own time this is a practical prescription for success. But in the 1940s, if the research groups had insisted on these as conditions of arrival into the university, it seems fair to guess that they would have been barred at the gate. Zealots they were, but they were also petitioners, with a sense of proportion and limitation. Their acceptance and effectiveness in the long run probably depended in some good part on the very modesty and ambiguity of their demands in the beginning.

9

The Bureau of Applied Social Research: The First Wave

> What made the Columbia department so exciting in those
> early days of the Lazarsfeld-Merton era was the sense that
> students had that they were in on the ground floor of an
> enterprise that believed it was about to remake social
> science, if not the world.
>
> *Seymour Martin Lipset*

> It was a Christmas skit at the Bureau. One of the boys
> plays me and I come in and distribute cigars and someone
> asks, "Is it a boy or a girl?" And this fictitious Lazarsfeld
> stops and says, "Gosh, I don't know—I'm only interested
> in the method."
>
> *Paul F. Lazarsfeld*

Applied Research on the Margins of the Academy

The Nature of the Innovation

The Bureau of Applied Social Research at Columbia was not the first
academic research center in sociology in an American university, but it
was the most significant and influential for the growth of quantitative
research in that discipline and the first of three organizations central to
the development of academic survey research.

The Institute for Research in Social Science (IRSS), founded at the
University of North Carolina by the sociologist Howard Odum in 1924,
was an early forerunner, but it had different roots and took different
directions. IRSS was dedicated to research into the cultural history and
social problems of the South as a region. It was reformist in spirit, concerned about race, poverty, and economic and political development,
and it was more an heir to the social survey tradition than a forerunner
of survey research.[1] Odum's Institute was a good distance in miles and
spirit from radio research, market research, and polling data—and especially from the clients of Madison Avenue, where Lazarsfeld found
some of his early research connections and funds for the Bureau.

Another development in empirical research which preceded the Bureau was social science at the University of Chicago in the 1920s and 1930s.[2] The Bureau differed from this set of interdisciplinary projects at Chicago by its identity as a standing organization, by its concentration on survey methods, and by its financing research in good part through applied contracts.

Barton finds Lazarsfeld's applied social research organizations (first in Vienna, and then at Columbia) to have been "social invention,"

> which gets contracts from clients, supports its staff of empirical researchers and students, tries out new methods, and feeds back the results into teaching and the dissertation work of students at the University.[3]

Lazarsfeld's research organization did not come full-blown. It had started as a research project on radio (see chapter four) which took on the character of an organization and then settled by degrees into Columbia University. It was financed by foundation grants, contracts for business and nonprofit organizations, and university subsidy. This mixture was not wholly new for research in business schools on university campuses (see chapter three), but it was indeed an innovation for sociology.

When Lazarsfeld came to Columbia he had traditional academic credentials and experience—a Ph.D. from the University of Vienna, work under the direction of well-known psychologists, scholarly publication, and a Rockefeller fellowship to study in the United States. His research experience was less traditional, in Vienna as well as in the United States, because of its combination of academic personnel and commercial clients. The commercial connection gave a special quality and complication to Lazarsfeld's research organization at Columbia in the early years.

In 1939, Lazarsfeld accepted a courtesy appointment in the Department of Sociology at Columbia. In 1940, he brought onto the edges of Columbia the radio research funded by the Rockefeller grant that had been obtained by Cantril and Stanton. There was, apparently, a mutual interest on the part of the Rockefeller Foundation and the Columbia administration in the development of educational radio.[4] In the spring of 1940, the Office of Radio Research (ORR) was included under the umbrella of the Council for Research in the Social Sciences and a governing board chaired by Robert S. Lynd, who was also chairman of the sociology department. Through Lynd's good offices, especially, ORR was provided with offices in the old College of Physicians and Surgeons (on

Amsterdam and 59th Street, some sixty blocks from the Morningside Heights campus)—which came complete with a surgical amphitheatre and rising and descending floors. Former students later recalled arranging appointments with Lazarsfeld or Merton to take the long cab ride up to the Columbia campus.[5]

ORR had no university budget. It came with the Rockefeller Foundation grant and added such contracts as it could from outside clients. In the early 1940s, that meant research on radio audiences and programs, along with readership studies for *Life* magazine, *Time*, and *Tide* and advertising studies for the manufacturers of toothpaste, Bisodol, vitamins, whiskey and wine, Sloan's Liniment, and greeting cards.[6] The budget records from these years are sketchy, but it appears that for four of the first five years (1941–46), the organization relied on "commercial" work for 50 percent or more of its income. The term *commercial* apparently encompassed not only contracts for business firms but also (in lesser quantity) work for nonprofit organizations such as the American Jewish Congress.[7] Never again was the percentage that high, but commercial work was always a part of Bureau financing, and it was a critical part in the first decade.[8]

By 1944, the original radio project had considerably broadened its research agenda, and it was given a new name, the Bureau of Applied Social Research, to indicate that greater scope, with the Office of Radio Research keeping its name as a department. By this time, the organization was receiving some funds from the university (first $5,000, then $10,000) which acknowledged its work training students, and from the beginning it had received the support of the university through office space, utilities, and building maintenance. In 1949, the Bureau moved to 117th Street, close to the Columbia campus.[9]

Lazarsfeld was appointed as an associate professor of sociology in 1941. He and Merton were *both* appointed, to resolve an argument in the department about who should replace statistician Robert E. Chaddock after his death.[10] In 1943, Merton took an official role in the Bureau as associate director, beginning a long friendship and professional association with Lazarsfeld and an involvement in the Bureau. Their interests converged in the effort to integrate theory and method, with Merton's "theories of the middle range" and Lazarsfeld's explorations in research design and data analysis. Lazarsfeld had the more dominant role in the Bureau itself, doing his best teaching in the informal seminars and on-the-job training of Bureau projects. Merton was less involved in the day-to-day direction of Bureau projects—although he was deeply involved in its planning—but was the more brilliant formal lecturer in the sociology department. Many students in the department became drawn into the orbit of one or the other scholar or both, as the two, especially, gave Columbia a new era of intellectual excitement and ascendance in the discipline.[11]

Under their leadership, the Bureau was intent on harvesting scientific fruit from contracts as well as grants. The radio studies, which cumulated as "Mass Communications," the Bureau's first research program, identified the class composition of the radio audiences, their self-selection to programs offering familiar themes rather than new information, the psychological appeals of programs (such as the fantasy "gratification" of the daytime radio serial), the limited audience available for serious "educational" programs, and the limited capacity of the media generally to effect political conversion. From market research for publishers of *True Story* and of *Time*, and for a consortium of drug companies, the Bureau explored the process of interpersonal influence in the community and the diffusion of innovation in a professional network—matters to which we will return later in this chapter.

The Issue of Commercial Work

LAZARSFELD'S ORIENTATIONS

Lazarsfeld's own valuations of applied work were complex. At times, he expressed the view that the contract work was a practical expedient by which to stay solvent and to try to build up funds for work of more significance in science. As he wrote in 1946,

> The Bureau is perpetually facing the well-known paradox that work has to be done on topics with low priorities, so that funds are available for the study of matters more scientifically important.[12]

Generally, this meant trying to get a profit markup of 20 to 25 percent over expenses, which could be set aside to finance nonfunded scholarly projects.

Years later, in a twentieth-anniversary celebration of the Bureau, Lazarsfeld reflected on how he had patched together the funds for the study of the 1940 election from miscellaneous commercial arrangements:

> This afternoon there was a dramatic discussion of the intellectual impact of this kind of study, [but] no one remembers that at some times the only prob-

lem which anyone was really concerned with was how to finance the thing. . . .
I had to get about $100,000 to finance the study, and I had only a $15,000
nest egg left to develop it [from a Rockefeller grant]. I had to go to *Life Magazine* and sell them the first reprint rights. That added something like $10,000
or $15,000. Then I had to get to all sorts of manufacturers of radio sets and
tell them, "We put in a few questions of whether people prefer this one make
rather than another make," and that added another $10,000, but that wasn't
enough. But people also bought refrigerators at the time, so I was willing to
put in a question of refrigerators.[13]

And so it went. Commercial work was sometimes a matter of pure
scrounging to make another project possible.

However, Lazarsfeld insisted on the value of contract work in its own
right. He himself found the practical problems of business intellectually
exciting, often a greater stimulus than many a grant-sponsored project.[14]
To Columbia administrators, he defended the equivalent value of academic and commercial projects:

Studies done for commercial sponsors are so budgeted that they cover part
of the Administrative Expenses and yield "profits" with which to conduct research development studies. One should keep in mind that we only accept
such contracts that provide us with material that is interesting for our own
purpose. Practically every commercial study so far has either yielded a publication or material needed for Dr. Merton's and my teaching in the Department. There is hardly any difference between the academic and the commercial study as far as methods and content go; they differ only with respect to
purpose and finances.[15]

(In this draft document, it is not clear whether the last two sentences
went forward with the rest; there is a penciled comment, "omit," beside
them.)

Lazarsfeld also taxed social scientists for blinding themselves with academic snobbery to the substantive potential of commercial studies. In
later years, he recalled addressing a class of Gordon Allport's in 1933:

After a few introductory remarks, I said: "Let me give you a first example
from a study of mouthwash." There was a roar of laughter, and I answered:
"I don't quite see why 'lifted weights' are so much more dignified than 'mouthwash.' "[16]

On other occasions, he rued the academic distinction between trivial and
"dignified" research, and he chided academics for being so ideologically

alienated from business that they even failed to study it as an institution.[17]

Lazarsfeld saw equivalent theoretical interest in individual decision making of various kinds, or "empirical analysis of action," as he called it—buying soap, choosing a career, voting for political candidates, committing a crime, joining a union, making investments. He viewed Parsons's use of the word *action* for his pattern variables and theory of social structure as something of a misnomer that had inhibited the growth of empirical study of individual human action and decision making.[18]

Applied contracts served some scientific purposes at the Bureau, but they also posed some problems. They meant living from hand to mouth because so much of the work was small-time and short-term and because Lazarsfeld was trying to do so much with so little. They meant delays in completion and publication, in part because of inadequate funds, and they meant continuing on the margins of academic respectability. In a memoir about Lazarsfeld and the Bureau, Lipset reflected wryly on his reaction as a student that Lazarsfeld's trafficking with commerce was a sellout to the "capitalist devils." Lazarsfeld's own view continued to be that the academic-commercial collaboration was not only essential to the Bureau's survival but was also a source of its intellectual quality.[19]

UNIVERSITY ORIENTATIONS

From the beginning, commercial work had disadvantages for dealing with Columbia administrators. It made them uneasy about money and reputation. They worried about unpaid bills and the possibility that Columbia's name might be used for commercial or political gain. M. Emerson Gentzler, the university bursar, probably epitomized the administration's hopes for the Bureau when he wrote to Lazarsfeld in 1944:

> You certainly have done very well in rounding up new research projects. All of them appear to be of a very good type, inasmuch as they are, first of all, non-commercial and secondly, non-controversial.[20]

In early 1944, as the office faced the end of Rockefeller support, Lynd and Lazarsfeld tried to interest Columbia in establishing a "revolving fund" of $15,000 to enable the ORR to develop sustained projects and survive between commercial contracts.[21] Without success. (Columbia never did agree to such a fund, although in later years it created a small publication fund, which was designed to serve something of the same purpose.) By the fall of 1944, the Bureau had accumulated a debt to the university.

Lazarsfeld tried to explain that the picture was not as bleak as it might seem. Columbia administrators might be concluding that there was a deficit of close to $8,000,

> but this impression would be erroneous. I have not included in my report about thirty thousand dollars worth of studies which are now in progress [which are estimated to be half-finished]. . . . Assuming that a "profit" of only 20% would accrue, this would mean an additional income of $3,000 for last year not accounted for in this report.

And this would have meant a debt of $4,600, regrettable but still only a small part of the $60,000 activity.[22]

The Bureau's books and the university's were in disagreement on this occasion, and they would be again. Furthermore, from the bursar's standpoint the Bureau should have turned to its *clients* for advance funding of the research rather than running up unauthorized advances from the university. While the sums seem small now, the university took a serious view of them then.[23]

Administrators were also uneasy when Lazarsfeld embarked on a series of thirteen articles for *The Nation* on the forthcoming national election of 1944. Because these articles were not signed by Lazarsfeld himself but rather by the "Bureau of Applied Social Research, Columbia University, New York," they raised directly the issue of university publicity and involvement. University Provost Fackenthal wrote various memos to Lynd in this season, none of them expressing much pleasure about Columbia's public association with this project:

> I wish we could set up some kind of management for the O.R.R. that would make it possible for some of the rest of us to give up worrying as to what may be happening. [And later:] Is the enclosed just the kind of thing on which we wish to issue reports from the University? . . . I think as an institution we should not take part in a political campaign.[24]

In this correspondence, Fackenthal was not hostile to the Bureau—Merton, in fact, recalls him as having been essentially sympathetic to empirical research[25]—but he was worried on this occasion. Lynd tried to reassure Fackenthal and sympathized with his concern about possible "political repercussions" from the "gathering of data on controversial issues," but he also supported the legitimacy of social scientists studying national elections. He noted that he found Lazarsfeld's commentary judicious almost to a fault, even colorless, in its resolute effort to be neutral.[26]

Some Official Links to Columbia: 1944–45

In the wake of these concerns about the Bureau, the sociology department went into action in November 1944 to show its support and responsibility for the Bureau and to stave off what was feared would be direct control by the administration. First, it reshaped a new governing committee, giving it closer ties to Columbia's sociology department.[27] The governing committee then wrote a new set of policies which, among other things, clarified officially the limitations on clients' proprietary rights. Scientific values were to hold sway over all commercial purposes, and the university was to be the sole judge of which was which. In this set of actions, Lynd and the others tried to protect the Bureau's most vulnerable flank: the relationships to business interests that might conflict with the university's interests.[28]

The university administration, meanwhile, had organized an external review committee, chaired by Elliot A. Cheatham of the Law School, which delivered a report in May 1945. Up until this point, as the Cheatham committee discovered, there had been nothing in writing to authorize the existence of the Bureau, and it had "acted with great informality in its undertakings with sponsors and others."[29] Henceforth, the committee recommended, the Bureau was to get it in writing, especially in binding clients to university policies; the governing committee was to oversee the Bureau's research policies and contracts; and the bursar was to control its finances.[30] The committee left to the director himself most personnel matters. By this time the Bureau already involved more than thirty-five individuals, many of them part-time: Lazarsfeld and Merton, a half dozen research assistants, another half dozen clericals, and twenty-three graduate students who had been averaging just under half time.[31]

The Cheatham committee supported the Bureau. It found this statement of the Bureau's objectives consonant with university purposes and guidelines:

1. Training of students in research techniques
2. The theoretical integration of empirical social research
3. The development of an institutional pattern for a social science laboratory

4. The collection of sociological data
5. Research in specific subject matters[32]

The committee recognized the values of methodological inquiries—a Lazarsfeldian position if ever there was one. It recommended better quarters, and it duly noted Lazarsfeld's own estimate that the Bureau's student training was a "contribution" to the university of approximately $20,000. Most important, it explicitly supported university funding for research organizations:

> The Committee believes that a research agency should have some measure of financial support from the University itself [and] not be wholly dependent on the funds solicited from year to year outside the University . . . an agency should be privileged to create a reserve fund for future years.[33]

The university did not implement that crucial recommendation, leaving the Bureau with only the "environmental" support (housing, maintenance, grounds, accounting services), but it accepted the basic legitimation by the Cheatham report, which declared in effect that this mixture— of grants and contracts, small university subsidy, faculty direction, and adult and student employment—was an acceptable hybrid, if in need of some tidying up. The Bureau could be trusted to carry out social research in ways that would not embarrass or unduly obligate the university. The Cheatham report thus made possible the continued existence of the Bureau.

Financial Support: The Partial Advantage

For years after the Cheatham report, the Bureau continued to seek university funding. Lynd lobbied for it in 1945.[34] Lazarsfeld argued in 1946 that the Bureau needed about $20,000 to sustain its mere existence, quite apart from the actual work load of research.[35] In that year, there was still a deficit to the university—a smaller one than the previous year's, as the Bureau noted optimistically—and the bursar wrote Lazarsfeld that "either the general expenses are too high or . . . you are not including in your estimates a large enough cushion for these general overhead expenses [or both]."[36] By 1950, the Bureau was in debt, according to university bookkeeping, by over $18,000. However, the Bureau had by this year obtained new contracts, and the financial issue had changed.

In 1949 and 1950, the Bureau had embarked on some large federal projects that paid administrative overhead costs. Kingsley Davis, who had been at Princeton, came to the Bureau as its director in 1948, and he brought in a large contract with the air force for the study of major cities of the world. In 1949, the Bureau undertook studies in the Near East for the Voice of America. Government work, which had represented only small proportions of Bureau income, now jumped swiftly to 36 percent and then to 75 percent of the overall budget, which in 1950–51 soared to a new high of $380,000.[37]

With sums of this sort, the Bureau could indeed begin to build a reserve fund, and in fact it had accumulated a surplus of approximately $30,000. It tried to negotiate an understanding with the university that there had always been an implicit policy that the Bureau would *keep* its overhead. In a report of March 1951, the Bureau invoked this "tradition":

> This difficulty is of recent origin and stems primarily from the fact that no decision has been reached regarding the disposition of overhead on contracts which the Bureau holds with several agencies of the Federal Government. Any allocation of this overhead other than to the Bureau's account will, of course, represent a deviation from the established policy.[38]

There was some logic to this, for the Bureau *had* been keeping its profits, in principle—it was just that there had not been any. But the argument did not wash. The university called in its chits, settled the Bureau's debt, claimed all the overhead, and put the Bureau on the university budget. The Bureau's letter to Vice President Grayson L. Kirk insisted to the last that there had been a policy change. But for this change, it argued,

> the Bureau would now be in a position both to retire its deficit of $18,316.35 and to have an uncommitted fund of $11,870.47 earmarked for basic research on problems for which other funds are not available.[39]

The new financial arrangements of 1951 offered the gain of some recognition and legitimacy within the university, but the Bureau still did not have reserves to develop new research projects and to keep body and soul together *between* projects. The Bureau was given the kind of budgetary burden of any university department, that of making a new case each year to the central administration for funds, but this was also a special burden because the Bureau had to *earn* that budget from its research contracts and grants. As Bureau people saw it, when they went in the red, they owed the university; when they stayed in the black, they *also* owed the university, because they had to turn the surplus back.[40] University administrators in general at this time saw it all quite differently, of course: every overhead penny they could get was not enough to balance the books of *their* administrative costs. (See chapter eight.)

From the Bureau's vantage point, 1951 was the year in which the university started making a profit from the Bureau. From then on, Bureau bookkeeping carefully showed not only the indirect cost allowances paid over to the university but the "net amount accruing" to the university—overhead funds paid by the Bureau minus whatever university funds were paid to the Bureau, a net amount that was always positive: from 1951 to 1960 it ranged from $7,000 to $70,000.[41] Bureau hands continued to feel that they paid dearly for being incorporated into the university system.

Growth and Constraints

Over the decade of 1951–60, the cash contribution of the university averaged only 7 percent of the Bureau's income, but the Bureau grew substantially in money, staff, and research productivity, nonetheless. When Lazarsfeld himself was director (1940–48), he was an indefatigable and ingenious money raiser, going out on the stump to business and foundations to "advertise" the Bureau—and digging into his own pocket when need be to piece out a project or pay a student's salary.[42] After he no longer functioned officially as director, he continued to raise substantial foundation grants and commercial contracts. His successors as director (Kingsley Davis [1948–51], Charles Y. Glock [1951–57], David L. Sills [1957–59], and Bernard Berelson [1960–61], who were aided late in the 1950s by the gifted administrator Clara Shapiro) managed to keep the budgetary balls in the air and to keep Bureau income rising, from approximately $100,000 to $600,000, with an average annual budget in the 1950s of close to a half million dollars.[43]

Staff expanded in similar fashion. The Bureau's report of 1960–61 lists 135 different names as staff members: 9 members of the directorial committee (mostly faculty), 45 senior staff, 39 research assistants and other research help, and 42 administrative and technical staff.[44] How many were employed at the same time and what their number represented in terms of full-time equivalents is not clear, but Barton estimates that soon after (in 1962), the Bureau involved about 100 individuals.[45] Publications and participation rose accordingly. In the first decade of the

Bureau, for example, 36 different individuals at the Bureau published articles—32 staff members and 4 faculty members (Cantril, Lazarsfeld, Merton, and C. Wright Mills). In the second decade, the comparable figures rose to 54 staff members and 10 faculty members. Over the period 1943–60, 35 dissertations were completed at the Bureau.[46]

While its projects provided valuable research vehicles for faculty members and rich research experience for sociologists in training, the Bureau could not offer its nonfaculty staff a professional career ladder. In the 1950s, the new role of "research associate" conferred security at the Bureau, but it was not really analogous to faculty standing. In this era, Bureau staffers could not act as official principal investigators of their own research projects without the collaboration of a faculty member.[47]

Could the Bureau principals have gathered more political support from central administrators, from the faculty, from the Department of Sociology? To consider such a question, we need more documentation from *all* sides than I have been able to gather. I can offer only some interesting recollections and interpretations by some principal witnesses within the Bureau.

In Merton's view of these years, there were two enduring policy obstacles to security for Bureau staff members. One, at the level of the administration, was the clear policy against conferring faculty status on researchers who were being financed by "soft" money. This was not just a matter of the Bureau. There were much bigger stakes involved in other institutes affiliated with Columbia, especially those in the physical sciences, with far larger budgets and staffs. Merton recalls that Lazarsfeld and he never really abandoned their efforts to change that policy, but he judges in retrospect that it was a hopeless endeavor. Had tenured research appointments been made available across the board, the financial burden would have been unbearable for the university.[48]

Could the Bureau have rounded up political support for empirical research from the wider faculty? Was the new administrative structure of 1951 an opportunity? In that year, the old four-man governing committee of sociologists was enlarged by another eight professors from other disciplines on campus (statistics, economics, psychology, international affairs, etc.). In principle, these arrangements were supposed to link the operations of the Bureau to an interdisciplinary network of Columbia scholars. In fact, the new board of governors remained largely on the periphery, detached from direct involvement in the Bureau itself.[49]

Sheridan, who was an administrator of the Bureau in the 1970s, concludes in her recent dissertation that by failing to involve board members more closely in its actual research program, the Bureau missed a chance to broaden its political base.[50] Barton, who was on the Bureau's staff from the 1940s and was its director in later years (1962–77), thinks that the opportunity was illusory. Engaging most board members in the work of the Bureau was virtually impossible in his view, because interest in empirical research was simply not widely enough shared among other social scientists at Columbia.[51]

What of the departmental level? For most of the staff who had major research roles at the Bureau, there was little prospect of becoming tenured in the Department of Sociology. The department was wary of the "laboratory" tail wagging the departmental dog—there were so many Bureau people—and it was concerned with maintaining a balance between the interests of quantitative researchers and sociological theorists. As Barton has noted, departmental personnel decisions are not commonly made to sustain the programs or personnel of research organizations[52]—and they were not made for this purpose at Columbia in this era, despite Merton's and Lazarsfeld's prominence in the department.

What of Lazarsfeld and Merton themselves? As Merton recalls his own views of this period, he "thought small" about the Bureau, feeling comfortable in his own work with projects utilizing one or two research assistants or a small group.[53] Lazarsfeld seems to have thought about the Bureau in more expansive terms—especially in two projects that we shall consider in the next section of this chapter—and was more missionary about the importance of the Bureau and empirical research. It seems, however, that Lazarsfeld's own hopes and frustrations made him at least occasionally impatient and resentful in public about the administration's failure to support the Bureau. In his speech at the celebration of the Bureau's twentieth anniversary in 1957, Lazarsfeld rejoiced that the Bureau had prevailed, but he stressed that it was not thanks to the likes of Jacques Barzun, eminent humanist, scholar of the arts, *and* Columbia administrator—then dean of the graduate faculties (1955–58) and later provost (1958–67).[54]

More extensive research into university archives and professional papers is necessary to trace the negotiations between Bureau scholars and central administrators. From my incomplete gleanings, I draw only three tentative conclusions. The Bureau achieved eminence *in spite of* Columbia administrators and other scholars by the force and diffusion of its publications and graduates. At high administrative levels the Columbia environment was a formidable one—not an easy place in which to create an organization for empirical social science. Bureau principals probably did not bring to university politics the same time, interest, and brilliance that they brought to their intellectual work.

The Institutional Context of the Intellectual Product

Early Aspirations for the Bureau

A NATIONAL CAPACITY

During these early years, Lazarsfeld tried to redesign the Bureau in two different ways: he sought a technical capacity for work of national scope and a professional school in social research. He pursued the first in the late 1940s by trying to incorporate NORC into the Bureau. Upon the death of founder-director Harry Field in 1946, NORC officials considered leaving the University of Denver and locating at another university. Lazarsfeld was one of seven social scientists who tried to attract NORC to his campus. A merger of the Bureau and NORC would offer mutual advantages, he wrote:

> Without wanting to sound boastful, we feel that our Bureau has been leading in a number of methodological advances. But we never had an opportunity to do steady large scale work because of a lack of a field staff. We frankly have felt that NORC in the past has missed some analytical opportunities. Many of the studies they have published were straight tabulations, and we felt that with our methodological tradition, we could have improved some of the publications. . . . This whole question of optimum balance between a polling and other techniques would really be the intellectual purpose of a NORC combination.[55]

Negotations between the Bureau and NORC apparently did not progress further, and for various reasons NORC relocated at the University of Chicago. (See chapter ten.)

By the mid-1950s, if not earlier, it became a part of Bureau culture that *not* having a national field staff was a distinct intellectual advantage, and according to Glock and Barton, Lazarsfeld shared that perspective.[56] The national component of the polls, NORC, and SRC came to provide a negative reference point as leading to descriptive work of no particular analytic interest. McPhee expressed the viewpoint in a Bureau memo, probably written in 1956:

Consider [why it is that the Bureau maintains] no national interviewing staff? Because we really aren't in the descriptive business. Which is to say, we don't really do the same sort of thing that NORC and Michigan do, even though we do use interviews a good deal. What we try to avoid, everyone would agree, is solely or chiefly a "static" kind of descriptive research, e.g., telling the state of opinion today on X topic.[57]

There was also the feeling at the Bureau that a standing field staff (and other permanent departments, such as sampling, coding, etc.) risked bureaucratic routinization, threatening to chop research into component operations and to take the life and insight out of it.[58] By the late 1950s this set of advantages was a leading, though not unanimous, view at the Bureau of its own strengths and of the reciprocal weaknesses of both NORC and SRC.[59] In any case, the overtures to NORC in the 1940s appear to have been Lazarsfeld's only concerted effort to develop a national capacity for the Bureau.

That capacity at NORC and SRC was a financial charge to maintain *and* an intellectual resource to develop, both constraining and focusing national survey programs at the two organizations. The Bureau was neither constrained nor focused to create national data sets, and instead it led the way in inventive and innovative designs in local communities and organizations, trying to capture the force of social interaction and a social context. All three organizations pursued the virtues of their own structural "necessities," generating projects and ideas within the frameworks of their specific technical capacities.

A PROFESSIONAL SCHOOL IN SOCIAL RESEARCH

Lazarsfeld's interest in a national field staff was apparently short-lived, but his hope to create a professional school for social scientists was a more enduring (apparently lifelong) ambition. In 1950, he and Merton wrote a "Proposal to Establish an Institute for Training in Social Research," in which a new institute and the ongoing Bureau were to complement each other. With cadres of advanced graduate students, postdoctoral students, practicing professionals, and adjunct and core professors, the institute would incorporate some of the key features of professional training in medicine, law, and business. The Bureau would provide the institute with live research projects and case materials as it obtained new foundation support and reduced the proportion of short-term commercial contracts.[60]

The professional school did not come to pass. Columbia did not want to support it, and the Ford Foundation money that Lazarsfeld hoped to attract went into, among other things, the Center for the Advanced Study of the Behavioral Sciences, established at Stanford in 1954. Both Lazarsfeld and Merton participated in the early planning for the center, but it adopted a very different approach of granting one-year fellowships to already established scholars. Lazarsfeld spent an unhappy year in the first "class" at the center, trying to convince other Fellows that this individualistic approach to development in the social sciences was a mistake.[61]

One key feature of the professional institute proposal was, however, salvaged: the Ford Foundation made a substantial grant to the Bureau of $60,000 for a project called the Planning Program in Advanced Training (PPAT), for codifying case materials, and the Rockefeller Foundation matched the funds.[62] The PPAT funds were used for seminars, a variety of research projects, publications, and for two major books in advanced training: Lazarsfeld and Rosenberg's *The Language of Social Research* and Hyman's *Survey Design and Analysis*, both published in 1955.[63] The former brought together a wide variety of articles by Bureau authors and others on analytic concepts and operations—for example, construction of indicators, classification, typologies, multivariate analysis, and trend and panel studies. Hyman's book, designed as a training text, included exercises, machine routines, and many examples. He focused especially on seven contemporary surveys, such as Lazarsfeld and Field's radio study, the Strategic Bombing Surveys, the Kinsey Report, the *Authoritarian Personality*, Richard Centers's study of class consciousness, and others.

Without any basic change in structure, the staff and the budget of the Bureau grew substantially in the 1940s and 1950s, through the force of Lazarsfeld's own fund-raising genius from the beginning and through the projects organized by later directors and staff. Without the standing departments of field, coding, and sampling, the Bureau had to organize these services anew for each study, employing students when possible or contracting for the field staffs of NORC, Roper, or other firms. There were recurring start-up costs to organizing work in this way, but there were also advantages for training when students were able to gain experience in all phases of a survey project.

The Multipurpose Shop: Opportunities and Limitations

LAZARSFELD'S LONG SHADOW

The Bureau of Applied Social Research had not been fashioned as a *survey* research center, as NORC and SRC/ISR both had been from the beginning, but it evolved from its radio research beginnings into a broad-scope research laboratory in sociology. A concentration on survey methods developed at the Bureau because Lazarsfeld used them in his early research and continued them with flair and high purpose in the 1940s and 1950s. After the late 1950s, he pursued some of his many other interests in social science, none of them entirely unrelated to survey research—mathematical sociology, research organization, utilization of sociology, and history of quantification—but without publishing any more major original work in survey research itself.

While Lazarsfeld's interest in surveys was strong, that work thrived at the Bureau, for although Merton was a commanding influence on sociological theory and the sociology of science, Lazarsfeld's own work had greater impact on the development of surveys. In the recollections of various students who worked with him, Lazarsfeld was the "star center" of the Bureau's social structure. Sills has stressed the community that also developed among those in Lazarsfeld's entourage:

> We joked endlessly about his impossible work habits, his outrageous demands upon our time, his nearly impenetrable Viennese accent, his ever-present cigar, his comments during hurried conferences in taxi rides downtown, his making three appointments for lunch at the Faculty Club and keeping them all by skillful table hopping, and his ability to juggle a dozen projects and research assistants simultaneously. And we joked about his jokes, for Paul was a very funny man who reveled in life's absurdities. But we learned from him how to construct statistical tables from survey responses and how to use these tables to understand behavior.[64]

Coleman's reflections point to an interaction process that kept Lazarsfeld at the center. Because he had a voracious curiosity and a huge intellectual agenda, he was continually in search of people who would take up some part of it,

> people who, as extensions of himself, could take the problem and carry it further. Yet he continued *himself* to be occupied with the problem, with strong and definite ideas about *how* the problem should be solved. . . .

> This was his personal style—he could not stand to have a bright person, whether colleague or student, whom he respected, in the vicinity and yet not working on problems *he* saw as important.[65]

In Coleman's view, Lazarsfeld's style was not teaching of a conventional sort but "something strange and different . . . a medium of *personal influence*," akin to a "magnetic force" making for a "charged atmosphere," both attracting and repelling, keeping people in orbit around him.[66]

Some students thrived and bloomed in this atmosphere charged with Lazarsfeld's intellectual and personal magnetism. Caplovitz recalls that students wrote seminar papers with even a reverse snobbery about publication, considering the Bureau's own work and mission more important than communication with the larger professional community.[67] If Lazarsfeld came to your home, as his son-in-law Bernard Bailyn later recalled, the onslaught of telephone calls and wires would soon follow, meaning that students had picked up the scent.[68]

The Bureau was at once Lazarsfeld's pride, a special source of intellectual and personal stimulation—he felt that he himself absolutely required the presence of students and a research organization to function as a scholar—and a source of personal frustration, because he wanted so much more for it. He especially regretted losing gifted students, feeling that as soon as he got them trained, they were up and away on their own careers.[69]

THE GENERATION OF STUDENTS

As the Bureau grew in size and diversity, small groups of young scholars also embarked on work together which was stimulated by the senior members but not closely organized or supervised by them. Coleman noted in the late 1950s that certain "Young Turks" took heart from each other and dared to undertake work in concert that they would not have had the courage to do alone.[70] This was the period of Glock's directorship, one that Lazarsfeld himself came to think of as the Bureau's golden era.[71]

Like the "managerial scholar" that Lazarsfeld wrote about, Glock was a "working" scholar who conducted his own research into religion as well as a "worrying" scholar who was concerned about the overall Bureau agenda, trying to match people who could work together and get the reports out to sponsors and clients. During Glock's directorship, Coleman, Katz, and Menzel developed their studies in the diffusion of innovation. McPhee and Glaser set out on a study of the 1950 congressional election. Under Glock's overall coordination, Bureau staff members cooperated in a multinational study of the Near East, a study that was later made into a book by Lerner at MIT.[72]

Certain students developed their own strengths sufficiently during this period that they came to feel constrained by Lazarsfeld's personal and intellectual dominance. They accepted his problems but then wanted to strike off in new directions with them, and Lazarsfeld resisted. Bureau researchers such as Coleman, Glock, Rossi, and Lipset experienced the need to break away in order to create their own intellectual agendas.[73]

In later years, Bureau alumni from the 1950s, students and staff, spread Bureau influence into other universities and businesses, some in directors' roles. Rossi and Coleman, for example, settled at NORC for a time, and Rossi was the director there from 1960 to 1967. Robert T. Bower founded the Bureau of Social Science Research, Inc.; Hans Zetterberg and Natalie Rogoff both directed research organizations in Europe; Glock left the Bureau to direct a new Survey Research Center at the University of California, Berkeley. Sills became editor of the *International Encyclopedia of the Social Sciences*. The quantitative and analytic culture of the Bureau was disseminated by new practitioners.

THE BUREAU'S RESEARCH STYLE

Research of the Bureau in these early years yielded work of invention, not the kind of replication that we have seen in *The American Soldier*. Bureau researchers were actually at some pains to avoid overgeneralizing, and they offered appropriate caveats that the study in question was exploratory and was not intended to be "representative."[74] Underscoring that point, Bureau researchers did not use tests of statistical significance, not even when using a probability sample of a community. The avoidance of statistical tests was Bureau policy, as explained by Merton, Reader, and Kendall in 1957. They argued that in these early stages of scientific work, it was desirable to assemble a wide array of evidence, even if some of it was not conclusive, lest "possibly productive lines of investigation" be cut short (that is, by losing interesting leads). Later, as they wrote, hypotheses could be subjected to more rigorous tests.[75]

Some critics noted that Bureau authors might well have been guided rather than constrained by nonsignificant but interesting leads, and they could have *reported* tests of significance on their findings without throwing data or ideas away. Scholars such as James A. Davis and Daniel Katz pointed out that the difficulty with abandoning such tests was finding something to place in their stead other than researchers' own judgment of relevance and interest.[76]

For scholars who believed that scientific work must be built conservatively on cautious inferences and replication, the Bureau corpus of research was not a model. At the time, some reviewers took Bureau researchers to task for freewheeling interpretation rather than developing ideas systematically from theory. The balance of coverage in prominent journals in sociology, social psychology, and public opinion research was nevertheless appreciative.[77] The Bureau's survey work was a shower of ideas and techniques showing that surveys could be shaped in ways that market researchers and pollsters had probably never dreamed of—or in any case would never have had the time and training to carry out. The Bureau's contribution was to invention; to demand of it replication and rigor as well could seem almost ungracious.

Contributions to the Field

Good Examples: Ideas and Productivity

The Bureau's contributions to survey research were formative in three areas: one, theoretical ideas emerging from and undergirding survey analysis of quantitative data; two, enrichment of analytic methods; and three, social organization exemplified not only by the Bureau itself but by other vehicles for participation and publication of academic and commercial researchers. We shall consider each in turn.

The Bureau's pilot and community studies were exploratory forays in pursuit of interesting ideas in theory and method, often conceived as work to be tested later by broader inquiry. But there was visible intellectual continuity too. The pioneering voting studies, mounted on large Ns and cross-section samples of single communities, extended ideas originating in communication/radio studies, such as the self-selection of audiences and taste groupings by class. The unexpectedly widespread phenomenon of effective *non*involvement in the campaign process suggested ideas about the structure and process of influence as well as a theory of voter apathy as a factor in political stability.[78] The voting studies did not gather much data about the specific communities at hand, but they linked ideas about the media and the "background" characteristics of respondents. They developed, for instance, the "index of political predisposition" (formed of religion, SES, and urban/rural residence) as the best predictor of party vote; a theory of "cross-pressures" on voters with dissonant components in these social factors; the "limited effects" model of media influences; the "two-step flow of communication"; and the horizontal existence of "influentials" at a given class level. As Katz and Lazarsfeld wrote in 1955, studies that expected to find massive media effects contributed to the "rediscovery" of the small group and the "part played by people."[79]

Merton's study of "Locals and Cosmopolitans" was a strong strand in the same skein of ideas. This small pilot in 1943 was based on informal, intensive interviews with thirty of the "influentials" who had been named by eighty-six residents of a town given the pseudonym "Rovere." *Personal Influence* (1955), by Elihu Katz and Lazarsfeld, was based on research conducted in Decatur, Illinois, and was designed in part to follow up on some of the processes of influence suggested by both the Rovere study and the election study of 1940. Studies among medical doctors in four midwestern communities by Coleman, Katz, and Menzel extended the analysis of influence still further into the study of innovation and diffusion. *The Academic Mind*, a special national study of social science professors' reactions to the McCarthy period of anticommunism, explored the "contextual" processes of the influence on individuals of the dominant political climate of their colleges.[80] Bureau research from these years still bears fruit, especially in voting behavior, network analysis (now more feasible with computer designs), mass-media influence studies, and the lively debates and critiques of the Bureau's "limited-effects" model.[81]

In these years, the Bureau was very productive. It became highly visible to social scientists through its series of volumes published by the Free Press, its reprints in the influential Bobbs-Merrill series (which were used heavily in college courses), and its volume of published articles.[82] In the years of interest to us here, 1937–1960, the Bureau published fifty-two books, of which thirty dealt in some major way with survey research, either focused on primary or secondary analysis of survey data or on a discussion of survey methods. Bureau authors were also responsible for more than 350 articles, book chapters, and other publications. (See chapter eleven.) And still, much of the Bureau corpus existed in unpublished reports, monographs, and master's and doctoral dissertations.[83]

Beyond Polls: Reforging the Survey Instrument

In these early years, the Bureau conducted secondary analysis on existing poll data (see chapter four). It also labored to expand and enrich survey data in the design of questionnaires, causal analysis, and variables of social process. In each case, the Bureau work pushed and pulled and stretched the polling form—sometimes successfully, sometimes straining and overloading it, and finally illuminating some of the powers as well as some of the apparent limits of the survey instrument.

Neither sampling nor questionnaire design per se was a major explicit emphasis at the Bureau. With the exception of one important article on questionnaire design,[84] Lazarsfeld's own work on field practice dealt with relatively informal, unstructured interviewing. He did not participate in the debate about probability sampling. When that debate was flourishing, the Bureau drew its sample for a 1945 study (which became *Personal Influence*) "according to usual probability methods" and deemed that "nothing special need be said about it."[85] Significantly, in their major book on methodology, *The Language of Social Research*, Lazarsfeld and Rosenberg eliminated material bearing on sampling, questionnaire construction, and other topics for which they felt a standardized literature already existed. They concentrated on "the analysis of material which has been properly collected"—examples and principles of research design, classification, index construction, and data analysis.[86]

In practice, however, Bureau studies tried to enrich poll questionnaires by using auxiliary data sets such as census information, content analysis of the media, observation and records of the community, and interviews with special subgroups *and* by trying new designs of the basic questionnaire itself. Two different such designs are of interest, not because they wholly succeeded but because they illuminate some of the virtues of "compromise" in more successful Bureau questionnaires.

QUESTIONNAIRES

Poll data in parallel. One such technique involved using poll data to complement intensive interviews. In this design, large-sample poll data were used as the quantitative parallel for smaller collections of qualitative data gathered by the Bureau. The book *Mass Persuasion* (1946) by Merton, Fiske, and Curtis is one example of the use of this technique.[87] (See also chapter seven.) A commercial firm interviewed a sample of nearly 1,000 respondents with a questionnaire presenting about fifteen questions of this sort:

> 5. If you had to describe Kate Smith, which one of these would you choose? She is: (which one of these would be your last choice?)
> Very patriotic
> All out to help others
> An entertainer
> A motherly kind of person
> Able to give advice and things to think about
> An average American woman

This questionnaire was designed to check hypotheses developed from interviews with 100 informants who had listened to Kate Smith's radio marathon, 75 of whom had telephoned in pledges. These intensive interviews, lasting some three to four hours, were conducted by the Bureau with an "interview guide" of topics such as these:

> 24. Were your feelings about [Kate Smith] when she was broadcasting about bond-buying any different from your usual opinion of her? In what way? Why did they change?[88]

The interpretation of the book was based much more heavily on the intensive interviewing than on the poll data (which were presented in just a few tables) or on a real integration of the two.

Sills's study in the 1950s of the National Foundation for Infantile Paralysis, *The Volunteers: Means and Ends in a National Organization*, was another variant on the Bureau's use of intensive interviews and extensive poll data in tandem. In an "intensive" interview, 234 of the foundation's volunteers were asked to reconstruct their individual goals and motivations as well as the immediate "trigger events" that brought them into the work of the foundation. Sills used Gallup Poll data on foundation volunteers (N = 520) primarily in order to provide quantitative comparisons with the more intensive research conducted by the Bureau.[89] The parallel tracks of poll and intensive interviews are clearer in *Mass Persuasion*, but the two books are alike in that most of the interpretation in each is based on qualitative insights and quotations from selected intensive interviews.

Unstructured interviews in mass publics. Another strategy practiced at the Bureau tried to *fuse* structured and unstructured techniques in the same questionnaire in an effort to apply the "art of asking why" to large samples. In the 1940 voting-study questionnaire, many questions were fully specified in the poll and attitude-measurement tradition of exact wording, and certain questions were repeated in a "panel" design so that analysts could track changes in respondents over the course of the campaign. But when interviewers discovered that a respondent had changed any political opinions, they too were to find out *why* with questions of their own devising. An "accounting scheme" set forth some major variables. Were respondents being "pushed away" from one candidate or "pulled toward" another? What information channels and events led to the change? And so on. A "graphic device" quite like a flowchart was drawn up to help interviewers understand how to proceed in gathering complete answers.[90]

In 1955, Lazarsfeld and Rosenberg included these instructions by Gaudet in *The Language of Social Research* as a chapter entitled "A Model for Assessing Changes in Voting Intention," to "show how the general ideas of action-analysis are applied to a concrete study and can be adapted to use by an average field interviewer."[91] What we know of the experience suggests that these ideas were *not* in fact very adaptable for the average field interviewer. The results from Gaudet's large pretest results were cautionary—only 7 percent of 632 responses were found to be complete[92]—and Rossi later wrote that because interviewers were not skillful enough to follow the elaborate instructions, the analysis of the reasons for change ("action-analysis") could not be undertaken.[93]

The "fusion" strategy also underlay the Bureau's exploratory surveys in the Near East for the Voice of America. The scope of this study is in marked contrast to another leading international venture of the era, the UNESCO "international tensions" project of 1947, which was a direct application of the standardized polling interview, conducted in about fifteen to twenty minutes, lending itself to simple tabulation of the results.[94] The Bureau studies were methodologically and analytically far more ambitious. The master questionnaire, which Lazarsfeld and Merton helped to design, was some 240 questions long, with substantial numbers of open-ended questions. Some required a good deal of information and imaginative projection:

> 42. If you were put in charge of a radio station, what kinds of programs would you like to put on? (*Probe here.*)

> 97a. How do you feel about the behavior of Russia in world affairs? How about its behavior towards our country? (*Probe also for changes.*) How long have you felt that way?

> 102. Suppose that you were made head of the government. What are some of the things you would do? (*If no answer, say:*) Many people have difficulty trying to answer this question. Why do you suppose that is?[95]

The questionnaire was translated for use in the six countries of the study (Turkey, Syria, Lebanon, Egypt, Iran, and Jordan), in each of which local interviewers gathered some 200 to 300 usable interviews. The interview ran from some one to six hours and went beyond the literal wording of questions in follow-up improvisations and explorations.

This was rough terrain for survey work. Working in the field was an "eighteen-hour-day and seven-day-week job," as Glock (overall coordinator of the project) wrote appreciatively of the Bureau supervisors' on-site work. Iraq posed such formidable field obstacles, in fact, that it was abandoned in favor of a study in Iran.[96] Analytic comparison across these countries was severely constrained by such variable field conditions as well as by melding of elite and mass interviewing techniques.

Two kinds of publications resulted from the studies. A book of some cross-national scope by Daniel Lerner, *The Passing of Traditional Society: Modernizing the Middle East* (1958), used opinion holding itself as a key variable in a psychological theory of the "modernizing" personality.[97] Lerner used the survey data as much in illustration as in thoroughgoing quantitative data analysis, however, calling upon historical analysis, high journalism, literary imagination, and judicious selection of interview quotes. The other publications were articles written by Bureau staff members—Ringer and Sills, Kendall—and based on national data. These articles did not capitalize on the cross-national design.[98]

Both the Bureau/MIT and the UNESCO studies were important stages in the American development of cross-cultural survey work, an expansion of survey research that we shall consider again in chapter twelve. But both were limited technically. The Bureau studies dared much more than the UNESCO project, as they tried to go beyond polling simplicities to exploratory interviewing and analytic complexities, but the largely unstructured interviewing could not support much comparative analysis.

The compromise questionnaires. The Bureau's efforts did not fully bridge the qualitative-quantitative divide. Nor did anyone else's efforts in this era. The breach would seem to be formidable still, in fact, as investigators in the 1980s continue to face the cost-benefit calculus of learning a lot "in depth" about a small group of people or learning much less "off the top" from a large one. In this context of such trade-offs, one can appreciate the sensible and artful compromise that various Bureau questionnaires represented at the time.

The compromises reduced the freedom and responsibility of the interviewer's "art" by increasing the share of fully standardized questions. The questionnaires used for *Union Democracy*, *The Academic Mind*, and other studies show these compromises, but the study of the 1948 election, *Voting*, provides an especially good example because of its contrast to the 1940 election study. In 1948, in the fourth questionnaire wave after the election, interviewers were no longer asked to devise their own questions to track the reasons for change, as they had been in the 1940 study. They were given, instead, specific questions to ask respondents, such as these:

8. Did anyone in your family or any of your friends change their minds about how to vote in the last week or so before the election? (Yes/no)

10a. A few weeks ago you were leaning toward ——, yet you actually voted for ——. What made you change your mind? (Open-ended)

13. Please tell me if any of these were particularly important in influencing you to make up your mind that way. (Card of thirteen items: radio broadcast, articles in newspaper, somebody I talked with, etc.)[99]

And so on, through a series of just over twenty questions, which were a mix of mostly closed questions and a few (four) fully open questions. The questionnaires in the other waves of the 1948 study incorporated a wide range of subjects (e.g., reactions to the candidates, the parties, the issues, contact with media, interest in politics, and discussion with friends and family). They were longer, conceptually richer, and more complex than polling questionnaires, but they were structured enough to be administered by interviewers who were not social scientists.

BEYOND "ATOMISM": VARIABLES OF
SOCIAL CONTEXT AND PROCESS

In another major approach to research design and analysis, Bureau researchers tried to go beyond the psychological "atomism" of the individual unit of analysis to the study of group context and process. It was this concern that led to such ventures as the snowball sample of *Personal Influence*, the sociometric design of the drug studies, and the "contextual" design of *The Academic Mind*.

The first, a complex and difficult project conducted in Decatur, Illinois, in 1945, was a dogged effort by the Bureau to wrest social theory from market research. Because of administrative problems and the intricacies of fieldwork, sampling, and analysis, ten years intervened before *Personal Influence* was published, but it successfully extended some of the ideas of influence that evolved from *The People's Choice*.

Using a "snowball" sample, the Decatur study tried to trace the social process of individual decision making. A sample of 800 women were first asked about their decisions in four areas of daily life (public affairs, movies, fashion, and household marketing). They were then asked to identify which individuals, if any, had influenced these decisions, and whether they themselves had been "influential" in these matters. The process was hard to capture. Influence itself was difficult to codify, for there were not only the influenced and the influential but also people who sought advice and specifically rejected it and others who were influential without being aware of it. Such complexities meant that standardized interviewing procedures could not be maintained. It is a tribute to Katz and Lazarsfeld that these and other difficulties were delineated in the book's excellent appendix—an admirable instance of the "biography" of a research project, which Lazarsfeld urged his students to construct and which he himself used in seminars on research projects.[100]

Given these problems, the data used in the analysis had to be restricted largely to the "influentials" who were self-designated and then corroborated by follow-up interviews with the people they thought they had influenced. That the full design proved too intricate may well have been an instance of "overload": a demand for precision measurement from an instrument that could not—and perhaps cannot—be that finely tuned for a large sample. At least the Decatur study put a considerable burden on respondents to reconstruct in great detail decisions and reasons that could well have been trivial, ephemeral, or difficult to recall for other reasons.[101] Matters like this:

> During the last month or so, have you bought any new product or brand that you don't usually buy? (I don't mean something you had to buy because it was the only one available.) . . . (Q8)

> Have you recently changed your opinion about any important social or political issue . . . like what to do in Europe, how the government should handle any problem at home, or anything like that? (Q44)

The interviewer, equipped with copies of an earlier panel interview, could detect change even if the respondent did not report it and was to inquire into the reasons. Respondents could thus be asked questions of this sort about a decision that was presumably minor enough that they had forgotten to mention it:

> When we spoke to you in June, you were using (insert old brand). Now you are using (insert new brand). Why did you stop using (insert old brand)? (Q1)

> How did you happen to start using (insert new brand)? (Q2)

> Before you started to use (the new brand) were you satisfied or dissatisfied with any of the other brand(s) you were using? (Q6)

And so on, through some forty questions exploring the change of purchase.[102]

Personal Influence was nevertheless a seminal project from a conceptual standpoint, and it led to another important project, the so-called drug study. Here, a sociometric design was used to study influence processes. This study had the advantage of dealing with decisions of a larger "size."

The project, which was the work of Menzel, Katz, and Coleman, investigated the diffusion of a new prescription drug among the doctors of four communities in a personal and professional network. The study integrated a sociometric sample with the theory of the two-step flow of communication, which had dated from *The People's Choice*. The idea was now generalized beyond the specific effects of the mass media—it became the more general case of a flow of information from outside the community to circulation within it—and it illuminated the general proposition and some of the processes of diffusion within a medical community. The drug study has been cited by Everett M. Rogers as one of the most important and influential diffusion studies.[103]

Why Families Move was another exploration of context, as individuals' plans and reasons for residential moving were examined in the context of the community *rate* of mobility. The community variable proved much less powerful than the individual data, but this was a finding of interest. *Union Democracy* was more successful in finding group properties (such as the size of the group, its isolation, and the off-duty social contacts of its members) that were predictors of individual attitudes.[104]

The adaptation of "contextual" design to *The Academic Mind* was another effort to incorporate variables of social structure. It was ambitious in its use of a national sample of college professors and successful in its isolation of group variables with predictive power. First, the sample stratified the academic community by measures of school size, which provided differing social contexts in a general way, and then the study generated other variables of group context (such as the rate of civil liberties incidents on campus) within which to explore the individual attitudes of apprehension. This design successfully integrated variables of group structure with individual interviews of the mass survey.[105]

These new ventures in survey design were never quite as "sociological" as some Bureau researchers had hoped.[106] *Voting*, for instance, obtained a sociological measure of the influence of friends by asking respondents about the political views of close friends without consulting those friends themselves. This was a far simpler approach to sociometry and group context than those we have mentioned—a step down in elegance and complexity, but a reasonable step in feasibility for mass survey design. And the fact probably bespeaks some of the practical limitations of surveys based on individual self-report, which are commonly vulnerable to the fallibility of individual memory, the manifold variety of social inter-actions, and the prodigious expense of sociometric designs on a mass basis. The Bureau designs nevertheless added richness and power to poll/survey design. They structured the interview of individual self-report within a more complex sampling and questioning framework, in ways that successfully revealed properties of the individual's interper-sonal and social environment.[107]

BEYOND DESCRIPTION: RESEARCH DESIGNS FOR CAUSAL ANALYSIS

Lazarsfeld took two approaches to causal inference: "reason analysis," an intuitive strategy to develop subjective materials, and "variable analy-sis," a logic of analysis to test causal relations objectively. These were not pure forms—Bureau studies sometimes mingled them in the same study—but they were distinguishable, and Lazarsfeld continued to set great store by both of them.

Reason analysis was an extension of the "art of asking why" from the Vienna days, and we have already seen a simple instance of it in the Gaudet memo for the 1940 election study. Respondents were expected to be insightful (as well as accurate) about the decisions and the influ-ences on them, and interviewers were to be capable of analyzing influ-ences in ways of which the respondents might not be aware. As Zeisel explained that process,

> Sometimes the very sequence of the interview will reveal something about the relevance of reasons: on issues which are discussed without embarrassment, the reason given first may be the most important one. On touchy issues the reverse might be true. An observer, or the analyst . . . may often do better in evaluating the relative importance of reasons than the actor himself.[108]

Lazarsfeld was not unaware, to be sure, that retrospective analysis posed problems. As he wrote in 1958,

> The shortcoming of this approach should not be overlooked. Skillful retro-spective interviewing can isolate the role of outside influences; but it cannot easily connect them with the dispositions and sentiments that prevailed at the time of the act. It is unlikely that a respondent can remember, or even know, that he followed a neighbor's advice because he reminded him of a person whom he trusted when he was a child. Thus, the retrospective reconstruction of an activity . . . will miss much of the "inner" elements of the process.[109]

He nevertheless retained his enthusiasm for reason analysis. He continued to advocate the practicality of such "qualitative" techniques in survey work, and on occasion he was rather dismissive of objections to it as representing narrow disciplinary boundaries of behavioral psychologists.[110]

Still, causal inference by the informal interviewing techniques of reason analysis probably remains of greater significance for a study of Lazarsfeld's own intellectual biography than for a history of survey research, for it did not have the formative impact on the field that the logical system of variable analysis did.

Variable analysis. Lazarsfeld's analytic penchant was for multivariate contingency tables based on attribute data. Far less often did he use techniques for continuous variables. While in fact he *created* much data at the ordinal level (in indices) which could have been adapted to the more quantitative techniques, he often resimplified the index into grosser categories (e.g., High/Low) and examined percentage differences rather than capitalizing on the ordinal property. Lazarsfeld felt that the analysis of attribute variables formalized by Yule had been rather neglected in recent years, eclipsed by the attention to Pearsonian correlation, regression, factor analysis, and other quantitative analysis.[111] Analysis of categorical data was a Lazarsfeld hallmark, and within it he labored to make survey data yield up causal relationships through his elaboration formula for successive testing of relationships.

Lazarsfeld and others at the Bureau disseminated simple, powerful procedures in data analysis as well as more complex ideas. Zeisel's book *Say It with Figures*, for example, a Bureau publication that appeared in 1947 and went through many editions, started with rules and conventions for how to design and read a table using percentages—"a statistic that has become so common that few authors considered it worthy of detailed treatment"[112] but which surely needed explication, a distinct service to students as well as to social scientists who had no analytic training or practice.

"Deviant case analysis" was another useful step. In a fourfold table, Kendall and Wolf advised, one should not only observe the pleasing cases along the diagonal that established a relationship of some strength or another but should also note the off-diagonal, or "deviant" cases, that diluted it. What was going on with those people? Reading the actual interviews of these deviant cases might well provide some hunches, and "deviant case analysis" was in essence the prescription that one should go back to the interviews in the hope of finding clues in order to construct and test other variables[113]—a way of starting to think analytically. And it was characteristic of the Bureau that one started with data—a table or a relationship rather than Grand Theory—to search for ways to refine the variables at hand or to conceptualize some new ones. Lazarsfeld also continued to stress the construction of indices that would capture the force of complex variables. (See also chapter four.)

What Lazarsfeld called "elaboration" was the most systematic approach to attribute data analysis, a model for approximating in survey analysis some procedures of controlled experiment. He introduced the germ of the model in 1946 in a paper to the American Sociological Association, and he and Kendall expanded it in a seminal article of 1950, which used examples from *The American Soldier*.[114] Elaboration was a procedure for "decomposing" an observed relationship between two variables by introducing a third, "test" variable (related to both the presumed causal variable, X, and the presumed effect, Y) and observing what happened to the original relationship.

Lazarsfeld's logic distinguished three basic kinds of elaboration procedures. In the first, a check for *spurious* causality (or "explanation"), there was no meaningful connection between two apparently related variables; they were linked by sheer accident because of their connections to another variable. Some vivid examples made the point. One was the observed relationship in Sweden between the number of storks and the number of children born in the area, with the inference in favor of the storks. Another was the conclusion that firemen were incendiaries because the more of them there were at a fire, the greater the damage. In both illustrations, the observed relationship could be reduced to zero by a third variable, which was associated with both the purported cause and effect (the abundance of both storks and babies, which was found only in rural areas; the proliferation of firemen and damage costs together only when the fire was a particularly large one). In both examples, the test factor was antecedent in time and was the cause of both the X and Y variables.

In contrast, the second type of elaboration procedure, *interpretation*, enabled the analyst to show meaningful links when the test factor was a variable intervening between the purported cause and the effect. An example from the housing study by Merton et al. makes the point. A relationship was observed between the race of respondents and their anticipation of conflict, with whites found to be more likely than blacks to expect tension and conflict in a biracial housing project. When the test factor of prior experience with integrated housing was introduced, the observed difference in expectations by race was not wholly erased, but it was greatly attenuated.

In a third type, *specification* (or what would now be called *interaction*), the analytic interest was in identifying the conditions or contingencies under which an observed relationship held. The study of Puerto Rican immigrants by C. Wright Mills et al. provides a good example of this type. The authors observed a relationship between occupational mobility and sex: among Puerto Rican immigrants, the proportion of men moving up occupationally was found to be twice that of women. But this relationship proved to be limited in time. When the test factor of time of arrival was introduced and men and women were further categorized into "early arrivals" and "late arrivals," only men who had arrived early showed a relative advantage over women. Among the late arrivals, the mobility was much more even, with men showing in fact somewhat greater downward mobility.[115]

Lazarsfeld's elaboration formula was the basic model for the analysis of survey data during the years of interest to us here. It was used in the major substantive works by Bureau authors, and it was explicated in major texts on analysis published by the Bureau: the Lazarsfeld-Rosenberg reader, *The Language of Social Research*; Zeisel's simpler text, *Say It with Figures*; Hyman's more detailed treatment, *Survey Design and Analysis*; and, later, Rosenberg's *Logic of Survey Analysis*.[116] The formula was widely disseminated in practice. In the view of some expert observers, it may have been Lazarsfeld's most important contribution.[117]

Panel analysis. The panel design combined the Bureau's concern with quantitative analysis and dynamic process. This was a stronger model than reason analysis, because in it change was observed by repeated measurements of the same respondents over time rather than reconstructed on the spot by the respondent or the interviewer. A major technical monograph on the panel which Lazarsfeld undertook in 1947 for SSRC did not materialize, but he, Glock, and others at the Bureau continued to experiment with the form, to write of its possibilities and problems, and to use it in major work.[118]

The election study of 1940, conducted in Sandusky, Ohio, was the first major panel study ever conducted in the field—forerunner panels by Rice, Newcomb, and Murphy and Likert had been based on students (see chapter two)—and was also the most complex large-scale panel ever tried by the Bureau. Seven interviews were conducted in as many months, with "control" panels (who were not reinterviewed) serving as baseline measures. *The People's Choice* (subtitled *How the Voter Makes Up His*

Mind in a Presidential Campaign) assumed that many voters would come to their voting decision in the course of the campaign and that these decisions would be heavily influenced by the political parties' use of the mass media. Both assumptions proved frail.

First, a good half of the electorate in Sandusky were found to have made up their minds before the campaign even started. In the main panel of 600 respondents, tracked by the study throughout the campaign, only 54 were found to have shifted completely from one candidate to another. Second, it seemed that the media did not have the impact of face-to-face contacts. These negative findings were something of a disappointment, but they were of capital importance—and they were the genesis for alternative ideas, such as the limited-effects model of media influence with a two-step flow of communication from opinion leaders to people in their own stratum.[119]

As Rossi has pointed out, the initial assumptions of the 1940 study reflected a model of market research, with voter choice looking very like a consumer choice between alternative products.[120] Lazarsfeld and his colleagues learned from experience that many voters in fact had strong "brand loyalties" to one political party or another. *The People's Choice* made clear that the civic (or consumer) decision model was not the way voters went about making their choices:

> The real doubters—the open-minded voters who make a sincere attempt to weigh the issues and the candidates dispassionately for the good of the country as a whole—exist mainly in deferential campaign propaganda, in textbooks on civics, in the movies, and in the minds of some political idealists. In real life, they are few indeed.[121]

The doubters were in fact more often drifters than seekers. The best-informed voters tended to be the stalwarts who voted loyalty to a party. The chief function of party work, campaign literature, and media coverage was not conversion but the activation and reinforcement of latent predispositions toward one party or another. Lazarsfeld et al. used the image of an exposed photographic negative; the image was not influenced by a developer, but it did not appear until the developer brought it out.[122]

Before the analysis of the 1940 study had been completed, Lazarsfeld embarked on another panel, this time with a Gallup Poll conducted in December 1941, and reinterviews conducted in February 1942. Gaudet, who had worked with Lazarsfeld on the 1940 study, was not enthusiastic about the new panel and she reminded him of the trouble they had had in trying to patch together enough "change" data in Sandusky to sustain an analysis.[123] Lazarsfeld nevertheless convinced Elmo Wilson that the subject matter bore sufficiently on national morale that the OWI Surveys Division should take over the project, and another reinterview of the Gallup panel was conducted in June. But panel mortality was high— some 37 percent of the initial 1,171 had been lost—and quite as Gaudet had expected, there was much stability of opinion among the survivors. Wilson concluded that the work could no longer be justified as a contribution to the war effort, and nothing further seems to have come of this effort.[124]

Lazarsfeld's interest in panel design persisted, nevertheless, and it led to a panel study of the 1944 election study conducted by NORC;[125] to an SSRC committee project of 1945 to study the panel, on which Lazarsfeld was to take the lead; and to national panels at SRC, starting in 1948. It also led to continued work at the Bureau, where the form flourished in the 1940s and 1950s, ranging from two waves used in the 1945 Decatur study to the very ambitious design of the medical sociology project of Merton, Reader, and Kendall. In the last, self-administered questionnaires were distributed annually or better to medical students over a five-year period (1952–56), for an average of seven waves at each of three medical schools.[126]

The panel in the hands of Lazarsfeld and his associates was an instrument under design, with a modest ration of questions repeated over time. The 1940 study relied on retrospective as well as observed measures of change, as we have noted. Even in the 1948 study, as Rossi has pointed out, few questions were repeated at all, and over the four waves no question was ever repeated more than twice.[127] And, in fact, *Voting* remains in certain respects a spotty record of changes which were calculated now on one time period (June to August), now on another (August to October). But there were some good reasons for this at the time. The intervals between interviews were quite short, and the authors were chary that respondents would become irritated or suspicious if they were "asked the identical question several times on various waves," and they were therefore cautious about reinterview effect.[128] They were still tinkering with how many waves were feasible and how much repeat questioning there really should be. Bureau researchers valued panels not only as instruments to measure change, by asking the *same* questions, but also as a means of getting more information by asking *different* questions, too.[129]

TABLE 2

VOTE INTENTION AND LIKING FOR WILLKIE

Republican +/Democratic − Attitude toward Willkie	Second Interview (October)				Total
	+ +	+ −	− +	− −	
First interview (August)					
(+ +) Republican for Willkie	129	3	1	2	135
(+ −) Republican against Willkie	11	23	0	1	35
(− +) Democrat for Willkie	1	0	12	11	24
(− −) Democrat against Willkie	1	1	2	68	72
Total	142	27	15	82	266

Lazarsfeld's major instrument for panel analysis was the so-called sixteenfold table. Bureau authors used this example from the 1940 Sandusky study in a 1954 exposition of the analytic technique (see table 2).[130] Such a table condensed a great deal of information. From the marginals one could observe that most voters were "consistent" in August, with Republicans favoring their party's candidate (Willkie) and Democrats opposing him. By October, even more voters were consistent. Within the cells of the table, along the diagonal, one could locate the "stable" opinions, the great majority, who had not changed at all in the two-month period; in the off-diagonal cells, one could find the "shifters." One could see, too, which people had changed parties and which had changed candidates. For example, in August there were thirty-five Republicans who did not like Willkie; in October, twenty-three of them still did not like Willkie, but eleven had come around to their party's choice, while only one had gone over to the Democratic party.

The exact findings are, of course, not the point—although the stability of opinion itself and especially the durability of party loyalty were not at all obvious in 1940—for the analytic device is of greater interest here. Lazarsfeld was drawn to it by the polls' use of "trend" data (gross changes over time, appearing in successive polls using different samples), for he wanted to explore the specific changes and why they had come about. In the course of working with panel design, he made more elaborate use of it than for simple comparisons to trend data, in more complex applications of the sixteenfold table.[131]

Critics at the time noted that Lazarsfeld and his colleagues did not fully exploit either the panel design or variables of community context. But this view should not serve to obscure the Bureau's innovation and contribution in applying the panel design to survey measurement. From the beginning of his American career, Lazarsfeld saw the potential of the polls and was intent on broadening their explanatory scope through a broader swath of subjects, a richer depth of inquiry, and a greater sweep of time. And more than any other single academic scholar, Lazarsfeld was active in trying to show pollsters and scholars that they had common technical and professional ground.

Social-Intellectual Organization

The Bureau itself was the foremost organizational contribution of Lazarsfeld and his colleagues, but Bureau researchers, and Lazarsfeld in particular, also spurred the formation of survey research as a "field" in two other ways; by promoting professional organization and publication in AAPOR and *POQ*, and by acting as an intellectual envoy between Americans' polls and the European scholarly tradition.

Lazarsfeld came to the founding meeting of AAPOR in 1947, and thereafter played a leading role in the association in these early years (as president in 1949–50 and as a frequent participant in the annual meetings). He appeared on ten of the fifteen annual programs of 1946–1960, and his participation was matched only by Gallup, Roper, Hart, Elmo Wilson, and J. Stevens Stock.[132] Bureau staff members appeared on the AAPOR program fifty-eight times in the period from 1947 to 1960 (more often than the staff of NORC [forty-six] or SRC [thirty-two]). This figure actually minimizes Bureau influence somewhat, because it does not include the Bureau alumni in business and university positions who came to the meetings and participated in the programs.[133]

Bureau authors published more often in *POQ* than in any other single publication, with forty articles in all during this period, thirteen of which were by Lazarsfeld. Bureau scholars made of the journal and the association a special vehicle for their work, and they were in turn the strongest scholarly force in this confluence of commercial, governmental, and academic research.

Three *POQ* articles in particular show Lazarsfeld's second role and special mission as diplomatic-intellectual envoy. The first was the thirty-page "expository review" of *The American Soldier*, lauding its merger of theoretical ideas and quantitative evidence, which we have already considered in chapter seven. In a second classic article, Lazarsfeld called survey researchers to their scholarly responsibilities. This was his presidential address of 1950, "The Obligations of the 1950 Pollster to the 1984 Historian"—1984, because the historians in Orwell's novel helped thought police to *erase* the past. In it, Lazarsfeld urged pollsters to help create data that would illuminate the past, present, and future.[134]

What light surveys might have cast on history, Lazarsfeld contended. What if attitude surveys had been conducted in fifteenth-century Florence, for instance? Had Machiavelli's *The Prince* been misunderstood as the politics of connivance and manipulation because (as Macauley claimed) we had lost the Florentines' sense of politics as the exercise of ingenuity under limited options? When did Americans become convinced that schooling for the young should be provided at public expense? How could scholars know? And what of the present? Anthropologists were bandying about big ideas on the nature of American culture, in an intellectual dialogue that was "distinguished equally by brilliance and by irresponsibility" in its lack of factual evidence. As accustomed as pollsters were to "asking for a better definition of terms and for more precise evidence," they should bring data to the test of some of these interesting notions, in research across cultures and across times.[135] Lazarsfeld asked,

> Who among us, either in this country or abroad, has collected answers to questions like these: To what extent do young people make their own occupational choices and to what extent do their parents influence their decisions? In what countries and in what groups does a young suitor still ask the girl's parents for consent to marriage? How are conflicts between father and son resolved when they both want the car or both want to use the living room? Where do children still spend their holidays with their families, and where do they go off on their own?[136]

These were not unlike the questions both Lazarsfeld and Cantril had raised in the early 1930s, but there was a larger professional constituency to consider them now.

In a third article, Lazarsfeld endeavored to link "Public Opinion Research and the Classical Tradition."[137] There was much to separate them, he conceded, but the clash between modern empiricists and classical scholars was almost always productive too. New empirical tools could reveal new implications of the classics, which could in turn enrich the intellectual base of empirical inquiry with ideas which might otherwise have been overlooked, either because of preoccupation with the work of the day, or because empirical researchers are likely to be guided too much by what is a manageable topic at the moment, rather than by what is an important one.[138]

Drawing on the political theories of Dicey, Bryce, and Lowell on the one hand and on contemporary attitude/opinion data on the other, Lazarsfeld called for exploring the many possible connections between government decisions and public opinion in the exercise of an "empirical-classical synthesis."

Lazarsfeld's own survey research did not wholly exemplify that synthesis, because he was so fascinated with what were called "methods" at the Bureau—the logic and construction of designs and analysis. However, he himself moved comfortably back and forth: he brought a richer culture in the scholarly tradition than many of his empirical colleagues did, and he was immersed in quantitative research that was quite foreign to many humanistic scholars. In the breadth of his interests and culture, he could move in both worlds, displaying some kinship with both, and he could argue forcefully that each had much to learn from the other.

10

The National Opinion Research Center: From the Margins of Commercial Polling

If the war were to end tomorrow, the peace would still have to be won. The need for the Center, therefore, would, I believe, increase rather than decrease because of the need for the voice of the "common" man to be heard by those in authority.

Harry H. Field

Maybe we are just getting accommodated to living on a shoestring, or maybe we are just incorrigible optimists, but the future still looks bright and challenging to us.

Clyde W. Hart

Denver: 1941–1947

In the summer of 1941, Harry H. Field (1897–1946) established the National Opinion Research Center (NORC) at the University of Denver. Field was an experienced founder. He had been Gallup's envoy abroad to help establish the first affiliate, the British Institute of Public Opinion, as well as the French Gallup Poll. After six years in the Gallup enterprises, Field set off in 1939 to establish and direct his own polling organization, the People's Research Corporation (PRC).[1]

Detailed information about PRC is hard to come by, but a few features are clear from NORC records. It had a national interviewing staff; it was active during the 1940 presidential campaign; and from a final preelection national sample of 2,500 respondents, it forecast a Roosevelt victory within 2.3 percent of the returns.[2] It did not make this forecast public, however, because Field had agreed not to compete with his former employer, who was, after all, selling election forecasts in his syndicated column to newspapers.[3] From these experiences, Field went on to the design of NORC.

In 1939 or 1940, Field wrote a proposal for a public opinion foundation that would bring commercial and academic opinion researchers into closer communication. Academics, he felt, brought much knowledge from fine-grained, closely analyzed studies that were based on inadequate samples. Commercial pollsters, for their part, were almost awash in national data and years of practical experience, but because of pressure to get the results out, they did not have the time to examine their data in detail. Field's proposal was the germ of the idea that evolved into plans for a university research center.[4]

Field had not done academic research or administration, but he had had broad experience in other realms—not only as ambassador abroad and as a founder-administrator but also as an advertising and public relations man, an editor, and a writer. Born in England in 1897, Field served in combat in the First World War as a captain. After the war, he came to the United States, where he had a variety of jobs, from door-to-door selling to high-level administration in advertising. He also published the book *After Mother India*, which defended an exposé of child marriages and other practices in India. He is remembered by early NORC staff members as a gallant, charming man, with dash, high energy, and a strong conviction that opinion polling had great promise in the service of democracy and world peace.[5]

Why did Field go to Denver? The city was a long train trip (and an overnight plane trip) from the Eastern seaboard, where the other polls were clustered. And the University of Denver was not in the mainstream of social science: it had an enrollment of about 8,000 students, mostly undergraduate, and it did not grant a Ph.D.[6] It is not clear whether Field considered other locations, but Gallup and Cantril had counseled Field to go West: a geographic separation, they argued, would be good for the field. Field himself judged that if NORC were located at Princeton, it might never establish its own identity as distinct from the Gallup enterprises. In this organization, too, Field wanted to avoid competition with Gallup.

Gallup was also concerned about competition. When Field sounded him out about the project in 1940, Gallup suggested that instead of using a national sample, NORC might do better to select six "representative" communities in the nation and do enumerations of their populations. Field did not like the idea and wanted to get on with the organization of a national field staff. Later, in 1941, with Roper and Crossley concurring, Gallup suggested that NORC shift from the study of opinion to the study of behavior.[7] This is not to say that competition was Gallup's only concern; his suggestions doubtless represented genuine methodological interests as well.

There was also encouragement from Denver. The new chancellor at the University of Denver, Caleb F. Gates, had been in high administration at Princeton University. Field wrote that Gates was sympathetic to the idea of a noncommercial poll as an aid to democracy and was a force in the negotiations. Field was probably also acquainted with Ben M. Cherrington (they had mutual interests in organizing for world peace), who became chancellor at Denver in 1943.[8]

Field got an agreement from the (Marshall) Field Foundation (the two were not related) to back the new center for three years, with an annual grant of about $35,000. For a brief period in the fall of 1941, NORC had the status of a department in the university. At some point, Chancellor Gates supported giving NORC academic rank, with Field as full professor and his associates in corresponding positions, but Field was diffident: "My own feeling is that we should not be given any such professorial ranks until we have earned them."[9]

For reasons not clear from the official records, NORC was soon organized as an independent, nonprofit corporation, with the board of trustees and the NORC corporation constituted as two legal entities, with perfect overlap of membership.[10] Among its members were official representatives from the University of Denver, other Denver figures, and three "outside" social scientists: Cantril, Stouffer, and Gordon Allport, all of whom were active and interested board members throughout the Denver period.[11] NORC had the blessings of the university in the form of rent-free space, other support (such as a part-time librarian), and an annual cash grant of $5,000.[12]

The small NORC staff was recruited directly from the polling business. Douglas Williams, associate director, had been working most recently with Elmo Roper; William Salstrom, statistician, had been with Gallup before going to Cantril's OPOR; and Anne Schuetz (Zanes), field director, had been a Gallup interviewer. In January 1942, Paul Sheatsley was recruited from Gallup's Audience Research Institute to run a NORC branch office in New York, replacing John F. Maloney from Gallup (who went into the armed services).[13]

Major Purposes and Practice

Field's conception of NORC was complex, and it evolved somewhat during the course of the Denver experience. The center was to measure public opinion in the service of the public interest. It was also to provide expert service and data to others, to experiment in new methods, to monitor the results and techniques of others' polls, and to train a new generation of professionals in a developing science of public opinion measurement. This first purpose was sometimes a difficult goal to explain:

> To establish the first non-profit, non-commercial organization to measure public opinion in the United States. Through a national staff of trained investigators, representative cross-sections or samples of the entire population will be personally interviewed on questions of current importance.[14]

Was there a need for such an organization when Gallup and Roper were already measuring public opinion on so many subjects? Was this not a duplication of effort? Marshall Field continued to be somewhat unsure about this, and his doubt accounted in part for his reluctance to endow NORC on a longer-term basis.[15] NORC's own official announcement did sound quite like Gallup:

> In a democracy, the personal preferences and opinions of the electorate are a fundamental part of the governmental process. . . . By giving the electorate an opportunity to express itself in the intervals between elections, *opinion polls provide a new means of making voters articulate, which in turn should increase public knowledge and public interest in political, social and economic questions.*[16] (Italics in original)

Field's purposes were indeed broader than Gallup's conception of polling as a popular referendum, but in the Denver years there was a quest to specialize in issues and projects that Gallup did not already dominate. Field also had the continuing concern of not competing with Gallup from the sanctuary of a tax-exempt status.[17]

From the beginning, with its second purpose of public service, NORC intended to make a staff of public opinion experts available to legislators, government agencies, academics, and nonprofit organizations.[18] Field expected legislators to be eager for data on their constituents' views:

> For example, suppose the Senators and some members of the House from a certain state desired to know where a majority of their constituents stand on the many vital questions concerning America's relations to the present world crisis. For no more than the actual out-of-pocket expenses, the Center would work out a questionnaire and then submit it to a representative cross-section in the particular state and report the results.[19]

Field learned that congressmen tended to feel threatened by poll data on their districts, but other organizations and individuals were responsive and sought data from NORC, with some hoping to get it at little or no cost. Academics, in fact, tended to be thunderstruck at how expensive surveys were to undertake.[20]

The three additional goals that NORC set for itself—auditing polls, conducting research into methods, and providing graduate training—were all aimed at increasing the precision and power of public opinion polling. NORC meant to audit or monitor the work of other polls in order to enhance public confidence in their integrity (e.g., Who pays for the polls? What methods do the various polls use? How do these differ?).[21] In 1944, as we have seen, an audit of this kind was conducted into the Gallup Poll by the technical experts assembled by the congressional investigation, and it occasioned some fireworks and hard feelings. Even before that, Field had thought better of the audit plan: he concluded that NORC could reduce public skepticism and confusion about the polls more effectively by commenting privately on others' work.[22]

Field aspired to creating a university research center "to discover, test and perfect new methods, techniques and devices for ascertaining the status of public opinion."[23] Considering the limits on NORC's resources during the Denver days, it conducted research into polling methods with some vigor, and we shall consider it later in this chapter.

The educational aim, to create a graduate department in public opinion measurement, was not achieved, but a graduate program was.[24] Don Cahalan was added to the staff on a joint teaching/research appointment in the winter of 1945–46 to get a program started. Research assistants were engaged, and small research stipends were developed; at least two Ph.D. candidates came to use NORC data for their dissertations.[25] A program geared to the master's degree offered the supervision of theses using NORC and OPOR data, and the survey practicum called the Denver Community Survey, which later carried out the well-known Denver validity study.[26]

Because NORC-Denver lacked a large enough endowment to permit full exploration of all these purposes, as a matter of survival NORC had to specialize in contract work of providing data for other organizations. During the war, the federal government became a prime contractor of NORC data collection (especially the OWI Surveys Division headed by Elmo Wilson, which had no field staff of its own). NORC undertook a contract to do OWI Surveys' fieldwork, and it set up a branch office in New York in the same office building in which Wilson's group had its headquarters. The federal work supported NORC's national field staff and took up most of its time, about 90 percent, in fact, by 1943,[27] first in work for the OWI Surveys Division and later for OPA. NORC collected data for more than 160 studies dealing with public opinion on various phases of the American war effort: morale, inflation, minorities, defense plant absenteeism, rationing, victory gardens, scrap metal salvage, the relocation of the Japanese. (See also chapters five, six, and seven.)[28]

Field, in Denver, was especially concerned about the financial strains that the government work posed. NORC had to borrow in order to afford the work at all—the federal government did not pay until the work was completed—and financially it was a break-even matter at best. Documents of the period suggest that NORC was doing the government work at immediate cost, not covering its total institutional investment, and certainly not accumulating any funds for its own surveys or future growth.[29]

Field did not use the language contrasting basic and applied research which later became so familiar—he spoke of NORC's *own* work versus its *work for others*—but the conflict was essentially the same. Field saw surveys on major social issues as NORC's basic mission, from which he anticipated important social benefits in the long run, and he needed a greater endowment to make any headway. He made his own stand clear to the board when he declared in December 1943:

> *Personally, I am not really very interested in working for half the salary I made in the commercial world in order to try to make a non-profit organization self-supporting, especially as I feel that if ever NORC is self-supporting it will have defeated its own purposes.*[30] (Italics in original)

And he wrote to Marshall Field in the same period:

> If NORC has to go commercial to survive, it will become so engrossed in earning its way that the more altruistic aspects of its work are bound to fade, and its original purposes will be obscured.[31]

The immediate cause for Field's concern was the impending loss of Field Foundation funds. By initial agreement, this support was a three-year proposition, and it was to terminate in August 1944. NORC did succeed in getting continued support from the foundation (through 1950), but it also had to rely heavily on the contract, service work. NORC's total budgets in these war years varied around a mean of just over $100,000—1942–43 was the biggest volume year, with $134,000—and the contract work was not profitable enough to support many basic surveys.[32]

Institutional Fortunes

THE BASIC SURVEYS

Data analysis and interpretation did not thrive in the Denver years. NORC did not have the resources to mount many surveys of its own design, and when it did, it presented data in the demographic break-downs that were typical polling practice, only occasionally presenting other patterns or other cross-tabulations. The open codes of NORC in this period were quite simple, without the logical structure that created new variables, as Lazarsfeld had advised. NORC staff did not fine-tune its coding of open materials or design closed questions to enhance the prospect of more complex analysis.[33]

Stouffer, Allport, and Cantril urged more interpretation on NORC, aware that more money and staff would be required to do the job, for there were too few people as it was.[34] But Field was wary about inter-pretation, and he wanted the facts to "speak for themselves." In this concern he reflected his own inexperience with sophisticated data analy-sis, but he also reflected his experience with the pressures on polling—always under scrutiny for political bias—which academics had faced less often. In these discussions between Field and the board, it appears that the board members meant analytic interpretation, while Field meant po-litical interpretation—or interpretation that would be given political meaning by others. Stouffer, Allport, and Cantril argued that data did not speak for themselves, but Field's own rejoinder was regularly in the context of political vulnerability.[35]

Field had an important point. There *were* political pressures on NORC, both direct and indirect. Its important client early in the war, the OWI Surveys Division, had been quaking in its boots in the spring of 1944 before a Congress that was bidding fair to kill it off with a zero budget appropriation—and did so. (See chapter five.) Before that ax had fallen, the OWI group was worried about how Congress might react to a study that NORC had done on its own, which showed national attitudes toward politicians as being anything but admiring. Julian Woodward, acting head of OWI Surveys, wrote Field in March 1944:

> I may say we were a bit worried about the NORC contract and afraid of questioning about it [from Congressmen during the budgetary hearings]. Your recent report on "Politics and Politicians" was very untimely from our point of view since it is not the sort of thing that members of Congress are going to be very pleased with.[36]

Granted, Field said to the board, we cannot let outsiders dictate our policy, but it would be foolish to pretend that there are not some real pressures out there.

Field also felt the political implications of NORC's surveys on racial attitudes. NORC began its pioneering research into black attitudes in 1942. NORC data of 1944 on white attitudes toward blacks showed that the majority of Americans did not think that many blacks suffered discrimination:

> Sixty percent of the white respondents thought Negroes were being treated fairly.

> Eighty-five percent thought Negroes in their town had the same chance as white people to get a good education.

But anti-Negro feeling was actually widespread in the sample:

> Forty-two percent said that they wouldn't like it to have a Negro nurse in a hospital.

> Forty-two percent said they thought they would not eat in a restaurant that served both Negroes and whites.

> Fifty-two percent thought that white people should have the first chance at any kind of job.

After the war, as 39 percent saw it, Negroes and white people were not going to get along as well as they had before the war.[37] This was new material. Racial attitudes of whites and blacks had not been displayed in the polls. Until the summer of 1943 and the riot in Detroit, neither Gallup nor Roper had paid much attention to racial attitudes, and the riot did not keep their attention for long.[38] Judging from the evidence in the 1951 Cantril/Strunk volume *Public Opinion: 1935–1946*, which included poll data from five American organizations, virtually no research other than the NORC studies was conducted into attitudes toward blacks.[39] Field's own concern in undertaking this research had been with helping to resolve tensions, but he worried that the results might instead exacerbate them. The writing of the NORC report deserved special care, he explained to the board.[40] In December 1944 a preliminary confidential report summarizing the data was sent out to seventy-five persons, asking them to comment on constructive uses for these findings and on the advisability of releasing them for general distribution.[41]

Later, while Field was arranging for publication of the results by the American Council on Race Relations, the council objected to a preliminary release:

> The danger of publishing such figures, without due caution and interpretation, lies in the fact that many persons reading the results of the poll would mistake figures published for actual facts.[42]

Indeed, the council's argument was that these opinions could not be left to speak for themselves. The controversy was fair indication that NORC was dealing with some very important social issues indeed, in the few basic surveys it could afford.

CONTRACT WORK

NORC came to feel its budgetary constraints keenly. The University of Denver appreciated NORC and expected it to contribute to the development of an academic program in social science. However, the university's financial contribution in this period was small, about 5 percent of the NORC budget. The center ran on about 40 percent grants and 60 percent contracts, but the grants were not large enough to support independent research on any scale (at no time was there even a single staff member assigned exclusively to independent research), and NORC did not make enough money from contracts to subsidize the basic research sector. It was forced to seek contracts to keep its staff employed, but as Field explained to the board, it could not go after the really lucrative kind: it was industry, not education and public interest groups, that spent real money on research, but NORC had to seek out the nonprofit organizations, which were perennially hard up. NORC could not sell its surveys to newspapers without competing with Gallup and with the other polls, something that Field himself wanted to avoid, as noted. To do so might also have meant risking the tax-exempt status of the center.[43]

Costs had risen steadily during the war, funds had remained stable, and NORC's activities had overflowed the channels of the original budget. The center's weekly news release, which had initially gone out to 90 newspapers, now went to 400. The weekly radio program "Your Opinion," written at NORC and aired on the new ABC network, was now costing $3,000 a year to prepare, and there was no budget item for it at all. The roundup of various polls' results, published as *Opinion News*, was not making money. Answering requests for data information, especially from academics, had taken about three to four hours a week in the beginning but was now taking about three to four hours a day.

NORC's work was clearly in demand, but it did not yield the income the center needed to sustain itself and embark on development. Some cracks were showing: In 1944–45, NORC spent $12,000 more than it took in. Something had to give. NORC had to cut down on services or find new money, and some of its contract money was going to dry up. The OPA, which had recently provided almost half of NORC's revenue from contracts, was probably going to shut down in June 1946. Government work was going to be hard to find, Field felt, because the Census Bureau and Program Surveys would probably put a drive on to get it.[44]

In response to these pressures, Field felt that NORC should try to do some work for profit-making firms after all. The Massachusetts Institute of Technology did contract work for Westinghouse, he pointed out, and Lazarsfeld had been making surveys for McFadden Publications. The legal counsel and the board essentially agreed that some work for business firms would be legitimate and would not risk NORC's tax-exempt status, stressing that NORC surveys should continue to deal with topics of "social significance."[45] A contract with CBS was the immediate issue, and it became the second-largest item in the budget for 1945–46, also yielding a 15 percent surcharge for NORC's own development.[46] The biggest item in the budget in 1944 was survey work for the State Department's Public Studies Division.[47]

With new projects for business and government, the center was able to survive the waning of the OPA work. NORC had bought some time, but no fundamental remedy was in sight, and the board continued to consider trying to get more money from foundations and universities. No promising leads had turned up for foundation support, and no decision had been reached to seriously consider the possibility of moving to another university—Cornell University and the Yale Institute of Human Relations had expressed interest as early as 1943[48]—but the issue of relocation remained a live one.

In his 1946 report to the board, Field assessed NORC's work thus far. He felt that the center had contributed to the "science of ascertaining public opinion"—he cited an interviewing manual, the Negro Survey, and some experimental projects—but he hoped that NORC could make a more substantial contribution. Perhaps in a year or two, with more clients who paid the 15 percent research tax, NORC could put together a fund to support some staff who did nothing but research.[49] Field reported these reflections to the board in April. The Central City Conference on Public Opinion Research was held in July (see chapter seven).

In September, while traveling in connection with a UNESCO project, Field was killed in a plane crash in Paris.[50] The recurrent issue of relocation became a high priority for the board and its new director.

Clyde W. Hart became the center's new director. Hart was a sociologist who had done graduate work at Chicago and then had taught for a number of years at the University of Iowa, where he had offered one of the first courses in public opinion and had coauthored a text in sociology.[51] Just before the war, he had corresponded with Louis Wirth at Chicago about his plans to write a dissertation and complete his Ph.D.[52] Instead, with the advent of the war, Hart went into governmental opinion research and research administration, especially at the OPA, where he contracted for NORC surveys and came to know Field well. Field wanted Hart to join the NORC staff. Upon Field's death, Hart became a candidate for the directorship, and he assumed the post in January 1947. He pressed the search for information about other possible universities which had already been under way in the fall.[53]

The Early Years at Chicago: 1947–1960

Making the Change

THE INTERESTED PARTIES

NORC had made a substantial impact in five years. In 1946–47, social scientists at seven major universities tried to bring it to their own campuses. Cantril hoped that NORC would come to Princeton and work closely with his own (now very small) organization, OPOR.[54] Likert wanted to merge it into the Survey Research Center, which he and a small group from Program Surveys were establishing at the University of Michigan. Lazarsfeld wanted NORC to become a division of the Bureau of Applied Social Research. Other social scientists at Cornell, Wisconsin, Pittsburgh, and Chicago put in their bids, and most expected their universities to be able to help out with $10,000 or $15,000 a year. Denver officials wanted NORC to stay, offering at the last to bring their subsidy up to $20,000 within two years.[55]

Of the seven bidding for NORC from other institutions, only Lazarsfeld and Likert were directors of ongoing research organizations that had similarity to NORC. Both men pointed to the ways in which they wanted to improve on NORC's polling tradition. Characteristically, Lazarsfeld stressed analysis and criticized the straight tabulations of the polls. Likert stressed data collection and criticized the polls' closed questioning.[56] Certain features of these two offers in particular suggested that NORC might be cannibalized for its field staff essentially, and the board was concerned with maintaining NORC as an organization in its own right.

The board also saw some special attractions in the research-minded community of scholars at Chicago. Most members thought that in this mainstream of prestigious social science NORC could develop into a broad-range university research center. Hart brought back a favorable report from his visit with Wirth, who was representing Chicago, that the Chicago subsidy would be "$10,000 or $15,000 or in substance 'whatever is necessary,'" as the minutes of the May 1947 meeting put it,[57] and that faculty status and tenure would be available at Chicago to professional members of the staff.[58] The board decided to accept the Chicago offer, and the organization moved in the fall.

THE CONVERGENT INTERESTS AT CHICAGO

Why was the University of Chicago interested in bringing NORC from Denver? The move has somewhat puzzled NORC directors of recent years,[59] but there is evidence of support for the idea at the highest levels of university administration as well as at the faculty level, in a context of enthusiasm and optimism about interdisciplinary research. A group of Chicago social scientists was interested in having NORC serve as a center for an interdisciplinary research program in mass communication and public opinion. Bernard Berelson had come to Chicago from the Bureau of Applied Social Research in 1946, and he wanted to develop a national capacity for communications research. Berelson, Wirth, and a number of faculty members in sociology, psychology, political science, library science, education, and business expressed interest in bringing NORC to Chicago, and they took a proposal to Ralph W. Tyler, then acting dean (and soon to be dean) of the Division of the Social Sciences.[60]

At the highest echelons of the university, as Tyler recalls the period, Marshall Field was concerned about the fate of the organization after Harry Field's death and consulted with Chancellor Robert M. Hutchins and Dean Tyler about relocating NORC at Chicago, and Tyler facilitated the move. Tyler, a professional educator of influence and a powerful figure in the Hutchins administration, had published on implications of polling for political democracy and educational change.[61] He and other administrators appear to have been responsive to NORC's move because they saw value in it *per se*, because certain faculty members were interested, and because Marshall Field was interested—and Field was on Chicago's own board of trustees. After NORC settled in, Tyler served not only as dean of the Division of the Social Sciences but also as president of the NORC board (as did successor deans). In 1950, Marshall Field began to reduce his commitment to NORC, as planned, with a final grant, but he remained on the NORC board for several more years.[62]

CHICAGO'S CONDITIONS

In surviving documents, it seems clear that the Chicago administration did not expect to be involved in finding funds for NORC; that was to be the purview of the Chicago faculty and NORC staff. Before the negotiations were completed, Tyler explained to Wirth and his faculty group that the university had three conditions for its interest in the project. First, NORC was to do mostly research, not service—meaning, surely, that it was to seek foundation grants rather than contracts. Second, some regular university faculty were to be involved in NORC work in order to integrate it into the regular university program. Third, the university itself intended a very specific, not flexible, financial contribution—as later became a matter of record, this contribution was to be $10,000 a year.[63] Dean Tyler actually did a great deal of fund-raising for faculty research programs in the social sciences, but he clearly was not committed to raising funds for NORC, too.[64]

The first two conditions were no barrier, for this was precisely what NORC wanted to do: conduct basic research in collaboration with Chicago faculty (rather than do service work on its own). But the implications of this in conjunction with the third condition seem to have been perceived differently by university administrators and NORC staff. There appears to have been an element of informality in the negotiations, and the fact that one of the major university administrators had left Chicago by the time NORC moved there may have made for some ambiguity.[65] In any case, these were new arrangements, and it is not surprising that they were a matter of continued discussion and clarification. When NORC had been in Chicago for almost a year, Tyler (who had not actually directed the negotiations) drew up a "memorandum of agreement" that established the general lines of obligation on both sides.[66]

The problem imbedded in the three conditions was how NORC was going to maintain itself and its national field staff *without* either the bread-and-butter work of contracts or substantial support by the university. Very probably, both the university and NORC expected regular Chicago faculty to bring substantial foundation grants to the conduct of research at NORC. This had been, after all, the mode of research financing at Chicago in the 1920s and 1930s, when research organizations began to proliferate under the aegis of the Local Community Research Committee and the funds from the Laura Spelman Rockefeller Memorial.[67] (See chapter eight.)

There seems to have been little explicit recognition on either side of the implications of the structural difference between NORC and most other social science research organizations at Chicago, in two aspects in particular. First, NORC had a much bigger staff, with a national field staff of about 200 who required continuity in employment, even if it was ordinarily part-time. And NORC's central staff was not small by the standards of academic research projects. The organization had grown from five to twenty-six people in the Denver period; only a half dozen people made the move to Chicago, but another dozen or so positions were to be filled soon.[68]

Second, and more important, unlike most academic research organizations NORC staff lacked faculty standing and thus the financial continuity that university faculty had from their teaching salaries. NORC had to include staff salaries and administrative expenses in grants and contracts, like any business; if business was down, staff had nothing to fall back on, such as teaching more courses in a university department.

Precisely how NORC would be linked to the university was not spelled out in detail when the move was negotiated (not unlike the vagueness characterizing the Bureau's early links to Columbia and SRC's arrangements with Michigan, as we shall see). Wirth's own statement at the time captures some of the ambiguity:

> My own feeling is that the NORC ought to be autonomous, but that in its research and educational and training functions it ought to be thoroughly integrated into the University, leaving its service function open for independent development in any direction that seems appropriate.[69]

That NORC would find it difficult to be "autonomous" for service work and "integrated" for research and teaching is, with hindsight, not surprising. Some kind of optimal mix of grants and contracts was not impossible, to be sure, but finding it was tricky and required negotiation and innovation over a span of years.

THE EARLY ARRANGEMENTS

In 1947–48, NORC staff found the situation at Chicago less favorable than they had hoped. There was less money—a flat $10,000 from the university, as noted—and fewer of the indirect subsidies and perquisites than they had had at Denver. NORC had in fact suffered a financial loss by moving.[70] Did the new connections in social science make up for the loss? Not immediately. Relationships with faculty had to be worked out, gradually.

Chicago faculty interested in empirical research did engage in some cooperative projects with NORC. In particular, Berelson, Wirth, and Philip M. Hauser were active in early projects involving NORC.[71] So while the organization was by no means isolated from the kind of collegial stimulation and support it had hoped for, there was not enough faculty involvement (or funds) to transform NORC quickly into a broad-gauge social research center. Despite the administration's condition against it, NORC was required to continue doing contract work in substantial amounts. And the tenured appointments that NORC expected were not forthcoming.

By academic traditions and strict construction, NORC staff members did not qualify for tenure in these early years. The director's role itself was not a tenured position: the departments considered scholarly publication and teaching, not administration. Shirley Star was the first member of the staff to complete the Ph.D., in 1950.[72] The lack of a doctorate was not itself an automatic bar to tenure at Chicago,[73] but the NORC staff had not brought from its wartime experience with contract work any long, scholarly publishing record, which could have provided another route to prestige. Hart and his group had experience, information, and some publishing in large-scale opinion research, which most Chicago social science faculty lacked, and in another institution this expertise might have been given more weight than it was given at Chicago. (Indeed, at the University of Denver, it had been given more.) NORC sought to relocate at Chicago precisely because the university's social science program had already been so largely built, and because it offered an environment of the intellectual culture and prestige of accomplished social scientists. Chicago and its social science faculty may in fact have been rather *too* eminent for NORC's purposes in the short run.

Quite like the other new organizations, NORC was located on the physical margins of its university. To be sure, its offices were not as far away as the old medical building that had given Lazarsfeld's group its first housing at Columbia nor as cramped and undesirable as the basement headquarters that SRC got on its arrival at Michigan. NORC was about a mile from the center of campus, in part of the old Rosenwald mansion, which had been deeded to the university. But the space, as it turned out, was not rent free, as NORC had anticipated: $3,000 of the $10,000 subsidy had to be turned back in rent.[74]

Within a few years, NORC managed to relocate in bigger headquarters very close to campus, but the housing issue continued to be a disappointment. A decade later, in 1957 testimony to a congressional subcommittee in another context, Hart still showed concern with this issue:

> *Congressman*: [The organization is now connected with the University of Chicago?] . . . Do you receive any funds from the University?
>
> *Hart*: Well, I could almost answer that No, but not quite. . . . We get a total of $10,000 per year from the university in lieu of the housing and other appurtenances that they agreed to furnish us and found they could not furnish us.[75]

The University of Chicago did not integrate NORC into its academic divisional structure, but there seems to have been a common assumption on this point. The NORC board, as we have seen, was actually at some pains to maintain the autonomy of the nonprofit organization. Did the board ever consider dissolving the independent corporation in order to become an integral part of the university? While this cannot be ruled out, I have found no evidence of such a plan.

Tyler, who had two roles, one as NORC board president and the other as social sciences dean, recalls his own belief that NORC had a mission of its own and did not have good reason to become a charge on the university budget. He and other members of the board agreed that NORC should be autonomous, and when they elected new members as needed, they sought people who shared that belief.[76] In effect, NORC was overseen by people *inside* Chicago's Division of the Social Sciences who continued to agree that NORC should function *outside* that division. Given this structural arrangement, NORC actually achieved a fair amount of contact and common activity with Chicago social scientists.

Converting to Social Research: In Search of Funds and Academic Prestige

WHERE THE MONEY WAS TO COME FROM

Expanding the financial base. NORC needed substantial funds to make the transition from contracts in polling to grants in social research. In 1947, when Leonard S. Cottrell, Jr., relayed Cornell's bid for NORC, he had estimated that foundation grants of some $75,000–$95,000 a year would be necessary for five years to establish the center in a primary research role. After that, he felt, NORC could seek and accept a certain amount of contract work to help support itself.[77] At the time, Hart thought that Cottrell's estimate was rather high[78]—and whether Cornell could have gotten the money is another matter entirely—but Cottrell's view about the costs of creating a financial base for basic research now seems to have been rather down-to-earth.

There was probably no realistic prospect of getting a large endowment to underwrite NORC at this time. But Hart saw problems with general-purpose subsidies in any case, feeling that subsidies that were not earmarked for a specific project tended to make researchers careless about cost overruns. He also felt that if NORC were known as a subsidized research center, others in the university community might press it to do work for them for little or nothing.[79] Hart had good reason to be concerned: NORC did indeed perform technical services for Chicago faculty and students which sometimes overburdened the staff without adding commensurately to income.[80]

Over the course of the 1940s and 1950s, NORC funds came in roughly equal thirds from three main sources: *foundation grants* for designated projects from Carnegie, Ford, SSRC, and others; *contracts for private nonprofit organizations*, such as the Fund for Adult Education and the National Association for Mental Health; and *contracts for federal agencies*, such as OWI, OPA, and the State Department, along with some military contracts. NORC also did occasional work for commercial firms.[81]

The total budget, which averaged around $300,000, was well over double the Denver high, with a range of $200,000 to $500,000.[82] NORC was thus doing a greater volume of business, but it was still very reliant on contracts. And for the stable employment of its national field staff, NORC was particularly dependent on contracts for the federal government. Its national work for the Public Studies Division of the State Department was a source of annual income for thirteen to fourteen years (1944–57), which added approximately a half million dollars, overall, to the budget. This contract had been an important one in the decision to retain NORC's New York office after the move to Chicago.[83]

The contract with the State Department was "confidential." The department did not make public either the findings or the fact of the contract itself. NORC published some results, with special permission, without identifying the sponsor.[84] In spring 1957, after a State Department official leaked to major newspapers some NORC data showing public support for foreign aid, a congressional subcommittee summoned spokesmen for both the department and NORC to public hearings. What were these polls? Why was the State Department paying for them from a discretionary fund designed and marked for "Emergencies in the Diplomatic and Consular Service"? An "emergency" of fourteen years— without the knowledge of most congressmen?

State Department officials squirmed, struggling to convince the committee that they had been trying to keep the work secret not from Congress but from international allies who might be offended by reports of certain American views. It did not wash. The congressmen were convinced—and the hearings amply confirm their suspicions—that the State Department had been trying to keep them in the dark, and they were furious.[85] A final congressional report castigated the Department of State for illegal use of funds, violation of security regulations, evasive testimony, and careless, propagandistic interpretation of poll data released to pressure Congress.[86]

NORC fared better. When Hart and Sheatsley testified at the hearings, they were not really the committee's quarry, and they dealt diplomatically and informatively with their interrogators. Hart admitted that when the *New York Times* story broke, his reaction was "one of weak knees," as he feared that NORC would come under public attack. Hart may not have made much headway with his technical explanations—his discussion of cluster sampling was translated in the committee's final report as "an error known as cluttering"—but he discussed many of the limitations and difficulties of surveys with candor, and for the most part he was treated respectfully by the congressmen, who reserved their fury largely for their political foes in the State Department.[87]

NORC certainly fared better than Gallup had in the inquiry of 1944, perhaps because polling in general had become more acceptable and better understood in the intervening years. NORC's connection to the University of Chicago and Hart's own performance also seemed to allay congressional suspicions that NORC itself had any political intentions. The most serious consequence for NORC was the loss of the contract, which the State Department canceled soon after the news story broke. This cut NORC's budget for national work in half.[88] Maintaining the invaluable national capacity on a stable basis was a continuing concern for the center in this era and later.

Service work and program development. In addition to the national surveys, much of NORC's other research in this period involved service for others: data design, collection, and tabulation for other organizations and scholars on campus; noncredit courses in data processing on the early IBM counter-sorter precomputers; and research contracts for data collection only or for collection, analysis, and a written report.[89] Some research continuity nevertheless developed in two areas, especially: survey methodology (which we shall consider later in this chapter) and research into health.

A number of studies bearing on health issues and measurement were directed by Paul N. Borsky, Jack Elinson, Jacob J. Feldman, Hart, Sheatsley, Star, and others: studies of mental health, chronic illnesses, health insurance, medical costs, dental care, preventive medicine, attitudes of doctors and patients, hospital admissions, and other health issues. In 1956, NORC published *Family Medical Costs and Voluntary Health Insurance: A Nationwide Survey*, by Anderson and Feldman; in 1957, it published *Voluntary Health Insurance in Two Cities*, by Anderson and NORC staff. NORC also organized a seminar in summer 1956 on health research methods.[90]

In its Chicago work, NORC's poll reports and press releases of the Denver period came to an end, but there was a rise in its publication of books and of articles in professional journals. NORC staff published a dozen books between 1941 and 1960, nine of these in the second decade (1951–1960). And of the more than 190 other publications (book chapters and journal articles), 80 percent were also published in the second decade.

There were factors in this output that contributed more to NORC's reputation as an important technical center than as a research center with intellectual interests of its own. Of the 203 publications listed in the NORC bibliography for 1941–1960, more than 25 percent were by authors not affiliated with NORC. And that figure somewhat underrepresents the unpublished share, for the NORC bibliography does not list most projects from which no publications were known to result.[91] NORC's continuing contract work that provided data or unpublished client reports was yeoman service, conducted for individuals and organizations that did not have research capacities of their own, but it was not calculated to enhance NORC's stock with social scientists in the local departments.

ARRANGEMENTS WITH THE FACULTY

The interdisciplinary plans. The plan to integrate NORC's national capacity into an interdisciplinary program in mass communication and public opinion had, as mentioned earlier, been a major reason for bringing NORC to Chicago.[92] There was some activity soon after NORC arrived. In the summer of 1949 a monthlong research seminar on communication and public opinion was codirected by Hart and Berelson and cosponsored by the faculty committee, NORC, and three departments (psychology, sociology, and political science). Lectures were given by such visitors as Merton, Lazarsfeld, Stouffer, Stephan, and others, including Hyman of NORC's New York office, and six of the lectures were published in the *American Journal of Sociology* in 1950.[93]

NORC continued to do some research in radio and television, but a vigorous interdisciplinary program did not develop in this period. It may be that changes in personnel mattered. Wirth died in 1952. Berelson left Chicago in 1951, and Tyler left in 1954 (both to work on social science projects of the Ford Foundation). In NORC Board minutes for the 1950s, there are only passing references to any NORC involvement in a communication program.[94] The interdisciplinary plans for NORC seem to have subsided, and certainly the departmental plans did not develop quite as the center had hoped.

The departments. Joint appointments between NORC and the departments had been another plank in the original plan for NORC. Before the 1947 move, the university had approved two such appointments. One was in psychology, a full professorship with a half-time appointment as research director at NORC, but the department did not succeed in filling the post with a candidate of its choice. NORC staff members later taught some courses in the department, but no substantial joint appointments were made in this period. The Department of Sociology, for its part, wanted a statistician-methodologist who would work half-time at NORC and half-time in the department for one year—clearly not a tenured position that might attract academics who were already established, and various people whom sociology approached turned it down. Neither did sociology fill its appointment with NORC immediately.[95]

Quite apart from the NORC appointment, in 1950 the sociology department was trying to recruit established people, such as the combination of Lazarsfeld and Merton or individuals such as Theodore F. Newcomb, John Dollard, and Stephan.[96] Had sociology landed any of these scholars, one or another might well have done substantial research with NORC and set an early precedent for joint appointments of tenured faculty.

As it was, by the mid-1950s at least four NORC staff members—Hart, Star, Elinson, and Eli Marks—were teaching courses in statistics, methods, and data analysis in the sociology department, for which the university reimbursed NORC through the initial $10,000 fund.[97] But the fact that these appointments were on a course-by-course basis, without tenure, meant that the NORC-sociology connection was an insecure career line that had limited appeal to academic "stars" from elsewhere. And the ongoing bread-and-butter contracts required to keep the organization functioning limited the NORC staff's own possibilities of becoming "stars" themselves, either through a large volume of distinguished research of their own or through a large cadre of graduate students who would extend their research agenda and influence.

Nevertheless, NORC did begin to collaborate in graduate training in research, as doctoral dissertations and master's theses were undertaken with NORC data and guidance. NORC also became a source of employment in fieldwork, coding, and data management and analysis for a much larger number of students with ongoing research projects. In 1958–59, for example, fifty-five students had on-the-job training of various kinds at NORC.[98]

New arrivals and new programs. By the late 1950s, NORC and the sociology department had some new links, as several new arrivals to the department also became study directors at NORC. These new study directors were not tenured faculty, but unlike the arrivals from NORC-Denver, they had a place in the department from the beginning and their course teaching reflected substantive interests in social psychology and political sociology as well as survey research methods. Their departmental appointments simply allowed them to work part-time in research at NORC, if they or others could find funds to support research projects there—and they found them. Donald J. Bogue, Ethel Shanas, Coleman, Davis, and Rossi undertook new studies on such topics as skid row, aging, adolescents in high school, Great Books discussion groups, and students' school achievement and career choices. Certain of these studies also contributed to ongoing work in survey methods and the study of health issues.[99]

This new current showed some influence from the Bureau of Applied Social Research. Rossi and Coleman had worked directly with Lazarsfeld; Davis, who had been attracted to NORC by its health methods seminar, had worked with Rossi at Harvard.[100] In 1957, Coleman wrote of hoping to capture at Chicago some of the esprit and camaraderie that a group of younger researchers had felt at the Bureau, and he hoped to enhance Chicago's impact on sociology by creating a new research institute. He envisaged a voluntary "federation" or "holding company" that would pool the resources of the three major centers doing sociological research at Chicago—NORC, the Population Center, and the Family Center—and he looked to NORC's special contribution as being that of providing expanded machine services and a full-time computing center.[101] Such a pooled research center did not materialize, but NORC itself consolidated and strengthened its own place on the campus.

New headquarters. In the early 1950s, NORC moved to headquarters that were closer to campus (less than a block from the quadrangle), but as its volume of research increased, the organization overflowed these headquarters into additional temporary offices. In 1958, NORC began negotiations for financing of a headquarters that would bring all of NORC under one roof. The basic negotiations were conducted during Hart's administration, before his retirement in 1960: building renovation and enlargement were under way that year, when Rossi succeeded Hart as director.[102]

For an expanded headquarters, the university was to contribute the site, valued at $10,000, and to make about another $75,000 available to NORC in loans payable over twenty years. The rest of the money was to be provided by NORC itself ($30,000) and by NIH, which made a $60,000 grant to the university for the NORC building.[103] The NIH grant, made in support of health-related facilities, reflected NORC's volume of work in the health area.

The good offices and affiliation of the university were crucial to landing the NIH grant, and the university's willingness to loan a substantial sum to NORC was new: a decade before, NORC had tried to get a university loan and had been turned down as a poor risk.[104] The new arrangements were recognition of NORC's value to the university. NORC staff members were indeed providing not only some formal teaching but also the informal teaching and expertise of a complex research facility: the creation of data, a vehicle for research by faculty and students; consultation in technical design and analysis; use and instruction in early IBM equipment for tabulation and analysis; and on-the-job training for students in survey research methods. Under the new financial arrangements, the outright contribution of the university was a small fraction of the NORC endeavor; NORC had hoped for more, to be sure.[105] With the loan, nevertheless, Chicago's investment was 50 percent of the whole and represented a new level of integration between NORC and the university.

Contributions to the Field

Continuity and Change in the Polling Tradition

NORC-Chicago in these years showed substantial change from the Denver days. The center grew financially, showed greater integration into the social science community, and expanded its intellectual agenda beyond the study of opinions in the polling tradition to include more complex work in opinions, attitudes, experiences, and behaviors as well as more complex designs involving groups, communities, and national samples of the population. Social scientists who worked at NORC also put their print on the analysis of data, going beyond the old marginals and demographic breakdowns of the pollsters to the pursuit of relationships, guided by concepts developing in the social sciences. Important changes were thus effected in the early Chicago years, but there was also continuity to polling in two important respects. The first concerned the national capacity itself.

THE NATIONAL STAFF

The national capacity was a direct transplant into the academic environment of a social invention of the pollsters: the national organization of subjective data. There is little reason for it to have developed indigenously. In an academic setting, who would have organized it, staffed it, paid for it? What academic department would have had the disciplinary mandate, the political clout, and the financial resources to rise up imperially above the other departments and set upon the creation of a truly national center that could gather data year-round on the national population—with a budget, for starters, that would surely be larger than that of any department? Or, perhaps a still more awesome task: what combination of existing departments could have come together in sufficient harmony of purpose, coordinated political power, and continued intellectual collaboration to raise the money and build the staff to share in an *interdisciplinary* center of national scope?

NORC clearly had struggles in these years in bringing a national organization in from the margins of business, but to have built it from the ground up from within, with entirely academic personnel and skills, looks now like the much more massive task. The Denver experience was probably a useful prelude and learning experience for NORC before it tried to scale the academic heights of Chicago. It may not be the case that NORC would have failed entirely if it had started at Chicago, but the speculation is hard to resist.

The wartime experience of the New York office in particular was probably critical in making the national capacity viable. The work for government agencies established a network of clients (especially OWI and OPA, and later the State Department). It involved social scientists who later joined the NORC staff: Hart and Hyman, from the wartime civilian agencies; Star and Elinson, from Stouffer's Research Branch in the army. And it probably facilitated NORC's participation in AAPOR, which usually met on the eastern seaboard. After NORC moved, Hart wanted to consolidate the organization in Chicago, but Sheatsley and Hyman and others resisted.[106] Some of NORC's most visible work was conducted by the New York office—projects for Stouffer, Lazarsfeld, and Hyman et al., which we shall discuss presently.

QUALITY WORK FOR OTHERS

There was a hope at NORC from the beginning that it could get down to more of its own work and be less dependent on the work for others. The center developed original work, but it also remained dependent on the contract work. This was disappointing to NORC, but from a broader perspective this service work was indeed an institutional contribution of major importance. It created an alternative as well as a complement to the market and polling firms, and it developed NORC's reputation not for beating market-firm prices but for doing more sophisticated work in the design and conduct of surveys, instituting more training, supervision, and quality control.

Some of the best-known survey research that NORC carried out in its first twenty years was national work for other social scientists. In 1960, NORC collected the United States data for the five-nation study by Almond and Verba which was published in 1963. Other landmark studies using NORC data were published in the 1947–60 period by North and Hatt, Lazarsfeld, and Stouffer, none of whom were based at NORC.

The North-Hatt study of occupational prestige was the most strongly identified with the organization, having been first reported in a 1947 issue of NORC's own publication on poll results, *Opinion News*, and it was sometimes referred to as the "NORC-North-Hatt" study. In this survey, NORC gathered data from a national quota sample of respondents who rated ninety occupational titles for their "general standing" on a five-point scale from Excellent to Poor, and the resulting prestige ratings had an enormous influence in sociological research.[107]

NORC also collected the data for other important national studies: for example, two radio surveys that were directed by Lazarsfeld, *The People Look at Radio* (1946), with Harry Field as coauthor, and *Radio Listening in America* (1948), by Lazarsfeld and Kendall.[108] It also helped in the data collection for two surveys that explored public reactions during the McCarthy period: *Communism, Conformity, and Civil Liberties* (1955), by

Stouffer, and *The Academic Mind* (1958), by Lazarsfeld and Thielens (see chapter nine). The surveys on the McCarthy era were widely reviewed as being contributions to national political information and to the scientific literature, as they addressed an important public issue with technical and analytical sophistication.[109]

The Stouffer work was a "mass-elite" study comparing the attitudes of a national cross-section and a sample of "community leaders" on the dangers of communism and the constitutional threat to civil liberties posed by fears of communism. Stouffer found that only a tiny fraction of the American public was "worried" about the domestic threat of communism, Senator McCarthy's alarms notwithstanding. Community leaders (generally better educated) showed more understanding and concern than did the cross-section regarding protecting the civil liberties of those holding unpopular political and religious ideas.

In each study, NORC and a commercial firm shared the fieldwork, Gallup in one case and Roper in the other. The doubling up was largely a practical expedient, but both studies made some scientific use of the academic-commercial comparison. Stouffer, in particular, was pleased to note that "for the first time in the history of public opinion polling, the work of two different agencies can be compared on an entire questionnaire."[110]

In *Communism, Conformity, and Civil Liberties*, Stouffer expressed pleasure with the comparability of results. NORC and the Gallup organization had each drawn a separate national cross-section probability sample of about 2,500, and Stouffer found the demographic characteristics and the attitudes reported to be in close agreement. This was a conclusion he supported with much quantitative evidence (see especially his first chapter).[111]

In *The Academic Mind*, Lazarsfeld and Thielens did not compare the results obtained by NORC and the Roper field staffs, and the fact that they did not do so is largely accounted for by the noncomparable field assignments: Roper interviewers were more often at colleges of lower quality and NORC at schools of higher quality. But the authors invited David Riesman to make an independent study of the interviewing, which he conducted by mail questionnaire and by interviewing, himself, a substantial number of the college-professor respondents as well as some of the interviewers.

Riesman's long field report, included in *The Academic Mind*, is full of appreciation for most interviewers in *both* houses. The best of these, in Riesman's view, brought good talent and training to their task and, in fact, more social science than did some of their respondents at the colleges of lower quality. He characterized two "house styles" of interviewers—Roper's prototypic "market research types" and NORC's "blue-stockings"—and found that NORC interviewers were younger, better educated, and more familiar with academic culture; they conducted longer interviews, probed more insistently, and wrote down more material. Riesman nevertheless found no compelling evidence that one house style was necessarily more effective than the other, as there were some pluses and minuses to each. The field report is limited to quite general and intuitive comparisons, but it is vintage Riesman and eminently worth reading today.[112]

Overall, the effect of both reports was to commend the interviewing competence of *all three* firms, NORC, Gallup, and Roper. Both questionnaires involved a fair ration of open-ended questions (15 to 18 percent), and although NORC interviewers tended to record *more* open-ended material, this did not seem to affect substantially the comparability of the data or the conclusions. Even though the comparisons of fieldwork were hardly exhaustive, the three organizations' willingness to be scrutinized by others was not without risks. The secondary house comparisons still stand as the only full academic-commercial comparisons.[113]

Taking Its Measurement Seriously

NORC took scientific responsibilities to monitor and experiment in data collection rather more seriously than its colleagues at either the Bureau or SRC seemed to.[114] Its research into methods was an effort to monitor its own quality, to develop higher standards for the field as a whole, and to establish itself in a role of scientific respectability in the academic world, an aspiration that shaped work in the Denver days and continued in Chicago. NORC staff paid attention to measurement issues from the beginning and built a reputation for quality data collection.

QUESTION WORDING

NORC's early experiments in alternative question wording, conducted in the split-ballot design, bore on practical decisions facing question writers (then and now): Should a question offer a choice of *ideas*, or just a yes/no question about a single proposal? Should there be a middle alternative, such as more, less, and *about the same*? Would changing the order of the alternatives show a position effect? Would open and closed forms of a question yield comparable answers?[115] In August 1944, Sheatsley commented on one of these problems in a letter to Gordon Connelly at the NORC home office:

I dislike intensely the practice of the Denver office (perhaps inherited from Roper) of constantly offering the negative alternatives when the issue is clear cut.

Sheatsley was not opposed to providing a choice between two policy ideas, but including the grammatical alternative "or not" struck him as pointless and awkward. (For example, "Do you think that Great Britain should or should not pay us for the war materials . . . ?") Connelly thought it a useful tactic for discouraging what researchers were already calling *acquiescence*.[116]

NORC had done an experiment in 1942 on the inclusion of the formal negative at Sheatsley's request, and it was this experiment to which he was alluding: whether or not the grammatical negative was included did not seem to matter, though the choice of a rival idea did.[117] And Sheatsley was doubtful more generally that principles to guide practice could be developed from these experimental results:

Re the further research, I'm not sure there are any cut and dried answers to such problems as whether or not to list the alternatives. Depends too much on the issue you're polling on, strength of feeling, amount of information, simplicity or complexity, how you're going to interpret the answers, etc. Thus, if a test showed that the alternative made no difference, that might be true only of that one question at that particular time. And if it showed it did make a difference, the same inference might hold true.[118]

Connelly wanted NORC to keep at it, conducting experiments on ten or twenty national surveys, not just one. Field was willing, but from indirect evidence it seems unlikely that NORC embarked on the many additional tests. Results were shaggy and uneven; changing the order or form of alternatives sometimes made for different results and sometimes did not, and it was hard to know why. NORC did not have the resources to undertake a large program in question wording, but it launched some experiments, circulated the findings, and in fact conducted more serious study of questions than the other groups did in these early years or have in fact done until quite recently. Some very recent work acknowledges the early NORC work.[119]

A SAMPLING EXPERIMENT

In another project, NORC conducted a comparison between area and quota control sampling in 1946.[120] The original plan had been to mount two different surveys simultaneously in the city of Denver, one of each design. This would have posed some problems in comparability because NORC interviewers, already trained in quota methods, would have required new training in area procedures.[121] But such a design would have had the advantage of yielding cost comparisons, and cost was the sticking point for commercial firms. But it was also the reason why NORC was skeptical about area probability sampling, and the design was not carried out because the experiment itself was too expensive to use for a single survey.[122]

Instead, NORC interviewers sampled by the usual quota controls (age, sex, and rental value) and replicated certain questions of the governmental *Monthly Report on the Labor Force*, which used an area sample. In the preliminary report of July 1946, NORC reported equivalent results on three measures of the civilian labor force taken by the two methods (numbers of employed, farm and nonfarm, male and female). NORC did not apparently pursue this analysis or conduct additional experiments in sampling until much later. By fall 1946, however, it had lost some of its skepticism, having profited from the discussions of probability sampling at the Central City Conference, and it planned to try a "modified" form of area probability sampling in its new contracts. In 1953, NORC designed a new sample that was a compromise: probability methods were used to select the segments, and quotas were used to select respondents at the block level.[123]

CHANGES IN PRACTICE: TOWARD STANDARDIZATION

NORC's field practice increased standardization of interviewer performance, both in the fieldwork of quota sampling and the asking of questions. In both domains, NORC made a trade-off: it diminished the scope of interviewer judgment and increased the amount of information asked directly of the respondent. This meant that interviewers were asked to intervene and interpret less, even when their judgments might have been better than a respondent's on a given occasion. But if they were given this freedom and responsibility, there was no telling what had gone on in the interview. This concern stands in marked contrast to the exploratory and elite interviewing conducted by staff of the Bureau of Applied

Social Research in the same period (see chapter nine). The intensive, unstructured interviewing underlying Lazarsfeld's "art of asking why" was not a feature of NORC practice. "Open" questions were used at NORC—very heavily in Star's mental health questionnaire—but as a rule the *questions* themselves were fully specified.[124]

Standardization had a strong practical imperative: the need to establish some central administrative control of a large, far-flung field staff, who were trained and paid at modest levels. NORC brought this kind of concern for standardization from its own prior experience with national polling and continued it from the imperatives of national work. From the outset, NORC required that questions be read exactly as written.[125] The "Basic Instructions to Interviewers," published in *POQ* in 1942, were very explicit:

> Always ask a question exactly as we have worded it, without any changes whatsoever. Even if you discover what you think is a better way of asking the question, still ask it as it is printed. In the first place, there is no certainty that your change would suit our purpose. Secondly—and very important—in order to analyze our results all over the country, on a comparable basis, we have to be sure that *all* our interviewers ask the questions in exactly the same way.[126]

These instructions actually governed the asking of opinion questions, for standardized wording of demographic questions was not yet typical poll practice. Age, education, and class were considered "sensitive" questions, and interviewers were trusted to find out the information indirectly if they could, judging for themselves whether respondents were under or over forty. If they felt unsure, they were to ask respondents to place themselves in one category or the other, without asking for their exact age.[127] In the mid-1940s, NORC began to provide interviewers with direct questions: "What is your approximate age?" and then more directly, "May I ask your age?"[128]

Education was another matter that pollsters had been approaching indirectly. Gallup did not publish education in cross-tabulations until 1942.[129] When polls asked the question at all, they relied on interviewers to get the answer without offending or embarrassing the respondent. In 1941, Cantril's organization, modeling its question after the fashion of Gallup, used a mixture of standardized and nonstandardized questioning:

> Can you remember the name of a teacher you had in your last year of schooling—who was it?

This was supposed to get the respondent talking and in the process to volunteer information that the interviewer would use to fill in blanks for the name of the teacher, the subject taught, the grade or year, and the name and location of the school[130]—indeed, a long way around to find out the respondent's educational attainment.[131]

NORC interviewers tried out that question, and Field wrote to Cantril that respondents became wound up in talking about that last teacher, telling the interviewers the "color of their hair, the year they were born, and their marital status"—it would be better, he thought, to ask more directly about the level of schooling.[132] Cantril's group soon did so:

    a. Do you remember the name of the last school you attended?
    b. How far did you go in that school?[133]

The respondent's socioeconomic status was a third matter usually left to the interviewer's judgment. NORC made that clear in the 1942 instructions:

At the risk of being obvious, let us caution you to use your own judgment as to which economic group a respondent should be classed in. Don't ask him.[134]

Indeed, it might well have seemed crass to ask respondents themselves if they should be classed as A,B,C, or D, a hierarchy based on perceived consumption which NORC had inherited from market research.[135]

NORC tried to make a more sophisticated assessment of class by adding five other factors that interviewers were to use in their judgment: rent, occupation, family status and size, income, and comforts and luxuries.[136] But this was a very complex and intuitive process, and NORC had been looking for more objective procedures. In 1945, after some field trials, NORC began to use rental levels to control quota selection on SES.

This was NORC's transition from the selection of individuals—in stores, parks, and on street corners, as well as at homes—to the selection of households. Interviewers were given rental information about cities (or were supposed to get it themselves) which was to govern their choice of neighborhoods. And rather than picking houses of their own choice, interviewers were to use some sort of system, such as approaching every fifth or tenth house in the neighborhood they had chosen.[137] In their assessment of their respondents' class level, they used a mixture of statistical data (when they had it), personal impression, and information obtained from the respondent.

This evolution did not solve the problem of quota selection itself, to be sure. NORC was forthright and concerned about underrepresenting less educated groups,[138] but the new sampling instructions were still another way in which NORC was trying to standardize field procedures, in a trade-off that had the effect of reducing the personal judgment of the interviewer and increasing the role of the respondent.[139]

Some of these changes appeared in NORC's manual, *Interviewing for NORC* (published in 1945). This manual was the most ambitious and complete set of instructions in this period for survey fieldwork. The commercial polls' own interviewing guides had not been published for widespread distribution. Bingham and Moore's well-known book, *How to Interview*, reflected the advent of the new polls when it incorporated into its third edition (1941) a new chapter on poll interviewing, but it was very brief and general.[140] Program Surveys had written fairly extensive instructions to interviewers, but its materials were classified as government documents. NORC's 150-page book was a well-organized, well-written text presenting the detailed instructions for conducting the interview, interacting with the respondent, filling the sample quotas, and handling all aspects of the personal encounter and the paperwork. It was indeed a signal service to the new field to have current and conscientious data-collection methods described in practical detail. (Lazarsfeld ordered fifty copies for the Bureau.)[141] A second edition was published in 1947.

INTERVIEWING EXPERIMENTS

In the Denver period, with Cantril's encouragement especially, NORC conducted various experiments on interviewer performance.[142] It also made a lively test comparing interviewing to the secret ballot in order to address skepticism about the validity of data collected in the face-to-face setting. Gosnell and de Grazia, for example, argued that the personal interviewing situation was likely to distort the opinions of low-income groups in particular.[143] NORC got permission to set up its own secret ballot boxes in all the polling places of Boulder, Colorado, on election day, and it conducted what is now called an "exit survey." Results from these ballots on two candidate races and three issues were compared with results from a sample of personal interviews done a few days earlier. The interviews predicted the ballot results on the candidates and on two of the three issues to within sampling error. Turnout itself showed the biggest discrepancy: of those who said they would vote, only 69 percent went to the polls.[144]

NORC's major research into interviewing involved analysis of data from other organizations and searching inquiry into its own staff and practice. *Interviewing in Social Research* (1954), by Hyman, Cobb, Feldman, Hart, and Stember, stood until very recently as the most ambitious research project ever on survey research interviewing.[145]

The project was started in 1947. Stouffer suggested such an inquiry to the group of academics, pollsters, and market researchers which SSRC/NRC had brought together right after the war, the Committee on the Measurement of Opinion, Attitudes, and Consumer Wants. (Stouffer was chair.) Of the three projects sponsored by the committee, the interviewing research was brought to the most timely successful conclusion. The interviewing project directed by Hyman became NORC's most important contribution to methodological research in this period. By 1952, NORC authors had published thirty articles on research into interviewing problems, many of which were summarized in the 1954 volume.[146] Two of those reported projects are of special note: Sheatsley's analysis of leading national field staffs and the Denver validity study.

Sheatsley's 1950–51 articles were an analysis of the characteristics and performance ratings of all interviewers on the NORC staff since 1941, along with more summary data from other major organizations (including the big three and the USDA organization that succeeded Program Surveys). NORC had kept excellent books on the attributes and ratings of its field staff, and Sheatsley's study is an invaluable historical document showing variations in composition and practice across major organizations at the time. The study summarized what was known about other aspects of interviewing, such as the effect of experience, the faking of interviews, the degree of matching interviewers and respondents by age, sex, and education, and tests of interviewer competence—important issues of quality control then (and still).[147]

Another component study, the Denver validity study of 1949, was directed by Cahalan in the survey practicum at the affiliated Opinion Research Center (ORC) that remained at Denver after NORC moved to Chicago. This study compared reports on a number of factual items with official records (voting and registration, contributions to Community Chest, possession of a driver's license and library card, etc.). Assuming that the official records were the true value, invalidity of reporting ranged from negligible amounts up to a high of almost 50 percent. The random assignment of interviewers in comparable sectors of the city also permitted analysis of interviewer differences. (Interviewers' field ratings and their handling of open questions showed the strongest differences.)[148] A comprehensive monograph of the study did not result, doubtless because the Denver ORC closed down in 1949, but several important papers were published. The study still stands as a classic inquiry into validity on a scale that has for the most part been unreplicated. Its excellent documentation makes it still useful for analysis.[149]

The book *Interviewing in Social Research* canvassed the existing literature and reported a series of its own laboratory experiments and field trials using NORC staff. Such a review involved a "dangerous confession" of error which might well be misinterpreted, the authors noted:

> Let it be noted that the *demonstration* of error marks an advanced stage of a science. All scientific inquiry is subject to error, and it is far better to be aware of this, to study the sources in an attempt to reduce it, and to estimate the magnitude[s] . . . than to be ignorant of the errors concealed in the data.[150]

Hyman et al.'s findings went against the grain of much educated common sense in the survey field. Training manuals of leading firms, including NORC, all assumed that interviewers' *ideology* was the main carrier of bias.[151] But the new evidence pointed to a more likely culprit in the *expectations* of interviewers for intellectual consistency or stereotyped behavior in their respondents, factors that the authors called "attitude structure" and "role" bias. They cautioned against exaggerating the interaction of "rapport" (highly praised in the literature) and recommended a balancing attention to professional involvement in the task. Their data led them to other nonobvious conclusions, including the view that much interviewer error was random in character and did not lend itself easily to solutions through training or recruitment.

The authors were not alarmed. They judged that the existing literature exaggerated the sins of interviewing: poorly designed studies did not randomize assignments and thus did not permit disentangling of the variability of interviewers from that of their respondents. When studies were properly designed to tackle that problem, as in the Denver study and other NORC work, they showed evidence of interviewer variability, but it was weaker, more complex, and somewhat more idiosyncratic than laboratory studies suggested. The authors did *not* really conclude that "the effect of the bias introduced by the interviewer is . . . practically negligible," as their dust jacket contended,[152] for they did indeed make recommendations for ways to reduce and control interviewer bias and error, and their analysis was far more qualified and complex.

Until very recent years, the NORC project has stood alone as the only broad program of research into interviewing, one that reconceptualized some of the basic problems of survey interviewing. (The book was reissued in 1975.) Recent work by the Bradburn and Sudman group at NORC and by the Cannell group at SRC has refocused inquiry into an emphasis that Hyman and his colleagues made many years back, that of placing more attention on the task of asking and answering than on the interpersonal relationship of "rapport."[153]

New Research Organization

In these early years, NORC initiated several projects to create new networks and structures for publicizing surveys and for making its national work more accessible and more affordable. Most of these ideas did not come to a more permanent form until later, when the pool of talent and interest had widened, the store of treasure for research had increased, and experience had accumulated.

Recognizing that surveys were often too expensive for a single client, NORC set out on time-sharing projects as early as the mid-1940s. By 1944, NORC had sold eighteen questions, at $250 each, to various clients (who probably bought space in the State Department surveys), and a brochure was sent to 200 nonprofit organizations to try to stimulate more question sales. Another NORC plan for "periodic surveys," for example, was approved in 1949, but it did not take shape until later (in the form of NORC's own "amalgam" series and SRC's "omnibus" studies of the 1970s, both of which addressed the problem of costs).[154]

NORC's "affiliates" program was another invention that was short-lived at the time but was later renewed. In 1947–48, representatives of several universities (chiefly those that had hoped to attract NORC to their own campuses) contributed $1,000 each and met with NORC to consider joint studies and data sharing, starting with some work in voting studies. The program apparently was not renewed after the first year.[155] The germ of this idea was expressed again, in 1961, when the Interuniversity Consortium for Political and Social Research was founded at ISR by Warren E. Miller and his associates to archive quantitative studies and make them available to members.

NORC's own General Social Survey (GSS), established by James A.

Davis in 1972, was another approach to national archiving and data sharing: the GSS made available to subscribers the data of an annual national survey that focused especially on the replication of questions over time. This, too, had been in the wind at NORC in 1959–60, as NORC sought NSF funding for a national survey facility and considered other plans that would make national surveys financially feasible and more widely accessible.[156]

Another NORC enterprise was discontinued in 1948 because of financial losses: the fortnightly publication *Opinion News*, which summarized various polls' results. But much the same function has been carried out by *POQ*, which since the 1940s has regularly presented a section called "The Polls;" and also by a more recent arrival, the monthly magazine *Public Opinion* (published by the American Enterprise Institute), which specializes in summarizing poll data.

Various ideas that were discussed or tried out by NORC in these early years were born again in later years, at NORC or elsewhere, as interest and training in survey research burgeoned, affecting the social science disciplines and attracting more money, more practitioners, and a new demand for social science data. Another organizational innovation by NORC during this period reflected its own hybrid character of commercial and academic experience. The professional association AAPOR, which represented the effort to bring commercial and academic interests together, actually took on a character very like the original foundation that Field had had in mind in 1939–40. AAPOR was NORC's most durable organizational innovation of this period (see chapter seven), providing a place outside of the traditional social science disciplines for the professional shelter and development of survey researchers from commercial and academic life.

11

The Survey Research Center at Michigan: From the Margins of Government

Ren had this fantastic ability to learn only from success. He experienced failures like everyone else, but he just sloughed them off—he didn't really know they had happened—and went on to the next thing.

Angus Campbell

Staking a New Place

By the end of the war, certain members of Congress had made perfectly clear that they were displeased with governmental opinion research. The temporary wartime agencies were gone or dismembered, and Program Surveys was on the chopping block, too. Conservative congressmen and farm interests had shown their suspicion of the liberalism of the Department of Agriculture in general and some of its surveys in particular. Some Southern congressmen had come upon what they interpreted as racial meddling in a departmental survey conducted in Coahoma County, Mississippi. Program Surveys was not, in fact, involved—Carl Taylor's Division of Farm Population and Rural Life had studied the county as part of an ambitious plan in the social survey tradition and had reported on the wretched living conditions of poor blacks—but hostile congressmen reacted by determining to abolish all "social surveys."

Embattled spokesmen for Agriculture tried to save some minimal capacity to gather survey data, and Congress relented enough to allow the department to do a little market research.[1] In August 1946, Program Surveys was officially dissolved and was replaced with another organization with a mission carefully circumscribed to studies of consumer attitudes and preferences about agricultural products, and its budget was pared back accordingly. By the end of the war, Likert himself had been out of academic life for a decade, but others at Program Surveys had only been out of university life for the duration of the war (Campbell,

340

Cannell, Kish, and Lansing, for example; Katona's academic career in Europe had been interrupted when he fled Hitler). The group's members were ready to take their research experience in government to a university as an interdisciplinary venture. They had been scouting around—Cottrell of Cornell and Wirth of Chicago had both shown interest—and they finally settled on the University of Michigan.[2]

The lure could not have been money or security. In two official actions over the summer of 1946, the university's board of regents approved the establishment of a Survey Research Center (SRC) on the condition that it be entirely self-supporting through grants and contracts, making no charge on the university budget. If the staff did any teaching in the departments, it was to be on one-year appointments, explicitly without tenure, and the whole "experimental" arrangement could be terminated at any time. The Michigan regents were taking few chances.

The Likert group found Michigan attractive for several reasons—the reputation of the university itself, Likert's familiarity with it from his days as a Michigan undergraduate, the desirability of a small college town (Ann Arbor) as a place to raise children—in spite of the university's lack of support. Likert agreed to the arrangements, and the group began to move from Washington in the winter of 1946–47, when space at the university became available.[3]

SRC's quarters befit its "marginal" arrival: a few offices in the basement of the elementary school of the university's School of Education, where the tallest of the new SRC staffers had to be careful not to crack their heads on the exposed heating pipes. The center later expanded somewhat into some other nearby offices, and in 1950 it was consolidated into larger headquarters, a short mile from the center of the campus at that time. This was the old West Hospital building, which still bore its external cylindrical chutes for dispatching patients on stretchers in case of fire.

By 1949, the Institute for Social Research (ISR) under Likert's direction had combined SRC, of which Angus Campbell was now director, and the Research Center for Group Dynamics, which Cartwright had brought to Michigan from MIT after the death of its founder, Kurt Lewin.[4] SRC remained much the bigger partner, usually accounting for about 80 percent of ISR income, and it is the organization of focal historical interest for us here. It will often be convenient to refer to SRC/ISR where SRC is our major concern but cannot be disconnected from ISR.

ISR's transition from Agriculture to the "elegance" of various local facilities at Michigan was regularly celebrated in the local culture of

Christmas skits, as in the rousing song, sung to the tune of "Old Mac-
Donald":

> Old Ren Likert had a barn—UMISR
> And in that barn he had some walls—UMISR
> With a crack-crack here, and a plaster there,
> Here a crack, there a crack,
> We don't have a crack lack.
> Old Ren Likert had a barn—UMISR
>
> Old Ren Likert had a barn—UMISR
> And in that barn he had some paint—UMISR
> With an eggshell blue, and a sheep dip brown,
> Here a blue, there a brown,
> Then the wall and all comes down!
> Old Ren Likert had a barn—UMISR.[5]

The Inheritance from Washington

Despite the tenuousness of the original arrangement in 1946, the move
to university territory for SRC/ISR was a more favored one in certain
respects than either the Bureau's or NORC's had been. The fact that
SRC represented a "second wave" that was arriving five or six years later,
when there were already precedents in university research, may have
been a help. It is easier to identify certain other factors, however, including the Washington experience. From this SRC brought prominent and
prestigious wartime service, a technical capacity to do work on a national
scale, and a network of useful contacts.

Likert himself had had considerable visibility in Washington as Pro-
gram Surveys' only director (1939–1946), as a technical consultant in the
Gallup hearings of 1944, and as director of the morale surveys for the
U.S. Strategic Bombing Surveys in 1945 (for which he was awarded the
Medal of Freedom), and he went back to university life in 1946 with
greater professional strength than he had had before the war.

In negotiating the transfer from Washington, Likert argued that universities had new responsibilities to undertake research of social and scientific importance, for the government's own research was constrained
to short-run, practical results.[6] In the immediate postwar years, Likert
publicized the work that he and his colleagues had done during the war,
especially the projects to increase war-bond purchases and to monitor
potentially inflationary spending. He continued to use the imagery of
wartime to argue for social research:

One of the most serious problems that we face . . . is mobilizing our economy to produce all that is needed for the defense of our basic freedom . . . the social sciences have research tools, such as the sample survey, which can provide important scientific results and valuable information to guide policy and program decisions.[7]

The rhetoric was not entirely anachronistic, for although the war itself ended in 1945, the Cold War followed in swift succession. Likert was addressing that political context, but his words effectively publicized the group's wartime achievements and credentials.

The technical capacity to do national surveys was clearly a resource for getting contracts with the federal government—a way of surviving in the beginning. SRC staff had experience in national work (Cannell in interviewing and Kish in sampling). They managed to keep most of their old interviewers and supervisory staff working for them under a university label, and they also wangled the sample itself out of the federal government.[8]

The wartime days also provided a network of contacts in government administration and social science. Likert consulted people in Washington on how best to hang onto the liquid assets study for which Program Surveys had done a pilot study.[9] The wartime network provided some kindred spirits in social science departments at Michigan, too: Donald Marquis, the new chairman of the psychology department, and psychologist Theodore Newcomb were both wartime colleagues. When the group came from Washington, they were not as interdisciplinary as they had been during the war—the anthropologists, for example, had moved on early—but SRC could still count social psychology, economics, and statistics among their number. They were short on political scientists (until Warren E. Miller came in 1951), and they remained short on sociologists, which was an intellectual and political disadvantage. But ties with the psychology department were especially useful. Under Marquis's expansionist administration, the psychology department was welcoming new specialties; it was growing at such a rate, in fact, that even five ISR teaching appointments were acceptable to the department in one unusual year (1955).[10]

The Key Advantage

The legacy from Washington days was a good one, allowing SRC a lifeline back to government money and some webs of political network in the new setting. But the fact that SRC was allowed to keep its overhead from the beginning was probably the prime resource, a view that is widely shared within the Michigan group and in the larger social science community. It was a singular arrangement for the time and ultimately became the envy of other university research organizations.[11] The arrangement was largely an informal understanding, the "logic" of which lay in the university's complete freedom from any financial responsibility for the center (except for the support of some office space, heat, light, and maintenance); if the university did not provide any money to the center, there was little reason for the center to give any *back*. Keeping the overhead was a by-product of the university's firm intention to keep its own budget safely unentangled from this experimental enterprise.

The great advantage of keeping the overhead was not really apparent until SRC/ISR survived its independence from university support and began to prosper. It was not entirely a fluke; Likert later recalled having known that there was at least a precedent with some engineering school contracts.[12] But Likert accepted the arrangement as the best that could be had and treated it as something of a challenge. Fine, he said: we'll do $250,000 worth of business in the first full year (1948) and $350,000 in the second. They got very close to that in the first year and a half, and they did better in the years following.[13] When ISR began to accumulate reserves, the overhead arrangement was not disturbed.[14]

Once SRC/ISR showed its capacity to make money, why didn't Michigan do what Columbia had done, calling in the overhead and putting the research institute on the university budget? (See chapter nine.) It is not entirely clear. It is not even clear whether the Michigan administration seriously considered taking that step, though the thought crossed at least one administrator's mind, as we shall see. We do have good evidence that ISR administrators went to a lot of trouble to become intellectually and politically as well as financially integrated into academic life.

The Political Process

In the early days, SRC people had the sympathetic interest not only of some colleagues in the social sciences but also of certain top administrators. James P. Adams, provost of the university, for example, told Likert to report directly to him. Just why Adams was interested is not clear, but Likert later recalled this as an important protection for the infant institute from other administrators who were *not* enthusiastic about this project.[15] An interdisciplinary executive committee was drawn from relevant schools and departments, which meant that from the beginning the center had an opportunity to cultivate allies in the disciplines, and it naturally made its nominations for this committee from among social scientists who were sympathetic to empirical research (e.g., Angell of sociology, Boulding of economics, Marquis of psychology).[16]

This moral support was valuable for the long run, but money was the immediate problem. In the beginning, SRC lived from hand to mouth, surviving through federal government grants and contracts, which provided almost 99 percent of the center's income during the first year. In the next several years, federal government monies still provided the lion's share of SRC income.[17] Income rose, but there was little stability, and financial officers of the university felt that ISR's bookkeeping style erred on the side of optimism. In a 1951 letter to Likert, Vice President Pierpont reminded him that none of his "tentative contracts" of the past year had become firm ones:

> I appreciate the fact that in many instances it is necessary to carry on a certain amount of effort before a contract is entered into and that in some instances this promotional work will not materialize in a contract. I am sure you will realize, however, that this is one of the easiest ways of dissipating all of your reserves and I think that your project people and other directors must be aware of the need to be extremely careful about incurring costs which will not be reimbursed.[18]

—shades of correspondence between the Columbia bursar and Paul Lazarsfeld.

Pierpont took an even darker view of the institute's use of its overhead. Cost overruns were piling up in both of its centers, he wrote. Overhead expenses and overhead-sponsored research expenses were currently running over a third of total revenue:

> Such a situation is entirely out of accord with my understanding of the reason that overhead revenues are retained by the Institute. In no other operation of the University to my knowledge can project directors use overhead revenues without the approval of the Committee on Budget Administration and I think that the freedom which you have had should be appreciated by your whole staff. It certainly is not my desire to decrease or modify or restrict your operations, but I think that the financial control of your operations must rest essentially with the directors if such freedom is to continue.[19]

The ISR executive committee noted that directors should be more vigilant about overruns, but it also took the position that putting staff on overhead temporarily was the only way it had of keeping people employed *between* projects.

ISR did not lose control over its overhead, but Pierpont appointed a business manager to keep things in better order.[20] Raymond R. Garlough, though appointed by the central administration, came to identify with the institute and became its advocate in financial dealings with the university. Garlough was an activist and an ingenious finance manager, whose alertness to keeping the wolf from the door inspired the kind of admiration at ISR that Clara Shapiro inspired at the Bureau. Through having a business manager of its own, albeit thrust upon it by the university, ISR actually came to take greater control over its own finances and bookkeeping.

Although the university had shown concern about ISR finances, the institute had in fact covered some good ground politically and financially by 1951. In 1948, at Campbell's suggestion, it organized a summer institute in survey research methods in the university summer session, which paid some summer salaries. With this exception, SRC/ISR staff taught courses only through teaching appointments with the departments and were intent on trying to be integrated into the departments, not competitive with them.

SRC/ISR also had a close relationship with the university's Detroit Area Study (DAS), a graduate practicum in survey research which was established in 1951 by sociologist Ronald Freedman, founding director. DAS was a two-semester course that conducted an annual survey in the Detroit metropolitan area. It was similar to and perhaps modeled on the ORC-NORC Denver Community Survey. Initially, DAS was supported by a grant from the Ford Foundation, and funds were administered through SRC and an interdisciplinary committee. In 1958, the university assumed full support for DAS and channeled funds through the sociology department. Throughout most of the 1950s, however, DAS was physically located within SRC, and DAS called upon SRC's technical resources in sampling and interviewing and linked its name to SRC in publications and press releases. SRC, for its part, felt that an interdisciplinary practicum was better equipped than SRC itself was to meet students' expressed demand for systematic instruction in survey research.[21]

SRC/ISR offered employment to students in ongoing research projects, which provided another point of some integration into university life. By 1950–51, more than fifty graduate students worked full- or part-time at the institute, and almost all were Ph.D. candidates. In 1951, as well, ISR was authorized to send a representative to meetings of the division of the social sciences.[22] And financially, ISR was doing well: its income had grown each year, reaching over $850,000 in 1951–52, of which the Survey Research Center's share was over $650,000.[23] After these first five years, SRC/ISR apparently felt strong enough to begin asking for some things. At least by the chronicle of the official minutes of SRC/ISR, 1951 was the first year in which ISR asked for some university funds.

The university was reimbursing ISR staff for teaching about a dozen courses in the departments, but reimbursement for this amounted to $30,000, less than 4 percent of ISR's income. An ISR committee recommended that the university allocate some general funds, a minimum of $10,000, which could be shown as a portion of the three directors' part-time salaries.[24] The institute did not get the money, but it kept trying. ISR minutes show a succession of memos, meetings, subcommittees, and personal visits to university administrators, especially on Likert's part—and some headway. In the course of 1953–56, the three directors' salaries were assumed by the university: first for Likert, then for Campbell and Cartwright, in turn.[25] After an "experiment" of about eight years, this was the first hard financial commitment that the university had made to the institute.

In the course of the next several years (1955–60), the staff's aspirations rose with their achievements, and little by little they got more security within the university system. They wanted tenure and university-paid sabbaticals for the directors, research salaries for their program directors—perhaps half-time for the present—and other perquisites of first-class citizenship for research personnel. They did not get the moon—but they did manage to get some pieces of it.

The role of director was not tenured, but some ISR staff got teaching on tenure-track appointments in psychology and economics and a position each in sociology and political science.[26] They got sabbatical leaves for their senior personnel—not through university general funds, as they had hoped, but through a Ford Foundation grant and university permission to allocate their own reserves. (These sabbaticals were labeled "off-campus duty assignments," lest the traditional prerogative of professors be seen as extending generally to researchers.)

In 1958, ISR made good progress on plans for a new building and began talks with university administrators about possible sites on the central campus and ways of funding. The institute was given permission to apply to NIH for building funds, just as NORC was doing in the same season, and, like NORC, it ultimately got some. ISR directors got promise of outright and substantial university funds to supplement the money they could obtain from government, private subscription, and their own reserves.[27]

ISR achieved a degree of real integration into the university during this decade (1951–1960). It did not receive everything it hoped for, to be sure, nor all the acceptance across the disciplines that it wished—the relationship with sociology continued to be unsatisfactory for both parties, and the relationship with political science was prickly, too[28]—but ISR managed to put down roots in the university's prestige-tenure system and to negotiate some university financial support. In both areas, it achieved more security as an organization than either the Bureau or NORC was able to in the same period. *Why* it managed to do this is impossible to say with any certitude: the situation at Michigan differed in so many ways from that prevailing at either Columbia or Chicago that we have nothing like a "natural experiment." Certainly, SRC had a more favorable environment to start with; in addition, it may well have had more administrative talent and have worked harder at institutional integration.

Neither the Bureau nor NORC had the advantage that was conferred at Michigan by sympathetic central administrators, first by Provost Adams and then by his successor, Marvin L. Niehuss. In 1951, Niehuss, a lawyer and an economist with research experience in business economics, rose to the position of vice president and dean of faculties, with still more responsibility than provost. Among his manifold duties, Niehuss carried the institute's message to the regents and brought back interpretations of the politically possible to the institute leadership. The minutes of the ISR and SRC executive committees show frequent consultation with Niehuss and continuing evidence that his support was carefully sought and his judgments clearly valued.[29]

If in his key position Niehuss had opposed the institute or even given it mere grudging assistance, he could have been a major roadblock. As we have seen, neither the Bureau nor NORC seems to have had the same support. At Columbia, Niehuss's counterpart in the early years, Frank Fackenthal, was supportive of social research, but his successors in the role were less sympathetic. At Chicago, NORC's chairman of the board, Ralph W. Tyler, was also the university dean of the social sciences, as we have seen, but this was not a remarkable political advantage for integrating NORC into the university. Tyler pushed NORC's cause with the university in certain ways, but he also approved of NORC's location outside it. (See chapters nine and ten.)

SRC had the resource of some good friends on high as well as supportive colleagues in the social sciences, and it cultivated them. Likert and Campbell met repeatedly with members of the central administration and the departments. Lazarsfeld and Merton, in particular, surely lavished no less devotion on their enterprise, but their gifts and aspirations were different and the conception and the practice of leadership in the two organizations were different, too. It seems fair to say that the priority at the Bureau was on scholar-administrators, with the emphasis on the first word; at ISR, Likert and Campbell were instead administrator-scholars. They did not bring the same range of interests to their own research or the same intellectual excitement to students that Lazarsfeld and Merton did—neither Michigan scholar had many graduate students, in fact—nor did they reach Lazarsfeld's and Merton's intellectual attainments. Rather, they took heavier administrative responsibilities and displayed more political talent in institution building, making sensitive and judicious use of the more favorable Michigan environment and attracting talented social scientists to an expanding decentralized organization.

The Institutional Context of Intellectual Products

The Internal Structure

THE LEADERSHIP

SRC/ISR was never "Likert's shop" in the sense that the Bureau was Lazarsfeld's. When SRC came from Washington, it was already a group of some psychological coherence that functioned in many ways as a committee—there was more consensus and less director dominance than in research organizations of the European tradition that Lazarsfeld had brought with him from Vienna. SRC/ISR had a collegial structure that rested intellectually on Likert's and others' ideas from industrial and small-group psychology (to which we shall return) and rested personally on a set of individuals who had first joined Likert in wartime as fully credentialed professionals, not as students. The consensual practice at ISR also rested on a particular division of labor between Likert and Campbell.

The way in which Likert and Campbell divided their administrative labor did not *conflict* with Likert's emerging theory of organization, but it did not flow from it, either. It suggests more readily Bales's theory of the two functions of leadership in the small group, the socio-emotional and task needs.[30] By temperament and conviction, Likert was the yea-sayer, the consummate optimist displaying confidence in himself, his colleagues, their organization, and the future of social science, exuding high energy and missionary zeal.[31] Not everyone was drawn to Likert's enthusiasm and salesmanship, but to many he was persuasive and imaginative. Those who had stayed at Program Surveys and then wanted to go on to Michigan tended to value his style.[32] Likert carried a socio-emotional approach to leadership not only because he was responsive to other people (quick to support others' ideas and quick to give praise and credit) but also because he conveyed an excitement, a verve and vision, about the enterprise itself. He used this ability to great effect in promoting the institute and its interdisciplinary mission, in raising money for its research, and in acting often as its ambassador of external affairs.

Campbell was the realist, more cautious, judicious, and prudent. He and Cartwright sometimes felt that they were trying to hang onto Likert with invisible kite strings as he soared up and away with another notion of dubious practicality. They also later admitted with amusement that on certain of the occasions that he got away from them, it was good that he had. So they did not succeed in leashing him entirely, although they sometimes tempered his hopes.[33] Campbell conveyed a personal strength, solidity, and principled integrity that inspired confidence, and in the committee deliberations of ISR it was a good thing to have Campbell on your side. (It was a good strategy to try an idea out first with Rensis, who would probably say "More power to you," and then to see if it would fly with Angus.)[34]

Close up, Campbell was valued by his colleagues for his sensitivity, warmth, and humor, but at a greater distance—tall and straight, with a mien of personal reserve, and sometimes dour—he could be forbidding in a way that Likert probably could not.[35] In this implicit division of labor, Campbell was more often the administrator of internal affairs. It was he who ferreted out the office sherry drinkers at Christmastime and invoked university rules. (When he joined them in later years, the rules had also changed.) Campbell was concerned about tasks within the SRC and within university politics, pressuring people to get their writing done, to seek teaching appointments, and to participate in university affairs through the faculty senate and the university committees—and he did these things himself.[36] He continued to feel that ISR's overhead arrangement had developed through some good luck as well as some prescience and wisdom and that it required protection. He believed in keeping in good political touch with administrators and colleagues in the university community, and Campbell did both well.[37]

ORGANIZATIONAL THEORY AND STAFF DEVELOPMENT

The structure of the institute was also modeled in some fashion after Likert's own adaptation of the "human relations" school of industrial management. During wartime, Likert's improvisational and consensual style at Program Surveys was not everyone's cup of tea; some found it loose, confusing, and inefficient; others thrived on the informality and committee structure. Those who thrived remember an esprit, a sense of social relevance and intellectual headiness in their work. The fact that this feeling was much like that remembered for the same years by others who had thrived in Stouffer's Research Branch, Lazarsfeld's Bureau, the Polls Division, and NORC suggests that it was not critically a function of a specific organizational structure. It was an exciting time—in the urgency of wartime, in the emergence of the social sciences, in new loyalties and commitments of younger lives—and these were probably more formative than any particular scheme of organization. After the war, however, Likert's theory and practice of decentralization of ISR probably made a difference.

Exactly how much the organizational theory of Likert and his colleagues shaped the structure of their own organization or guided the day-to-day practice at the institute is impossible to say. The institute did not study itself—when there were internal aggravations and conflicts, it was felt that such a study would be divisive; efforts were made instead to involve contending parties in common projects.[38] But two core ideas from the theory were unmistakably part of the institute's structure: group decision making and decentralized responsibility (that is, committees and program directors).

From the beginning, the research program was decentralized at SRC, which was consonant not only with a democratic, decentralized theory but also with the traditional independence of academic scholars—as well as with the practical fact that nobody was able to raise enough money for everybody. Staff could do research if they could find enough money to pay their own salaries, hire other staff, pay for central services (interviewing, coding, analysis, etc.), and pay for other study expenses. This, in conjunction with some staff security through part-time teaching appointments, powered a mechanism for entrepreneurial expansion. Projects could be added on and enlarged as other entrepreneurs—not just the institute directors but other study directors as well—found money. The budget did indeed expand. From 1946–47 to 1959–60, it rose almost linearly from $234,000 to $1,517,000, with a mean of $897,000 over the fourteen years.[39]

If senior project directors at ISR could not maintain research money at a steady state for themselves and their project staffs, they could ask to dip into the overhead fund for short periods until the next grant or contract came through. But "going on overhead" for any length of time threatened the organization's future, and it was discouraged. ISR nevertheless had the advantage of being able to use overhead flexibly to maintain its senior staff and their projects. Very self-consciously, the institute leadership tried to build loyalty and commitment—it became policy that staff members with split research-teaching appointments should work *more* than half-time at the institute—and tried to protect its senior staff.[40]

At the outset, SRC, like NORC, set forth methodological research as one of its prime purposes, but that objective subsided somewhat. Staff members repeatedly tried and failed in these early days to get foundation support for research into sampling and interviewing.[41] In the face of this failure, there was thought of committing some of ISR's own reserves to such work. A subcommittee report in 1957 commended the idea, noting that the institute's very future was in the development of methods of greater technical sophistication and power. But this committee report was revised to say that the institute's greatest resource for the future was its senior staff.[42] Instead of investing its capital in methodological experiment and development, senior staff decided to invest in the senior *people* of their organization—themselves, and those to come—by financing sabbaticals out of reserves and tiding senior people over between projects. The basic purpose of the policy was to blunt some of the business pressures and sharpen some academic advantages, notably the freedom to do work that was intellectually interesting under conditions of some security.[43]

The Applied/Basic Mix

The dichotomy between applied and basic research was not thought to be "useful" at the institute, Stanley E. Seashore wrote later, because preference was given to research programs "which in some fashion join[ed] theory development with issues of societal effectiveness and human values."[44] But this was something of a gloss. The issue was lively, even so. The institute researchers felt the familiar tensions between the client's short-run imperatives (with their own compelling short-run need for support) and the scientist's long-term intellectual hopes. How much of a given study could the individual scientists build to suit themselves, in the pursuit of science itself and of their own reputations and careers? And how could they and the institution as a whole steer clear of any charge of commercialism that would jeopardize their standing as scientists? These questions had some meaning in all three major programs that developed at SRC in this period—economic, organizational, and political behavior.

THE ECONOMIC BEHAVIOR PROGRAM

SRC functioned during its first year as something of an outpost of the federal government, gathering descriptive data. As we have seen, almost all of its first-year income was federal money, the lion's share of which came from a contract with the Federal Reserve Board to gather national financial data on savings, assets, and spending, the outgrowth of work directed by Dorwin Cartwright and then by George Katona during the war. The first full survey of liquid assets was conducted in 1946 before the group left Washington and was continued from Michigan as the Survey of Consumer Finances (SCF), the core of the Economic Behavior Program. Campbell later reflected that if at any time during the first five years that contract had been canceled, SRC/ISR probably would not have survived.[45] The Economic Behavior Program remained a workhorse of the institute throughout this period (1947–60). It was always the biggest program in SRC, with a budget that was always bigger than the whole budget of Group Dynamics.[46]

Katona had Ph.D.'s in both economics and psychology, and he differed from mainstream economists because of his theory of the "powerful consumer," as he later entitled a book.[47] In this view, it was no longer sufficient to track the fluctuations in the economy through aggregate financial statistics, as resultants of decisions made by government and business, with consumers playing a largely responsive role. Katona saw consumers in the postwar era as having a new dynamic impact on the economy because they had more discretionary income than ever before. He believed that consumers' attitudes of optimism or pessimism about the economy influenced their saving and spending decisions just as businessmen's attitudes influenced *their* behavior, and Katona's group tried to measure those consumer attitudes.

The governors of the Federal Reserve Board were not particularly taken with the theory of the consumer or the use of the subjective measures, so the SRC economists were able to repeat only eight questions from survey to survey—and not because of the theory. As Morgan has explained,

> Questions on buying plans and expectations and attitudes, urged by the Survey Research Center on theoretical grounds, were accepted only because they were necessary to keep a financial survey from being too dull and uninteresting to the respondent.[48]

The first of these questions was the old "can opener" of Program Survey days, designed to start the conversation in a relaxed and natural style, well in advance of asking respondents their actual income:

We are interested in how people are getting along financially these days. Would you say that you and your family are better off or worse off financially than you were a year ago? . . . Why is that?

Other questions inquired into optimism/pessimism about the future:

Now looking ahead—do you think that a *year from now* you people will be better off financially, or worse off, or just about the same as now? . . .

Now, turning to business conditions in the country as a whole—do you think that during the next twelve months we'll have good times financially, or bad times, or what? . . . Why do you think that?

Additional questions asked respondents their more specific *buying intentions*: was it a good or bad time to buy a house, furniture, a car, a refrigerator, a stove?[49]

The "psychological economists" worked to develop this Index of Consumer Sentiment as a leading indicator of "turning points" in the economy in annual trend cross-section studies. These were complicated matters of definition and measurement—the index was predictive of some short-run changes in the economy in this period but not in others—and other economists were by no means convinced *en masse* of the merit of collecting household data on attitudes. James Tobin used SRC panel data, for example, to compare attitudes of households at one point with their behavior at a later point, and he concluded that the more specific buying intention questions were a good deal more predictive of behavior than were the more diffuse attitude questions about the economy in general. Attitudes were probably seen by most economists as, at best, supplements to standard aggregate measures of income, wealth, savings, and spending.[50]

The Federal Reserve Board remained lukewarm about the attitudinal measures but contracted for the economic surveys from 1946 to 1959. In 1959, the board considered slowing down the SCF to a biennial rhythm. SRC decided that if a Ford Foundation grant came through, along with business support (about $72,000 from General Motors and Ford) and sales of special tabulations, it could get along without the Federal Reserve—and the Ford grant did come through (for $300,000).[51] The program's theory and data of consumer attitudes, intentions, and motives penetrated the profession. Economists found it difficult to incorporate attitudes into their models using "objective" measures of income, wealth, and savings, but the issue was joined, and the theoretical argument was continued with benefit of data.[52]

Support in the commercial sector. The program's contract with the Federal Reserve Board had been for an *annual* SCF. This was sufficient for the government's purposes, but national consumer surveys at this rhythm were not sufficient intellectually or financially for the psychological economists at SRC. The field office needed approximately four studies a year to sustain its national staff, and the analysts thought that the winds of change in consumer sentiment were more variable than an annual measure could capture.

In 1951, the program made a major expansion in its repertoire of consumer surveys with a series of "interim" surveys, conducted before and after the SCF. These surveys were financed by private industry—General Motors, manufacturers of major home appliances, Bell Telephone, the life insurance industry, and others—and they duly inquired not only into consumers' intentions to buy cars, washers, dryers, and other consumer durables but also into their preferences and reactions concerning matters of price, safety, design, and color, their feelings about long-distance telephoning, their intentions to travel, and other topics.

The continuing Index of Consumer Sentiment was a small part of the consumer surveys. Much the greater part of the data gathered in these supplemental consumer surveys was designed to meet the needs of corporate clients. Data were also sold to national magazines. *Business Week* was particularly important to the program. With a long-standing contract, the magazine gave regular—and very respectful—coverage to the ups and downs of consumer intentions and attitudes recorded in SRC consumer surveys. This was probably the single most important source of publicity for the program and SRC/ISR. There were times, however, when SRC staff felt that they might be too closely linked to the business community.

Keeping an eye on commercialism. The strong link to business was a worry at ISR. Some people at the institute regarded the consumer surveys as dull bread-and-butter work that offered to the organization little life of the mind—an impression that Katona was quick to try to counter.[53] But even within the program, there was concern that "the holy grail not be traded in for the tin cup" and that SRC researchers be seen as "professors, not marketers."[54] No perfect clarity of policy was achieved, but SRC tried to keep vigilant. It tried to create data that would be useful for the industry as a whole rather than for just a single company—that is, the market for cars in general rather than for General Motors in particular—and it sold advance tabulations from the surveys to subscribing companies and industrial associations alike. When SRC took contracts that seemed almost wholly without scientific interest for them, it tried to tack on some methodological work, though it did not always succeed in doing so.[55] In great part, SRC rejected clients' proprietary rights to withhold data from publication for any longer than six months. And of course, the staff themselves made use of these market data in professional publications of their own. Katona and his younger associates (such as Eva Mueller, John B. Lansing, Lawrence R. Klein, and James N. Morgan) published in journals of economics, business, and marketing— rarely in psychology.[56]

The SRC psychological economists were able to obtain large *national* data sets throughout this period through the combination of governmental and commercial funding, with some support from foundations. Their intellectual interests were a small but continuous part of the consumer surveys, and the contracts permitted them to keep working on the theory of "psychological economics" by frequently monitoring consumer attitudes on a national scale. Morgan later reflected in a festschrift to Katona that the program that developed

> had to be forged out of the available research funds in a persistent application of the principle of second-best. Funds were never free, or unrestricted, or ample, and a good deal of negotiation, and mutual education, had to take place.[57]

The economic group yearned for freedom from "applied" funds, but they stayed solvent, and they managed to create a program of intellectual substance that challenged reigning economic theory.

THE HUMAN RELATIONS PROGRAM

The Human Relations Program brought together somewhat different tensions between basic and applied science. While the psychological economists had to settle for saving small portions of the client questionnaire for their own theoretical interests, the balance in the Human Relations Program was tipped the other way. Here, the mission of the scientists was to make their own theoretical explorations of sufficient practical appeal to the clients that they would put up with the work and, if possible, put up some of the money as well. The psychologists were convinced, along with Kurt Lewin, that in the long run there was "nothing so practical as a good theory"—but in the short run, the scientists were asking a good deal of their clients in the effort to build that theory.

This had implications for the way in which they conducted their research, funded it, and reported it.

Conducting the research. This program was not prototypic survey research—it spanned SRC and Group Dynamics in the use of some survey techniques and some experimental design in an organizational setting— and it did not provide work for the national staff. Regular survey interviewers lacked the education, training, and probably the status (when dealing with top management) to carry out the various tasks: the conducting of interviews that were sometimes long and intensive, skilled observation, psychological testing, and the gathering of productivity measures from company records.[58] Individual data were usually sampled within the organization, but the organization itself was chosen when it was feasible—that is, when the company was not currently plagued by strife and when both management and labor unions, if there were any, were willing to cooperate—and when it offered an interesting case study, such as a different industry, technology, new kinds of workers, new kinds or layers of hierarchy, or other features. The program studied groups in business and industry, such as clerical workers in the Prudential Insurance Company, maintenance-of-way crews in the C&O Railroad, and personnel at various levels in Studebaker Auto, the Maytag Corporation, Caterpillar Tractor, Standard Oil of New Jersey, and the United Parcel Service, and it also investigated other kinds of organizations (e.g., scientific and voluntary associations, labor unions, and military units).[59] The program tried to develop standardized measurement techniques and to build theory that would generalize across diverse settings offering different constraints and contingencies.

Funding: old and new foundations. Not surprisingly, given its low immediate payoff for businesses, the Human Relations Program got started with government funding. Likert established the program in 1947 as a ten-year project, with a grant from the Office of Naval Research. Individual businesses ranged widely in their willingness or ability to pay for the research, and together they paid about half of the research costs— goodly amounts, but not enough. Likert created the Foundation for Research on Human Behavior (FRHB) in part to help get more. The foundation offered research publications, research-report meetings, and informal seminars in which social scientists and industrialists discussed researchable business problems (there were more than fifty such seminars in these early years). Also invited to participate were scientists from outside the foundation, such as Stouffer, Merton, Glock, Conrad Taeuber, James G. March, John W. Bennett, Ithiel de Sola Pool, Everett M.

Rogers, Herbert A. Shepard, and M. Brewster Smith, as well as institute
staff. In addition, representatives from many different companies participated.[60]

The foundation was close to ISR—next door, in fact. Likert got university permission for the foundation to locate in the old hospital complex. While ISR neither directed the foundation (economist Samuel P.
Hayes, Jr., did) nor had a controlling membership on its board, it was
the dominant force and the foundation's largest beneficiary. In the years
from 1952 to 1959, the foundation spent about $250,000 (a third of its
income) on research conducted at a dozen different research centers,
but the money to Michigan researchers amounted to almost 60 percent
of the research disbursements.[61]

The foundation was never a source of big money, but it was a help,
not only in public relations for ISR but also in funding the "interim"
surveys of the Economic Behavior Program and in some Human Relations Program research, too. It was Likert's idea (one of those times, in
fact, when Campbell and Cartwright remember trying to hang onto the
kite strings),[62] and it served to keep researchers in some touch with potential sponsors and users—an effort, indeed, to fuse theory and application. Likert functioned in still another way, as communicator and publicist for social research, which shows more clearly how the tension
between applied and basic research continued.

Reporting: generalizing in the interest of intelligibility. The basic theory
with which the Human Relations Program started stated a relationship
among these three variables:

Organization: supervision (independent)		Individual: worker morale (intervening)		Product: effort (dependent)
	$\rightarrow$		$\rightarrow$	

This was to say that if supervisors valued their workers and treated them
with consideration as human beings rather than as cogs in the production machine, workers would feel appreciated for themselves as persons
as well as for their work. They would in turn feel a sense of relationship
with and loyalty to the supervisor and the company, which would motivate them to exert more initiative and greater effort. The end product,
higher productivity, could be measured in familiar "hard" units of cost
accounting, but the actual process was a psychological one. This "human
relations" approach had roots in the work of Mayo, Roethlisberger, and
others in the 1920s and 1930s (see chapter two).

This was the core theory of the Human Relations Program, which in the next ten to fifteen years guided much research. As director of SRC and then of ISR, Likert was engaged more as ambassador in fund-raising, publicity, and promotion than he was in day-to-day conduct or direction of research. Daniel Katz and (later) Robert L. Kahn were the first two program directors; Floyd C. Mann, Donald Pelz, Stanley Seashore, Arnold Tannenbaum, and others were active in the research. In the hands of these colleagues, the theory grew in contingency and qualification.

Humane supervision did not always predict high morale, they found, and high morale did not always predict high productivity. "Morale" itself proved too global a concept. Supervision also needed a more precise definition, and it was only one aspect of the total organization, in any case. It was imbedded in an ascending structure of management, and style was not enough. To be effective with their subordinates, supervisors had to be able to represent their group's interest to higher levels of authority. The dynamics of the small group became of concern, and here too was complexity. Cohesive work groups were not always the higher-producing groups; rather, they showed the greatest variance, tending to operate at higher or lower levels of productivity than did less cohesive groups.[63]

Theory in the Human Relations Program was explored and enriched with new variables and contingencies. The original statement remained of interest—the organizational style of supervision affected individual morale, which in turn affected effort for productivity. But it now involved a much more complex set of possibilities at each of the three levels:

Organizational Factors:	Individual Factors:	Product:
Immediate Job Situation	Morale (kinds of satisfaction)	Behavioral Outcome: staying with company
Supervision	Goals, motives	doing adequate work
Work group cohesion	Strength of needs	doing more work
Participation	Perceptions	(high productivity)
Skill level of job	Expectations	
Total organization	Available alternative ways of satisfaction	
Interlocking roles		
Distribution of power and control		
Higher management styles		

This new complexity was a scientific essence, but it offered few mandates for clear and immediate application on the job. In fact, the change of the name from Human Relations to Organizational Behavior and Change reflected two things: a desire to be more distant from the old "school" of Human Relations, which was seen by some as industry dominated, and a desire to put more emphasis on the exploration of a theory of organization than on the practical goals of productivity.[64] While this greater qualification and sophistication had the great advantage of not making rash and unrealistic promises, it was likely to be less clear and *intelligible* to businessmen. Likert continued to take on the hard work not only of relaying to the business community the findings of organizational research but also of convincing them of the wisdom of undertaking research and funding it, a process of generalizing which was not unlike *resimplifying* the caveats and qualifications of the research process.[65]

THE POLITICAL BEHAVIOR PROGRAM

Avoiding and escaping applied work. A third program in election studies was able to reduce a good deal of the basic/applied tension by getting large foundation grants. The Political Behavior Program started rather by accident in 1948, as one of the rather miscellaneous surveys grouped together as the Public Affairs Program—surveys of attitudes toward foreign policy, atomic energy, domestic issues, cancer, and public use of the library, along with descriptive studies (for various clients), all of which lacked any obvious theoretical coherence. In a study dealing with attitudes toward foreign policy issues, in October 1948, two questions were tacked on as measures of political interest and participation:

> In the presidential elections next month, are you almost certain to vote, uncertain, or won't you vote?

> (If certain or uncertain) Do you plan to vote Republican, Democratic, or something else?

The national sample was a small one (610 interviews), and there was no intention of making a forecast. But watching the horse race was pretty irresistible, even so, and a hand tally was kept on a blackboard in the elementary school basement offices. The race was indeed neck-and-neck, with some 20 percent of the voters still undecided about how they were going to vote.

This most modest of election studies proved of commanding interest in November when the pollsters missed the presidential forecast. It was an independent source of data, and, unlike the polls, it was based on a national probability sample. With a grant from the Social Science Research Council (SSRC), SRC promptly went back into the field for a *post*election study, reinterviewing most of the initial sample (83%), this time with many more questions about the election:

> Why do you think people voted for Truman?
> Do you think there was anything special about Truman that made some people vote against him?
> Why do you think people voted for Dewey?
> Do you think there was anything special about Dewey that made some people vote against him?
> Whom did you vote for?
> How long before the election did you decide that you were going to vote the way you did?
> Had you ever thought during the campaign that you might vote for somebody else?

Still other questions probed voting intention and behavior.[66] Material from this survey was incorporated into the technical report on the 1948 election commissioned by SSRC, and SRC continued to stay in good touch with SSRC's Committee on Political Behavior. Pendleton Herring had organized this committee in 1945; he became president of SSRC in 1948, and he was an invaluable source of support for SRC. Largely through Likert's good offices, Campbell was put on the committee, and a conference on political behavior was held in Ann Arbor in late summer 1949. The conference was attended by an interdisciplinary mix of social scientists: various political scientists, including Pendleton Herring (chair), Samuel Eldersveld, James K. Pollock, V. O. Key, Jr., David Truman, and Avery Leiserson, and social scientists from other fields, such as Paul Lazarsfeld, George Murdock, and Frederick Stephan.[67] SRC was later able to obtain funds for a study of the 1952 election from a Carnegie Corporation grant channeled through SSRC.

In research into voting behavior and attitudes, it was difficult to be "just a little bit applied." There were clients who were likely enough; political candidates and parties would have been interested. But the researchers could not offer much data of "general" interest to politicians of both or all parties, for that set of people needed data when they were hot; if the data had cooled off for six months, they were of little use. But neither did researchers want to offer data to a specific candidate or party, lest this compromise their scholarly reputation for nonpartisanship and evenhandedness.

Campbell himself was concerned enough about nonpartisanship that as late as 1955 he wanted his ISR colleagues to keep mum about their individual political allegiances. They did not submit. The institute was no longer so fragile, some said; others twitted him that the sensitive political situation he faced did not mean that all of ISR's political liberties should be infringed—only *Angus Campbell's*.[68] They were all of a mind, however, about the wisdom of avoiding election forecasts and any public association with them. In 1952, they turned down an invitation to be on a panel on election polls at the American Sociological Association, and they generally watched journalistic coverage to make sure they were not quoted as forecasting.[69] As part of a scholarly program, the election study people resisted the excitement, the journalistic publicity, and the risks of the horse race, permitting themselves, at the last, only sealed predictions on election eve—to each other.

In the mid-fifties, the program obtained more foundation funding to continue studying national elections, this time from Rockefeller. Foundation support did not exempt the election studies from the labors and struggles of trying to find that money—proposal after proposal, for election after election—but it reduced the strain of trying to merge the practical interests of business or government with the theoretical interests of science. The election study's enviable situation obviously owed something to the solvency and reputation of the institute itself, as well as to the other two programs that did straddle the two worlds. Each of these two programs almost always brought in more money than did the Public Affairs Program, which initially housed the election studies. Because the election study analysts did not have to be as concerned about blending the needs of business and science, they did not have to justify and clarify results to clients bent on practical application and could concentrate somewhat more on following their own conceptual interests.

Building on Lazarsfeld. In their first published election study, SRC researchers acknowledged the pioneering role of Lazarsfeld and his colleagues, and they announced their own intention to extend their analysis to national realms:

> During the 1940 presidential campaign Paul Lazarsfeld and his associates undertook a series of sample surveys in Erie County, Ohio, which demonstrated for the first time something of the range of possibilities which this research method promises in the analysis of political behavior. . . . This remarkable project, though limited in geographical scope, set the stage for the application

of the survey method to a national study of the presidential election—an investigation which would illuminate many aspects of the perceptions, attitudes, and behavior of the national electorate. As yet, such a study has not been done.[70]

In fact, NORC had first walked on that stage with the first national study in 1944, conducted in some cooperation with Lazarsfeld (see chapter ten). That enterprise had not gone beyond Korchin's dissertation and Ziff's thesis, however, and the SRC researchers had hopes of broader scope and longer range. Campbell and his colleagues continued to acknowledge Lazarsfeld's "pioneering work" as a "model" for their own work,[71] but as scientists they were intent upon scrutiny, criticism, and the search for new trails that might mark the map of discovery with their own claims to originality. To that end, they were different in three major ways. The first difference came with SRC's own *national* capacity: with national samples of the electorate, it could explore whether the results of the single communities (Sandusky, Erie County, Ohio, and Elmira, New York) held up on the national scene. The second, the *historical* study over time, emerged as SRC was able to fund repeated election studies of national scope. The third difference was in disciplinary tradition, as the institute put on voting studies its own stamp of *psychological* variables.

Whether or not SRC scholars paid full acknowledgment seems something of an imponderable—Lazarsfeld apparently came to feel that they rather slighted his contribution[72]—but it is clear that they paid him scientific tribute in two kinds of coin. They sought his advice: Miller and Gurin went East to interview Lazarsfeld during the planning stage of their 1952 study.[73] And they followed his trail, testing his sociological categories and his Index of Political Predisposition. They also found reason to criticize. With national data, the index showed differences that were in the predicted direction but were not statistically significant; the index worked better for Republicans in 1948 than for Democrats, and in certain respects Erie County voters were not a microcosm of the nation's voters. Janowitz and Miller acknowledged that the index was "a significant point of departure for the empirical development of a theory of political behavior in the United States."[74]

SRC *departed* in its national, historical studies, with a special emphasis on the intervening variables of attitudes, expectations, and group loyalties, which were set forth in the 1954 book *The Voter Decides*, by Campbell, Gurin, and Miller:

1. personal identification with one of the political parties
2. concern with issues of national governmental policy

3. personal attraction to the presidential candidates
4. conformity to the group standards of one's associates
5. a sense of personal efficacy in the area of politics
6. a sense of civic obligation to vote[75]

The authors confronted the sociological approach quite directly by noting that the power of group and class interests in predicting the vote varied over time. It had been potent during the Roosevelt years, but it was less so when General Eisenhower became the Republican candidate in 1952:

> The experience of the last two presidential elections has shown us . . . that the simple classification of voters into sociological categories does not have the explanatory power that at first appeared. It has been demonstrated that the application of the Lazarsfeld index to the national electorate in 1948 resulted in a prediction of the vote not remarkably better than chance. In 1952, the great shifts in group preferences . . . would have been very difficult to predict on the basis of previous voting records . . . the movement toward Eisenhower occurred in virtually all of the groups represented.[76]

SRC's apparent satisfaction with these psychological variables, especially party identification, was nevertheless somewhat mystifying to sociologists. Was it really much of a triumph to predict, for example, that people who considered themselves Democrats would tend to vote Democratic and hold a recognizably "Democratic" cluster of attitudes about public issues? It seemed rather obvious. Not really, argued the social psychologists. Not everyone displayed this kind of attitude-behavior consistency—it had to be explained. And these variables not only served as better predictors of a given election than did such factors as income, occupation, education, and sex but they were also far more useful for understanding *historical changes* in party fortunes. The electorate's social characteristics changed only slowly, while the vote was sometimes volatile indeed—with the election of a Democratic president for a long period (1932–1948), mostly under Roosevelt's aegis, and the election of a Republican president (1952–1956) when Eisenhower was the candidate. Could that shift be explained by *class?*

The American Voter. The authors of the 1960 book *The American Voter*, Angus Campbell, Philip E. Converse, Warren E. Miller, and Donald E. Stokes, were an interdisciplinary mix of social psychologists (Campbell and Converse) and political scientists (Miller and Stokes), and they addressed again the interpretations in sociology and psychology:

From initial efforts to understand voting behavior two major currents have emerged, one primarily sociological, the other more psychological in emphasis. . . . It has been unsatisfactory, however, to leave these two approaches as independent and competing bodies of theory. They are addressed to the same reality, and conflict between them is hardly a matter of contradictory findings. Rather, they are attacking the problem at different levels, and consequently in different languages.[77]

It was wasteful, they argued, to choose between the sociologist's social factors of, say, religion and class, and the psychologist's political attitudes; it was important to use both, in some conceptual order. They proposed the metaphor of a "funnel of causality," narrowing on a time dimension from its wide mouth to the small stem through which the flow of events relevant to understanding the dependent behavior, voting, were progressively focused. At the narrow end of the funnel, one could observe attitudes. Because they had already been given personal and political meaning, attitudes provided the advantage of high predictive power but low coverage of the funnel. At wider points in the funnel, one could observe events more remote in time, with less personal, politicized meaning, such as social class and religion. These factors predictably accounted for less of the variance in voting behavior, but they offered a longer view back into the chain of events.[78] This theoretical orientation did indeed guide the book in the exploration of social, economic, political, and legal contexts in which the voting decision was taken, in addition to its focus on matters at the narrower end of the funnel—attitudes and feelings of "party identification" and the role of the party in providing a frame of reference for confusing political stimuli.

The American Voter established that a liberal/conservative ideology was a framework used by only a small part of the electorate (at most, 15%). What more people brought to their political attitudes was a sense of self or group interest (45%); a more nebulous collection of opinions with some political content but no real structure (23%); and, finally, at most, a sense of party or candidate, without any issue content at all (17%), as in this example:

(Like about Republicans?)
    No, I don't know about the *party*. I like Ike. . . .
(Like about Eisenhower?)
    I just like him, the way things have gone.
(How do you mean?)
    That's really all I know.[79]

These four levels were a summary version of a more elaborate ten-category coding of open-ended questions on parties and candidates, which were used repeatedly in election studies. This set of questions and the Index of Consumer Sentiment represented the most long-term and illuminating analytic use of open-ended questioning by SRC.

With the publication of *The American Voter*, the program in "political behavior" had spanned the elections of 1952, 1954, 1956, and 1958, after its small opener in the 1948 election, and it had extended V. O. Key, Jr.'s, classification of critical elections as "maintaining," "deviating," and "realigning" elections. The book generated prompt responses of both criticism and enthusiasm, adding weight to the thrust of the "behavioral movement" in political science[80] and demonstrating the conceptual power of survey research. The program was on a rising tide of achievement for SRC.

Contributions to the Field

Continuity in the National Data Base

Two SRC programs, Economic Behavior and what came to be named the National Election Study, gathered large national cross-section data sets over time. They were able to gather data of "objective" demographic character, such as those which government surveys gathered, in combination with the subjective measures of attitudes, intentions, and self-reported behavior which the polls gathered. And they did so in a combination of certain technical advantages that the polls did not offer.

SRC did not have the resources to match either the great *size* of surveys conducted by agencies of the federal government or the great *frequency* of the commercial polls, but it created national data sets annually or biennially with a more sophisticated technical base than the polls, as it used a national probability sample and longer, more detailed interviews. The consumer studies gathered national data annually or better, from 1946 on, using independent cross-section samples rather than panel data. The election studies conducted a national survey of six national elections from 1948 to 1960 (they missed the congressional election of 1950), using independent cross-sections at first and then a panel design. There was much of sheer description in these studies, especially in the consumer studies that took detailed measures of income and assets, but their national scope provided the comparability for analysis over time—the stuff, finally, of historical record and analysis. In the late 1950s, Miller began to seek support in the institute for the idea of archiving and distributing these and other data to the wider community of scholars, a notion that came into being as the Interuniversity Consortium for Political and Social Research in 1961.[81] The consortium developed directly from the trend and panel data built by the consumer and electoral studies. The national time series were a data base for policymakers of the present and historians of the future as well as a source for the economic and political theory that we have just discussed. In its more immediate effects, SRC made contributions to survey methodology.

Methods: Questions and Samples

OPEN-ENDED QUESTIONING

Over the postwar years (1946–60), SRC maintained but modified its practice of open-ended questioning. SRC staff were probably more dogmatic about the virtues of the technique than a mere jot of experimental evidence could support, but their practice of the art was a distinct contribution to the survey repertoire. The issue of open versus closed questions presented the familiar qualitative/quantitative tension that pervades all of social science, raising important problems in measurement, analysis, and valid inference in large-scale surveys. No one provided very good answers to these questions—neither SRC nor anyone else did sustained experimental work addressing these problems—but "qualitative" data were made viable in an era when closed questions and questionnaires were being generated in great profusion.

In later years, Lazarsfeld expressed his feeling that SRC members vaunted their own work in open questioning at the expense of his own, slighting his contribution. Gallup agreed, for one. In a congratulatory wire to Lazarsfeld to be read aloud at his fiftieth birthday party, Gallup wrote that Lazarsfeld deserved more credit for the development of the open question than Likert and his group did,[82] and indeed Lazarsfeld had published on the asking and classification of open-ended materials many years before the SRC people had done so. But as we have seen, these early writings on open questioning assumed the good offices of a small staff of elite interviewers (well educated, well informed about the study, and in close touch with the inner councils of research), who were free to use an interview schedule not only as a literal document of written questions but also as a "guide" to questioning. The "Art of Asking Why"

(1935) and "The Controversy over Detailed Interviews—An Offer for Negotiation" (1944) have provided valuable insight and counsel to survey researchers and have been frequently cited, but neither fully addressed the problems of a large staff of interviewers doing work at a great physical distance and some fair intellectual-educational distance from the study directors (see chapters four and nine).

SRC's originality was in applying open-ended questioning to mass data collection by a national staff: a far-flung staff of people working in their own communities, usually part-time, most with educational backgrounds of some college, and a few with college degrees—a field staff much like the other large-scale survey organizations such as NORC and Gallup. And the typical interview schedule had grown greatly in size. SRC systematized a form of open questioning for this kind of interviewing staff, with these features:

> Written questions to be read exactly as written.
> "Neutral probes" designed to elicit meaning and clarification.
> Written "specifications" setting forth the objectives of the question to guide interviewers in the use of probes.
> Personal training in the specific study.
> Verbatim transcription of the open-ended responses.
> Classification of the open-ended materials created from a sample of interviews.
> Coding reliability measures through independent "check-coding" of some percentage of the interviews.

That was the ideal, and there were deviations in practice. Completely verbatim transcription was impossible with most respondents, for instance. There were limits on how complete the question "specifications" could be. What was freedom for respondents could often be burdens for interviewers—to listen and evaluate with intelligence and sensitivity, to transcribe with great conscientiousness, to use probes that did not bias—and burdens for coders and analysts as well. The risk was always that a respondent's open-ended answer might be so fragmentary, unintelligible, idiosyncratic, or irrelevant to the study objectives that it could not be used to advance the analysis and perhaps not even coded at all (or coded with low reliability), as Campbell discussed in his 1946 article, "Two Problems in the Use of the Open Question."[83] The great scientific strength of the technique lay in the taking of those risks: investigators allowed the possibility of finding out the bad news that what they wanted to learn was not what all respondents had to teach.

SRC investigators took these sterner risks and learned from them, but they did not publish much about the experience. A 1947 article by Crutchfield and Gordon reported on an experimental probing of a closed Gallup question and showed the variations in the frame of reference that respondents had assumed.[84] But this article, based on Program Surveys work during the war, was the only real experimental comparison. A collection of methodological experiments, memos, and plans from the wartime period has been preserved at ISR, but no full open/closed experiment survives, and there is evidence that by 1944, at least, none had been conducted.[85]

In 1946, as SRC was getting established, it collaborated on a study of attitudes toward the atomic bomb, under the auspices of SSRC and Cornell University, which commissioned two surveys: Gallup's commercial firm, Benson and Benson, which was to use closed questions and quota sampling, and SRC, which was to use open questions and probability sampling. This would seem to have been a classical comparison in the making, but there was no exploitation of the comparative design. The two studies were reported separately, and the report spanning them summarized only that the supplementary studies raised important methodological problems that would be dealt with in time—but which apparently never were.[86] SRC authors later conducted a couple of experiments that bore somewhat on the open/closed issue, but not centrally.[87]

In this period, open questioning was not restricted to pretesting but remained a substantial part of the final questionnaire. SRC interviewers also typically reported much verbatim material that accompanied answers to closed questions, and the "thumbnail sketch" of the interview and respondent was another indication of the interest in qualitative materials.[88] But open questioning ebbed from the wartime levels. *Americans View Their Mental Health* (1960), by Gerald Gurin, Joseph Veroff, and Sheila Feld, represented a high point for SRC: 65 percent of the 295 discrete items in the questionnaire were open-ended, and, probably because this was a pioneering, exploratory venture, SRC's first major study of mental health.[89]

In other studies where experience had been cumulating, the proportion of open questions shrank. The consumer surveys, for example, showed about one-third of their questionnaires in open form; the share of open questions in the National Election Studies was averaging a bit less[90]—while it was still very high indeed compared to standard polling practice, it represented a downward trend since the war.[91]

Why was this so? In certain cases, investigators had learned from experience with open-ended materials and continuing data analysis how to get what they wanted from closed questions, which were generally easier and more satisfactory to analyze. They no longer had to explore as much. In almost all cases, closed questions were cheaper—they took less interviewer time to ask and record in the field, less investigator time to construct code categories, and less coder time. Cost was of particular concern, as the size of the schedule had grown to an interview that usually took about an hour.

Open questioning held a strong (if shrinking) place in the reigning ideology of SRC/ISR, and not everyone who had some history with SRC seemed to be aware that there had been a downward trend. In the course of interviews, I talked with people who still seemed to feel that open questioning was as strong an institute practice as ever. Campbell was aware of the change. When asked why it had happened, he said, in effect, Why else?—meaning money. Converse, too, was aware, and he stressed analytic strategy.[92] It was surely both.

Methodological research into question form, coding reliability, and interviewing techniques did not get off the ground at SRC in these years. SRC staff had been trying to fund a research project into interviewing, but when the Hyman group at NORC got the SSRC grant, SRC withdrew its proposal instead of trying for joint research, which SSRC suggested.[93]

SRC authors typically were scrupulous about reproducing their whole questionnaire or the exact wording of questions used in the analysis, but they did not always report other important technical matters, such as interviewer characteristics and training or measures of coding reliability. These matters were heeded at SRC—staff took a serious view of interviewer training and training materials, and they gathered some data on interviewer performance—but such information was not routinely incorporated into research reports. Researchers (or publishers) may have been unwilling to clutter the reports with methodological details, just as the pollsters were, although this seems less likely, given the social scientists' professional audience. Whatever the reason, a fuller kind of methodological reporting simply did not get systematized in the field as a canon of respectable survey research, either through the enforcement of journal standards or the practice of organizations. SRC did not lead the way here as it had done in reporting sample response rates.

PROBABILITY SAMPLING

The end of the debate. SRC became the single most important academic practitioner of area probability sampling, second in influence only to the sampling statisticians in government (Hansen, Hurwitz, Madow, Deming, Snedecor, Cochran, and others).[94] SRC staff may have been more fervent, in fact, than some statisticians, who were not unanimous in rejecting quota sampling out of hand. Everyone agreed that quota sampling had no standing in probability theory—sampling error could not be measured with quota samples, except by very complex experimental designs[95]—but there was disagreement about the importance of that fact. If one was not in the business of making real population estimates, did one have to make the greater investment in probability sampling? How important was it to be able to measure sampling error and establish confidence limits?

Stephan and McCarthy, who undertook the sampling project for the SSRC/NRC Committee on the Measurement of Opinion, Attitudes, and Consumer Wants established in 1945, went in search of empirical studies, not because these could blunt criticism of quota sampling on a theoretical basis, but because empirical studies could be more persuasive than theoretical arguments to people who were not well acquainted with probability theory.[96] The data they could find were not very conclusive on the issues of costs or results. The data on costs generally contained too many uncontrolled variables. For results, sometimes they found close agreement (for example, in NORC's comparison with the *MRLF*), and sometimes they did not. Even with the most carefully designed experimental comparison they could find (by Moser and Stuart), they came to the same conclusions: quota data sometimes showed agreement with outside sources; they also showed instances of bias related especially to SES controls, as well as other sources of bias which were difficult to assign. There was no way to place quota sampling on a sound theoretical basis.[97]

Were quota studies worth continued experimental study? Stephan and McCarthy argued that they were, although they cautioned that researchers would probably soon find themselves in "an impenetrable mass of details."[98] Quota samples were going to continue, in any case:

> There are great quantities of data that were obtained by quota methods in the past for which important uses will be found, and it is likely that some kind of quota methods will be used quite frequently in the future. Hence we believe that further study of interviewer-selected samples will be worth while, though the work will be difficult and the results not always conclusive.[99]

Probability samples could not be recommended across the board of survey research, they concluded. There were problems here, too: discrepancies between plans and performance and problems in nonresponse (15 to 20% at this time), and further research was needed. In any case, there were occasions on which purposive samples could be very useful or simply the only practical recourse (purposive selection of a single community for study, for example, or the use of clinical patients), and the choice depended on the level of accuracy that was required, a determination that in itself was not an easy matter.[100]

It is not hard to see in the Stephan-McCarthy book a purpose of "compromise"—not to stir something together from each side but to cut down the trade in criticism and increase the barter in information. The book projects, throughout, the "research temper." An SRC colleague who was a firm advocate of probability sampling recently commented, still reflecting the spirit of contention, "Fred Stephan never gave up on quota samples—he should have known better." Stephan and McCarthy clearly "knew better," but their book seems to have featured some effort in research diplomacy, as though they were trying to bring the debaters down off the stump to the discussion table in order to consider the problems and the realities on both sides. Stephan and McCarthy had much contact with research organizations in the course of writing the book (as well as during the work for the 1948 SSRC postelection report, in which they both participated), and they got cooperation and access to data from real people in commercial, academic, and governmental work. They clearly got an insider's view of problems in all three realms, and it seems likely that they were looking for the ways of conflict resolution.

By the time the book was published in 1958, the SSRC committee representing those three realms had been disbanded for about four years, and the debate about sampling had subsided somewhat.[101] In 1957, Stephan himself observed that there had been increased understanding and adoption of probability sampling, and he credited the leadership of the government agencies and SRC.[102] The polls had in fact made some adaptation to probability designs, with a compromise of the mixture called "probability down to the level of the block," meaning that blocks were selected by probability methods and that respondents within the block were selected by interviewers with quotas.[103] So, while the polls' conversion was hardly complete, probability methods had attained great legitimacy. SRC, as strong advocate, critic, and practitioner, helped spread that word.

SRC's special contributions. SRC professionals contributed to the designs and diffusion of probability sampling in several ways. They published descriptions of their samples and analysis of sampling problems;

they taught area probability sampling from the beginning in their summer institute; and in research writing they regularly provided information about their sample design and response rate. Furthermore, as we have noted, the fact that their time series in consumer economics and the election studies had their base in national probability samples gave these surveys special utility and importance, allowing repeated empirical tests and historical trend analysis.

The probability sample of the Survey of Consumer Finances, based on the sample that SRC had brought from Washington, was put to use in 1947 and provided some three to six national studies every year from then on. It was described in the *Federal Reserve Bulletin* and then again in *IJOAR* in 1948 by Goodman and Maccoby.[104] The latter article was the single most complete description of a multistage probability sample in that journal's five-year history. In 1952, Kish reviewed the basic steps of area probability sampling in the *ASR* article "A Two-Stage Sample of a City." The following year, in the 1953 methodological text, he included in his chapter on sampling a description of the SRC sample. Kish had already invented the household selection table that bears his name (see chapter seven). He published several other articles bearing on the general practice of multistage sampling, most notable of which was probably "Confidence Intervals for Clustered Samples" (1957). Here he provided data from recent *ASR* articles to show how widespread the practice still was of using a simple random sampling formula for confidence intervals for data gathered from complex samples—and how much the practice could inflate apparent statistical significance. SRC's own complex national surveys usually showed variances of one to two times the *srs* formulas, and the appropriate adjustments were made in published work. Kish's 1959 article "Some Statistical Problems in Research Design," which set forth different advantages and disadvantages of experiments, surveys, and "controlled investigations," was one of the rare SRC/ISR entries in the Bobbs-Merrill reprint series (Kish's second).[105] Starting in 1960, Kish organized a second summer institute for scholars of underdeveloped countries especially to spread instruction on probability sampling, another source of diffusion and influence for SRC.

Social Organization of the Field

LINKS BETWEEN COMMERCIAL AND UNIVERSITY RESEARCH

SRC staff contributed less to the communication between commercial and academic research, through AAPOR and *POQ*, than the Bureau and

NORC did. SRC's relationship to the polls during the war had been financially competitive and intellectually critical, and the academic staff had been eager to distinguish themselves *from* the polls. For a time after the war, they still wanted to. Their publications criticizing polling practice were not the stuff of common cause.

The criticisms were actually rather mild mannered compared to the clarion calls to *ad hominem* slaughter which sound now and then in the social science literature, and they might not have had much impact on the polls but for two factors. First, the coalition was under construction, and debate was being managed across the divide with a good deal of care. Second, in 1948–49 the pollsters were vulnerable and sensitive, and Likert published articles in that season that infuriated them. Campbell and Katz had both published articles in 1946 which praised SRC practice at the expense of the polls,[106] but Likert's criticism was published immediately after the election, when it particularly stung.

Many years later, Likert pointed out that he had written the article appearing in the December 1948 *Scientific American* months before the election; he felt that he had been quite misunderstood about the whole thing. But the article had been updated to deal with the election misforecast, and Likert attributed it to the pollsters' failure to use probability sampling, intensive interviewing, and open-ended questioning. In the same month, two shorter versions of the same interpretation were published in *U.S. News and World Report* and *American Psychologist*.[107] Likert may have come to regret his published pieces, but he was not misunderstood at the time. Gallup was angry. He wrote a rejoinder to *Scientific American*, and the following fall he published an article entitled, "Should We Set Up Standards for Poll Critics?" in which Likert was the only critic he named by name.[108]

In January 1949, a small group gathered in Iowa City (at Norman Meier's initiative) to review the problems of the pollsters. Berelson, Cahalan, Crossley, Gallup, Hansen, Hart, Lazarsfeld, Meier, Stouffer, and others discussed general problems in social science prediction. They expressed appreciation and good-humored support for the pollsters' "blood, sweat, and tears" and for their prescience in understanding before academics did that polling provided "one of the great opportunities for developing an effective social science," as Stouffer put it. No one from ISR was there. Likert had been invited, and his absence from the gathering was pointedly noted by Meier.[109]

The misforecast was only briefly on the AAPOR agenda, but some discussion at the June 1949 meetings showed the tension between SRC and the pollsters. Kahn reported on SRC's panel work on the 1948 election, noting the importance of turnout, last-minute shifts, and the behavior of the undecideds, who voted disproportionately for Truman—in sum, the vagaries of the electorate in this campaign, more than the failure of general polling methods of sampling, interviewing, or question wording. The contrast between the emphasis of Kahn's report at the summer meetings and that of Likert's articles right after the election was not lost on Gallup, who chided:

> In the light of the [Survey Research Center] study . . . I am not sure that Mr. Likert should have rushed into print with his criticisms of our poll and others immediately after the election.[110]

Campbell and Katz rose to Likert's defense.

After this season of acrimony, SRC/ISR participation in AAPOR lagged. Likert was no longer active in executive councils, and, with one exception (Daniel Katz), no one from ISR served on the executive committee or was ever appointed or elected to major office (until later years). SRC people continued to participate in AAPOR meetings but at a visibly lower rate than the people at the Bureau and NORC, and they did not publish as much in *POQ*, either.[111] Of thirty-three individuals who published with relative frequency in *POQ* between 1937 and 1960 (five or more articles), only one was a long-term staff member from SRC (Katz), and another was a short-term member (William A. Scott).[112]

There were several barriers to SRC/ISR's joining the academic-commercial confluence of AAPOR. Geography was one. The AAPOR coalition was centered around New York, and SRC was on this circuit less than NORC was, with its New York office. (Travel at this time was not the casual matter it became in the 1960s and 1970s, when social science began to enjoy affluence.) These were disciplinary waters, too, for the dominant academics of AAPOR were sociologists. The uncomfortable, competitive relationship between SRC and pollsters during the war had not faded from memory, and this tension, now exacerbated by the pollsters' plight and SRC's criticism, reinforced the most important barrier, a cultural-ideological one, for overall, the commercial-academic alliance was not attractive to SRC staff members. It was not that they were strangers to business and industry: from an almost total dependence on the federal government in 1947, they had gradually increased their money from business-industry and foundations, and by 1960 the three realms provided roughly equal shares of the ISR budget.[113] They had in fact become good businessmen themselves, as "research entrepreneurs." But they nevertheless saw themselves exclusively as scientists, were distrustful of commercial researchers, and saw the future of survey research not in breaking down the barriers between researchers in business and academic life but in breaking down the barriers between disciplines. They tended to their own organization at Michigan, and they tried to make their links with the departments and the disciplines. SRC/ISR did not contribute much to the "fusion" movement, but because it published a great deal it accounted for much diffusion of survey research to the disciplines.

DIFFUSION TO THE ACADEMIC DISCIPLINES

All three organizations logged an impressive publication record in these early years, as shown in table 3. The figures represent the *total* writings through 1960 which are listed in the basic bibliographies of the three organizations, not specifically *survey* writings. The figures are noncomparable in certain ways, because the criteria of inclusion in the three bibliographies differ. The Bureau's bibliography, for example, gives more complete coverage to its unpublished materials, including short reports, memos, and other unpublished categories that were specifically excluded from the 1946–60 ISR document. The Bureau's corpus of unpublished work was probably greater than that of the other two organizations, just not as great (by some unknown amount) as the comparison of the bibliographies would suggest. The NORC bibliography differed from the other two in that it listed publications by non-NORC authors which were based on data collected by NORC. Even so, this listing probably underestimates the visibility of NORC, because there must have been still more publications based on NORC data which were not entered here; surely, for example, only a small portion of the publications using the NORC-North-Hatt measures of occupational prestige found its way into this bibliography.[114]

From this gross count, it is apparent that the Bureau published many more books than the other centers, ISR published more "mainline" journal articles, and NORC, which provided so much survey data to other groups and individuals, published fewer books and articles of its own. ISR authors published in journals with some interdisciplinary span, such as *IJOAR, POQ*, and journals of industrial psychology, business management, and education. But they also appeared with fair frequency in what we are calling "mainline" journals. These are the journals published by

TABLE 3

NUMBER AND KINDS OF WRITINGS LISTED IN OFFICIAL BIBLIOGRAPHIES

	Bureau (1937–60)	NORC (1941–60)	ISR (1946–60)
Publications:			
Books	52	12	22
Mainline journal articles[a]	62	29	103
Book chapters	45	9	94
Other	267	153	426
Unpublished writings:			
Dissertations	35	6	73
Master's essays	45	7	—
Monographs	24	82	26
Other	375	144	144

[a] "Mainline" journals, taken to be the high-prestige journals for these research organizations at this time, are defined as journals published in these years by the seven associations comprising SSRC in this period, with three additional inclusions: (1) *AJS* and *Social Forces*, as journals of comparable prestige to *ASR*, which were included to balance somewhat the large number of journals sponsored by the American Psychological Association; (2) reprints in the Bobbs-Merrill series (an article reprinted there was thus counted twice); and (3) papers presented at meetings or published in the proceedings of any of seven component associations.

the seven disciplinary associations that were members of the Social Science Research Council (sociology, psychology, history, economics, statistics, anthropology, and political science), plus two additional sociological journals considered to be of comparable prestige (see footnote to table 3). ISR authors were visible in mainline journals of four fields—psychology, sociology, political science, and economics—publishing five or more articles in *JASP, JASA, ASR, Sociometry, APSR, Psychological Review, American Economic Review,* and *AJS*. Bureau authors appeared in fewer mainline journals, publishing five or more articles only in the *Journal of Applied Psychology, ASR,* and *AJS*. The journal in which the most Bureau articles appeared was *POQ*.[115]

Was SRC/ISR, then, a truly interdisciplinary center that brought scholars from different disciplines together to work on "problem-oriented" research? Or was it a multidisciplinary center that housed scholars from different disciplines in the same building in which they worked on their separate disciplinary concerns? It was something of both. The Economic Behavior Program was an intellectual blend of economic and psychological ideas, but it was conducted mostly by economists, who published in economic journals, rarely in psychological ones. The Human

Relations Program, conducted by social psychologists, was already established as industrial psychology with links to industrial management, and the group published in both disciplinary and "problem-oriented" vehicles. The election studies were a mix of scholars from social psychology and political science who published in both disciplines.

But this was no longer the "problem-centered" research of wartime Washington days. SRC people had taken on university ways once again, identifying with disciplines, departments, course teaching, graduate training, and the journals of their associations, trying to get money to pursue problems in basic research as defined by their intellectual tradition. The fact that many SRC scholars focused on basic research and published in their disciplinary journals was presumably a loss for policy research, but it helped survey research to gain respectability among academics. Survey research of the Bureau and NORC made deeper penetrations into sociology, through books and articles, and SRC's work began to spread itself more broadly across social psychology, economics, and political science. Together, the effect was to spread the quantitative culture of survey research in major social science disciplines.

12

The Academic Establishment of Survey Research: A Summary and Evaluation

What assumptions did sociology's reformers [of the 1930s and 1940s] make about the nature of true science? However brilliant, the individual scholar could accomplish little. Scientific progress was made in "knowledge factories," staffed not by intellectuals but by technicians, who need not be persons of considerable ability, for they employed precise, easily mastered techniques to fulfill their assigned tasks.

Henrika Kuklick

Survey analysis is much akin to artistic creation. There are so many questions which might be asked, so many correlations which can be run, so many ways in which the findings can be organized. . . . Beyond his technical responsibility for guaranteeing accuracy and honest statistical calculations, the real job of the study director is to select and integrate . . . to simplify but not gloss over, to be cautious without pettifoggery, to synthesize without distorting the facts, to interpret but not project his prejudices on the data. These, I submit, are ultimately aesthetic decisions, and the process of making these decisions is much like aesthetic creation.

James A. Davis

The Postwar Period: 1945–1960

The End of an Era

The year 1960 provided something of a watershed. Survey research organizations had been established in universities. There was new recognition for early leadership, some changing of the guard, new activity of a younger generation. And certain revolutionary changes had *not* happened.

In 1960, Lazarsfeld became president-elect of the American Sociolog-

379

ical Association. In 1956, Herbert Blumer had devoted his presidential address to a critique of "variable analysis," meaning Lazarsfeld's work very particularly.[1] Four years later, on his third try for the office, Lazarsfeld won his own place in the association hierarchy.[2] In 1959, the American Sociological Association approved the formation of a section on methodology. It was not a section on *survey* methodology, but survey researchers such as Patricia Kendall, Leslie Kish, Peter Rossi, and Shirley Star were prominent in its council.[3] In 1959, Rensis Likert served as president of the American Statistical Association. This honor did not have quite the same symbolic meaning that a presidency of the American Psychological Association would have had—with the new prestige in that discipline for social psychology and subjective measures—but it was welcome recognition from statisticians, and ISR enjoyed its first presidency of a professional association.

By 1960, a changing of the guard was in progress. In that year, Clyde Hart retired and Samuel Stouffer died. Thus, with Harry Field's early death in 1946, three important figures of the wartime cohort of survey researchers were gone. The interest of certain others had waned. Stouffer had not been as active in survey research after the war as he had been during it, in any case (though he remained active in AAPOR), and Cantril and Lazarsfeld no longer had the same involvement in the survey field.

After the war, Cantril's organization, OPOR, had shrunk into a small office operation devoted to creating an archive for poll data, with no field capacity to collect new data. In 1955, it was discontinued, as Cantril resigned from Princeton to accept a lifetime research grant from Rockefeller for policy research. He continued to work on surveys—*The Politics of Despair* (1958), for example, analyzed the Communist voter from data collected by Gallup affiliates in France and Italy, and *The Pattern of Human Concerns* (1965) brought together data on human aspirations from a number of countries—but these works did not feature much survey data analysis and, with the exception of the "self-anchoring" scale, did not bring any new methodology or analysis. Cantril was the single most prolific contributor to *POQ* from the journal's beginning in 1937 until 1967 (the year in which he died), but these articles, with one exception, were all published before 1950. Thereafter, other interests, such as problems in perception ("transactional analysis"), claimed much of Cantril's attention in the 1950s and 1960s. His greatest influence on survey research was felt during the 1940s.[4]

Lazarsfeld's impact on the formation of American survey research was more central and long-lasting, as he remained directly influential from the mid-1930s to the late 1950s, some twenty to twenty-five years, and indirectly beyond that period. Though he lived until 1976, his last major book in survey research was *The Academic Mind*, published in 1958; after 1960 he did not publish any more articles in *POQ*.[5] Berelson noted in 1955 that Stouffer and Lazarsfeld had both effectively left public opinion work, an exodus he suspected was a response to the low prestige of the field.[6] That may well be, though in the case of Stouffer we are left with merest speculation. In Lazarsfeld's case, it is clear that he chafed at the low prestige of quantitative sociology and tried to change it. His interest in the history of quantification in social science was in part an effort to endow it with some of the commanding prestige that *theory* had in the history of sociology.[7] Lazarsfeld had catholic interests in science and culture, however, and great capacities, and he may simply have moved on to some of the other things on his mind. The best truth of the matter may be in Jahoda's borrowing of Isaiah Berlin's bestiary: for whatever reasons, Lazarsfeld's many interests made him a fox, fascinated by many things, rather than a hedgehog, working on one big thing (Talcott Parsons, for example, was considered a hedgehog).[8] Merton did not proceed into much further survey work after his explorations into housing and medical sociology, the bulk of which were conducted in the 1940s and 1950s.[9]

By 1960, many in the generation of social scientists that had worked on surveys during the war (e.g., Field, Hart, Stouffer, Cantril, Lazarsfeld, Merton, Likert, and Cartwright) were no longer active in survey work, through death or through the ascendance of other interests or responsibilities. Likert continued as director of ISR, but his intellectual work centered on organizational theory and research. Cartwright, director of the Research Center for Group Dynamics, did not continue survey work after the war.

Of that wartime generation, only Hyman and Sheatsley of NORC and Campbell, Katona, Katz, Cannell, and Kish of SRC pushed on in full pursuit of careers in survey research in the 1960s and 1970s, in collaboration with younger-generation scholars. Campbell undertook election studies with the collaboration of Cooper, Gurin, Miller, Converse, and Stokes. Katona continued work in psychological economics with Mueller, Klein, Lansing, and Morgan. These research programs, especially, gave to SRC/ISR the ascendancy in survey research in the 1960s and 1970s that the Bureau of Applied Social Research had had in the 1940s and 1950s. Lazarsfeld's influence on survey research continued through the work of some of his heirs at the Bureau, such as Barton, McPhee, and Glaser, and of some who had gone out from the Bureau, especially Coleman, Rossi, Lipset, and Glock. In 1960, Rossi became NORC's director. Glock and Lipset were now both at the University of California, Berkeley, where Glock had become director in 1958 of a new Survey Research Center—the name reflecting the influence of the Michigan group, but Glock himself reflecting the more direct influence of the Bureau.

The end of this era saw a golden yield of books from all three organizations based on primary or secondary analyses of survey data. From the Bureau, there were Merton, Reader, and Kendall, *The Student Physician* (1957); Lazarsfeld and Thielens, *The Academic Mind* (1958); and, all in 1960, Lipset, *Political Man*; Hyman, *Political Socialization*; Berelson, *Graduate Education in the United States*; and Klapper, *The Effects of Mass Communication*. At NORC, projects of Rossi, Coleman, and Davis which had been initiated in the late 1950s came to major publication in 1961, with Coleman et al.'s *The Adolescent Society*, Davis's *Great Books and Small Groups*, and a variety of articles by Rossi. For ISR, 1960 was a vintage year, with Gurin, Veroff, and Feld, *Americans View Their Mental Health*; Katona, *The Powerful Consumer*; and Campbell et al., *The American Voter*.[10] And journal articles based on surveys had begun to flourish in all three organizations.

This published research was largely the fruit of the precomputer era. Data analysis was crafted with paper and pencil, desk calculators, the counter sorter of Hollerith cards, and the IBM 101, which could be programmed by wiring a simple board to carry out various cross-tabulations. This technology was the most advanced equipment in the "machine rooms" of all three major organizations during most of these early years. Correlation, regression, analysis of variance, and factor analysis were only rarely carried out on the desk calculator. Giant computers, which began to be installed in major universities in the late 1940s and early 1950s, did not accommodate analytic routines for social science data until the late 1950s and early 1960s. A few intrepid social scientists, well counseled by their statisticians, set upon the giant central computers (such as the IBM 650) to wrest from them a few key analyses, such as some multiple regressions,[11] but computer technology was still forbidding and inhospitable for social science use. The books and articles these researchers published around 1960 were, indeed, the last of the handcrafted work.

What Was Coming

Three new features were to come in the future. First, there would be *machine technology*: the computer models that would revolutionize the kinds of analysis that could be performed on survey data, as well as the speed. Prodigious new programs would be devised that could "ransack" data for relationships and test elaborate causal models. Computer technology, for all its power, had the major defect in the 1960s and 1970s of intruding between the analyst and the data. Analysts delivered their "batch" to the queue at a computing center, and if all went well they got their output a few hours or a day later. This put a crimp in the style of those artists in data analysis who liked to work with data as Stouffer did, turning at once to the counter-sorter to try out an idea or resolve an argument, intent upon the immediate detective work of survey analysis. In the 1980s, the hands-on approach to analysis provided by the old counter-sorters would become possible once again with the advent of small terminals and then microcomputers. Three new eras in computer technology were actually in prospect: the giant computer, or mainframe, as it is now called; the microcomputers; and direct data entry, in which telephone interviewers were equipped to record survey responses instantaneously into the computer.

New kinds of *archives* were coming, a second innovation in data storage and data diffusion made practical by machine-readable data. In 1951, Cantril and Strunk produced from the OPOR archive of poll data in the old style a large bound volume of marginal percentages, question by question and poll by poll. The new archives would be able to disseminate the data for whole studies in the form of magnetic tapes and disks that could be used for secondary analysis. Elmo Roper started the first archive in 1946 at Williams College, in honor of a son who had been killed in the war. (This resource has since been divided between Yale University and the University of Connecticut at Storrs.)

In 1961, after germination and discussion in the late 1950s, an Interuniversity Consortium for Political and Social Research (ICPSR) was established at ISR. Within a few years, the ICPSR archive would provide machine-readable data to hundreds of subscribing universities and colleges and would have its own computing installation obtained with NSF funds.[12] NORC would establish another unique data archive in the early 1970s, in the General Social Survey (GSS), an idea that had circulated in various forms at NORC since the late 1950s. The GSS was an annual survey designed to provide data replication and diffusion to a subscribing community of social scientists. With the consultation of some fifty social scientists, GSS designed a national questionnaire that replicated many questions of the past—from NORC's own studies, from Stouffer's work, from SRC/ISR, from other academic research, and from the polls. (Gallup was in fact the single most important source of questions.)[13] Together, the archives of ICPSR and GSS would provide a treasure house of survey data for students and scholars and a source of income for the parent organizations.

A third change was coming in *research organization*. Academic survey research centers mushroomed in universities. As of the early 1980s, about fifty university organizations had listed themselves as "academic survey research organizations" in *Survey Research*, a newsletter edited by Mary Spaeth at the University of Illinois. The directory is not complete because of nonresponse from various organizations, but the data at hand show that some seventeen new organizations were founded in the 1960s, another sixteen in the 1970s, and eight more in the 1980s, for a total of 55 extant in 1983, and 58 in 1985.[14] Starting in the 1970s, survey organizations of a quasi-academic character also developed, the "not-for-profits" built on something of an academic model but operating outside the university (for example, Westat in the Washington, D.C., area).

With the expansion of scientific organizations, the entrepreneurial role that emerged in this early period would acquire new importance and complexity. In the late 1970s and 1980s, as federal funds for research shrank, the research entrepreneurs of social science would organize for informal and even formal lobbying of Congress and would seek harmony for the "applied" purposes of business/industry and the "basic" research of university science, just as had been done in the 1940s and 1950s.[15] In these later years, the research entrepreneurs would be anything *but* "marginals" trying to span the cultures and contradictions of science and government/business. In the realms of highest scientific eminence, they would become scientific "statesmen" (and a few women) charting broad areas of scientific policy and politics[16]—mainline.

These coming developments in "big" social science—the dazzling new capacities of computer technology, the growth of data archives, and the complex politics and economics of research administration to build and sustain these organizations—would be particularly visible in survey research. It was already "big science" for its time in the 1950s, and it would loom larger and spread in new institutional forms. The complexities of the more recent years are beyond our scope here, except in these most general terms that we have just been considering. The continuity is nevertheless clear, for in these earlier years survey researchers achieved *consolidation* as legitimate research organizations in social science, and they also achieved some *diffusion* of survey methods to the traditional disciplines. We shall review both briefly.

Consolidation

The Local Cultures

> Geology is a parochial science: rocks collected in familiar terrain always seem more important than rocks collected elsewhere by someone else.[17]

Just like geologists, the survey organizations especially valued their local rocks. Their members generally had an esprit, a loyalty, and a strong sense of the history and impact of their own organizations. In this sense, they rather resembled scientists in industry, likely to feel more identification with and loyalty to their company than to their discipline, in contrast to their counterparts in the universities, who were more likely to identify more strongly with their discipline.[18] Or perhaps it is more accurate to say that the emerging survey professionals identified with both. They continued their disciplinary and departmental orientation as sociologists, social psychologists, economists, and so on, but their day-to-day identification with their research organization was also strong.

Citation patterns, for example, reflected the intellectual culture of the given organizations. ISR produced its manual in 1953, *Research Methods in the Behavioral Sciences*, edited by Leon Festinger and Daniel Katz and written by nineteen authors, almost all of whom were at the University of Michigan, with more than half at ISR. Of the 458 publications cited in the bibliographies of the book, 25 percent were by ISR authors. Bureau authors accounted for only 3 percent of the citations—not invisible, but not much of a presence, either.

In the Bureau's 1955 volume, *The Language of Social Research*, edited by Lazarsfeld and Rosenberg, the authorship was more diverse: of the sixty-four chapters, fewer than half (44%) were written by Bureau authors. Neither did Bureau authors entirely dominate in the much shorter bibliography: only 10 percent of the eighty-five works recommended for further reading were by current Bureau writers. But the recent Michigan volume by Festinger-Katz was cited only once (a chapter written by Cartwright on the coding of qualitative materials). In the Bureau book, ISR was not entirely invisible, but it was not much of a presence, either.[19]

Were there plots to ignore the competition? That seems unlikely. There was much to separate these organizations without introducing a conspiracy theory—notably, the distance of geography, the fences of disciplines, and the internal concerns of organizations. The Bureau was the empirical arm of the Columbia Department of Sociology, and while it had interdisciplinary ties, these tended to be temporary and project based, linked to Lazarsfeld himself more than to ongoing programs.[20] SRC/ISR had only one staff member (Leslie Kish) on a tenured appointment in the sociology department during this period. While certain classes were cross-listed in sociology, SRC's teaching links were basically with psychology, economics, political science, business. Not surprisingly, the editors of each book looked to their own. The volumes produced in the two centers also had quite different purposes, and the editors wanted to show what their organizations had learned and would gladly teach. The visibility of the local "rocks," however, was an interesting comment on the state of the field. The communication and influence were probably still more local and organizational than professional, national, and interdisciplinary. Not surprisingly, there was some muted competition as well—for money, place, priority.

A MEASURE OF COMPETITION

SRC and NORC both vied for NIH support of a study of mental health, and NORC got it. NORC also got the interviewing project of SSRC. SRC and the Bureau came into some competition in their voting studies. SRC started election work in earnest on the presidential election of 1952, when the Bureau was analyzing data from the congressional election of 1950. SRC continued to capitalize on its national capacity, in election studies of 1954, 1956, 1958, and 1960, using both cross-section and panel design.[21] The Bureau did not gather data on American elections after 1950, for reasons that are unclear, but SRC's investment was perhaps a contributing factor.

Among all three organizations, there was a mild current of competition for prestige and priority. To a certain extent, this was handled by the organizations' staking out of different claims in this period. NORC defined itself as the first academic center in public opinion research (see chapter ten), and SRC/ISR laid claim to being the first interdisciplinary center in survey research. The Bureau saw itself as a "general social research center and training laboratory," second in time only to Odum's Institute for Research in Social Science, and the first academic "applied" social research laboratory.[22]

Members in each organization felt their differences from the others. For example, there was sentiment in the Bureau that both NORC and SRC were too "poll-like" and descriptive, without much analytic flair. Certain figures in NORC and SRC felt the same way—that the *other* organization was too close to polling or to "assembly-line research." In later years, at least, there was some sentiment at SRC/ISR that Lazarsfeld was brilliant as an intellect but chaotic as a director. At NORC, there was some feeling that SRC disdained the contract work that others did—just not *its* contract work.[23] The invidious comparisons were mild-mannered, however, and did not preclude cooperation across organizations—more between the Bureau and NORC, especially through AAPOR, than between SRC/ISR and either of the other two. According to some brief reflections recently published by Pasanella, Lazarsfeld came to regret the competitiveness that developed among these organizations, especially SRC/ISR and the Bureau.[24] With separate groups striving to build viable organizations; creating their own histories, loyalties, and morale; vying for scarce resources in money and prestige—how could it have been otherwise?

THE ANCESTRY AND THE INFLUENCE

Survey research still has a local culture. Within the ranks of the academic research organizations that started early, lasted long, *and* specialized in surveys—notably the three that are of special interest to us here—the past tends to be reconstructed in ways that emphasize the particular originality and priority of that group. As one talks to people in each organizational setting, one has a sense that "survey research"—or at least a special aspect of it—was indeed invented *here*.

In the literature, there are some quite different accounts. Babbie, a sociologist in the Bureau tradition, considers that Stouffer and Lazarsfeld "must be regarded as the pioneers of survey research as we know it today" and that the Bureau must be seen as the first in the "development of the permanent research center supporting survey methods."[25] Barton and Glock focus on Lazarsfeld. Barton traces Lazarsfeld's career as the inventor of the applied academic research center. Glock sees him as the founder of survey research methodology—or, more properly, survey analysis—as well as organizational innovator.[26] Aubrey McKennell, however, in a historical article contrasting the academic development of survey research in Britain and America, sees ISR and NORC as "where it all began." With still another view, Edward A. Shils sees these organizations—at least the Bureau and ISR—as having been rather independent developments.[27] In all of these accounts, the case is essentially assumed rather than argued, so it is difficult to know what are considered to be "the facts" on which these different interpretations are based.

Two kinds of distinctions would seem to be useful for understanding these differing accounts. The first is the distinction between survey *methodology* and survey *organizations*. In this dichotomy, Lazarsfeld's contribution to survey research seems to be greater in the development of the instrument than in the development of the survey organization itself. Lazarsfeld was surely the first great *practitioner* of survey research methodology, as he enlarged the analytic scope and power of the survey/poll technique being used in market research and commercial polling. What Lazarsfeld wanted for the Bureau itself, however, as an organization, was really much grander than for it to be simply a survey research center. He saw the Bureau as a laboratory in social science, organized for scholarship, research, and training, not just as a research center organized around the conduct of surveys. There was a time, as we have seen, when he wanted to equip the Bureau with a national field staff and tried to acquire NORC for that purpose (see chapter ten). But this appears to have been a brief aspiration. Had he successfully obtained or organized permanent staffs for sampling, fieldwork, coding, and data management, it would surely have cramped his "foxy" style, for it would have been hard to sustain a survey research center *without* becoming a survey "hedgehog."

The very technical capacities at issue here comprise the *organizational* model for academic survey research, and this is surely what McKennell referred to when he credited NORC and ISR with a pioneering role: university-based organizations with the ongoing technical capacity for the conduct of surveys. The Bureau improvised the academic conduct of survey research, from study to study; NORC and later SRC undertook the ongoing, institutional conduct of surveys in the academic setting. The Bureau's innovative role is clearest in methodology; the innovation of the other two organizations is clearest in the institutional organization of surveys.

The second distinction is between *priority* and *influence*. Whatever the founding date of the Bureau is considered to be—1937, when the Cantril-Stanton-Lazarsfeld radio research project was funded by the Rockefeller Foundation, or 1940, when Lazarsfeld brought the Office of Radio Research under the administrative umbrella of Columbia University—it was clearly prior in time to NORC's founding at Denver in 1941 and SRC's at Michigan in 1946. Whether the Bureau was a *formative example* for NORC and SRC bears on the other matter, that of influence.

In recent histories of their organizations, neither NORC nor SRC/ISR offers Lazarsfeld or the Bureau as a model of their practice or a formative influence in their founding. In Sheatsley's account of NORC, he cites Lazarsfeld as one of several academics who were supportive and helpful to Field in his plan to found NORC as an academic center, but the idea itself is seen as evolving out of Field's own experience and aspirations for commercial polling, not as a response to Lazarsfeld's work in radio research with Stanton and Cantril.[28] Cannell and Kahn trace the origins of ISR to Likert's survey organization in the federal government, starting in the Department of Agriculture in 1939 and expanding during World War II. Lazarsfeld does not figure in their account as a formative influence on the founding of SRC/ISR.[29]

Apart from these organizations' own accounts of their origins, however, it seems clear that the taproot of both NORC and SRC goes first to the commercial polls. Each organization was designed to be a "full service" facility for the conduct of public opinion research. In their beginnings, they seemed to have been motivated less by following the example of Lazarsfeld than by improving on the example of Gallup—conducting polls in the public and scientific interest, with more precision, more scope, and more complexity in their coverage. Over time, in the academic setting, each took on broader mandates for social research as well.

Was Lazarsfeld's organization their model for becoming *academic* organizations? In Field's case, the timing seems to have been a little tight. Lazarsfeld's research project with Stanton and Cantril from 1937–39 had academic connections, but mostly on paper; its incarnation as a center with primary university affiliation started at Columbia in 1940. By that time Field's activities to create a nonprofit poll were already under way, with his People's Research Corporation, begun in 1939. Did Field proceed from that to the idea of a university-based poll because of Lazarsfeld's example? This cannot be ruled out, but there is no direct evidence for it in the surviving record of Field's own deliberations and consultations with pollsters and social scientists. It may nevertheless be the case that the Office of Radio Research in 1940 constituted for Field a general example of feasibility—evidence that a research organization that did polling could be mounted in an academic setting—but this is neither self-evident nor clear from the record.

By 1946, when Likert and his group went to the University of Michigan, the examples of both NORC and the Bureau must have been more vivid and influential. Lazarsfeld's academic organization had become very visible, it had produced major published work, and Lazarsfeld himself had been in direct contact with Likert and his colleagues. The ORR/Bureau must surely have been a formative example as an academic research organization.

It seems a fair claim indeed that the Bureau was the first of a new generation of academic organizations engaged in empirical social research. As we have noted, it was original in three respects. First, it was constituted as a *standing research organization*, unlike the great range of research projects funded by the Local Community Research Committee at the University of Chicago in the 1920s. Second, it was original in commissioning or collecting *primary survey data* (unlike Odum's IRSS, which relied on published Census Bureau data and smaller-scale empirical investigations) and in making use of precollected poll and market research data in secondary analysis. Third, it was *applied*—it relied on contracts as well as grants.

In the fusion of these three features, the Bureau has clear priority to being the first academic social research organization that used and developed the instrument—the method—of survey research. Lazarsfeld's creative use and development of survey designs surely had great intellectual influence on scholars in both NORC and SRC. But in their origins, the two organizations do not seem to have been an intellectual or organizational spin-off of the Bureau, because they were modeled so closely on the polls. In the 1940s and 1950s, in fact, the two organizations were regarded by Lazarsfeld and others at the Bureau as a rather negative reference point, as too close to the practice of the polls, too mechanical and descriptive. Lazarsfeld's paternity of the organizations as survey research centers seems to have been a recent one, of adoption.

A New Discipline?

Could it be said that by this point, circa 1960, these new organizations had crystallized a new discipline? Probably not. Survey research was a complex research instrument that could be put into use only with the coordination of hundreds of people linked in an elaborate division of labor and with the expenditure, often, of hundreds of thousands of dollars. So, while it was no garden-variety tool, it was still something less than a discipline, for academic survey practitioners kept one foot in their traditional disciplinary associations and departments as sociologists, psychologists, and the like. They kept the other foot in their research organizations, where the practice of their trade made them *different* from their disciplinary colleagues by opening up certain kinds of problems (and not others) and by facilitating certain kinds of thinking (and not others). But this activity did not organize them intellectually or socially as a distinctly new discipline.

Survey research nevertheless was consolidated as a method of research, and its influence was diffused into social science disciplines. In these few postwar years, the new survey researchers made significant changes in the four criteria we considered in chapter seven: theory, methods, good examples, and social organization. We have already seen changes in methods and "good examples" of the practice, in the foregoing chapters on the three major research organizations. To see the developments in theory and social organization, we need to take a broader view across organizations and disciplines.

Interstitial Theory of Attitudes

Survey researchers did not develop a unique core of theory which entirely distinguished their endeavor from that of their mainline disciplines; rather, survey researchers emerged from one discipline and encroached upon another, weaving together some conceptual strands from each one, creating new subdisciplinary specialties supported by quantitative analysis. Lazarsfeld, for instance, worked on surveys of radio audiences, endowing them with new analytic power, and he opened up new interest among social scientists in "communication research." The "two-step flow of influence" was a conceptual link between the influence of the media, individuals, and small groups.[30] The early voting work of the Lazarsfeld group came to be labeled "political sociology"—honoring the fact, aptly enough, that sociologists had been turning their attention to political attitudes and behavior. The implicit theory was, of course, that the voting behavior of individuals could not be understood without reference to their attitudes, and attitudes could not be understood without reference to their formation and transmission in group structures and membership. The Campbell group at SRC took the concept of group identification from the fields of personality and social psychology and wove it into the study of voting behavior as "party identification." "Psychological economics" (or economic behavior) wove the borders of the two disciplines, positing that consumer attitudes could be one of the leading indicators of business cycles.

The specialists aspired to integrating the study of attitudes and behavior and called their work "political behavior," "economic behavior," and "organizational behavior." While certain studies in behavior were appropriately named, such as Kinsey's study of self-reported sexual behavior, in much the greater part survey researchers were intent upon attitudes as independent, intervening, or dependent variables, primarily because their instruments were a better fit for attitudes—a short self-report by interview or questionnaire. There was some use of behavioral measures, which complemented the special techniques of survey research. In studies of organizations, for example, measures of physical productivity were gathered from records, and measures of group process and morale were gathered by observation. But these studies did not develop any special techniques that were fine-tuned for the study of the behavior of individuals or of group process beyond the techniques of small-group dynamics.

In this era, whatever the aspirations of psychologists and political scientists to illuminate the behavior of interest in their disciplinary realm or of sociologists to cast new light on behavior within the context of social structure and group process, all of these disciplines were doing a better job of gathering and analyzing attitudes. By 1960, survey research had not revolutionized the theory of attitude change or development, but it had stamped the major social science disciplines with the study of opinions and attitudes and had established some interdisciplinary organizations of its own.

Social Organization

THE IMPERFECT, DURABLE UNION

AAPOR, officially constituted in 1947, was a successful effort to span the academic/commercial divide of survey research. The bridging had its trials. First, there was difficulty in building a constitution in 1947. Then, by the next year, the misforecast of the polls resonated the same conflicts between academic and commercial survey researchers and threatened all of opinion research. In that emergency, AAPOR itself was sore beset because it had not yet constructed a durable coalition, but those who were interested in forging that alliance tried to help and used SSRC to good advantage. Certain academics went into immediate action to review the pollsters' problems, and the pollsters cooperated in making their records available. In time, the tensions of 1948–49 subsided and the polls survived and went on—and AAPOR, along with *POQ,* continued to provide professional forums for discussion and research for both commercial and academic wings.

AAPOR's difficult constitutional debate of 1947 was on professional standards—"the rock on which the AAPOR craft almost foundered before it was well out of the ways," as Hart and Cahalan described it in their 1957 review of AAPOR's history.[31] The issue was whether AAPOR should have the power to expel wrongdoers, and this in turn depended on the definitional matter of whether AAPOR was to be considered an organization solely of individuals or also one of organizations that *could* be expelled for unethical practices. The 1947 debate was not perfectly polarized between academic versus commercial attitudes, but the sides were visible—more of the vocal academics pushed for specific rules and tough enforcement, while more of the vocal commercials argued for general principles and the encouragement of cooperation.

The debate was not always that polarized. In 1948, for example, academic Frederick Stephan argued that sound practice would develop not through formal statements but through informal processes that stimulated consensus on striving for higher standards. He cautioned that formal standards at this point, when AAPOR had so little experience, might actually shield "shady characters" who might advertise conforming to the letter of the law, but actually "engage in slipshod research." And he noted that AAPOR had company in these problems: the American Psychological Association had been struggling with the issue of standards and enforcement for some time. An accommodation was reached with the creation of the Committee of Standards, whose mission was "to contribute to the elevation of professional standards"—without power of enforcement.[32]

AAPOR has hardly been alone in struggling with professional standards—it was the 1950s and beyond before either sociologists or psychologists managed to create a code—or in laboring to create a common culture and a shared past across a heterogeneous membership.[33] But the 1948 failure of the pollsters put another strain on the coalition. AAPOR leadership acted quickly to try to help. Hart, in particular, went into immediate action to organize a scientific review of the polls' procedures.[34] Arrangements were made right away with SSRC, which appointed the Committee on Analysis of Preelection Polls and Forecasts, to be led by academics S. S. Wilks and Stephan. Foundation grants were obtained from Carnegie of New York and from Rockefeller, and a technical staff was put to work. Just after Christmas, the committee released a preliminary report (which was followed in 1949 by a full book). Haste was of the essence, as Pendleton Herring of SSRC explained in his foreword to the book:

> Appointment of the committee rested upon the judgment that extended controversy regarding the pre-election polls among lay and professional groups might have extensive and unjustified repercussions upon all types of opinion and attitude studies and perhaps upon social science generally. . . . Quick action seemed necessary after the election for several reasons. An authoritative factual inquiry was needed to terminate the growing controversy or to focus discussion upon specific issues at the earliest possible moment.[35]

Academics and commercials alike were running scared. Campbell, who was not ordinarily given to purple prose, reviewed the SSRC book in language that conveyed some of that emotion and fear:

> The detailed post-mortem which this volume presents needs to be seen in some historical perspective as it represents the dénouement in as lurid a melodrama as American social science has ever seen.

> Rising phoenix-like from the ashes of the *Literary Digest*, the pollsters burst on the national scene in 1936 with a dramatic entry that has few equals. From their original success in predicting the 1936 election, they went on for ten years from one triumph to the next. Their names became household words, not only in this country but abroad. They became in some sense the vanguard of the infant social sciences and were seen by some as proof that the study of society, like the study of less diffuse and more controllable phenomena, could also be scientific. Then, finally, flushed with success and too over-confident to heed the portents of disaster, they plunged down together to public humiliation and ridicule. Now, with the melancholy chorus of the SSRC committee to explain the tragedy, the drama is complete.[36]

AAPOR endorsed research into the matter, trying to stem the controversy. In September of 1948, *POQ* had become the official organ of AAPOR while remaining under the editorial sponsorship of Princeton University, and in 1949 it did not dwell on the fateful forecast. It would not, in fact, have been entirely difficult to skim the four issues of *POQ* in 1949 and remain largely innocent of the news that there had even been a polling "debacle" in 1948. There was one lead article that year which analyzed the reactions of a sample of newspaper editors to the polls' failure, "Election Polling Forecasts and Public Images of Social Sciences: A Case Study in the Shaping of Opinion among a Strategic Public," by Merton and Hatt. There was another by Alfred M. Lee, a polemic piece that denounced those academics who rose to defend the polls, probably referring to Cantril and Meier and perhaps also to Hart's organizing efforts.[37] These were the only full-length *POQ* articles in 1949 that dealt centrally with the pollsters' misforecast.

This was a vivid contrast to *IJOAR*, the other leading journal of opinion research, which had just started in 1947 and was publishing many interesting reports on survey methods. In the wake of the election, that journal launched a series entitled, "The Opinion Polls and the 1948 U.S. Presidential Election: A Symposium," which coursed on for five issues, forty-three articles strong. Cantril's was the lead article, a judicious consideration of probable sources of error which should be the subjects of research but also a support of the polls against the "malicious glee" of their fellow journalists:

> Newspaper editors and reporters along with radio commentators have finally been able to make the pollsters their whipping boy. Their use of the pollsters as the scapegoat for their own unanimously wrong predictions shows the extent to which they themselves had begun to rely on polls even though many of them had always been irritated by the intrusion of scientific forecasting into a field of prediction traditionally regarded by them as their own special province.[38]

At the other extreme in this series, Krech invoked the pollsters' failure as a "grand opportunity" for social scientists to get shut of "the notorious pollsters."[39] It was also in this series that Gallup asked that there be standards for critics; that Roper called the issue of sampling a red herring; that Bernays argued that pollsters should not be allowed to practice without a license; and that market researcher Coutant tried to distinguish carefully between market research and polling.[40] It could hardly be said that *IJOAR* failed to confront the hot topic of opinion/attitude research in 1948. AAPOR/*POQ* leadership may well have felt that *IJOAR* was covering the issue well enough and that they were making their contribution by supporting the SSRC study. It also seems likely that AAPOR leadership felt that further deliberations on the pollsters' failure threatened the association.

Protecting the coalition had advantages for academics as well as for commercial researchers. Notwithstanding Lee's view that scientists had nothing to fear—that indeed "social science gains from every such situation as the November affair"[41]—social scientists in opinion research did have something to lose from a breakup of AAPOR: the association itself and especially the avenue for publication in *POQ*. The latter became the more important because *IJOAR*, the main alternative, ceased publication at the end of 1951.[42]

THE DIVISION OF LABOR

By agreement, from the beginning AAPOR alternated its presidency between academics and commercials. Hart of NORC was followed by Elmo Wilson of CBS, and the succession proceeded in orderly fashion, alternating academic Lazarsfeld, commercial Woodward of Roper, Inc., Berelson of the University of Chicago, Crossley, Stouffer of Harvard, Gallup, and later Hyman of NORC and the Bureau.[43] AAPOR also seems to have kept its meeting participation carefully apportioned. From 1946 through 1960, the number of participants in the AAPOR meetings grew, but the share of participation stayed in delicate oscillation between its two major sectors (table 4).

Information about AAPOR membership over the years is more fragmentary. What *is* easily accessible suggests that the commercial sector was carrying more of the membership, and thus more of the financing, of the association, as shown in table 5. Academics, for their part, were writing more of the *POQ* articles. Over this period, as another set of numbers shows, academics gradually took over more of the pages of *POQ*. In the graph in figure 2, the decline of governmental representation reflects the end of the war and the return of many academics to universities. Over and above that adjustment in the 1940s, academics increasingly showed more authorship in the journal than the business sector did.

THE LEADERSHIP

AAPOR remained a small outfit of several hundred members, very junior to the major disciplinary groups, which numbered in the many thousands, and its journal was comparatively low in prestige. The various editors over the early years had a good deal of freedom to publish what they thought best, without much refereeing.[45] The association and the journal nevertheless offered an intellectual forum and a point of consolidation for survey researchers which was not available in their original disciplinary associations.

TABLE 4

AAPOR Participation: AAPOR Programs 1946–1960[a]

		Number of Conference Participants by Affiliation			
		Academic	Commercial	Other[b]	Total
Year:	1946	13	24	7	44
	1947	19	16	6	41
	1948	18	29	9	56
	1949	25	17	6	48
	1950	17	23	11	51
	1951	28	20	19	67
	1952	19	16	7	42
	1953	30	24	12	66
	1954	26	25	7	58
	1955	36	44	8	88
	1956	60	55	11	126
	1957	43	37	14	94
	1958	47	44	9	100
	1959	33	31	8	72
	1960	39	43	19	101
Total		453	448	153	1,054

[a] "Participants" are panelists or presenters of papers. Most of these counts are taken from the printed programs; they do not reflect such last-minute changes as there may have been or the participation of panel audiences. For 1950, 1951, and 1952, the data were taken from *Proceedings*.
[b] Governmental workers are the largest part of this category. It also includes those coded as Other and Affiliation Unclear.

TABLE 5

AAPOR Membership: Selected Years

	Conference registration 1947	Membership directory 1956	Response to mail questionnaire 1959[a]
Percent:			
Commercial	46	55	61
Academic[b]	39	28	33
Government	10	9	6
Other	5	8	—
	100	100	100
N	(194)	(380)	(329)

[a] A response rate of 60 percent: 329 of 545 responded.
[b] "Academic" includes nonprofit organizations.[44]

The leadership for AAPOR and *POQ* came from both wings. From the commercial side, the AAPOR regulars were Elmo Wilson, J. Stevens Stock, Gallup, Roper, and Louis Harris, all of whom appeared on half or more of the annual programs. The list of academic regulars featured the Bureau and NORC, especially: Lazarsfeld, Berelson, and Zeisel, with Bureau roots; Hart, Sheatsley, Hyman, and Cahalan, of NORC stock; and Stephan, Stouffer, Dodd, and John Riley, from other places—all appeared on half or more of the AAPOR programs. There was a little overlap between being on the AAPOR program and being published in *POQ*. A few of the conference mainstays were also frequent publishers in *POQ*, notably Roper, Gallup, Lazarsfeld, Sheatsley, Hyman, Dodd, Wiebe, and Davison.[46] There was rather more specialization. Cantril, for instance, was the single most prolific author in *POQ*, but he faded early from the programs of AAPOR meetings. Stouffer's situation was the reverse: he published only one article in *POQ*, but he was on every program from 1953 through 1960.

Diffusion and Expansion

The practice of American survey research spread from 1940 to 1960 along four routes. First, it was *taught*, through on-the-job training, courses, and texts. Second, surveys were *used* more frequently, and publications based on surveys gained greater visibility in the social science literature. Third, surveys spread into *new subject matter*, and fourth, they expanded in *cross-cultural* scope.

On Teaching the Trade

Survey organizations provided some on-the-job training just in the course of getting the work out. There were jobs in coding, machine work

Fig. 2. Public Opinion Quarterly Articles, Thirteen Volumes, 1937–1961, Proportion Written by Authors of Academic and Business Affiliation

Note: The two categories do not sum to 100%. The remaining proportion not shown includes authors with governmental affiliation, independent writers, those with double affiliation, and affiliation NA. The only substantial group in that miscellany is the government group during the war years, when their contribution in 1941–1945 ranged from 12 to 24%. The coding unit is the article, not the author. In the case of multiple authors, the first author's affiliation is coded. Authors of news notes and editors of journal departments are not coded.

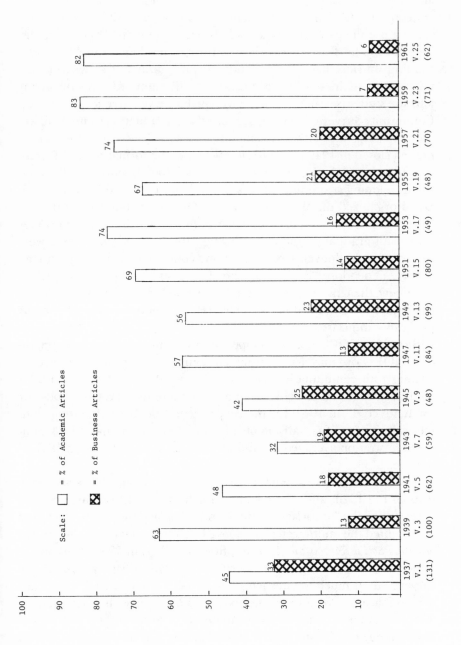

Scale: ☐ = % of Academic Articles

◪ = % of Business Articles

and data analysis, and some in interviewing. These jobs provided an avenue for professional recruitment of students as well as support for graduate students who were already training in the field and doing dissertations. The Bureau was the most active teaching "shop": it had a training mission, it employed students, and Lazarsfeld's own teaching was exciting in this on-the-job context.[47] NORC and SRC provided many jobs for students, too, and each developed a survey practicum. NORC's Community Survey of Denver, organized as a graduate class in 1946, was the first. (This was not transplanted to Chicago-NORC after the Denver branch closed in 1949.) In 1951, at Michigan, the formation of the graduate practicum, the Detroit Area Study, took the pressure off SRC itself for developing a training program. And there were others: in 1947, Dodd organized the Washington Public Opinion Laboratory at the two major state universities at Seattle and Pullman, which integrated survey work with graduate training up through the Ph.D. level.[48] There were survey organizations or frequent surveys conducted at Washington University (Theodore F. Lentz), the University of Minnesota (R. O. Nafziger), the University of Miami (Ross C. Beiler), Iowa State University (Raymond Jessen), Purdue University (H. H. Remmers), as well as many programs and classes.[49]

SRC and NORC both developed summer institutes in survey methods. NORC organized two sustained summer programs, one in 1949 dealing with communication and another in 1956 dealing with health methods.[50] SRC undertook a summer institute in survey methods for graduate credit in 1948, for the very practical purpose of getting summer salaries for SRC staff members, and it became annual. SRC's summer registration averaged around fifty in this period, diffusing SRC influence.[51]

Texts in methods of survey research developed in the 1950s. Sociology texts of the 1920s and 1930s had set forth the "statistical" method, the "case study," the "historical" method, and so on, and the "survey" method represented the multifaceted and loosely defined *social survey*. In Young's *Scientific Social Surveys and Research*, first published in 1939, one can see something of a turning point in that the book dealt briefly with sample surveys but at much greater length with social surveys. In 1942, Lundberg published a revision of his text *Social Research*, with a new chapter on the questionnaire as one of the methods of sociological investigation. He, too, dealt with sampling in a general way, but he did not deal with surveys as a composite, complete method. Blankenship's book *Consumer and Opinion Research* (1943) was too early to reflect wartime developments, especially area probability sampling.[52]

Parten's 1950 book *Surveys, Polls, and Samples* was the first text in contemporary survey research.[53] A student of Chapin's, Parten had done survey work early in the 1930s using systematic samples. Her book remains a very ambitious and particularly useful historical document, combining "how to" instruction with a historical overview and a generous bibliography of nearly 1,150 items.

Other important texts appeared in the 1950s that gave survey techniques considerable space. The two-volume work *Research Methods in Social Relations* (1951), by Jahoda, Deutsch, and Cook, covered social research generally and a variety of techniques (field observation, small-group analysis, sociometry, content analysis of media, etc.), but much of the material bore on the techniques of survey research. (The chapter "Community Self-Surveys" evoked the old social survey movement in its focus on community participation and political action.)

Nineteen fifty-one also saw the publication of Payne's book *The Art of Asking Questions*, which summarized 100 guidelines for the writing of poll/survey questions. It has long been the single most informative book on the subject, reflecting the sophistication of Payne's experience in governmental and commercial work and some experimental evidence, aided by his sprightly writing.

The 1952 volume by Goode and Hatt, *Methods in Social Research*, represented a more general text that tried to sweep across all methods relevant to "the new sociology." Much of its content was especially relevant to survey research (although the term itself was used rarely, if at all). In 1953, ISR made its contribution to research methodology in the volume edited by Festinger and Katz (*Research Methods in the Behavioral Sciences*), a good half of which had special reference to survey research methods. In 1955, there were two strong offerings from the Bureau: Hyman's case studies in *Survey Design and Analysis* and the Lazarsfeld-Rosenberg volume *The Language of Social Research*. Both had rich implications for the sophisticated design, conduct, and analysis of surveys. In 1957, Kahn and Cannell of SRC/ISR published a major book on survey interviewing, *The Dynamics of Interviewing*, reflecting especially psychological theory and the practice of open-ended questioning.

In 1958 there were two more books of importance. Stephan and McCarthy's *Sampling Opinions* appeared in that year, having been planned initially as one of the three main projects of the SSRC Committee on the Measurement of Opinion, Attitudes, and Consumer Wants. From England, another text appeared that was devoted exclusively to survey research, although it reflected the British social survey emphasis on "factual" measures: *Survey Methods in Social Investigation*, by Claude Moser of the London School of Economics. Texts in elementary statistics for social scientists appeared with growing frequency in this period: among others were Hagood and Price's 1951 revision of their 1942 text *Statistics for Sociologists*; Wallis and Roberts, *Statistics: A New Approach* (1956); and Blalock, *Social Statistics* (1960).[54] Technical counsel for survey research began to flow into *POQ* and into the sociology journals.

Diffusion to the Disciplines

By 1949–50, survey research was very visible in the *Public Opinion Quarterly*: 43 percent of its articles in those two years were based on survey data. This is not to be wondered at, from one standpoint: if surveys had not resonated in *POQ* by this time, where would we have heard them? But in fact, this represented some real change. *POQ* was not a journal of survey research at the outset. It had been established for the study of public opinion and thus drew articles on public relations, advertising, propaganda and censorship, radio, film, the press, and public opinion generally, many of which had little or nothing to do with surveys. Of academic journals, *POQ* showed the strongest increase in the use of survey data in general.

In the major disciplines, survey research had the greatest impact on sociology. Economics showed increased use of surveys, most of it in government surveys. The impact on political science was a later phenomenon; psychology reflected a rather steady 10 percent of articles based on survey data. Table 6, showing this change over time, uses and extends Presser's recent data on the diffusion of survey research. I have included Presser's data for 1964–65 because they show the continuing growth in the use of surveys in the mid-1960s; in the 1979–80 data (not shown), that growth is shown to have leveled off in the journals of sociology and economics but to have continued upward in political science journals and in *POQ*.

Subject Matter: The Luxuriant Fields of Self-Report

Early poll-survey questioning now seems like a curious mixture of daring and caution. Gallup, for instance, asked opinion questions about vene-

TABLE 6

PERCENTAGE OF ARTICLES USING SURVEY DATA
BY FIELD AND YEAR[a]

	1939–40	1949–50	1959–60	1964–65
Sociology	17.6	24.1	42.6	54.8
	(277)	(282)	(291)	(259)
Political Science	2.6	2.6	10.5	19.4
	(113)	(114)	(152)	(160)
Economics	10.2	5.7	16.1	32.9
	(175)	(141)	(167)	(155)
Social Psychology	20.5	22.0	17.0	14.6
	(34)	(59)	(229)	(233)
Public Opinion	27.5[b]	43.0	57.8	55.7
	(51)	(86)	(64)	(61)

[a] The journals used in this analysis were: *ASR*, *AJS*, and *Social Forces*; *APSR*, *Journal of Politics*, and *American Journal of Political Science* (formerly the *Midwest Journal of Political Science*); *American Economic Review*, *Journal of Political Economy*, and *Review of Economics and Statistics*; and *Journal of Personality and Social Psychology* (formerly *Journal of Abnormal and Social Psychology*). For the rationale of these choices, see Stanley Presser, "The Use of Survey Data in Basic Research in the Social Sciences," in *Surveying Subjective Phenomena*, ed. Charles F. Turner and Elizabeth Martin, vol. 2 (New York: Russell Sage Foundation/Basic Books, 1984), pp. 93–114, esp. pp. 94–95.
[b] The coding rules for this table, which exclude symposia and research notes, happen to minimize the figure for *POQ* in these years because reports on poll data were introduced to the journal through its research note "Departments" and because a special issue was devoted to the polls. With the inclusion of these two types of articles, 35.7 percent of 126 articles were devoted to poll/survey data.

real disease and birth-control information in the 1930s, but he and other pollsters did not ask respondents their educational attainment until the 1940s. Pollsters generally thought that inquiry into education, occupation, and income was "sensitive" enough that they had to proceed cautiously. Well into the 1940s, investigators were getting only very gross demographic measures at best, sometimes asking interviewers to make estimates and sometimes avoiding the issue entirely. Survey professionals had to feel their way and *learn* what things people were willing to discuss and what they were not.

In the course of the 1935–60 years, investigators pushed at the borders of inquiry, and they learned that most people were willing to discuss *almost anything*. For good or ill, people were in general willing to express opinions and attitudes not only on innumerable impersonal topics but also on subjects very close to the bone of personal revelation, emotion, and intimacy. Whether they did so with candor and completeness was an ongoing question, but survey research did indeed expand the realms of inquiry.

Not all of these topics were new to social science. Many had been touched on before at some point, in some study or another. But survey investigators dealt with new explorations of old topics as well as with new topics, not only in the more secluded environments of clinics, small groups, or classrooms but also in the mass population. The reporting of income, savings, and assets, for example, was a "sensitive" issue, especially at higher income levels. And it proved feasible for surveys. The study of racial attitudes, for another example, was not an entirely new preoccupation of social scientists—Bogardus and Park had studied Oriental-Caucasian relations in the mid-1920s (see chapter two)—but black-white attitudes had been touched on only lightly by the polls. Survey investigators embarked again on this subject and on the subject of anti-Semitism as well.

Large-scale surveys were used to explore attitudes toward marriage, mental illness, occupational prestige, political socialization, child-rearing, and national character. There was new survey work on attitudes in the context of groups and institutions, such as housing units, industrial organizations, volunteer groups, unions, the medical profession, college departments, the sick, the elderly, and mental hospital patients. Some of this work used self-report of attitudes in conjunction with other methods of *observing* behavior, but it was in the use of *self-report* of behavior that investigators pushed surveys further still into "sensitive" areas of inquiry.

The most dramatic of these areas was sexual behavior. The so-called Kinsey Reports on American males (1948) and American females (1953) did not use a standardized interviewing schedule.[55] Like Lazarsfeld's early market research work and some of Likert's early questionnaires in Agriculture, the interviewer was allowed to vary the language in the judgment that only thus could meaning be standardized across very different groups. The topics of the interview were specified (some 300 to 500, depending on the individual's kinds and ranges of sexual experience). But the language of the questioning was shaped to the particular sexual vernacular—of prison inmates, marriage counselors, farmers, housewives, headmasters, prostitutes, physicians, bootleggers, and so on. Kinsey, a zoologist at the University of Indiana, used an unorthodox and fascinating mix of methods to try to obtain individual candor and mass data. These were something of an amalgam of survey research and the field methods of anthropology.

Feeling that they could not get enough cooperation from a national sample of individuals, Kinsey and his colleagues tried to reach many different kinds of groups of varying class, age, ethnicity, occupation, intelligence, and region and to interview as many people as they could in that group. This was not unlike Bogardus's efforts in his mass study of social distance, but it was more ambitious. Kinsey and his associates got acquainted with members of the community. They tutored themselves in local customs and language, and they made friends with people who would vouch for the research to their friends and acquaintances.

The interviews were relatively short (from one to two hours) because it was found that beyond that length of time, fatigue diminished the quality of the information. The interviewing style assumed that all respondents had engaged in every kind of sexual activity; interviewers asked not *whether* respondents had engaged in homosexual practices, masturbation, extramarital intercourse, and so on but *when* they had done so for the first time. They elicited the *straightest* kind of talk and were free to contradict respondents when they sensed any falsity, but they also tried to convey in some wordless way (i.e., with a glance or a facial expression) that they understood and sympathized when the sexual history was a record of "hurt, of frustrations, of pain, of unsatisfied longings, of disappointments, of desperately tragic situations, and of complete catastrophe."[56] They recorded data in the presence of the respondent in a quick check-off system, using a code that the six interviewers had memorized and which was never written down. Kinsey's standards for confidentiality could hardly have been more scrupulous. He and his small group of colleagues were also tireless. By the publication of the 1948 book, they had conducted more than 18,000 interviews. Kinsey and Wardell Pomeroy had each done 8,000.[57]

As Kinsey et al. emphasized, human sexual behavior had inspired a mountain of graphic art and print—probably more thought, more talk, and more books than any other subject in the human repertoire, and goodly amounts of scientific inquiry, too. But there had been little systematic work of broad coverage that allowed statistical treatment. Kinsey located twenty-three studies published between 1915 and 1947, most of which had no pretensions to being a sample of any population, the largest set of which were based on college students. Kinsey's work was not a real sample, either, which he recognized full well and for which his work was duly criticized by social scientists, but it had gone way beyond the college classroom in its inquiry into very intimate human experience.[58]

As a hotel manager said when he refused to allow Kinsey and his group to conduct any interviews on his premises, "I do not intend that anyone should have his mind undressed in my hotel."[59]

Kinsey traveled farther into the "sensitive" areas of human experience than anyone else did in this period, but other surveys also pushed at the boundaries. Studies of self-reported drinking behavior were undertaken—Jellinek's survey of Alcoholics Anonymous, for instance; "polls of drinking" conducted by the Washington Public Opinion Laboratory; and Riley and Marden's surveys of alcohol users and social drinkers, for which NORC did the fieldwork.[60] Reports of personal "worrying" behavior were gathered by Stouffer for his communism study. More intense inquiry into worries, fears of "nervous breakdown" and mental illness, and the incidence of seeking professional help for personal problems was done with a national sample in the Gurin, Veroff, and Feld study of mental health, along with self-reports of personal problems in marriage, feelings of inadequacy, and marital happiness and unhappiness.[61]

It appears that surveys in this period did not explore mystical or religious experience or personal trauma such as the immediate impact of divorce, the experience of grief and death in the family, or the onset and course of terminal illness, but all of these experiences would be the subject of surveys in a later epoch.[62] Psychologists began to use survey techniques in conjunction with indirect and projective measures to study personality in adult populations outside the classroom.

The Authoritarian Personality (1950), by Adorno, Frenkel-Brunswik, Levinson, and Sanford, one of the several books in the Studies in Prejudice series sponsored by the American Jewish Committee, was the source of the famous "F-scale" designed to measure the potentially Fascist personality. The other scales used in the book (on anti-Semitism, ethnocentrism, and political-economic conservatism) were also influential, but the F-scale had special impact and wide circulation. These items were among the large set comprising the F-scale:

Obedience and respect for authority are the most important virtues children should learn.

Young people sometimes get rebellious ideas, but as they grow up they ought to get over them and settle down.

Homosexuals are hardly better than criminals and ought to be severely punished.

Most of our social problems would be solved if we could somehow get rid of the immoral, crooked, and feebleminded people.

Human nature being what it is, there will always be war and conflict.[63]

The book can be viewed now as a fine point of comparison to the Kinsey Reports, for both represent interesting variants on the survey method. *The Authoritarian Personality* used the direct measures of survey questions and the indirect methods of "depth" interviews and thematic apperception tests of the clinical tradition; the Kinsey group relied on straightforward self-report of surveys, with variants on interviewing and coding practice. Both used members of groups rather than large-scale samples of individuals. Kinsey had much better scientific warrant for doing so, for the sensitive nature of his subject matter argued for the use of special measures to elicit the cooperation and confidence of his respondents. The Adorno group apparently used special groups for entirely practical reasons. Confronted with a scarcity of resources, they started their study with college students; as they expanded the study, they collected questionnaires from a variety of adult groups. But, overall, it was a far less heterogeneous set of groups than the Kinsey collection and used a variety of questionnaire forms. One hundred ten San Quentin State Prison inmates, 121 psychiatric clinic patients, and another group were given one form; 343 merchant marine officers and 106 veterans were given another; and a variety of groups identified by the authors as middle-class or working-class were given still another, and so on.

The Authoritarian Personality had problems in sampling bias, along with problems in coding and analysis, which Hyman and Sheatsley explained in a long review article. The most striking defect of analysis was the failure to subject the hypothesis of an authoritarian *personality* systematically to a thoroughgoing test of a rival idea, namely, that differences in formal education might account for much of the variation in expressed "authoritarianism." Hyman and Sheatsley marshalled compelling illustrations from the Adorno protocols in support of the education hypothesis. They also adduced results from more than a dozen relevant attitudinal items drawn from national NORC surveys (five of which were abbreviated F-scale items) that showed strong differences by education.[64]

Their critique was the work of sophisticated survey researchers who were experienced in survey sampling, questioning, coding, and analysis and who also could call upon cogent national survey data to argue their case. The critique did not argue against using projective tests in a survey context—indeed, this was a perfectly appropriate and feasible expansion of survey techniques, which others were also using.[65] It was, rather, an indication of the resources available by the mid-1950s—sophisticated researchers and a wealth of survey data on a national scope.

The Cross-Cultural Expansion

At the end of the 1950s, a new and ambitious international survey conducted in five nations went into the field; it was published in 1963 as *The Civic Culture*, by Almond and Verba.[66] While the authors traced their intellectual roots back to Charles E. Merriam and University of Chicago political science, they cited both of the international studies we have discussed in chapter nine. Their study yielded data of greater richness than the Buchanan-Cantril UNESCO report and greater comparability than the Bureau-Lerner studies.

The so-called Five-Nation Study by Almond and Verba went through two pretests and seven separate versions—the first interviews lasted no less than a whole day!—as the investigators progressively whittled their vast aspirations down to an instrument that could be administered with fair comparability in cross-section national samples of 1,000. (Wilson's International Research Associates did the fieldwork in England, Germany, Italy, and Mexico, and NORC did it in the United States.) The rich explorations of unstructured questions and elite interviewing were sacrificed in favor of less complete, more comparable measures. The questionnaire itself was 90 percent closed; on the open-ended questions, interviewers were leashed in:

> It was necessary . . . to specify precisely the number of times an interviewer could probe for further information in an open-ended question, as well as the content of that probing. In this way, the extent to which a sophisticated interviewer could obtain a full response in a particular area through extensive follow-up questions was circumscribed, but the comparability of the results was increased.[67]

The Almond/Verba study also tried to incorporate some "in-depth" materials from small "life-history" subsamples in each country (with Ns ranging from 45 to 135). From the cross-section samples, respondents were selected who had special interest as political types or as "deviant cases" in the Lazarsfeld tradition (e.g., poorly educated women who were politically active). The study nevertheless relied most heavily on the mass questionnaires. For national and international studies of this scope, "mass" and "elite" techniques and goals were not wholly fused, in some fifty-fifty blend. Rather, the enduring compromise from this period favored the standardized and quantitative survey instrument that could be administered to large samples by large field staffs.

The Power and the Limits

The Historical Ascendance of the Subjective Realm

The survey data amassed by academics in the postwar period were dominantly subjective: beliefs, ideologies, preferences, feelings, and, especially, opinions and attitudes. As we have defined it from the outset of this book, survey research as a technology encompassed anything that could be stored and analyzed by the individual record, as *reported by* or *observed of* individuals—for example, "facts" of income, amounts of spending, space of residence, amounts of nutrition, reactions of physiology, states of disease or health—and much survey work in government in particular continued to gather data in these *less* subjective realms. In principle, in the same survey one could also gather data of the respondent's self-report and the observational measures of the interviewer, as in the "schedules" with which the social survey movement had tried to systematize an investigator's observations of a community. In practice, the role of the interviewer-as-observer dwindled to the making of a few estimates, such as the class level of the neighborhood, the condition of the house, and the general intelligence of the respondent.

In university-based survey research, self-report and subjective measures quite overshadowed the observation of "objective" conditions. This happened for two main reasons. In general, much of the survey work reporting on community conditions became institutionalized in realms of government. These surveys of "objective" conditions, which took on special visibility with Charles Booth's study of London and which persisted in the American social survey movement, were absorbed by agencies of local, state, and federal government work, especially as the role of the federal government burgeoned during the New Deal. Furthermore, academic work was formatively influenced in this period by the preoccupations of opinion pollsters, social psychologists, and sociologists—people interested in attitudes. This was not an intrinsic limitation of the method but a historical one that made the scope of survey research in this period even narrower than subjective phenomena generally.

If other people had been the first captains of survey research, attitudes surely would not have been as ascendant and more data would have been collected on self-report of experience, behavior, and information. Historians and anthropologists of a certain stripe, for example, might well have tried to bring the self-report of individuals' life experiences to the fore, and we would now have a richer record of the human impact of wars, refugee flight, the Nazi experience, depressions, unemployment. Political economists might have been drawn to individuals' experience with industrial technology, the lateral spread and high-rising of cities, the impact of the bulldozer, the onset of computers, the rise of affluence, the endurance of poverty. If social biologists, anthropologists, or demographers had been in charge, survey research might have been put into first service for studies of culture and class, migration and assimilation, sex roles, generational strain, life phases, fertility, child-rearing, and aging. If educators had been dominant, we would presumably know much more about the kinds and distribution of public information, ignorance, understanding, and belief—not just an occasional question aimed at testing knowledge or interest in politics. Since 1960 surveys have been spreading into these areas. Still, the early period had its own richness, in its concentration on attitudes and some extensions into behavior. It demonstrated unequivocally that attitudes were indeed "facts" of life and that much so-called factual data had vivid and intractable attitudinal components. The limited content of surveys in this period also provided a powerful focus.

Survey research of these early years was critically shaped by social psychologists in psychology and sociology. More than other disciplinary groups, social psychologists were prepared to undertake large-scale surveys, for they had an interest and experience in subjective measurement which economists, for instance, did not share. They also had quantitative skills from their training in psychology which most political scientists still lacked. Without interested and prosperous clients, however, who had money to commission this expensive, broad-scale work, social psychologists would have continued to study attitudes in the low-cost populations of students and small groups.

For the kind of support that provided access to the broad population, the social scientists were indebted, indirectly, to the pollsters. It was the commercial pollsters, especially, who provided the most dramatic and persuasive example to prospective clients that it was feasible and affordable to sample opinions and attitudes of great economic and political importance, with results that could be generalized to vast populations. During World War II, the federal government was the greatest client of them all, with urgent political and administrative needs to know about soldiers and civilians, their "morale," their support of the war and of the government. This federal use was a prime factor in steering survey research in the direction of opinions and attitudes.

The Relentless Need for Big Money

Funding was, and continues to be, a vital factor in the origins and development of survey research, simply because by the standards of social science this research is such expensive work. This is not to say that the content of surveys is rigidly determined by economic interests. Even in very specific "applied" contract work, scientists are usually at pains to try to widen the research agenda of clients or sponsors to admit more of their own intellectual interests, in the practice wryly called "bootlegging." Furthermore, as science has gained in cultural prestige and political power, scientists have been more successful in garnering resources for their own intellectual pursuits. Rather, it is to say that the "entrepreneurial" efforts of survey researchers in this early period were not only the struggles of an infant industry but also reflected an enduring tension between social scientists who wanted to be free to list where Truth led them (or at least intellectual Beauty) and the people who paid for their work. The latter expected from social research some payoff, as they defined it, in practical benefit for some objective, as they sighted it. And funders still do.

As Stouffer reflected about these matters during World War II, it was necessary for social scientists to come out now and then and show what they could "do." But showing what they could (or can) do inevitably raises the question of doing *what* and for *whom*. The wartime work was performed in a spirit of patriotic national consensus, so this question was not an acute one. The question was muted, too, by the more general funding of foundation and governmental grants that asked no immediate practical payoff, and survey researchers in these early years were of course intensely interested in trying to get this more ample and generous funding. The question is nevertheless raised, as a chronic condition, by even the most disinterested and generous kind of support.

If social science is not required to come out now and then and show what it can *do*, as its practical benefits are defined in some fashion or another, there is an alternative justification: namely, that basic science is another facet of human intelligence and creativity, equivalent in value and meriting the kind of public support given to museums, orchestras, repertory theater, libraries, and other resources for a cultivated, intellectual life. The contemporary attack on positivism by a new generation of historians and sociologists of science of the post-Kuhnian era would suggest that social scientists might well argue for support on such cultural rather than practical grounds. They do not tend to, however, and they probably do not because these cultural institutions are usually mendicants, struggling to stay alive. Rather, social scientists tend to argue that support of their basic research will bring benefits in application to the society as a whole—with world enough and time.

Survey research is not peculiar in needing money, but it vivifies the issues of basic/applied research simply because it usually requires so much of it. If survey research is not to be funded by the personal fortune of a Charles Booth, it is to be subsidized from the coffers of foundations or governments, or it must make its own way in work for business, industry, labor, political groups, and other large sectors. The applied/basic tension will not go away.

As an instrument of social science, survey research grew in power and precision in this early period and also showed some sophistication concerning the limits of its methods. It aroused vocal criticism in a series of complaints which we have already reviewed briefly in chapter eight; some of these complaints still flourish. The advent of survey research certainly leaves other empirical methods alive and well, with their own characteristic advantages and disadvantages: participant observation and community studies of sociology and anthropology, aggregate data analysis of macroeconomics and political science, laboratory experiment and clinical interviews of psychology, documentary studies of history, and so on. In principle, these various strategies can even be used together. In practice, however, it has become increasingly difficult to mix methods, because the use of any one of them has come to involve professional specialization of a high order, with vast educational preparation and ongoing intellectual commitment. And the various methodologies of social science are to a certain extent in competition with one another as they vie for scarce resources, striving to become attractive to government and foundation funding. Just because the practice of survey research is especially expensive for social science inquiry—even if for no other reason—it is especially likely to inspire criticism from other wings of social science.

Of Time, Structure, and Self-Report

Certain criticisms of survey research in this early period pointed then, and continue to point, in my view, to specific weaknesses or limits of survey research that are also its peculiar strengths. The first feature is the constraint on *time*. A survey typically averages not much more than an hour of an individual's life, a limit that is dictated largely by respondents themselves. An hour or so of survey questioning is about as much as most people in the general population will concentrate on, enjoy, or put up with. *Special populations* will submit to much longer, more intensive, and more frequent interviews or observation because they have special desires or special pressures—for example, clinical populations, prisoners, college students, schoolchildren, and paid respondents. Such special groups can provide much more detailed information, "in depth," but their very specialness limits the generalizability of the data they provide. If one works with samples of the broad population—people who are much freer to refuse to cooperate—a researcher is largely constrained to the brief and necessarily rather superficial encounter. This is true almost regardless of the money available for the total size of the survey. The great weakness of brevity is the counterpart of its great strength, generalizability to people in general.

A second constraint is *standardized questions*. All three of the early organizations tried to enrich survey questions with inquiry into detail and "depth," using open-ended and qualitative material, profiting from interviewer insight and flexibility. NORC, however, relied more heavily on standardized wording from its beginning, out of the experience of its own polling tradition; in the course of the 1940s and 1950s the Bureau and SRC also converged in the practice of greater standardization. In using structured questionnaires, the survey researchers banked on two assumptions. First, they assumed that interviewers could and would deliver the same questions, whatever the variety of conditions they found. Second, and still more basic, they assumed that English-speaking respondents in the United States shared common culture *enough* that they could all be addressed in the same vocabulary: not, to be sure, an identical culture, education, or interpretation, but close enough that survey questions did not have to be "translated" or selected for the special cultures of region, class, or community.

There was some scientific warrant for these bets. Survey investigators could not insure that each respondent would *receive* the same meaning, but they aspired to *send* the same literal message, trying to word that message in such a way that it would communicate much the same meaning to the mass public without being insulting to elites. (Pretests were aimed especially at finding that language.) There was an even stronger practical warrant. Survey investigators could not allow a flexible and intuitive style when the data collection was out of their hands, conducted by large groups of interviewers who were not professionally trained in the social sciences and who were paid modest wages. Standardized questions represented an instrument of administrative control, offering some hope that interviewers would not simply use their own (highly variable) judgment of what was appropriate in the given situation.

The highly stylized *closed* question that "puts people in little boxes" was a part of the same constraint posed by large-scale data collection for statistical analysis. If one is to do quantitative research of any sort, data must be put into boxes, and a limited number of them at that. All the rich material of an entirely open-ended interview, recorded verbatim, will either be put to no systematic analytic use at all or it will be put into boxes, by somebody—either analysts, who design codes for the open-ended material, or respondents, who try to find from among the boxes offered those that best fit their lives and souls. In either case, one hopes for artful, realistic, valid choices.

Are there alternatives? There are no simple ones, in any case. The most obvious remedies would tax enormously both the resources of survey organizations and the tolerance of respondents. What about using highly educated, intensively trained interviewers who would be paid at truly professional levels? This solution would cost a fortune. Or highly detailed, intensive questioning of respondents over several hours and repeated visits? This would likely be at a high cost in response rates; the willingness of respondents to provide data for social science is another special constraint on surveys.

A third factor is *self-report*, which also constrains surveys with certain limits and particular powers. The validity of survey reporting has been in vigorous question from the beginning, offering a rich and contentious history of its own which I have slighted here in favor of other topics. Do people mean what they say? Do they know what they mean? Can they say it? Do survey questions even give them a chance to speak plainly? The adequacy of both questions and answers has repeatedly been called into question. The validity of self-report has probably aroused more skepticism in surveys than it has in other areas of applied science. The practice of medicine, for instance, would be hobbled indeed if professionals could not put some credence in the data of self-report, although medical histories must rely on much retrospective measurement and are probably still gathered with little attention to even such principles of interviewing and question wording as survey research has developed. There are obviously differences, however, for medicine generally goes beyond self-report to physical examination of patients and the assays of the biochemical laboratory as primary data.

Survey researchers rarely go beyond self-report. Validity studies are not only expensive but amazingly complex as well. One can compare the "subjective" self-report of surveys to the "objective" data of official records, but most of the documents that one can consult to validate surveys are also constructed of self-report and thus are usually vulnerable to the same kinds of measurement error and bias that surveys themselves are prey to. In some situations, the survey information may be better than the records: samples are likely to be more accurate than censuses, and contemporary data management by computer can monitor error more successfully than the paper-and-pencil systems still governing much of official record keeping of the past.

Even so, self-report has left a record of some ingloriousness. In the 1980s, the distribution of ignorance has come to seem quite awesome, as documented by surveys and as interpreted by social science elites. On issues of manifest importance to the culturally well educated or the politically sophisticated, a substantial fraction of the general public has scored low. For all the goodwill and pliability that many of the American public have shown in their willingness to be interviewed, there is much that social scientists want to learn about people which a substantial part of the mass public cannot teach—they don't know.

This datum itself is one we have learned from polls and surveys, and it illustrates one of their great strengths. With no other instrument can we gather data from the broad public in some semblance of their natural setting. And there is no other method of data collection and analysis that so successfully forces social scientists to contemplate the narrow limits of their own construction of social reality.

George Gallup was long sensitive to the democratic potential of polls: that polls at their best could permit mass publics to speak for themselves rather than being interpreted by political pressure groups or cultural elites who spoke *for* them. Academic survey researchers can also be forced by their data to consider a question that is a variant of Gallup's guarded, qualified populism, with respect not only to politics but to science as well: If The People do not know, are survey researchers asking the right questions?

Notes

Notes

Introduction

1. A. F. K. Organski, *The Thirty-Six Billion Dollar Bargain: Why Does the U.S. Give Aid to Israel?* (in preparation); V. O. Key, Jr., *Public Opinion and American Democracy* (New York: Knopf, 1961); E. E. Schattschneider, *The Semi-Sovereign People: A Realist's View of Democracy in America* (New York: Holt, Rinehart, and Winston, 1960).

2. James R. Beniger, "Speaking Your Mind without Elections, Surveys, or Social Movements" (comment on Charles Tilly), *Public Opinion Quarterly* 47 (1983): 479–484.

3. Barnes and Shapin note regarding an internal/external dichotomy: "The intense concern of earlier generations with the special status of science and its allegedly distinctive characteristics has begun to ebb away . . . [yielding to] a real interest in our natural knowledge as a product of our way of life, as something we have constructed rather than something which has been, so to speak, revealed to us.

"If this tendency continues . . . the contrast of 'internal' and 'external' factors in the history of science will cease to be a major source of interest or controversy. That external procedures, representations, or even standards of judgment become taken up into the esoteric subculture of 'science' will simply be something to be noted and treated as seems fit to the interpretive task at hand. External factors would then be dealt with as they presently are when taken up into the subcultures of painters or musicians. Nobody expects a subculture to be capable of complete independence of its environment or general setting" (Barry Barnes and Steven Shapin, *Natural Order: Historical Studies of Scientific Culture* [Beverly Hills, Calif.: Sage Publications, 1979], introduction).

4. Thomas S. Kuhn, "The History of Science," *International Encyclopedia of the Social Sciences* (New York: Macmillan Co., 1968), vol. 14, pp. 74–83.

5. Daniel S. Greenberg, *The Politics of Pure Science*, 2d ed. (New York: New American Library, 1971).

6. Harry Levin, review of Jerome Bruner, *In Search of Mind: Essays in Autobiography*, *Science* 224 (May 18, 1984), p. 720.

1. The Reformist Ancestor of Policy: The Social Survey

1. The various editions of the Booth work can be confusing. The first volume, published in 1889, was entitled *Life and Labour of the People*; the second, published

in 1891, was called *Labour and Life of the People* because there was another copyright claim to the first title. These two volumes constituted the Poverty Series. In the definitive revised edition, which reissued all seventeen volumes as *Life and Labour of the People in London* (London and New York: Macmillan Co., 1902–03), the Poverty Series was expanded to four volumes. There were also five volumes on industries and trades, seven on religious influences, and a final volume entitled *Notes on Social Influences and Conclusion*. See T. S. Simey and M. B. Simey, *Charles Booth, Social Scientist* (London: Oxford University Press, 1960), p. 115; *Charles Booth's London*, ed. and with an introduction by Albert Fried and Richard M. Elman (New York: Random House, 1968), p. xxvii.

2. Pauline V. Young, *Scientific Social Surveys and Research*, 2d ed. (New York: Prentice-Hall, 1949); Mildred Parten, *Surveys, Polls, and Samples* (New York: Harper, 1950); Mark Abrams, *Social Surveys and Social Action* (London: Heineman, 1951); C. A. Moser, *Survey Methods in Social Investigation* (London: Heinemann, 1958); Charles Y. Glock, "Introduction," in *Survey Research in the Social Sciences*, ed. Glock (New York: Russell Sage Foundation, 1967); James S. Coleman, "Sociological analysis and social policy," in *A History of Sociological Analysis*, ed. Tom Bottomore and Robert Nisbet (New York: Basic Books, 1978); Duane Alwin and Susan A. Stephens, "The Use of Sample Surveys in the Social Sciences" (Paper presented at the national meetings of AAAS, Houston, Jan. 1979). Richard W. Boyd and Herbert H. Hyman consider the tradition of Booth and Rowntree in "Survey Research," in *Strategies of Inquiry*, ed. Fred I. Greenstein and Nelson W. Polsby (Reading, Mass.: Addison-Wesley, 1975), but they decide to exclude it because it did not incorporate sampling.

3. Robert C. Davis, "Social Research in America Before the Civil War," *Journal of the History of the Behavioral Sciences* 8 (1972):69–85.

4. The term *social survey* is retained as the generic term by Stephen E. Fienberg and Judith M. Tanur, "Large-scale Social Surveys: Perspectives, Problems, and Prospects," *Behavioral Science* 28 (1983):135–153. The Library of Congress classification "social survey" includes contemporary work as diverse as texts on survey sampling and portraits of individuals based on informal interviewing.

5. Mary Booth, *Charles Booth: A Memoir* (London: Macmillan & Co., 1918); Simey and Simey, *Booth*, p. 157. Booth clearly needed an editor, and two have emerged in recent books: *Charles Booth's London* (see note 1 above) and *Charles Booth On the City: Physical Pattern and Social Structure*, ed. and with an introduction by Harold W. Pfautz (Chicago: University of Chicago Press, 1967).

6. Abrams, *Social Surveys*, pp. 39–40.

7. Bernard Lécuyer and Anthony R. Oberschall, "The Early History of Social Research," in *The International Encyclopedia of the Social Sciences* (*IESS*), ed. David L. Sills (New York: Macmillan/Free Press, 1968), pp. 36–53; Davis, "Social Research"; Sir John Sinclair's *The Statistical Account of Scotland Drawn Up from the Communications of the Ministers of the Different Parishes* (Edinburgh: no publisher listed, 1791–1799) is described by D. Caradog Jones, *Social Surveys* (London and New York: Hutchinson, 1949); Sir Frederick Morton Eden, *The State of the Poor: A History of the Labouring Classes in England, with Parochial Reports*, abridged and ed. by A. G. L. Rogers (New York: E. P. Dutton, [1797] 1929) (see esp. chap. 2); Nathan Glazer, "The Rise of Social Research in Europe," in *The Human Meaning*

of the Social Sciences, ed. Daniel Lerner (New York: Meridian, 1959), pp. 43–72; David Landau and Paul F. Lazarsfeld, "Adolphe Quetelet," *IESS* 13:247–257; Paul F. Lazarsfeld, "Notes on the History of Quantification in Sociology—Trends, Sources and Problems," *Isis* 52 (1961):277–333; Edwin G. Boring, "The Beginning and Growth of Measurement in Psychology," *Isis* 52 (1961):238–257.

8. R. K. Webb, *Modern England* (New York: Dodd, Mead, & Company, 1975), pp. 27–32. Eden in *The State of the Poor* notes a survey made by the Lord Mayor of London in 1595 showing 4,132 poor householders (p. 21). See also Thomas Beames, *The Rookeries of London* (London: Frank Cass, [1850] 1970); Rev. Andrew Mearns, *The Bitter Cry of Outcast London: An Inquiry into the Condition of the Abject Poor* (London: James Clarke, 1883); Ruth Glass, "Urban Sociology in Great Britain: A Trend Report," *Current Sociology* IV (1955):5–76; Parten, *Surveys, Polls, and Samples*, pp. 5–9; Young, *Scientific Social Surveys*, chaps. 1 and 2; Stephen Cole, "Continuity and Institutionalization in Science: A Case Study of Failure," in *The Establishment of Empirical Sociology*, ed. Anthony Oberschall (New York: Harper & Row, 1972).

9. Statistical Society of London, "Report of a Committee on the Statistical Society of London, on the State of the Working Classes in the Parishes of St. Margaret and St. John, Westminster," *Journal of the Statistical Society* III (1840):14–24; David Elesh, "The Manchester Statistical Society: A Case of Discontinuity in the History of Empirical Social Research," in *The Establishment of Empirical Sociology*, ed. Oberschall; Paul J. Fitzpatrick, "Statistical Societies in the United States in the Nineteenth Century," *American Statistician* XI (Dec. 1957):13–21.

10. Data on the incidence and causes of poverty early in the nineteenth century were measured by counting cases of people receiving public assistance rather than by field studies on the actual standard of living, according to Raymond A. Mohl, *Poverty in New York 1783–1825* (New York: Oxford University Press, 1971), esp. chap. 2; the YMCAs of St. Louis and Washington had committees on statistics in the 1850s which undertook surveys. A New York survey of 1866 was recommended by the YMCA as a model for communities to organize a "reconnoitering party" of young men who would make continuous surveys of their city conditions, such as tenements, sanitary facilities, saloons, brothels, and the moral conditions of the community. See Charles Howard Hopkins, *History of the Y.M.C.A. in North America* (New York: Association Press, 1951); idem, *The Rise of the Social Gospel in American Protestantism 1865–1915* (New Haven: Yale University Press, 1940), pp. 274–279; Leah Hannah Feder, *Unemployment Relief in Periods of Depression: A Study of Measures Adopted in Certain American Cities, 1857 through 1922* (New York: Russell Sage Foundation, 1936); Davis, "Social Research."

11. Simey and Simey, esp. pp. 69–116.

12. E. P. Hennock, "Poverty and Social Theory in England: The Experience of the Eighteen-eighties," *Social History* 1 (1976): 67–91.

13. Booth, *Labour and Life of the People*, 3d ed. (London: William and Norgate, 1891), Poverty Series, vol. 1, pp. 131–132, 146–155, and vol. 2, pp. 20–22, 40–45.

14. Beatrice Webb, *My Apprenticeship* (London: Longmans, Green, 1926), pp. 215–217. A 1823 New York survey based on data from 22,111 recipients of

public poor relief concluded that drink produced two-thirds of the permanent poor and more than half of the temporary poor (Davis, "Social Research," pp. 81–82). As Davis notes, temperance workers rushed rather easily from an apparent correlation to causal inference. The concern about alcoholism and drunkenness, especially the physical abuse of women and children, was a spur to middle-class women's involvement first in the temperance movement and later in the women's suffrage movement. See Ruth Bordin, *Woman and Temperance: The Quest for Power and Liberty, 1873–1900* (Philadelphia: Temple University Press, 1981). The concern to separate the "deserving" from the "undeserving" poor shows not only in Booth's work but in other investigations early in the century (see Mohl, note 10 above), but Booth saw in public houses little actual drunkenness and much companionship: "*Public-houses* play a larger part in the lives of the people than clubs or friendly societies, churches or missions, or perhaps than all put together" (*Labour and Life*, vol. 1, pp. 113–114).

15. Booth, *Life and Labour of the People in London*, Religious Influences Series, vol. 1, p. 7.

16. Simey and Simey, p. 201.

17. Hanan C. Selvin, "Durkheim, Booth and Yule: The Non-Diffusion of an Intellectual Innovation," *European Journal of Sociology* 17 (1976):39–51; A. L. Bowley and A. R. Burnett-Hurst, *Livelihood and Poverty: A Study in the Economic Conditions of Working-Class Households in Northampton, Warrington, Stanley, and Reading* (London: G. Bell, 1915).

18. Webb, *My Apprenticeship*, p. 196.

19. Ibid., p. 201.

20. Booth, *Life and Labour*, Poverty Series, vol. 2, p. 2.

21. B. Seebohm Rowntree, *Poverty: A Study of Town Life*, 2d ed. (London: Macmillan, [1901] 1902), p. viii.

22. Ibid.

23. Ibid., pp. 117–118, 216, 295–300.

24. Rowntree asked thirty-five working-class families to keep family budgets, which he recapitulated in copious detail, including all food consumed. See *Poverty*, pp. 222–294. The lack of fruits and vegetables is conspicuous, for their importance was not understood in this era. Research into vitamins in the United States was an outgrowth of nutrition research begun in 1894 by the U.S. Office of Experiment Stations. See Jane M. Porter, "Experiment Stations in the South, 1877–1940," *Agricultural History* 53 (1979):84–101; Charles E. Rosenberg, "Science Pure and Science Applied: Two Studies in the Social Origin of Scientific Research," in *No Other Gods: On Science and American Social Thought* (Baltimore and London: Johns Hopkins University Press, [1961] 1976).

25. Rowntree, *Poverty*, pp. 107–108.

26. Ibid.

27. In publicity included in the back of the Rowntree volume, Booth's work is subtitled "An Economic and Industrial Survey." Booth himself used the word *survey* occasionally, as in *Survey and Conclusions* (*Life and Labour*, Industries Series, vol. 5).

28. See Noah Webster, *An American Dictionary of the English Language*, Vol. II (New York: S. Converse [1828], 1838) and subsequent editions of 1861, 1898;

The New American Encyclopedic Dictionary (New York: J. A. Hill, 1907), and 2d ed., 1947; the *Oxford English Dictionary* (Oxford: Clarendon Press, [1933] 1970).

29. Walter L. Goldfrank, "Reappraising Le Play," in *Empirical Sociology*, ed. Oberschall, pp. 130–151, notes that Le Play used the family budgets as a basis for intensive questioning but did not use the data systematically as a basis for conclusions. In *Frederic Le Play On Family, Work, and Social Change*, ed., transl., and with an introduction by Catherine Bodard Silver (Chicago and London: University of Chicago Press, 1982), Silver points out that neglect and criticism of Le Play is explained in part by the polemical, antiscientific temper of the second edition of *Les Ouvriers Européens*, published in 1877–79.

30. According to Goldfrank, Le Play said that he had made 300 detailed studies, but no more than 30 of his ever appeared in print ("Reappraising Le Play," p. 139).

31. Hugh S. Hanna, "Adequacy of the Sample in Budgetary Studies," *JASA* 29 (1934): March 1934 Proceedings, no. 185A; Jerome Cornfield, "On Certain Biases in Samples of Human Populations," *JASA* 37 (1942):63–68; Faith M. Williams and Carle C. Zimmerman, *Studies of Family Living in the United States and Other Countries* (Washington; D.C.: USDA Misc. Publication no. 223, Dec. 1935). In their review of approximately 1,500 studies of family living, all of which present some data on income or expenditure, Williams and Zimmerman conclude that "in the last seventy years . . . there has never been a comprehensive study of the living of all the groups in the population" nor even of all groups in any one state or city (p. 13). Thus, indeed, the need for *surveys* of broad scope.

32. Helen Campbell, *Prisoners of Poverty: Women Wage-Workers, Their Trades and Their Lives* (New York: Garrett Press [1887], 1970; Jacob Riis, *How the Other Half Lives* (New York: Scribner, 1890) and *The Children of the Poor* (New York: Scribner, 1892); and Robert Hunter, *Poverty* (New York: Macmillan Co., 1905). Arthur Weinberg and Lila Weinberg, eds., *The Muckrakers* (New York: Simon & Schuster, 1961) is a selection of significant muckraking magazine articles fom 1902 to 1912.

33. *Nation* 53 (1891):244–245; *Century Magazine* XLV (1892–93):245–256; *Review of Reviews* 28 (1903):331–334; *Outlook* 76 (1904):1038–1040; *Annals of the American Academy of Political and Social Science* 2 (1892):854–865; *Political Science Quarterly* 5:507–519; 7:149–153; 10:727–729; 12:719–723. In "The Statistical Study of Causes of Destitution," *JASA* 11 (1908):273–285, Gustav Kleene criticized Booth's "case-counting" for its loose assumptions about causality.

34. Residents of Hull House, *Hull-House Maps and Papers: A Presentation of Nationalities and Wages in a Congested District of Chicago* (New York and Boston: Thomas Y. Crowell, 1895), p. 11. This was part of the study by U.S. Commissioner of Labor Carroll D. Wright, *The Slums of Baltimore, Chicago, New York, and Philadelphia* (New York: Arno [1894], 1970). Certain slum districts thought to be "representative" were selected and then fully canvassed for every individual living in them (p. 23).

35. W. E. B. Du Bois, *The Philadelphia Negro: A Social Study* (Philadelphia: Ginn, 1899).

36. The Scottish sociologist and urban planner Patrick Geddes was also of some influence on Kellogg and others involved in *The Survey* (see note 38, first reference, and note 40), but I have not traced the connections. Mairet notes

Geddes's awareness of Booth's work: see Philip Mairet, *Pioneer of Sociology: The Life and Letters of Patrick Geddes* (London: Lund Humphries, 1957), p. 118.

37. Allen Eaton and Shelby Harrison, *A Bibliography of Social Surveys* (New York: Russell Sage Foundation, 1930).

38. "To Change the Name of Charities and The Commons," *Charities and The Commons* XXI (1909):1251–1253; Harriett M. Bartlett, "The Social Survey and the Charity Organization Movement," *AJS* 34 (1928):330–346.

39. Paul Underwood Kellogg, ed., *The Pittsburgh Survey: Findings in Six Volumes* (New York: Russell Sage Foundation, 1914).

40. *Charities and The Commons* XXI (Mar. 1909):1251–1253; *The Survey* 22 (Apr. 1909):3. See also *Survey Graphic* 85 (Jan. 1949):4–5 for a short account of the magazine's evolution.

41. Paul U. Kellogg, "The Spread of the Survey Idea," *Proceedings of the Academy of Political Science* II (1912):475–491; George Walter Fiske, *The Challenge of the Country: A Study of Country Life Opportunity* (New York: Association Press, 1912).

42. Shelby M. Harrison, *Social Conditions in an American City: A Summary of the Findings of the Springfield* [Ill.] *Survey* (New York: Russell Sage Foundation, 1920).

43. Carl C. Taylor, *The Social Survey, Its History and Methods* (University of Missouri Bulletin, vol. 20, 1919), pp. 62–63.

44. Clayton S. Ellsworth, "Theodore Roosevelt's Country Life Commission," *Agricultural History* 34 (1960):155–172; David B. Danbom, "Rural Education Reform and the Country Life Movement," *Agricultural History* 53 (1979):462–474; William L. Bowers, *The Country Life Movement in America: 1900–1920* (Port Washington, N.Y.: Kennikat Press, 1974).

45. Wayne E. Fuller, "The Rural Roots of the Progressive Leaders," *Agricultural History* 42 (1968):1–14.

46. Liberty Hyde Bailey, "Why Do the Boys Leave the Farm?" *Century Magazine* 72 (1906):410–416; idem, "Why Some Boys Take to Farming," *Century Magazine* 72 (1906):612–617; Bowers, *Country Life Movement*, chap. 4.

47. Bowers, *Country Life Movement*, pp. 24–25.

48. *Report of the Commission on Country Life* (New York: Sturgis and Watson, 1911); also as Senate Document no. 705, 60th Congress, 2d sess., 9 February 1909. The tabulations of the final "most important single thing" question were lost (Ellsworth, "Country Life Commission").

49. Ellsworth, *Country Life Commission*.

50. Ellsworth finds that "The history of a better rural America has been, to a significant extent, the history of the adoption of the recommendations of the Commission" (p. 171), and he notes these outcomes: the Rockefeller Sanitary Commission to combat hookworm in 1909, the growth of county health boards, the commercial effort to sell labor-saving devices to the farm, the growth of church departments concerned with rural life in all the major Protestant denominations, and the development of a national extension education program based on agricultural agents (the Smith-Lever Act of 1914).

51. "Farm Wives Tell of Further Needs," *New York Times*, April 4, 1915, IV:6; "Farm Women Find Life Hard," *New York Times Magazine*, May 30, 1915, pp. 14–15. An earlier state study had focused on the reports of farm women: W. L. Nelson, "The Farmers on Farm Life," *World's Work* 23 (Nov. 1911):77–79.

52. Carl C. Taylor, "The Work of the Division of Farm Population and Rural Life," *Rural Sociology* 4 (1939):221–228.

53. Ellsworth, "Country Life Commission."

54. Charles F. Sarle, "Development of Partial and Sample Census Methods," *Journal of Farm Economics* 21 (1939):838–845; Conrad Taeuber, "Some Recent Developments in Sociological Work in the Department of Agriculture," *ASR* 10 (1944):169–175.

55. W. J. Spillman, "Validity of the Survey Method of Research," USDA Bulletin no. 529 (Washington, D.C., Apr. 5, 1917).

56. Louise O. Bercaw, *Rural Standards of Living: A Selected Bibliography*, USDA Misc. Publication no. 116 (Washington, D.C., July 1931). See, e.g., items 46, 151a, 260, 261, 261a, 262 on farm women's labor and time use.

57. Julius Rosenwald of Sears Roebuck offered $1,000 to each of 100 countries that would organize for extension teaching and hire a county agent. Farmers apparently accepted the offer, but some argued against the advertising purposes of a mail-order house. See Russell Lord, *The Agrarian Revival: A Study of Agricultural Extension* (New York: American Association for Adult Education, 1939), p. 87; Bowers, *Country Life Movement*, p. 18.

58. Interchurch World Movement of North America pamphlets *World Survey Conference Booklet, World Survey: A Statistical Mirror*, and *The Findings of the World Survey Conference Held at Atlantic City, New Jersey, January 7–10, 1920*.

59. H. N. Morse and Edmund De S. Brunner, *The Town and Country Church in the United States* (New York: George H. Doran, 1923), pp. vii–viii.

60. C. Luther Fry, *Diagnosing the Rural Church: A Study in Method* (New York: George H. Doran, 1924). Fry notes that social science professors from institutions in Iowa, Colorado, Wisconsin, West Virginia, Minnesota, and Missouri were given released time to participate as supervisors (p. ix).

61. Edmund De S. Brunner, *Surveying Your Community: A Handbook of Method for the Rural Church* (New York: Institute of Social and Religious Research, 1930), pp. 21–22.

62. *Literary Digest* 80 (Jan. 12, 1924):33. For the political controversy see "The Church as a Critic of Industry," *Literary Digest* 66 (Sept. 4, 1920):40–41; "Why the Interchurch Movement Failed," *Literary Digest* 66 (Aug. 7, 1920):42–43; Edwin L. Earp, "Sociological Evaluation of the Interchurch Movement," *Papers and Proceedings of the American Sociological Society* 15–16 (1920–21):74–89; and David Brody, *Labor in Crisis: The Steel Strike of 1919* (Philadelphia: J. B. Lippincott, 1965). Karl and Katz note that Rockefeller's own social activism involved a liberal meliorism about poverty and educational opportunity, especially for Negroes, and a conservative, even brutal, policy toward organized labor. See Barry D. Karl and Stanley N. Katz, "The American Private Philanthropic Foundation and the Public Sphere 1890–1930," *Minerva* 19 (1981):236–270.

63. ISRR, *The Institute of Social and Religious Research, 1921–1934: A Sketch of Its Development and Work* (New York, 1934), p. 26. See also H. Paul Douglass, *1,000 City Churches: Phases of Adaptation to Urban Environment* (New York: George H. Doran, 1926), pp. vi–ix, passim; Morse and Brunner, *Town and Country Church*, introduction, and chap. 1.

64. *The Institute of Social and Religious Research*, pp. 23–26, 53–59; Robert E.

Park, "A Race Relations Survey: Suggestions for a Study of the Oriental Population of the Pacific Coast," *Journal of Applied Sociology* VIII (1924):195–205; Robert S. Lynd and Helen Merrell Lynd, *Middletown: A Study in Contemporary American Culture* (New York: Harcourt, Brace and Company, 1929); Hugh Hartshorne and Mark A. May, *Studies in Deceit* (New York: Macmillan Co., 1928); Hugh Hartshorne and Frank K. Shuttlesworth, *Studies in the Organization of Character* (New York: Macmillan Co., 1930).

65. Fred H. Matthews, *Quest for an American Sociology: Robert E. Park and the Chicago School* (Montreal and London: McGill–Queen's University Press, 1977), pp. 112–115.

66. See note 63 above. These works by H. Paul Douglass show a transition from Interchurch methods to more sophisticated attitude measurement: *1,000 City Churches; The Springfield Church Survey* (New York: George H. Doran, 1926); and *Protestant Cooperation in American Cities* (New York: Institute of Social and Religious Research, 1930).

67. Edmund De S. Brunner, *The Growth of a Science* (New York: Harper and Bros., 1957), p. 145.

68. Shelby M. Harrison, *Community Action through Surveys* (New York: Russell Sage Foundation, 1916), p. 27.

69. Kellogg, *The Pittsburgh Survey*, vol. 1, p. 515.

70. Manuel C. Elmer, *Technique of Social Surveys*, 3d ed. (Los Angeles: Jesse Ray Miller, [1917] 1927).

71. Ibid., esp. pp. 12–27. See also Carol Aronovici, *The Social Survey* (Philadelphia: Harper Press, 1916). Jesse Frederick Steiner, *The American Community in Action: Case Studies of American Communities* (New York: Henry Holt & Co., 1928), provides a useful bibliography, pp. 373–387.

72. George A. Lundberg, *Social Research: A Study in Methods of Gathering Data* (New York: Longmans, Green, 1929), p. 162.

73. Elmer, *Technique of Social Surveys*, p. 47.

74. Ibid., p. 53.

75. F. Stuart Chapin, *Field Work and Social Research* (New York: Century, 1920), pp. 148–149.

76. Ibid., p. 175.

77. Ibid., chaps. 3 and 4.

78. Ibid., pp. 178–185; John R. Commons, "Standardization of housing investigations," *JASA* XI (1908):319–326.

79. F. Stuart Chapin, "A Quantitative Scale for Rating the Home and Social Environment of Middle-Class Families in an Urban Environment: A First Approximation to the Measurement of Socio-Economic Status," *Journal of Educational Psychology* XIX (1928):99–111.

80. Walter Scott Athearn, *The Malden Survey* (New York: Interchurch World Movement of North America, 1920); Morse and Brunner, *Town and Country Church.*

81. Teer and Spence state that Bowley's work in sampling "was very quickly followed by social researchers in the United States and the development of a large and expanding market for consumer goods stimulated the application of Bowley's methods in marketing research" (p. 19). It may be that the sometime use of selecting every *n*th household in marketing research was influenced by

Bowley, but if so, the American practice was a loose adaptation because interviewers were free to make their own selections. Parten's sample of households from a list in 1931 reflects Bowley's influence and may be the first American effort at true systematic selection; Margaret Hogg, a collaborator of Bowley's who came to the Russell Sage Foundation, used this sample for her study of unemployment. Stephan links Hogg to the transmission of Bowley's ideas into American practical application. See Frank Teer and James D. Spence, *Political Opinion Polls* (London: Hutchinson, 1973), p. 19; Parten, *Surveys, Polls, and Samples*, pp. 12–13; Frederick F. Stephan, "History of the Uses of Modern Sampling Procedures," *JASA* 43 (1948):12–39, p. 23.

    82. Chapin, *Field Work*, chap. 5.

    83. Margaret F. Byington, *Homestead: The Households of a Mill Town*, vol. 4 in *The Pittsburgh Survey*, ed. Kellogg, esp. pp. 194–195; Shelby M. Harrison, *Social Conditions in an American City: The Springfield Survey* (New York: Russell Sage Foundation, 1920); Harrison, "Syracuse, Survey of a Typical American City," *Academy of Political Science* 4 (1912):18–31.

    84. Kellogg, "The Spread of the Survey Idea"; Aronovici, *The Social Survey*; Elmer, *Technique of Social Surveys*; C. Luther Fry, *Diagnosing the Rural Church* (New York: George H. Doran, 1924).

    85. C. J. Galpin, "Gentlemen Preferring Farms," *Rural America* 7 (1929):5–6.

    86. Eaton and Harrison, *A Bibliography of Social Surveys*.

    87. Bercaw, *Rural Standards of Living*; Williams and Zimmerman, *Studies of Family Living*.

    88. Ellsworth, "Country Life Commission"; Harry H. Moore, "Health and Medical Practice," in U.S. President's Research Committee on Social Trends, *Recent Social Trends in the United States* (New York: McGraw-Hill, 1933), 2 vols., pp. 1061–1113; J. H. Kolb and Edmund De S. Brunner, "Rural Life," in *Recent Social Trends*, pp. 497–552; D. Clayton Brown, "Health of Farm Children in the South, 1900–1950," *Agricultural History* 53 (1979):170–187.

    89. Eaton and Harrison, *A Bibliography of Social Surveys*.

    90. Porter, "Experiment Stations in the South"; Kolb and Brunner, "Rural Life."

    91. Jesse Frederick Steiner, "Community Organization," *AJS* 40 (1935):788–795, p. 790. See also Seba Eldridge, "Two Major Ills of the Social Survey," *Journal of Applied Sociology* 8 (1924):223–232; and Carl C. Taylor, "Rural Life," *AJS* 47 (1941–42):841–853.

    92. Kate Holladay Claghorn, "Social Surveys to Date," *The Survey* 70 (July 1934):217–218.

    93. Compare the activism in E. W. Burgess, "The Social Survey: A Field for Constructive Service by Departments of Sociology," *AJS* 21 (1916):492–500, with his later emphasis on long-term patient data collection in "Basic Social Data," in *Chicago: An Experiment in Social Science Research*, ed. T. V. Smith and Leonard D. White (Chicago: University of Chicago Press, 1929), esp. p. 66. Robert E. Park and Ernest W. Burgess, in *Introduction to the Science of Sociology*, 2d ed. (Chicago: University of Chicago Press, 1924), credited the social survey reformism with arousing interest *in* the community but saw greater scientific promise in the social analyses *of* the community (esp. pp. 211–212).

    94. Vivien M. Palmer, *Field Studies in Sociology: A Student's Manual* (Chicago:

University of Chicago Press, 1928), distinguished the social survey as interested in "pathological conditions" and "practical reform and amelioration" from the sociological survey that was concerned with "normal phenomena" and the "scientific discovery of how human societies function" (pp. 48–51).

95. Carle C. Zimmerman in "The Trend of Rural Sociology," in *Trends in American Sociology*, ed. George A. Lundberg, Read Bain, and Nels Anderson (New York: Harper, 1929), pp. 221–260, reflected that the "mania" for achieving reform before thorough analysis had been conducted was not constructive for rural sociology. Lundberg was also a strong spokesman for that viewpoint. See Gary Easthope, *A History of Social Research Methods* (London: Longman, 1974), esp. chap. 7.

96. Charles P. Loomis and Zona Kemp Loomis, "Rural Sociology," in *The Uses of Sociology*, ed. Paul F. Lazarsfeld, William H. Sewell, and Harold L. Wilensky (New York: Basic Books, 1967), pp. 674–675. See also Dwight Anderson, "Status of and Prospects for Research in Rural Life under the New Deal," *AJS* 41 (1935–36):180–193.

97. As Secretary of Commerce in 1926, Hoover tried to interest industry in supporting basic research. The plan was to raise $20 million over a decade, but less than $400,000 was raised, and no mechanism was ever set up for making grants to scientists. Dupree thinks that the plan was dormant before the New Deal, which Hoover blamed (A. Hunter Dupree, *Science in the Federal Government* [Cambridge, Mass.: The Belknap Press of Harvard University Press, 1957], pp. 340–343). See also Gene M. Lyons, *The Uneasy Partnership: Social Science and the Federal Government in the Twentieth Century* (New York: Russell Sage Foundation, 1969), chap. 2.

98. U.S. President's Research Committee on Social Trends, *Recent Social Trends in the United States*, 2 vols. (New York: McGraw-Hill, 1933); Martin Bulmer, "The Methodology of Early Social Indicator Research: William Fielding Ogburn and 'Recent Social Trends,' 1933," *Social Indicators Research* 13 (1983):109–130. Dwight Sanderson, director of the rural research of FERA, estimated that FERA expenditures for 1934 (approximately $2.5 million) were equivalent to those for all of the state experimental stations for the five preceding years ("Research in Rural Life under the New Deal," *AJS* 41 [1935–36]:180–193, esp. 181).

99. See the titles and annotations of research projects in Works Progress Administration, Administrator Harry L. Hopkins, *Index of Research Projects* (3 vols.) (Washington, D.C., 1938–39).

100. S. H. Hobbs, Irene Link, and Ellen Winston, *Plan for Cooperative Rural Research: Organization, Scope, Results* (Washington, D.C.: Works Progress Administration, Division of Social Research, 1938). Between 1935 and 1943, the Division of Research (Works Progress Administration/Work Projects Administration) produced twenty-six research monographs from the rural surveys and other data, such as *Urban Workers on Relief, Farmers on Relief and Rehabilitation, Migrant Families*, and *Getting Started: Urban Youth in the Labor Market*. These were based on large data sets, ranging from Ns of about 1,000 to more than 285,000 (cases selected from relief rolls in the largest sets). In the three-volume *Index of Research Projects* compiled by WPA (1938–39), 5,137 studies are briefly annotated, representing projects undertaken by the Civil Works Administration, Economic Recovery Administration, WPA, and public planning agencies. Approximately

2,000 bear on social topics rather than on topics of land use, natural resources, regional history, and so on. Only about 70 seem to bear centrally on attitudes, preferences, and other subjective measures. The word *survey* is used variously to mean a review of existing case records, fresh data collection by questionnaire or interview, "social surveys" of a community's resources, and combinations of these.

101. John N. Webb and Malcolm Brown, *Migrant Families*, Research Monograph XVIII (Washington, D.C.: Works Progress Administration, Division of Social Research, 1938).

102. Personal communication, Tracy R. Berckmans, Assistant Head, Field Section, Survey Research Center, Institute for Social Research, University of Michigan, June 11, 1982; see also chap. 10 of this book. For an example of the fully formatted questionnaire, see Carl A. Jessen and H. Clifton Hutchins, "Community Surveys," U.S. Bureau of Education Bulletin no. 18–VI (Washington, D.C., 1936), pp. 91–96.

103. You Poh Seng, "Historical Survey of the Development of Sampling Theories and Practice," *Journal of the Royal Statistical Society* 114A (1951):214–231; William Kruskall and Frederick Mosteller, "Representative Sampling, IV: The History of the Concept in Statistics, 1895–1939," *International Statistical Review* 48 (1980):169–195.

104. Kruskall and Mosteller, "Representative Sampling, IV," pp. 169–179.

105. Ibid., p. 176; Seng, "Historical Survey," p. 218.

106. Seng, pp. 215–219.

107. Kruskall and Mosteller, p. 175.

108. A. L. Bowley, "Address to the Economic Science and Statistics Section of the British Association for the Advancement of Science," *Journal of the Royal Statistical Society* 69 (1906):540–558; Morris H. Hansen and William G. Madow, "Some Important Events in the Historical Development of Sample Surveys," in *On the History of Statistics and Probability*, ed. D. B. Owen (New York: Dekker, 1976), pp. 75–102, esp. pp. 78–80.

109. A. L. Bowley and A. R. Burnett-Hurst, *Livelihood and Poverty* (London: G. Bell, 1915).

110. George W. Snedecor, "Design of Sampling Experiments in the Social Sciences," *Journal of Farm Economics* 21 (1939):846–855; "Discussion on Dr. Neyman's paper," *Journal of the Royal Statistical Society* 47 (1934):607–625, esp. p. 607; Hansen and Madow, "Some important events," p. 79.

111. Kruskall and Mosteller, "Representative sampling, IV," pp. 186–187; Hansen and Madow, "Some important events," pp. 78–80.

112. The Neyman paper appeared in *Journal of the Royal Statistical Society* 97 (1934):558–606; discussion, pp. 607–625. For much of its interpretation, I have relied on the other sources I cite in this section, "Some of the Intellectual Ground." For its seminal character see Fienberg and Tanur, "Large-Scale Social Surveys: Perspectives, Problems, and Prospects"; Kruskall and Mosteller, "Representative Sampling, IV," pp. 187–191.

113. Jerzy Neyman, "Some Statistical Problems in Social and Economic Research: Part 1, Sampling Human Populations, General Theory," *Lectures and Conferences on Mathematical Statistics and Probability*, 2d ed. (Washington, D.C.: Graduate School, USDA, [1938] 1952), pp. 103–128.

114. Ibid., p. 106.

115. Kruskall and Mosteller, p. 188. Neyman's 1934 article did not have much impact on U.S. government statisticians until the 1937 lectures, arranged by W. Edwards Deming, head of the statistical program at the USDA Graduate School, according to Joseph W. Duncan and William C. Shelton, *Revolution in United States Government Statistics, 1926–1976* (Washington, D.C.: U.S. Department of Commerce, 1978), p. 45.

116. M. S. Bartlett, "R. A. Fisher," *IESS* 5 (1968):485–491.

117. Ibid.; Jerzy Neyman, "R. A. Fisher (1890–1962): An Appreciation," *Science* 156 (1967):1456–1462.

118. M. S. Bartlett, "R. A. Fisher and the Last Fifty Years of Statistical Methodology," *JASA* 60 (1965):395–409, p. 405; Wei-Ching Chang, "Statistical Theories and Sampling Practice," in Owen, *On the History of Statistics and Probability*, pp. 297–316, esp. p. 308.

119. Chang, "Theories and practice," pp. 308–309.

120. Ibid.; F. Yates, "A Review of Recent Statistical Developments in Sampling and Sampling Surveys," *Journal of the Royal Statistical Society* 109 (1946):12–30; Hansen and Madow, "Some Important Events," pp. 83–84; Stephan, "History of Sampling," pp. 29–31.

121. Samuel E. Wood, "Henry A. Wallace and the General Welfare," *Journal of Politics* 3 (1941):450–485; George W. Snedecor and Arnold J. King, "Recent Developments in Sampling for Agricultural Statistics," *JASA* 37 (1942):95–102; "An Editorial View of Sampling at Iowa State," *Des Moines Register* reprint of articles appearing Nov. 4, 7, and 11, 1946; Stephan, "History of Sampling," p. 32; Hansen and Madow, "Some Important Events," p. 83.

122. Thomas McCormick, *Comparative Study of Rural Relief and Non-Relief Households*, Research Monograph no. 2 (Washington, D.C.: Works Progress Administration, Division of Social Research, 1935), p. 117.

123. Duncan and Shelton, *Revolution in Statistics*, chap. 2.

124. Ibid.

125. Interview with Morris H. Hansen, June 6, 1979.

126. Margaret H. Hogg, "Sources of Incomparability and Error in Employment-Unemployment Surveys," *JASA* 25 (1930):284–294; Duncan and Shelton, *Revolution in Statistics*, pp. 18–19, 24.

127. Herbert H. Hyman, "Samuel Andrew Stouffer," *Dictionary of American Biography*, Supplement Six, 1956–1960, ed. John A. Garraty (New York: Scribner), pp. 604–606; Samuel A. Stouffer, "Karl Pearson—An Appreciation on the One Hundredth Anniversary of His Birth," *JASA* 53 (1958):23–27.

128. Ibid.; Anthony Oberschall, "The Institutionalization of American Sociology," in *The Establishment of Empirical Sociology*, Oberschall, ed. (New York: Harper & Row, 1972), esp. pp. 225–232. Columbia was one of the early schools that first established courses in descriptive statistics in the 1880s. See Paul J. Fitzpatrick, "The Early Teaching of Statistics in American Colleges and Universities," *American Statistician* IX (Dec. 1955):12–18.

129. Duncan and Shelton, *Revolution in Statistics*, chap. 2.

130. Ibid.

131. Samuel A. Stouffer, "Statistical Induction in Rural Social Research," *Social Forces* 13 (1935):505–515, esp. p. 508. Stouffer was among a number of social

scientists becoming interested in sampling in the 1930s. Stephan cites work by Chaddock, Ross, Ogburn, Lundberg, D. Thomas, and Stephan ("History of Sampling," p. 23).

132. Stouffer, "Statistical Induction"; Edmund De S. Brunner and J. H. Kolb, *Rural Social Trends* (New York: McGraw-Hill, 1933).

133. Edmund De S. Brunner, Gwendolyn S. Hughes, and Marjorie Patten, *American Agricultural Villages* (New York: Doran, 1927), esp. Appendix A.

134. Stouffer, "Statistical Induction," p. 514.

135. U.S. Public Health Service, Division of Public Health Methods, National Institutes of Health, *The National Health Survey 1935–1936* (Washington, D.C., 1938); Jessen and Hutchins, "Community Surveys"; U.S. National Resources Committee, *Consumer Incomes in the United States: Their Distribution in 1935–1936* and *Consumer Expenditures in the United States: Estimates for 1935–1936* (Washington, D.C.: U.S. Government Printing Office, 1938 and 1939); Erika Schoenberg and Mildred Parten, "Methods and Problems of Sampling Presented by the Urban Study of Consumer Purchases," *JASA* 32 (1937):311–322. For references to other large-scale surveys in the 1930s, see Parten, *Surveys, Polls, and Samples*; Stephan, "History of Sampling"; and Duncan and Shelton, *Revolution in Statistics*.

136. David B. Danbom, "Rural Education Reform and the Country Life Movement, 1900–1920," *Agricultural History* 53 (1979):462–474; Roy V. Scott, *The Reluctant Farmer* (Urbana: University of Illinois Press, 1970); Carl C. Taylor, "The Contribution of Sociology to Agriculture," in *Farmers in a Changing World: Yearbook of Agriculture 1940* (Washington, D.C.: U.S. Government Printing Office, 1940), pp. 1042–1055; Pitirim Sorokin and Carle C. Zimmerman, *Principles of Rural-Urban Sociology* (New York: Henry Holt & Co., 1929), esp. pp. 309–331. See also references in chap. 2 of this book.

137. Robin M. Williams, "Rural Youth Studies in the United States," *Rural Sociology* 4 (1939):166–178; Russell Lord, *The Agrarian Revival: A Study of Agricultural Extension* (New York: American Association for Adult Education, 1939); Webb and Brown, *Migrant Families*. An attempt at national coverage of political attitudes, involving 8,149 respondents in thirty-seven states, was conducted in conjunction with the League of Women Voters. See Edward S. Robinson, "Trends of the Voter's Mind," *JSP* 4 (1933):265–284, and Samuel P. Hayes, Jr., "Voters' Attitudes toward Men and Issues," *JSP* 7 (1936):164–182; E. Pendleton Herring, "How Does the Voter Make Up His Mind?" *POQ* 2 (1938):24–35. Herring's findings anticipated the importance of party affiliation: "Our findings suggest that party connection may in some instances be more important than occupation in determining opinion" (p. 35).

138. Hornell Hart, "Changing Social Attitudes and Interests," in *Recent Social Trends*, pp. 382–442.

139. National Industrial Conference Board, Inc., *A Statistical Survey of Public Opinion Regarding Current Economic and Social Problems as Reported by Newspaper Editors in August and September 1934*, Final Report (New York, 1934).

140. Samuel A. Stouffer and Paul F. Lazarsfeld, *Research Memorandum on the Family in the Depression* (New York: SSRC, 1937), p. 65.

141. Henry A. Wallace's candidacy for the presidency under the Progressive Party in 1948 has probably eclipsed for contemporary readers the high regard

in which he had been held for nonpolitical accomplishments, such as the marketing of the first hybrid corn on a commercial basis and the publication of a text with George C. Snedecor, *Correlation and Machine Calculation* (Ames, Iowa: Iowa State College, 1931), along with many books on applications of national planning and democratic philosophy. Wallace's father, Henry C., had been Secretary of Agriculture before him and with Henry C. Taylor had established the Bureau of Agricultural Economics (BAE). BAE became the center of reform ideas developed in the 1920s, some of which were applied in the 1930s. The germ of the domestic allotment program with which M. L. Wilson became identified developed in BAE, especially under the leadership of W. J. Spillman. For a picture of the powerful Wallace family, see Russell Lord, *The Wallaces of Iowa* (New York: Da Capo Press, [1947] 1972).

142. Richard S. Kirkendall, *Social Scientists and Farm Politics in the Age of Roosevelt* (Columbia: University of Missouri Press, 1966), chap. 9; Paul Appleby, *Big Democracy* (New York: Knopf, 1945), pp. 11–27. Even in 1933, USDA was the largest research organization in the world, and within the next few years it was given enormous new responsibilities. The 1933 Agricultural Adjustment Administration was invalidated by the Supreme Court in 1936 for its tax on grain processors to finance payments to farmers. It was replaced in 1936 by the Soil Conservation and Domestic Allotment Act. This and another 1938 act gave greater emphasis to increasing farm income through soil conservation and land-use practices and less to production quotas alone, which had aroused vigorous political opposition. The 1938 act, like the 1933 version, called for democratic participation by the farmers affected. See Wayne D. Rasmussen and Gladys L. Baker, *The Department of Agriculture* (New York: Praeger, 1972).

143. In 1935, Wilson set up a program of discussion groups with Agricultural Extension workers, which came to be called "Schools of Philosophy." These were seminar discussions in the social sciences, history, and philosophy for local Agriculture administrators whose training in the agricultural colleges had been limited to physical science and technology. Some 200 social scientists and philosophers participated in leading the four-day program, first in Washington and then throughout the nation. See Carl F. Taeusch, "Schools of Philosophy for Farmers," *Farmers in a Changing World*, pp. 1111–1124; M. L. Wilson, "Rural America Discusses Democracy," *POQ* 5 (1941):288–294.

144. To Whitson from Wilson, Nov. 2, 1936, RG 16, Outgoing Correspondence, NA.

145. To Skott from Wilson, June 16, 1937, RG 16, Outgoing Correspondence, NA.

146. Gladys Baker, "The County Agent," Ph.D. diss., University of Chicago, 1939; Thelma A. Dreis, "The Department of Agriculture's Sample Interview Survey as a Tool of Administration," Ph.D. diss., American University, Washington, D.C., 1950, pp. 32–40. This was by no means the first use of field-workers in USDA, for the department had long employed people to check on the actual operation of one program or another. But this new program was to feature more two-way communication. Interviewers were to learn what problems the farmers were encountering with AAA programs and what solutions they could suggest. See W. J. Spillman, "The Validity of the Survey Method of Research," USDA

Bulletin no. 529 (Washington, D.C., 1917); Rensis Likert, "Democracy in Agriculture—Why and How?" *Farmers in a Changing World*, pp. 994–1002; and H. W. Henderson, "An Early Poll," *POQ* 6 (1942):450–451.

147. Telephone interview with Gladys Baker, June 8, 1979. Supporting documents of the Dreis dissertation kindly given to me by Dr. Dreis show specific questions that resemble poll questions: "1. Do you consider the Conservation Program of the AAA a better program for agriculture than was the old Corn-Hog program? 2. Do you favor the Reciprocal Trade Agreement program?" In a total of 318 interviews logged by Whitson, the "No Report" ranged from 68 up to 192, and the notes record that "a surprisingly large number of farmers contacted knew little or nothing of the policy and as a result were in no position to comment."

148. Dreis dissertation, p. 36; telephone interview with Baker, June 8, 1979.

149. "Report on Attitude of Farm Families in South Benton County, Iowa," Oct. 17, 1936, in Dreis supporting documents.

150. To Whitson from Wilson, Nov. 2, 1936, RG 16, Outgoing Correspondence, NA.

151. Interview with F. F. Elliott, conducted by Dreis, April 8, 1948, Dreis supporting documents.

152. Dreis dissertation, p. 30.

153. M. L. Wilson, *Democracy Has Roots* (New York: Carrick and Evans, 1939).

2. The More Elegant Ancestor of Science

1. Christian A. Ruckmick, "The Uses and Abuses of the Questionnaire Procedure," *JAP* 14 (1930):32–41.

2. Thomas and Znaniecki's contribution is credited by Carle C. Zimmerman, "Farmers' Marketing Attitudes," Ph.D. diss., University of Minnesota, Oct. 1925; G. W. Allport, "Attitudes," in *A Handbook of Social Psychology*, ed. Carl Murchison (Worcester, Mass.: Clark University Press, 1935), pp. 798–844; Ellsworth Faris, "The Concept of Social Attitudes," in *Social Attitudes*, ed. Kimball Young (New York: Holt, 1931), pp. 3–16; D. D. Droba, "The Nature of Attitude," *JSP* 4 (1933):444–462; Donald Fleming, "Attitude: The History of a Concept," *Perspectives in American History* 1 (1967):287–365.

In a brilliant elaboration of Gordon Allport's history of the concept of attitude, Fleming credits Thomas with having cut the link between a *motor* meaning for the term, as a state of physiological readiness (for danger, flight, attack, etc.), which Darwin had meant, and a purely *mental* state, without intrinsic physiological content. Fleming interprets the changes in the meaning of attitude as a pulling back by scientists from excesses of materialism, implying a new concept of the individual as a thinking-feeling organism, adapting to the environment and integrating it through mental attitudes.

3. Ellsworth Faris, "The Concept of Social Attitudes," *Journal of Applied Sociology* 9 (1925):404–409; L. L. Bernard, "Social Attitudes," in *Encyclopaedia of the Social Sciences*, ed. E. R. A. Seligman and A. Johnson (New York: Macmillan Co., 1930), vol. 2, pp. 305–306; Daniel H. Kulp II, "Concepts in Attitude Tests with

Special Reference to Social Questions," *Sociology and Social Research* 19 (1934–35):218–224.

4. W. I. Thomas and F. Znaniecki, *The Polish Peasant in Europe and America* (Boston: Richard G. Badger, 1918), Vol. I, Methodological Note, pp. 22–86; Vol. III, pp. 5–18. Thomas and Znaniecki distinguished between attitudes of temperament, which were innate, and those of character, which were acquired, but they paid little attention to the innate branch. Attitudes that could change with personal experience and social interaction were of much greater interest.

5. Stuart A. Rice, "Measurements of Social Attitudes and Public Opinion," USDA BAE Bulletin (Washington, D.C., Feb. 1930), pp. 11–30.

6. Allport, "Attitudes," p. 801.

7. Read Bain, "Theory and Measurement of Attitudes and Opinions," *Psychological Bulletin* 27 (1930):357–379, p. 359.

8. Cited by Rice, "Statistical Studies of Social Attitudes and Public Opinion," in *Statistics in Social Studies*, ed. Stuart A. Rice (Philadelphia: University of Pennsylvania Press, 1930), esp. pp. 177–181.

9. Emory S. Bogardus, *Essentials of Social Psychology*, 2d ed. (Los Angeles: University of Southern California Press, 1920), esp. pp. 25–27.

10. Edwin G. Boring, "The Beginning and Growth of Measurement in Psychology," *Isis* 52 (1961):238–257.

11. Grace E. Manson, "Bibliography on Psychological Tests and Other Objective Measures in Industrial Personnel," *Journal of Personnel Research* 4 (1925–26):301–328.

12. G. Allport, "Attitudes," p. 828.

13. Gardner Murphy, Lois Barclay Murphy, and Theodore M. Newcomb, *Experimental Social Psychology*, rev. ed. (New York: Harper, 1937), chap. 13; Gardner Murphy and Lois Murphy, *Experimental Social Psychology* (New York: Harper, 1931), chap. 11.

14. Daniel Katz and Floyd H. Allport, *Student Attitudes* (Syracuse: Craftsman Press, 1931).

15. Sturges and Young both explored student attitude change from the college experience itself, but Rice noted that Young's study of attitude change from an academic class was almost unique. Newcomb's well-known study of attitude change in the course of Bennington College experience was not started until the 1930s. See Herbert A. Sturges, "The Theory of Correlation Applied in Studies of Changing Attitudes," *AJS* 33 (1927):269–275; Donald Young, "Some Effects of a Course in American Race Problems on the Race Prejudice of 450 Undergraduates at the University of Pennsylvania," *JASP* 22 (1927):235–242; Stuart A. Rice, "Undergraduate Attitudes toward Marriage and Children," *Mental Hygiene* 13 (1929):788–793; Theodore M. Newcomb, *Personality and Social Change* (New York: Dryden, 1943).

16. Walter R. Miles, "Age and Human Ability," *Psychological Review* 40 (1933):99–123, 106–107.

17. George B. Vetter and Martin Green, "Personality and Group Factors in the Making of Atheists," *JASP* 27 (1932–33):179–194; Edward S. Robinson, "Trends of the Voter's Mind," *JSP* 3 (1933):265–284; Richard L. Schanck, "A

Study of Change in Institutional Attitudes in a Rural Community," *JSP* 5 (1934):121–128.

18. The Katz/Allport census of Syracuse University students' attitudes stressed consultation with student power groups and the voluntary cooperation of the student body, but classes were dismissed for two hours to enable students to take the questionnaire, and those who did not show got double cuts (Katz and Allport, *Student Attitudes*, p. 2).

19. Martin Bulmer and Joan Bulmer, "Philanthropy and Social Science in the 1920s: Beardsley Ruml and the Laura Spelman Rockefeller Memorial, 1922–1929," *Minerva* 19 (1981):347–407.

20. Ernest W. Burgess, "Statistics and Case Studies as Methods of Sociological Research," *Sociology and Social Research* 12 (1927–28):99–120; Stuart A. Rice, "Behavior Alternatives as Statistical Data in Studies by William F. Ogburn and Ernest W. Burgess," in *Methods in Social Science: A Case Book*, ed. Rice (Chicago: University of Chicago Press, 1931), pp. 586–613.

21. Nels Anderson, *The Hobo: The Sociology of the Homeless Man* (Chicago: University of Chicago Press, 1923); Frederic M. Thrasher, *The Gang: A Study of 1,313 Gangs in Chicago* (Chicago: University of Chicago Press, 1927); Carle C. Zimmerman, "Types of Farmers' Attitudes," *Social Forces* 5 (1927):591–596; Robert E. Park, "Methods of a Race Survey," *Journal of Applied Sociology* 10 (1926):410–415; Ernest W. Burgess, "Is Prediction Feasible in Social Work? An Inquiry Based upon a Sociological Study of Parole Records," *Social Forces* 7 (1929):533–545; Emory S. Bogardus, *Immigration and Race Attitudes* (Boston: D. C. Heath, 1928); Pauline V. Young, "Occupational Attitudes and Values of Russian Lumber Workers," *Sociology and Social Research* 12 (1928):543–553; William Albig, "Opinions Concerning Unskilled Mexican Immigrants," *Sociology and Social Research* 15 (1930–31):62–72; Carle C. Zimmerman and C. Arnold Anderson, "Attitudes of Rural Preachers Regarding Church Union and Science: A Methodological Study," *Sociology and Social Research* 12 (1927–28):144–150.

22. Zimmerman, "Types of Farmers' Attitudes."

23. Richard T. LaPiere, "Race Prejudice: France and England," *Social Forces* 7 (1928):102–111.

24. Richard T. LaPiere, "Attitudes vs. Actions," *Social Forces* 13 (1934):230–237. LaPiere did not debunk questionnaire measurement; he thought it a valuable indicator of ideology to use in conjunction with measures of experience and behavior. See LaPiere, "The Sociological Significance of Measurable Attitudes," *ASR* 3 (1938):175–182.

25. Schanck's study of public and private attitudes bore on the problem even though they were both verbal measures (see note 17). In the Hartshorne/May studies of student cheating, the focus was on behavior. See M. A May and H. Hartshorne, "First Steps toward a Scale for Measuring Attitudes," *Journal of Educational Psychology* 17 (1926):145–162.

26. E. C. Lindeman, *Social Discovery* (New York: Republic, 1924); Harvey Zorbaugh, *The Gold Coast and the Slum: A Sociological Study of Chicago's Near North Side* (Chicago: University of Chicago Press, 1929); Thrasher, *The Gang*; Anderson, *The Hobo*.

27. George A. Lundberg, "The Demographic and Economic Basis of Political Radicalism and Conservatism," *AJS* 32 (1927):719–732; W. F. Ogburn and N. S. Talbot, "A Measurement of the Factors in the Presidential Election of 1928," *Social Forces* 8 (1929):175–183; Stuart A. Rice and W. W. Weaver, "The Verification of Social Measurements involving Subjective Classifications," *Social Forces* 8 (1929):16–28; Rice, *Farmers and Workers in American Politics* (New York: Columbia University Press, 1924); Hornell Hart, "Changing Social Attitudes and Interests," in the U.S. President's Research Committee on Social Trends, *Recent Social Trends in the United States* (New York: McGraw-Hill, 1933), Vol. I, pp. 382–442.

28. Zorbaugh, *Gold Coast*; Emory S. Bogardus, "Personal Experiences and Social Research," *Journal of Applied Sociology* 8 (1923–24):294–303; E. T. Krueger, "The Technique of Securing Life History Documents," *Journal of Applied Sociology* 9 (1925):290–298.

29. Floyd H. Allport, "The Group Fallacy in Relation to Social Science," *AJS* 29 (1923–24):688–703; Emory S. Bogardus, "Discussion," pp. 703–704.

30. Thomas E. Lasswell, "Emory S. Bogardus," *IESS* 18 (1979):65–68.

31. Daniel Katz, "Floyd H. Allport," *IESS* 1 (1968):271–274; F. H. Allport, "Toward a Science of Public Opinion," *POQ* 1 (1937):7–23.

32. Robert E. Park, "The Concept of Social Distance," *Journal of Applied Sociology* 8 (1924):339–344.

33. Bogardus, *Immigration and Race Attitudes*, pp. 27, 210–213.

34. Bogardus later had a set of judges evaluate statements to determine scale steps in a modification of the Thurstone procedures and revised the middle steps somewhat. He also changed the language that focused so directly on immigration; see Emory S. Bogardus, "A Social Distance Scale," *Sociology and Social Research* 17 (1932–33):265–271. There were several editions of the social distance scale.

35. Emory S. Bogardus, *The New Social Research* (Los Angeles: Jesse Ray Miller, 1926), pp. 212–213.

36. Eugene L. Hartley, *Problems in Prejudice* (New York: King's Crown Press, 1946).

37. Bogardus, *Immigration and Race Attitudes*, p. 23.

38. Floyd H. Allport and D. A. Hartman, "The Measurement and Motivation of Atypical Opinion in a Certain Group," *APSR* 19 (1925):735–760, p. 752.

39. An intensity measure appears in the psychological literature as early as 1898. See F. B. Sumner, "A Statistical Study of Belief," *Psychological Review* 5 (1898):616–631.

40. Katz, "Allport," *IESS*.

41. See, for example, George A. Lundberg, *Social Research: A Study in Methods of Gathering Data* (New York: Longmans, Green, 1929), chap. 9; Bain, "Theory and Measurement"; D. D. Droba, "Methods Used for Measuring Public Opinion," *AJS* 37 (1931–32):410–423; Murphy and Murphy, *Experimental Social Psychology*, chap. 11.

42. W. G. Binnewies, "A Method of Studying Rural Social Distance," *Journal of Applied Sociology* 10 (1926):239–242; F. Wilkinson, "Social Distance between Occupations," *Sociology and Social Research* 13 (1929):234–244; R. Zeligs and G. Hendrickson, "Checking the Social Distance Technique through Personal Inter-

views," *Sociology and Social Research* 18 (1934):420–430; R. Zeligs and G. Hendrickson, "Racial Attitudes of Two Hundred Sixth-Grade Children," *Sociology and Social Research* 18 (1933):26–36.

43. E. F. Shideler, "The Social Distance Margin," *Sociology and Social Research* 12 (1928):243–252; Willard C. Poole, Jr., "Distance in Sociology," *AJS* 33 (1927–28):99–104.

44. Stuart C. Dodd, "A Social Distance Test in the Near East," *AJS* 41 (1935–36):194–204. Judges' ratings would have been interesting cross-cultural comparisons in themselves. These were not the judgments only of firebrand student ideologues, as Dodd also used a panel of Beirut businessmen. Would students and businessmen in other cultures construct a comparable scale that positioned personal marriage at one pole and wishes for genocide at another, equidistant from a midpoint of speaking acquaintance?

45. Bogardus, "Personal Experience and Social Research"; idem, *Immigration and Race Attitudes.*

46. Bogardus, *The New Social Research,* p. 192; idem, "The Social Research Interview," *Journal of Applied Sociology* 10 (1925–26):69–82.

47. Kimball Young, ed., *Social Attitudes* (New York: Holt, 1931), p. vii.

48. Ibid.

49. Arnold M. Rose, "Discussion [of Bogardus's Paper, 'Measuring Changes in Ethnic Reactions']," *ASR* 16 (1951):52–53.

50. Hartley's study of racial attitudes of students used Bogardus scales to explore personality characteristics of individuals rather than intergroup relations. The work for *Problems in Prejudice* was conducted in 1938 and published in 1946. For psychologists in general, the Bogardus scale lacked psychometric legitimacy; its design was such that it could not be tested for reliability by any means except test-retest.

51. Katz and Allport, *Student Attitudes.*

52. Schanck, "A Study of Change."

53. Daniel Katz and Kenneth Braly, "Racial Stereotypes of One Hundred College Students," *JASP* 28 (1933–34):280–290.

54. L. L. Thurstone, "Autobiographical Note," in *A History of Psychology in Autobiography,* ed. Edwin G. Boring, Herbert S. Langfeld, Heinz Werner, and Robert M. Yerkes (Worcester, Mass.: Clark University Press), vol. 4 (1952):295–321; L. L. Thurstone and E. J. Chave, *The Measurement of Attitude* (Chicago: University of Chicago Press, 1929), p. 19.

55. L. L. Thurstone, "The Measurement of Social Attitudes," *JASP* 26 (1931–32):249–269; "Thurstone," in *Psychology in Autobiography,* p. 310.

56. For example, if just as many judges perceived that A was more favorable than B as perceived that B was more favorable than A, the two statements could not be discriminated and were given equal scale values. Differing proportions in the judgments yielded different scale positions. The method of paired comparisons was originated by G. T. Fechner. See D. D. Droba, "Methods for Measuring Attitudes," *Psychological Bulletin* 29 (1932):309–323.

57. Gordon W. Allport, "Discussion of 'Methods of Studying Social Attitudes' by Stuart A. Rice," USDA, BAE Bulletin (Washington, D.C., Feb. 1930), pp. 20–23. Guilford had been working on the method of paired comparisons at the same

time that Thurstone was, in the measurement of racial attitudes. Guilford credited the Bogardus scale as the only one up to that time that had tried to measure racial attitudes as a form of social distance, although a very rough one. Thurstone published "An experimental study of nationality preferences," *Journal of General Psychology* 1 (1928):405–423, before J. P. Guilford finished his study "Racial Preferences of a Thousand American University Students," *JSP* 2 (1931):179–202.

58. Thurstone and Chave, *The Measurement of Attitude*, pp. 23–29.

59. E. A. Rundquist and R. F. Sletto, *Personality in the Depression: A Study in the Measurement of Attitudes* (Minneapolis: University of Minnesota Press, 1936), p. 6.

60. Thurstone and Chave, *The Measurement of Attitude*, passim.

61. Droba, "Methods for Measuring Attitudes."

62. Bogardus, "A Social Distance Scale."

63. Thurstone and Chave, *The Measurement of Attitude*, p. 9.

64. H. T. Moore, "Innate Factors in Radicalism and Conservatism," *JASP* 20 (1925):234–244; Rice, "Undergraduate Attitudes."

65. Stuart A. Rice, *Quantitative Methods in Politics* (New York: Knopf, 1928).

66. Rice, *Farmers and Workers*; Rice, "Measurements of Social Attitudes."

67. Rice, "Statistical Studies of Social Attitudes," p. 190. Newcomb reported persisting difficulties in trying to use Thurstone-type scales with people who had had relatively little education. See Theodore M. Newcomb, "Labor Unions as Seen by Their Members: An Attempt to Measure Attitudes," in *Industrial Conflict: A Psychological Interpretation*, ed. George W. Hartmann and Theodore M. Newcomb (New York: Cordon, 1940), pp. 313–338.

68. Some experiments in this period seemed to vindicate the Thurstone judging process, since judges holding very different attitudes showed high agreement on the placement of statements. See E. D. Hinckley, "The Influence of Individual Opinion on Construction of an Attitude Scale," *JSP* 3 (1932):283–295; Leonard W. Ferguson, "The Influence of Individual Attitudes on Construction of an Attitude Scale," *JSP* 6 (1935):115–117. Later work has cast some doubt on the generality of those findings, however. See W. A. Scott, "Attitude Measurement," in *The Handbook of Social Psychology*, 2d ed., ed. Gardner Lindzey and Elliott Aronson (Reading, Mass.: Addison-Wesley, 1968), vol. 2, pp. 204–273.

69. Rice, "Statistical Studies of Social Attitudes," p. 188.

70. Samuel A. Stouffer, "Experimental Comparison of a Statistical and a Case History Technique of Attitude Research," *Publications of American Sociological Society* 25 (1931):154–156; Ruth Shonle Cavan, Philip M. Hauser, and Samuel A. Stouffer, "Note on the Statistical Treatment of Life-History Material," *Social Forces* 9 (1930–31):200–203.

71. Thurstone, in *History of Psychology*, ed. Boring, vol. 4, p. 312.

72. Daniel Katz, "Attitude Measurement as a Method in Social Psychology," *Social Forces* 15 (1937):479–482; Quinn McNemar, "Opinion-Attitude Methodology," *Psychological Bulletin* 43 (1946):289–374; Bert F. Green, "Attitude Measurement," in *Handbook of Social Psychology*, ed. Gardner Lindzey (Reading, Mass.: Addison-Wesley, 1954), pp. 335–369; "Attitude Measurement," in *Handbook*, 2d ed.

73. Gardner Murphy and Rensis Likert, *Public Opinion and the Individual* (New York: Harper, 1938), pp. 34–39.

74. Rundquist and Sletto, p. 5. In *item analysis*, the correlation of the item score to the total score was used as an index of the discriminating power of the item; a low correlation meant that the item did not capture enough of the single common factor that was in principle underlying all the items. More than one factor could be isolated by correlating every statement with every other. In tests of *internal consistency*, an "undifferentiating" statement was one that would not discriminate between two groups that scored high and low on the total score. Likert used this criterion of internal consistency in constructing his scales because it was less laborious to compute and had yielded, experimentally, results comparable to item analysis. See Appendix B in *Public Opinion and the Individual*.

75. Rensis Likert, Sydney Roslow, and Gardner Murphy, "A Simple and Reliable Method of Scoring the Thurstone Attitude Scales," *JSP* 5 (1934):228–238.

76. R. H. Seashore and K. Hevner, "A Time-Saving Device for the Construction of Attitude Scales," *JSP* 4 (1933):366–372; H. H. Remmers and Ella Belle Silance, "Generalized Attitude Scales," *JSP* 5 (1934):298–311.

77. Leonard W. Ferguson, "A Study of the Likert Technique of Attitude Scale Construction," *JSP* 13 (1941):51–57; A. L. Edwards and K. C. Kenney, "A Comparison of the Thurstone and Likert Techniques of Attitude Scale Construction," *JAP* 30 (1946):72–83.

78. O. Milton Hall, "Attitudes and Unemployment: A Comparison of the Opinions and Attitudes of Employed and Unemployed Men," *Archives of Psychology* 25, no. 165 (1934); Rundquist and Sletto, *Personality in the Depression*.

79. Murphy and Likert, *Public Opinion*, p. 200, p. 3.

80. Ibid., pp. 264, 278–279.

81. Murphy, Murphy, and Newcomb, *Experimental Social Psychology*, p. 992.

82. Murphy and Likert, *Public Opinion*, p. 252.

83. Ibid., pp. 208, 226–245.

84. Ibid., p. 264.

85. J. David Houser, *What the Employer Thinks: Executives' Attitudes toward Employees* (Cambridge, Mass.: Harvard University Press, 1927); A. W. Kornhauser, "The Technique of Measuring Employee Attitudes," *Personnel* 9 (1933):99–107; Albert B. Blankenship, "Methods of Measuring Industrial Morale," in Hartmann and Newcomb, *Industrial Conflict*, pp. 299–312; Rensis Likert and J. M. Willits, *Morale and Agency Management*, 4 pts. (Hartford, Conn.: Life Insurance Sales Research Bureau, 1940).

86. Houser, *What the Employer Thinks*, p. 178.

87. G. A. Pennock, "Industrial Research at Hawthorne: An Experimental Investigation of Rest Periods, Working Conditions, and Other Influences," *The Personnel Journal* 8 (1930):296–313; M. L. Putnam, "Improving Employee Relations: A Plan Which Uses Data Obtained from Employees," *The Personnel Journal* 8 (1929–30):314–325; Elton Mayo, "Changing Methods in Industry," *The Personnel Journal* 8 (1929–30):326–332; Elton Mayo, *The Human Problems of an Industrial Civilization* (New York: Macmillan Co., 1933). Only as the program continued did the researchers realize that the kind of conversational interview they had

been conducting (and the personal material it generated) was not their own discovery and that, indeed, it had a history in the clinical work of Janet, Freud, and Jung. See Mayo, chaps. 3–5.

88. In a political study in the field, Beyle found that the use of a scale stimulated people's interest in talking about politics—they did not want to stick to the scale measurement. See H. C. Beyle, "A Scale for the Measurement of Attitude toward Candidates for Elective Governmental Office," *APSR* 26 (1932):527–544.

89. W. V. Bingham and B. V. Moore, *How to Interview* (New York: Harper, 1931), p. 83.

90. A. W. Kornhauser and A. A. Sharp, "Employee Attitudes," *The Personnel Journal* 10 (1932):393–404.

91. Leonard D. White, *The Prestige Value of Public Employment in Chicago* (Chicago: University of Chicago Press, 1929). White did a larger study in eleven U.S. cities (N = 7,168), *Further Contributions to the Prestige Value of Public Employment* (Chicago: University of Chicago Press, 1932), which replicated some of the findings. Data collection was administered mostly by colleagues in political science. Like the Chicago sample, this study overrepresented younger age groups and student and professional occupational groups, and even more heavily the native-born (87%).

92. White, *Prestige Value*, p. 9.

93. Ibid., chaps. 2 (esp. p. 35) and 11.

94. Charles E. Merriam and Harold F. Gosnell, *Non-Voting: Causes and Methods of Control* (Chicago: University of Chicago Press, 1924); Harold F. Gosnell, *Getting Out the Vote: An Experiment in the Stimulation of Voting* (Chicago: University of Chicago Press, 1927).

95. *Non-Voting*, p. 279.

96. See *Getting Out the Vote*, pp. 9–10.

97. Gabriel A. Almond, "Harold Dwight Lasswell (1902–1978)," manuscript prepared for publication by the National Academy of Sciences, *Biographical Memoirs*, vol. 57.

98. *Getting Out the Vote*, p. 119.

99. Ibid., p. 120. See also the instructions to interviewers on pp. 121–126.

100. Ibid., pp. 100–101.

101. Ibid., p. 119.

102. Ibid., p. 11.

103. Martin Bulmer, "Quantification and Chicago Social Science in the 1920s: A Neglected Tradition," *Journal of the History of the Behavioral Sciences* 17 (1981):312–331, 320–321. Bulmer does not cite the histories of survey research he has in mind.

104. *Non-Voting* and *Getting Out the Vote* are discussed briefly by Heinz Eulau in "Political Behavior," *IESS* 12 (1968):203–214.

105. Albert Somit and Joseph Tanenhaus, *The Development of Political Science: From Burgess to Behavioralism* (Boston: Allyn and Bacon, 1967), pp. 122–133; Heinz Eulau, "Political Science," in *A Reader's Guide to the Social Sciences*, ed. Bert F. Hoselitz (Glencoe, Ill.: The Free Press, 1959), pp. 89–127; Angus Campbell,

Philip E. Converse, Warren E. Miller, and Donald E. Stokes, *The American Voter* (New York: Wiley, 1960), p. 14; Almond, "Lasswell."

106. Harold F. Gosnell, *Machine Politics: Chicago Model* (Chicago: University of Chicago Press, 1937).

107. Almond, "Lasswell." See also Martin Bulmer, *The Chicago School of Sociology* (Chicago and London: University of Chicago Press, 1984), pp. 203–205.

108. Harold F. Gosnell, "The Polls and Other Mechanisms of Democracy," *POQ* 4 (1940):224–228; idem, "The Improvement of Present Public Opinion Analyses," in *Print, Radio, and Film in a Democracy*, ed. Douglas Waples (Chicago: University of Chicago Press, 1942).

109. The independent candidate John Anderson was deemed eligible to participate with the two major party candidates (Carter and Reagan) on the basis of his having logged 15 percent in various preelection polls.

110. Charles Edward Merriam and Harold Foote Gosnell, *The American Party System*, 4th ed. (New York: Macmillan Co., 1949), p. 416.

3. The Most Direct Line, Business

1. Claude E. Robinson, in *Straw Votes: A Study of Political Prediction* (New York: Columbia University Press, 1932), esp. chap. 4, dates straw votes back to the late 1800s. George Gallup and S. F. Rae, in *The Pulse of Democracy* (New York: Simon and Schuster, 1940), p. 35, note specific straw polls as early as 1824.

2. W. Phillips Shively, "A Reinterpretation of the New Deal Realignment," *POQ* 35 (1971–72):621–624.

3. Frank R. Coutant, "The Difference between Market Research and Election Forecasting," *IJOAR* 2 (1948):569–574, esp. p. 572.

4. Henry C. Link, "Some Milestones in Public Opinion Research," *IJOAR* 1 (1947):36–46, esp. p. 36.

5. On the whole, social scientists of a later era (especially the 1950s and 1960s) have probably underestimated the sophistication of the market research tradition of the 1920s and 1930s. In the interest of distinguishing their own work from that of the polls, especially from the polls' misforecast of 1948, academic social scientists have made the pollsters' methods sound quite wrongheaded. The relentless references to the event as a "debacle" or "fiasco" suggest vaguely that if the pollsters had only had their scientific wits about them, they would have known better. In fact, the pollsters' heritage from market research work was sophisticated applied social science for its time, reflecting much involvement and counsel from academic social scientists, and some of the issues that market researchers wrestled with fifty years ago have by no means been entirely laid to rest.

6. Irving Crespi, "The Case of Presidential Popularity," in *Polling on the Issues*, ed. Albert H. Cantril (Cabin John, Md.: Seven Locks Press, 1980), pp. 28–45, esp. p. 29. Crespi notes that the standardized questions on presidential popularity were not used systematically for comparisons and trends until the Eisenhower administration in the early 1950s.

Intermittent use of the measure occurred much earlier. Claude E. Robinson, "Recent Developments in the Straw-Poll Field," _POQ_ 1 (1937):45–46. Gallup gathered data every month from Feb. 1934 to Aug. 1936 and every two weeks during the campaign.

7. "Advertising News and Notes," _New York Times_, Nov. 5, 1936, p. 50; Charles E. Egan, "Straw Polls Help Market Research," _New York Times_, Nov. 8, 1936, III, p. 9; "Market Guide Seen in Election Polls," _New York Times_, Nov. 29, 1936, III, pp. 1, 7.

8. Frank G. Coolsen, "Pioneers in the Development of Advertising," _Journal of Marketing_ 12 (1947):80–86. Harlow Gale was interested in advertising as a study of involuntary attention. His questionnaire was sent out to 200 businessmen in 1895 and was returned by only 20. Walter Dill Scott was more successful in appealing to advertising men, and he worked as a consultant to members of an advertising club. Scott studied newspaper readership with questionnaire and sampling techniques. See Coolsen, "Pioneers," pp. 82–84; Paul D. Converse, "The Development of the Science of Marketing—An Exploratory Study," _Journal of Marketing_ 10 (1945):14–23.

9. William J. Reilly, _What Place Has the Advertising Agency in Market Research?_ University of Texas Bulletin no. 2916 (Austin, Tex., April 22, 1929). In "The Evolution of Marketing Research Technique," _National Marketing Review_ (1935–36), pp. 268–272, Albert Haring writes that the problem of distribution became apparent in the 1910–20 decade, but work on it was delayed until the 1920s by World War I. "Sounder research" was developed during the depression years.

Advertising developed certain organizations in the 1910–20 decade, namely, the Association of National Advertisers in 1910, the Audit Bureau of Circulation in 1914 (which verified circulation figures), and the American Association of Advertising Agencies, 1917. The national expenditure for magazine advertising increased from 1900 to the 1920s by about sixfold, from 25 million to about 140 million. See Paul T. Cherington, _The Consumer Looks at Advertising_ (New York: Harper, 1928), esp. chap. 6; Robert Bartels, _The Development of Marketing Thought_ (Homewood, Ill.: Richard D. Irwin, 1962), pp. 106–124; Lawrence C. Lockley, "Notes on the History of Marketing Research," _Journal of Marketing_ 14 (1950):733–736; Daniel Starch, "Research Methods in Advertising," _Annals of the American Academy of Political and Social Science_ 110 (1923):139–143; William J. Reilly, _Marketing Investigations_ (New York: The Ronald Press, 1929), esp. pp. 3–30.

10. Lockley, "Notes," pp. 734–735; Converse, "An Exploratory Survey," 1945, pp. 19–20.

11. Charles Coolidge Parlin, _The Merchandising of Automobiles, An Address to Retailers_ (Philadelphia: Curtis Publishing Co., 1915).

12. Cited by Lockley, "Notes," 1950, p. 734.

13. Converse, "An Exploratory Survey," 1945, p. 19; Lockley, "Notes," 1950; Cherington obituary, _New York Times_, Apr. 25, 1943, p. 35.

14. "Predetermining the Size of a Sample," chap. 20 in the American Marketing Society, _The Technique of Marketing Research_ (New York: McGraw-Hill Book Co., 1937), is an adaptation of Theodore H. Brown, _The Use of Statistical Techniques_

in Certain Problems of Market Research, Harvard University Graduate School of Business Administration, Bureau of Business Research, Business Research Studies, no. 12 (Cambridge, Mass., 1935); Neil H. Borden and Osgood S. Lovekin, *A Test of the Consumer Jury Method of Ranking Advertisements*, Harvard University Graduate School of Business Administration, Bureau of Business Research, Business Research Studies no. 11 (Cambridge, Mass.: 1935); Henry C. Link, "How Many Interviews Are Necessary for Results of a Certain Accuracy?" *Journal of Applied Psychology* 21 (1937):1–17.

15. The American Marketing Society and the National Association of Marketing Teachers were merged in 1937 as the American Marketing Association, which continued to publish the *Journal of Marketing*; Hugh E. Agnew, "N.A.M.T.—a Survey," *Journal of Marketing* 1 (1937):305–309.

16. Lyndon O. Brown, *Market Research and Analysis* (New York: The Ronald Press, 1937), pp. 431–432; R. O. Eastman, Inc., *Zanesville and Thirty-Six Other American Communities* (New York: Literary Digest, 1927); R. O. Eastman, Inc., *Marketing Geography* (New York: Alexander Hamilton Institute, 1930); True Story Publishing Co., *The New Housewives Market* (New York, 1927); Reilly, *Marketing Investigations*, 1929, pp. 18–21.

17. Fred E. Clark, *Readings in Marketing* (New York: Macmillan Co., 1924), p. 20.

18. Henry C. Link, *The New Psychology of Selling and Advertising* (New York: Macmillan Co., 1932), pp. 21–22.

19. Daniel Starch entry in *Who's Who in America*, 40th ed. (Chicago: A. N. Marquis, 1978–79), p. 3093. Starch's 1928 study of radio broadcasting, published by the National Broadcasting Company, is called the "granddaddy of all radio surveys and the first attempt at an evaluation of audience size, habits, and general program preferences," by E. P. H. James in "The Development of Research in Broadcast Advertising," *Journal of Marketing* 2 (1937):141–145.

20. Ibid.

21. Ibid.; Howard T. Hovde, "Recent Trends in the Development of Market Research," *American Marketing Journal* 1 (1936):3–19, esp. p. 4. White, in *Marketing Research Technique*, reports that the depression of 1921 "started a phenomenal interest in marketing research" (p. 4); Haring, in "The Evolution of Marketing Research Technique," notes that problems in selling manufactured merchandise "burst upon troubled business executives late in 1920" (p. 268).

22. Committee on Research, "Progress in Marketing Research," *Journal of Marketing* 2 (1937):68–71; Vergil D. Reed, "The Census of Business as an Aid to Market Measurement," *American Marketing Journal* 3 (1936):38–40; Wilford L. White, "Market Research Activities in the Department of Commerce," *American Marketing Journal* 3 (1936):25–31.

23. "Wrong 42% of the Time," *Business Week*, Sept. 12, 1936, pp. 30 ff.

24. Ibid.; N. H. Engle, "Gaps in Marketing Research," *Journal of Marketing* 4 (1940):345–351. Engle's analysis of the number of marketing research projects reported to the *Journal of Marketing* (1935–39) shows the largest share originating with university faculty members—more than half of the total of 676 projects, counting a small group conducted by university bureaus of business research.

Government agencies ranked second and business, third. Business was highly underrepresented because so much market research was proprietary and thus not published.

25. L. O. Brown, *Market Research*, p. 86. Consumer research also used *unobtrusive measures* of consumer behavior, such as attention given to advertising and to products in stores.

26. Elmo Roper, "Problems and Possibilities in the Sampling Technique," *Journalism Quarterly* 18 (1941):1–9, esp. p. 2.

27. Hovde, "Recent Trends," 1936, p. 12; Weaver wrote in 1935 that there were "thousands of textbooks on statistical analysis" but a "dearth of literature on questionnaire technique" and a tendency in practice to overstress mechanics to the neglect of "what we might call the art of extracting information." See Henry G. Weaver, "The Use of Statistics in the Study of Consumer Demands," *JASA* 30 (1935):183–184, and "Consumer Questionnaire Technique," *American Marketing Journal* 1 (1934):115–118. However, the Committee on Research of the American Association of Advertising Agencies expressed concern about the inadequacy of market sampling. Quoted in Coutant and Doubman, *Simplified*, p. 148.

28. W. Edwards Deming, *Sample Design in Business Research* (New York: Wiley, 1960), p. 32.

29. Market decisions were, of course, based on various kinds of data besides survey data. See L. O. Brown, *Market Research*, pp. 421–428 for a discussion of various indices obtainable from business and government sources. The Curtis Index was a well-known single index based on so-called Curtis units (i.e., the sale of one copy of any of its three magazines) and calculated for states, counties, and cities. General Motors developed a purchasing power index by counties based on aggregate figures on income tax returns, population, number of retail outlets, and total value of products, all statistics that were obtainable from government sources. See Henry G. Weaver, "The Development of a Basic Purchasing Power Index by Counties," *Harvard Business Review* 4 (1926):275–289. This research was awarded the Harvard Award for Scientific Research in Advertising of 1925.

30. Henry G. Weaver, "Proving Ground on Public Opinion," *Journal of Consulting Psychology* 5 (1941):149–153.

31. *Oxford English Dictionary* (London: Oxford University Press, 1933), 7:420.

32. Marjorie Fleiss, "The Panel as an Aid in Measuring Effects of Advertising," *Journal of Applied Psychology* 24 (1940):685–695.

33. One of the best-known market panels was set up by the *Woman's Home Companion* in the fall of 1935: 1,500 readers were selected from 3 million to serve as readers-editors, and for their trouble in answering questionnaires they received a special communication, "Companion Piece." See Paul F. Lazarsfeld and Marjorie Fiske, "The 'Panel' as a New Tool for Measuring Opinion," *POQ* 2 (1938):596–612. General Foods constituted a panel in the same years, but the beginnings went back to 1926, when it had assembled a jury of consumer testers who were paid a small sum for filling out questionnaires and sending in samples of jelly and jam they had prepared with its product Certo. The initial list of 200 women soon grew to 2,000. In other developments of testing procedures, response rates to mail questionnaires proved to be a spectacular

60–90 percent instead of the expected 20–25 percent. See Marie Sellers, "Pretesting of Products by Consumer Juries," *Journal of Marketing* 6 (Supplement) (1941–42):76–80. R. A. Robinson, in "Use of the Panel in Opinion and Attitude Research," *IJOAR* 1 (1947):83–86, noted that *Woman's Home Companion* panelists tended to grow more articulate over time, forming a "psychological upper-crust," as those who did not develop dropped out. To cope with this problem, a rotating membership was developed, in which people served for only three years and one-third of the memberships were replaced each year.

34. The first substantial treatment of panel/change analysis was Lazarsfeld and Fiske, "The 'Panel' as a New Tool"; Hans Zeisel, *Say It with Figures*, 4th ed. (New York: Harper & Row, [1947] 1957), chap. 10, "The Panel."

35. Theodore Henry Brown, *Problems in Business Statistics* (New York: McGraw-Hill Book Co., 1931); Theodore Henry Brown, "Interpretation of Market Data," *American Marketing Journal* 2 (1935):217–223. Curtis maps were published showing the average value of properties in the block, colored much as Charles Booth's maps of London had been. Red and yellow areas were higher income and blue areas were the poorest, and agents were instructed to "refrain from selling Curtis circulation in any of the areas colored blue." Parlin, *Passenger Car Industry*, p. 114.

36. Starch, "Research Methods in Advertising"; L. O. Brown, *Market Research*, pp. 456 ff.; White, *Marketing Research Technique*, esp. pp. 14–42.

37. Paul T. Cherington entry, *Who's Who in America* 16 (1930–31):505–506 (Chicago: Marquis, 1930).

38. Paul T. Cherington, "Statistics in Market Studies," *Annals of the American Academy of Political and Social Science* 115 (1924):130–135.

39. See C. M. Chester, "Measuring the Public's Attitude toward Business," *Market Research* 4 (Jan. 1936):3–6.

40. A. M. Crossley, "Theory and Application of Representative Sampling as Applied to Marketing," *Journal of Marketing* 5 (1941):456–461, esp. p. 458.

41. L. O. Brown, in *Market Research*, pp. 258 ff., used the term *proportionality* in much the same way in which market researchers and pollsters used *microcosm* or *representativeness*, by which "each significant class which exists in the universe must be represented in the sample in exactly the same proportion as it exists in the universe" (p. 260). In 1957, Crossley reflected on the use of the word *scientific* with sampling as a pretentious "gilding of the lily" and "the first of a long string of competitive catchwords which has so thoroughly characterized claims about sampling and interviewing methods" (p. 162). That "scientific" sampling became something of a magical term there is little doubt, but it is also the case that Crossley and his generation had no opportunity to become schooled in sampling theory. See A. M. Crossley, "Early Days of Public Opinion Research," *POQ* 21 (1957):159–164.

42. The "stabilizing" method was also called "series" sampling (Link, *New Psychology*, p. 60), and the "cumulative frequency" method (L. O. Brown, *Market Research*, pp. 312–319). See also T. H. Brown, "Interpretation of Market Data"; Kenneth Goode, *Manual of Modern Advertising* (New York: Greenberg, 1932), pp. 483 ff.; Frank R. Coutant and J. Russell Doubman, *Simplified Market Research* (Philadelphia: Walther, 1935), p. 28.

43. T. H. Brown, "Interpretation," p. 218. Brown also noted in *Statistical Techniques* (p. 11) that the process left open the question of what degree of stabilization was necessary for the problem at hand.

44. T. H. Brown, *Statistical Techniques*; Borden and Lovekin, *A Test of the Consumer Jury Method.*

45. Rensis Likert, "Democracy in Agriculture—Why and How?" in *Farmers in a Changing World: 1940 Yearbook of Agriculture*, USDA (Washington, D.C.: U.S. Government Printing Office, 1940), pp. 994–1002; American Institute of Public Opinion, *The New Science of Public Opinion Measurement* (Princeton, n.d., but probably 1938), p. 7; Link, "Milestones," pp. 38–39; George Gallup and Saul F. Rae, *The Pulse of Democracy* (New York: Simon & Schuster, 1940), p. 69. *The Journal of Applied Psychology* had published such a table in the mid-1920s, but it appears not to have received the same attention: Harold A. Edgerton and Donald G. Paterson, "Table of Standard Errors and Probable Errors of Percentages for Varying Numbers of Cases," *Journal of Applied Psychology* 10 (1926):378–391.

46. As Reilly put it in *Marketing Investigations*, pp. 221–222, "The use of the above formula . . . does not assume that the market data being tested satisfy the conditions of simple [random] sampling. The formula is used merely to find out whether or not market data have variation greater than simple [random] sampling data."

47. T. H. Brown, in *Statistical Techniques*, reviewed briefly several methods for selecting random samples—selecting homes "at random"; listing homes on slips of paper and shuffling; selecting every nth name from a directory or telephone book; selecting listed residents by a table of random numbers—each of which provided some difficulty in considerable labor or expense. Brown concluded that "practical difficulties of selection make compromises necessary" (p. 16).

48. S. S. Wilks, "Representative Sampling and Poll Reliability," *POQ* 4 (1940):260–269, p. 262.

49. Walter Van Dyke Bingham and Bruce Victor Moore, "The Interview in Marketing Studies and Commercial Surveys," in *How to Interview* (New York: Harper, 1931), esp. pp. 101–107; True Story Publishing Co., *The New Housewives Market.*

50. White, *Marketing Research*, p. 144, quoting Eastman, without complete citation. This view of the interviewing process is very like that used today by Cannell and his associates in experimental work. See Charles F. Cannell, Lois Oksenberg, and Jean M. Converse, *Experiments in Interviewing Techniques: Field Experiments in Health Reporting, 1971–1977* (Ann Arbor: Survey Research Center, Institute for Social Research, University of Michigan, 1979).

51. Bingham and Moore, *How to Interview*, pp. 104–108; L. O. Brown, *Market Research*, p. 175.

52. White, *Marketing Research Technique*, pp. 153–155.

53. Ibid., pp. 116 ff.; L. O. Brown, *Market Research*, p. 388.

54. White, *Marketing Research Technique*, pp. 103–110.

55. Ibid., p. 113. See also Harold E. Burtt, *Psychology of Advertising* (Boston: Houghton Mifflin Co., 1938), p. 46; R. B. Alspaugh, "Present Status and Future Outlook of Consumer Research in Commercial Firms," *American Marketing Journal* 2 (1935):80–84; Reilly, *Marketing Investigations*, pp. 104–105. Reilly discussed

"getting men with the proper ability and training background" as skilled interviewers—meaning, at best, men trained in marketing, economics, and engineering. Not surprisingly, Reilly reported that men with such training often preferred higher-paying jobs to interviewing.

56. White, *Marketing Research Technique*, p. 117.

57. Manuel N. Manfield, "The Status of Validation in Survey Research," pp. 61–85 in *Current Controversies in Marketing Research*, ed. Leo Bogart (Chicago: Markham, 1969). See esp. pp. 76–77.

58. Coutant and Doubman, *Simplified*, pp. 110–111.

59. Link, *New Psychology*, p. 56.

60. L. O. Brown, *Market Research*, pp. 295–296. See, for example, White, *Marketing Research Technique*, pp. 76, 185; and American Marketing Society, *Technique*, pp. 130, 140, 144, 173.

61. White, *Marketing Research Technique*, p. 225. L. O. Brown, in *Market Research*, makes the same point, that opportunities for dishonesty so abound that "personal reliability is regarded as one of the most important single qualifications for field investigators" (p. 287).

62. See Jean M. Converse and Howard Schuman, *Conversations at Random: Survey Research as Interviewers See It* (Ann Arbor, Mich.: Institute for Social Research, 1974).

63. American Marketing Society, *Technique*, p. 174. See also n. 15.

64. Elmo Roper, "Three Weaknesses of Market Research," *Market Research* 8 (1938):16–19.

65. One author in our references was rather less than scandalized to note that interviewers sometimes posed as census takers: "The ethics of this method is open to question, but it is used because it does get results. Fancy titles on questionnaires, such as 'American Survey Council,' hint at an authority which some people will respect" (L. O. Brown, *Market Research*, p. 219).

66. Ibid., p. 105; American Marketing Society, *Technique*, p. 125.

67. American Marketing Society, *Technique*, p. 150.

68. Coutant and Doubman, *Simplified*, pp. 110–111.

69. Starch, "Research Methods," p. 141.

70. An experiment involving users vs. nonusers is summarized in White, *Marketing Research Technique*, pp. 79 ff. Coutant and Doubman, *Simplified*, p. 90, reported that the use of mail questionnaires was on the decline, as did Haring in "The Evolution of Marketing Research Technique." In a postmortem of the 1936 election, Weld commented that mail questionnaires were known to be so likely to yield a biased return that "leading research men have largely given up this method of gathering information" (L. D. H. Weld, "Those Election Straw Votes," *Printers' Ink* 177 [Nov. 12, 1936]:6 ff.). The American Association of Advertising Agencies (AAAA) was on record by the mid-1930s as critical of mail questions (Coutant and Doubman, *Simplified*, pp. 148–149).

71. L. O. Brown, *Market Research*, p. 242; Burtt, *Psychology of Advertising*, p. 43; Hovde, "Recent Trends," p. 8; Burtt, *Psychology of Advertising*, p. 43; Ferdinand C. Wheeler, "New Methods and Results in Market Research," *American Marketing Journal* 2 (1935):35–39; John G. Jenkins, *Psychology in Business and Industry* (New York: Wiley, 1935), p. 323. Weaver wrote that General Motors could increase its

return rate by 50 percent by sending out questionnaires in duplicate, because respondents wanted to keep a copy, tribute indeed to the appeal of the questionnaire design (Henry G. Weaver, "Consumer Questionnaire Technique," *American Marketing Journal* 1 [1934]:115–118).

72. Link, *New Psychology*, p. 11.

73. These generalizations about questionnaire design and wording are based on actual questionnaires reproduced (in whole or in part) in leading texts as examples of good practice. Seventy-five questionnaires in all were featured in the following texts:

Daniel Starch, *Principles of Advertising* (thirteen questionnaires)
Percival White, *Market Research Technique* (twenty-five)
A. T. Poffenberger, *Psychology in Advertising* (one)
American Marketing Society, *The Technique of Marketing Research* (seventeen)
Frank R. Coutant and J. Russell Doubman, *Simplified Market Research* (nine)
Henry C. Link, *The New Psychology of Selling and Advertising* (four)
John G. Jenkins, *Psychology in Business and Industry* (one)
L. O. Brown, *Market Research and Analysis* (five)

74. Starch, "Research Methods," pp. 140, 143.

75. Jenkins, *Psychology in Business and Industry*, pp. 354–355.

76. Coolsen, in "Pioneers," noted that as early as 1906 texts discussed "reason why" advertising copy. Parlin stressed that automobile advertising depended for its effectiveness on attractive display and "reason why" copy (*The Passenger Car Industry*, pp. 107, 109).

77. American Marketing Society, *Technique*, p. 173.

78. Ibid., p. 186. See also Link, *New Psychology*, p. 283.

79. Franzen noted in 1937 that asking general whys and hows "without any formal limitation to the inscription of response" led to much comment which was largely irrelevant and certainly difficult to analyze. See Raymond Franzen, "Technical Responsibilities Involved in Consumer Research," *Market Research* 5 (Oct. 1936):3–7.

80. Crossley, "Early Days," p. 162. The "thermometer test" first appeared in *Literary Digest*, *The Lord of Telephone Manor* (New York, 1925), pp. 26–33.

81. Daniel Katz, "The Measurement of Intensity," in *Gauging Public Opinion*, ed. Hadley Cantril and Associates (Princeton: Princeton University Press, 1944), pp. 51–65. Katz notes that the thermometer device was suggested by OPOR, Hadley Cantril's research organization at Princeton, of which Katz was an associate. See *American National Election Study* (Ann Arbor: Center for Political Studies/Survey Research Center, University of Michigan, 1968).

82. A mail questionnaire reproduced in American Marketing Society, *Technique*, p. 137, asked for a five-point agree-disagree reaction to fourteen statements about advertising, e.g., "Advertising is valuable consumer education" and "Advertising is the life blood of quackery." Wheeler, "New Methods," p. 36, describes such a study conducted by Market Research Corporation in association with Lazarsfeld and explains the procedure of scoring the agreement/disagreement items from $+2$ to -2.

83. American Marketing Society, *Technique*, p. 169; L. O. Brown thought it important not to use questions on personal prejudices, personal health and mor-

als, and racial and religious prejudices. Age, income, and personal habits were all personal questions, and if rent had to be determined, he advised, one should ask the neighbors! (Brown, *Market Research*, p. 236).

84. In the total of seventy-five questionnaires on hand, level of education is not asked once. There are instances in this collection of direct questioning into home owning and occupation, along with a set of rather probing financial questions (White, *Marketing Research Technique*, p. 66; American Marketing Society, *Technique*, p. 124). There are also a few examples in which age is asked directly, although there are more in which the interviewer was apparently to estimate age (American Marketing Society, *Technique*, pp. 130, 137).

85. Carson S. Duncan, *Commercial Research: An Outline of Working Principles* (New York: Macmillan Co., 1919), p. 180.

86. Jenkins, *Business and Industry*, p. 343. See also Burtt, *Psychology*, p. 47, and Henry C. Link, "A New Method for Testing Advertising and a Psychological Sales Barometer," *JAP* 18 (1934):1–26.

87. See White, *Marketing Research Technique*, p. 66, where these questions appear in sequence: "Do you own? rent? Family head's occupation?" Harold E. Burtt and H. V. Gaskill, "Suggestibility and the Form of the Question," *JAP* 16 (1932):358–373, based experiments on B. Muscio's work, which appears to be the earliest work on question wording, "The Influence of the Form of a Question," *British Journal of Psychology* 8 (1916):351 ff. Both limit inquiry to such comparisons as definite vs. indefinite article and positive vs. negative, as in "Did you see *a* . . ." vs. "Didn't you see *the* . . ." Link, in "A New Method," pp. 13–14, describes two experiments in very general terms: (1) for a questionnaire of about twenty-five questions, the order was completely reversed for half the sample, without significant effects; (2) half the sample were given questions on both advertising and use of a given product, with such related questions completely avoided in the other half, also without significant difference. See also p. 25. Bingham and Moore's *How to Interview*, 2d ed., 1934, p. 101, reports a Psychological Corporation experiment comparing an "increase in prices" and "a *reasonable* increase in prices," which shows an 11 percent difference.

88. A. T. Poffenberger, "The Conditions of Belief in Advertising," *JAP* 7 (1923):1–9, and "Measuring the Comprehension of Advertisements," ibid., pp. 364–369.

89. The experiments are described in A. T. Poffenberger, *Psychology in Advertising* (New York: McGraw-Hill Book Co., [1925] 1932), pp. 140–143. The advisability of open vs. checklist questioning elicited contradictory advice from other sources. For example, Coutant and Doubman (*Simplified*, p. 94) reported from experiment that "it was comparatively easy to get five or six choices" from a checklist as opposed to only two or three from an open question, and they appeared to favor the use of checklists for that reason. L. O. Brown (*Market Research*, p. 234) thought such checklists were likely to elicit *over*reporting by stimulating "the imagination."

90. Jenkins, *Business and Industry*, pp. 348–351.

91. Starch, *Principles of Advertising*, p. 197; Poffenberger, *Psychology*, p. 144; L. O. Brown, *Market Research*, p. 237; Franzen, in "Technical Responsibilities," p. 6, stated flatly that "rating scales have been discredited for general use. Individ-

uals are unable to rate a set of factors for importance." There were, nevertheless, exceptions. White reproduced a General Motors questionnaire that was even more difficult, involving, in effect, a ratio scale: the respondent was to rate the most important factor in a list as 10 and to rate as 5 the factor that had "about half as much influence with you" (White, *Marketing Research Technique*, p. 80). There was recognition in the 1920s that ranking ("order of merit") was difficult when the number of items was large. Franken proposed assigning scores from 0 to 3 and determining the rank-order from the mean scores (Richard B. Franken, "Advertising Appeals Selected by the Method of Direct Impression," *JAP* 8 (1924):232–244.

92. Starch, *Principles*, pp. 272–274. Starch's instructions read in part: "Consider the strength and importance of these motives or incentives to action from the standpoint of your own personal life and behavior as a whole. Ask yourself in connection with each one how important it is in determining your own actions from day to day. Write 10 after the very strongest motives . . ." (p. 272). According to Jenkins, *Business and Industry*, p. 326, Starch's list of motives got wide circulation among advertisers. See also Melvin T. Copeland, "Consumers' Buying Motives," *Harvard Business Review* 2 (1923–24):139–153, which identifies thirty motives.

93. Henry C. Link, "How to Prepare Questions for Consumer Research," *Printers' Ink* 166 (Jan. 11, 1934):37–41. See also Poffenberger, *Psychology*, pp. 147–148; Franzen, "Technical Responsibilities"; Reilly, *Marketing Investigations*, pp. 82, 128; Alspaugh, "Consumer Research," p. 80.

94. Starch, *Principles*, pp. 150–151, 205. For example, Starch later advocated wording questions to focus on a specific *time or condition*: "What newspapers were received in your home or bought outside by some member of your family *yesterday?*" See Daniel Starch, "Factors in the Reliability of Samples," *JASA* Supplement 27 (1932):190–201.

95. Poffenberger, *Psychology*, p. 147; Reilly, *Marketing Investigations*, p. 129; L. O. Brown, *Market Research*, p. 229.

96. Percival White, "New Deal in Questionnaires," *Market Research* 4 (June 1936):23.

97. Crossley, in *Watch Your Selling Dollar!*, counseled simplification and brevity, noting that most consumer investigations were needlessly long (p. 311).

98. White, *Marketing Research Technique*, pp. 196–199; L. O. Brown, *Market Research*, p. 344.

99. Ibid., p. 174; Weaver, "Questionnaire Technique," p. 117; John G. Jenkins, "Customer Research," in *Handbook of Applied Psychology*, ed. Douglas H. Fryer and Edwin R. Henry (New York: Rinehart and Co., 1950), vol. 1, pp. 371–374, provides the example of a comment inspiring the analysis of the data by age.

100. Raoul Blumberg and Carroll Rheinstrom, "How Advertising Techniques Are Rated by Gallup Survey," *Printers' Ink* 158 (Mar. 24, 1932):17–20.

101. Wheeler, "New Methods," p. 36.

102. Ibid., p. 39.

103. G. Udny Yule, *An Introduction to the Theory of Statistics* (London: Charles

Griffen, [1910] 1927); Mordecai Ezekiel, *Methods of Correlation Analysis* (New York: Wiley, 1930); Horace Sechrist, *An Introduction to Statistical Methods* (New York: Macmillan Co., [1917] 1925); Frederick C. Mills, *Statistical Methods Applied to Economics and Business* (New York: Henry Holt Co., 1924); Robert E. Chaddock, *Principles and Methods of Statistics* (Boston: Houghton Mifflin Co., 1925).

104. T. H. Brown, *Problems in Business Statistics*, p. 185.

105. Coutant and Doubman, *Simplified*, p. 117. See also L. O. Brown, *Market Research*, p. 341, in which he urges simple cross-tabulation: "Those who think of correlation in terms of the Pearsonian *r*, or something more complex, would regard this as a very crude statement . . . [but] even the simpler tables are for the fundamental purpose of showing relationships."

106. White, *Marketing Research Technique*, pp. 206–207.

107. Ibid., pp. 207–208; L. O. Brown, *Market Research*, pp. 332–333.

108. Weaver, "Questionnaire Technique," p. 116.

109. Robert K. Merton, "Science and the Social Order," in Merton, *Social Theory and Social Structure*, rev. ed. (New York: The Free Press, 1957), originally published in *Philosophy of Science* (1938); Robert K. Merton, "Science and Democratic Social Structure," ibid., originally published in *Journal of Legal and Political Sociology* (1942); Herbert A. Shepard, "Nine Dilemmas in Industrial Research," in *The Sociology of Science*, ed. Bernard Barber and Walter Hirsch (New York: The Free Press, 1962), pp. 344–355; Donald C. Pelz, "Some Social Factors Related to Performance in a Research Organization," ibid., pp. 356–369.

110. Alspaugh, "Present Status and Future Outlook," p. 83.

111. F. R. Coutant, "Copy Testing Technique," *Printers' Ink* 170 (Jan. 10, 1935):57–62.

112. Leo Bogart, "Opinion Research and Marketing," *POQ* 21 (1957):129–140, esp. p. 135. Bogart's career has combined academic training and commercial research. He also stressed the intellectual differences between those with business or economics backgrounds and those with general backgrounds in social science. See also Leo Bogart, "The Researcher's Dilemma," in *Current Controversies in Marketing Research*, ed. Bogart (Chicago: Markham, 1969).

An academic survey researcher in my own ken, whose career started in the 1940s, has reported ruefully that even in the 1970s he had to guard against a reflex to "talk down" to market research professionals, despite the fact that their field had long since become a technically very sophisticated one. He also recalled the regret that he and his academic colleagues felt in the early days upon learning that one of their number had abandoned *scientific work* of importance for mere *business* success. See also Coutant, "Copy Testing," p. 58.

113. H. L. Hollingworth, "Memories of the Early Development of the Psychology of Advertising Suggested by Burtt's *Psychology of Advertising*," *Psychological Bulletin* 35 (1938):307–312.

114. "Report on the Activities of the Psychological Corporation, 1941," *JAP* 26 (1942):151–158, esp. p. 153.

115. Sokal argues that Cattell had little experience or conception of how applied psychology ought to be organized or directed and conceived of the Psychological Corporation in part as an effort to bolster his lagging prestige in the

profession. See Michael M. Sokal, "The Origins of the Psychological Corporation," *Journal of the History of the Behavioral Sciences* 17 (1981):54–67.

116. R. S. Woodworth, "Some Personal Characteristics," *Science* 99 (Feb. 25, 1944):160–161.

117. Paul S. Achilles, "The Role of the Psychological Corporation in Applied Psychology," *American Journal of Psychology* 56 (1937):229–247, esp. p. 230.

118. Paul S. Achilles, "Report on the Activities of the Psychological Corporation 1939," *JAP* 24 (1940):109–121, esp. pp. 120–121; idem, "The Psychological Corporation," *Science* 99 (Feb. 25, 1944):161–162.

119. George Burton Hotchkiss and Richard B. Franken, *The Measurement of Advertising Effects* (New York: Harper, 1927). The 1917 experiment was reported by L. R. Geissler, "Association-Reactions Applied to Ideas of Commercial Brands of Familiar Articles," *JAP* 1 (1917):275–290.

120. The earliest opinion questions published by the corporation in *JAP* were asked in October 1932. Among the early questions were these: "From what you have seen of the N.R.A. in your neighborhood, do you believe it is working well?" "Who should take care of unemployment relief?" (Link, "A New Method," pp. 23–24). Business interest in public perception of corporate and related government policy made an extension from market research into public opinion research a very easy and natural one. See, for example, C. M. Chester, "Measuring the Public's Attitude toward Business," *Market Research* 4 (Jan. 1936):3–6. Five questions were asked by return postcards, e.g., "Do you think wages paid by large companies to their employees are too low? about right? too high?" and others dealing with treatment of employees, taxes paid by business, and government regulation of business.

121. Henry C. Link, "Some Milestones in Public Opinion Research," *IJOAR* 1 (1947):36–46. In "News and Notes" of *JAP* 23 (1939):310, a bulletin of the Psychological Corporation was quoted as having given to Gallup the accolade, "probably the greatest national figure among psychologists, in fact one of the greatest figures in any field today," and it went on: "Members of the Psychological Corporation are especially proud because his work has helped to vindicate the studies of public opinion, buying habits, etc., which they have been developing since 1931." It is not clear who wrote this material, but in a 1941 review of a book by Gallup, Link expressed almost as much enthusiasm: "No single development in the history of social psychology—probably no development anywhere in the history of psychology—has produced such a wealth of scientifically important material in so short a time as have these polls" (*Psychological Bulletin* 38 [1941]:117–118).

122. "A large number of naive interviewers doing about twenty-five interviews each was generally more desirable than a small number of sophisticated interviewers doing two or three hundred interviews each. The former were less likely to become stereotyped or biased in their work. The spread of the sample was also facilitated" (Link, "Milestones," p. 38).

123. The Psychological Corporation, "A Study of Public Relations and Social Attitudes," *JAP* 21 (1937):589–601; Leonard W. Doob, "An 'Experimental' Study of the Psychological Corporation," *Psychological Bulletin* 35 (1938):220–222.

124. This was probably the pamphlet published by the corporation in 1934.

See Jenkins, *Business and Industry*, p. 344. It appeared in the journal literature in 1937: Henry C. Link, "How Many Interviews Are Necessary for Results of a Certain Accuracy?" *JAP* 21 (1937):1–17.

125. Link, "A New Method," p. 13.

126. Ibid., p. 25.

127. Link, "Milestones," p. 43.

128. Ibid.

129. Henry C. Link, "The Ninety-fourth Issue of the Psychological Barometer and a Note on Its Fifteenth Anniversary," *JAP* 32 (1948):105–117, esp. p. 106.

130. Henry C. Link and A. D. Freiberg, "The Problem of Validity vs. Reliability in Public Opinion Polls," *POQ* 6 (1942):87–98.

131. "Many psychologists still fail to see that, from the standpoint of progress in techniques, advertising and market surveys have far more to offer than do political opinion surveys. To measure people's buying behavior requires far more exacting methods than to measure their voting behavior" (Link, "Ninety-fourth Issue," p. 108).

132. Cherington combined academic and commercial careers, teaching at Harvard, Stanford, and New York University, directing research at J. Walter Thompson (1922–1931) and consulting in a number of firms. Among his publications were *Advertising as a Business Force* (New York: Doubleday Page, 1913), *The Elements of Marketing* (New York: Macmillan Co., 1920), and *The Consumer Looks at Advertising* (New York: Harper, 1928).

133. Interview with Archibald Crossley, April 7, 1977, conducted by Richard Baxter under the auspices of AAPOR. Literary Digest, *The Lord of Telephone Manor* (New York, [1925] 1927) provided county-by-county figures for all the states of population and families with telephones (almost 10 million telephone homes).

134. James, "Broadcast Advertising," p. 142.

135. Link, *New Psychology*, pp. 156–160. The CAB was sponsored by the Association of National Advertisers, Inc. See Neil H. Borden, "The Harvard Advertising Awards," *Harvard Business Review* 3 (1925):257–264; Crossley, *Watch Your Selling Dollar!*

136. Robinson, "Recent Developments," pp. 48 ff.

137. See Crossley, "Early Days," 1957; *Proceedings of the American Association for Public Opinion Research, POQ* 13 (1949–50):764–768; ibid. 14 (1950):826–831. Crossley was president of AAPOR in 1952–53. In 1953 he was among 122 individuals named to the Hall of Fame in Distribution at the twenty-fifth annual Boston Conference on Distribution ("Action Urged Now to Avert Setback," *New York Times*, Oct. 20, 1953, pp. 41, 45).

138. Interview with Elmo Roper, Aug. 14, 1968, conducted by Robert O. Carlson, to be deposited in an AAPOR archive being established at the University of Chicago, Regenstein Library.

139. Ibid.

140. Ibid.

141. Ibid.; *Proceedings of AAPOR, POQ* 13 (1949–50):768. Roper felt that academics reacted very badly in 1948 when the polls misforecast a Dewey victory,

in part because the political scientists felt that the pollsters were invading their field. He imagined their saying, "Roper? He doesn't have a degree in political science? Gallup doesn't. . . . Neither does Crossley. . . . What are they doing this for?" Economists went through the same distrustful reaction, he felt (Carlson's interview with Roper).

142. Ibid.

143. Interview with George Gallup, Mar. 22, 1978, conducted by Paul B. Sheatsley, to be deposited in an AAPOR archive being established at the University of Chicago, Regenstein Library. George Gallup, "An Objective Method for Determining Reader Interest in the Content of a Newspaper" (Ph.D. diss., State University of Iowa, 1928). Gallup later used the same method in much larger readership studies of newspapers and magazines. In George Gallup, "What Do Newspaper Readers Read," *Advertising and Selling* 18 (March 31, 1932):22 ff., a study of fourteen metropolitan dailies, the great appeal of photographs and comics was again stressed. See also Link, *New Psychology*, pp. 51–52; Haring, "The Evolution of Marketing Research Technique," p. 270; "The Gallup Method of Advertising Research," *Advertising and Selling* 18 (March 16, 1932):30 ff.; Blumberg and Rheinstrom, "How Advertising Techniques Are Rated." Gallup tested validity by observing, unobtrusively, what thirty-three students read in a newspaper posted on a university bulletin board and later by interviewing the students on what they had read. Reliability was tested in various repeated measurements involving the same newspaper, and same/different stories, at various time intervals.

144. Sheatsley's interview with Gallup, 1978.

145. Ibid.; see also *Current Biography* (New York: H. W. Wilson, 1940), pp. 319–321.

146. Richard Jensen, in "Democracy," p. 59, notes that the Greek language added a word, "*to Gallup*." Paul Lazarsfeld noted humorously in 1949 that the Norwegians tried to keep track of all the Gallups: "Has Crossley's 'Gallup' been better than Roper's 'Gallup?'" (Norman C. Meier and Harold W. Saunders, *The Polls and Public Opinion* [New York: Henry Holt & Co., 1949], p. 194).

147. "Poll: Dr. Gallup to Take the National Pulse and Temperature," *Newsweek*, Oct. 26, 1935, pp. 23–24; "Poll: Dr. Gallup Closes a Gap between People and Government," *Newsweek*, Nov. 14, 1936, pp. 14–16; "News and Notes: Research News," *AJS* 42 (1936):256.

148. Gallup published in such trade publications as *Advertising and Selling* ("What Do Newspaper Readers Read?") and *Market Research* ("How America Was Made to Speak," 4 [April 1936]:6–7); in popular magazines, such as *Scribner's* ("Putting Public Opinion to Work," 100 [1936]:36–39 ff.); and in academic journals, such as *JASA* ("Government and the Sampling Referendum," 33 [1938]:131–142), *POQ* ("Is There a Bandwagon Vote?" 4 [1940]:244–249), and *Sociometry* ("Question Wording in Public Opinion," 4 [1941]:259–268). In 1939, Gallup delivered the Stafford Little Lecture at Princeton University, "Public Opinion in a Democracy" (University Extension Fund, Herbert L. Baker Foundation, Princeton). See note 151 for Gallup's major books on polling.

149. George Gallup, *The Sophisticated Poll Watcher's Guide* (Princeton: Princeton Opinion Press, 1972), pp. 230–232.

150. J. J. O'Malley, "Black Beans and White Beans," *New Yorker* 16 (March 2,

1940):20–24. The article notes that *institute* had become fashionable among businessmen over the past decade as a synonym for *organization* or *company*. See also Williston Rich, "The Human Yardstick," *Saturday Evening Post* 211 (Jan. 21, 1939):8–9 ff.

151. In Gallup and Rae, *The Pulse of Democracy*, the authors point to research methods in market analysis which provided "yardsticks by which surveys of public opinion could be checked" (p. 45). Gallup concentrated on a chronicle of journalism in "The New Science of Public Opinion Measurement," 1938; "Sampling Referendum," 1938; *A Guide to Public Opinion Polls*, 1944; and esp. in *The Sophisticated Poll Watcher's Guide*, 1972 (pp. 221–227).

152. See Robinson, *Straw Votes*, esp. pp. 65–85; Robinson, "Recent Developments." Robinson's work on the early straw polls may well still be the most ambitious and comprehensive treatment of the subject. He was respectful of the methods of *Columbia Dispatch* and *Cincinnati Enquirer*, but these remained local polls and were an exception to generally crude sampling methods, in his view.

153. Gallup, "How America Was Made to Speak." His congressional election forecast missed the total congressional vote by 1 percent.

154. Robinson, "Recent Developments," pp. 47–50; Daniel Katz and Hadley Cantril, "Public Opinion Polls," *Sociometry* 1 (1937):155–179; Archibald M. Crossley, "Straw Polls in 1936," *POQ* 1 (1937):24–35.

155. Hadley Cantril, in his preelection article "Straw Votes This Year Show Contrary Winds," *New York Times*, Oct. 25, 1936, IV, p. 3, used quotation marks to distinguish "scientific" from "practical" polls such as the *Digest*, but without invidious effect. V. O. Key, Jr., saw the pollsters as using "scientific sampling" methods in both his 1942 and 1947 editions of *Politics, Parties, and Pressure Groups* (New York: Thomas Y. Crowell, 1942, p. 640; reprinted 1947, p. 562).

156. "Dr. Gallup Chided by *Digest* Editor," *New York Times*, July 19, 1936, p. 21. See also letter from W. J. Funk, editor of the *Literary Digest* (*New York Times*, Sept. 7, 1936, p. 16) in which Funk, without naming Gallup directly, assails his poll as "so-called 'scientific' " and "unseasoned" because it has "never had to forecast a national election."

157. Institute of Public Opinion, "Results Today Point to Close November Race," *Washington Post*, July 12, 1936, III, 1, 2; Harwood L. Childs, "Rule by Public Opinion," *Atlantic Monthly* 157 (June 1937):755–764; Cantril, "Straw Votes This Year."

158. Rich, "Human Yardstick," p. 9.

159. Robinson, *Straw Votes*, p. 51.

160. In 1930, 20,227,370 ballots were sent out and 4,806,464 were returned, a return rate of 23.8% (*Literary Digest*, May 24, 1930, pp. 7–9); Walter F. Willcox, "An Attempt to Measure Public Opinion about Repealing the Eighteenth Amendment," *JASA* 26 (1931):243–261.

161. See *Literary Digest*, Aug. 22, 1936, p. 4; ibid., Nov. 4, 1916, pp. 1155–1156.

162. *New York Times*, Oct. 8, 1924, p. 5; ibid., Oct. 19, 1928, p. 4; ibid., Oct. 17, 1930, p. 4; *Literary Digest*, Oct. 31, 1936, p. 5.

163. *Literary Digest*, Apr. 3, 1926, p. 9; *New York Times*, Apr. 2, 1930, p. 20; ibid., Apr. 1, 1930, p. 13.

164. *Literary Digest*, Nov. 1, 1924, pp. 5–8; *New York Times*, Oct. 4, 1924, p. 12;

ibid., Oct. 16, 1936, p. 24; ibid., Oct. 28, 1936, p. 24. William L. Crum, "Crum's Analysis Shows Election in Balance," *Wall Street Journal*, Oct. 30, 1936, pp. 5 ff., adjusted 1936 state forecasts by 1932 figures. Crum's final forecast was 241 for Landon, 199 for Roosevelt, with 91 borderline; he considered the election too close to call (*Literary Digest*, Oct. 31, 1936, pp. 5–6).

165. Gallup, "Putting Public Opinion to Work," p. 38.

166. The figures I cite here are those used by Harold F. Gosnell in "How Accurate Were the Polls?" *POQ* 1 (1937):97–105, in which both Gallup and Crossley show 54 percent for Roosevelt.

167. *Detroit Sunday Times*, Nov. 1, 1936, pt. 2, p. 2. Also "Voter Swing Aids Landon, Poll Shows," *Detroit Times*, Nov. 2, 1936, p. 5. At the very end, the article forecast 55 percent of the major party vote for Roosevelt. The first paragraphs showed Landon gaining "new impetus" and contained other circuitous statements.

168. *Fortune* 14 (Oct. 1936):130–132 ff.

169. *Fortune* 14 (Dec. 1936):86–87 ff.

170. O'Malley, "Black Beans and White Beans"; *Fortune* 21 (May 1940):34.

171. *Printers' Ink*, Nov. 12, 1936, pp. 46–47.

172. *Washington Post*, July 12, 1936, III, pp. 1–2. Elmo Roper noted in October 1936 that it was "axiomatic" that upper income levels returned mail ballots more frequently than lower income (Roper, "Forecasting Election Returns," *Review of Reviews* 94 [Oct. 1936]:58–59).

173. Kristi Andersen, "Generation, Partisan Shift, and Realignment: A Glance Back to the New Deal," in *The Changing American Voter*, ed. Norman H. Nie, Sidney Verba, and John R. Petrocik (Cambridge, Mass.: Harvard University Press, 1976), pp. 74–95; Jerome M. Clubb, William F. Flanigan, and Nancy H. Zingale, "The Dynamics of Partisan Change," in *Partisan Realignment: Voters, Parties, and Government in American History* (Beverly Hills: Sage Publications, 1980), pp. 251–272; Shively, "A Reinterpretation of the New Deal Realignment."

With regard to the *Digest*'s failure, Bryson argues (1) that sampling frame bias did not account for it; (2) that response bias from mail questionnaires did; and (3) that almost nobody has noted response bias. (See Maurice C. Bryson, "The *Literary Digest* Poll: Making of a Statistical Myth," *American Statistician*, Nov. 1976, pp. 184–185.)

Response bias has in fact been cited repeatedly for many years in explanation of the *Digest*'s misforecast. Bryson cites only Rensis Likert ("Public Opinion Polls," *Scientific American* 179 [1948]:7–11), but there are many additional references. See *Newsweek*, Oct. 26, 1935, pp. 23–24; Cantril, "Straw Votes"; Katz and Cantril, "Polls," p. 167; Crossley, "Straw Polls," p. 29; Robinson, "Recent Developments," p. 54; Gosnell, "How Accurate," p. 103; Don Cahalan and Norman C. Meier, "The Validity of Mail Ballot Polls," *Psychological Record* 3 (1939):3–11; Frederick F. Stephan, "Representative Sampling in Large-Scale Surveys," *JASA* 34 (1939):343–352; Gallup and Rae, *Pulse of Democracy*, p. 48; Wroe Alderson, "Trends in Public Opinion Research," in *How to Conduct Consumer and Opinion Research*, ed. Albert B. Blankenship (New York: Harper, 1946), pp. 289–309; Frederick Mosteller et al., *The Preelection Polls of 1948* (New York: SSRC, 1949), p. 10; Mildred Parten, *Surveys, Polls, and Samples: Practical Procedures* (New York: Harper, 1950), p. 393.

In support of the basic argument, Bryson discusses the *Digest*'s own explanation of Nov. 14, 1936, that in two cities where voter registration lists had been sampled, Republicans showed higher response rates than Democrats did. The returns from Allentown and Chicago do indeed show, as Parten noted in 1950, that even with a better sample source (e.g., registered voters instead of telephone lists and car registration) the *Literary Digest* poll would have failed "because of the unrepresentative character of mail respondents" (p. 393). But the great bulk of the *Digest*'s sample was gathered from phone and car registration lists, not from voter registration lists. The example from two cities seems insufficient warrant for rejecting the most common interpretation that *both* sample bias and response bias were operating, that both favored upper- and middle-income respondents, and that both biases were exacerbated by a growing political realignment that attracted lower-income voters to the Democratic party and upper-income voters to the Republican party in 1936. The *Digest*'s own argument against sample bias was an interested and defensive one, for the editors had long claimed to their advertisers that they were reaching a broad *national* market, not just a middle-class or upper-middle-class one. Unfortunately, the *Digest* provided only two examples of response bias and only very general information about its sample.

What the Bryson article serves to emphasize is the fact that in recent years certain *statistics* texts have neglected response bias in giving exclusive attention to sampling-frame bias. Bryson's own case for this is somewhat flawed: of the five authors he cites, two—and possibly three—are under the misapprehension that the *Digest* conducted its poll *by* telephone, which would of course have made mail questionnaire bias logically impossible, and they do indeed fail to mention it (see references 4 and 5 in Bryson's article; 2 is ambiguous). I have located four other sources that are more accurate about *Digest* matters and that also concentrate almost exclusively on sampling-frame bias: W. Allen Wallis and Harry V. Roberts, *Statistics: A New Approach* (Glencoe, Ill.: The Free Press, 1956), p. 74; Morris Zelditch, Jr., *A Basic Course in Sociological Statistics* (New York: Holt, Rinehart and Winston, 1959), p. 232; Frederick E. Croxton and Dudley J. Cowden, *Applied General Statistics* (New York: Prentice-Hall, 1939), p. 32; Albert B. Blankenship, *Consumer and Opinion Research* (New York: Harper, 1943), passim.

174. Gallup, "Putting Public Opinion to Work"; Crossley, "Early Days."

175. Gallup, *Sophisticated*, p. 224.

176. *Time*, Mar. 7, 1938, p. 55; May 23, 1938, pp. 46–47; *Newsweek*, June 26, 1937, pp. 23–24.

177. Crossley, "Straw Polls," pp. 34–35.

178. Gallup, "Sampling Referendum," p. 141.

179. James Bryce, *American Commonwealth* (New York, 1919 edition), vol. 2, pp. 262–263 (italics added). See Gallup, "Sampling Referendum," and "Public Opinion in a Democracy."

180. Gallup, *A Guide to Public Opinion Polls*, 2d ed., p. x; Walter Lippmann, *Public Opinion* (New York: Harcourt, Brace and Company, 1922) and *The Phantom Public* (New York: Macmillan Co., 1925); Ronald Steel, *Walter Lippmann and the American Century* (Boston: Little, Brown & Co., 1980), esp. pp. 180–184 and 211–216.

181. David L. Sills, ed., *International Encyclopedia of the Social Sciences*, Bio-

graphical Supplement (New York: The Free Press, 1979), vol. 18, pp. 226–228 and 675–678.

182. Ibid. (1968), vol. 13, p. 189.

183. Robinson, *Straw Votes*; William L. Crum, "On Analytical Interpretation of Straw-Vote Samples," *JASA* 28 (1933):152–163; Walter F. Willcox, "An Attempt to Measure Public Opinion about Repealing the 18th Amendment," *JASA* 26 (1931):243–260.

184. Doob, "An 'Experimental' Study of the Psychological Corporation."

185. "Fortune Survey II: Preview," *Fortune* 12 (Sept. 1935):84 ff.; "A New Technique in Journalism," *Fortune* 12 (July 1935):65–68 ff.

186. Page numbers and results are from George Gallup, *The Gallup Poll: Public Opinion 1935–1971*, 3 vols. (New York: Random House, 1972).

187. The Gallup Poll in fact provides the largest single source of questions replicated in the NORC General Social Survey, a national survey established in 1972 as an annual source of trend analysis and data diffusion (*General Social Surveys, 1972–80: Cumulative Codebook* [Chicago: NORC, University of Chicago, July 1980]).

188. Rensis Likert, "Democracy in Agriculture"; Morris H. Hansen and William G. Madow, "Some Important Events in the Historical Development of Sample Surveys," in *On the History of Statistics and Probability*, ed. D. B. Owen (New York: Dekker, 1976), p. 80.

189. Interview with Paul B. Sheatsley, April 12, 1977.

4. The Prewar Years

1. Hadley Cantril and Gordon W. Allport, *The Psychology of Radio* (New York: Peter Smith, [1935] 1941).

2. This was included in *Jugend und Beruf* (Jena, Germany: Gustav Fischer, 1931). Lazarsfeld reviewed the literature on occupational choice of adolescents and found that it was based almost exclusively on children of the middle class. See Paul F. Lazarsfeld, "An Episode in the History of Social Research: A Memoir," in *The Intellectual Migration: Europe and America 1930–1960*, ed. Donald Fleming and Bernard Bailyn (Cambridge, Mass.: The Belknap Press of Harvard University, 1969), pp. 275–277.

3. Sills dates the advent of the Wirtschaftspsychologische Forschungsstelle as 1925, the same year as Lazarsfeld's degree. See David L. Sills, "Paul F. Lazarsfeld," *IESS* (New York: The Free Press, 1979), vol. 18, pp. 411–427. So does Zeisel, who worked with Lazarsfeld in the research center. See Hans Zeisel, "The Vienna Years," in *Qualitative and Quantitative Social Research: Papers in Honor of Paul F. Lazarsfeld*, ed. Robert K. Merton, James S. Coleman, and Peter H. Rossi (New York: The Free Press, 1979), pp. 10–15. Lazarsfeld himself notes 1927 as the beginning and refers to a fortieth anniversary of the center in 1967. See Lazarsfeld, "A Memoir," p. 286.

4. Ibid, p. 279; see also published interview with Mark Abrams, *Market Research Society Newsletter* 149 (1978):8–10.

5. Zeisel, "The Vienna Years"; Hans Zeisel, "L'école viennoise des récherches

de motivation," *Revue Française de Sociologie* 9 (1968):3–12, esp. 8. In 1934, Zeisel described the interviewing of the center as " 'conversations' with individuals taken from the various classes of potential buyers. These 'conversations' are conducted by its trained research staff working according to detailed instructions, and their results are recorded in diagrammatic form and supplemented by verbal reports in periodical conferences." See Hans Zeisel, "Market Research in Austria," *The Human Factor* 8 (1934):29–32.

6. Marie Jahoda, Paul F. Lazarsfeld, and Hans Zeisel, *Marienthal: The Sociography of an Unemployed Community*, trans. from the German by the authors with John Reginall and Thomas Elsaesser (Chicago: Aldine, Atherton, [1933] 1971).

7. Ibid., chap. 7.

8. Sills, "Lazarsfeld." Lazarsfeld seemed slightly puzzled by the waning of his political involvement, or at least he labored somewhat to understand it. He concluded that he sublimated expressions of political concerns into his research work, seeing his interest in voting behavior as a substitute for political participation and linking his directorship of research to youthful political fervors that he could not express by running for office because he was Jewish. It seems just as plausible that Lazarsfeld recognized that socialism was not as much of a leading current in American intellectual or political life as it had been in Vienna. His comments in the oral history interviews that he consciously changed his writing style to be less passionate, more detached—as Charlotte Bühler had strongly advised—suggest the same kind of adaptation to norms of scientific writing.

9. Lazarsfeld, "A Memoir," pp. 293–295.

10. Interview with George H. Gallup, 1962, Oral History Collection, Butler Library, Columbia University; American Marketing Association, *The Technique of Marketing Research* (New York: McGraw-Hill Book Co., 1937).

11. Neither Lazarsfeld nor his bibliographers specify any European publications from the Vienna market research, although Cantril and Allport cite a radio study, "Hörerbefragung der Ravag," 1932. See Cantril and Allport, *The Psychology of Radio*, pp. 34, 95. Presumably, the work in Vienna was generally proprietary.

12. Paul F. Lazarsfeld, "Psychological Approach in the Development of Conclusions," in American Marketing Society, *Technique*, pp. 271, 273.

13. Zeisel, "L'école viennoise."

14. Paul F. Lazarsfeld, "The Psychological Aspect of Market Research," *Harvard Business Review* 13 (1934):54–71, esp. p. 56.

15. Ibid., p. 62.

16. Zeisel, "L'école viennoise," p. 11.

17. Paul F. Lazarsfeld, *Qualitative Analysis: Historical and Critical Essays* (Boston: Allyn and Bacon, 1972).

18. Merton, Coleman, and Rossi, eds., *Qualitative and Quantitative Social Research*; Jennifer Platt, "Whatever Happened to the Case Study? or, From Znaniecki to Lazarsfeld in One Generation" (unpublished paper, 1981).

19. Paul F. Lazarsfeld, "The Art of Asking Why in Marketing Research," *National Marketing Review* 1 (1935):32–43, reprinted in *Public Opinion and Propaganda*, ed. Daniel Katz, Dorwin Cartwright, Samuel Eldersveld, and Alfred McClung Lee (New York: Dryden, 1954), pp. 675–686; Elias Smith and Edward

A. Suchman, "Do People Know Why They Buy?" [1940], reprinted in *The Language of Social Research*, ed. Paul F. Lazarsfeld and Morris Rosenberg (Glencoe, Ill.: The Free Press, 1955), pp. 404–419. ("Elias Smith" is an alias that Lazarsfeld took to obscure his authorship of various articles that he was including in the *Journal of Applied Psychology* as guest editor [see "A Memoir," p. 308].) To test validity, Lazarsfeld and Suchman proposed judges' classifications, supplemented by field experiments on the impact of advertising: "The number of people who, on the basis of interviews such as the one discussed in this paper, are finally considered to have been influenced by the program, should be equal to the difference in customers between the campaign city and the control city" (*Language of Social Research*, p. 410). The analysis of the relationship between exposure and effect in advertising was further explained in another article, reprinted in *The Language of Social Research* (pp. 411–420): Paul F. Lazarsfeld, "Evaluating the Effectiveness of Advertising by Direct Interview," *Journal of Consulting Psychology* 5 (1941):170–178. The procedure is basically the same as that presented in an article by Rensis Likert, "A Method for Measuring the Sales Influence of a Radio Program," *JAP* 20 (1936):175–182.

20. John G. Jenkins, *Psychology in Business and Industry* (New York: Wiley, 1935), pp. 329–337; telephone interview with Sydney Roslow, July 6, 1979; Abrams, published interview, p. 8.

21. Lazarsfeld, "The Art of Asking Why," p. 681.

22. Paul F. Lazarsfeld, "The Use of Detailed Interviews in Market Research," *Journal of Marketing* 2 (1937):3–8.

23. The other three chapters by Lazarsfeld included in the American Marketing Society/Association, *The Technique of Marketing Research* (New York: McGraw-Hill Book Co., 1937), are "Psychological Aspect of Questionnaire Development," "Further Considerations of Psychological Aspects," and "Psychological Approach in the Development of Conclusions." Paul F. Lazarsfeld and Allen H. Barton, "Qualitative Measurement in the Social Sciences: Classification, Typologies, and Indices," in *The Policy Sciences: Recent Developments in Scope and Method*, ed. Daniel Lerner and Harold D. Lasswell (Stanford: Stanford University Press, 1951), pp. 155–192.

24. Samuel A. Stouffer and Paul F. Lazarsfeld, *Research Memorandum on the Family in the Depression* (New York: SSRC, 1937).

25. Lazarsfeld oral history interview, Columbia, p. 145.

26. *JAP* 23 (Feb. 1939); *JAP* 24 (Dec. 1940).

27. Paul F. Lazarsfeld, *Radio and the Printed Page* (New York: Arno Press and New York Times, [1940] 1971), pp. 157–169.

28. Paul F. Lazarsfeld, "Interchangeability of Indices in the Measurement of Economic Influences," *JAP* 23 (1939):33–45. See also Hortense Horwitz and Elias Smith, "The Interchangeability of Socioeconomic Indices," in *The Language of Social Research*, pp. 73–77.

29. Lazarsfeld, *Radio and the Printed Page*, pp. 13–14.

30. Paul F. Lazarsfeld, "Radio Research and Applied Psychology: Introduction by the Guest Editor," *JAP* 23 (1939), pp. 1–7.

31. Stouffer and Lazarsfeld, *Family in the Depression*, p. 199.

32. Paul F. Lazarsfeld, "The Change of Opinion during a Political Discussion," *JAP* 23 (1939):131–147, esp. p. 144.

33. Marjorie Fleiss, "The Panel as an Aid in Measuring Effects of Advertising," *JAP* 24 (1940):685–695.

34. Paul F. Lazarsfeld and Marjorie Fiske, "The 'Panel' as a New Tool for Measuring Opinion," *POQ* 2 (1938):596–612.

35. Hazel Gaudet, "The Favorite Radio Program," *JAP* 23 (1939):115–126; Isabelle F. Wagner, "Articulate and Inarticulate Replies to Questionnaires," *JAP* 23 (1939):104–115; Hadley Cantril and Hazel Gaudet, "Familiarity as a Factor in Determining the Selection and Enjoyment of Radio Programs," *JAP* 23 (1939):85–94. The last involved some observation of experimental change.

36. Lazarsfeld, "Change of Opinion." The two instances are Paul F. Lazarsfeld, "'Panel' Studies," *POQ* 4 (1940):122–128, and Paul F. Lazarsfeld, "Repeated Interviews as a Tool for Studying Changes in Opinion and Their Causes," *American Statistical Association Bulletin* 2 (1941):3–7.

37. Lazarsfeld, "'Panel' Studies."

38. Telephone interview with Richard Centers, Dec. 7, 1979; personal interview with Lloyd A. Free, March 7, 1979; telephone interviews with Free, July 13 and July 17, 1979; personal interview with Albert H. Hastorf, Dec. 4, 1979.

39. A. Lawrence Lowell, *Public Opinion and Popular Government* (New York: Longmans [1913], 1926); James Bryce, *The American Commonwealth* (New York: Macmillan Co., [1888], 1931–33).

40. Hadley Cantril, *The Human Dimension: Experiences in Policy Research* (New Brunswick, N.J.: Rutgers University Press, 1967), p. 167.

41. Ibid., p. 22.

42. Hadley Cantril, "General and Specific Attitudes," *Psychological Monographs* 42 (1932), no. 5, whole no. 192; Gordon W. Allport and P. E. Vernon, *A Study of Values* (Boston: Houghton Mifflin Co., 1931).

43. Hadley Cantril, "The Social Psychology of Everyday Life," *Psychological Bulletin* 31 (1934):297–330.

44. These questions are published in George Gallup, *The Gallup Poll: Public Opinion 1935–1971* (New York: Random House, 1972), vol. 1, pp. 576, 560, 562, 625, 632, 689, 696, 700, 726, 729.

45. See also Paul F. Lazarsfeld, presidential address, "The Obligations of the 1950 Pollster to the 1984 Historian," *POQ* 14 (1950):617–638. Most of his suggestions bore on political topics, but he too commended including the concerns of anthropologists about American family structure, generations, resolution of conflict, occupational choice, complaints of children within and across cultures, etc.

46. Hadley Cantril, *The Pattern of Human Concerns* (New Brunswick, N.J.: Rutgers University Press, 1965).

47. Cantril and Allport, *Psychology of Radio*, p. 90.

48. Hadley Cantril, Hazel Gaudet, and Herta Herzog, *The Invasion from Mars: A Study in the Psychology of Panic* (Princeton: Princeton University Press, 1940).

49. Hadley Cantril, "The Bombardment of Ballots," *New York Times Magazine*, June 14, 1936, p. 22.

50. Cantril, *The Human Dimension*, p. 23.

51. This chronology is established in Lazarsfeld, "A Memoir." The project is occasionally identified as the Office of Radio Research before this change, but for the far greater part that name is associated with the Columbia University period from 1940, with the Princeton Radio Research Project title identifying it in 1937–39.

52. Personal interview with Lloyd A. Free, Mar. 7, 1979; telephone interview with John Harding, Oct. 22, 1979.

53. Lazarsfeld, "A Memoir," p. 310.

54. Personal interview with Marjorie Fiske, May 11, 1978.

55. Personal interview with Free, Mar. 7, 1979. Free's work is acknowledged in Lazarsfeld, *Radio and the Printed Page*.

56. Lazarsfeld, "A Memoir," p. 317.

57. Ibid., p. 313.

58. Theodore M. Newcomb and Eugene L. Hartley, *Readings in Social Psychology*, rev. ed. (New York: Henry Holt & Co. [1947], 1952), pp. 198–207.

59. Cantril, Gaudet, and Herzog, *Invasion from Mars*, pp. 55–63.

60. Ibid., pp. 155 ff.

61. Hadley Cantril, "Identification with Social and Economic Class," *JASP* 38 (1943):74–80.

62. Richard Centers, *The Psychology of Social Classes: A Study of Class Consciousness* (Princeton: Princeton University Press, 1949).

63. Cantril, Gaudet, and Herzog, *Invasion from Mars*, pp. xiii–xiv.

64. Hadley Cantril, *The Psychology of Social Movements* (New York: Wiley, 1941). Cantril's last article on radio was "The Role of the Radio Commentator," *POQ* 3 (1939):654–662.

65. Personal interview with Free, Mar. 7, 1979.

66. Barry D. Karl and Stanley N. Katz, "The American Private Philanthropic Foundation and the Public Sphere 1890–1930," *Minerva* 19 (1981):236–270, esp. p. 268.

67. Gerard B. Lambert, *All out of Step: A Personal Chronicle* (Garden City, N.Y.: Doubleday & Co., 1956). Lambert quotes letters from President Roosevelt thanking him for funding OPOR studies. See esp. pp. 270–272.

68. Hadley Cantril, "Public Opinion in Flux," *Annals of the American Academy of Political and Social Science*, 22 (March 1942):136–152. These questions were asked by Gallup's AIPO or Cantril's OPOR.

69. Ibid.

70. Personal interview with Free, Mar. 7, 1979.

71. Personal interview with Rensis Likert, Oct. 19, 1976. Sydney Roslow was a graduate student at Columbia at the time and worked at the Psychological Corporation. He suspects that the chairman objected more to Likert's making extra money outside the department than to graduate students working or manifesting enthusiasm for the research project (telephone interview with Sydney Roslow, July 6, 1979).

72. The organization is now known as the Life Insurance Agency Management Association, Hartford, Connecticut.

73. Leonard W. Ferguson, "A Look across the Years 1920 to 1950," in *Appli-*

cations of Psychology: Essays to Honor Walter V. Bingham, ed. L. L. Thurstone (New York: Harper, 1952), p. 5.

74. Rensis Likert and J. M. Willits, *Morale and Agency Management*, 4 pts. (Hartford, Conn.: Life Insurance Sales Research Bureau, 1940), pt. 1, pp. 14–17.

75. Ibid., pt. 3, pp. 11–12.

76. Rensis Likert, *New Patterns of Management* (New York: McGraw-Hill Book Co., 1961).

77. Likert and Willits, *Morale and Agency Management*, pt. 1, pp. 28–38 and Appendix.

78. Ibid., pt. 1, p. 10.

79. Rensis Likert, "Democracy in Agriculture: Why and How?" in *Farmers in a Changing World: 1940 Yearbook of Agriculture*, USDA (Washington, D.C., 1940), p. 1000.

80. Rensis Likert, "The Sample Interview Survey: A Fundamental Tool of the Social Sciences," in *Current Trends in Psychology*, ed. W. D. Dennis (Pittsburgh: University of Pittsburgh Press, 1947), pp. 196–225.

81. Interview with F. F. Elliott, conducted by Thelma A. Dreis, Apr. 8, 1948, Dreis supporting documents (a collection of materials that Dr. Dreis had used in preparing "The Department of Agriculture's Sample Interview Survey as a Tool of Administration" [Ph.D. diss., American University, Washington, D.C., 1950], and which she kindly gave to me).

82. To Edward De S. Brunner from M. L. Wilson, July 10, 1939, and to Robert S. Lynd from M. L. Wilson, July 10, 1939, both RG 16, Outgoing Correspondence, NA. Interview with Likert, Oct. 19, 1976.

83. *Annual Report 1939–40*, draft, DPS, p. 4, Dreis supporting documents.

84. Likert, "Democracy in Agriculture," p. 1001.

85. Ibid., pp. 1000–1001.

86. To Rensis Likert from S. J. Haycraft, Dec. 19, 1941, RG 83, BAE General Correspondence 1936–40, Likert folder, NA; Baker interview June 9, 1979. Other comments by old-line division personnel such as Jay Whitson and Ben Owens quoted in the Dreis dissertation reflect much the same objection.

87. *Annual Report 1939–40*, draft, DPS, Dreis supporting documents.

88. Henry A. Wallace and James L. McCamy, "Straw Polls and Public Administration," *POQ* 4 (1940):221–223.

89. *Annual Report 1939–40*, draft.

90. See also Goodwin Watson, ed., *Civilian Morale* (Boston: Houghton Mifflin Co., 1942). The Harding measure of morale was taken into the field before Pearl Harbor. See John Harding, "The Measurement of Civilian Morale," in *Gauging Public Opinion*, ed. Cantril, pp. 233–258. The governmental concern with morale inspired in part the very formation of the Office of Facts and Figures and its successor, the Office of War Information (OWI).

91. Graph entitled "Appropriations Received by the Division of Program Surveys 1940–1946," the Rensis Likert Collection, Box 7, unprocessed folder, Bentley Historical Library, University of Michigan.

92. "Interviewing for Program Surveys," Oct. 13, 1942, p. 8, Historical files, ISR Library, University of Michigan.

93. Interview with Angus Campbell, Apr. 5, 1977.

5. The Wartime Experience in Policy Research

1. The *Public Opinion Quarterly* 1943 is a special issue on OWI. See also Elizabeth G. Herzog, "Pending Perfection: A Qualitative Complement to Quantitative Methods," *IJOAR* 1 (1947):31–48.

2. Terminology varies in the war years, with a number of terms used interchangeably: *attitude surveys, public opinion surveying, sample surveys,* and *sample interview surveys,* as well as *public opinion polling* and *attitude research.* The first use of *survey research* that I have come upon is a passing one in a memo of Oct. 10, 1944, Program Surveys, "The Growth of Sample Surveys as a Science," in this sentence: "Survey research will be fully scientific only when interpretations are tied down at every critical point to empirical findings" (Division of Program Surveys Memo File, ISR, p. 3). This was not yet a routine use. In a 1946 publication, Nielsen, who had been field director of Program Surveys, was still searching for a better term than *attitude surveys* to convey inquiry through personal interviews into a "wide range of data bearing on public attitudes, expectations, information, and activities as well as many items of a socio-economic character regarding each respondent." See Waldemar A. Nielsen, "Attitude Research and Government," *Journal of Social Issues* 2 (1946):2–13, p. 2, footnote.

3. John McDiarmid, "The Mobilization of Social Scientists," in *Civil Service in Wartime,* ed. Leonard D. White (Chicago: University of Chicago Press, 1945), pp. 73–96; Donald G. Marquis, "Social Psychologists in National War Agencies," *Psychological Bulletin* 41 (1944):115–126.

4. The *main* governmental organizations conducting opinion research were these seven: (1) Division of Program Surveys, Department of Agriculture; (2) Surveys Division, OWI; (3) Office of Civilian Requirements, Civilian Relations Branch, War Production Board; (4) Research Branch, Morale Division, War Department; (5) Committee on Food Habits, National Research Council; (6) Special Surveys Division, Bureau of the Census; and (7) Surveys Division, Information Department, Office of Price Administration (Julian L. Woodward, "Making Government Opinion Research Bear upon Operations," *ASR* 9 (1944):670–677.) There were others: a survey group in the Psychological Warfare Division of the Supreme Headquarters Allied Expeditionary Force (SHAEF); and a Public Affairs Division in the Department of State, for which NORC did fieldwork.

5. This is a rough estimate of reports, not of separate surveys put into the field, which is a considerably smaller number. The Research Branch produced more than 300 "manuscript reports." NORC lists 160 wartime studies, many of which were done for OWI. The Division of Program Surveys produced several hundred reports and memos.

6. Samuel A. Stouffer, Edward A. Suchman, Leland C. DeVinney, Shirley A. Star, and Robin M. Williams, Jr., *The American Soldier,* vol. 1, *Adjustment During Army Life* (New York: Wiley, Science Editions, 1949), p. 19.

7. Marquis, "Social Psychologists"; Stouffer et al., *American Soldier,* vol. 1, chap. 1, esp. p. 26.

8. Charles S. Hyneman, "The Political Scientist and National Service in War Time," *APSR* 36 (1942):931–945; Major Harvey Walter, "Political Scientists in the War," *APSR* 36 (1942):728–733. The Chicago political science tradition was

a source of personnel. Harold F. Gosnell, David Truman, Gabriel A. Almond, Harold Lasswell, and others became connected with government opinion research in one way or another during the war. According to Somit and Tanenhaus, Merriam's influence on the discipline was somewhat played out by 1930, when a countercurrent emphasizing public policy, public service, and popular political education competed successfully with Merriam's interest in empirical research into politics. Not until well after the war did quantitative research again prosper in political science, despite Gosnell's prewar work *Non-Voting*, 1924; *Getting out the Vote*, 1927; *Negro Politicians*, 1935; and *Machine Politics: Chicago Model*, 1937. See Albert Somit and Joseph Tanenhaus, *The Development of Political Science: From Burgess to Behavioralism* (Boston: Allyn and Bacon, 1967). The dominance of sociologists and social psychologists was later seen by the political scientist V. O. Key, Jr., as having somewhat slowed the growth of the political field and the understanding of government. See V. O. Key, Jr., *Public Opinion and American Democracy* (New York: Knopf, 1961), preface, p. vii.

9. Somit and Tanenhaus, *Political Science*, p. 110; Harold D. Lasswell, *Psychopathology and Politics* (Chicago: University of Chicago Press, 1930); Harold D. Lasswell, *Politics: Who Gets What, When, How* (New York: Meridian, [1936] 1958).

10. In 1943, Roosevelt aides found in some data provided by Cantril ominous signs about Roosevelt's 1944 prospects for reelection, and they asked Cantril if these data gathered by Gallup could be kept out of print. Cantril cautioned them against pressuring Gallup in any way, but he agreed to call no attention to their implications. See Michael Leigh, *Mobilizing Consent: Public Opinion and American Foreign Policy, 1937–1947* (Westport, Conn.: Greenwood Press, 1976), pp. 81–82. It is interesting to note, however, that the data were indeed published. See George Gallup, *The Gallup Poll: Public Opinion 1937–71* (New York: Random House, 1972), vol. 1, p. 371, "March 1, Franklin Roosevelt."

11. Sheldon Menefee, "Recruiting an Opinion Field Staff," *POQ* 8 (1944):262–299, describes the field staff as OPOR's, but Free says that it was operated through the Research Council (personal interview with Lloyd A. Free, Mar. 7, 1979). After the war, OPOR's main task was compiling an archive of public opinion data: Hadley Cantril, ed., with Mildred Strunk, *Public Opinion: 1935–1946* (Princeton, N.J.: Princeton University Press, 1951).

12. To Gen. George C. Marshall, from Elmo Roper, Apr. 9, 1941. AG. 353.8, RG 407, Modern Military History, Modern Military Branch, Military Archives, NA.

13. The organizational name changes are confusing. A morale organization was created in the Adjutant General's Office on July 20, 1940, and reorganized on Mar. 14, 1941, as the Morale Branch, under the jurisdiction of the Chief of Staff. On Sept. 5, 1941, Gen. Frederick H. Osborn was named chief of the Morale Branch. This took on a succession of names—Special Services Branch, Special Service Division, Morale Services Division, and, finally, Information and Education Division (see War Department Special Staff, "History of Research Branch, Information and Education Division," Feb. 1946, Appendix I, unpublished, on file at Center of Military History, Department of the Army, 20 Massachusetts Ave., Washington, D.C. A Xeroxed copy can be requested of MMB, NA).

Frederick H. Osborn, "Recreation, Welfare, and Morale of the American Soldier," the *Annals of the American Academy of Political and Social Sciences* 220 (1942):50–56; Gene M. Lyons, *The Uneasy Partnership: Social Science and the Federal Government in the Twentieth Century* (New York: Russell Sage Foundation, 1969), pp. 102–108.

The formation of the Research Branch was facilitated by the Joint Army and Navy Committee for Welfare and Recreation, which had been set up in February 1941 and of which Frederick H. Osborn was chairman. With a grant obtained from the Carnegie Corporation of New York, this committee performed various good offices, including paying Samuel Stouffer's salary in the early months and paying for civilian consultants. See "History of Research Branch," p. 13; Osborn, "Morale of the American Soldier," p. 54.

The Department of the Navy's opinion research appears to have been modest in scope. A private advertising agency was used to develop its recruiting and informational problems. The navy conducted surveys among civilian employees in navy docks and yards, but whether it did so among military personnel is not clear. See Harwood L. Childs, "Public information and opinion," *APSR* 37 (1943):56–68; Harold F. Gosnell and Moyca C. David, "Public Opinion Research in Government," *APSR* 43 (1949):564–572.

14. To Assistant Chief of Staff from Gen. E. B. Gregory, Apr. 22, 1941; to Chief of Staff from Gen. Wade H. Haislip, Apr. 25, 1941, AG 353.8, RG 407, MMB, NA; Memorandum for the Adjutant General from Lt. Col. S. R. Mickelson, May 23, 1941, AG 014.35, RG 407, MMB, NA.

15. Stouffer et al., *American Soldier*, vol. 1, p. 12.

16. The euphemisms *planning survey* and *panel survey* were used to circumvent the prohibition. "History of Research Branch," 1946, pp. 18–19; "Planning Survey," report no. 1, Feb. 5, 1942, RG 330, Box 989, MMB, NA.

17. "Planning Survey," ibid.

18. Interview with Elmo Roper, Aug. 14, 1968, conducted by Robert O. Carlson (to be deposited in the AAPOR archive being established at the University of Chicago, Regenstein Library). I am indebted to Burns W. Roper for making a copy of the taped interview available to me. See Stouffer et al., *American Soldier*, vol. 1, p. 19; memo to Gen. Osborn from Samuel Stouffer, Aug. 27, 1942, Samuel A. Stouffer Collection, Nathan Pusey Library, Harvard University, 31.8 Box 1, 1942–45. In consultation with Roper and Stanton, a plan was developed to conduct studies by "remote control," i.e., with personnel attached to the units in question. This was abandoned in favor of using branch personnel dispatched from headquarters, which recruited local staff on a temporary basis.

19. Robin W. Williams, Jr., "Field Observations and Surveys in Combat Zones," *Social Psychology Quarterly* 47 (1984):186–192, esp. p. 187. See also "History of Research Branch," p. 9.

20. Frederick H. Osborn and Gladys C. Schwesinger, eds., *Heredity and Environment* (New York: Macmillan Co., 1933); Frank Lorimer and Frederick H. Osborn, *Dynamics of Population* (New York: Macmillan Co., 1934). Harold F. Gosnell, "Development of Public Opinion Research in the Domestic Field 1941–43," Jan. 31, 1944, RG 51, Series 41.3, Unit 156, NA.

21. Personal interview with John A. Clausen, May 30, 1980. General Mac-

Arthur went over the questionnaire personally and deleted questions bearing on officers and leadership. See also John A. Clausen, "Research on the American Soldier as a Career Contingency," *Social Psychology Quarterly* 47 (1984):207–213, esp. p. 209. On Stouffer's role see "History of Research Branch," p. 12.

22. Personal interview with Jack Elinson, May 16, 1977; interview with John A. Clausen, May 30, 1980.

23. Interview with M. Brewster Smith, May 27, 1980.

24. Stouffer et al., *American Soldier*, vol. 1, p. 30.

25. Ibid., pp. 8, 309–311. Also, Stouffer et al., *Measurement and Prediction*, esp. chaps. 15 and 16 by Clausen on postwar plans and chap. 14 by Star on psychoneurotic screening.

26. Samuel A. Stouffer, Arthur A. Lumsdaine, Marion Harper Lumsdaine, Robin M. Williams, Jr., M. Brewster Smith, Irving L. Janis, Shirley A. Star, and Leonard S. Cottrell, Jr., *The American Soldier: Combat and Its Aftermath*, vol. 2 (Princeton, N.J.: Princeton University Press, 1949), p. 548.

27. Stouffer et al., *American Soldier*, vol. 1, pp. 379–382.

28. United States Government Historical Reports on War Administration, Bureau of the Budget, *The United States at War* (Washington, D.C., June 1946), chap. 8, "Informing the Public," pp. 203–233. (E. Pendleton Herring was chairman of this committee, which included, among others, Harold F. Gosnell and V. O. Key, Jr.; see p. xi.) Nelson Rockefeller headed the Office of Coordinator of Inter-American Affairs, and Donovan headed the Office of Coordinator of Information. The two other major domestic agencies were the Office of Emergency Management (1941–42) and the Office of Government Reports (1939–42). See William E. Daugherty, "U.S. Psychological Warfare Organizations in World War II," in *A Psychological Warfare Casebook*, ed. Daugherty and Morris Janowitz, published for Operations Research Office (Baltimore, Md.: Johns Hopkins University Press, 1958), pp. 126–135. See also references in note 58.

29. Archibald MacLeish, well-known poet and Librarian of Congress for the previous two years, was a vigorous spokesman for American intervention in the war. Much of the design for the Bureau of Intelligence had been developed by Harold D. Lasswell, who suggested to MacLeish that Keith Kane head the Bureau of Intelligence. See Childs, "Public Information and Opinion"; Gosnell, "Development," pp. 14–17. See also three memos to Herring from Gosnell, Jan. 16, 1943, re interview with Elmo Wilson; Dec. 22, 1942, re interview with Samuel Stouffer; and, same date, re interview with John Fleming, RG 51, Unit 153a, NA.

30. The organizational names can be rather confusing here. The Polls Division was also known as the Polling Division and the Extensive Surveys Division; the Surveys Division was also known as the Intensive Surveys Division. When the contract with the Surveys Division/Program Surveys was canceled, the single remaining opinion research organization in OWI was named the OWI Surveys Division. Program Surveys continued to function in its home base, the Bureau of Agricultural Economics, Department of Agriculture.

31. Marquis, "Social Psychologists," p. 118; to Herring from Gosnell, Dec. 26, 1942, re interview with Leonard Cottrell, RG 51, Unit 153c, NA.

32. To Keith Kane from Paul F. Lazarsfeld, June 18, 1942, and July 1, 1942, DPS Memo File, ISR. A "production flow chart" of the Bureau of Intelligence after the severing of the Program Surveys contract shows the market research organizational model. See Alan Barth, "The Bureau of Intelligence," *POQ* 7 (1943):75. Social scientists tended to show strong interest in *direct* contact with the client or user. See indications in the Research Branch writings, e.g. Samuel A. Stouffer, "Studying the Attitudes of Soldiers," *Proceedings of the American Philosophical Society* 92 (1948):336–340; William McPeak, "Problems of Field Management in Army Opinion Research," *JASA* 40 (1945):247–248; Robin M. Williams, Jr., "Some Observations on Sociological Research in Government during World War II," *ASR* 11 (1946):573–577.

33. Gosnell, "Development," p. 36; personal interview with Daniel Katz, Jan. 28, 1977; personal interview with Herbert Hyman, June 27–28, 1977.

34. Personal interview with Leslie Kish, June 28, 1979; personal interview with Angus Campbell and Dorwin P. Cartwright, Apr. 5, 1977.

35. Interview with Dorwin P. Cartwright, Apr. 5, 1977; interview with Ernest R. Hilgard, May 8, 1978. Among those transferring to Wilson's division were Daniel Katz, Herbert Hyman, Julian L. Woodward, John W. Riley, Jr. and Ernest Hilgard.

36. To Herring from Gosnell, Nov. 13, 1942, re interview with Gardner Cowles, RG 51, Unit 153a, NA. Cowles reported that he had independent advice from Gallup, Roper, and Cantril that the Likert operation was more extensive than was necessary; that he (Cowles) supported Kane also to show confidence in his subordinates; and that Likert had asked him to look over his work more carefully but that he (Cowles) had not had the time to do so.

Kane apparently wanted the Surveys Division to come as a body into the Bureau of Intelligence, severing its connection with BAE, USDA. Minutes taken on a staff discussion of the problem report that both Kane and Likert felt that their respective organizations would probably continue after the war (neither Kane nor Likert was at the meeting). Likert was thought to have hopes that Program Surveys would become a central research agency of the government after the war, serving all administrators ("Meeting on Future of Program Surveys," July 2, 1942, Rensis Likert Collection, Box 7, unprocessed, Bentley Historical Library, University of Michigan).

The new OWI Surveys Division had a central staff of forty-three and a field staff of twenty-five, about twice the size that it had been before the reorganization; Program Surveys was cut to about seventy-five, less than half its former size. The new Surveys Division continued to be located in New York, "because the polling people were there, Roper and Gallup," and because it was deemed easier to get coders, locate office space, and conduct pretesting there. It was located in the same building as the NORC New York office. See memo to Herring from Gosnell, Jan. 16, 1943, re interview with Elmo Wilson, RG 51, Unit 153c, NA.

Wilson later went on to a very successful career as director of research for CBS and as the organizer of an international network of market research firms. Rensis Likert went on to a very successful career as the director of the Institute for Social Research, with a research specialty in organizational theory.

37. Elmo C. Wilson and Daniel Katz, "Absenteeism in War Industry," *Survey*

Graphic 32 (1943):345–347; Daniel Katz and Herbert Hyman, "Industrial Morale and Public Opinion Methods," *IJOAR* (1947):13–30.

38. Robert K. Merton, Marjorie Fiske, and Alberta Curtis, *Mass Persuasion: The Social Psychology of a Bond Drive* (New York: Harper, 1946); Dorwin Cartwright, "Some Principles of Mass Persuasion: Selected Findings of Research on the Sale of United States War Bonds" [1949], in *Public Opinion and Propaganda*, ed. Daniel Katz, Dorwin Cartwright, Samuel Eldersveld and Alfred McClung Lee (New York: Dryden, 1954), pp. 382–393; Cartwright, "Surveys of the War Finance Program," in *Measurement of Consumer Interest*, ed. C. West Churchman, Russell L. Ackoff, and Murray Wax (Philadelphia: University of Pennsylvania Press, 1947), pp. 198–209. See also Peter H. Odegard and Alan Barth, "Millions for Defense," *POQ* 5 (1941):399–411. Advertising efforts and the organization of local and state committees were both already in place in 1941; Daniel Katz, "The Surveys Division of OWI: Governmental Use of Research for Informational Problems," in *How to Conduct Consumer and Opinion Research*, ed. Albert B. Blankenship (New York: Harper, 1946), pp. 241–250.

39. United States Strategic Bombing Survey, Morale Division, *The Effects of Strategic Bombing on German Morale*, vol. 1 (Washington, D.C.: U.S. Government Printing Office, May 1947), p. 1. The idea of assessing the bombing originated within the Army Air Force. Such a postbattle evaluation was not unusual in the military; what was novel was the civilian direction and the status as a presidential commission. See David MacIsaac, *Strategic Bombing in World War Two: The Story of the United States Strategic Bombing Survey* (New York: Garland, 1976), p. 22.

40. The morale studies called upon other data as well, such as written questionnaires from 2,000 foreign workers in Germany, the content analysis of captured German letters, and other interviews, documents, and statistical studies. See also Helen Peak, "Observations on the Characteristics and Distribution of German Nazis," *Psychological Monographs* 59 (1945):1–44; H. L. Ansbacher, "The Problem of Interpreting Attitude Survey Data: A Case Study of the Attitudes of Russian Workers in Wartime Germany," *POQ* 14 (1950):126–138.

41. George H. H. Huey, "Some Principles of Field Administration in Large-Scale Surveys," *POQ* 11 (1947–48):254–263, esp. p. 256.

42. Rensis Likert was one of the twelve-man USSBS Board, and he organized the staff for Germany and Japan. Harold Nisselson and Morris Hansen of the Census Bureau directed the sampling in Japan. See Huey, "Principles of Field Administration"; also, staff members listed in Richard Boyd and Herbert Hyman, "Survey Research," in *Strategies of Inquiry*, Handbook of Political Science, vol. 7, ed. Fred I. Greenstein and Nelson W. Polsby (Reading, Mass.: Addison-Wesley, 1975), p. 313.

43. The United States Strategic Bombing Survey, Morale Division, *The Effects of Strategic Bombing on Japanese Morale* (Washington, D.C.: U.S. Government Printing Office, June 1947), p. 56; USSBS, *German Morale*, vol. 1, p. 1. Irving L. Janis, in *Air War and Emotional Stress: Psychological Studies of Bombing and Civilian Defense* (New York: McGraw-Hill, 1951), reviews some evidence on the British experience; see pp. 127–128, 139, 153–179. The "trekking" described on p. 139 was the response of Londoners who in the spring of 1941 left the city every night by the thousands but came back to work the next morning.

Mark Abrams, a well-known British market researcher, has recently observed that "what was needed urgently was to know [what] the impact of this bombing [was] on the civilian behaviour. And so, I did surveys. . . . The conclusion I arrived at . . . was that if you bomb civilians who think they are making an important contribution to their country's victory, you'll get nowhere; you'll kill some of them; the others will go away for a few nights, but then they will come back and work harder. If you bomb a civilian body which thinks it's making no contribution to the war, they will clear away in three nights, but it will make no difference to the nation's ability to fight the war, because they were not contributing anyway. This proved true in Korea and it proved true in Vietnam; I think in every major conflict where someone has attempted to bomb the civilian population that has held true. It was not a particularly popular finding as far as British Bomber Command was concerned (they wanted to use their bombs)" (*Market Research Society Newsletter*, no. 149, Aug. 1978, p. 9). I have been unable to obtain copies of the wartime surveys Abrams refers to.

44. See Boyd and Hyman, "Survey Research," pp. 312–315, which builds on the morale reports; Harrison E. Salisbury, *Without Fear or Favor* (New York: Times Books, 1980), p. 190; and Anthony Lewis, "For the Sake of Israel," *New York Times*, July 26, 1981, p. E-21, are probably both building on John Kenneth Galbraith's memoir, *A Life in Our Times* (Boston: Houghton Mifflin Co., 1981). Galbraith was on the USSBS Board and was responsible for assessing overall economic effects. He notes wryly that "it could be argued that the effect of the air attacks was to increase German airplane output," because the attacks resulted in the replacement of the incompetent Goering with the more able Speer (p. 215; see also pp. 204–205). Galbraith is trying to puncture two claims that he thinks were exaggerated: one, the claim that Germany was a well-managed economy; two, the Air Force's implicit claim that saturation bombing virtually won the war singlehandedly. He acknowledges that morale was damaged by the bombing, however.

A persisting confusion involves the definition of morale, which in the Morale Reports themselves was largely a psychological, attitudinal one. In other reports of USSBS, morale is sometimes treated as a behavioral variable. MacIsaac found the Morale Division's definition of morale to be essentially trivial, yielding findings of "little more than academic interest" (*Strategic Bombing*, p. 115, note 32), a view that does not seem warranted but that shows the difference in measures and interpretations.

45. The Japanese morale report also presents a measure of personal loss but does not use it in the published analysis (USSBS, Morale Division, *The Effects of Strategic Bombing on Japanese Morale* [Washington, D.C., June 1947], Appendixes J and M).

46. USSBS, Morale Division, *The Effects of Strategic Bombing on German Morale*, vol. 1 (Washington, D.C., May 1947), p. 1. Cities were classed into four categories of average tonnage dropped: IV: None (unbombed); III: 500 tons; II: 6,000 tons; and I: 30,000 tons or more. In Germany (only), the sharpest decline in morale was observed between the first and second categories, after which increased bombing affected morale at sharply diminishing rates. At the highest levels of bombing tonnage, on the step up from 6,000 to 30,000 tons, there was

no observable effect on morale on four of fourteen different measures; on nine of the measures there were very slight increases in morale. See USSBS, *German Morale*, chap. 3, tables 23, 24, 25, 26, 27, 28A, 28B, 29, 30, 31A, 31B, 32A, 32B, and 33. Morale declined linearly only in table 32B.

47. USSBS, *German Morale*, vol. 1, pp. 23–24.

48. USSBS, *Overall Report (European War)*, Office of the Chairman (Washington, D.C., Sept. 30, 1945), p. 74; USSBS, *German Morale*, vol. 1, p. 30.

49. USSBS, *German Morale*, pp. 30–31.

50. Ibid., p. 1. David MacIsaac, a leading scholar of USSBS, notes that "most of the widely read reports are in that sanitized style wherein we of the twentieth century have learned to describe the indescribably horrible." He points to a notable exception in the photographs in one USSBS report, *The Effects of Bombing on Health and Medical Care in Germany*, which equal or exceed the horror of photographs from Dachau or Auschwitz (MacIsaac, *Strategic Bombing*, p. 215, note 13). Irving L. Janis, in *Air War*, pp. 138–152, cites evidence from the morale reports themselves to demur from the conclusion advocating lighter raids.

51. Boyd and Hyman, "Survey Research," pp. 313–315. These are complex matters. MacIsaac notes that airmen knew that "enemy civilian morale could be affected decisively only when the extent and weight of attack reached proportions altogether unacceptable to the humanitarian instincts of the governments and peoples the bombers were *defending*." His own considered conclusion from the World War II bombing was that "decisive results can be expected only when bombing attacks are repeated, sustained, and heavy," not from sporadic attacks (MacIsaac, *Strategic Bombing*, p. 164). Stewart Alsop, in *The Center: People and Power in Political Washington* (New York: Harper & Row, 1968), reflected on the "humanitarian instincts" that MacIsaac refers to: "Production declined and morale began to disintegrate only after the really brutal—and morally repugnant—bombing of population centers began" (p. 163).

John Kenneth Galbraith recalls that his own reactions to bombing in Germany were not as distressed because "one still had feelings of fear and relief that [Hitler and the Nazis] were vanquished. For Japan one had only sympathy and sorrow. . . . [In a first draft of my comments on the bombing of Japan] I had described it as 'this appalling business,' which was how anyone of any sensitivity would have felt" (Galbraith, *A Life in Our Times*, p. 233). It seems very likely that Galbraith's reaction was shared by many because of the atomic bombing in particular and also because even the conventional bombing had caused more massive loss of life and property in Japan. The one-volume morale report on Japan is longer than the two-volume report on Germany. Most of the photographs do not show evidence of damage, but some of the prose does, because a fair amount of open-ended material is included which conveys civilian terror and loss. James Stern's book *The Hidden Damage* (New York: Harcourt, Brace and Company, 1947) conveys some of the same personal accounts from the German experience.

52. Across thirteen morale measures, nine showed fairly regular declines in morale across five strata of increasing tonnage/damage/city size. One of these showed a sharp decline of 34 percent (table 44). The other eight showed declines of from 9 to 15 percent (tables 29, 33A, 35, 36, 38, 40, 42, and 46). The remain-

ing four tables showed irregular patterns. The city bombing measure in Japan was constructed by arranging cities in five strata indexing bomb tonnage, estimated damage, and city size (USSBS, *Japanese Morale*, chap. 5).

53. See tables 38, 30, 32A, 32B, 34, 37, 39, 41, 43, 45, 47A, and 47B in chap. 5. On all twelve measures, the Personally Bombed showed levels of morale lower than those of the Unbombed; on ten of the measures those differences ranged from 4 to 10 percent.

54. USSBS, *Japanese Morale*, pp. 54–57; the USSBS *Summary Report (Pacific War)*, Office of the Chairman, points to *excessive* bombing: "We underestimated the ability of our air attack on Japan's home islands, coupled as it was with blockade and previous military defeats, to achieve unconditional surrender without invasion" (p. 29). The report cites inadequate intelligence on Japan's economy and morale.

55. USSBS, *Japanese Morale*, p. 4. USSBS morale findings in Japan after the war were in agreement with evidence collected by the Foreign Analysis Morale Division (FMAD) of OWI during the war, especially from interviews with Japanese prisoners of war. After the war, Alexander H. Leighton published key findings of the FMAD report—distrusted and delayed by higher-level policymakers—alongside USSBS findings to show their close comparability. See Alexander H. Leighton, *Human Relations in a Changing World: Observations on the Use of the Social Sciences* (New York: E. P. Dutton, 1949), esp. chap. 3.

56. USSBS, Office of the Chairman, *The Effect of Atomic Bombs on Hiroshima and Nagasaki* (Washington, D.C., June 30, 1946), p. 23. Only 3 of the 108 reports on the Pacific war were issued by the Office of the Chairman: this, the *Summary Report (Pacific War)*, and *Japan's Struggle to End the War*. Only three of the 208 reports on the European war were from that office.

57. As Lauder notes, "There is no common agreement on what the Survey says, let alone how its findings should be applied to contemporary situations" (p. 773). The USSBS was cited by opposing sides in the 1949 controversy on the B-36 bomber (the navy and the air force). See John A. Lauder, "Lessons of the Strategic Bombing Survey for Contemporary Defense Policy," *Orbis* 18 (1974):770–790. See also MacIsaac, *Strategic Bombing*, p. 168.

58. Sydney Weinberg, "What to Tell America: The Writers' Quarrel in the Office of War Information," *Journal of American History* 55 (1968):73–89, p. 83; Allan M. Winkler, *The Politics of Propaganda: The Office of War Information 1942–1945* (New Haven, Conn.: Yale University Press, 1978), pp. 66–69; Harold F. Gosnell and Moyca C. David, "Public Opinion Research in the Government," *APSR* 43 (1949):564–572, p. 567. See also note 59.

59. The OWI Domestic Branch's request for $8.9 million was cut to $2.9 million. OWI's difficulties in winter-spring 1943 were compounded of several factors: (1) congressional distrust of wartime propaganda in general, which had been centralized during World War I under the Creel Committee and which had come under much criticism; (2) a genuine desire of congressmen to cut wartime budgets; (3) a new conservative majority in Congress from the 1942 election, with a determination to end the New Deal; (4) conflicts within OWI; and (5) personnel problems. None of the four directors of the OWI Domestic Branch served a full twelve months (see Jones, below, p. 447). See Winkler, *Politics of*

Propaganda, esp. chap. 2; Weinberg, "Writers' Quarrel"; Richard W. Steele, "Preparing the Public for War: Efforts to Establish a National Propaganda Agency, 1940–41," *American Historical Review* 75 (1970):1640–1653; David Lloyd Jones, "The U.S. Office of War Information and American Public Opinion during World War II, 1939–45" (Ph.D. diss., State University of New York at Binghamton, 1976); Harold F. Gosnell, "Obstacles to Domestic Pamphleteering by OWI in World War II," *Journalism Quarterly* 23 (1946):360–369.

60. L. E. Gleeck, "Ninety-six Congressmen make up their minds," *POQ* 4 (1940):3–24; Winston Allard, "Congressional Attitudes toward Public Opinion Polls," *Journalism Quarterly* 18 (1941):47–50; George F. Lewis, Jr., "The Congressmen Look at the Polls," *POQ* 4 (1940):229–231; Martin Kriesberg, "What Congressmen and Administrators Think of the Polls," *POQ* 9 (1945):333–337.

61. Congress appropriated $2 million less than OWI had requested, and it was decided that the Bureau of Intelligence should take a large share of the reduction. Cowles had been advised by pollsters that the government polls were too expensive and that more reliance could be placed on the commercial agencies. Cowles felt that OWI should not get into survey work that bore on policy and should avoid contention with Congress by limiting itself to information problems. Julian Woodward, Assistant Chief of the reorganized OWI Surveys Division, felt that it had not publicized its work sufficiently and had failed to gather support from those congressmen who would have been sympathetic. See Gosnell and David, "Public Opinion Research," pp. 567–569; memos to Herring from Gosnell dated July 7, 1943 (re interview with Woodward), and Mar. 18, 1943 (re Bureau of the Budget Hearings), RG 51, Unit 153c, NA. Earlier that spring, writers and advertising men had come into conflict in another bureau of OWI. The outcome was a public resignation in April 1943 of a group of writers, including Henry Pringle, Arthur M. Schlesinger, Jr., and others, with a statement to the press that "the activities of OWI on the home front are now dominated by high-pressure promoters who prefer slick salesmanship to honest information. . . . They are turning this Office of War Information into an Office of War Bally-hoo" (quoted in Winkler, *Politics of Propaganda*, p. 65).

Twenty years later, Schlesinger noted, "I [did not] recognize that the conservative gains in the congressional elections of 1942 were forcing the administration to retreat all along the line and to abandon exposed and expendable positions like, I fear, the writer's bureau of OWI" (quoted in Weinberg, "Writers' Quarrel," p. 88).

62. Report no. 1511, May 25, 1944, National War Agencies Appropriations Bill, 1945, pp. 21–27, *House Miscellaneous Reports III*, 78th Cong. 2d sess., 1944. The budget for the Domestic Branch OWI was cut to $2.2 million, down $502,000 from the 1944 funds. The item for the Surveys Division was eliminated.

When the Surveys Division was transferred to the Bureau of Special Services, its small field staff for intensive interviewing was eliminated (Gosnell and David, "Public Opinion Research," p. 569).

63. John W. Riley, Jr., "Opinion Research in Liberated Normandy," *ASR* 12 (1947):698–703; M. I. Gurfein and Morris Janowitz, "Trends in Wehrmacht Morale," *POQ* 10 (1946):78–84; obituary of Elmo C. Wilson by Helen Dinerman, *POQ* 32 (1968):319–320.

64. Report no. 653, June 1, 1945, National War Agencies Appropriation Bill, 1946, pp. 7–9, *House Miscellaneous Reports III*, 79th Cong., 1st sess., 1945.

65. Program Surveys was succeeded immediately by the Division of Special Surveys, which was authorized to conduct studies for USDA and other agencies to "help increase the effectiveness of agricultural activities or improve services to farmers" (to assistant chiefs and division heads, from O. V. Wells, August 1, 1946 [Rensis Likert Collection, Box 7, unprocessed, Bentley Historical Library, University of Michigan]). See also Richard S. Kirkendall, *Social Scientists and Farm Politics in the Age of Roosevelt* (Columbia: University of Missouri Press, 1966), chaps. 12 and 13, esp. pp. 248–252. Late in 1945, a cultural survey project in Coahoma County, Mississippi, came to congressional attention; Secretary Anderson said that such sociological work had not had his permission, and Howard Tolley, head of BAE, stated that the work had been stopped and would not be resumed. In the spring budgetary hearings, Tolley succeeded in getting a Senate prohibition against all "social surveys" changed to "cultural surveys." But this was generally a victory for conservative farm forces, and Tolley resigned from BAE.

66. Anna J. and Richard L. Merritt, *Public Opinion in Occupied Germany: The OMGUS Surveys, 1945–1949* (Urbana: University of Illinois Press, 1970); Richard L. Merritt and Donald J. Puchala, *Western European Perspectives on International Affairs: Public Opinion Studies and Evaluations* (New York: Praeger, 1968); Leo P. Crespi, "The Influence of Military Government Sponsorship in German Opinion Polling," *IJOAR* 4 (1950):151–178; Herbert Passin, "The Development of Public Opinion Research in Japan," *IJOAR* 5:20–30; James R. Thayer, "Japanese Opinion on the Far Eastern Conflict," *POQ* 15 (1951):76–88; John W. Bennett, "Social and Attitudinal Research in Japan: The Work of SCAP's Public Opinion and Sociological Research Division," *University of Manila Journal of East Asiatic Studies* 2 (1952):21–33. An annotated bibliography of English-language studies of the occupation of Japan is extremely useful and provides other references to archives and publications of the Public Opinion and Sociological Research Division described by Bennett and Passin: Robert E. Ward and Frank Joseph Schulman, *The Allied Occupation of Japan 1945–1952* (Chicago: American Library Association, 1974).

Lloyd A. Free was the first director of the Office of International Information, which was taken over by USIA.

67. Julian L. Woodward, "Public Opinion Polls as an Aid to Democracy," *Political Science Quarterly* 61 (1945):238–246, p. 245. In January 1944, the State Department set up a public information service, which commissioned surveys from NORC, an operation that remained in place until 1957 (Gosnell and David, "Public Opinion Research," p. 571). A Troop Attitude Research Branch remained to succeed the Research Branch. See also notes 65 and 66.

68. Rensis Likert, "Opinion Studies and Government Policy," *Proceedings of the American Philosophical Society* 92 (1948):314–350. The thesis of this article was that the "sample interview survey" could make government "more responsive to the needs of those who are governed" and more efficient, especially in permitting the kind of criticism from below that Nazi Germany thwarted (p. 349); David Truman, "Public Opinion Research as a Tool of Public Administration," *Public Administration Review* 5 (1945):65–72; Hans E. Skott, "Attitude Research in the

Department of Agriculture," *POQ* 7 (1943):280–292; Woodward, "Aid to Democracy."

69. Thelma A. Dreis, "The Department of Agriculture's Sample Interview Survey as a Tool of Administration" (Ph.D. diss., American University, 1950). Dreis reviews evidence of use and nonuse of Program Surveys data by federal agency administrators.

70. Leonard W. Doob, "The Utilization of Social Scientists in the Overseas Branch of the Office of War Information," *APSR* 49 (1947):649–667; Woodward, "Operations."

71. If the morale researchers expected their findings or recommendations to be crucial in future bombing policy, they must have rather minimized the complexity of the *total* USSBS report as well as the process by which the parts were brought together. MacIsaac's judgment was that USSBS "performed a most difficult task as well as could reasonably be expected"—one that was limited by the complexity of its mandate and its organization as a "huge committee, subject to all the advantages and disadvantages that accrue to committee processes. . . . The members are always aware that a report unacceptable to the appointing authority, usually the President, will serve no useful purpose whatever; it will either be suppressed, played down, or ignored" (MacIsaac, *Strategic Bombing*, p. 163).

72. Richard Jensen, "Method and Philosophy of Early Public Opinion Polls," unpublished manuscript, 1978, pp. 16–17.

73. Key, *Public Opinion and American Democracy*, p. vii.

74. Lasswell, *Politics: Who Gets What, When, How.*

75. Samuel A. Stouffer, "Some Afterthoughts of a Contributor to *The American Soldier*," in *Continuities in Social Research: Studies in the Scope and Method of "The American Soldier*," ed. Robert K. Merton and Paul F. Lazarsfeld (Glencoe; Ill.: The Free Press, 1950), pp. 197–211.

6. The Wartime Experience in Science (I)

1. Paul F. Lazarsfeld, Bernard Berelson, and Hazel Gaudet, *The People's Choice: How the Voter Makes up His Mind in a Presidential Campaign* (New York: Columbia University Press [1944], 1948), p. vii. This book stressed the contribution. Dorwin Cartwright, in "Basic and Applied Social Psychology," *Philosophy of Science* 16 (1949):198–208, stressed the learning and the first large-scale funding of applied social psychology.

2. Robert Ford, quoted by John A. Clausen, "Research on the American Soldier as a Career Contingency," *Social Psychology Quarterly* 47 (1984):207–213, esp. p. 209.

3. Robin M. Williams, Jr., "Field Observations and Surveys in Combat Zones," *Social Psychology Quarterly* 47 (1984):186–192, esp. p. 187.

4. Samuel A. Stouffer, Edward A. Suchman, Leland C. DeVinney, Shirley A. Star, and Robin M. Williams, Jr., *The American Soldier: Adjustment during Army Life*, vol. 1 (New York: Wiley, Science Editions, 1949), pp. 37–38; Samuel A. Stouffer, "Studying the Attitudes of Soldiers," *Proceedings of the American Philosophical Society* 92 (1948):336–340.

5. Lazarsfeld et al., *The People's Choice*, pp. ix–x, 2.

6. Guttman scaling during the war simplified work he had done in the logic of measurement published in 1941. See Louis Guttman, "The Quantification of a Class of Attributes: A Theory and Method for Scale Construction," in *The Prediction of Personal Adjustment*, ed. Paul Horst (New York: SSRC, 1941), pp. 319–348.

7. Louis Guttman, "An Outline of Some New Methodology for Social Research," *POQ* 18 (1954):395–404, esp. 398.

8. Edward A Suchman, "The Utility of Scalogram Analysis," in *Measurement and Prediction*, vol. 4 in *Studies in Social Psychology in World War II*, ed. Samuel A. Stouffer, Louis Guttman, Edward A. Suchman, Paul F. Lazarfeld, Shirley A. Star, and John A. Clausen (Gloucester, Mass.: Peter Smith, [1950] 1973), p. 152.

9. The approximate nature of the single dimension is clarified by an article on scaling by Scott: "The ideal model of scalogram analysis assumes unidimensional items, which probably do not exist (since this implies that responses depend on a single attribute only, which is contrary to most psychological concepts) [p. 224]. . . . [The assumption of unidimensionality] is patently unrealistic if one takes seriously the widely held psychological principle that any response is multiply determined. At best, it is possible to construct a set of items each of which reflects the intended trait more than it reflects any other trait [p. 250]." See William A. Scott, "Attitude Measurement," in *The Handbook of Social Psychology*, 2d ed., vol. 2, ed. Gardner Lindzey and Elliot Aronson (Reading, Mass.: Addison-Wesley, 1968), pp. 204–273.

10. Samuel A. Stouffer, "An Overview of the Contributions to Scaling and Scale Theory," in *Measurement and Prediction*, ed. Stouffer et al., pp. 9–11.

11. Edward A. Suchman, "The Intensity Component in Attitude and Opinion Research," in *Measurement and Prediction*, ed. Stouffer et al., pp. 213–276, esp. p. 266 ff. See also Edward A. Suchman and Louis Guttman, "A Solution to the Problem of Question 'Bias,'" *POQ* 11 (1947):445–455, esp. p. 452. This work was done during the war; see "'Experiments on the Measurement of the Intensity Function and Zero-Point in Attitude Analysis" and "Questions and Answers about Scale Analysis," July 24, 1945, both in RG 330, Box 1004, Modern Military Branch, Military Archives Division, NA.

12. Edward A. Suchman, "The Scalogram Board Technique for Scale Analysis," in *Measurement and Prediction*, ed. Stouffer et al., pp. 91–121. The method involved making "successive approximations which will converge anyhow to the proper scale ordering—if a scale exists" (p. 102). Criteria included a coefficient of reproducibility of .85 (later .90), meaning that if 100 respondents answered 10 questions, providing a total number of responses of 1,000, a reproducibility of .90 would correctly predict from the scale scores of the respondents 900 of those answers. In addition to the criteria of a range of marginal frequencies and a scatter of error, the "number of answer categories" was a factor: "The more categories that can remain uncombined, the more credible is the inference that the universe is scalable" (p. 117). If fewer than ten items were used, it was thought important not to have only dichotomized items. *Quasi-scales* showed lower reproducibility than .90 but a scatter of error, indicating a "single dominant factor," and they could be used to explore relationships between the attitude area

and an outside variable. See also Suchman, "The Utility of Scalogram Analysis," in *Measurement and Prediction*, ed. Stouffer et al., esp. pp. 159–163.

13. Suchman, "Scalogram Technique," p. 121.

14. Suchman, "The Intensity Component," pp. 214–215. An alternative was to cast the content question as a Likert-type item (Strongly Agree . . . Strongly Disagree), which had the advantage of not lengthening the questionnaire as much as the separate intensity measures did. There were other variants on the wording of the intensity question.

15. Ibid., p. 259.

16. Daniel Katz, "The Measurement of Intensity," in *Gauging Public Opinion*, ed. Cantril et al., pp. 51–65.

17. Suchman, "The Intensity Component."

18. Stouffer, "How These Volumes Came to Be Produced," in *The American Soldier*, by Stouffer et al., vol. 1, pp. 3–53, esp. p. 46.

19. George Gallup, *A Guide to Public Opinion Polls* (Princeton: Princeton University Press [1944], 1948), p. 55.

20. *POQ* published twelve articles on Guttman scaling in the 1945–55 period; *IJOAR* published six in its five-year existence (1947–51). Stouffer's variant on Guttman scaling, called the "H" technique, involved combining three or more items in a "contrived" item to be used in the scale. See Samuel A. Stouffer, Edgar F. Borgatta, David G. Hays, and Andrew F. Henry, "A Technique for Improving Cumulative Scales," *POQ* 16 (1952):273–291. Robert N. Ford, in "A Rapid Scoring Procedure for Scaling Attitude Questions," *POQ* 14 (1950):507–532, is one of the few (besides the original writers in *Measurement and Prediction*) to make clear that Guttman scaling uses very generalized items, explaining that "the research worker prepares 10 or 12 questions bearing on one attitude. If he is interested in a general measure of Job Satisfaction, for instance, he does not ask about pay, hours, supervision, safety hazards, vacations, etc., but sticks to a more general theme, [e.g.,] 'Do you like your job,' 'Are you treated well,' etc. He expects and hopes to get a variety of percentage splits from these questions, even though they are essentially restatements of the same general questions" (p. 509). Festinger makes the same kind of clarification (see note 21).

Guttman procedures have been used not only with attitudes but also with information or *knowledge* (Suchman, "Utility of Scalogram Analysis," p. 139); *physiological symptoms* (ibid., pp. 141 ff.; Shirley A. Star, "The Screening of Psychoneurotics: Comparison of Psychiatric Diagnoses and Test Scores at All Induction Stations," in *Measurement and Prediction*, ed. Stouffer et al., pp. 548–567); reports of *behavior* (Paul Wallin, "A Guttman Scale for Measuring Women's Neighborliness," *AJS* 59 [1953]:243–246); and "collective" scales of *group behavior* (Matilda White Riley, John W. Riley, Jr., and Jackson Toby, *Sociological Studies in Scale Analysis* [New Brunswick, N.J.: Rutgers University Press, 1954]). See also Angus Campbell, Gerald Gurin, and Warren E. Miller, *The Voter Decides* (Evanston, Ill.: Row, Peterson, 1954); Samuel A. Stouffer, *Communism, Conformity, and Civil Liberties* (New York: Wiley, Science Editions [1955], 1966).

21. Leon Festinger, "The Treatment of Qualitative Data by 'Scale Analysis,'" *Psychological Bulletin* 44 (1947):149–161; Ivan D. Steiner, "Scalogram Analysis as a Tool for Selecting Poll Questions," *POQ* 19 (1955):415–424; Helen Peak,

"Problems of objective observation," in *Research Methods in the Behavioral Sciences,* ed. Leon Festinger and Daniel Katz (New York: Dryden, 1953), pp. 243–299, esp. pp. 263–266.

22. Louis Guttman, "On Festinger's Evaluation of Scale Analysis," *Psychological Bulletin* 44 (1947):451–465, esp. p. 461; Louis Guttman, "The Basis for Scalogram Analysis," in *Measurement and Prediction,* ed. Stouffer et al., pp. 60–90, esp. pp. 82–83. Changes over time in a Guttman scale of political efficacy were shown by Campbell and Converse, 1972, as one component of four pulled out of line with the others in the 1960s: "Our analysis of these trends would have been greatly muddied if we had proceeded with the composite [Guttman] scale taken as a whole" (Angus Campbell and Philip E. Converse, "Change in the American Electorate," in *The Human Meaning of Social Change,* ed. Angus Campbell and Philip E. Converse (New York: Russell Sage Foundation, 1972), p. 328.

23. This brief summary glosses over the complexities of the basic theory. Certain reviewers of Lazarsfeld's initial explanation of the model criticized the exposition and turned gratefully to Stouffer's summary, which provided some illustrations and examples, and I have done so, as well. Lazarsfeld's own summary in 1954 is a clearer version for the mathematically limited than is the initial presentation. See Ethel Shanas, review, *AJS* 57 (1952):386–388; F. Stuart Chapin, review, *ASR* 15 (1950):811–813; Stouffer, "An Overview of the Contributions to Scaling and Scale Theory," in *Measurement and Prediction,* ed. Stouffer et al.; also Stouffer, "Scaling Concepts and Scaling Theory," in *Research Methods in Social Relations,* ed. Marie Jahoda, Morton Deutsch, and Stuart W. Cook, 2 vols. (New York: Dryden, 1951); Lazarsfeld, "A Conceptual Introduction to Latent Structure Analysis," in *Mathematical Thinking in the Social Sciences,* ed. Paul F. Lazarsfeld (Glencoe, Ill.: The Free Press, 1954); Scott, "Attitude Measurement," 1968; C. A. Moser and G. Kalton, *Survey Methods in Social Investigation* (London: Heinemann, 1971), p. 372.

24. Paul F. Lazarsfeld, "The Controversy over Detailed Interviews: An Offer for Negotiation," *POQ* 8 (1944):38–60. The article is based on Lazarsfeld's own experience and admittedly brings no research to bear on any of the argument. Lazarsfeld identified Rensis Likert and certain "poll directors." The references in the article specified Hans Skott's 1943 article "Attitude Research in the Department of Agriculture," *POQ* 7 (1943):280–292, and Henry C. Link's "An Experiment in Depth Interviewing on the Issue of Internationalism vs. Isolationism," *POQ* 7 (1943):267–279. (Skott was an interviewer at Program Surveys, and Link was with the Psychological Corporation.) Lazarsfeld himself had argued about question form with Link, but probably not lately (see chap. 4).

25. "A Study of Liquid Assets: Sample Interviews Collected in Birmingham, Alabama, and Douglas County, Illinois," originally issued in Feb. 1945, DPS, USDA, p. 56, DPS Questionnaire file, ISR.

26. Carl R. Rogers, "The Nondirective Method as a Technique for Social Research," *AJS* 50 (1945):279–283. Rogers was not very involved personally, but Charles F. Cannell was, and he soon joined Program Surveys, later becoming field director.

27. See Walter Van Dyke Bingham and Bruce Victor Moore, *How to Interview,* 3d ed. (New York: Harper, 1941), chap. 10, "Public Opinion Polls and Commer-

cial Surveys," pp. 162–179, esp. the three-page treatment of "Polling public attitudes," pp. 162–164. Commercial field practice at this time was still supervised largely by mail. Joseph Bevis of the Opinion Research Corporation wrote in 1945, "In the kind of work we do—opinion surveys—there is little need for long, comprehensive instructions. The assignment sheet tells the interviewer the number and types of people he is to interview, and the questionnaire itself contains most of the instructions necessary to make the interview. In fact, we feel that the fewer instructions, the better. As a general rule, we don't want our interviewers to interpret or elaborate on the questions" (Joseph C. Bevis, "Management of Field Staffs in the Opinion Research Field," *JASA* 40 [1945]:245–246).

28. Early in 1942, Program Surveys interviewers were described as experienced in clinical psychology, market research, social casework, and anthropology. As a matter of policy, all staff members except clerical workers went into the field at some point to get personal interviewing experience ("The Role of the Division of Surveys in the Office of Facts and Figures," Apr. 20, 1942, p. 3, Rensis Likert Collection, Bentley Historical Library, University of Michigan, Box 7, unprocessed).

29. "Appraisal of the Sixth War Loan: Part I: Solicitation and Buying," Feb. 1, 1945, Study no. 118–I, and "Types of Codes Used in Program Surveys," Dec. 18, 1944, DPS Memo Collection, ISR. Two other kinds of codes were commonly used: in *scale* codes, an office coder classified the respondent's answer into one of these scale types, for example: Yes, Yes with reservations, Undecided, No with reservations, No ("Farmers' Views on Postwar Programs for Wheat," Oct. 1945, p. 24, DPS Questionnaire Collection, ISR). The *whole interview* or a subgroup of questions could be classified for the respondent's attitude or information.

30. Memo to Planning Committee from Richard Crutchfield, "Methodological Proposals Concerning Extension and Enrichment of the Studies of the Division," May 22, 1942, DPS Memo Collection, ISR.

31. Interview with Daniel Katz, Jan. 28, 1977. See, for example, "Public appreciation of the problem of inflation," Aug. 12, 1943, Surveys Division, Bureau of Special Services, OWI, on file at NORC as Study T-26. Of fifty-four questions, fifteen were cast in open format.

32. Interview with Rensis Likert, Oct. 19, 1976.

33. Dorwin P. Cartwright, "Analysis of Qualitative Material," in *Research Methods in the Behavioral Sciences*, ed. Leon Festinger and Daniel Katz (New York: Dryden, 1953), pp. 421–470; Eleanor E. Maccoby and Robert R. Holt, "How Surveys Are Made," *Journal of Social Issues* 2 (1946):45–57. The latter, which was based on Program Surveys experience, dealt with coding in a single paragraph. Lazarsfeld and his colleagues published earlier and more fully on open coding. See, for example, Paul F. Lazarsfeld and Allen H. Barton, "Qualitative Measurement in the Social Sciences: Classification, Typologies, and Indices," in *The Policy Sciences: Recent Developments in Scope and Method*, ed. Daniel Lerner and Harold D. Lasswell (Stanford: Stanford University Press, 1951), pp. 155–192. There appears to be little basic overlap in the structure of content analysis developed by Harold Lasswell and in the codes used to classify answers in survey research.

34. "The Nature of the Free-Response Interview," Research Methodology Section, DPS, June 2, 1942, DPS Memo Collection, ISR. While this is the most

enthusiastic exposition of open interviewing that the archives reveal, there are ample indications from other in-house memos and interview transcriptions that this was a key to the main doctrine and to much of the practice of Program Surveys in the early 1940s. In 1944, Cartwright reflected that there had been an exaggerated "devotion to the so-called open interview," which was often "excessively defensive in its nature" because of the competition with Polls Division (memo to Rensis Likert from Dorwin Cartwright, "Random Thoughts about the Division of Program Surveys," July 10, 1944, p. 2, DPS Memo Collection, ISR). According to the June 2 memo, the questioning gave enough leeway to the interviewer that the style verged on the unstructured, "expert" form. In order to ward off context effects and other distortions, for example, the interviewer could allow greater time to elapse between questions, introduce irrelevant questions to change the respondent's train of thought, change the order of questions, and change the wording of questions to fit the respondent's vocabulary—"To question people uniformly does not mean to ask them a question made up of an invariant set of words: it means to ask them a question *understood* in the same way by all" (p. 3). This was precisely the view of interviewing which Lazarsfeld had assumed and advocated in the mid-1930s. Neither he nor Program Surveys staff explained how permitting interviewers to vary the language would insure uniformity of meaning for respondents, but both relied on interviewers' intelligence and judgment to make these translations.

35. A presidential order of Feb. 19, 1942, gave the military the authority to designate special restricted zones, and in March of that year Congress gave statutory approval for relocating Japanese in these zones (*Dictionary of American History*, rev. ed. [New York: Scribner, 1976], vol. 3, p. 491).

36. "Pacific Coast Attitudes Toward the Japanese Problem," Survey P.C. (NORC, University of Denver, Feb. 28, 1942), NORC Archives, Chicago.

37. "Exploratory Study of West Coast Reactions to Japanese" (Feb. 4, 1942), Division of Intensive Surveys, OFF, DPS Questionnaire Collection, ISR.

38. A letter to Likert from "Bob" (probably Robert S. Lynd, Jr.), Mar. 11, 1942, interpreted Lazarsfeld's reactions to that effect (Rensis Likert Collection, Bentley, Box 7, unprocessed).

39. June 23, 1942, Likert Collection, Bentley, Boxes 9–13.

40. Memorandum, "The Role of Different Types of Interviews in an Integrated Research Operation: Documentation of Suggestions Made in Letter to Mr. Kane," July 1, 1942, p. 3. The initial suggestions were made in a letter to Kane from Lazarsfeld on June 18, 1942 (DPS Memo Collection, ISR). Members of the Surveys Division published only one comparison with poll data; this showed that 63 percent of a sample assumed what was probably the intended frame of reference by a Gallup question concerning postwar changes in U.S. domestic policy (Richard S. Crutchfield and Donald A. Gordon, "Variations in Respondents' Interpretations of an Opinion-Poll Question," *IJOAR* 1 [1947]:1–12).

41. Interview with Rensis Likert, Angus Campbell, and Dorwin P. Cartwright, Oct. 19, 1976.

42. Interview with Daniel Katz, Jan. 28, 1977. Several memos in RG 51, series 41.3, NA to E. Pendleton Herring from Harold F. Gosnell bear on these various

reactions. See in Unit 153a a memo of Feb. 16, 1943, re interview with Waldemar Nielsen; in Unit 153c, memo dated Apr. 15, 1943, re interview with Samuel Stouffer; Feb. 23, 1943, re interview with Elmo Wilson; Apr. 20, 1943, re interview with Simon Lesser.

43. See note 31.

44. Robert K. Merton, Marjorie Fiske, and Alberta Curtis, *Mass Persuasion: The Social Psychology of a War Bond Drive* (New York: Harper, 1946).

45. Cartwright, "Random Thoughts," July 10, 1944; memo to Research Committee from Clements and Cartwright, Mar. 26, 1945, DPS Memo Collection, ISR. Crutchfield's experiments with question form had shown, for example, that personal savings was *volunteered* by 28 percent when the question read, "As you see it, what are the purposes of war bonds?" but *endorsed* by 89 percent when the question read, "What do you think of war bonds as a method of savings?" A measure of Salience (S) was constructed from the percent difference between volunteered and endorsed, but there is no surviving evidence of the systematic use of S.

46. Memo to all members of the division from Angus Campbell, Mar. 12, 1945, re "Questionnaire Construction in Program Surveys," DPS Memo Collection, ISR.

47. Lazarsfeld, "Detailed Interviews." The other four functions he discussed were clarifying the meaning of an answer, singling out decisive aspects of an opinion, interpreting motivation, and determining complex attitude patterns.

48. Campbell, "Questionnaire Construction"; Cartwright, "Random Thoughts," pp. 9–10.

49. Rensis Likert, "Public Opinion Polls," *Scientific American* 179 (Dec. 1948):7–11; Rensis Likert, "The Sample Interview Survey as a Tool of Research and Policy Formation," in *Policy Sciences*, ed. Lerner and Lasswell, pp. 223–251.

50. Angus Campbell, "Polling, Open Interviewing, and the Problem of Interpretation," *Journal of Social Issues* 2 (Nov. 1946):67–71. See also Albert A. [Angus] Campbell, "Two Problems in the Use of the Open Question," *JASP* 40 (1945):340–343.

51. Interview with Angus Campbell and Dorwin P. Cartwright, Apr. 5, 1977.

52. In a memorandum to Stouffer, in 1945, Cottrell expressed the hope that there would be "systematic integration of intensive interviewing techniques with extensive questionnaire techniques," noting that "we lack experience and skill in intensive interviewing and in analyzing results of such interviews. . . . I strongly suspect that many of our analytical puzzlements would have been greatly clarified and our hypotheses regarding the problems we have dealt with would have been more fruitful had we made more adequate use of intensive techniques in conjunction with our usual questionnaire procedures" (memo to Stouffer from Leonard S. Cottrell, Jr., re "Gaps in the Research Program," Jan. 30, 1945, p. 2, Samuel A. Stouffer Collection, 31.8, Box 2, Nathan Pusey Library, Harvard University). John A. Clausen's 1950 summary of the advantages and disadvantages of open/closed questions remains a valuable reflection on actual work with the two forms. See chap. 16 in *Measurement and Prediction*, esp. pp. 676–688.

53. Frederick F. Stephan, "History of the Uses of Modern Sampling Procedures," *JASA* 43 (1948):12–39; Joseph W. Duncan and William C. Shelton, *Rev-*

olution in United States Government Statistics 1926–1976 (Washington, D.C.: U.S. Department of Commerce, 1978), esp. chap. 2; C. A. Moser and G. Kalton, Survey Methods of Social Investigation, 2d U.S. edition (New York: Basic Books, 1972), pp. 118–121.

54. Leslie Kish, Survey Sampling (New York: Wiley, 1965), chap. 9.

55. Stuart A. Rice, "Quantitative Methods in Politics," JASA 33 (1938):126–130; Duncan and Shelton, Revolution in Statistics, p. 47.

56. Duncan and Shelton, Revolution in Statistics, pp. 47–55; Lester R. Frankel and J. Stevens Stock, "On the Sample Survey of Unemployment," JASA 37 (1942):77–80. The Current Population Survey is still in operation in the 1980s. For a description of the first supplemental sample of the Census enumeration in 1940, see Philip M. Hauser, "The Use of Sampling in the Census," JASA 36 (1941):369–375.

57. Morris H. Hansen and William N. Hurwitz, "A New Sample of the Population," Estadistica 2 (1944):483–497; Max A. Bershad and Benjamin J. Tepping, "The Development of Household Sample Surveys," JASA 64 (1969):1134–1140; P. V. Sukatmé, "Major Developments in Sampling Theory and Practice," in Research Papers in Statistics, ed. F. N. David (New York: Wiley, 1966); Morris H. Hansen and William G. Madow, "Some Important Events in the Historical Development of Sample Surveys," in On the History of Statistics and Probability, ed. D. B. Owen (New York: Dekker, 1976). Two articles are considered central contributions, both by Morris H. Hansen and William N. Hurwitz, "Relative Efficiencies of Various Sampling Units in Population Inquiries," JASA 37 (1942):89–94; and "On the Theory of Sampling from Finite Populations," Annals of Mathematical Statistics 14 (1943):333–362. For interpretation of these mathematically difficult articles, I have relied on Duncan and Shelton.

58. Sukatmé, in "Major Developments," considers the recognition of nonsampling error the most important development since Neyman's 1934 paper (p. 387); W. Edwards Deming, "On Errors in Surveys," ASR 9 (1944):359–369.

59. George H. Gallup, "Government and the Sampling Referendum," JASA 33 (1938):131–142; Elmo Roper, "Sampling Public Opinion," JASA 35 (1940):325–334.

60. Rice, "Quantitative Methods," p. 130.

61. Harold F. Gosnell, "How Accurate Were the Polls?" POQ 1 (1937):97–105.

62. Frederick F. Stephan, "Representative Sampling in Large-Scale Surveys," JASA 34 (1939):343–352. See also Rensis Likert, "Democracy in Agriculture—Why and How?" in Farmers in a Changing World: 1940 Yearbook of Agriculture (Washington, D.C.: U.S. Government Printing Office, 1940), pp. 994–1002, esp. p. 1000. Quinn McNemar's review of sampling in education and social psychology, "Sampling in Psychological Research," Psychological Bulletin 37 (1940):331–365, was quite tolerant of quota methods (see esp. pp. 348–350). McNemar was apparently unfamiliar with Bowley's sampling work, misinterpreting him as registering "extreme skepticism of sampling" generally (see p. 339).

63. Daniel Katz and Hadley Cantril, "Public Opinion Polls," Sociometry 1 (1937):155–179, esp. p. 157.

64. Samuel A. Stouffer, "Some Notes on Sampling and Questionnaire

Administration by the Research Branch," in *Measurement and Prediction*, ed. Stouffer et al., Appendix, p. 709.

65. Ibid., p. 715.
66. Ibid., pp. 710, 713.
67. "Interviewing for Program Surveys," Oct. 13, 1942, DPS Memo Collection, ISR; memo to field interviewers from sampling section, re "Grid Sampling and Block Sampling," May 10, 1943, ibid. It was considered very desirable but not routinely practical to compute sampling errors because it was "a complicated and time-consuming job and has been carried out for only a few past studies. It is hoped that in the future more work will be done in this field" ("Consideration of Sampling in Report Writing," July 9, 1945, p. 7, DPS Memo Collection, ISR).
68. Leslie Kish, "A Procedure for Objective Respondent Selection within the Household," *JASA* 44 (1949):380–387.
69. Arnold J. King, "The Master Sample of Agriculture," *JASA* 40 (1945): 38–45.
70. The characteristic feature of a "master" sample is its complete mapping and counting—in effect, a complete enumeration from which samples are drawn.
71. Interview with Morris H. Hansen, June 6, 1979.
72. Interview with Leslie Kish, June 28, 1979.
73. For research into sampling, see "A Comparison of Frequency Distributions Obtained in Two Surveys Conducted for the Treasury Department," June 15, 1943, and memo to Research Committee from James A. Bayton, re "Corrections for Bias in Study 107," Dec. 9, 1944, DPS Memo Collection, ISR.
74. Norman C. Meier and Cletus J. Burke, "Laboratory Tests of Sampling Techniques," *POQ* 11 (1947):586–593, esp. p. 586; *Hearings* before the Committee to Investigate Campaign Expenditures, House of Representatives, 78th Cong., 2d sess., on H. Res. 551, pt. 12, Dec. 28, 1944.
75. Interview with Leslie Kish, Oct. 14, 1981. The 1946 report "A National Survey of Liquid Assets," *Federal Reserve Bulletin* (June, July, Aug. 1946) provided a response rate (90%); the pilot study reported in 1945, "Surveys of Liquid Asset Holdings," *Federal Reserve Bulletin* (Sept. 1945), did not.
76. *Hearings*, esp. pp. 1235–1252 written report, and pp. 1256, 1271–1281 of personal testimony.
77. Ibid., p. 1266; Leonard Doob, *Public Opinion and Propaganda* (New York: Henry Holt & Co., 1948), p. 169. Doob saw the hearings as having "vindicated" the Gallup organization. In a letter to Edward Benson of AIPO, Stouffer mentioned his impression that Gallup had come out of the hearings "with flags flying" (Feb. 21, 1945, Series 31.8, Box 1, Stouffer Collection, Nathan Pusey Library, Harvard University).
78. *Hearings*, 1944, p. 1298.
79. Ibid., pp. 1241–1242.
80. Ibid., pp. 1294–1295.
81. Ibid.
82. Ibid., p. 1296.
83. Ibid., p. 1280.
84. Ibid., pp. 1298–1299.
85. Eric F. Goldman, "Poll on the Polls," *POQ* 8 (1944):468–467.

86. Daniel Katz, "The Polls and the 1944 Election," *POQ* 8 (1944):468–488 ff., esp. p. 468.

87. Goldman, "Poll on the Polls."

88. Katz, "The Polls, 1944"; Edward G. Benson, "Notes in Connection with Professor Katz's Article," *POQ* 8 (1944):483.

89. Katz, "The Polls, 1944," p. 606. The differing approaches of businessmen and academics in the wartime agencies were visible in other situations. For example, psychological warfare early in the war endeavored to inspire defections by persuasion that did not offend the "consumer" by portraits of Hitler's sadism or cruelty; later in the war it shifted to a more moralistic, evangelical tone of indignation and condemnation (Donald V. McGranahan, letter, *POQ* 10 [1946]:446–450). See also chap. 6.

90. Edward G. Benson, C. C. Young, and C. A. Syze, "Polling Lessons from the 1944 Election," *POQ* 9 (1945):467–484. Defenders of quota sampling were sometimes frustrated by what they considered to be the technical jargon used by area samplers. See book review by Joe Belden, *IJOAR* 1 (1947):102–103; comments by A. N. Watson in *Measurement of Consumer Interest*, ed. C. West Churchman, Russell L. Ackoff, and Murray Wax (Philadelphia: University of Pennsylvania Press, 1947), pp. 163–166.

91. Morris H. Hansen and Philip M. Hauser, "Area Sampling—Some Principles of Sample Design," *POQ* 9 (1945):183–193, esp. p. 192.

92. Daniel Katz, "Survey Techniques in the Evaluation of Morale," in *Experiments in Social Process: A Symposium on Social Psychology*, ed. James Grier Miller (New York: McGraw-Hill Book Co., 1950), pp. 65–77; Daniel Katz, "Survey Technique and Polling Procedure as Methods in Social Science," *Journal of Social Issues* 2 (1946):62–66.

93. United States Strategic Bombing Survey, *The Effects of Strategic Bombing on German Morale*, vol. 1 and (esp.) vol. 2 for supplementary studies (Washington, D.C.: U.S. Government Printing Office, May 1947 and Dec. 1946, respectively) [*sic*]; Daniel Katz, "Survey Techniques in the Evaluation of Morale"; Helen Peak, "Observations on the Characteristics and Distribution of German Nazis," *Psychological Monographs* 59 (1945):1–44. The Japanese report, USSBS, *The Effects of Strategic Bombing on Japanese Morale*, June 1947, includes twenty appendixes on various methodological issues.

94. USSBS, *German Morale*, vol. 1, Appendix A, pp. 109–131. A later independent reading of the interview protocols reported by Janis found that more hatred of the Allies was expressed in the course of the interview as a whole than in response to the specific questions on the subject (Irving L. Janis, *Air War and Emotional Stress: Psychological Studies of Bombing and Civilian Defense* [New York: McGraw-Hill Book Co., 1951], pp. 130–133).

95. David MacIsaac, *Strategic Bombing in World War II: The Story of the United States Strategic Bombing Survey* (New York: Garland, 1976), p. 115.

7. The Wartime Experience in Science (II)

1. Hadley Cantril and Associates, *Gauging Public Opinion* (Princeton: Princeton University Press, 1944), p. viii.

2. According to John Harding, who was a graduate student at OPOR, Cantril thought that a good deal of experimental psychological research was a waste of time and wanted to debunk it, thinking that much of the perceptual work was largely *suggestion*, in any case. To that end, he got a student to do an analysis of "ortho-sonority," an entirely fake attribute (telephone interview with John Harding, Oct. 22, 1979). The tone of Cantril's preface, cited in note 1, was more likely to appeal to pollsters than to academics, e.g., "The dizzy speed with which [the field of public opinion research has developed] left the social scientist momentarily breathless. Vaguely he sensed that something important was happening in a domain he had come to regard as his own" (p. vii).

3. Hadley Cantril and Edrita Fried, "The Meaning of Questions," in Cantril et al., *Gauging Public Opinion*, p. 22.

4. Donald Rugg, "How Representative are 'Representative Samples'?" and J. Stevens Stock, "Some General Principles of Sampling," both in Cantril et al., *Gauging Public Opinion*.

5. Cantril acknowledged the greatest debt to Gallup, for having made interviewing facilities available and for having encouraged him "to experiment with the Institute's research tools without restriction or stipulations concerning the publication of results" (p. x). Gallup conducted almost 400 split-ballot experiments between Sept. 1936 and Nov. 1949, which are on file at the Roper Public Opinion Research Center. Some of these (but apparently not all) were designed by Cantril. See Williams College, *The Roper Public Opinion Research Center Study Inventory, American Surveys* (Williamstown, Mass.: Williams College).

6. A. B. Blankenship, ed., *How to Conduct Opinion and Consumer Research* (New York: Harper, 1946); C. West Churchman, Russell L. Ackoff, and Murray Wax, eds., *Measurement of Consumer Interest* (Philadelphia: University of Pennsylvania Press, 1947).

7. For such work, after long hiatus, see Charles F. Turner and Elissa Krauss, "Fallible Indicators of the Subjective State of the Nation," *American Psychologist* 33 (1978): 456–470.

8. Quinn McNemar, "Opinion-Attitude Methodology," *Psychological Bulletin* 43 (1946):289–374, esp. p. 289.

9. Donald Rugg and Hadley Cantril, "The Wording of Questions," in Cantril et al., *Gauging Public Opinion*, p. 25.

10. McNemar, "Opinion-Attitude," p. 318.

11. Daniel Katz, "The Interpretation of Survey Findings," *Journal of Social Issues* 2 (1946):32–43.

12. Vol. 3 concerns experiments conducted in the Research Branch with instructional films, such as the "Why We Fight" series, and other teaching devices and situations. Vol. 4 treats Guttman scaling, Lazarsfeld's latent structure analysis, Star's work on psychoneurotic testing, and Clausen's work on prediction of soldiers' postwar plans.

13. Paul F. Lazarsfeld, "*The American Soldier*—An Expository Review," *POQ* 13 (1949):373–404.

14. Samuel A. Stouffer, "Some Afterthoughts of a Contributor to *The American Soldier*," in *Continuities in Social Research: Studies in the Scope and Method of "The American Soldier*," ed. Robert K. Merton and Paul F. Lazarsfeld (Glencoe, Ill.: The Free Press, 1950), pp. 200–201.

15. Ibid., pp. 198–199.
16. Ibid., pp. 199–200.
17. Ibid., p. 204.
18. Ibid., p. 202; see also Samuel A. Stouffer, Edward A. Suchman, Leland C. DeVinney, Shirley A. Star, and Robin M. Williams, Jr., *The American Soldier: Adjustment during Army Life*, vol. 1 (Princeton, N.J.: Princeton University Press, 1949), pp. 29–30.
19. Stouffer et al., *The American Soldier*, vol. 1, pp. 40–41.
20. Arthur M. Schlesinger, Jr., "The Statistical Soldier," *Partisan Review*, Aug. 1949; Ethel Shanas, review, *AJS* 55 (1950):590–594.
21. Stouffer et al., *The American Soldier*, vol. 1, pp. 29–30.
22. Ibid., vol. 2, pp. 130–149.
23. Ibid., vol. 2, pp. 380–382.
24. Ibid., vol. 2, pp. 242–289.
25. Ibid., p. 123.
26. Ibid., vol. 1, pp. 593–595.
27. Ibid., p. 251.
28. Ibid., p. 256.
29. Stouffer, "Some Afterthoughts," p. 199.
30. Stouffer et al., *The American Soldier*, vol. 1, pp. 561–564.
31. Robert K. Merton and Alice S. Kitt, "Contributions to the Theory of Reference Group Behavior," in *Continuities*, pp. 40–105.
32. Daniel Katz, review, *Psychological Bulletin* 48 (1951):512–519.
33. Daniel Lerner, "*The American Soldier* and the Public," in *Continuities*, pp. 212–251.
34. Lazarsfeld, "Expository Review," p. 380.
35. Ibid., p. 404.
36. Theodore M. Newcomb reviewed it as the most "sophisticated treatment of principles of ordering of variables which can be isolated from survey data" (review, *AJS* 57 [1951–1952]:90–92).
37. Stouffer, "Some Afterthoughts," p. 211.
38. John W. Riley, Jr., review, *ASR* 14 (1949):557–559. The chart is in vol. 1, p. 228.
39. Interview with M. Brewster Smith, May 27, 1980.
40. In the selection of his writings made by Stouffer himself, *Social Research to Test Ideas: Selected Writings of Samuel A. Stouffer* (Glencoe, Ill.: The Free Press, 1962), he included a few pages of analysis from the *Communism* study but considerably more material from *The American Soldier*.
41. Dorwin P. Cartwright, in "Basic and Applied Social Psychology," *Philosophy of Science* 16 (1949):198–208, did not mention relative deprivation. The book by Jerome S. Bruner, *Mandate from the People* (New York: Duell, Sloan, and Pearce, 1944) used poll data to interpret American culture and politics during the war, especially, but the data were cited more in illustration of generalizations than in true data analysis.
42. Dorwin P. Cartwright, "Some Principles of Mass Persuasion," *Human Relations* 2 (1949):253–268, esp. pp. 266–267.
43. Peter H. Odegard and Alan Barth, "Millions for Defense," *POQ* 5 (1941):399–411.

44. George H. Gallup, *The Gallup Poll* (New York: Random House, 1972), vol. 1, p. 307. This is the highest percentage that I have observed on any Gallup information item. See also Cartwright, "Some Principles," pp. 254–255.

45. Ibid., passim.

46. Daniel Katz and Herbert Hyman, "Industrial Morale and Public Opinion Methods," *IJOAR* 1 (1947):13–30.

47. Herbert Hyman, "Do They Tell the Truth?" *POQ* 8 (1944):557–559.

48. Ernest R. Hilgard and Stanley L. Payne, "Those Not at Home: Riddle for Pollsters," *POQ* 8 (1944):254–261.

49. Angus Campbell, "Factors Associated with Attitudes toward Jews," in *Readings in Social Psychology*, rev. ed., ed. Guy E. Swanson, Theodore M. Newcomb, and Eugene L. Hartley (New York: Henry Holt & Co., 1952), pp. 582–591; Joseph A. Kershaw and Harry Alpert, "The Invalidation of Food Ration Currency, December 1944," *Journal of Social Issues* 3 (1947):40–48; Saul B. Sells, "Questionnaire Control in a Civilian War Agency," *Psychological Bulletin* 40 (1943):448–450; Arnold M. Rose, "Army Policies toward Negro Soldiers: A Report on a Success and a Failure," *Journal of Social Issues* 3 (1947):26–31.

50. Interview with W. Phillips Davison, Dec. 15, 1978.

51. Princeton University was heavily represented by six members, including Hadley Cantril, S. S. Wilks, and DeWitt Clinton Poole. The other seven members came from a sprinkle of places along the Eastern seaboard: Pendleton Herring (Harvard), Harold Lasswell (Washington, D.C.), Peter Odegard (Amherst), and others, such as Lloyd Free and Daniel Katz. There were no members from the commercial field.

52. The community of interest was actually somewhat broader, for it recognized the concerns of governmental workers in the "rapidly developing scientific methods of measuring public attitudes and opinions" and also of those involved in product testing and standards, such as Agnew, Warwick, and Shewhart, who had already made notable contributions to sampling in industrial quality control (Proposal I, Joint Committee of the National Research Council and Social Science Research Council on Measurement of Opinion, Attitudes, and Consumer Wants, n.d., National Academy of Sciences Archives, Joint Committee, 1945–1954). The full list of the committee is as follows: Samuel A. Stouffer, chairman, University of Chicago and War Department; S. S. Wilks, vice chairman, Princeton University; P. G. Agnew, American Standards Assn.; Edward Battey, Compton Advertising Inc.; Hadley Cantril, Princeton University; Archibald M. Crossley, Crossley, Inc.; W. Edwards Deming, Bureau of the Budget; Robert F. Elder, Lever Bros. Co.; George H. Gallup, AIPO; Philip M. Hauser, Dept. of Commerce; Carl I. Hovland, Yale University and War Department; Paul F. Lazarsfeld, Columbia University; Rensis Likert, Dept. of Agriculture; Darrell B. Lucas, New York University; Elmo Roper, New York City; Walter A. Shewhart, Bell Telephone Laboratories; Frank Stanton, Columbia Broadcasting System; and C. L. Warwick, American Society for Testing Materials.

53. Stouffer was a notoriously poor correspondent, but the Samuel A. Stouffer Collection shows cordial correspondence from various figures in commercial research such as Frank Stanton, Claude Robinson, Edward Benson, Albert B. Blankenship, Elmo Roper, and George Gallup. In a 1945 letter, Roper wrote Stouffer concerning the new SSRC/NRC Committee, expressing the hope that

the committee would agree that there was not just one way of doing research but several ways suited to different problems. Roper was concerned about Likert's claims for open interviewing and others' claims for area sampling: "Maybe we could decide that marketing research and opinion research had many tools, each suited for certain purposes, each unsuited for others" (to Stouffer from Roper, Aug. 22, 1945, Stouffer Collection, Series 31.8, Box 2, Nathan Pusey Library, Harvard University).

54. "Preliminary Draft: Memorandum on the Problem of Investigating Reliability of Various Sampling Methods," Sept. 27, 1945, NAS Archives, Joint Committee.

55. "Appendix B, Annual Report, 1945–46," ibid.

56. *Proceedings of the Central City Conference on Public Opinion Research*, Central City, Colo., July 29–31, 1946 (Denver, Colo.: NORC, University of Denver).

57. Duncan and Shelton, p. 52.

58. *Proceedings*, pp. 106–108.

59. Ibid., pp. 14–15.

60. Interviews with Anne Schuetz Zanes, July 3, 1978, and Feb. 12, 1982; Clyde W. Hart and Don Cahalan, "The Development of AAPOR," *POQ* 21 (1957):165–173; *Proceedings*, passim.

61. Gordon Allport, review of George Gallup, *A Guide to Public Opinion Polls, JASP* 40 (1945):113–114.

62. E. Pendleton Herring, "Political Science in the Next Decade," *APSR* 39 (1945):757–766, esp. p. 761.

63. Herbert S. Conrad, "Some Principles of Attitude Measurement: A Reply to 'Opinion-Attitude Methodology,'" *Psychological Bulletin* 43 (1946):570–589, esp. p. 584.

64. Quinn McNemar, "Opinion-Attitude Methodology," *Psychological Bulletin* 43 (1946):289–374, esp. p. 326.

65. Ibid., p. 368.

66. Ibid., p. 369.

67. Dorwin P. Cartwright, personal communication, Dec. 16, 1981.

68. John A. Clausen, "Research on the American Soldier as a Career Contingency," *Social Psychology Quarterly* 47 (1984):207–213, esp. p. 208.

69. Ibid., pp. 210–211.

70. Ibid., p. 211.

71. Ibid.

72. Ibid., p. 212. See also M. Brewster Smith, "*The American Soldier* and Its Critics: What Survives the Attack on Positivism," *Social Psychology Quarterly* 47 (1984):191–198 for a critical appraisal of the strengths and weaknesses of Stouffer et al.'s empirical work.

8. General Perspectives and Anticipations

1. Phyllis Sheridan, "The Research Bureau in a University Context: A Case History of a Marginal Institution" (Ph.D. diss., Columbia University Teachers College, 1979); Allen H. Barton, "Paul Lazarsfeld and Applied Social Research,"

Social Science History 3 (1979):4–44; Charles Y. Glock, "Organizational Innovation for Social Science Research and Training," in *Qualitative and Quantitative Social Research: Papers in Honor of Paul F. Lazarsfeld,* ed. Robert K. Merton, James S. Coleman, and Peter H. Rossi (New York: The Free Press, 1979); Paul B. Sheatsley, "NORC: The First Forty Years," in *Report 1981–82 NORC* (Chicago: NORC, 1982), pp. 6–21; Charles F. Cannell and Robert L. Kahn, "Some Factors in the Origins and Development of the Institute for Social Research, the University of Michigan," *American Psychologist* 39 (1984):1256–1266.

2. See Thomas S. Kuhn, "The History of Science," *IESS* 14 (1968):74–83, and idem, "The Relations between History and the History of Science," in Kuhn, *The Essential Tension: Selected Studies in Scientific Tradition and Change* (Chicago and London: University of Chicago Press, 1977), pp. 127–161. See also the discussion of the internalist/externalist orientations in A. R. Hall, "Merton Revisited," *History of Science* 2 (1963):1–16. Ben-David traces the origins of bacteriology and psychoanalysis to the practical concerns of academically marginal persons, such as Pasteur, Koch, and Freud, who evolved hybrid roles between theory and practice. See Joseph Ben-David, "Roles and Innovations in Medicine," *AJS* 65 (1960):557–568, and Joseph Ben-David and Randall Collins, "Social Factors in the Origins of a New Science: The Case of Psychology," *ASR* 31 (1966):451–465; Joseph Ben-David and Abraham Zloczower, "Universities and Academic Systems in Modern Society," *European Journal of Sociology* 3 (1962):45–84. Weinberg argues that nearly every pure science started as an applied one or is at least motivated from outside of science, and he cites thermodynamics, bacteriology, and branches of mathematics. See Alvin M. Weinberg, "But Is the Teacher Also a Citizen?" in *Science and the University,* ed. Boyd R. Keenan (New York and London: Columbia University Press, 1966).

3. Vannevar Bush, *Science, the Endless Frontier,* Report to the President on a Program for Postwar Scientific Research, July 1945 (Washington, D.C.: U.S. Government Printing Office, 1945); James L. Penick, Jr., Carroll W. Pursell, Jr., Morgan B. Sherwood, and Donald C. Swain, *The Politics of American Science: 1939 to the Present* (Chicago: Rand-McNally, 1965), pp. 54–89; Gene M. Lyons, *The Uneasy Partnership: Social Science and the Federal Government in the Twentieth Century* (New York: Russell Sage Foundation, 1969), esp. chaps. 4 and 5.

The total volume of OSRD funds was less than that of either the army or the navy; the significance was in the arrangements that brought leading scientists into wartime research, which offered much freedom in the conduct of research and established a new pattern of relationship between science and government. See Don K. Price, *Government and Science: Their Dynamic Relation in American Democracy* (New York: New York University Press, 1954), and idem, "Money and Influence: The Links of Science to Public Policy," *Daedalus* 103 (1974):97–113.

Talcott Parsons, "The Science Legislation and the Role of the Social Sciences," *ASR* 11 (1946):653–666. Senator Kilgore's design would have incorporated social sciences and merged basic and applied work under a traditional governmental organization headed by a presidential appointee, with advisers drawn not only from science but also from the military and cabinet posts. See Daniel S. Greenberg, *The Politics of Pure Science* (New York: New American Library, 1967). Certain eminent scientists, such as Oppenheimer and Conant, favored inclusion of the social sciences in NSF, and according to a *Fortune* poll there was widespread support in the scientific community (mathematics, physics, chemistry, and biology) for having social science share in federal funds ("The Scientists: A Sympathetic Portrait," *Fortune* 38 [Oct. 1948]:106–112 ff.).

In Greenberg's view, the new links between government and science during the war provided an "intoxicating and traumatic" experience "that was formative of personal and institutional relationships, many of which endure to this day in the politics of science." Even more important, in his view, was the scientific community's conviction that its contributions to victory were indispensable and would have been impossible if scientists themselves had not had much administrative responsibility (Greenberg, *The Politics of Pure Science*, pp. 81–82). Price, in contrast, concludes that scientists were fearful for the future and were much less impressed with their accomplishments than many others were: "The rest of us were inclined to believe that the fantastic discoveries of World War II could be continued indefinitely if only enough money were provided to pay for the research." Scientists, for their part, thought that they had run through much of their stockpile of basic knowledge, and they wanted to get back to the universities to undertake basic science (Price, *Government and Science*, p. 32). Clearly, it was difficult to know what "most" scientists were feeling. Curiously, Price speculates about how it might be "if it were possible to take some sort of Gallup poll on the political opinions of scientists and people in related professional fields"—as if it were not! (Price, *Government and Science*, p. 120).

4. Bird Dogs, "The Evolution of the Office of Naval Research," *Physics Today*, Aug. 1961. (A group of young naval officers wrote collectively as the "Bird Dogs.") See also Lyons, *Uneasy Partnership*, esp. chaps. 5 and 8. Alan T. Waterman, the first director of NSF, had been Chief Scientist of ONR, and during the war he had been one of the top administrators of OSRD (Greenberg, *The Politics of Pure Science*, p. 133). The scientists' ideology of freedom from governmental control had been adopted so thoroughly by navy personnel that they were not convinced at the outset that the scientists would welcome ONR support. In Greenberg's view, the military motives for supporting basic science were the development of better weapons and good relations wtih the newly prestigious men of science. Certain scientists were opposed to the reliance on military funds (e.g., Norbert Wiener, Philip Morrison, and Albert Einstein). Those scientists who favored government support were apparently motivated chiefly by a zeal for basic science. ONR research was open to publication in scientific journals. See Greenberg, *The Politics of Pure Science*, esp. chap. 7; Donald F. Hornig, "The evolving federal role," in *Science and the University*, ed. Keenan, pp. 40–58.

5. For example, in a 1953 SRC Human Relations Program proposal to the air force, the military implications were specific: "To wage war successfully and to maintain a strong military position, it is not only necessary that we as a nation know how to build powerful military units but it is also essential that we be able to combine civilian and military personnel into integrated, productive organizations" ("Technical Information Regarding a Research Proposal for a Study of the Effect of Managerial Personnel Changes on the Productivity and Motivation of Civilian and Military Personnel in the Air Material Command," Mar. 10, 1953, p. 1, ISR program files, ISR). A major infusion of government funds came to

the Bureau from contracts with the air force obtained by Kingsley Davis in 1950. (See Sheridan, "The Research Bureau," p. 127.) Sponsors for the following series of unpublished reports are not identified in the Bureau bibliography, but it seems a reasonable inference that reports by Davis, Blake, Iklé, and others were a part of the air force project: for example, series B-0390, reports 1–6 and 14–25 bear on a World Urban Resource Index, the demographic structures of certain cities, and the effects of bombing in European cities during World War II. Some of the NORC studies for the U.S. Army Chemical Center are summarized in Charles E. Fritz and Eli S. Marks, "The NORC Studies of Human Behavior in Disaster," *Journal of Social Issues* 10 (1954):26–41. Field trips were conducted to communities that had experienced airplane crashes, a series of house explosions and fires, a coal mine explosion, and an earthquake.

6. Harry Alpert, "The National Science Foundation and Social Science Research," *ASR* 19 (1954):208–211; idem, "The Government's Growing Recognition of Social Science," *Annals* of the American Academy of Political and Social Science 327 (1960):59–67. After the war there was great expansion in the appropriations and program of NIH, from about $3 million in 1946 to $81 million in 1955 and $324 million in 1959. See Greenberg, *The Politics of Pure Science*, p. 129; Hornig, "The Evolving Federal Role," p. 47.

7. The first appropriations to NSF for overall operations were tiny: it received approximately $230,000 the first year, and in the first three years, the organization's funds permitted it to do little more than stay in existence. By 1960, its budget had grown to just under $160 million. In that year, just over $2 million, or 1.3 percent of the total budget, was allocated to "basic research in the social sciences." For fiscal year 1961, the comparable figure had risen slightly to 1.9 percent of a total budget of roughly $176 million (National Science Foundation, *Tenth Annual Report*, for fiscal year ending June 30, 1960, p. 168; *Eleventh Annual Report*, for fiscal year ending June 30, 1961, p. 173).

8. Krohn calls the peer-review system a "brilliant device to mesh hierarchical agencies with specific purposes with the individualist-equalitarian pattern and open goals of science" (p. 55) in Roger G. Krohn, "Patterns of the Institutionalization of Research," in *The Social Contexts of Research*, ed. Saad Z. Nagi and Ronald G. Corwin (New York: Wiley-Interscience, 1972). Prestige of in-government work was low, according to a survey conducted for the President's Scientific Research Board, even among in-government researchers and especially among university researchers. See Bernard Barber, *Science and the Social Order* (Glencoe, Ill.: The Free Press, 1952), esp. chap. 8; Simon Marcson, "Research Settings," in *The Social Contexts of Research*, ed. Nagi and Corwin.

9. Robert L. Hall, "Agencies of Research Support: Some Sociological Perspectives," in *The Social Contexts of Research*, ed. Nagi and Corwin, p. 208. Hall also notes that "some analysts have commented on the scientific community as a remarkable establishment which has drawn massive federal funds while maintaining a maximum of control over these funds through the system of governing boards and advisory boards," and cites Don K. Price, "The Scientific Establishment," *Proceedings of the American Philosophical Society* 106 (1962):235–245, and Greenberg, *The Politics of Pure Science*.

10. Governmental laboratories received somewhat more than this; industries

received four times as much as universities did. See Leonard Silk, *The Research Revolution* (New York: McGraw-Hill, 1960). For fiscal 1960, federal expenditures for research and development were estimated at just over $8 billion, over three-quarters of which was allocated to agencies outside the government ("extramural" research). Ninety-three percent of the extramural monies were expended by the direct military agencies, AEC, and NASA. Domestic agencies shared the remaining 7 percent. HEW (including NIH) distributed 3.8 percent and NSF, 1.1 percent of the total "extramural" research money. See J. Stefan Dupré and Sanford A. Lakoff, *Science and the Nation: Policy and Politics* (Englewood Cliffs, N.J.: Prentice-Hall, 1962), p. 14.

11. Peter H. Rossi, in "Researchers, Scholars and Policy Makers: The Politics of Large-Scale Research," *Daedalus* 93 (1964):1142–1161, notes that the research organization serving the humanist scholar has become entirely incorporated into the structure of the university, namely the library. (By now, of course, the same can be said for mainframe computers.) Rossi stresses the tension between researchers and professors over status (higher for professors) and grant/contract money (higher for researchers), and the hierarchical organization of the research center vs. the collegial individualism of the departments. Weinberg shares Rossi's general perspective that hierarchical structure is necessary for the conduct of research and that this structure in a university setting makes for more tenuous ties with university departments. See Alvin M. Weinberg, "Scientific Teams and Scientific Laboratories," *Daedalus* 99 (1970):1056–1075. Cf. James A. Davis's view that the collegial relationships *within a research center* are more supportive and less problematic than they are within a department because the criteria for status are clearer in the research organization. Researchers who bring in money are valued; in the department, status ambiguity and anxiety hamper collaboration and mutual support (interview with James A. Davis, May 24, 1979). David Riesman makes a similar point in observing the individualism and status concerns of Harvard scholars (interview with David Riesman, May 24, 1979). Riesman has analyzed the disciplines as "making large-scale reorganization of large-scale universities almost as difficult as comparable reorganizations in the political realms," while "stabilizing the market for ideas, policing it to some extent and controlling the worst charlatanry" (pp. 109–110). See David Riesman, "The Intellectual Veto Groups," in *Constraint and Variety in American Education* (Garden City, N.Y.: Doubleday Anchor, 1958). See also Kenneth Prewitt, "Management of Survey Organizations," in *Handbook of Survey Research*, ed. Peter H. Rossi, James D. Wright, and Andy B. Anderson (New York: Academic Press, 1983). There is often central administrative pressure, according to Ikenberry and Friedman's empirical study, to insure that permanent staff not be developed in a research institute. Also, the department is considered to be the "normal unit" of the university, with a center or institute considered to be the deviant (Stanley O. Ikenberry and Renée C. Friedman, *Beyond Academic Departments: The Story of Institutes and Centers* [San Francisco: Jossey-Bass, 1972], pp. 88–89).

12. Martin Bulmer, "The Early Institutional Establishment of Social Science Research: the Local Community Research Committee at the University of Chicago, 1923–30," *Minerva* 18 (1980):51–110. From 1923 to 1932, the Chicago committee produced 84 books and monographs and 120 articles, from projects sup-

ported by it and its successor, the Social Science Research Committee. See Wilson Gee, *Social Science Research Organizations in American Universities and Colleges* (New York: Appleton-Century, 1934), p. 90. In 1933, Gee conducted a survey of 567 institutions of higher education; 539 returned the questionnaire, and 80 schools indicated that they had one or more "definitely organized bodies" representing the cause of social science. Gee classified 24 of these as social science councils and committees that allocated funds to faculty research projects, such as those at Chicago, allocating $200,000; at Columbia, $125,000; and at Yale, $105,000. He listed another 35 as "bureaus and similiar research organizations." These were typically institutes of public administration, bureaus of business research, and bureaus of government. They involved faculty members conducting research, some secretarial help, graduate student or other paid assistants, and—rarely—field staff who were employed temporarily as needed.

Lazarsfeld's Bureau of Applied Social Research differed from these organizations in its size as a standing organization and in its early reliance on commercial contracts for sociological work. Bureaus of business research also had business clients, for which they did service work, but the organizations tried to keep these contracts to a minor share of the total budget. Harvard's Bureau of Business Research, which was established in 1911 and with which Paul T. Cherington was affiliated (see chap. 3), stressed in its policy statement of 1932 that it carried out studies for business for the main purpose of obtaining case materials for teaching and did not accept studies that did not "contribute directly or indirectly to this purpose." The Harvard Bureau's policy was not to conduct "private investigations for the benefit of individual companies" (Gee, *Social Science Research Organizations*, pp. 133–134). The Bureau of Business Research at the University of Michigan was at pains to explain the same educational use of its applied work (Gee, *Social Science Research Organizations*, p. 144). How rigorously this policy was applied cannot be determined from Gee's study. The policy statements of these organizations are of interest for their concern to be seen as not working *for* business but instead as availing themselves of business materials for educational purposes.

For details of Odum's organization, founded in 1924, see Guy Benton Johnson and Guion Griffis Johnson, *Research in Service to Society: The First Fifty Years of the Institute for Research in Social Science at the University of North Carolina* (Chapel Hill: University of North Carolina Press, 1980).

13. Joseph Ben-David, *The Scientist's Role in Society* (Englewood Cliffs, N.J.: Prentice-Hall, 1971), p. 147.

14. Ibid., pp. 147–152.

15. The University of Michigan Department of Sociology allocation for 1946–47 was just over $50,000, and the Department of Psychology, $78,000. The two departments were growing in this period, for in 1950–51 psychology's budget had risen to over $200,000, and sociology's, to $93,000. But by then the ISR budget was growing faster still, and in that year it was over $850,000. Comparable figures could not be obtained from Columbia University, which does not make such figures available, or from the University of Denver, which at the time did not maintain separate social science departments. (The Michigan figures are from the Literature, Sciences, and Arts Records, Budgets 1946–1947, Box 74,

Michigan Historical Collections, Bentley Library, University of Michigan.) The figures themselves are not entirely comparable, of course, because the departmental allocations were almost entirely to pay teaching staff, whereas the research center had a far greater range of costs for technical personnel and equipment. The respective sizes of the budgets had political implications, in any case, even if the research center's monies were largely from outside the university.

16. Universities had typically lost money when the trifling amount of overhead paid by certain foundations before the war meant that the universities had to assume the overhead burdens themselves. According to Price, they had been willing to do so when these sums were not an important fraction of their budgets. Some scientists opposed higher overhead rates because they felt that the more money went to the university, the less went to their project. Price says that this interpretation was sometimes correct, but that if this line of reasoning had been applied across the board, it would have bankrupted universities all over the country (Price, *Government and Science*, pp. 81–82).

Charles V. Kidd, in *American Universities and Federal Research* (Cambridge: Belknap Press of Harvard University Press, 1959), esp. chap. 5, summarizes some of the complexities of the argument, including the fact that indirect-cost receipts (which were centrally controlled by a university administration) were often used in some part to provide support for research in the arts and humanities (p. 102). "Many scientists see the payment of indirect costs to the university as legalized robbery, with the business officer, financial vice-president, or whoever it may be, as the thief and they themselves as the victims" (p. 100). This was surely the viewpoint of the staff of the Bureau of Applied Social Research.

The figures in these references show indirect cost rates of 15 percent for NIH and 20 percent for NSF in the late 1950s.

17. Laurence R. Veysey, *The Emergence of the American University* (Chicago: University of Chicago Press, 1965), pp. 32–50, 346–356.

18. A Harvard report of 1961 estimated that 20 percent of the total expenditures in higher education came from federal sources (excerpted in Penick et al., *Politics of American Science*, p. 253).

19. Ibid., esp. pp. 271–273; Frederick Seitz, "The University: Independent Institution or Federal Satellite?" in *Science and the University*, ed. Keenan, pp. 149–161.

20. The distinction between basic and applied work is not neat or satisfying, and it may have become fuzzier with the advent of the RFP (Request for Proposal) by government agencies. Some scientists try to answer the RFP in ways that are at once "applied" enough to satisfy the client and "basic" enough to satisfy their own intellectual interests. The difference is clear at the extremes, however, and it probably was so during these early years.

21. This was a greater issue for the Bureau than for SRC or NORC. SRC's market research certainly had implications for Madison Avenue, but the link was not usually as close. NORC did a little work for business, avoiding it for the most part out of concern for its tax-exempt status.

The festschrift to Lazarsfeld features one short chapter on his market research work, dealing only with the Vienna experience: Hans Zeisel, "The Vienna Years," in *Qualitative and Quantitative Social Research*, ed. Merton et al.

Riesman observed among many of his own students and those at other leading universities "a posture of contempt for business and a belief that, in contrast, teaching offers respectability and even integrity (. . . not a political contempt, for these students are very rarely directly political; it is rather a cultural, moral, or intellectual contempt)." See David Riesman, "The Spread of 'Collegiate' Values," in *The Intellectuals: A Controversial Portrait*, ed. George B. de Huszar (Glencoe, Ill.: The Free Press, 1960), pp. 507–508. Riesman saw the attitude as originating in two groups: aristocratic students, who disdained "the trade" in an English style; and students who were children of small businessmen, seeking intellectual and social mobility into the professions.

A blending of academic and business culture was achieved at the top of the academic hierarchy as early as 1910, according to Veysey, in *The Emergence of the American University*, esp. pt. 6.

22. Norman W. Storer, *The Social System of Science* (New York: Holt, Rinehart, and Winston, 1966); Robert K. Merton's "A Note on Science and Democracy," *Journal of Legal and Political Sociology* 1 (1942):115–126, was the seminal article on the norms of science; Bernard Barber, in *Science and the Social Order* (Glencoe, Ill.: The Free Press, 1952), extended the essential characteristics of science analyzed by Merton.

23. Anselm L. Strauss and Lee Rainwater, *The Professional Scientist: A Study of American Chemists* (Chicago: Aldine, 1962), p. 109. Theodore Caplow and R.J. McGee, *The Academic Marketplace* (New York: Basic Books, 1958), find some greater dissatisfaction levels in the four universities they studied with highest salaries than in the four with lowest salaries (p. 99), which is consonant with theories of expectation and relative deprivation discussed in other chapters here. See also Logan Wilson, *The Academic Man: A Study in the Sociology of a Profession* (New York: Oxford University Press, 1942), pp. 136–139. Paul F. Lazarsfeld and Wagner Thielens, Jr., in *The Academic Mind: Social Scientists in a Time of Crisis* (Glencoe, Ill.: The Free Press, 1958), note that social science professors (and the higher-ranking ones, more so) "seem to consider themselves an occupational minority toward which significant sectors of the community hold relatively contemptuous attitudes" (p. 14). However, Seymour Martin Lipset, "The Real Status of American Intellectuals," in *The Intellectuals*, ed. de Huszar, concludes that "professors, like the lawyers who become judges or elective officials rather than corporation counselors, really believe that the non-economic rewards of the job are better than monetary gains" (p. 516).

24. Charles E. Rosenberg, *No Other Gods: On Science and American Social Thought* (Baltimore, Md.: Johns Hopkins University Press [1961], 1976), pp. 3, 15. The metaphor of building the cathedral is still salient for modern scientists. See Herbert A. Shepard, "Basic Research and the Social System of Pure Science," *Philosophy of Science* 23 (1956):48–57; Donald Hornig, "A Look Ahead," in National Academy of Sciences, *Science, Government and the Universities* (Washington, D.C., 1966); Roger G. Krohn, "Patterns of the Institutionalization of Research," in *The Social Contexts of Research*, ed. Nagi and Corwin, finds "strong continuity of

motives between religion and science" (p. 52). The heroic model of the scientist is similar. See Gerald Holton, "Modern Science and the Intellectual Tradition," in _The Intellectuals_, ed. de Huszar, esp. p. 185. Norman W. Storer, in "Some Sociological Aspects of Federal Science Policy," _American Behavioral Scientist_ 6 (1962):27–30, argues that the social system of science has continued for the last 100 years in good part because scientists were unable to acquire the power or the money circulating in other systems, and the system thus flourished, in effect, because it was ignored by other realms.

25. Rosenberg, _No Other Gods_, p. 139. Rosenberg notes that "Images of isolation and moral heroism appear with illuminating frequency in the writings of would-be American scientists in this generation" (mid- to late nineteenth century). Twentieth-century scientists show a paler, somewhat different asceticism, for example, expressing little interest in social life because it diminishes available work time. See Anne Roe, _The Making of a Scientist_ (New York: Dodd, Mead, 1952). Kaplan reminds us, however, that we tend to generalize about all scientists from studies of particularly outstanding ones: Norman Kaplan, "Organization: Will It Choke or Promote the Growth of Science?" in _The Management of Scientists_, ed. Karl Hill (Boston: Beacon Press, 1964), pp. 103–127.

26. William F. Ogburn, "The Folkways of a Scientific Sociology," 1929 presidential address, _Publications of the American Sociological Society_ 24 (1930):1–11.

27. Storer, _The Social System of Science_, chap. 7. Shepard, in "Basic Research," makes much the same point, that the value systems of scientists and those of the larger society were becoming congruent. He notes, however, that the notion of a social system of pure science was something of a myth, with little empirical evidence on how much it corresponded to the reality or on whether it was indeed the system under which great strides of scientific creativity were taken.

28. Charles Dollard, "A Middleman Looks at Social Science," _ASR_ 15 (1950):16–20. In 1955, the _Journal of Social Issues_ devoted a special issue to "Anti-Intellectualism in the United States." Eight of the eleven articles were by professors; the only clearly "anti-intellectual" piece was a foolish one by the columnist Westbrook Pegler. Bernard Barber's article "Sociological Aspects of Anti-Intellectualism," pp. 25–30, was rare in questioning the premise of the topic. All criticism of intellectuals, he cautioned, should not be lumped together as anti-intellectualism. Herbert Stember, in "Why They Attack Intellectuals," pp. 22–24, considered the intellectual to be a deviant "in a society dominated by material and commercial values" (p. 24). Elsewhere, and in contrast, von Mises viewed intellectuals' hostility to business as an "anticapitalistic mentality" of those who fail in a system that rewards achievement rather than hereditary privilege (Ludwig von Mises, "The Resentment and the Anticapitalistic Bias of American Intellectuals," in _The Intellectuals_, ed. de Huszar, pp. 365–370).

29. Orlans shows empirical evidence of faculty members' feeling that those who got research funds would be treated with more respect by university administrators (Harold Orlans, _The Effects of Federal Programs on Higher Education: A Study of 36 Universities and Colleges_ [Washington, D.C.: Brookings Institution, 1962], pp. 201–203).

30. Shepard, "Basic Research."

31. Alfred M. Lee, "Sociological Theory in Public Opinion and Attitude Studies," *ASR* 12 (1947):312–323.

32. To Samuel Stouffer from Jessie Bernard, May 2, 1950 (the Stouffer Collection, Nathan Pusey Library, Harvard University, File 31.6, Box 2).

33. Paul F. Lazarsfeld, "An Episode in the History of Social Research: A Memoir," in *The Intellectual Migration: Europe and America 1930–1960*, ed. Donald Fleming and Bernard Bailyn (Cambridge: Belknap Press of Harvard University Press, 1969) p. 298.

34. Paul F. Lazarsfeld, "Reflections on Business," *AJS* 65 (1959):1–31.

35. Warren O. Hagstrom, *The Scientific Community* (New York: Basic Books, 1965), note 43, pp. 239–240; Norman Kaplan, "The Role of the Research Administrator," *Administrative Science Quarterly* 4 (1959):20–42. Kaplan finds that there was little tradition for the research institute or its director, and that as the complexity of research grew, the model of imitation was big-business enterprise. See also Norman Kaplan, "Research Administration and the Administrator: U.S.S.R and the U.S.," *Administrative Science Quarterly* 6 (1961):51–72; Marcson, in "Research Settings," in *The Social Contexts of Research*, ed. Nagi and Corwin, p. 167, notes academic antipathy to "management."

36. Rebecca Adams, "An Organization and Its Uncertain Environment: A Case Study of the National Opinion Research Center" (master's thesis, University of Chicago, 1977). I am indebted to Adams's formulation of the uncertainty of those flows in both prestige and money.

37. Storer's discussion puts the distinction between applied and basic science in the context of other creative professions and of the "temptation" to "go commercial" in engineering, fiction, and music (*The Social System of Science*, pp. 91–97).

38. Consider some negative reactions by social scientists. In a review of *The American Soldier* in *AJS* 55 (1950):590–594, Ethel Shanas chided the authors for their indulgence in colloquialism as well as for atheoretical inquiry; Nathan Glazer, in "*The American Soldier* as Science," *Commentary* 8 (1949):487–496, saw questionnaires as "fodder" for IBM machines; in a 1959 review, Morton Grodzins wrote that *The American Mind* by Lazarsfeld and Thielens was "a pretentious and awkward way to state the obvious" (*Ethics* 70 [Apr. 1959]:200). One of the most interesting criticisms of this period was Riesman and Glazer's analysis of the public opinion interviewer as a "pervasive symbol of the demand to be opinionated." The authors made artful use of a character in *Anna Karenina* who had no special interest in science, art, or politics but who, to quote Tolstoy, "held those views on all these subjects which were held by the majority and by his paper, and he only changed them when the majority changed them—or, more strictly speaking, he did not change them, but they imperceptibly changed of themselves within him." See David Riesman and Nathan Glazer, "The Meaning of Opinion," *POQ* 12 (1948):633–648.

39. Robert Alun Jones and Sidney Kronus, "Professional Sociologists and the History of Sociology: A Survey of Recent Opinion," *Journal of the History of the Behavioral Sciences* 12 (1976):3–13; Pitirim A. Sorokin, *Fads and Foibles in Modern Sociology and Related Sciences* (Chicago: Regnery, 1956), chap. 7. Sorokin had oth-

ers just as firmly in mind, such as Kurt Lewin, Stuart C. Dodd, Louis Guttman, Edward Suchman; C. P. Snow, *The Two Cultures and the Scientific Revolution* (New York: Cambridge University Press, 1961); Henrika Kuklick, "Boundary Maintenance in American Sociology: Limitations to Academic 'Professionalization,'" *Journal of the History of the Behavioral Sciences* 16 (1980):201–219.

40. Sophia Peterson, personal communication, June 19, 1982.

41. Herbert Blumer, "Public Opinion and Public Opinion Polling," *ASR* 13 (1948):542–549; discussion by Theodore M. Newcomb and Julian Woodward, pp. 549–554.

42. Interview with Peter H. Rossi, May 23, 1979; conversations with Angus Campbell.

43. Interview with John A. Clausen, May 30, 1980; Stouffer wrote to Percy Black that he was not surprised that some of his "friends around the University of Chicago don't think very much of *The American Soldier*. They would not be running true to form if they did" (letter to Black from Stouffer, Dec. 17, 1949, in Stouffer Collection, Nathan Pusey Library, Harvard University, File 31.6, Box 2).

44. C. Wright Mills, "Abstracted Empiricism," chap. 3 in *The Sociological Imagination* (New York: Grove Press [1959], 1961), esp. pp. 71–72.

45. Lindsay Rogers, *The Pollsters: Public Opinion, Politics, and Democratic Leadership* (New York: Knopf, 1949), pp. 11, 15, 125, 190–194.

46. Arthur M. Schlesinger, Jr., "The Statistical Soldier," *Partisan Review* 16 (1949):852–856.

47. Howard Mumford Jones, in "A Humanist Looks at Science," *Daedalus* 87 (1958):102–110, noted how scientists and humanists had their own particular language or jargon, and Jones thought communication was difficult but very important. Fiedler noted that the humanist's image of the sociologist was "that of a heavily subsidized, much-touted and honored scholar, torn at each moment between offers from industry and government—scarcely knowing, indeed, whether to take the rewards offered by the Coca Cola Company or the Air Force" for another documentation of the obvious. Fiedler felt the humanist's case had merit but had to be "discounted a little for the professional pique of the excluded which lies behind it" (pp. 186–187). See Leslie A. Fiedler, "Voting and Voting Studies," in Eugene Burdick and Arthur J. Brodbeck, *American Voting Behavior* (Glencoe, Ill.: The Free Press, 1959), pp. 184–196.

48. Joseph Wood Krutch, "The Average and the Norm," chap. 5 in *Human Nature and the Human Condition* (New York: Random House, 1959), p. 78.

49. Alfred C. Kinsey, Wardell B. Pomeroy, and Clyde E. Martin, *Sexual Behavior in the Human Male* (Philadelphia: W. B. Saunders, 1948).

50. Lionel Trilling, "The Kinsey Report," in Trilling, *The Liberal Imagination: Essays on Literature and Society* (Garden City, N.Y.: Anchor Books, Doubleday, [1950] 1953), p. 223.

51. Joseph Wood Krutch, "Are the Humanities Worth Saving?—II," *Saturday Review*, June 11, 1955, pp. 22–23.

52. Paul F. Lazarsfeld, "The Obligations of the 1950 Pollster to the 1984 Historian," AAPOR presidential address, *POQ* 14 (1950–51):617–638, esp. p. 636. NORC embarked on a pilot study of psychological well-being in 1960 or 1961

(the so-called happiness study), using probability samples in four communities of varying degrees of economic prosperity and depression. See Norman M. Bradburn and David Caplovitz, *Reports on Happiness* (Chicago: Aldine, 1965), and Norman M. Bradburn, *The Structure of Psychological Well-Being* (Chicago: Aldine, 1969). Gallup first asked about marital happiness in 1950; see *The Gallup Poll*, vol. 1, pp. 890, 898.

53. James B. Conant, "The Role of Science in Our Unique Society," presidential address, American Association for the Advancement of Science, Dec. 1947, *Science* 2769 (Jan. 23, 1948):77–83.

54. Stuart C. Dodd, "A Barometer of International Security," *POQ* 9 (1945):194–200; Hadley Cantril, ed., *Tensions That Cause Wars* (Urbana: University of Illinois Press, 1950).

55. Lazarsfeld, "A Memoir," pp. 294, 305 passim.

56. Donald G. Marquis, "Research Planning at the Frontiers of Science," presidential address, *The American Psychologist*, Oct. 1948, pp. 430–438.

57. Robert E. Park, "Human Migration and the Marginal Man," *AJS* 33 (1928):881–893; E. V. Stonequist, *The Marginal Man* (New York: Scribner's, 1937).

58. Ben-David and Collins, "Social Factors in the Origins of a New Science."

59. Lazarsfeld reflected on marginality: "According to his gifts and external circumstances, [the marginal man] may become a revolutionary, a surrealist, a criminal. In some cases his marginality may become the driving force for institutional efforts; the institution he creates shelters him and at the same time helps him crystallize his own identity. In my case there was a general convergence toward institutional innovation" (Lazarsfeld, "A Memoir," p. 302).

60. Sheridan uses the concept centrally in "The Research Bureau." Lazarsfeld himself saw the status of being "marginal" in both a positive and negative sense—as a source of innovation and as a source of difficulties in stabilizing funds for his organization in an academic setting. Sheridan does as well. See also Barton, "Paul Lazarsfeld and Applied Social Research," esp. the last section, "Problems of an unspecialized research organization." Lazarsfeld came to take particular pride in himself as an institutional innovator, and probably most leading alumni of the Bureau interpret his various directorships as stages of innovation (and perhaps many other social scientists do who do not have specific Bureau loyalties). There is an alternative view within the Bureau group, probably held by a minority, which sees an element of failure, even tragedy, in the failure of the 1950 professional school proposal and the ending of the Bureau in 1977. An outside observer, MacRae, suggests that "perhaps Lazarsfeld got himself wrong," because his greatest contribution may have been not in creating organizations but in "creating scholars" (Donald McRae, "The Master Surveyor," *Times Literary Supplement*, Sept. 26, 1980, p. 1073).

Gieryn and Hirsh find that the concept of marginality itself is so poorly defined as to be very difficult to use. Within that limit, they find that so-called marginal scientists in X-ray astronomy are no more likely to be innovative than others. See Thomas F. Gieryn and Richard F. Hirsh, "Marginality and Innovation in Science," *Social Studies of Science* 13 (1983):87–106.

61. Lazarsfeld, "A Memoir," p. 298. Edge and Mulkay consider scientific in-

novation in such fields as bacteriology, physical chemistry, crystallography, and others, emphasizing innovation emerging on the margins between disciplines and between basic and applied research communities. They cite T. Burns's work on the greater importance of the movement of people than the passage of information in technological transfer (note 21, p. 400). See David O. Edge and Michael J. Mulkay, *Astronomy Transformed: The Emergence of Radio Astronomy in Britain* (New York: Wiley, 1976).

62. R. W. Gerard, "Problems in the Institutionalization of Higher Education: An Analysis Based on Historical Materials," *Behavioral Science* 2 (1957):134–146.

63. Rensis Likert, "Behavioural Research: A Guide for Effective Action," in *Some Applications of Behavioural Research*, ed. Rensis Likert and Samuel P. Hayes, Jr. (Paris: UNESCO, 1957), p. 43; Rensis Likert, "The Sample Interview Survey as a Tool of Research and Policy Formation," in *The Policy Sciences: Recent Developments in Scope and Method*, ed. Daniel Lerner and Harold D. Lasswell (Stanford: Stanford University Press, 1951), p. 233; Rensis Likert, "The Sample Interview Survey: A Fundamental Research Tool of the Social Sciences," in *Current Trends in Psychology*, ed. Wayne Dennis (Pittsburgh: University of Pittsburgh Press, 1947), pp. 196–225.

64. Conversation with Charles F. Cannell, Sept. 5, 1983.

65. Press release, NORC, Sept. 24, 1946, NORC materials, ISR Library.

66. Hadley Cantril, "The Human Sciences and World Peace," *POQ* 12 (1948):236–242; idem, *The Pattern of Human Concerns* (New Brunswick, N.J.: Rutgers University Press, 1965).

67. Lazarsfeld, "A Memoir," pp. 286, 310.

68. Charles Y. Glock, "Some Implications of Organization for Social Research," *Social Forces* 30 (1951):129–134; Angus Campbell, "Administering Research Organizations," *American Psychologist* 8 (1953):225–230; Clyde W. Hart, "Some Factors Affecting the Organization and Prosecution of Given Research Projects," *ASR* 12 (1947):514–519.

69. Peter B. Clark and James Q. Wilson, "Incentive Systems: A Theory of Organizations," *Administrative Science Quarterly* 6 (1961–62):129–166.

70. Telephone interview with Lloyd A. Free, July 17, 1979.

71. Hadley Cantril, *The Human Dimension: Experiences in Policy Research* (New Brunswick, N.J.: Rutgers University Press, 1967), chap. 19.

72. See chaps. 9 and 11.

73. Rensis Likert and J. M. Willits, *Morale and Agency Management*, 4 pts. (Hartford, Conn.: Life Insurance Sales Research Bureau, 1940). See esp. pt. 3, pp. 79–80.

74. *Entrepreneur* is somehow more allusive and interesting than *businessman*, and it may offer the same kind of elegance-with-vagueness that other imports from the French seem to (e.g., *rapport, rapprochement, esprit*). Writing in 1949, Cartwright reflected, "Ten years ago it was the rare social psychologist who felt at home in the business world, in governmental agencies, in a union hall, or even among social workers. Furthermore, there existed very few institutional arrangements providing a basis for cooperative work. It is no accident that the men who made the earliest advances in the application of social psychology, who worked

out a *modus vivendi* in relation to practical men, were often regarded by their 'pure' colleagues as unusually smooth and polished 'operators.' Nor is it surprising that frequently they displayed social values closely similar to those held by their clients. Today the number of social psychologists working on 'even terms' with men of practical affairs has greatly increased, and those who are particularly skillful in developing good working relations are no longer viewed as peculiar deviates" (Dorwin Cartwright, "Basic and Applied Social Psychology," *Philosophy of Science* 16 [1949]:198–208, p. 199).

The role of the entrepreneur is vividly reconstructed by Rosenberg. The directors of the state agricultural experiment stations had to mediate between their lay constituency in the state legislature and farm population and the world of science, while also protecting their Hatch Act funds as best they could from university administrators who were trying to charge off teachers' funds to the federal funds allocated to the station. Only a handful of men successfully handled this complex and demanding role. See Charles E. Rosenberg, "Science, Technology, and Economic Growth: The Case of the Agricultural Experiment Station Scientist, 1875–1914," in Rosenberg, *No Other Gods*.

75. Shepard, "Basic Research," p. 56.

76. "The Reminiscences of Paul Felix Lazarsfeld," 1961–62, Oral History Collection, Butler Library, Columbia University, pp. 120–121.

77. Glock observed wryly in 1951, "Even though it is apparently regarded by some sociologists as too indelicate a subject to mention, the need for financial support must be recognized as the first of these organizational attributes" (Glock, "Some Implications of Organization," p. 130).

78. Personal interview.

79. Don Cahalan, personal communication, Sept. 12, 1982.

9. The Bureau of Applied Social Research

Note: "University Archives" refers to the permanent cataloged records of Columbia University at the Office of the Secretary, Low Library. The "Bureau Collection" refers to a small set of documents and papers of the Bureau (perhaps four linear feet) which were housed temporarily in the Office of the Secretary, Low Library, at the time that I consulted them. Copies of unpublished Bureau reports have been on file at the Lehman Library of Columbia University and are now available on microfiche. See n. 6.

1. Guy Benton Johnson and Guion Griffis Johnson, *Research in Service to Society: The First Fifty Years of the Institute for Research in Social Science at the University of North Carolina* (Chapel Hill: University of North Carolina Press, 1980); SSRC, *Minutes of the Conference of University Social Science Research Organizations*, Sept. 5–7, 1934, Lake George, N.Y., Appendix H, report by Dr. Odum on the University of North Carolina Institute for Research in Social Science. Odum's institute had predecessors in academic research in government, business, and industry. At the SSRC meetings of 1934, J. H. Willits, representing the Department of Industrial Research, founded in 1921 at the University of Pennsylvania, reported on the

problem of maintaining intellectual direction of applied research undertaken for industry: "Even though the research group is left completely independent, this independence is not apparent to outsiders" (*Minutes*, p. 53).

2. Martin Bulmer, *The Chicago School of Sociology* (Chicago and London: University of Chicago Press, 1984).

3. Historical accounts of the Bureau appear in Paul F. Lazarsfeld, "An Episode in the History of Social Research: A Memoir," in *The Intellectual Migration: Europe and America 1930–1960*, ed. Donald Fleming and Bernard Bailyn (Cambridge, Mass.: The Belknap Press of Harvard University Press, 1969); Phyllis Sheridan, "The Research Bureau in a University Context: A Case History of a Marginal Institution," Ph.D. diss., Columbia University Teachers College, 1979; and Allen H. Barton, "Paul Lazarsfeld and Applied Social Research," *Social Science History* 3 (1979):4–44. A fuller version of Barton's paper is published as "Paul Lazarsfeld and the Invention of the University Institute for Applied Social Research," in *Organizing for Social Research*, ed. Burkhardt Holtzner and Jiri Nehnevajsa (Cambridge, Mass.: Schenckman, 1982), pp. 17–83. This stresses a dynamic interplay between new research methods and theoretical findings, stimulating in turn still further methodological innovation. In "A Memoir," Lazarsfeld reflected that he could "keep the Bureau maneuvering between the intellectual and political purist and an industry from which I wanted cooperation without having to 'sell out'" (p. 321). On Lazarsfeld's social invention and applied contracts for business, see Barton, "Lazarsfeld and Applied Social Research," esp. pp. 9–14.

4. To Lynd from Frank D. Fackenthal (Provost), Sept. 26, 1940, University Archives, Lynd folder.

5. David L. Sills, "Paul Lazarsfeld . . . 'He Taught Us What Sociology Is—or Should Be,'" *Columbia Today*, Dec. 1976, pp. 41–42.

6. Unpublished reports to these clients and others are listed in the *Bibliography 1937–1977*, Bureau of Applied Social Research, compiled by Judith S. Barton. The bibliography has been published as Judith S. Barton, *Guide to the Bureau of Applied Social Research* (New York: Clearwater Publishing Co., 1984). The unpublished reports are available on microfiche from Clearwater Publishing Co., 1995 Broadway, New York, NY 10023.

7. Complete budget records were not preserved for the Bureau until 1944–45. Some earlier financial records survive in the Bureau Collection, especially in the folder labeled "Miscellaneous Financial Records, 1942–1960," which permit rough estimates of Bureau activity in the early 1940s. The range of income appears to have been $50,000–75,000, with the fraction attributable to "commercial work" ranging from about 35 to 75 percent. These figures somewhat overestimate the role of business because by Bureau convention before 1944, "commercial studies" referred to "all studies that are done upon request of a sponsor who is willing to pay all the expenses and necessary overhead"—which included work commissioned by nonprofit as well as business organizations. The Bureau's report for 1944 shows 81 percent of its total income ($68,989) from "commercial studies," for example. But if what appear to be nonprofit organizations are excluded, the fraction of the budget provided by work for profit-making organizations is 55 percent. I am assuming that the projects identified as Expert Poll,

NBC, Opinion Leaders, Superman, Subscription Radio, Station WNEW, True Story, Time, Schenley, and Chrysler represent research for profit-making firms, totaling $56,000, with $13,000 income coming from these organizations that I take to be nonprofit: the Lavanburg Foundation, the Jewish Social Service Association, the American Jewish Committee, Races of Mankind, and ADL (Anti-Defamation League). There is some ambiguity here, because neither the identity of the sponsors nor the nature of the research conducted for them is entirely clear. However, the financial statement does clearly distinguish two other categories: "Research Development" means income of $15,000 from the Rockefeller grant ($10,000) and the university ($5,000 to reimburse training costs), and another $5,460 comes from "Partially Endowed Studies." (The latter category lists income amounts ranging from $360 to $1,500 for five studies in radio, magazines, national stereotypes, the election study, and the articles for the *Nation*.)

As of 1944, the Bureau distinguished between business and nonprofit organizations. For 1944–45, Barton shows these percentages: business, 68 percent, nonprofit, 17 percent, and foundations, etc., 15 percent. From 1944–50, the business share ranged from 15 to 68 percent (mean 42.8%); from 1951 to 1960, it ranged from 3 to 24 percent (mean 13.6%).

8. Barton, "Lazarsfeld and Applied Social Research," pp. 14–15.

9. See note 3.

10. The atmosphere and structure of the Department of Sociology at Columbia before the appointments of Lazarsfeld and Merton are treated by Robert Bierstedt, "Robert M. MacIver: Political Philosopher and Sociologist," in *Sociological Traditions from Generation to Generation*, ed. Robert K. Merton and Matilda White Riley (Norwood, N.J.: Ablex, 1980), pp. 81–92. MacIver and Robert S. Lynd clashed over the replacement of Chaddock. MacIver wanted a focus on social structure and argued for Merton; Lynd advocated an orientation to practical service and expected Lazarsfeld to provide it. The resolution was to appoint both.

11. Merton estimates that he and Lazarsfeld discussed, planned, and talked about the Bureau and its intellectual directions some ten to fifteen hours per week, on the average, over the years 1942–1965 (interview with Robert K. Merton, Jan. 23, 1979). For the complementary influences of Merton and Lazarsfeld, see James S. Coleman, "Paul F. Lazarsfeld: The Substance and Style of His Work," in *From Generation to Generation*, ed. Merton and Riley; Hanan C. Selvin, "On Formalizing Theory," in *The Idea of Social Structure: Papers in Honor of Robert K. Merton*, ed. Lewis A. Coser (New York: Harcourt Brace Jovanovich, 1975), pp. 339–354; Seymour Martin Lipset, "Some Personal Notes in Tribute to Paul Lazarsfeld, a Great Methodologist and Teacher," in *A Handbook of Social Science Methods*, ed. Robert B. Smith and Peter K. Manning (Cambridge, Mass.: Ballinger, 1982).

12. "Report to the Council for Research in the Social Sciences," Dec. 11, 1946, p. 5, Bureau Collection, Robert MacIver Correspondence folder.

13. Talk by Paul Lazarsfeld at twentieth-anniversary celebration of Bureau, Bureau Collection, Twentieth-Anniversary folder.

14. Lazarsfeld reflected in 1961–62, "You see, to get a commercial contract is much more difficult than to get a government contract, because with a govern-

ment contract you know what the sources are, you know what the agencies are, and it's just a question of, so to say, getting into the stream of this available money. But for commercial contracts, you have to have new ideas, you have to know who needs what. It's infinitely more difficult. . . . It's more diversified. There's an element of laziness, intellectual laziness, that gets in. I don't want to argue free enterprise, but . . . I don't believe at all in this distinction between basic research and applied research. There's a lot of basic research which is quite trivial, and a lot of applied research which is quite ingenious. . . . I remember vividly a study we did for the Schenley Company, which bought the Roma Wine Corporation, and the question was, Why is it that Americans don't drink wine, and what can be done about it? Now, this is an extremely interesting and challenging problem. It just sounds so horrible, taking money from a whiskey company, and who cares whether people drink wine? (pp. 114–115). . . . I was in the game of free enterprise, because I could go on getting contracts, making money, or occasionally or very often making deficits. I had the full game of the market, without personal risk, and also without the excessive rewards. I have always known that that was a very important part of my enjoying the directorship so much. . . . It's selling, you see; it's not soliciting. A president begs. A bureau director sells. In addition, to invent what he sells on the spot . . . " (Reminiscences of Paul F. Lazarsfeld, Nov. 1961–Aug. 1962, Oral History Collection, Butler Library, Columbia University, p. 119).

In 1961, Lazarsfeld and Spivack wrote, "No observations in the field of organized research justify the distinction between 'applied' and 'basic.' A number of very important theoretical ideas grew out of research done for the purpose of solving a specific problem, while many studies originated without a practical goal but just because they seemed feasible have led nowhere. In the absence of good criteria, it is difficult to assess the present situation. But a review of the output by major institutes as compared to the papers published by academic journals gives the impression that attending to concrete problems has a stimulating effect on the creativeness of many scholars" (Paul F. Lazarsfeld and Sydney S. Spivack, "Observations on the Organization of Empirical Social Research in the United States," *Social Science Information* 29 [Dec. 1961]:3–37, p. 29).

15. "The activities of the Bureau of Applied Social Research as reflected in its budget," p. 3, Nov. 1944, Bureau Collection, Robert MacIver Correspondence folder.

16. Lazarsfeld, "A Memoir," p. 298. The lifted weights refer to psychophysical experiments (see chap. 2).

17. Paul F. Lazarsfeld, "Reflections on Business," *AJS* 65 (1959):1–31; Elihu Katz and Paul F. Lazarsfeld, *Personal Influence* (New York: The Free Press, 1955), pp. 6–7. Lazarsfeld felt that some members of the Bureau were a good deal less comfortable with the contract research for business than he was (Oral History, pp. 127–133). According to Miller, Lynd became estranged from the Bureau's orientation to method, theory, and pragmatic approach (S. M. Miller, "Struggles for Relevance: The Lynd Legacy," *Journal of the History of Sociology* 2 [1979–80]:58–63). See also Lynd's review of *The American Soldier* in the *New Republic*, Aug. 29, 1949, pp. 22–25, in which he decried the use of social science as an instrument of mass control.

18. Paul F. Lazarsfeld, "Historical Notes on the Empirical Study of Action: An Intellectual Odyssey" (1958), chap. 2 in *Qualitative Analysis: Historical and Critical Essays*, ed. Lazarsfeld (Boston: Allyn and Bacon, 1972), esp. p. 98.

19. Lipset, "Personal Notes"; Lazarsfeld, twentieth-anniversary talk, Bureau Collection; Oral History, pp. 114–122, passim.

20. To Lazarsfeld from Gentzler, July 12, 1944, University Archives, Bureau 1944–47 folder. See also memorandum to Philip Hayden (Secretary of the University) from Lynd, May 16, 1941, University Archives, Lynd folder. University administrators were also uneasy about the "Expert Poll" conducted by Arthur Kornhauser, identified with the Bureau and Columbia, published in *The American Magazine*. See memo to Lynd from Lazarsfeld, Feb. 1, 1944, University Archives, Lazarsfeld folder; to Lynd from Philip Hayden, June 19, 1945, University Archives, Lynd folder.

21. To bursar, from trustees and director of O.R.R, re a revolving fund of $15,000, Jan. 31, 1944. The memo explains that the development of ORR work "justifies the hope that within a few more years the Office will be completely self-supporting, while also continuing to provide training and research facilities for the Department of Sociology." The Rockefeller Foundation had been eager to see ORR become self-supporting, and the new three-year $60,000 grant awarded in 1941 was made with that understanding. See memo to Hayden from Lynd, May 16, 1941, and letter to Dr. Frank D. Fackenthal, provost, from Norma S. Thompson, secretary of the Rockefeller Foundation, May 20, 1941, both in University Archives, Lynd folder.

22. "The Activities of the Bureau of Applied Social Research as Reflected in Its Budget," Nov. 1944, p. 7, Bureau Collection, Robert MacIver Correspondence folder.

23. To Lazarsfeld from Gentzler, Aug. 15, 1944; to Lazarsfeld from Gentzler, Jan. 19, 1946, both in University Archives, Bureau 1944–1947 folder.

24. To Lynd from Fackenthal, Sept. 26, 1944, and Oct. 7, 1944, University Archives, Lynd folder. Lynd wrote to Fackenthal on Sept. 23, 1944, that he was uneasy about the use of Columbia University's name in the forthcoming *Nation* series.

25. Interview with Merton, Jan. 23, 1979.

26. To Fackenthal from Lynd, Oct. 11, 1944, University Archives, Lynd folder.

27. Stanton of CBS was kept on as the former codirector of ORR, but Lyman Bryson of Teachers College, who was also connected to CBS, was dropped so that "in this ticklish time of fighting off University criticism" there could be no accusation that ORR was "being dominated by one of the broadcasting chains." Stouffer, and Herbert Brucker of the Journalism School, were replaced by Robert M. MacIver, former chairman of the Columbia Department of Sociology and Edmund De S. Brunner, of the Columbia School of Education, who was closely identified with the department. (Brunner was a rural sociologist at Teachers College who had studied rural church and community through the Institute of Social and Religious Research. See chap. 1.) Lynd continued as the new chairman. (See letter to Lyman Bryson from Lynd, Nov. 22, 1944, Bureau Collection, Robert MacIver Correspondence folder.)

28. To Hayden from Lynd, Dec. 7, 1944, University Archives, Lynd folder.

29. "The Bureau of Applied Social Research, Report no. 1, by the Committee on Social Research Agencies to the Council for Research in the Social Sciences," May 15, 1945, p. 4, Bureau Collection, Cheatham folder.

30. The Cheatham report noted the expenses incurred by the director, adding that "if the burden of raising funds is lifted from the Director and the Bureau moves to the campus, these expenses will be greatly reduced" (report no. 1, p. 7).

31. Cheatham report no. 1, pp. 7–11.

32. Ibid., pp. 7–8.

33. Cheatham reports no. 1, p. 13; no. 2, pp. 2, 6; no. 3, p. 1.

34. To President Fackenthal from Lynd, Nov. 30, 1945, University Archives, Lynd folder.

35. "Materials for the Feb. 6, 1946 meeting, Board of Governors, Bureau of Applied Social Research," University Archives, Bureau 1944–1947 folder.

36. To Lazarsfeld from Gentzler, Jan. 2, 1946, University Archives, Bureau 1944–1947 folder.

37. The Bureau's statement of estimated income and expenditures for 1950–51 lists $97,000 for the U.S. Air Force and $40,000 for the Voice of America. The Bureau's statement of financial position for 1952–53 shows an income of almost $588,000: two contracts with the air force are shown to have totaled almost $269,000, with overhead paid at 25 percent; another $27,000 project for the Office of Naval Research paid overhead of 42.2 percent. See "Miscellaneous Finances 1942–1960," Bureau Collection; Barton, "Lazarsfeld and Applied Social Research," esp. pp. 14–15.

38. "An Historical Review and Current Report on the Operations of the Bureau of Applied Social Research, Prepared for the Information of the Board of Governors," Mar. 1951, p. 28, Bureau Collection.

39. To Grayson L. Kirk, Vice President, from BASR, re retirement of Bureau's deficit, Aug. 8, 1951, University Archives, Lazarsfeld 1951–52 folder.

40. Just before Glock left the Bureau, he tried to effect a more favorable financial arrangement for it. Bureau minutes reported his meeting with Vice President John A. Krout: "Dr. Glock pointed out that present fiscal policy places an undue strain on the Director and makes no provision for fiscal rewards for the successful operation of the Bureau. He indicated that he thought it was important that the University review its fiscal policy towards the Bureau and perhaps work out some arrangement whereby part of the earned surplus each year might be returned to the Bureau for its use. Dr. Krout expressed understanding for the situation and promised to bring it to President Kirk's attention" (Minutes of the meeting of the Administrative, Finance, and Policy Committee, Board of Governors, Dec. 1, 1958, p. 3, Bureau Collection, Board of Governors meeting minutes 1956–1958 folder).

41. Barton, "Lazarsfeld and Applied Social Research," pp. 14–15; interview with Clara Shapiro, Jan. 24, 1979. In the late 1950s, it was Shapiro's regular responsibility to point up the Bureau's contribution to the university.

42. Lazarsfeld was known to have put income from royalties or honoraria

back into the Bureau and to have paid students out of his pocket (interviews with Barton, Dec. 12, 1978; and Ann Pasanella, Dec. 13, 1978).

43. Barton, "Lazarsfeld and Applied Social Research," pp. 14–15.

44. "A Report on the Years 1960–61," Bureau of Applied Social Research, May 1962, pp. iii–vi.

45. Barton estimates that 100 people were "connected with"—a "deliberately loose term"—the Bureau, about half of them full time (Barton, "Lazarsfeld and Applied Social Research," p. 16). As a measure of potential influence, the absolute number of people involved is probably of greater interest than an estimate of full-time equivalence.

46. These figures are counts from the Bureau's *Bibliography*.

47. Interview with Barton, Dec. 12, 1978.

48. Interview with Merton, Jan. 23, 1979.

49. Sheridan, "The Research Bureau," pp. 28–32. In the Bureau's own Hanover (N.H.) Conference, June 28–29, 1956, staff members tried to evaluate present tendencies and chart future directions. One suggestion for improving the Bureau's position in the university was to take advantage of all opportunities to do service research for other university agencies. See the Bureau Collection, Hanover Conference folder.

50. Sheridan, "The Research Bureau," pp. 28–32.

51. Barton, interview Jan. 22, 1979. Continued efforts to interest other departments in the Bureau's work are apparent in the Bureau's minutes. See Bureau Collection, Minutes of the meeting of the Board of Governors folder, esp. May 2, 1955.

52. Barton, "Lazarsfeld and Applied Social Research," p. 36.

53. Interview with Merton, Jan. 23, 1979.

54. At the twentieth-anniversary celebration, Lazarsfeld hailed the Columbia Department of Sociology as "the leading department of any department anywhere in sociology at any university" and credited its eminence to the Bureau and to Merton: "From one point of view, it's due to the Bureau; the relation between the department and the Bureau has been imitated at other universities but certainly not equalled. But it is further made possible by the fact that the Bureau has never become a statistical mill, or whatever other terms the friends of Dean Barzun occasionally might use for our kind of activity. And this fact that the Bureau has been part of the core of the social sciences and not, as it is called at other universities, the research facilities, is due to the role of Bob Merton." Lazarsfeld also referred to Barzun's defining lower middle classes in his book on Berlioz—*Berlioz and the Romantic Century* (Boston: Little, Brown & Co., 1950)— as "those people who know enough to want more but don't know enough to want the right things. And I think that's a way the Bureau was looked at at Columbia for the first few years." The speech is preserved in the Bureau Collection, Twentieth-Anniversary folder.

In these years, the dean of the graduate faculties at Columbia had responsibility for overseeing three faculties (political science, pure science, and philosophy, which included the humanities); there was no dean of the social sciences. While Barzun was not sympathetic to quantitative social science or to the Bureau's work, Barton thinks it likely that the Bureau directors did not present him with a serious proposal for a more institutionalized, program-based Bureau. (See Barton, "Lazarsfeld and Applied Social Research"; personal interviews, Dec. 12, 1978, and Jan. 22, 1979.) Charles Y. Glock feels that Bureau research in this period nevertheless had attained considerable programmatic coherence, as shown in the *Twentieth-Anniversary Report* (personal communication). In that report, 513 Bureau publications and unpublished reports were arranged under fourteen major topics. Sixty percent of the items were grouped in four topics: Communication and the Mass Media (27%), Methodology (15%), Interpersonal Relations (9%), and Population and Manpower (9%). The remaining 40 percent of the listing was shared among ten topics, accounting for 1 to 7 percent each. So there was indeed both cumulation in mass communications and methodology and scatter in many other subjects.

Jacques Barzun's most pointed published objections to quantitative social science appeared in the 1960s. In *Science, the Glorious Entertainment* (New York: Harper & Row, 1964), Barzun identified Lazarsfeld as "leader of American quantitative sociology," and he cited a statement of Lazarsfeld's as an instance of behavioral research being "naturally imperialistic" (p. 178). In Barzun's *The American University* (New York: Harper & Row, 1968), he rued the "extension of government science in the academy" to the social sciences and the humanities that had adopted the "scientific fashion" out of envy not only of the money but also of the administrative attention that was lavished on scientists (pp. 145–146). In the 1950s, Barzun was apparently sympathetic to Lazarsfeld and Merton as intellects but chilly to their quantitative research (interviews with Charles Y. Glock, May 10, 1978; David L. Sills, Dec. 12, 1978; Robert K. Merton, Jan. 23, 1979). The Bureau's direct negotiations with Barzun were probably infrequent; at least, direct contact with other administrative figures is more visible in surviving Bureau records.

55. "Reply by Columbia University to Questions of Interest to the Trustees of the National Opinion Research Center," by Paul F. Lazarsfeld, p. 2, n.d., but questionnaires were sent out in fall-winter 1946–47 (Trustees' Correspondence 1941–1952, Director's Files, NORC). In 1946–47, Columbia's contribution to the Bureau had risen from $5,000 to $10,000 as new money was channeled to sociology for the Bureau's student training. (See memo to Lynd from Lazarsfeld re "Summary of Bureau's Budgetary Situation," May 29, 1947, in Bureau Collection, Miscellaneous Correspondence 1947–1950 folder.) Lazarsfeld was sanguine about more support from Columbia; he wrote that NORC's coming to the Columbia campus would be "a welcome occasion to approach the administration for a larger contribution" (Reply to NORC, p. 2).

56. Barton, "Lazarsfeld and Applied Social Research," p. 40; Glock, "Organizational Innovation," p. 27. Glock notes that Lazarsfeld believed that employing permanent staffs in interviewing, coding, and sampling "would heighten the necessity of accepting contracts of no research interest" to keep them occupied. Glock writes that while the policy was both a blessing and a handicap, "the net effect of the policy was to enlarge more than to limit the capacity to engage in cumulative research along theoretical and methodological lines being developed in the Bureau" (p. 27).

Glock's and Barton's interpretations of the Bureau are quite different. Glock stresses its continuity in both theory and methods; Barton emphasizes that methodological innovation thrived at the expense of programmatic continuity. Barton writes, "If [the Bureau] specialized in anything, it was initiating new research methods, because that was what Lazarsfeld specialized in" (p. 35). Barton thinks that one of the Bureau's major options was indeed to have created a permanent field staff. The disadvantages, in his view, would have included the need to hustle for contracts, but on the positive side, "the Bureau would have been in a better position to refine and develop survey techniques, including its own specialties of panel, sociometric, and contextual surveys" (Barton, "Lazarsfeld and Applied Social Research," pp. 36–37). These differing perspectives may represent their different eras as director—Glock from 1951 to 1957, and Barton from 1962 to 1977—and Barton's greater interest in understanding why the Bureau closed in 1977.

57. Memo to committee on programs and projects from Bill McPhee, n.d., probably 1956, Bureau of Applied Social Research Documents, Lehman Library, Columbia University.

58. Memorandum for discussion to members of department and others from James Coleman, Sept. 19, 1957. Coleman wrote these reflections when he was a member of the staff of NORC and of the Department of Sociology at Chicago. The document is probably filed at the Department of Sociology, University of Chicago. I obtained a Xeroxed copy from Rebecca Adams.

59. Bernard Berelson's "Reflections on the Bureau," April 1960, was sharply critical of the Bureau's atmosphere and research improvisation and recommended, among many changes, a focus on national and international policy research (Bureau Collection, Bernard Berelson Correspondence—Memos folder).

60. Paul F. Lazarsfeld and Robert K. Merton, "A Professional School for Training in Social Research" [1950], in *Qualitative Analysis: Historical and Critical Essays*, ed. Paul F. Lazarsfeld (Boston: Allyn and Bacon, 1972), pp. 361–391.

61. Interview with Patricia L. Kendall, Jan. 24, 1979.

62. The "codification of social research" project dates from the early or mid-1940s. Lazarsfeld sent a description of it to the Cheatham committee in Jan. 1945 and included it in his reply to NORC of 1946–47.

63. Paul F. Lazarsfeld and Morris Rosenberg, eds., *The Language of Social Research: A Reader in the Methodology of Social Research* (Glencoe, Ill.: The Free Press, 1955); and Herbert H. Hyman, *Survey Design and Analysis: Principles, Cases and Procedures* (Glencoe, Ill.: The Free Press, 1955).

64. Sills, "Paul Lazarsfeld." See also Anthony Oberschall, "Paul F. Lazarsfeld and the History of Empirical Social Research," *Journal of the History of the Behavioral Sciences* 14 (1978):199–206.

65. Coleman, "Lazarsfeld: The Substance and Style," in *Sociological Traditions*, ed. Merton and Riley, pp. 167–168.

66. Ibid.

67. Interview with David Caplovitz, Dec. 12, 1978.

68. Bernard Bailyn, "Recollections of PFL," in *Qualitative and Quantitative Social Research*, ed. Robert K. Merton, James S. Coleman, and Peter H. Rossi (New York: The Free Press, 1979).

69. Interview with Clara Shapiro, Jan. 24, 1979; Lazarsfeld, Oral History interview, 1961–62, passim. At that time Lazarsfeld complained about losing students but also took pride in the fact that Bureau alumni, notably Glock, Rossi, and Robert T. Bower, were directing other research organizations.

70. Coleman memorandum, Sept. 19, 1957.

71. Lazarsfeld, Oral History interview, pp. 132–134; personal interview with Patricia L. Kendall, Jan. 24, 1979.

72. William N. McPhee and William A. Glaser, eds., *Public Opinion and Congressional Elections* (New York: The Free Press, 1962); Daniel Lerner, *The Passing of Traditional Society: Modernizing the Middle East* (Glencoe, Ill.: The Free Press, 1958).

73. This theme recurs in the personal interviews or writings of all four: interview with Charles Y. Glock, May 10, 1978; interview with Peter H. Rossi, May 23, 1979; the reminiscences of Lipset and Coleman, cited in notes 11 and 65. Barton makes the same point more broadly (interview, Jan. 22, 1979). Shapiro points out that Lazarsfeld also developed people to the point at which they could strike out for themselves; she observed certain students who, under Lazarsfeld's direction, rose to achievements that they did not duplicate afterward (interview, Jan. 24, 1979). Lazarsfeld's dominance in publication is apparent in the first years of the Bureau. In the first decade, approximately 100 published articles are listed in the Bureau's *Bibliography*, and 44 percent of these were written by Lazarsfeld alone or with collaborators. In the second decade, the comparable figure is 14 percent of approximately 155 articles. In the Bureau *Bibliography* submitted to the Cheatham Committee in 1945, 51 articles were listed; Lazarsfeld was the sole author of 18, senior author of 9, and junior author of 2—accounting for 57 percent of the total.

74. Seymour Martin Lipset, Martin A. Trow, and James S. Coleman, *Union Democracy* (Glencoe, Ill.: The Free Press, Anchor edition, 1956), explained the omission of significance tests as appropriate to studies that were "exploratory" rather than "confirmatory" (p. 483). In "Lazarsfeld and Applied Social Research," Barton deals with the Bureau's work generally as explorations that focused on methodological rather than substantive specialization. Lazarsfeld saw his own work on voting as exploratory, and he recommended much more of the same. In a 1949 talk, "A Sociological Approach to Politics," he recommended developing perhaps 300 studies of voting behavior in various parts of the United States from which to begin to develop organizing concepts of what would be applicable to other fields of research. (See SSRC, Conference on Research into Political Behavior, Aug. 29, 1949, Ann Arbor, Mich. This talk is filed in a temporary archive of historical materials at the Institute for Social Research.) The interpretive thrust of the published political studies goes considerably beyond variables of the community, which are not fleshed out much, into implications for national politics, such as the last-minute shift to Truman and the theory of voter apathy. For the 1948 study (Bernard Berelson, Paul F. Lazarsfeld, and William N. McPhee, *Voting* [Chicago: University of Chicago Press, 1954]), Elmira, New York, was chosen as a "labor town" in anticipation that labor-management issues would be central in the campaign. (See letter to Charles Dollard, Carnegie Corporation, from Bernard Berelson, Jan. 29, 1948, in Stouffer Collection, Na-

than Pusey Library, Harvard University.) But in fact the Elmira area proved to be "so solidly Republican that the AF of L's Labor League for Political Education and the CIO's Political Action Committee sent neither money nor trained men to try to influence the election there" (Berelson et al., *Voting*, p. 38). Local leaders in the area tended to feel that political activity by unions should be nonpartisan (Ibid., p. 40). Rossi observes that the authors and the observers from Cornell were unprepared to deal analytically with the level of political activity the unions did engage in because they expected so much more (Rossi, "Four Landmarks," pp. 30–32). Some analytic use is made, nevertheless, of effects on both Republicans and Democrats in a heavily Republican "climate of opinion" (ibid., pp. 100–106).

75. Robert K. Merton, George G. Reader, and Patricia L. Kendall, *The Student Physician: Introductory Studies in the Sociology of Medical Education* (Cambridge, Mass.: Harvard University Press, 1957), pp. 301–305. See also Lipset et al., *Union Democracy*, pp. 480–485; Hanan Selvin, "A Critique of Tests of Significance in Survey Research," *ASR* 22 (1957):519–527.

76. James A. Davis, review of Merton et al., *The Student Physician, AJS* 63 (1957–58):445–446; Daniel Katz, review of Berelson et al., *Voting, POQ* 19 (1955):326–328.

77. Among reviews critical of Bureau books bearing on survey research see *IJOAR* 5 (1951):422–423; *ASR* 21 (1956):508–509; *ASR* 18 (1953):465–466; *APSR* 53 (1949):887; *Rural Sociology* 20 (1955):328; *Contemporary Psychology* 1 (1956):137–140. For positive reviews, see *ASR* 21 (1956):395–396; *POQ* 15 (1951):161–163; *AJS* 57 (1951–52):90–92; *AJS* 64 (1958–59):197; *ASR* 14 (1949):178–179; *POQ* 22 (1958–59):167–168; *POQ* 20 (1956–57):730–732; *AJS* 62 (1956–57):339–340.

78. Paul F. Lazarsfeld, Bernard Berelson, and Hazel Gaudet, *The People's Choice* (New York: Duell, Sloan, and Pearce, 1944); Berelson et al., *Voting*. Chap. 14 of *Voting*, "Democratic Practice and Democratic Theory," relates voter apathy and political stability.

79. Elihu Katz and Paul F. Lazarsfeld, *Personal Influence* (New York: The Free Press, 1955), pp. 32–34.

80. Robert K. Merton, "Patterns of Influence: Local and Cosmopolitan Influentials," in *Social Theory and Social Structure*, rev. enlarged ed. (Glencoe, Ill.: The Free Press [1949], 1957) pp. 387–420; Elihu Katz, "The Two-Step Flow of Communication: An Up-to-Date Report on an Hypothesis," *POQ* 21 (1957):61–78; James Coleman, Elihu Katz, and Herbert Menzel, "The Diffusion of an Innovation among Physicians," *Sociometry* 20 (1957):253–270; Herbert Menzel, "Planned and Unplanned Scientific Communication," [1959] in *The Sociology of Science*, ed. Bernard Barber and Walter Hirsch (New York: The Free Press, 1962), pp. 417–441; Herbert Menzel, "Innovation, Integration, and Marginality: A Survey of Physicians," *ASR* 25 (1960):704–713; Paul F. Lazarsfeld and Wagner Thielens, *The Academic Mind: Social Scientists in a Time of Crisis*, with a field report by David Riesman (Glencoe, Ill.: The Free Press, 1958).

81. Heinz Eulau, "The Columbia Studies of Personal Influence," *Social Science History* 4 (1980):207–228; Carl A. Sheingold, "Social Networks and Voting: The Resurrection of a Research Agenda," *ASR* 38 (1973):712–720; Maxwell E.

McCombs and D. L. Shaw, "The Agenda-Setting Function of the Mass Media," *POQ* 36 (1972):176–187; Steven H. Chaffee, "Asking New Questions about Communication and Politics," Foreword in *Political Communication: Issues and Strategies for Research*, ed. Chaffee, *Sage Annual Reviews of Communication Research*, vol. 4 (Beverly Hills: Sage Publications, 1975); Todd Gitlin, "Media Sociology: The Dominant Paradigm," *Theory and Society* 6 (1978):205–253; Elihu Katz, "On Conceptualizing Media Effects," *Studies in Communication* 1 (1980):119–141; Gabriel Weimann, "On the Importance of Marginality: One More Step into the Two-Step Flow of Communication," *ASR* 47 (1982):764–773.

82. Bobbs-Merrill reprinted twenty-seven articles written by Bureau authors between 1944 and 1960. See the Bureau *Bibliography*, p. 68A.

83. Approximately 375 unpublished reports are listed in the Bureau *Bibliography* for the years 1937–1960, as well as forty-five master's theses, thirty-five Ph.D. dissertations, and twenty-four monographic studies. Almost all of the reports are available from Clearwater Publishing Co. (see n. 6). The dissertations are available from University Microfilms.

84. Paul F. Lazarsfeld, "The Controversy over Detailed Interviews: An Offer for Negotiation," *POQ* 8 (1944):38–60.

85. Katz and Lazarsfeld, *Personal Influence*, p. 339.

86. Lazarsfeld and Rosenberg, *The Language of Social Research*, p. 5; the quote is italicized in the original.

87. Robert K. Merton, Marjorie Fiske, and Alberta Curtis, *Mass Persuasion: The Social Psychology of a War Bond Drive* (New York: Harper, 1946).

88. Ibid., pp. 192, 195. The guide was an instance of the "focused" interview, in which the objective content of a media communication was analyzed first and then the respondent's subjective response to that content was evoked by intensive, freely devised questioning. An important purpose of the focused interview was to aid retrospection—respondents' recall of what they had experienced at the time rather than their considered, later reactions. The qualitative data of focused interviews were to aid quantitative data analysis in heuristic (pilot/pretest) inquiry and interpretation—indeed, the very purposes Lazarsfeld saw as critical for open-ended questions in his 1944 article cited in note 84. See Robert K. Merton, Marjorie Fiske, and Patricia L. Kendall, *The Focused Interview: A Manual of Problems and Procedures* (Glencoe, Ill.: The Free Press, 1956).

89. Five different sources of data were gathered, but the book's tables were based largely on three sources: national poll data gathered by Gallup and two Bureau surveys, one of which was an intensive interview with the 234 volunteers. See David L. Sills, *The Volunteers: Means and Ends in a National Organization* (Glencoe, Ill.: The Free Press, 1957), esp. pp. 275–282.

90. Hazel Gaudet, "A Model for Assessing Changes in Voting Intention," in Lazarsfeld and Rosenberg, *The Language of Social Research*, pp. 428–438.

91. Ibid., p. 428.

92. Ibid., p. 435.

93. Rossi, "Four Landmarks," p. 24.

94. William Buchanan and Hadley Cantril, *How Nations See Each Other: A Study in Public Opinion* (Urbana: University of Illinois Press, 1953).

95. Lerner, *The Passing of Traditional Society*, questionnaire, pp. 415–433.

96. Ibid., p. 80.

97. Ibid.

98. Patricia L. Kendall, "The Ambivalent Character of Nationalism among Egyptian Professionals," *POQ* 20 (1956):277–292; Benjamin B. Ringer and David L. Sills, "Political Extremists in Iran: A Secondary Analysis of Communications Data," *POQ* 16 (1952–53):689–701.

99. Berelson et al., *Voting*, pp. 363–366.

100. Katz and Lazarsfeld, *Personal Influence*, Appendix C, "On Follow-up Interviewing and Analysis"; personal interview with David Caplovitz, Dec. 12, 1978. A brief account of the administrative difficulties appears in Irving Louis Horowitz, *C. Wright Mills: An American Utopian* (New York: The Free Press, 1983), pp. 77–82.

101. The concept of respondent "burden"—that survey questions can tax respondents with heavy tasks of recall and abstraction—is a recent one, to which Bradburn and Sudman, especially, have given attention. See Norman N. Bradburn, Seymour Sudman, and Associates, *Improving Interview Method and Questionnaire Design* (San Francisco: Jossey-Bass, 1979).

102. Katz and Lazarsfeld, *Personal Influence*, pp. 341–343. For recent research on underreporting of even personal hospitalization, presumably of far greater salience than small consumer purchases, see Charles F. Cannell, Peter V. Miller, and Lois Oksenberg, "Research on Interviewing Techniques," in *Sociological Methodology 1981*, ed. Samuel Leinhardt (San Francisco: Jossey-Bass, 1981).

103. Everett M. Rogers, *Diffusion of Innovations*, 3d ed. (New York: The Free Press, 1983). The other classic study cited by Rogers is Bryce Ryan and Neal C. Gross, "The Diffusion of Hybrid Seed Corn in Two Iowa Communities," *Rural Sociology* 8 (1943):15–24.

104. Peter H. Rossi, *Why Families Move* (Glencoe, Ill.: The Free Press, 1955); Lipset et al., *Union Democracy*.

105. Lazarsfeld and Thielens, *The Academic Mind*. The report by David Riesman on the fieldwork by Roper and NORC interviewers is discussed briefly in chap. 10.

106. In 1958–59, Coleman anticipated that the Bureau efforts to study social organization and process—such as networks of friends, coworkers, housing residents, paired medical students, and cliques—was a frontier that was just opening with computers (James S. Coleman, "Relational Analysis: The Study of Social Organization with Survey Methods," *Human Organization* 17 [Winter 1958–59]:28–36). In recent years he has concluded that Lazarsfeld's work did not capitalize on group properties. Coleman finds that Lazarsfeld's dominant influence on sociology has been in the analysis of individual action and that he neither fully understood sociological concepts nor successfully brought methods to bear on them: "Even when a community was the setting [as in the voting studies and in *Personal Influence*], the analysis was not of a community but of individual decision-making in a social context. This direction of work Paul Lazarsfeld so impressed upon the discipline of sociology that we all do it now, not just those in a 'Lazarsfeld tradition' or a 'Columbia tradition'" (Coleman, "Lazarsfeld, Substance and Style," p. 164).

Coleman speculates that Lazarsfeld was influenced critically by his migration (from closed communities such as Marienthal) to America where, suddenly, mass media seemed so powerful. Coleman's emphasis on the hiatus between Lazarsfeld's Viennese and American experience neglects two other influences from the Vienna days which suggest continuity in attention to the social psychology of the individual: Lazarsfeld's disciplinary training as a *psychologist* with the Bühlers and his experience in *market research* in consumer preferences.

In 1968, Barton urged that sociologists develop further some of the Bureau's sample designs for "including social structure": "For the last thirty years, empirical social research has been dominated by the sample survey. But as usually practiced, using random sampling of individuals, the survey is a sociological meatgrinder, tearing the individual from his social context and guaranteeing that nobody in the study interacts with anyone else in it" (Allen H. Barton, "Bringing Society Back in Survey Research and Macro-Methodology," *American Behavioral Scientist* XII [1968]:1–9 [quote is from p. 1]).

107. Eulau notes that network analysis has developed not only through computer technology that was not available until recent years but also through different concepts and a unit of analysis as the *communication* rather than the individual. See note 81.

108. Hans Zeisel, *Say It with Figures*, rev. 4th ed. (New York: Harper & Row, 1957), p. 161.

109. Lazarsfeld, "Historical Notes on the Empirical Study of Action: An Intellectual Odyssey," p. 81.

110. Lazarsfeld came to view "action" research as something of a "homeless skill or art," rejected by disciplinary bias: "In the American structure, at that time especially, academic psychology was so strongly behaviorist-oriented that this study of people's decisions had too much of an introspective element and was not acceptable. On the other hand, I think that beginning with the statistical study of people's decisions was too optimistic [atomistic?] for sociologists. It was too individual for sociologists, and too introspective for academic psychologists; therefore, it became necessary to look for a new form of academic setting where one could do such work"—referring to the founding of the Bureau (Nico Stehr, "A Conversation with Paul F. Lazarsfeld," *The American Sociologist* 17 [1982]:150–154). With the exception of the material quoted earlier in this chapter, I have not found general discussions by Lazarsfeld of problems in recall and validity posed by this kind of research nor systematic discussion of the problems he experienced in trying to use it in the election study of 1940. In *The Volunteers*, Sills pointed to difficulties that respondents had in reconstructing what goals they had initially had in mind when they joined the foundation, sometimes because the experience of being a volunteer swamped their recollection of what had moved them to become one (see Sills, *The Volunteers*, pp. 94–95). The applicability of Lazarsfeld's techniques to market research was called into question by Harry Henry, "We Cannot Ask 'Why'" [1953], in *Perspectives in Management, Marketing and Research*, ed. Henry (London: Crosby Lockwood, 1971), pp. 293–311, who argued from his own research that people did not know why they used particular products; cited by Catherine Marsh, *The Survey Method* (London and Boston: Allen & Unwin, 1982). Nisbett and Wilson's current experimental work suggests that people report poorly on their own thought processes; respondents are usu-

ally found not to engage in real introspection but instead to consider their own behavior in the light of implicit causal theories that they apply to other people's behavior. See Timothy De Camp Wilson and Richard E. Nisbett, "The Accuracy of Verbal Reports about the Effects of Stimuli on Evaluations and Behavior," *Social Psychology* 41 (1978):118–131; Richard E. Nisbett and Timothy De Camp Wilson, "Telling More than We Can Know: Verbal Reports on Mental Processes," *Psychological Review* 84 (1977):231–259.

111. Paul F. Lazarsfeld, "Survey Analysis: The Analysis of Attribute Data," in *The International Encyclopedia of the Social Sciences (IESS)*, ed. David L. Sills (New York: MacMillan/Free Press, 1968), 15:419–429; Hanan C. Selvin, "Survey Analysis," *IESS* 15:411–419. In "The Shortcomings of Tabular Analysis," a short chapter in their book *Delinquency Research: An Appraisal of Analytic Methods* (New York: The Free Press, 1967), pp. 162–174, Travis Hirschi and Hanan C. Selvin saw in tabular analysis four basic defects: interminable analysis, wastefully large samples, ambiguous causal inferences (especially because one is likely to run out of cases), and inefficient search procedures. They highly recommended multiple regression (for continuous or ordinal dependent variables) and discriminant analysis (for categorical dependent variables). But they thought that tables would continue to have utility—for summarizing the results of a long and complicated analysis and for providing ease of understanding to both lay readers and professional social scientists.

112. Zeisel, *Say It with Figures*, p. 3.

113. Patricia L. Kendall and Katherine M. Wolf, "The Analysis of Deviant Cases in Communications Research," in *Communications Research 1948–1949*, ed. Paul F. Lazarsfeld and Frank N. Stanton (New York: Harper, 1949), pp. 152–179.

114. Paul F. Lazarsfeld, "Interpretation of Statistical Relations as a Research Operation," in *Language of Social Research*, ed. Lazarsfeld and Rosenberg, pp. 115–125; Patricia L. Kendall and Paul F. Lazarsfeld, "Problems of Survey Analysis," in *Continuities in Social Research: Studies in the Scope and Method of "The American Soldier,"* ed. Robert K. Merton and Paul F. Lazarsfeld (Glencoe, Ill.: The Free Press, 1950), pp. 133–196.

115. This discussion condenses the treatment in references given above (notes 112 and 114); in chap. 7 by Patricia L. Kendall in Hyman, *Survey Design and Analysis*; and in Charles Y. Glock, *Survey Research in the Social Sciences* (New York: Russell Sage Foundation, 1967), chap. 1.

116. Morris Rosenberg, *The Logic of Survey Analysis* (New York: Basic Books, 1967), extends elaboration into a more complex system of "distorter," "suppressor," and other types of variables.

117. James S. Coleman, introduction, in *The Varied Sociology of Paul F. Lazarsfeld*, ed. Patricia L. Kendall (New York: Columbia University Press, 1982); Glock, introduction, *Survey Research in the Social Sciences*.

118. Paul F. Lazarsfeld, "The Use of Panels in Social Research," *Proceedings of the American Philosophical Society* 92 (1948):405–410; Charles Y. Glock, "Some Applications of the Panel Method to the Study of Change" [1951], in *The Language of Social Research*, ed. Lazarsfeld and Rosenberg, pp. 242–250. Two Bureau dissertations dealt specifically with the panel: Charles Y. Glock, "Participation

Bias and Re-Interview Effect in Panel Studies" (1952), and Lee M. Wiggins, "Mathematical Models for the Interpretation of Attitude and Behavior Change: The Analysis of Multi-Wave Panels" (1955).

119. Evidence for the "limited effects" model was brought together by the Bureau's Joseph T. Klapper, *The Effects of Mass Communication* (Glencoe, Ill.: The Free Press, 1960). It provided the context in which massive, hypodermic-like effects were expected to operate on atomized individuals in a mass society; limited effects were discovered instead, as the impact of the media was seen to be mediated by such intrapersonal and interpersonal factors as selective perception, group norms, and patterns of leadership. Elihu Katz's article "On Conceptualizing Media Effects," *Studies in Communication* 1 (1980):119–141, brings the theory up to date, setting forth nine different perspectives (agenda setting, diffusion of information, limited vs. powerful effects, etc.), and pointing up the conceptual and analytic difficulties in measuring long-term effects.

120. Rossi, "Four Landmarks," p. 17.

121. Lazarsfeld, Berelson, and Gaudet, *The People's Choice*, 3d ed. (New York: Columbia University Press [1944], 1968), p. 100.

122. Ibid., pp. 75–84.

123. To Lazarsfeld from Gaudet, Feb. 3, 1942, Washington National Records Center, Suitland, Md., RG 44, Entry 160, Box 1764, Panel-Sandusky folder.

124. To Lazarsfeld from Wilson, July 23, 1942, WNRC, RG 44, Entry 161, Box 1777, Gallup-Lazarsfeld Panel folder. Results of this study appear in Paul F. Lazarsfeld and Ruth Durant, "National Morale, Social Cleavage and Political Allegiance," *Journalism Quarterly* 19 (1942):150–158.

125. NORC conducted a before-and-after national panel of the 1944 election with some collaboration with Lazarsfeld, but what the arrangement was is not entirely clear. In the preface to the 1948 edition of *The People's Choice*, the Bureau appears to have had the initiating role (p. xxvii); in the preface to the 1968 edition, however, there is a comment that "because of the war we could not carry out a second voting study in 1944" (p. vii). NORC records this study in its bibliography but does not identify a sponsor or associate the study with Lazarsfeld or the Bureau. The study was designed in part by Sheldon J. Korchin, who used the data for his dissertation, under Gordon Allport's supervision at Harvard, "Psychological Variables in the Behavior of Voters" (1946). One conceptual concern was why voters so largely abandon party hostilities immediately after the election. Korchin remembers that Lazarsfeld read a draft of his dissertation, but he does not recall other contact (personal interview with Sheldon J. Korchin, May 30, 1980). Ruth Ziff wrote a master's thesis at Columbia with the 1944 data, which NORC made available to the Bureau (see *POQ* 12 [1948]:326–328).

126. Merton, Reader, and Kendall, *The Student-Physician*.

127. Rossi, "Four Landmarks," p. 26.

128. Morris Rosenberg, Wagner Thielens, and Paul F. Lazarsfeld, "The Panel Study," in *Research Methods in Social Relations*, ed. Marie Jahoda, Morton Deutsch, and Stuart W. Cook (New York: Dryden, 1951), vol. 2, p. 608.

129. Zeisel noted in *Say It with Figures* (rev. 4th ed.) that the panel surpassed the ordinary field survey not only in the quantity of information (p. 218) but also

in the quality, because of the steadily improving rapport between interviewer and respondent (p. 241).

130. Seymour M. Lipset, Paul F. Lazarsfeld, Allen H. Barton, and Juan Linz, "The Psychology of Voting: An Analysis of Political Behavior," in *Handbook of Social Psychology*, ed. Gardner Lindzey (Cambridge, Mass.: Addison-Wesley, 1954), vol. 2, pp. 1124–1175, esp. p. 1161.

131. Paul F. Lazarsfeld and Robert K. Merton, "Friendship as Social Process: A Substantive and Methodological Analysis," in *Varied Sociology*, ed. Kendall, pp. 298–348.

132. Stock and Wilson participated in eleven meetings.

133. Jean M. Converse, "Strong Arguments and Weak Evidence: The Open/ Closed Questioning Controversy of the 1940s," *POQ* 48 (1984):267–282, esp. p. 276.

134. This 1950 address is reprinted in *Qualitative Analysis*, ed. Lazarsfeld, pp. 278–299.

135. Ibid., pp. 290–291.

136. Ibid., p. 291.

137. This 1957 article is reprinted in *Qualitative Analysis*, ed. Lazarsfeld, pp. 300–317.

138. Ibid., p. 302.

10. The National Opinion Research Center

ABBREVIATIONS

Burgess Papers. The Papers of Ernest W. Burgess, Department of Special Collections, Regenstein Library, University of Chicago.

Director's Files. Files of NORC Director, NORC Library, University of Chicago.

Materials Relevant. Materials Relevant to the Trustees' Meetings 1941 through 1950, Director's Files, NORC Library, University of Chicago.

Wirth Papers. The Papers of Louis Wirth, Department of Special Collections, Regenstein Library, University of Chicago.

1. "Harry Hubert Field, 1897–1946," *IJOAR* 1 (Mar. 1947):93–95; *POQ* 10 (1946):399.

2. *NORC Brochure*, untitled, n.d. but probably summer or fall 1941, NORC Library, University of Chicago. Another brochure entitled "Announcement of Purposes" was probably published in 1943.

3. To James H. Causey from Harry Field, n.d., filed with NORC documents of 1941, NORC Library.

4. "A Proposal for a Public Opinion Foundation, Prepared by Harry H. Field, New York, President, People's Research Corporation, 1939–41" (n.d. but probably 1940–41), Materials Relevant.

5. Personal interviews with Anne Schuetz Zanes, July 3, 1978, and Feb. 12, 1982; with Paul B. Sheatsley, Apr. 12, 1977; and with Don Cahalan, Jan. 20, 1978. Harry Hubert Field, *After Mother India* (London: Jonathan Cape, 1929).

6. These figures are taken from *American Colleges and Universities* for 1947–48 (Washington, D.C.: American Council on Education), so they are approximations for the early 1940s.

7. See "Notes of Series of July 1941 Conferences with Dr. George Gallup of the American Institute of Public Opinion," H. Field, Director's Files, NORC, and "Minutes of a Special Meeting of the Board of Trustees of NORC, Sept. 21, 1946," p. 4, Materials Relevant. While various professional reasons motivated the move West, it also seems likely that the poor health of Field's wife made the climate of Colorado an attraction. She died in 1944.

8. Chancellor Gates's role is discussed in "Report on Where the Proposed Opinion Research Center Should Be Located," H. Field, June, 1941, Materials Relevant. The connection between Cherrington and Field is recalled by Paul B. Sheatsley (personal communication, Feb. 1, 1985). (Ben M. Cherrington should not be confused with Paul T. Cherington [in chap. 3, esp.].)

9. Report no. 1 to the Directors of the Field Foundation from NORC, Sept. 1941, p. 5, Director's Files. It is not clear from the record whether Gates intended that the university pay academic salaries to the researchers. It was symbolic support, in any case, and may have been more.

10. See the two sets of minutes of the meeting of the NORC Corporation and NORC Board of Trustees, Director's Files.

11. Hadley Cantril, *The Human Dimension: Experiences in Policy Research* (New Brunswick, N.J.: Rutgers University Press, 1967), esp. pp. 165–166. Cantril writes that he put Harry Field in contact with Marshall Field.

12. "Report on Where the Proposed Opinion Research Center Should Be Located," June 1941; letter to Harry Field from Louis S. Weiss, Secretary of Field Foundation, July 17, 1941, Materials Relevant.

13. "Notes on Discussions with Elmo Roper," July 1941, Materials Relevant; *NORC Brochure*, p. 2.

14. *NORC Brochure*, p. 1.

15. To Marshall Field from Harry Field, Dec. 8, 1943, Director's Files; "Report to NORC Trustees for Meeting of June 20, 1944," p. 6, Materials Relevant.

16. *NORC Brochure*, p. 3. See also the booklet *The New Science of Public Opinion Measurement* (Princeton, N.J.: American Institute of Public Opinion, n.d. but probably 1941). The first edition was published in 1938.

17. "Report to NORC Trustees for Meeting of June 20, 1944," pp. 5–6; "Report for Special Meeting of the Board of Trustees, Sept. 21, 1946," Director's Files.

18. *NORC Brochure*, p. 1.

19. Ibid., p. 7.

20. As NORC became better known, the number of inquiries from academicians and others mounted, and many were time-consuming requests that could not be billed. See "Agenda and Report for NORC's Trustees Meeting, Oct. 15, 1945," Materials Relevant.

21. *NORC Brochure*, p. 8.

22. "Report to the Board of Trustees, Dec. 17, 1943," p. 3, Materials Relevant.

23. *NORC Brochure*, p. 1.

24. The graduate program was not listed with the other purposes, as of early

1943, on official publications. NORC prepared a special brochure, *Graduate Study in Public Opinion Measurement and Analysis*, probably circulated in 1943–44, publicizing research topics for which it had data and small research stipends. The scope of the graduate program proved to be smaller than had originally been hoped, in good part because of the war. The program resurfaced in publications after the war and figured in the negotiations for moving NORC to Chicago.

25. Sheldon J. Korchin, "Psychological Variables in the Behavior of Voters" (Ph.D. diss., Harvard University, 1946); Albert B. Udow, "The 'Interviewer Effect' in Public Opinion and Market Research Surveys," *Archives of Psychology*, no. 277, New York, Columbia University, 1942.

26. The graduate program at Denver is described in Don Cahalan, "Opinion Research Training at the University of Denver," *IJOAR* 2 (1948):341–348. For other references to the Denver Community Survey, see n. 148.

27. "Confidential Report to NORC Trustees as of March 1943," p. 4, Director's Files.

28. Paul B. Sheatsley, "NORC: The First Forty Years," in *NORC Report 1981–82* (Chicago: NORC, 1982); interview with Paul B. Sheatsley, Apr. 12, 1977.

29. Field's memorandum of May 3, 1943, explains that NORC's own work would be cut down by just that fraction spent on others, "unless we change our present basis of making surveys for others for *not more than actual out-of-pocket expenses*" (italics in original) (pp. 3–4). The first reference to overhead, calculated as 60 percent of hourly salaries, appears to be that in the minutes of the board of trustees meeting for Oct. 15, 1945, p. 5, Materials Relevant.

30. Memorandum, May 3, 1943, p. 4, Materials Relevant.

31. To M. Field from H. Field, Dec. 8, 1943, p. 4, Director's Files.

32. Financial reports are usually included with minutes of the board of trustees meetings, Director's Files.

33. See NORC Report no. 18, "Should Soldiers Vote?" Jan. 1944, NORC Library.

34. It is not oversimplifying their respective suggestions much to say that Cantril wanted NORC to do more government policy research (he advised getting "tips" on what was coming up in Congress), Allport wanted it to focus on race relations and postwar problems, and Stouffer wanted it to get more social scientists who were mathematically trained—something of a projective test of their own professional interests. See minutes of the meeting of the board of trustees, April 9, 1943; Dec. 17, 1943; and May 25–26, 1945, Materials Relevant.

35. Some typed notes are not dated but are filed with NORC meeting materials for 1943 and reflect the concerns of that year. "Report to NORC Trustees for Meeting of June 20, 1944," Materials Relevant.

36. Ibid., p. 4.

37. The 1942 data were gathered in Survey No. S-1, Apr. 15, 1942; they are reported in Hyman et al., *Interviewing in Social Research*, pp. 159–161 (see below n. 145). These marginal percentages appear on a file copy of the May 1944 questionnaire (S–225), NORC Library.

38. George Gallup, *The Gallup Poll: Public Opinion 1937–1971*, 3 vols. (New York: Random House, 1972), and *Gallup Poll Reports 1935–1968* (Princeton, N.J.: American Institute of Public Opinion, 1969). There are occasional discrepancies

in the two sources, but it is useful to consult them together. The antilynch law question read, "Should Congress enact a law that would make lynching a federal crime?" and was asked Jan. 31 and Nov. 14, 1937, and Feb. 6, 1940. White voters in Southern states were asked on Apr. 24, 1941, and again on Aug. 25, 1943, whether people should have to continue paying a poll tax in order to vote. A racial-unrest question, asked on July 28, 1943, read, "What do you think is the real cause of *race riots* such as the one Detroit has had?" Another question asked whether "the present administration in Washington has done a good job, a fair job, or a poor job in dealing with the Negro problem?" (Aug. 28, 1943). Roper asked even fewer questions on racial issues. See Hadley Cantril and Mildred Strunk, *Public Opinion: 1935–1946* (Princeton, N.J.: Princeton University Press, 1951).

39. Ibid.

40. "Report to NORC Trustees for Meeting of June 20, 1944," p. 7, Materials Relevant.

41. This study went into the field in May 1944; an earlier study was reported in April of that year, which provided results for two questions: "Do you think Negroes have the same chance as white people to make a good living in this country?" followed by a "Why?" question; 85 percent of the Negroes said No; Whites were split 50–50. The April report gave more space to the half that said that Negroes did *not* have the same chance, and added: "The individual comments . . . are honest reactions and should be respected as such, even though many of them reveal areas of serious prejudice and misapprehension. The existence of these attitudinal areas constitutes a challenge to liberal educators and to all intelligent people seriously concerned with the expansion of democracy. . . ." NORC Report no. 22, "Do Negroes Have Equal Opportunities? Why?" April 1944, p. 3, NORC Library.

42. "Report for Special Meeting of the Board of Trustees, Sept. 21, 1946," p. 16, Materials Relevant.

43. "Agenda and Report for NORC Trustees Meeting, Oct. 15, 1945," passim, Materials Relevant.

44. Ibid., p. 2.

45. Ibid., p. 14; "Minutes of a Special Meeting of the Trustees of NORC, Oct. 15, 1945," pp. 2 and 4, Materials Relevant.

46. "Financial Statement to Supplement Report to the Trustees, Sept. 21, 1946," Materials Relevant.

47. The project had originally been Cantril's and had been carried out with Jerome Bruner's help, starting in 1943. By 1945, Cantril wanted to unload it, and he arranged for NORC to take it over (to Field from Cantril, Oct. 1, 1943, and June 7, 1945, Director's Files).

48. To M. Field from H. Field, Dec. 8, 1943, Director's Files.

49. "Report to the NORC Trustees for Annual Meeting, April 8, 1946," p. 7, Director's Files.

50. Field went to Europe to visit family and to consult with UNESCO people on the use of public opinion research to reduce international tensions. See note 1. See also *Denver Post*, Sept. 4, 1946, p. 1.

51. E. B. Reuter and C. W. Hart, *Introduction to Sociology* (New York: McGraw-Hill, 1933).

52. To Wirth from Hart, Jan. 11, 1940, Wirth Papers, Box 4, Folder 7.

53. Field had been in consultation with Hart for several months before his death and had asked Hart to become an associate director of NORC upon his retirement from government work. See memo to Tyler and Redfield from Hart, Dec. 15, 1947, Wirth Papers, Box 18, Folder 5.

54. Cantril's organization was at this time principally engaged in archiving data and preparing the compilation of poll results, *Public Opinion: 1935–1946*. Richard Centers's dissertation in the summer of 1945 involved the last use of the field staff, which was discontinued (telephone interview with Richard Centers, Dec. 7, 1979).

55. Their answers to a NORC questionnaire are included in a document labeled "University Questionnaire and Replies," filed in "Trustees' Correspondence 1941–1952" of the Director's Files, NORC, dated from late 1946 to early 1947. See also "Minutes of the Annual Meeting of Trustees of NORC, May 8, 1947," p. 9, Materials Relevant. A questionnaire was designed and distributed after several schools expressed interest in NORC.

56. Lazarsfeld's reply, n.d.; Likert's reply, Oct. 28, 1946. See note 55.

57. "Minutes of Annual Meeting of Trustees of NORC, May 8, 1947," pp. 5–10. See also Wirth's reply, p. 7, in the questionnaires cited in note 55.

58. In the minutes of May 8, 1947, Hart reported that "Chicago, as well as Cornell and Denver, was willing to give faculty status and tenure to professional members of the NORC staff." Wirth had commented in his questionnaire that "Presumably the Director of the Center would have an academic connection with the University . . ." (p. 5). But he had also written that "The key personnel in the NORC should have suitable academic appointments such as research associateships or lecturers in appropriate departments of the University" (p. 1). This written statement does not suggest tenured positions, but in Hart's understanding the personal conversations did. See Trustees' Correspondence, 1941–52, Director's Files.

59. Interview with Peter Rossi, May 23, 1979; with James A. Davis, May 24–25, 1979; conversation with Norman M. Bradburn, June 15, 1982. I am especially indebted to Bradburn for suggesting that I interview Ralph W. Tyler.

60. To Tyler and Redfield from Hart, Dec. 15, 1947; to Tyler from Wirth, Berelson, de Grazia, Goldhamer, and Leiserson, Nov. 2, 1946; to Tyler from Wallis, Nov. 5, 1946; to Tyler from Cox, Nov. 5, 1946—all in Wirth Papers, Box 18, Folder 5. See also Communication Committee, University of Chicago, "Tentative Report, Oct. 1947" and "Final Report, Feb. 1948," in Burgess Papers, Box 33, Folder 8. Among those signing the proposal to Tyler were Sebastian de Grazia, Herbert Goldhamer, Philip Hauser, Avery Leiserson, David Riesman, Edward A. Shils, and Douglas Waples.

61. Ralph W. Tyler, "Implications of Communications Research for the Public Schools," in *Print, Radio and Film in a Democracy*, ed. Douglas Waples (Chicago: University of Chicago Press, 1942), pp. 149–158.

62. This was, properly speaking, Marshall Field III; he resigned from the

board in 1954 and died in 1956 ("Minutes of Meeting of Board of Directors, Nov. 10, 1956," Materials Relevant).

63. The conditions were set forth by Tyler in a memo to Wirth, Berelson, de Grazia, Goldhamer, and Leiserson, Nov. 4, 1946, Wirth Papers, Box 18, Folder 5. Wirth relayed the conditions to Hart confidentially (to Hart from Wirth, Nov. 4, 1946, Wirth Papers, Box 18, Folder 5).

64. There were various research organizations on the Chicago campus, which, as Tyler has indicated, "were affiliated but retained their own identity," such as the Public Administration Clearing House, funded by the Laura Spelman Rockefeller Memorial. Tyler took responsibility for finding "donors" to support certain centers and committees that conducted research in the social sciences, such as the Family Study Center, the Chicago Community Inventory, the Committee on Communication, the Committee on International Relations, and others. Tyler explained that it "was never my intention, nor that of the Central Administration of the University, to have NORC become a legal part of the University. We wished to avoid establishing it in any way that would make it dependent on the University for financing, for this would be difficult when times are tight" (telephone interview with Ralph W. Tyler, Aug. 24, 1982).

65. Lawrence A. Kimpton, then dean of faculties, had a role in the negotiations. (See letter to Dean Kimpton from Edwin R. Embree of the Julius Rosenwald Fund, June 20, 1947, Wirth Papers, Box 18, Folder 5.) The secretary's report to NORC Trustees of May 28, 1949 (Materials Relevant), sounds in fact as though Kimpton were the main negotiator. If so, the fact that he left Chicago in 1947 for a three-year stay at Stanford may have injected some uncertainty into the agreement. Kimpton returned to Chicago in 1950 and became chancellor in 1951, replacing Robert Maynard Hutchins. Kimpton's 1955 speech "The Social Sciences Today," honoring the twenty-fifth anniversary of the Social Science Research Building, hardly seems very sympathetic to quantitative social science, as in observations of this sort: "There has developed another school among the social scientists, and they gather facts with a vengeance. They count things and correlate things and obtain medians and means and standard deviations. This school flourishes most among, though it is not limited to, the educationalists; and, though Johnny may not be able to read, he has been well counted and correlated. The psychologists and sociologists gather vast quantities of data which fail somehow to add up to an important conclusion or a conclusion of any kind" (Lawrence A. Kimpton, "The Social Sciences Today," in *The State of the Social Sciences*, ed. Leonard D. White [Chicago: University of Chicago Press, 1956], p. 351).

66. The memorandum of agreement committed the university to contribute $10,000 "to the salary payments of staff members of NORC whose academic standing is appropriate to the faculties of the University." The university also agreed, among other things, to give library privileges to NORC staff and to make faculty members available for consultation without charge insofar as time permitted. NORC agreed to help provide instruction in public opinion research, to work closely with faculty in furthering their research interests, to take on graduate students as apprentices and interns, and to take part in other, related activ-

ities. See "Memorandum of Agreement," Presidents' Papers, 1950–1955, NORC Folder, Department of Special Collections, Regenstein Library, University of Chicago.

67. Martin Bulmer, "The Early Institutional Establishment of Social Science Research: The Local Community Research Committee at the University of Chicago, 1923–30," *Minerva* 18 (1980):51–110.

68. Memo to Tyler and Redfield from Hart, Dec. 15, 1947, Wirth Papers, Box 18, Folder 5.

69. To Hart from Wirth, Dec. 6, 1946, Wirth Papers, Box 18, Folder 5. Wirth added, "If there is one thing that I would like to emphasize about Chicago in its relation to NORC it is that we have, I think, rich resources in the social sciences which will be at the disposal of the NORC."

70. Memorandum to Hart from Sheatsley, summary of trustees' meeting, July 21, 1948, Director's Files.

71. Memorandum to trustees from Hart, Nov. 13, 1954, pp. 20–22, Materials Relevant.

72. Star's dissertation on intergroup tension was based on data from a collaborative research project with NORC and Philip Hauser's and Louis Wirth's organizations. A condensed version of the dissertation, "An Approach to the Measurement of Interracial Tension," appears in *Contributions to Urban Sociology,* ed. Ernest W. Burgess and Donald J. Bogue (Chicago: University of Chicago Press, 1964), pp. 346–372.

73. There were Chicago scholars of obvious distinction who did not have Ph.D.s in social science (e.g., David Riesman). The Chicago system of the interdisciplinary committee, to which faculty members could be appointed without the full endorsement of a specific department, was a dean's way of keeping such scholars at Chicago, according to Tyler (telephone interview with Ralph W. Tyler, Aug. 24, 1982).

74. "Minutes of Special Meeting of Trustees of NORC," Nov. 21, 1947, Materials Relevant, p. 4.

75. State Department Public Opinion Polls: Hearings Before a Subcommittee of the Committee on Government Operations, House of Representatives, 85th Cong., 1st sess., June 21–July 11, 1957, p. 129.

76. Tyler interview, Aug. 24, 1982.

77. See Leonard S. Cottrell, Jr.'s reply to the NORC questionnaire, Oct. 10, 1946 (note 55). Cottrell suggested that NORC discontinue its conduct of "routine surveys," purchase national data as needed from the commercial polling organizations, and maintain a small staff that would work on more fundamental research. Cottrell wrote that these faculty members were expected to play an active part in NORC's work: Frederick F. Stephan, Louis Guttman, Robin M. Williams, Alexander Leighton, and William Feller, along with others, including himself. He also wrote that Julian L. Woodward might serve as director.

78. "Minutes of Annual Meeting of Trustees of NORC, May 8, 1947," Materials Relevant.

79. In 1947, Hart advised the affiliated ORC at the University of Denver not to seek a general grant that was not earmarked for specific studies, arguing that

it built up deficits every year and encouraged a psychology of overspending. See "Minutes of 1947 Meeting of NORC Trustees, Abercrombie's Notes"; memorandum to Hart from Sheatsley, summary of trustees' meeting, July 21, 1948, p. 3, Director's Files.

80. Memorandum to trustees from Hart, Nov. 13, 1954, pp. 20–22, Director's Files.

81. State Department Hearings, p. 130. Mention is made here of research for the Ford Motor Co. by NORC, SRC, and the Bureau, under the major direction of the Bureau. The NORC bibliography also lists a few other corporations. See *NORC Social Research 1941–1964: An Inventory of Studies and Publications in Social Research* (Chicago: National Opinion Research Center, University of Chicago, 1964).

82. Treasurer's reports are usually included in the minutes of trustees' meetings. See Materials Relevant.

83. Paul B. Sheatsley, personal communication, Feb. 1, 1985.

84. Herbert H. Hyman and Paul B. Sheatsley, "Some Reasons Why Information Campaigns Fail," *POQ* 11 (1947):412–423. (Katz considers this to be the classic paper on the mediation of media effects by selectivity and interpersonal relations: Elihu Katz, "On Conceptualizing Media Effects," *Studies in Communications* 1 [1980]:119–141.)

85. A classic example of congressional suspicion of polling is provided by Congressman Victor A. Knox's interrogation of the State Department spokesman: "Are you inclined to believe that the members of Congress are not representing the people who elected them to Congress . . . ? Congress is not enough. You feel you should go beyond that. You don't think the opinion of Congress represents the American people. . . ." See State Department Hearings, pp. 206–208.

86. House Report 1166, Eleventh Report by the Committee on Government Operations, Subcommittee on International Relations, 85th Cong., 1st sess., Aug. 14, 1957, vol. 11990. The contract was canceled by the State Department very promptly after the story broke. See State Department Hearings, p. 64.

87. State Department Hearings, pp. 142–143. Hart was worried that congressional critics of the State Department would do everything they could to discredit the NORC surveys. See also House Report no. 1166, p. 9.

88. Rossi's memorandum to trustees (Nov. 12, 1960, p. 10, Materials Relevant) provides indirect evidence of concern about the loss.

89. Hart reported that by 1952, NORC had provided informal consultation to twenty-two research grants under ten research units of the university (apparently not reimbursed) and had assisted altogether in sixty-five university and city research projects, twenty-nine of which were chiefly machine work in punching and tabulating (memorandum to Tyler from Hart, Oct. 31, 1952, Materials Relevant). See also memorandum to trustees of NORC from Hart, Nov. 13, 1954, and Director's Report, Nov. 9, 1957, Materials Relevant.

90. Odin W. Anderson and Jacob J. Feldman, *Family Medical Costs and Voluntary Health Insurance: A Nationwide Survey* (New York: McGraw-Hill, 1956); Odin W. Anderson and NORC Staff, *Voluntary Health Insurance in Two Cities* (Cambridge, Mass.: Harvard University Press, 1957); Clyde W. Hart, "Survey Methods

in Research on Health Problems: A Report on the Summer Research Training Institute," SSRC *Items* 11 (1957):16–19.

91. A research center's work is commonly undercited. The borrowing of questionnaire items from a given study or institution is often not acknowledged, for example, and technical support is sometimes acknowledged in only a very general way, at best.

92. To Tyler from Wirth et al., Nov. 2, 1946, Wirth Papers, Box 18, Folder 5; "Final Report, University of Chicago Committee on Communication, Feb. 1948," Burgess Papers, Academic, Box 33, Folder 8.

93. "Seminar on Communication and Public Opinion," Burgess Papers, Box 33, Folder 8. See also articles by six of the participants in the Jan. 1950 issue of the *American Journal of Sociology*.

94. In a 1959 article, "The State of Communication Research," Berelson wrote that "the Committee on Communication at my own university is in process of dissolution" (*POQ* 23 [1959]:1–17, p. 4). It has since been revived, but what its relationship with NORC has been over the years is not clear, except that NORC was expected to take part in a master's program established in 1954. See *AJS*, "News and Notes," Mar. (p. 474) and May (p. 580), 1954.

95. Daniel Katz was sought for the Psychology/NORC position (to Tyler from Wirth, Feb. 6, 1947, Wirth Papers, Box 4, Folder 7). From Katz's perspective, the Chicago position was unrealistically ambitious, involving responsibility for creating a program in social psychology and directing research at NORC. This constituted two different jobs at the University of Michigan, where Katz accepted an appointment (conversation with Katz, Apr. 5, 1982). Four people (unnamed) were approached for the sociology position, after which the position itself was changed into two lower-level positions ("Report to Trustees, July 17, 1948," by Hart, Materials Relevant).

96. To Blumer from Burgess, Oct. 30, 1950, Burgess Papers, Box 3, Folder 1.

97. Memorandum to trustees from Hart, Nov. 13, 1954, pp. 26–29. Marks was also teaching in psychology.

98. See "Director's Report, Nov. 14, 1959," Materials Relevant.

99. Memorandum to trustees from Rossi, Nov. 12, 1960, p. 7. See titles by Rossi, Coleman, Bogue, Shanas, and Feldman, as well as the project subject matter in *NORC Social Research 1941–1964*; interview with James A. Davis, May 24–25, 1979.

100. Ibid.

101. Memorandum for discussion to members of department and others from James Coleman, Sept. 19, 1957, p. 7. Rossi's term as director of NORC (1960–67) was one of financial overextension. See Rebecca Adams, "An Organization and Its Uncertain Development: A Case Study of the National Opinion Research Center" (master's thesis, University of Chicago, 1977).

102. The first address was 4901 South Ellis. In 1953, a new headquarters was leased at 5711 South Woodlawn. The Annex, 5720 South Woodlawn, was renovated and expanded starting in July 1960. See "Director's Report, Nov. 14, 1959"; "Minutes of Board of Trustees," Nov. 8, 1958; and memorandum to trustees from Rossi, Nov. 12, 1960, p. 8, Director's Files.

103. NORC's share proved to be somewhat higher; ibid.

104. NORC did obtain a special loan from the Field Foundation, but the university itself did not make the loan. See "Treasurer's Report, May 28, 1949," p. 9, Materials Relevant.

105. In 1958–1959, NORC conducted thirty-five new jobs for machine services, one-third of which were for members of the sociology department ("Director's Report, Nov. 14, 1959," Materials Relevant). NORC budget categories are labeled somewhat differently over the 1947–1960 years, but the University of Chicago contribution seems to have been unvarying, at $10,000. As the NORC budget approached a half million dollars in the late 1950s, this represented 2 to 3 percent of NORC's total income.

106. Interview with Sheatsley, Apr. 12, 1977.

107. Gabriel A. Almond and Sidney Verba, *The Civic Culture: Political Attitudes and Democracy in Five Nations* (Princeton, N.J.: Princeton University Press, 1963). The original North-Hatt-NORC study is reprinted in *Class, Status, and Power*, ed. Reinhard Bendix and Seymour Martin Lipset (Glencoe, Ill.: The Free Press, 1953), pp. 411–426. See also Albert J. Reiss, Otis Dudley Duncan, Paul K. Hatt, and Cecil C. North, *Occupations and Social Status* (Glencoe, Ill.: The Free Press, 1961); Peter M. Blau and Otis Dudley Duncan, *The American Occupational Structure* (New York: Wiley, 1967); David L. Featherman and Robert M. Hauser, "Prestige or Socioeconomic Scales in the Study of Occupational Achievement?" *Sociological Methods and Research* 4 (1976):403–422.

108. Harry Field and Paul F. Lazarsfeld, *The People Look at Radio* (Chapel Hill: University of North Carolina Press, 1946); Paul F. Lazarsfeld and Patricia L. Kendall, *Radio Listening in America—The People Look at Radio Again* (New York: Prentice-Hall, 1948); Samuel A. Stouffer, *Communism, Conformity, and Civil Liberties* (New York: Wiley [1955], 1966).

109. At least two other publications used data from the Stouffer study: Herbert H. Hyman and Paul B. Sheatsley, "Trends in Public Opinion on Civil Liberties," *Journal of Social Issues* 9 (1953):6–16; Herbert Stember made a limited comparison between AIPO and NORC data in "The Effect of Field Procedures on Public Opinion Data" (Ph.D. diss., Columbia University, 1955).

110. Stouffer, *Communism, Conformity, and Civil Liberties*, p. 15.

111. Ibid., chap. 1.

112. Assignments were made on practical bases, according to which organization had the best supervisor in the vicinity of the selected college. When a field staff was not within eighty miles, substitutions in selected colleges were made. See David Riesman, "Some Observations on the Interviewing in the Teacher Apprehension Study," and Appendices, in *The Academic Mind*, ed. Paul F. Lazarsfeld and Wagner F. Thielens (Glencoe, Ill.: The Free Press, 1958).

113. Riesman gave special thanks to Roper and to Hart and Star of NORC for facilitating a novel inquiry "which not only probed their staffs' adequacy but intervened between the field and the home office in a way which few institutions cheerfully encourage" (ibid., p. 351).

114. SRC/ISR took probability sampling very seriously but did not conduct much systematic research into other aspects of data collection until later years. The Bureau displayed little interest in *research* into research methods.

115. Eleven Confidential Reports are listed in the NORC Library; three of

these are missing and may involve wording experiments. Gallup's early split-ballot experiments are listed by the Roper Public Opinion Research Center, in the *Study Inventory: American Surveys*: 396 Gallup Polls archived there are identified as split ballots, which were conducted from Sept. 1936 to Nov. 1949. (These are numbered from 53 through 450, with a few discontinuities.) There are no listings of Gallup split-ballot forms after 1949.

116. To Connelly from Sheatsley, Aug. 2, 1944, Director's Files, NORC. Connelly was reporting from personal field experience with Southern blacks who had almost no formal education. For references to "acquiescence," see Theodore F. Lentz, "Utilizing Opinions for Character Measurement," *JSP* 1 (1930):536–542; Gardner Murphy and Rensis Likert, *Public Opinion and the Individual* (New York: Harper, 1938); Theodore F. Lentz, comments at Question Wording Panel, *Proceedings of the Central City Conference on Public Opinion Research*, July 29–31, 1946 (Chicago: NORC, University of Denver); and G. Lenski and J. Leggett, "Caste, Class and Deference in the Research Interview," *AJS* 65 (1960):463–467.

117. Confidential Report VI, "Question Wordings," Jan. 26, 1943, NORC Library.

118. To Connelly from Sheatsley, Oct. 10, 1945; to Sheatsley from Connelly, Oct. 16, 1945, Director's Files, NORC.

119. Howard Schuman and Stanley Presser, in *Questions and Answers in Attitude Surveys* (New York: Academic Press, 1981), make special mention of a master's thesis conducted at NORC by Valerie Tamulonis, "The Effects of Question Variations in Public Opinion Surveys" (University of Denver, 1947).

120. The comparison had been suggested by the OWI Surveys Division and planned for 1944 as the major NORC research project for that year, but manpower shortages made for delay. See "Report to NORC Trustees for Meeting of June 20, 1944," p. 9; "Interim Report, Nov. 1944," p. 2, Director's Files.

121. This proved to be a difficulty in a study reported by Dean Manheimer and Herbert Hyman, "Interviewer Performance in Area Sampling," *POQ* 13 (1949):83–92.

122. Comments by Harry Field, Sampling Panel, *Proceedings of the Central City Conference on Public Opinion Research*, July 29–31, 1946 (Chicago: NORC, Denver), p. 63.

123. "Preliminary Report: Experimental Comparison of Data Gathered through Two Sampling Methods," July 26, 1946, NORC Library; "Report for Special Meeting of Board of Trustees, Sept. 21, 1946," p. 3, Materials Relevant. For a description of the 1953 sample, see memorandum to NORC trustees from Hart, Nov. 13, 1954, Materials Relevant.

124. See final questionnaire for Survey 272, May 1950, NORC Library. The open-ended materials and the coding are referred to in papers Star presented to various professional meetings: "What the Public Thinks about Mental Health and Mental Illness," Nov. 1952; "The Public's Idea about Mental Illness," Nov. 5, 1955; and "The Place of Psychiatry in Popular Thinking," May 9, 1957, all on file at the NORC Library.

125. Social scientists generally have been very critical of polls' reliance on single questions but have accepted the use of a single questionnaire for a large, culturally diverse population as a practical matter. See chap. 12.

126. Douglas Williams, "Basic Instructions for Interviewers," *POQ* 6 (1942):634–641, p. 637.

127. Ibid., p. 640.

128. See, for example, questionnaires S–9 (Dec. 1942) and S–225 (May 1944), NORC Library.

129. George H. Gallup, *The Gallup Poll: Public Opinion 1935–1971*, 3 vols. (New York: Random House, 1972), vol. 1, p. 321.

130. Cantril, *Gauging Public Opinion*, p. 282.

131. Stouffer suggested that NORC use educational level as a check for comparing its quota samples with Census figures, as this would be more durable over time than income level would. "Notes on Meeting with Dr. Samuel Stouffer of Chicago University at Thetford, Vt., Aug. 2 and 3, 1941" (Field), Materials Relevant.

132. To Cantril from Field, Dec. 3, 1941, Director's Files, NORC.

133. Cantril, *Gauging Public Opinion*, p. 285. By 1943, NORC had modified this pair of questions as its staple measure of education. Asking the name of the school was designed to "put the respondent in a factual frame of mind"—that is, less likely to exaggerate educational attainment to the interviewer. The second question was changed to read, "What was the last grade (or year) you completed in school?" as this was deemed a more gentle way of finding out than asking "How far did you go . . . ?" Only if interviewers did not learn enough from these two questions to classify a respondent were they to resort to informal questions of their own devising. See *Interviewing for NORC* (Denver, Colo.: National Opinion Research Center, 1945), p. 111.

134. Williams, "Basic Instructions," p. 640.

135. The language used in "Basic Instructions" is very like that used by Elmo Roper in "Classifying Respondents by Economic Status," *POQ* 4 (1940):270–272. Sheatsley recalls that during his first job as interviewer with Gallup he got his Poor/On Relief quota by visiting WPA work crews during their lunch break. (See chap. 3.) Anne Schuetz Zanes recalls her own first interviewing for NORC as something of a shock, for she had not realized that one was to ask the question exactly as written when she had done interviewing for the polls (interview, July 3, 1978).

136. *Interviewing for NORC*, pp. 65–67.

137. Ibid., p. 82. Interviewers were expected to exercise a good deal of initiative in obtaining relevant data from cities for which they were not given rental data; they were also expected to be competent about digging into rows and columns of numbers. For the transition to household selection, compare Williams, "Basic Instructions," p. 635, and *Interviewing for NORC*, p. 79.

138. "How NORC Builds Its Cross Section," July 1946, pp. 7–8, NORC Library.

139. NORC continued to use rental quotas for their objectivity and ABCD classifications for the interviewer's judgment of all the factors that entered into the standard of living. See quota sheet in *Interviewing for NORC*, p. 87.

140. W. V. Bingham and B. V. Moore, *How to Interview*, 3d ed. (New York: Harper, 1941), pp. 162–179.

141. A voucher of the order is filed with Bureau materials, University Archives, Low Library (I failed to note the specific folder).

142. In 1943, Cantril proposed a comparison of respondents' economic levels obtained by the interviewing staffs of the two firms, Gallup and NORC. Field responded positively to the idea, but whether the experiment was carried out is not clear. In this proposed experiment, Larry Benson of AIPO asked that interviewers' ratings be returned to the AIPO office rather than to Cantril's OPOR. Field made the comparable request that NORC data be returned to the NORC office. This may have been an internal matter of wishing to have interviewers report to their own headquarters, perhaps to obscure the fact that an experiment was being conducted. To Field from Cantril, Apr. 26, 1943; to Cantril from Field, Apr. 29, 1943, Director's Files, NORC.

143. Harold F. Gosnell and Sebastian de Grazia, "A Critique of Polling Methods," *POQ* 6 (1942):378–390.

144. Harry H. Field and Gordon M. Connelly, "Testing Polls in Official Election Booths," *POQ* 6 (1942):610–616.

145. Herbert H. Hyman, William J. Cobb, Jacob J. Feldman, Clyde W. Hart, and Charles Herbert Stember, *Interviewing in Social Research* (Chicago: University of Chicago Press, 1954, reissued 1975).

146. Memorandum to trustees from Hart, Nov. 8, 1952, pp. 7–9, Materials Relevant.

147. Paul B. Sheatsley, "An Analysis of Interviewer Characteristics and Their Relationship to Performance," 3 parts, *IJOAR* 4 (1950):473–498; 5 (1951):79–94; 191–220. NORC began to match interviewers and respondents by race when it redesigned its national sample in 1953. All Negro cases were concentrated in eleven primary sampling units, which were selected with probability proportional to the size of the Negro population (Memorandum to NORC trustees from Hart, Nov. 13, 1954, pp. 17–19, Materials Relevant).

148. Hugh J. Parry and Helen M. Crossley, "Validity of Responses to Survey Questions," *POQ* 14 (1950):61–80; Helen M. Crossley and Raymond Fink, "Response and Nonresponse in a Probability Sample," *IJOAR* 5 (1951):1–19; J.J. Feldman, Herbert Hyman, and C. W. Hart, "A Field Study of Interviewer Effects on the Quality of Survey Data," *POQ* 15 (1951):734–761; Don Cahalan, "Correlates of Respondent Accuracy in the Denver Validity Study," *POQ* 32 (1968–69):607–621.

149. Stanley Presser, "Is Inaccuracy on Factual Survey Items Item-Specific or Respondent-Specific?" *POQ* 48 (1984):344–355. ORC research and training was discontinued Sept. 1, 1949; the University of Denver was reported to be absorbing a $600,000 budget cut. See "Minutes of Meeting of Members and Trustees, May 28, 1949"; letter to Weiss from Hart, May 19, 1949, Materials Relevant.

150. Hyman et al., *Interviewing in Social Research*, p. 4.

151. Ibid., pp. 304 ff. and p. 405 n. 35.

152. Review by Stanley Payne, *POQ* 19 (1955):328–330.

153. Norman M. Bradburn and Seymour Sudman, with the assistance of Edward Blair, William Locander, Carrie Miles, Eleanor Singer, and Carol Stocking, *Improving Interview Method and Questionnaire Design* (San Francisco: Jossey-Bass,

1979); Seymour Sudman and Norman M. Bradburn, *Asking Questions: A Practical Guide to Questionnaire Design* (San Francisco: Jossey-Bass, 1982). See also the program of experimental studies in interviewing in Charles F. Cannell, Peter V. Miller, and Lois Oksenberg, "Research in Interviewing Techniques," in *Sociological Methodology* (San Francisco: Jossey-Bass, 1981).

154. The brochure is filed with 1944 documents in Materials Relevant. See *NORC 1981–82*, p. 12; and "Secretary's Report and Minutes of the Trustees' Meeting, May 28, 1949," Materials Relevant. For the "amalgam" studies, see the NORC bibliography, p. 61. The "omnibus" studies of SRC/ISR grew out of the consumer behavior studies (see chap. 11).

155. Gordon Allport and Stouffer represented Harvard; Merton and Lazarsfeld, Columbia; Williams, Cornell; McCormick, Wisconsin; and Cahalan, Denver. See "Report to Trustees, July 17, 1948"; "Report to Trustees from Hart and Abercrombie, Mar. 8, 1949"; letter to Weiss from Hart, May 19, 1949; "Director's Report, Annual Meeting, May 28, 1949"—all in Materials Relevant.

156. Efforts were under way in 1960 (memorandum to trustees from Rossi, Nov. 12, 1960, Materials Relevant). The Survey Research Service was created at NORC in 1963 (NORC bibliography).

11. The Survey Research Center at Michigan

1. Richard S. Kirkendall, *Social Scientists and Farm Politics in the Age of Roosevelt* (Columbia, Mo.: University of Missouri Press, 1966), chap. 11.

2. Interview with Rensis Likert, Oct. 19, 1976.

3. Rensis Likert, *ISR: Part I: The University Setting* (Ann Arbor, Mich.: ISR, 1966), pp. 2–3. A Social Science Surveys Project was approved in June 1946; in Sept. 1946, the name was changed to the Survey Research Center, effective the month before.

4. Group Dynamics was guaranteed an allocation from the university of $10,000 as reimbursement for teaching (minutes of the ISR executive committee, Jan. 15, 1948, ISR files).

5. Lyrics by Martin G. Gold, professor of psychology and research scientist, Research Center for Group Dynamics, ISR.

6. One rationale for the Human Relations Program in 1947 was expressed in terms of "the capacity of a nation to survive" (*ISR 1946–1956*, p. 24, ISR Library).

7. Rensis Likert, "Using America's Full Power," talk presented at the American Association for the Advancement of Science, Cleveland, Dec. 27, 1950; "Motivational Dimensions of Administration," paper read at the Institute of Manpower Utilization and Government Personnel, Stanford University, Aug. 1951, ISR Library.

8. Interview with Charles F. Cannell, Mar. 31, 1977; with Leslie Kish, Oct. 14, 1981.

9. Likert had useful contacts with a number of agencies, such as the Federal Reserve Board and the Department of the Treasury. See also Thelma A. Dreis, "The Department of Agriculture's Sample Interview Survey as a Tool of Admin-

istration" (Ph.D. diss., American University, Washington, D.C., 1950), for both positive and negative reactions of various federal administrators. Likert recalled being pointed to Office of Naval Research funding possibilities by Merle Tuve, a leading physicist who was central in the development of the proximity fuse (interview with Rensis Likert, July 26, 1979).

10. SRC Executive Committee Minutes, May 3, 1955, ISR files. Psychology proposed five appointments—two associates and three assistant professors; sociology proposed Kish for an associate professorship.

11. Interview with Peter H. Rossi, May 23, 1979; James A. Davis, May 24, 1979; Donald Alan Riley, May 7, 1978.

12. Interview with Rensis Likert, July 26, 1979.

13. Interview with Rensis Likert, Oct. 19, 1976.

14. *SRC Progress Report 1948*, p. 2, ISR Library, shows total contracts for $589,000 as of Jan. 1, 1948; ISR Financial Records, ISR Business Office.

15. Interview with Rensis Likert, July 26, 1979.

16. The executive committee of SRC in 1948: Dean R. A. Sawyer (graduate school), Dean R. A. Stevenson (business school), Gardner Ackley (economics), Robert C. Angell (sociology), Arthur L. Brandon (university relations), Arthur W. Bromage (political science), Donald G. Marquis (psychology), and Rensis Likert (*Progress Report*, p. 10).

17. "Analysis of Institute Revenue by Source by Percentage, 1947–60," ISR Financial Records, ISR Business Office. The federal government's share of revenue in 1947 was almost 99 percent. It declined steadily and fell below 50 percent for the first time in 1952. It remained the largest source of income in most years, ranging in the late 1950s around 30 to 40 percent. Industry-business shares ranged roughly from 20 to 40 percent in the 1950s and foundations, from 10 to 35 percent. The university's contribution varied from around 5 to 15 percent.

18. To Likert from Pierpont, Sept. 21, 1951, filed in Financial Statements 1947–52 in the ISR Business Office.

19. Ibid.

20. Minutes of SRC/ISR Executive Committee, Dec. 21, 1951.

21. Interview with Angus Campbell, Apr. 18, 1977; Ronald Freedman, "The Detroit Area Study: A Training and Research Laboratory in the Community," *AJS* 59 (1953):30–33; Howard Schuman, "The Detroit Area Study after Twenty-Five Years," *American Sociologist* 12 (1977):130–137; memo from Angus Campbell, "Administration of the Detroit Area Study," July 9, 1958, filed at Detroit Area Study, University of Michigan.

22. SRC/ISR Executive Committee minutes, Mar. 4, 1948, and Apr. 24, 1951; "Report to the President of the University for 1950–1951," p. 22, document 00328, ISR Library.

23. ISR Financial Records, ISR Business Office.

24. SRC/ISR Executive Committee minutes, June 7, 1951.

25. See minutes of SRC/ISR Executive Committee, e.g., Sept. 30, Oct. 28, and Dec. 22, 1952; March 8 and May 3, 1955; and Nov. 19, 1957. All three directors' part-time salaries were paid in full as of 1955–56; reimbursement for their teaching was separate. In the 1960s, four "full-time equivalents" were spread around six appointments. Under this new arrangement, only Likert's sal-

ary was paid 100 percent; Campbell and Cartwright were paid 75 percent. By 1970, these arrangements of partial support were being made available to nine staff members (Financial Records, ISR Business Office).

26. SRC/ISR Executive Committee minutes, May 3, 1955 and Nov. 19, 1957.

27. ISR's new building was completed in 1965 at a cost of $2.1 million, and the University of Michigan contributed about $500,000. Federal grants from the U.S. Public Health Service and NSF yielded $579,000; ISR used $664,000 from its own reserve fund; and the balance was raised from other contributors. See Financial Records, 1965–66, ISR Business Office.

28. Interview with Charles F. Cannell, May 1, 1978; with Angus Campbell, March 29, 1977.

29. Niehuss's support of ISR's goals cannot be confirmed from Proceedings of the Board of Regents because discussion is not preserved, but it is clear from ISR minutes that Niehuss was seen as sympathetic and was later remembered that way in interviews.

30. Robert Freed Bales, "Task Roles and Social Roles in Problem-Solving Groups," in *Role Theory: Concepts and Research*, ed. Bruce Biddle and E. J. Thomas (New York: Wiley, 1966).

31. Interview with Angus Campbell and Dorwin Cartwright, Apr. 5, 1977; with Leslie Kish, June 28, 1979; with Charles F. Cannell, Feb. 8, 1979.

32. Some found Likert's enthusiasms too buoyant and unrealistic and felt that he indirectly and unintentionally drove his staff by overpromising and overcommitting slender resources.

The pollsters felt Likert's criticisms so keenly in 1948 that it would probably be difficult for them to credit the interpretation that he disliked and avoided conflict. However, this was a consistent theme among the ISR staff whom I interviewed. Some felt that in his participation in the Gallup 1944 hearings, Likert was *too* accommodating and not critical enough. The resolution of these differing perceptions may be in Likert's capacity for strong opinion when the issue bore on something that was of virtually religious significance to him. His views on polling methods came to have something of that character, and he took positions that were stern and quite moralistic in tone. Within the organization he did not often display such attitudes, although he was known for some time as a nondrinker, and he also reportedly once summarily fired a male interviewer for traveling around with a female companion. Nevertheless, within the organization he apparently tended to damp down conflict rather than confront it, and in his own writing and research it took him some years to incorporate the inevitability of conflict into his theory.

Likert's lack of concern with hierarchy was clear in many incidents, as was his genuine liking for many, many people (interviews with Angus Campbell and Dorwin Cartwright, Apr. 5, 1977).

33. Interview with Dorwin Cartwright and Angus Campbell, Mar. 18, 1977.

34. Interviews with Leslie Kish, July 20, 1977, and June 28, 1979.

35. Campbell, in "Administering Research Organizations," conveys some surprise that administrators (such as himself) carried as much influence as they did. See note 43. See also interview with Campbell, June 29, 1977.

36. Interview with Roe Goodman, July 2, 1979; interview with Leslie Kish, July 20, 1977; address by Philip E. Converse, Memorial Service, Dec. 1980.

37. Interview with Angus Campbell, Apr. 18, 1977.

38. When tensions were high between SRC and Group Dynamics, it was thought that small intercenter committees might publish together or otherwise collaborate without embarking on large joint studies and that this would be more useful than gathering data on the institute's problems. See SRC/ISR Executive Committee minutes for Mar. 28 and 31, 1952.

Likert in these years was developing a model of organizational authority structure ranging from the most authoritarian ("system 1") to the most consensual and participative ("system 4"). His first book developing these ideas was published in 1961: *New Patterns of Management* (New York: McGraw-Hill).

39. Annual Reports, ISR, ISR Business Office.

40. Interview with Charles F. Cannell, May 1, 1978.

41. See SRC/ISR Executive Committee minutes; for example, Mar. 31, 1952; Jan. 18, 1955; May 14, 1957; Apr. 8 and Sept. 23, 1958.

42. Ibid., Feb. 12 and May 15, 1957.

43. Angus Campbell, "Administering Research Organizations," *American Psychologist* 8 (1953):225–230.

44. Stanley E. Seashore, *ISR: Part II: The Internal Organization* (Ann Arbor: ISR, 1966), p. 27, ISR Library.

45. Interview with Angus Campbell and Dorwin Cartwright, Mar. 18, 1977.

46. The income of the program rose steadily, going from about $100,000 to a high of over $500,000. *Business Week* covered the consumer surveys regularly and did a special three-part series on the consumer surveys and the Human Relations Program in its issues of August 14, 21, and 28, 1954. *Nation's Business* and the *New York Times* also reported the economic work regularly.

47. George Katona, *The Powerful Consumer: Psychological Studies of the American Economy* (New York: McGraw-Hill, 1960).

48. James N. Morgan, "Contributions of survey research to economics," in *Survey Research in the Social Sciences*, ed. Charles Y. Glock (New York: Russell Sage Foundation, 1967), p. 224.

49. Survey Research Center, *1960 Survey of Consumer Finances* (Ann Arbor: ISR, 1961), pp. 174–175, 271–296.

50. James Tobin, "On the Predictive Value of Consumer Intentions and Attitudes," *Review of Economics and Statistics* 41 (1959):1–11; Harold Shapiro, "The Index of Consumer Sentiment and Economic Forecasting—A Reappraisal," in *Human Behavior in Economic Affairs*, ed. Burkhard Strumpel, James N. Morgan, and Ernest Zahn (San Francisco: Jossey-Bass, 1972).

51. SRC Executive Committee minutes, Aug. 4, 1959, and Oct. 6, 1959.

52. SRC, "Fifteen Years of Experience with Measurement of Consumer Expectations," *Proceedings of the Business and Economic Statistics Section* (Washington, D.C.: American Statistical Association, 1962), pp. 169–177.

53. SRC/ISR Executive Committee minutes, Nov. 17, 1950.

54. Ibid., Oct. 31, 1950; Nov. 4, 1955.

55. Ibid., Dec. 28, 1954.

56. *ISR Publications 1946–1960* (ISR, 1965), ISR Library.

57. James N. Morgan, "A Quarter Century of Behavioral Research in Economics, Persistent Programs and Diversions," in *Human Behavior in Economic Affairs*, ed. Strumpel, Morgan, and Zahn, p. 17.

58. Angus Campbell, "Development and Future Plans of the Human Relations Program," in *Groups, Leadership and Men*, ed. Harold Guetzkow (New York: Russell and Russell [1951], 1963), pp. 100–105.

59. Nancy C. Morse, "An Experimental Study in an Industrial Organization," in *Groups, Leadership and Men*, ed. Guetzkow, pp. 96–99; Eugene Jacobson, W. W. Charters, Jr., and Seymour Lieberman, "The Use of the Role Concept in the Study of Complex Organizations," *Journal of Social Issues* 7 (1951):18–27; Robert L. Kahn, "An Analysis of Supervisory Practices and Components of Morale," in *Groups, Leadership and Men*, ed. Guetzkow, pp. 86–89; Basil S. Georgopoulos and Arnold S. Tannenbaum, "A Study of Organizational Effectiveness," *American Sociological Review* 22 (1957):534–540; Floyd C. Mann, "Changing Superior-Subordinate Relationships," *Journal of Social Issues* 7 (1951):56–71; Daniel Katz, "An Overview of the Human Relations Program," in *Groups, Leadership and Men*, pp. 68–85; Guetzkow, Robert L. Kahn, Floyd C. Mann, and Stanley E. Seashore, eds., "Human Relations Research in Large Organizations," special issue, *Journal of Social Issues* 12 (1956), seven articles; Robert L. Kahn and Daniel Katz, "Leadership Practices in Relation to Productivity and Morale," 1952, reprinted in *Group Dynamics: Research and Theory*, ed. Dorwin Cartwright and Alvin Zander (Evanston, Ill.: Row, Peterson, 1960).

60. Interview with Angus Campbell and Dowrin P. Cartwright, Apr. 5, 1977; Foundation for Research on Human Behavior, *Seven-Year Report: 1952–59*, ISR Library, Appendices.

61. Ibid., pp. 46–47, 57, Appendices.

62. Interview with Angus Campbell and Dorwin Cartwright, Apr. 5, 1977.

63. Daniel Katz and Robert L. Kahn, "Some Recent Findings in Human Relations Research," in *Readings in Social Psychology*, ed. Guy E. Swanson, Theodore M. Newcomb, and Eugene L. Hartley, rev. ed. (New York: Henry Holt & Co., 1952), pp. 650–656; Donald C. Pelz, "Leadership Within a Hierarchical Organization," *Journal of Social Issues* 7 (1951):49–55; Arnold S. Tannenbaum, "The Concept of Organizational Control," *Journal of Social Issues* 12 (1956):50–60; Stanley E. Seashore, *Group Cohesiveness in an Industrial Work Group* (ISR, 1954).

64. Strong criticisms of a promanagement bias in industrial psychology and applied work generally appears in Loren Baritz, *Servants of Power: A History of the Use of Social Science in American Industry* (New York: Wiley, [1960] 1965). SRC authors are cited. I have found no evidence that they replied to Baritz. There was a general acknowledgment that management could make better use of research findings than unions could in the rare case in which the two groups had equal access to funds, time, and personnel for utilization. See Eugene Jacobson, Robert L. Kahn, Floyd C. Mann, and Nancy C. Morse, "Research in Functioning Organizations," *Journal of Social Issues* 7 (1951):64–71.

65. Rensis Likert (interview), "How to Raise Productivity 20%," *Nation's Business* 47 (1959):44.

66. Angus Campbell and Robert L. Kahn, *The People Elect a President* (ISR,

1952); Frederick Mosteller, Herbert Hyman, Philip J. McCarthy, Eli S. Marks, and David B. Truman, *The Pre-Election Polls of 1948* (New York: SSRC, 1949), Appendix G, pp. 373–379. The pre- and postelection samples were not identical; 577 respondents were interviewed in both.

67. "SSRC Conference on Research into Political Behavior" (Ann Arbor, Aug. 29, 1949), ISR historical materials, ISR Library; Robert A. Dahl, "The Behavioral Approach in Political Science: Epitaph for a Monument to a Successful Protest," *APSR* 55 (1961):763–772; interview with Angus Campbell, Mar. 29, 1977. Campbell believed that Lazarsfeld was hampered in continuing election studies because he was not well connected in political science.

68. SRC Executive Committee meeting, Nov. 8, 1955, ISR files.

69. Ibid., Oct. 14, 1952; June 22, 1954.

70. Campbell and Kahn, *The People Elect*, p. 2.

71. Angus Campbell, Gerald Gurin, and Warren E. Miller, *The Voter Decides* (Evanston, Ill.: Row, Peterson, 1954), p. vi.

72. Paul Lazarsfeld, in Oral History Collection, Butler Library, Columbia University, 1961–62, p. 102, makes an indirect allusion. Peter H. Rossi agreed (interview, May 23, 1979), but Warren E. Miller felt that Lazarsfeld influenced the SRC studies in only a general way (interview, June 19, 1979)—all of which suggest organizational interpretations. Assessing influence is a very difficult matter; priority is clearer, and Lazarsfeld and his group were clearly prior in time. A valuable contrast between the two kinds of political studies is provided by Carl A. Sheingold, "Social Networks and Voting: The Resurrection of a Research Agenda," *ASR* 38 (1973):712–720. Sheingold points out that the kind of network analysis the Bureau tried to do was virtually impossible without the computer.

73. Interview with Warren E. Miller, June 19, 1979.

74. Morris Janowitz and Warren E. Miller, "The Index of Political Predisposition in the 1948 Election," *Journal of Politics* 14 (1952):710–727.

75. *The Voter Decides*, p. 86.

76. Ibid., p. 85.

77. Angus Campbell, Philip E. Converse, Warren E. Miller, and Donald E. Stokes, *The American Voter* (New York: Wiley, 1960), p. 18.

78. Ibid., chap. 2.

79. Ibid., p. 248.

80. Dahl, "The Behavioral Approach in Political Science." V. O. Key, Jr., wrote a special review article for *POQ* 24 (1960):54–61. The book was widely reviewed, but never in *ASR* and *AJS*.

81. Interuniversity Consortium for Political and Social Research, *Guide to Resources and Services 1985–86* (Ann Arbor: ISR, 1986).

82. Paul Lazarsfeld, Oral History Collection, pp. 103–106. When Likert read this document, he contended that he had been working with open questioning before he met Lazarsfeld (interview, July 26, 1979).

83. Angus Campbell, "Two Problems in the Use of the Open Question," *JASP* 40 (1945):340–343.

84. Richard S. Crutchfield and Donald A. Gordon, "Variations in Respondents' Interpretations of an Opinion-Poll Question," *IJOAR* 1 (Sept. 1947):3–12.

85. Richard S. Crutchfield, "Ratings," Feb. 10, 1944, DPS Memo File, ISR.

Two unpublished memos on coding are on file at the ISR Library, documents no. 758 (by Eleanor Maccoby) and 780 (by William A. Scott). Kermit K. Schooler, in "A Study of Error and Bias in Coding Responses to Open-End Questions" (Ph.D. diss., University of Michigan, 1955) reported more error from coders' expectations than from their ideology, apparently following the lead of Hyman et al., *Interviewing in Social Research* (see chap. 10).

86. SSRC, *Public Reaction to the Atomic Bomb and World Affairs* (Ithaca, N.Y.: Cornell University, Apr. 1947); Leonard S. Cottrell, Jr., and Sylvia Eberhart, *American Opinion on World Affairs in the Atomic Age* (Princeton, N.J.: Princeton University Press, 1948).

87. Robert L. Kahn, "A Comparison of Two Methods of Collecting Data for Social Research: The Fixed-Alternative Questionnaire and the Open-Ended Interview" (Ph.D. diss., University of Michigan, 1951); Helen Metzner and Floyd C. Mann, "A Limited Comparison of Two Methods of Data Collection: The Fixed-Alternative Questionnaire and the Open-Ended Interview," ISR, 1951.

88. I am indebted to Jennifer Platt, University of Sussex, for pointing out the connection between the two kinds of qualitative materials. It is my impression that thumbnail sketches are used only very occasionally to resolve coding problems. They have also been of some use in detecting interviewer cheating—as has open questioning itself—but they probably survive as an interviewing task because they tend to be of intrinsic interest to study staff members.

89. Gerald Gurin, Joseph Veroff, and Sheila Feld, *Americans View Their Mental Health* (New York: Basic Books, 1960).

90. A sample of questionnaires drawn from the consumer surveys shows the following proportions of fully open questions: Jan. 1949, .17; June 1952, .43; July 1956, .34; Oct. 1960, .30. A sample of National Election Study questionnaires also shows a decline over time in the use of fully open questions: 1952, .33; 1956, .09; 1960, .22. The coding procedures were somewhat different for the two studies, so the proportions should be compared only within series. It is of interest that at least some staff members did not detect change toward more closed questioning. This may be because even with questions of closed format, interviewers were instructed to write down much verbatim material, and they did so. It may also reflect SRC's ideology on open questioning. On an impressionistic basis, it would seem that the SCF remained more open than the "interim" consumer surveys. See Jean M. Converse and Howard Schuman, "The Manner of Inquiry: An Analysis of Survey Question Form across Organizations and over Time," in *Surveying Subjective Phenomena*, ed. Charles F. Turner and Elizabeth Martin (New York: Russell Sage Foundation, 1984), vol. 2, pp. 283–316.

91. Jean M. Converse, "Strong Arguments and Weak Evidence: The Open/Closed Questioning Controversy of the 1940s," *POQ* 48 (1984):267–282.

92. Interview with Angus Campbell and Dorwin Cartwright, Mar. 18, 1977. There were other informal conversations of which I kept no record.

93. "Conference, Field Methods in Sample Interview Surveys, 1951," ISR Library; SRC/ISR Executive Committee minutes, Apr. 1, 1947.

94. Morris Hansen and Benjamin Tepping taught probability sampling at the first SRC Summer Institute in 1948 as guest lecturers.

95. Alan Stuart, "Nonprobability Sampling," *International Encyclopedia of the Social Sciences* (*IESS*) (New York: The Free Press, 1968), 13:612–616.

96. Frederick F. Stephan and Philip J. McCarthy, *Sampling Opinions: An Analysis of Survey Procedure* (New York: Wiley, 1958), p. 319.

97. Ibid., p. 190.

98. Ibid., p. 325.

99. Ibid., p. 323.

100. Ibid., pp. 376–377.

101. By 1952, Harry Alpert had found that probability sampling had become "fashionable" (Alpert, "Some Observations on the Sociology of Sampling," *Social Forces* 31 [1952]:30–33).

102. Frederick F. Stephan, "Advances in Survey Methods and Measurement Techniques," *POQ* 21 (1957):79–90.

103. In 1960, Paul Perry of the Gallup Organization did not report on the detailed procedure of selection in the household ("Election Survey Procedures of the Gallup Poll," *POQ* 24 [1960]:531–542, esp. p. 533), but in later Gallup releases, the probability down to the block is routinely referred to.

104. Roe Goodman and Eleanor E. Maccoby, "Sampling Methods and Sampling Errors in Surveys of Consumer Finances," *IJOAR* 2 (1948):349–360; Leslie Kish, "Selection of the Sample," in *Research Methods in the Behavioral Sciences*, ed. Leon Festinger and Daniel Katz (New York: Dryden, 1954), pp. 175–239; Leslie Kish and Irene Hess, *The Survey Research Center's National Sample of Dwellings* (ISR, 1965).

105. Leslie Kish, "A Two-Stage Sample of a City," *ASR* 17 (1952):761–769; Leslie Kish and Irene Hess, "On Noncoverage of Sample Dwellings," *JASA* 53 (1958):509–524; Leslie Kish, "Confidence Intervals for Clustered Samples," *ASR* 22 (1957):154–165.

106. Angus Campbell, "Polling, Open Interviewing, and the Problem of Interpretation," *Journal of Social Issues* 2 (1946):67–71; Daniel Katz, "Survey Technique and Polling Procedure as Methods in Social Science," *Journal of Social Issues* 2 (Nov. 1946):62–66. See also Daniel Katz, "Survey Techniques in the Evaluation of Morale," in *Experiments in Social Process*, ed. James Grier Miller (New York: McGraw-Hill, 1950), pp. 65–77.

107. Interview with Rensis Likert, Sept. 21, 1977; Rensis Likert, "Public Opinion Polls," *Scientific American* 179 (Dec. 1948):7–11; idem, "Why Opinion Polls Were So Wrong," *U.S. News and World Report*, Nov. 12, 1948; idem, "The Polls: Straw Votes or Scientific Instruments?" *American Psychologist* 3 (1948):556–557.

108. George Gallup, "Should We Set Up Standards for Poll Critics?" *IJOAR* 3 (1949):348–354.

109. Norman C. Meier and Harold W. Saunders, *The Polls and Public Opinion* (New York: Henry Holt & Co., 1949), pp. 37, 214, 243.

110. *Proceedings* of AAPOR, *POQ* 13 (1949):765; SRC/ISR's low involvement in AAPOR was noticed and interpreted, by some at least, as a boycott (interview with Herbert Hyman, June 27, 1977).

111. Daniel Katz served as conference chair for the 1957 meetings. In 1947–60, participants in the AAPOR program who were currently at the Bureau num-

bered fifty-eight; at NORC, forty-six; and at SRC, thirty-two. This count under-estimates the influence of the Bureau because it does not include participating Bureau *graduates.* See Jean M. Converse, "Strong Arguments and Weak Evidence," p. 276.

112. In 1958, Frederick Stephan, editor of *POQ,* asked if SRC/ISR would be interested in taking responsibility for the publication; the Michigan group declined. See SRC/ISR Executive Committee minutes for Mar. 18, 1958. There is no discussion surviving of the reasons for the decision.

113. "Analysis of Institute Revenues by Source of Dollar Value," ISR Financial Reports, ISR Business Office.

114. All listings in these three bibliographies were coded up through 1960: *Bureau of Applied Social Research Bibliography from Its Founding in 1937 to Its Closing in 1977* (Bureau of Applied Social Research, 1979); *NORC Social Research 1941– 1964* (NORC, University of Chicago, 1964), and *ISR List of Publications 1946– 1960* (ISR, 1965). As noted in the text, the three bibliographies vary in their criteria for inclusion, so the figures for unpublished material are not entirely comparable. Nor can they be deemed entirely accurate or exhaustive, for I have observed at least occasional omissions. But they are surely useful approximations of the respective organizations' output. Monographs published by the organization itself are considered "unpublished." "Frequent" publication in mainline journals means five or more articles.

115. The Bureau *Bibliography* lists forty articles published in *POQ* for 1937– 1960; NORC lists fifteen for 1941–1960, but almost as many AAPOR papers (twelve); and ISR lists twenty for 1946–1960.

12. The American Establishment of Survey Research

1. Herbert Blumer, "Sociological Analysis and the 'Variable,'" *ASR* 21 (1956):683–690.

2. Lazarsfeld's presidential address to the American Sociological Association, "The Sociology of Empirical Social Research," *ASR* 27 (1962):757–767, argued for the importance of academic research organizations and, among other things, criticized universities for not developing coherent support for them.

Lazarsfeld lost the presidential election in 1958 to Howard Becker and in 1959 to Robert E. L. Faris; in 1960, he won against Thorsten Sellin. *ASR* carries these notes on ASA committees and elections. Lazarsfeld's role as a sociologist remained rather anomalous for a time by one indicator. In a tally of citations of sociologists cited five times or more in at least four of the "leading" texts published in 1958–1962, Ralph Linton and Robert Merton tied for first place, with 208 mentions. Among others in the top twenty-five high scorers were W. L. Warner (92), T. Parsons (90), C. W. Mills (77), K. Davis (74), S. M. Lipset (69), and Stouffer (28). Lazarsfeld was not among the top twenty-five. (See Read Bain, "The Most Important Sociologists?" *ASR* 27 [1962]:746–748.) Far greater recognition of Lazarsfeld's attainments came later, in his election to the National Academy of Sciences in 1975 and other honors. See David L. Sills, "Paul F. Lazarsfeld," *IESS* 18: 411–427.

3. *ASR* 25 (1960):959.

4. Hadley Cantril, *The Politics of Despair* (New York: Basic Books, 1958); idem, *The Pattern of Human Concerns* (New Brunswick, N.J.: Rutgers University Press, 1965).

5. Lazarsfeld's major books after 1960: with Sam D. Sieber, *Organizing Educational Research: An Exploration* (Englewood Cliffs, N.J.: Prentice-Hall, 1964); with Neil W. Henry, eds., *Readings in Mathematical Social Science* (Chicago: Science Research Associates, 1966); with William H. Sewell and Harold L. Wilensky, *The Uses of Sociology* (New York: Basic Books, 1967); with Neil W. Henry, *Latent Structure Analysis* (New York: Houghton Mifflin Co., 1968); with Ann K. Pasanella and Morris Rosenberg, eds., *Continuities in the Language of Social Research* (New York: Praeger, 1972); with Jeffrey G. Reitz, *An Introduction to Applied Sociology* (New York: Elsevier, 1975).

6. Bernard Berelson, "The Study of Public Opinion," in *The State of the Social Sciences*, ed. Leonard D. White (Chicago: University of Chicago Press, 1955), pp. 299–318.

7. Anthony Oberschall, "Paul F. Lazarsfeld and the History of Empirical Social Research," *Journal of the History of the Behavioral Sciences* 14 (1978):199–206.

8. Marie Jahoda, "PFL: Hedgehog or Fox?" in *Qualitative and Quantitative Social Research: Papers in Honor of Paul F. Lazarsfeld*, ed. Robert K. Merton, James S. Coleman, and Peter H. Rossi (New York: The Free Press, 1979), pp. 3–9.

9. The major publication from the medical sociology project, which started in 1952, was Robert K. Merton, George G. Reader, and Patricia L. Kendall, eds., *The Student Physician: Introductory Studies in the Sociology of Medical Education* (Cambridge, Mass.: Harvard University Press, 1957). See also Robert K. Merton, "The Social Psychology of Housing," in *Current Trends in Social Psychology*, ed. Wayne Dennis (Pittsburgh: University of Pittsburgh Press, 1948), pp. 163–217; and Robert K. Merton, Patricia Salter West, Marie Jahoda, and Hanan C. Selvin, *Social Policy and Social Research in Housing*, special issues of *Journal of Social Issues* 7 (1951), nos. 1 and 2.

10. Other volumes in this period: Merton et al., eds., *The Student Physician*; Paul F. Lazarsfeld and Wagner Thielens, Jr., *The Academic Mind* (Glencoe, Ill.: The Free Press, 1958); Seymour Martin Lipset, *Political Man: The Social Bases of Politics* (Garden City, N.Y.: Doubleday, 1960); Herbert H. Hyman, *Political Socialization: A Study in the Psychology of Political Behavior* (Glencoe, Ill.: The Free Press, 1959); Bernard Berelson, *Graduate Education in the United States* (New York: McGraw-Hill, 1960); Joseph T. Klapper, *The Effects of Mass Communication* (Glencoe, Ill.: The Free Press, 1960); James S. Coleman, John W. C. Johnstone, and Kurt Jonassohn, *The Adolescent Society: The Social Life of the Teenager and Its Impact on Education* (New York: The Free Press, 1961); James A. Davis, *Great Books and Small Groups* (New York: The Free Press, 1961); Gerald Gurin, Joseph Veroff, and Sheila Feld, *Americans View Their Mental Health* (New York: Basic Books, 1960); George Katona, *The Powerful Consumer* (New York: McGraw-Hill, 1960); and Angus Campbell, Philip E. Converse, Warren E. Miller, and Donald E. Stokes, *The American Voter* (New York: Wiley, 1960).

11. Warren Miller recalls that the first multiple regression carried out at SRC (eleven predictors to the vote) took roughly three months of work (interview, June 16, 1979).

12. The growing interest at SRC and NORC for data archiving and diffusion

and grant money to expand them was the context of Angus Campbell's article "The Archival Resources of the Survey Research Center," *POQ* 24 (1960):686–688.

13. Jean M. Converse and Howard Schuman, "The Manner of Inquiry: An Analysis of Question Form across Organizations and over Time," in *Surveying Subjective Phenomena*, ed. Charles F. Turner and Elizabeth Martin (New York: Russell Sage Foundation, 1984), vol. 2, pp. 283–316.

14. *Survey Research*, published by Survey Research Laboratory, University of Illinois, maintains a list of "academically based organizations engaged primarily in sample survey research," Summer-Fall 1985, p. 13. I am grateful to Mary Spaeth for additional information on these listings.

15. Barbara J. Culliton, "Academe and Industry Debate Partnership," *Science* 219 (Jan. 14, 1983):150–151; Katherine Bouton, "Academic Research and Big Business: A Delicate Business," *New York Times Magazine*, Sept. 11, 1983, pp. 62 ff., focuses on bioengineering and biomedical research, but the institutional arrangements and the policy problems are general ones; Leon Lindsay, "Universities + Business = ," *Christian Science Monitor*, Oct. 29, 1982, pp. B–1 ff.

The University of Michigan decided in the fall of 1983 to invest $200,000 in start-up funds for a Michigan Research Corporation, "a profit-making company to develop and market research generated by U-M faculty" (*University Record* 39 [Oct. 24, 1983]:1).

16. Daniel S. Greenberg, *The Politics of Pure Science* (New York: New American Library, 1967). As early as 1951, Lee thought that group research had become so dominant that it was individual researchers who had become Park's "marginal men" (Alfred McClung Lee, "Individual and Organizational Research in Sociology," *ASR* 16 [1951]:701–707).

17. Mott T. Greene, review, *Science* 219 (1983):959.

18. Norman Kaplan, "Sociology of Science," in *Handbook of Modern Sociology*, ed. Robert E. L. Faris (Chicago: Rand-McNally, 1964), pp. 852–881; William Kornhauser, *Scientists in Industry: Conflict and Accommodation* (Berkeley and Los Angeles: University of California Press, 1962).

19. In contrast, a 1951 book on research methods had shown catholic tastes in authors. The two-volume book edited by Marie Jahoda, Morton Deutsch, and Stuart W. Cook, *Research Methods in Social Relations* (New York: Dryden, 1951), had special reference to research into prejudice and was published for the Society for the Psychological Study of Social Issues. Here, there was a mix among the nineteen contributors and editors—there were four from the Bureau, two from ISR, one from NORC, two from Cornell, two from Michigan State, four from the Research Center for Human Relations at New York University, and four other authors. The large bibliography of approximately 350 items showed a wide range of sources. The Bureau was represented by nineteen citations, ISR by nine.

The volume by William J. Goode and Paul Hatt, *Methods in Social Research* (New York: McGraw-Hill, 1952), provides something more of comparability to the Festinger-Katz volume in that both dealt much more with methods of data collection than the Lazarsfeld-Rosenberg volume did. Goode and Hatt acknowledged Bureau influence and showed it somewhat in their bibliography. Of 125 items, thirteen were by Bureau authors and none by ISR authors.

20. The Bureau's Professional Program in Advanced Training and its program to construct inventories of scientific findings were both interdisciplinary (interview with Herbert H. Hyman, June 27, 1977).

21. Angus Campbell, Gerald Gurin, and Warren E. Miller, *The Voter Decides* (Evanston, Ill.: Row, Peterson, 1954); Angus Campbell and Homer C. Cooper, *Group Differences in Attitudes and Votes: A Study of the 1954 Congressional Election* (Ann Arbor: ISR, 1956); Angus Campbell, Philip E. Converse, Warren E. Miller, and Donald E. Stokes, *The American Voter* (New York: Wiley, 1960).

22. In *A Directory of Social Science Research Organizations in Universities and Colleges* (New York: SSRC, 1950), the Bureau was described as a "general social research center and training laboratory, with divisions of communications and political behavior, urban research, population, advertising and marketing, research training, and development of methods and techniques" (p. 15). ISR was described as "economic behavior and motivation, human relations in organizations, public understanding of national and international issues, leadership and communication within groups, intergroup relations, community life, and the development of sampling survey methodology. Includes the Survey Research Center . . . and the Research Center for Group Dynamics . . . " (p. 24). NORC was described as "research on methodological and technical problems in the field of attitude and opinion study and on various substantive aspects of opinion and its development, from both a theoretical and a practical point of view" (p. 14). The Bureau's program emphasized the somewhat broader goals of "general" social research and training; all three centers noted their methodological interests as well as substantive programs.

In its ten-year anniversary brochure, *Institute for Social Research 1946–1956*, ISR was described in this way: "In the course of its development since 1946, the Institute has become a significant and, in some respects, a unique feature of mid-century social science. Because of the volume and scope of its work and its interdisciplinary character, it has attracted the attention of social scientists in many disciplines. . . ."

In the booklet *Bureau of Applied Social Research: Twentieth-Anniversary Report*, the Bureau's evolution was traced from the Office of Radio Research, which, "upon moving to Columbia University in 1940, became the social research laboratory of the Graduate Department of Sociology" (p. 3).

23. Memorandum to members of department and others from James Coleman, Sept. 19, 1957 (probably in sociology department files, Chicago); interview with Charles Y. Glock, May 10, 1978; interviews with Herbert H. Hyman, June 27, 1977; Angus Campbell, Mar. 29, 1977; James A. Davis, May 24, 1979; and David L. Sills, Dec. 12, 1978.

24. Ann Pasanella, "The Open/Closed Questioning Controversy—A Postscript," *POQ* 48 (1984):817–819.

25. Earl R. Babbie, *Survey Research Methods* (Belmont, Calif.: Wadsworth, 1973), pp. 43–44.

26. Charles Y. Glock, "Organizational Innovation for Social Science Research and Training," in *Qualitative and Quantitative Social Research: Papers in Honor of Paul F. Lazarsfeld*, ed. Robert K. Merton, James S. Coleman, and Peter H. Rossi (New York: The Free Press, 1979), esp. pp. 32–34; Allen H. Barton, "Paul Lazarsfeld and Applied Social Research," *Social Science History* 3 (1979):4–44.

27. Aubrey McKennell, "On the Academic Development of Survey Research," MS, n.d.; Edward A. Shils, "Tradition, Ecology, and Institution in the History of Sociology," *Daedalus*, 1970, pp. 760–825. Shils apparently sees NORC as deriving from the Bureau, and he specifically notes SRC as an exception to Lazarsfeld's influence (p. 794), but he does not explain either viewpoint. The case for Lazarsfeld's influence on Field is not clear. Glock's 1979 chapter (n. 26) states that since Field was acquainted with Lazarsfeld before 1941, he must have known about his Vienna research center. The influence on Field of Gallup and Cantril is direct and clear in NORC documents, but the only reference to Lazarsfeld is on the occasion when Stouffer commends to Field an article by Lazarsfeld in the *Journal of Applied Psychology* (notes on meeting with Stouffer, Aug. 2 and 3, 1941, NORC Director's Files).

28. Paul B. Sheatsley, "The First 40 Years," in *NORC Report 1981–82* (Chicago: NORC, 1982), pp. 6–21.

29. Charles F. Cannell and Robert L. Kahn, "Some Factors in the Origins and Development of the Institute for Social Research, the University of Michigan," *American Psychologist* 39 (1984):1256–1266.

30. See Steven H. Chaffee and John L. Hochheimer, "Mass Communication in National Election Campaigns: The Research Experience in the United States," paper presented to the German Association for Journalism and Communication Research, Munster, West Germany, June 1982.

31. Clyde W. Hart and Don Cahalan, "The Development of AAPOR," *POQ* 21 (1957):160–173.

32. *Proceedings* of AAPOR, Sept. 12–15, 1948, *POQ* 12 (1948–49):815–816.

33. Robert T. Bower, in his AAPOR presidential address, "Caveat Venditor: Some Observations on Research Sponsors and Professional Standards," *POQ* 34 (1970):432–441, pointed out that psychologists adopted their first code in 1953, anthropologists in 1967, and sociologists in 1970.

Warren O. Hagstrom, in *The Scientific Community* (New York: Basic Books, 1964), discusses the strain of heterogeneity of an emerging discipline, noting that it must "create a history for itself—it must discover its past" (p. 214). Hagstrom quotes from a 1958 presidential address of the American Statistical Association which addressed the "cleavages" between mathematical statisticians and applied statisticians (p. 216). The 1948 misforecast was clearly an occasion of dispute and distrust within AAPOR, making that creation of a common history more difficult. The effort to harmonize differences seems apparent in Bernard Berelson's presidential comments in 1952: "Perhaps this spirit of our meetings is best expressed in the recognized dichotomy in the membership between academic and commercial interests—with people from government offices serving as a kind of Troisième Force. There are probably few professional organizations with such a split membership, yet such a unified morale. Perhaps we have succeeded in having the best of both possible worlds." (I am indebted to Don Cahalan for a copy of the 1952 *Proceedings*, which were not published in *POQ*.)

In a history of a chemical engineering association, Reynolds notes that a voluntary association must avoid policies that provoke internal controversy if it is to retain the loyalty of a heterogeneous membership. See Terry S. Reynolds, *Seventy-Five Years of Progress: A History of the Institute of Chemical Engineers 1908–1983* (New York: American Institute of Chemical Engineers, 1983).

Roper summarized the general problems in academic/commercial perceptions and conflicts in 1950 in *"Proceedings* of AAPOR, June 15–20, 1950," *POQ* 14 (1950–51):836–837. Don Cahalan, in "Reflections on the History of Survey Research in America," a paper presented at AAPOR on May 22, 1983, expressed the hope that old feuds would not return, referring to disputes about open/closed questioning, probability/quota sampling, "and the attacks on 'the pollsters' for misprediction of the 1948 elections."

34. Don Cahalan, personal communication, Oct. 25, 1982. He reports that he corroborated his own memory with that of Archibald Crossley.

35. Frederick Mosteller, Herbert Hyman, Philip J. McCarthy, Eli S. Marks, and David B. Truman, *The Pre-Election Polls of 1948* (New York: SSRC, 1949), pp. vii–viii.

36. Angus Campbell, review of Mosteller et al. (note 35), *IJOAR* 4 (1950):27–36, esp. p. 27.

37. Alfred McClung Lee, "Implementation of Opinion Survey Standards," *POQ* 13 (1949–50):645–652. Cantril had written a rejoinder to criticism of the pollsters in *The American Psychologist* 4 (Jan. 1949):23, defending their integrity: "For us to condemn them now when they are temporarily in the doghouse seems to me to reflect much more on us than on them." Norman C. Meier was the chief organizer of the Iowa City meeting of a small group of pollsters and academics in 1949. *POQ* reproduced the SSRC report in the December 1948 issue.

38. Hadley Cantril, "Polls and the 1948 U.S. Presidential Election: Some Problems It Poses," *IJOAR* 2 (1948):309–320.

39. David Krech, "Social Science's Grand Opportunity," *IJOAR* 2 (1948):531–536.

40. George Gallup, "Should We Set Up Standards for Poll Critics?" *IJOAR* 3 (1949):348–354; Elmo Roper, "Some Comments on Election Polls," ibid., pp. 1–5; Edward L. Bernays, "Should Pollsters Be Licensed?" ibid., pp. 6–12; Frank R. Coutant, "The Difference between Market Research and Election Forecasting," *IJOAR* 2 (1948):569–574.

41. Lee, "Implementation of Opinion Survey Standards," p. 650.

42. Why *IJOAR* ceased publication is not clear. There were rumors at the time that Radvanyi, the editor, left Mexico for the Soviet Union, but whether this was fact or a fiction bred of the Cold War atmosphere of the times is not clear (conversation with Daniel Katz, n.d.).

43. The American Chemical Society also alternates its presidency between academic and nonacademic members (Anselm L. Strauss and Lee Rainwater, *The Professional Scientist: A Study of American Chemists* [Chicago: Aldine, 1962], p. 8).

44. I am indebted to Don Cahalan for the 1956 and 1959 figures.

45. Interview with W. Phillips Davison, Dec. 15, 1978; with Lloyd A. Free, Mar. 7, 1979.

46. The ten authors most published in *POQ* from 1937 to 1960 were Cantril (seventeen articles), Lazarsfeld (thirteen), Payne (twelve), Dodd (eleven), Hyman (eleven), O. W. Riegel (ten), Gallup (ten), Roper (nine), Cedric Larson (eight), and Morris Janowitz (eight). This does not count reviews.

47. Interview with David Caplovitz, Dec. 12, 1978.

48. Stuart C. Dodd, "The Washington Public Opinion Laboratory," *POQ* 12 (1948):118–124.

49. Research and professional news in both *IJOAR* and *POQ* provide irregular notice of organizations, conferences, and courses.

50. Papers from NORC's Seminar on Communication and Public Opinion were published in *AJS* 55 (1950). The 1956 institute was reported by Clyde W. Hart in SSRC *Items* 11 (1957):16–19.

51. Programs are on file at the director's office, ISR.

52. Pauline V. Young, *Scientific Social Surveys and Research*, 2d ed. (New York: Prentice-Hall [1939] 1949); George A. Lundberg, *Social Research: A Study in Methods of Gathering Data*, 2d ed. (New York: Longmans, Green [1929] 1942); A. B. Blankenship, *Consumer and Opinion Research* (New York: Harper, 1943).

53. Mildred Parten, *Surveys, Polls, and Samples* (New York: Harper, 1950).

54. Jahoda, Deutsch, and Cook, *Research Methods in Social Relations*; Stanley L. Payne, *The Art of Asking Questions* (Princeton, N.J.: Princeton University Press, 1951); Goode and Hatt, *Methods in Social Research*; Leon Festinger and Daniel Katz, eds., *Research Methods in the Behavioral Sciences* (New York: Dryden, 1953); Herbert Hyman, *Survey Design and Analysis* (Glencoe, Ill.: The Free Press, 1955); Paul F. Lazarsfeld and Morris Rosenberg, *The Language of Social Research* (Glencoe, Ill.: The Free Press, 1955); Robert L. Kahn and Charles F. Cannell, *The Dynamics of Interviewing* (New York: Wiley, 1957); Frederick F. Stephan and Philip J. McCarthy, *Sampling Opinions: An Analysis of Survey Procedure* (New York: Wiley, 1958); C. A. Moser, *Survey Methods in Social Investigation* (London: Heinemann, 1958); Margaret Jarman Hagood and Daniel O. Price, *Statistics for Sociologists*, rev. ed. (New York: Henry Holt & Co., [1941] 1952); W. Allen Wallis and Harry V. Roberts, *Statistics: A New Approach* (Glencoe, Ill.: The Free Press, 1956); and Hubert M. Blalock, Jr., *Social Statistics* (New York: McGraw-Hill, 1960).

55. Alfred C. Kinsey, Wardell B. Pomeroy, and Clyde E. Martin, *Sexual Behavior in the Human Male* (Philadelphia: W. B. Saunders, 1948); Alfred C. Kinsey, Wardell B. Pomeroy, Clyde E. Martin, and Paul H. Gebbard, *Sexual Behavior in the Human Female* (Philadelphia: W. B. Saunders, 1953).

56. Kinsey et al., *Human Male*, p. 42.

57. Wardell B. Pomeroy, *Dr. Kinsey and the Institute for Sex Research* (New York: Harper & Row, 1972).

58. William G. Cochran, Frederick Mosteller, and John W. Tukey, *Statistical Problems of the Kinsey Report on Sexual Behavior in the Human Male* (Washington, D.C.: American Statistical Association, 1954). James A. Davis notes that a Kinsey-type inquiry was conducted on a national sample by NORC but was not brought to completion (interview, May 24, 1979).

59. Kinsey et al., *Human Male*, p. 13.

60. E. M. Jellinek, "Phases of Alcohol Addiction," in *Society, Culture, and Drinking Patterns*, ed. David J. Pittman (New York: Wiley, 1962); M. A. Maxwell, "Drinking Behavior in the State of Washington," *Quarterly Journal of Studies on Alcohol* 13 (1952):219–239; John W. Riley, Jr., and Charles F. Marden, "The Social Pattern of Alcoholic Drinking," *Quarterly Journal of Studies on Alcohol* 8 (1947):265–273.

61. Gurin, Veroff, and Feld, *Americans View Their Mental Health*.

62. Norman M. Bradburn, Seymour Sudman, and Associates, *Improving Interview Method and Questionnaire Design: Response Effects to Threatening Questions in*

Survey Research (San Francisco: Jossey-Bass, 1979); J. D. DeFrain and L. Ernst, "The Psychological Effects of Sudden Infant Death Syndrome on Surviving Family Members," *Journal of Family Practice* 6 (1978):985–989; Barbara Snell Dohrenwend and Bruce P. Dohrenwend, *Stressful Life Events: Their Nature and Effects* (New York: Wiley, 1974); James S. House, *Work Stress and Social Support* (Reading, Mass.: Addison-Wesley, 1981); Herbert H. Hyman, *Of Time and Widowhood: Nationwide Studies of Enduring Effects* (Durham, N.C.: Duke University Press, 1983); Robert Kastenbaum, "'Healthy Dying': A Paradoxical Quest Continues," *Journal of Social Issues* 35 (1979):185–206; Richard A. Kulka and Helen Weingarten, "The Long-Term Effects of Parental Divorce in Childhood on Adult Adjustment," *Journal of Social Issues* 35 (1979):50–78; W. C. McCready and A. M. Greeley, *The Ultimate Values of the American Population* (Beverly Hills, Calif.: Sage Publications, 1976); Camille B. Wortman and Christine Dunkel-Schetter, "Interpersonal Relationships and Cancer: A Theoretical Analysis," *Journal of Social Issues* 35 (1979):120–155.

63. T. W. Adorno, Else Frenkel-Brunswik, Daniel J. Levinson, and R. Nevitt Sanford, *The Authoritarian Personality* (New York: Harper, 1950), pp. 255–257.

64. Herbert H. Hyman and Paul B. Sheatsley, "*The Authoritarian Personality*— A Methodological Critique," in *Studies in the Scope and Method of "The Authoritarian Personality*," ed. Richard Christie and Marie Jahoda (Glencoe, Ill.: The Free Press, 1954), pp. 50–122.

65. Joseph Veroff, John W. Atkinson, Sheila C. Feld, and Gerald Gurin, "The Use of Thematic Apperception to Assess Motivation in a Nationwide Interview Study," *Psychological Monographs: General and Applied* 74 (1960):1–32; Irving R. Weschler and Raymond E. Bernberg, "Indirect Methods of Attitude Measurement," *IJOAR* 4 (1950):209–228.

66. Gabriel A. Almond and Sidney Verba, *The Civic Culture: Political Attitudes and Democracy in Five Nations* (Princeton, N.J.: Princeton University Press, 1963).

67. Ibid., pp. 48–49.

Index

Designer:	U.C. Press Staff
Compositor:	Wilsted & Taylor
Text:	Baskerville
Display:	Baskerville
Printer:	Bookcrafters, Inc.
Binder:	Bookcrafters, Inc.